Retreat from Gettysburg

To Jim

With all my best wishes

[signature]

Gettysburg
June 7, 2012

CIVIL WAR AMERICA

Gary W. Gallagher, editor

Retreat from Gettysburg

Lee, Logistics, and
the Pennsylvania Campaign

Kent Masterson Brown

The University of North Carolina Press
Chapel Hill and London

Designed by Charles Ellertson
Set in Janson by Tseng Information Systems, Inc.
Manufactured in the United States of America

⊗ The paper in this book meets the guidelines for
permanence and durability of the Committee on
Production Guidelines for Book Longevity
of the Council on Library Resources.

Library of Congress Cataloging-in-Publication Data
Brown, Kent Masterson, 1949–
Retreat from Gettysburg : Lee, logistics, and the
Pennsylvania campaign / by Kent Masterson Brown.
p. cm. — (Civil War America)
Includes bibliographical references and index.
ISBN-13: 978-0-8078-2921-9 (cloth : alk. paper)
ISBN-10: 0-8078-2921-8 (cloth : alk. paper)
1. Gettysburg Campaign, 1863.   I. Title.   II. Series.
E475.51.B76 2005
973.7′349—dc22
2004011781

10 09 08 07 06   8 7 6 5 4

To my dear wife, Genevieve,

and our three precious little ones:

Annie Louise, Philip, and Thomas

Contents

Maps

Illustrations

Acknowledgments

I remember my first lesson about an army on retreat. I was, maybe, fourteen years old. While traveling with my family through the North Carolina mountains toward the seashore, my late father, Henry Pell Brown, a decorated veteran of the World War II campaigns in North Africa, Italy, and southern France, began explaining to me why mountains and even rivers and driving rains were advantageous to a retreating army. He must have been thinking then about his own pursuit of the retreating Germans across the swollen Rapido River and the mountains of Cassino. Retreats, he told me, need not be the last chapters of otherwise sad stories; instead, they can regain for armies advantages that had been lost on battlefields. My father was a wonderful man and a great soldier and patriot. I will never forget our discussions.

My father's "better half" helped me too. My late mother, Dorothy Franz Brown, and her sister, Elizabeth Franz Davis of Martinsburg, West Virginia, spent considerable time driving me to battlefields and historic sites in northern Virginia, Maryland, and West Virginia as a youth. Those memories are precious to me. Many of the sites we visited are found in this book. The time my mother and aunt devoted to me did more to encourage my interest in the Civil War than they could ever imagine.

My longtime friend Gary Gallagher took an early interest in this project. He encouraged me all through the years with his great knowledge of the war and his enthusiasm for the subject. He read my manuscript, offering many insightful suggestions, and, in the end, he even furnished the subtitle. Gary's assistance was absolutely decisive; he is a wonderful friend. William H. Freehling, like Gary Gallagher, read the manuscript and provided timely help in its organization. Likewise, Charles P. Roland and his lovely wife Allie Lee read portions of the draft and offered valuable suggestions. I am very, very grateful.

There are others who provided encouragement and assistance. One of them was Matthew Hodgson, director emeritus of the University of North Carolina Press. As early as 1985 Matt asked me to write this book for the Press. Even though it took more than twenty years for me to finally produce it, he was ever patient. He always believed that I would accomplish the task. David Perry, editor in chief at the Press, has been encouraging and patient as well.

All along the way I was helped by others. Barbara Wright of Charlottesville, Virginia, Alan Nolan, and the late William Woods Hassler encouraged me when it seemed as though the project would never get off the ground, and then they cheered me on as the work progressed. Thank you for your friendship and all the wonderful memories.

Countless individuals contributed a steady stream of documents for me to refer to, including Fletcher L. Elmore Jr. of Louisville, Kentucky; William Turner of Lanham, Maryland; James and Judy Philpot of Lexington, Kentucky; Ken Lawrence M.D. of Orwell, Ohio; Loring Shultz of Gettysburg, Pennsylvania; Lieutenant Colonel Hans Henzel of Fairfield, Pennsylvania; B. F. Moore of Cincinnati, Ohio; John H. Krohn Jr. of Wilmington, North Carolina; Richard Keith Irish of Marshall, Virginia; J. J. Fraboni of Myrtle Beach, South Carolina; David Schwartz of Staunton, Virginia; Michael S. Saks of Providence, Rhode Island; William C. Blackwell of Hagerstown, Maryland; Georgie Lee Blackwell Heizer of Danville, Kentucky; Bob Lurate of Lexington, Virginia; Gary Hendershott of Little Rock, Arkansas; Hunt B. Jones M.D. of Louisville, Kentucky; John Michael Priest of Hagerstown, Maryland; Clyde Wilson at the University of South Carolina; James McClellan of Farmville, Virginia; Michael A. Gureasko of Cincinnati, Ohio; Lewis Leigh Jr. of Leesburg, Virginia; B. Seward Totty of Lexington, Kentucky; and Sam and Wes Small of Gettysburg, Pennsylvania.

Robert Rosen of Charleston, South Carolina, and Marshall Krolick of Chicago, Illinois, sent me material on such personalities as Dr. Simon Baruch, Dr. Alexander Bear, Major Raphael Moses, and Major John Medill. General William A. Tidwell of Fairfax, Virginia, graciously gave me copies of Captain George M. Emack's letters, family history, and photographs. Likewise, my friend Ben Ritter of Winchester, Virginia, copied rare diaries for me and helped me find some unknown sources that were of great help in the development of this narrative. The late David V. Young M.D. of Washington, D.C., helped me understand the world of nineteenth-century medicine and the diagnosis and treatment of diseases. Todd Bowman and Jane Hershey of Williamsport, Maryland, helped me solve the mystery surrounding the location of Otho Williams's farm at Williamsport, and Ms. Hershey graciously copied many Williams documents and even provided a photograph of the Williams house, Rose Hill, as it looked in the nineteenth century. I am very grateful.

One cannot write about the Gettysburg campaign without consulting

Kathleen Georg, senior historian at the Gettysburg National Military Park. Her enthusiasm for the study of the campaign and battle of Gettysburg is only surpassed by her generosity. Kathy copied for me Dr. John W. C. O'Neal's journal of Confederate burials in and around Gettysburg and inventories of Gettysburg area hospitals. She even collated the damage claims of Adams County, Pennsylvania, residents. Those items were indispensable to the production of this book. Ted Alexander at the Antietam National Military Park and Eric Whittenberg of Columbus, Ohio, also gave me letters and reminiscences that added to the narrative.

Of course, to write a book on any aspect of the Confederate armies the author must consult, at a minimum, two repositories: the Southern Historical Collection at the University of North Carolina and the Museum of the Confederacy in Richmond, Virginia. Not only do these two collections contain a wealth of remarkable documents and records, but also they are managed by some of the nicest people I know. John E. White at the University of North Carolina and John and Ruth Coski at the Museum of the Confederacy are wonderful. Without them, this book could never have taken shape. John White would locate documents on his own and forward copies to me. John Coski uncovered all of the June and July 1863 quartermaster records of Lee's army in the holdings of the Museum of the Confederacy. Ruth patiently copied them and many other records, diaries, letters, and memoirs. What a difference the quartermaster records made in my understanding of Lee's invasion of Pennsylvania and his retreat from Gettysburg! As always, my old friends Richard Sommers and Jay Luvaas at the U.S. Army Military History Institute at Carlisle, Pennsylvania, supplied wonderful archival material and ideas.

Jason Tomberlin and the North Carolina Division of Archives and History, Raleigh, provided great assistance and material. Jennifer Bean Bower of the Old Salem/Museum of Early Southern Decorative Arts was most helpful. A wealth of material and aid were available at the special collections of the University of Georgia, Duke University, the University of Virginia, Washington and Lee University, Emory University, the University of South Carolina, Gettysburg College, the University of Michigan, Michigan State University, Western Michigan University, the College of William and Mary, the Virginia Military Institute, the University of Alabama, Tulane University, Louisiana State University, the University of Colorado at Boulder, Virginia Polytechnical Institute, Brown University, the Virginia Baptist Historical Society in Richmond, the University of Kentucky, and the Medical University of South Carolina in Charleston.

Helping me locate and copying innumerable documents, records, and illustrations critical to the production of this book were the Martinsburg–Berkeley County Historical Society and Public Library in Martinsburg, West Virginia; the Winchester–Frederick County Historical Society in Winchester, Virginia; the Clear Spring, Maryland, Historical Society; the Hagerstown–Washington County Historical Society in Hagerstown, Maryland; the Connecticut Historical Society in Hartford; the Pennsylvania Historical and Museum Commission in Harrisburg; the Virginia State Library in Richmond; the South Carolina Confederate Relic Room and Museum in Columbia; the Camden, South Carolina, Public Library; the Greensboro, North Carolina, Historical Museum; the Historical Society of Pennsylvania in Philadelphia; the Rochester, New York, Public Library; the Delaware Historical Society in Wilmington; the American Antiquarian Society in Worcester, Massachusetts; the Indiana State Library in Indianapolis; the Western Reserve Historical Society in Cleveland, Ohio; the Detroit, Michigan, Public Library; the New York Public Library; the Maine Historical Society in Portland; the Chesapeake and Ohio Railroad Historical Society in Clifton Forge, Virginia; and even the National Baseball Hall of Fame in Cooperstown, New York.

The staffs at the Library of Congress and the National Archives, particularly my friend, Michael Musick at the Archives, were of tremendous help. Mike would have the collections ready for me on my arrival there, making the whole effort as smooth as possible. Nelson Dawson, editor of the *Filson History Quarterly*, superbly copyedited drafts of the manuscript and my assistant, Jeremy Music, typed draft after draft of the book and then helped me create the maps.

I want to thank all of the foregoing people and institutions for their interest, assistance, and material.

Bob Maher, an old friend in Winchester, Virginia, showcased the retreat from Gettysburg as a tour for his Civil War Education Association many times over the past decade. The attendees were always wonderful. Giving those tours helped me crystallize facts and thoughts. I am very grateful.

My good friend Gabor Boritt, at Gettysburg College, expressed an interest in this project more than a decade ago. Always encouraging, he gave me the first chance to publicly present some of the critical theses of this book at his Civil War Institute in June 2003. That opportunity not only showcased my years of research, but it also tested some of my conclusions before a well-read and enthusiastic audience. Thank you, Gabor.

Finally, my deepest thanks are reserved for my dear wife, Genevieve, and my children, Annie Louise, Philip, and Thomas. They were patient, under-standing, and loving all through the ordeal of collecting the resources for and writing this book. One has to experience writing a book while his two- and three-year-old children are playing under the desk or sitting on his lap to ap-preciate the challenge. I love them more than words could ever tell. Thank you for bringing such joy to my life.

Kent Masterson Brown
Lexington, Kentucky
25 July 2004

Retreat from Gettysburg

This has been a sad day for us

Gettysburg, 3 July 1863, approximately 3:50 P.M.[1]

Through the heavy smoke and enemy artillery fire, the tattered remnants of the commands of Major General George E. Pickett, Brigadier General James Johnston Pettigrew, and Major General Isaac R. Trimble streamed down the bloody slope of Cemetery Ridge. Their attack against the center of the Union Army of the Potomac had been a disaster. "The whole field," wrote a Confederate officer, "was dotted with our soldiers, singly and in small groups, coming back from the charge, many of them wounded, and the enemy were firing at them as you would a herd of game."[2]

Losses had been appalling. In the commands of Pickett, Pettigrew, and Trimble, more than 6,700 officers and men were casualties. Nearly 5,000 were killed or wounded. Along the stone wall on Cemetery Ridge the dead and wounded lay in "heaps." The bodies of many of those who fell near the Union lines were literally set on fire by the flames from the blasting artillery pieces.[3]

In Pickett's Division, the severe loss was told by the staggering number of casualties among general and field-grade officers. Brigadier General Lewis A. Armistead was mortally wounded and in enemy hands. Brigadier General Richard Brooke Garnett was dead and his body unrecovered. Only Garnett's frightened, wounded, and riderless horse had been seen cantering to the rear prior to the climax of the attack. Brigadier General James Lawson Kemper was savagely wounded; a musket ball had entered his groin and ranged up his spinal column. Thirteen regimental commanders were killed or wounded; three lieutenant colonels were killed and eight were wounded. Of nine majors, one was killed and seven were wounded.[4]

Not only Virginia but also North Carolina, Mississippi, Alabama, and Tennessee had sent their sons into that maelstrom of death. In those fields,

General Trimble was badly wounded and the remnants of nearly all of General Pettigrew's regiments returned without their field-grade officers or acting regimental commanders. More than 3,500 officers and men were killed, wounded, or missing in Pettigrew's and Trimble's commands.[5]

The brigades of twenty-two-year-old Colonel James Keith Marshall and Brigadier General Joseph R. Davis suffered a ghastly casualty rate of 74 percent; Marshall was killed after two bullets struck him in the head. Ten regimental commanders fell in Pettigrew's and Trimble's commands. Some companies lost over 90 percent of their effective strength, while two companies —the University Greys of the Eleventh Mississippi and the color company of the Thirty-eighth North Carolina—lost 100 percent of their officers and men. After the attack the Thirty-eighth North Carolina consisted of only forty soldiers commanded by a first lieutenant. The Eleventh Mississippi had lost 341 of its 394 officers and men, a staggering 87 percent. Company A of the Eleventh North Carolina consisted of only eight men and a single officer.[6]

Out near the Emmitsburg Road General Trimble stood next to his horse, badly wounded. His aide, Captain Charles Grogan, remarked: "General, the men were falling back, shall I rally them?" Trimble looked to his right and observed Pickett's columns reduced to "a few men in squads moving to the rear." He turned to Grogan and said: "No, Charley, the best thing these brave fellows can do is to get out of this." Trimble and his aide mounted up and followed the men to the rear. As Trimble neared Seminary Ridge, his horse, Jinny, collapsed and died, having been struck by the same shot that wounded the general.[7]

Along the stone wall on Cemetery Ridge, from the whitewashed house and barn of free African American Abraham Brian to below the clump of trees, the attacking columns lost thirty-three battle flags. Many of the flags had not been fought over by the contending sides but, rather, were picked up off the ground after the attack had been repulsed, mute testimony that in many of the attacking regiments the color companies had been so shredded by the horrendous gunfire that when the flags fell to the ground, no one remained to bear them farther.[8]

Observing the melancholy scene was the commander of the Army of Northern Virginia, General Robert E. Lee. He had led the army only since the wounding of General Joseph E. Johnston at Seven Pines on 31 May 1862. On assuming the post, Lee turned the army into an offensive machine; the Seven Days, Second Manassas, Sharpsburg, Fredericksburg, and Chancellorsville were his battle honors thus far. Since he had taken charge, the

Army of Northern Virginia had suffered more than sixty thousand casualties. Lee was all army; he reveled in command and was good at it. He was exacting and expected those around him to be the same. He lectured others constantly, and his orders, letters, and telegrams reveal a leader who, for some, had an irritating propensity to micromanage. Added to that, Lee was quick to lose his temper, and no one wanted to be near him when he did. Lee could drive an army; he was relentless. If his men were hungry or short of supplies, Lee would seize necessities from civilians. If he believed that he must take an enemy position, he would hurl all he had at it and not mourn the lost men if the attack failed. In addition to all of this, correspondents of the Southern press were "not tolerated" at his headquarters and he refused them permission to see any official reports. In a year, though, Lee had achieved more with the Army of Northern Virginia than one could have ever imagined given the army's terrible supply problems and its inferior numbers.[9]

Lee was a family man. He deeply loved his wife, the former Mary Custis, a victim of rheumatoid arthritis, and his three sons and four daughters, one of whom, Annie Carter Lee, lay buried in North Carolina, a victim of typhoid in the fall of 1862. All of his sons were in the army. One of them, General William Henry Fitzhugh Lee, one of Major General J. E. B. Stuart's brigade commanders, had been wounded near Richmond and captured on 26 June. General Lee had become religious about ten years earlier, and his faith now deeply affected the way he viewed success and tragedy.[10]

At fifty-six years of age, Lee was well built and rather robust; he stood just under six feet tall, although his feet were rather small. His dark brown—almost black—penetrating eyes and finely chiseled features made him exceedingly handsome. But the burden of command had taken its toll; his once pitch-black hair and beard had turned snow-white, and he showed signs of stress and fatigue. In early April Lee had complained of "a good deal of pain" in his "chest, back and arms." He had been suffering from a heavy cold and fever, but the pain seemed different. Lee had experienced a heart attack. Although he was able to return to duty, Lee remarked how "differently" he had felt since his "attack last spring"; he felt that he had never really recovered.[11]

Beyond enduring the slow constriction of his coronary arteries, Lee had complained of another malady that was of more immediate concern, diarrhea. He had been stricken with it like virtually everyone in the army. The previous evening, Major William W. Blackford of General Stuart's staff rode to Lee's headquarters to present Stuart's report of his operations. While Blackford waited for him to read it, Lee hurried to the rear of his tent at least three

General Robert E. Lee as he appeared after Gettysburg. National Archives, Washington, D.C.

times. Finally, Lee's staff officers admitted that the commander had a bad case of diarrhea. Indeed, Blackford noticed that Lee "walked . . . as if he was weak and in pain." Lieutenant Colonel Moxley G. Sorrel, of Lieutenant General James Longstreet's staff, who had a close view of General Lee, later wrote of his "extreme agitation" on the afternoon of 3 July.[12]

Dressed in a long gray coat bearing only the three stars on the collar and wearing a black felt hat, Lee looked more like a civilian than a commander. He always carried a red bandana. From a position near Spangler Woods, Lee, seated on a large oak stump and holding the reins of his horse, Traveller, in one hand and his head resting in the other with his elbow supported by his knee, had observed the last great disaster at Gettysburg unfold along the fields in front of the distant Cemetery Ridge.[13]

Lee and his "old war horse," General Longstreet, feared that the enemy would counterattack while the center of the Army of Northern Virginia appeared to be in a state of collapse. From their vantage point in the Spangler Woods, they ordered their staff officers to ride ahead into the fields west of the Emmitsburg Road and rally the broken survivors of the attack along a ridgeline east of Seminary Ridge, marked by the massed artillery batteries of Longstreet's Corps and Lieutenant General Ambrose Powell Hill's Corps.[14]

Union cannoneers continued to pour galling salvos into the retreating butternut-and-gray soldiers, killing and wounding many. Some bloodied Confederates turned around to fire back, but Union artillery and small arms fire became so heavy that many of the wounded who littered the ground begged their comrades to stop shooting for fear of being killed in the crossfire, out of which they were helpless to extricate themselves. Such appeals were rarely heeded.[15]

The fields in front of Seminary Ridge were filled with battered veterans of the attack. Private Robert W. Morgan of Company C, Eleventh Virginia, had been wounded in both feet. Unable to walk, Morgan used his own musket and one he picked up on the battlefield as crutches and began hobbling back to Seminary Ridge.[16]

Farther to the rear was Colonel William R. Aylett of the Fifty-third Virginia. Blood poured from his mouth. He had been hit in the chest by a shell fragment during the bombardment that preceded the attack. Like most regimental officers, he had entered the attack wearing not only his frock coat and vest but also a blanket roll across his left shoulder. Aylett always wore a blanket roll into battle, believing that if he were wounded he could wrap himself in it and the warmth would ward off shock. On inspection, he discovered that the shell fragment had failed to penetrate the folds of the blanket roll, coat, vest, and shirt. It left him with a terrible hematoma, internal bleeding, and intense pain, but nothing more serious.[17]

Thousands who fell along Cemetery Ridge could not follow their comrades back to Seminary Ridge; they were too badly wounded. One of them was Lieutenant John E. Dooley of the First Virginia. He was shot through both thighs about thirty yards from the Union batteries. His eyes and face were slathered with the blood of those on either side of him who had been hit by shellfire and canister as they marched toward the Union lines. Dooley was in "excessive pain"; he feared that he was bleeding to death. As he was immobile and blinded by the blood, smoke, and dust, only the shouts of jubilant Union soldiers told him the result of the attack. He was left behind, ten yards from his colonel, Lewis B. Williams, who had been shot in the neck and was in "intense agony"; the bullet, after it hit the colonel, had ranged down his spinal column. Nearby were two of Williams's classmates from the Virginia Military Institute, Colonel Robert C. Allen, of the Twenty-eighth Virginia, who had been shot in the head, and Williams's first cousin, Colonel Waller Tazewell Patton, of the Seventh Virginia, whose jaw had been ripped away by artillery fire.[18]

All around the dismal fields, appeals for assistance and cries of "water, water" from the wounded joined the chorus of blasting guns and bursting shells. The smoke was dense, canister whirred about, shells shrieked through the acrid air and exploded above the confused and terrified returning soldiers. Efforts at rallying them failed; the scant line, which began to take form east of Seminary Ridge in the face of the hideous artillery fire, collapsed, and a general "stampede" commenced. The situation along Seminary Ridge became tense and precarious. Save for some units in Trimble's demidivision, virtually all distinction of regiments had disappeared.[19]

Countless ambulances, with brigade names stenciled across their canvas covers, clattered along bearing the wounded from temporary aid stations to the division hospitals in the rear. Litter bearers and ambulance drivers, most of whom were detailed soldiers, others slaves who also served as cooks and laborers, scurried about, their hats and caps "conspicuously displaying the badge of red cloth with white letters, reading 'Ambulance Corps.'" The aid stations were chaotic; they were overflowing with wounded. Each station consisted of little more than an assistant surgeon, a "knapsack toter," and some nurses (usually musicians or convalescent soldiers) with "a large collection of apple butter pots filled with water to be used for the wounded"; they were marked by a red flag attached to a stick planted in the ground.[20]

Standing on Seminary Ridge not far from General Lee was the Reverend Dr. Francis Milton Kennedy, a Methodist minister and chaplain of the Twenty-eighth North Carolina. Kennedy was appalled at the losses. He mounted up and rode across the fields west of Seminary Ridge to try to locate his brigade hospital but was unsuccessful. All he witnessed was agony and confusion. "By some means," Kennedy wrote in his diary, "the Medical Department was badly managed today causing a good deal of unnecessary pain and trouble to the wounded."[21]

Lieutenant Colonel Arthur J. L. Fremantle of Her Majesty's Coldstream Guards, an observer traveling with the Army of Northern Virginia, recalled:

> I soon began to meet many wounded men returning from the front. Many of them asked in piteous tones the way to a doctor or an ambulance. The further I got, the greater became the number of the wounded. At last I came to a perfect stream of them flocking through the woods . . . some were walking alone on crutches composed of two rifles, others were supported by men less badly wounded than themselves, and others were carried on stretchers by the ambulance corps; but in no case did I see a sound man helping the wounded to the rear, unless he carried the red badge of the ambulance corps. They were still under a heavy fire; the shells were continually bringing down great limbs of trees, and carrying further destruction amongst this melancholy procession.[22]

Fremantle rode up to Lee. The general turned to him and said, "This has been a sad day for us, Colonel, a sad day; but we can't always expect to win victories." Beside Lee and Fremantle were Colonel E. Porter Alexander and Lieutenant Fred M. Colston of Alexander's staff. Suddenly, loud cheering from the enemy lines was heard above the moaning and mutter of the returning veterans. Lee immediately turned to young Colston and ordered him to ride out into the fields to determine what the enemy was doing.[23]

The Herculean task facing Lee was to rally his bloodied veterans and to keep the center of his army from disintegrating. He ordered the brigades of Brigadier Generals Ambrose R. Wright, William Mahone, and Carnot Posey of Major General Richard H. Anderson's Division forward from their reserve positions in the Long Lane and along Seminary Ridge to support what was left of the attack force.

General Longstreet became alarmed. After conferring with Lee, he quickly mounted up and rode over to General Anderson and directed him to halt his men, explaining that an advance was "useless and would only involve unnecessary loss." Longstreet then told Anderson to have Brigadier General

Cadmus M. Wilcox and Colonel David Lang, whose brigades had entered the attack just to the right and several minutes behind Pickett's columns, pull back their shattered commands to Seminary Ridge. Anderson ordered his staff to inform his brigade commanders of the decision; all of the brigades were to re-form along the lines they had previously held and prepare for a counterattack. Lee had run out of tactical options to defeat the enemy at Gettysburg.[24]

While the remnants of the brigades of Wilcox and Lang withdrew to Seminary Ridge, Union guns poured heavy fire into their backs. Captains C. Seton Fleming and William E. McCaslin, both of the Second Florida, were walking side by side toward the rear. McCaslin remarked to Fleming that no matter how one escaped the dangers of any particular battle, he was exposed to the same perils in the next engagement, and it seemed impossible to pass through them all in safety. Just then, a shell shrieked by, striking McCaslin in the head, killing him instantly, and splattering his blood and brains over Fleming.[25]

Back along Seminary Ridge, Lee conferred with Longstreet about where the survivors of the assault might rally. Lee then rode unattended among the broken troops in front of the woods. He addressed every soldier he met, giving words of encouragement. "All this will come right in the end; we'll talk it over afterwards; but in the meantime, all good men must rally. We want all good and true men just now," he said. He urged the wounded, "Bind up [your] hurts and take up a musket."[26]

Lee clearly felt his most important duty at that moment was to encourage his disheartened and tattered veterans. He lowered his field glasses and rode out among the men again. Lee asked Lieutenant Randolph Abbott Shotwell, of the Eighth Virginia, whom he saw sink down on a pile of fence rails after returning to Seminary Ridge, "Are you wounded?"

"No, General," was the reply, "not hurt I believe, but completely exhausted."

Lee then responded, "Ah, yes, it was too much for you. We were not strong enough. It was my fault, and I am very sorry, but we will try to repair it."[27]

Shotwell recalled: "There was the saddest imaginable expression in [Lee's] voice and upon his features, yet with all a calm intrepidity marvelous to see, in view of the fact that the enemy had advanced his skirmishes already as far as the Emmitsburg Road, and should according to every lesson of military science have retaliated by launching a counter assault against our crippled center."

"Well, my poor boy," Lee said to Shotwell, "try and get on to the rear; those people seem to be moving. Your division is ordered to rendezvous at the wagon camp on Marsh Creek. Try to get back there, and take a good night's rest."[28]

Lee turned his iron gray horse around to face his returning soldiers. Some badly wounded men took off their hats and cheered him. Few failed to answer him when he spoke. Major Edmund Berkeley, of the Eighth Virginia, who was carried to the rear by a few of his men, observed Lee near the Spangler Woods. The general was directing the formation of a line of slightly wounded men along the crest in front of Seminary Ridge. Berkeley heard him comfort the thin line of survivors. "My men," Lee said, "it was not your fault."[29]

Lee saw Pickett and his men along the banks of Pitzer's Run west of Seminary Ridge and rode up to them. The soldiers crowded around Lee asking what they should do. Some begged him to attack again. After comforting them, Lee extended his hand to their leader. "General Pickett," he said, "place your division in rear of this hill, and be ready to repel the advance of the enemy should they follow up their advantage."

"General Lee," Pickett replied, tears flowing down his face, "I have no division now, Armistead is down, Garnett is down, and Kemper is mortally wounded."

"Come, General Pickett," Lee said soothingly, "this has been my fight and upon my shoulders rests the blame. The men and officers of your command have written the name of Virginia as high today as it has ever been written before."[30]

Presently, a litter was seen moving through the tattered veterans. "Captain," Lee asked one of Pickett's staff officers, "what officer is that they are bearing off?"

"General Kemper," was the reply.

Hearing Lee's voice, Kemper slowly pulled the blanket from over his face. Only moments before, his ambulance had been hit and overturned by Union artillery fire. A wounded veteran from the Fourteenth Virginia had helped carry him to safety.

"I must speak to him," Lee said. He rode over to the wounded general's side. "General Kemper, I hope you are not seriously wounded."

"I am struck in the groin," Kemper responded, "and the ball has ranged upward; they tell me it is mortal."

"I hope it may not prove to be so bad as that; is there anything I can do for you, General Kemper?"

Painfully lifting himself on one elbow, Kemper said, "Yes, General Lee, do full justice to this division for its work today."

Lee calmly answered, "I will," and Kemper was carried on.[31]

Lee turned back toward the crest of Seminary Ridge. He received word from Captain Colston, who had just returned from the front, that the cheering was for some Union officers who had ridden along the enemy lines. General Wilcox rode up, wearing his round shell jacket and battered straw hat. Like Pickett, he had been moved to tears by the events of the day. Lee and Wilcox shook hands. With emotion, Lee said, "Never mind, General, all this has been my fault—it is I that have lost this fight, and you must help me out of it the best way you can."[32]

Lee paused to observe the enemy through his field glasses; he could see a forward movement of Union skirmishers toward the Emmitsburg Road. It was threatening. From the far right, heavy gunfire arose; there was cheering. There General Elon J. Farnsworth's Union cavalry brigade recklessly attacked General Longstreet's advanced brigades and artillery batteries along the western base of Round Top. Farnsworth was mortally wounded, and his brigade was repulsed by infantry volleys and artillery fire. The sounds of the attack, though, were ominous to those on Seminary Ridge. Many believed that a counterattack was under way, but the heavy gunfire subsided as quickly as it occurred.[33]

Lee remained near the battlefield for more than an hour after the survivors of Pickett's, Pettigrew's, and Trimble's commands had returned to Seminary Ridge. Often in the presence of General Longstreet and Colonel Alexander, Lee rode out into the clearings in front of the ridge where the wounded continued to be evacuated and near where sweating cannoneers, blackened with powder and dirt, watched the front and grimly waited for the enemy to go on the offensive.[34]

Before long, couriers informed Lee of other ominous developments. His artillery chief, Brigadier General William Nelson Pendleton, reported that all of his long-range artillery ammunition was exhausted and that there was still no word of the whereabouts of a reserve ammunition train Lee had ordered from Richmond four weeks earlier. Furthermore, General Stuart's horse brigades had been badly cut up in fighting east of Gettysburg, and General Wade Hampton severely wounded. Even more worrisome, elements of the Sixth U.S. Cavalry of Brigadier General Wesley Merritt's Union Reserve Brigade had reached Fairfield, Pennsylvania, eight miles in Lee's rear, in an attempt to destroy an immense reserve wagon train of purchased, impressed, and confiscated quartermaster and subsistence stores that lined the road from Cashtown to Fairfield. The two gray horse brigades of Brigadier Generals William E. "Grumble" Jones and Beverly H. Robertson, however, had arrived just in time to crush that Union force at about the same hour that Pickett's, Pettigrew's, and Trimble's columns were repulsed along Cemetery Ridge and Stuart's horsemen were being worsted on the far left flank. The advance of Union cavalry into Lee's rear and onto his principal artery of communication, supply, and retreat was alarming.[35]

For Lee, the only remaining option was to withdraw his army; he had to return to Virginia. Lee had done this once before—in September 1862—but then his army was only three miles from the Potomac River. The present retreat would call upon him to muster not only all of his talents but also all of his nerve. The army's quartermaster and subsistence trains carrying stores seized in Maryland and Pennsylvania were very long; they had to be safely returned to the army's base of supply in the lower Shenandoah Valley along with the vast herds of seized horses, mules, cattle, sheep, and hogs. If this could not be done, the invasion of Pennsylvania would become a complete strategic loss. The large number of wounded also posed a major challenge; those who could stand the journey had to be taken back with the army; others would have to be left behind. Then there was the geography to contend with. The battle at Gettysburg had lured Lee away from the security of the South Mountain range; those 700-foot peaks stood between him and the Potomac River, forty-five difficult miles south. His enemy had just tasted victory. Over the last three days it had proved to be a formidable force; it would not remain idle. Moreover, two more Union armies were moving toward Lee's left flank from the north and toward his rear from the west. Only rain and mud could make the operation Lee faced more challenging than it already appeared to be.

One

Take what is necessary for the army

The logistical problems attendant to any retreat from Gettysburg by Lee's army were acute. The mountains, the distance to the Potomac River, the thousands of sick and wounded, the size of the army, and the capability of the victorious enemy made such an operation extremely difficult. The most profound logistical challenge facing Lee on the afternoon of 3 July 1863, however, was safely moving his enormous quartermaster and subsistence trains — and all the horses, mules, cattle, sheep, and hogs traveling with them — back to Virginia. Those trains consisted of thousands upon thousands of wagons and their horse and mule teams; they extended for miles when on the road. The livestock accompanying them numbered in the tens of thousands. The nature and size of those trains, and the resulting logistical concerns they presented, can only be comprehended by examining Lee's purpose in invading Pennsylvania in the summer of 1863.

The idea for the Pennsylvania campaign arose many months before. It was born in a desperation caused by the looming collapse of the Army of Northern Virginia if it remained in war-ravaged central Virginia without adequate food and supplies for its men and fodder for its horses and mules. Lee's army had suffered from shortages of quartermaster stores all through the winter of 1862–63. The shortages were mostly the result of few manufactures being available for the army and a woefully inadequate supply system in the Confederacy. Clothing and shoes were desperately needed yet difficult to obtain. The soldiers were mostly dirty, ragged, and barefooted. Worse than that, the supply of fodder had run out in the early months of 1863. In February General Trimble had recorded that large numbers of horses in his division were dying every day due to "want of food and disease." For that reason Lee scattered his mounted units, including many artillery batteries, to distant areas behind his lines to allow them to find fodder. On 16 April he wrote to Jefferson Davis of his anxiety over "the present immobility of the army owing to the condition of our horses and the scarcity of forage and provisions." He reminded the Confederate president that the army was scattered and that he was "unable to bring [it] together for want of proper subsistence and forage."[1]

Equally difficult had been the supply of subsistence stores. Virginia had virtually run out of surplus food for Lee's army. Shipments of food by rail from North Carolina and farther south were notoriously unpredictable and inadequate. The government informed Lee in the winter of 1863 that meat rations had to be reduced. Lee balked at the suggestion, demanding that the government respond to the crisis by providing his army with more food. He refused to reduce his men's rations and thus quickly ran out of food. From January to March 1863 only 400,000 pounds of meat reached Lee's army. By April the soldiers were forced to exist on a ration of one-fourth pound of salt meat a day.[2]

The miserably poor rations led to another problem—sickness. By the end of March, scurvy had become widespread in the army, and Dr. Lafayette Guild, its medical director, was ordering corps, division, and brigade surgeons to aid the men in the collection of all sorts of vegetables and wild greenery like wild mustard, garlic, onions, watercress, sassafras, lamb quarter, vinegar, coleslaw, sauerkraut, horseradishes, peas, potatoes, turnip greens, and pickles to supplement their diets.[3]

To try to address the issue of supply of forage and subsistence stores, Lee detached Longstreet's Corps to Suffolk in southeastern Virginia in April to collect food and supplies for the men and forage for the army's nearly 36,000 horses and mules. Colonel Sorrel recalled that at the time the "army was in want of all supplies. The subsistence department lacked fresh meat. In southern Virginia and eastern North Carolina there were said to be large quantities of cattle. There were also large stores of bacon and corn."[4]

In the midst of the horrific problems of supply facing Lee's army, another difficulty surfaced in the winter and spring of 1863. With Confederate armies on the defensive everywhere, President Davis and Secretary of War James S. Seddon sought to detach elements of Lee's army and send them to less successful fronts.[5]

As early as March 1863, at the request of President Davis, Lee traveled to Richmond to discuss the question of sending elements of his army west, but he put up stiff resistance to the idea. The issue arose again in early April. Lee again resisted, convincing Davis and Seddon that because Major General Joseph E. Hooker's Army of the Potomac had shown increased activity in his front, he could not afford a reduction of strength.[6]

Lee's predictions of an enemy advance in Virginia were realized in late

April, when Hooker's army, then north of Fredericksburg, crossed the Rappahannock River in an attempt to reach Lee's rear. Without Longstreet's command, Lee held back a feint by Hooker against his lines at Fredericksburg and Salem Church and, at the same time, divided his remaining force in the face of the enemy and defeated it in the clearings and dense thickets near Chancellorsville on 2 and 3 May. But the victory was costly. The Confederate casualties were very high, and General Thomas J. "Stonewall" Jackson, Lee's "right arm," was seriously wounded and died on 10 May.[7]

In the wake of Chancellorsville, Davis and Seddon renewed their insistence on severing elements of Lee's army. On 9 May Seddon asked Lee to send Pickett's Division westward to reinforce Lieutenant General John C. Pemberton at Vicksburg. Once more, Lee resisted. War clerk John B. Jones reported on 14 May that Lee was in Richmond "closeted" with the president and the secretary of war. In the end, it was resolved, Jones recorded, to send Pickett's Division back to Lee.[8]

It had become apparent to Lee that unless he made a move, Davis and Seddon would ultimately strip his army of some of its best fighting men to assist armies whose generals had not shown any capability of winning. Though he had prevailed thus far, he could not expect to do so through the summer if his army remained idle. Moreover, if he did not try to move the army to a region where it could obtain the critical quartermaster and subsistence stores, it would collapse. An invasion of Pennsylvania was accordingly planned.

Feeding and equipping his men and feeding his horses and mules represented Lee's most pressing challenge. The lack of subsistence and fodder had reached crisis proportions in June 1863. By then, Lee had been campaigning continuously in and around central Virginia for almost nine months. During the past two years only the invasion of Maryland in September 1862 had taken his army out of that area for about thirty days. Union troops had pillaged every town and farm they overran in Virginia. Central Virginia, wrote William Alexander Gordon, one of Lee's engineer officers, in June 1863, was a "stripped and desolate country." The armies had devoured everything edible by man and beast. A serious drought had gripped Virginia in 1862, and in the spring of 1863 it had been too wet. Little had been harvested in 1862, and there had been little planting of wheat, grasses, or feed grains thus far in 1863. Horses, mules, and cattle had no place to graze. And northern Virginia was no better. Colonel Fremantle noted in June 1863 that that part of the state "is now completely cleaned out. It is almost uncultivated, and no animals are grazing where there used to be hundreds." As early as February, Lee had claimed that his horses and mules were in such a "reduced state" that they might be unable to pull the artillery. So difficult had the supply problem become that the Confederate Congress, as early as 26 March 1863, had authorized quartermasters and commissary of subsistence officers to impress private property in the Confederate states for the use of the armies.[9]

According to war clerk Jones, 140,000 bushels of corn were sent from Richmond to Lee's army in May. Even with that, the horses and mules were feeding on less than three pounds of corn a day when they required ten pounds. Lee and his quartermasters knew that late June and early July was harvest time in south central Pennsylvania for hay, oats, and feed corn. It was also when grasses for grazing animals were at their peak.[10]

Beyond fodder, Lee's army had run out of other necessary supplies and equipment. Horseshoes and muleshoes, for instance, were difficult to procure. Blacksmith forges, bellows, anvils, hammers, and the steel to make shoes and other artillery and wagon hardware and the coal to fire the forges had become almost nonexistent. Horses and mules were breaking down because of the lack of shoes as well as the lack of forage.[11]

Lee's men were in need of food; his army had virtually run out of cattle. Without adequate beef the soldiers would not be able to continue in the field. Sheep and hogs were not to be found. Central Virginia, wrote Brigadier General John B. Gordon, "was well-nigh exhausted. How to subsist was becoming a serious question." One quartermaster remembered going from farm to farm not far from Richmond actually begging the occupants for meat, as it could not be obtained otherwise.[12]

In late May Lee was notified that some cattle might be available in southwestern Virginia and the upper Shenandoah Valley. On 1 June he wrote Major General Samuel Jones of the Department of Western Virginia: "I am very anxious to secure all the cattle which can be obtained for the use of this army. I must beg you, therefore, to let me have the 1,250 head brought out . . . on the [latest] expedition. . . . It is reported to me there are already 3,000 head in Greenbriar and Monroe Counties. I hope, indeed, you will be able to spare some of these in addition to the 1,250." On the same day Lee informed the secretary of war that Brigadier General John D. Imboden, whose independent command of cavalry had been foraging in western Virginia, had reported that 3,176 head of cattle were brought out of southwestern Virginia. Lee was anxious to secure all of them for his army, as well as all of those obtained by General Grumble Jones in Pocahontas and Augusta Counties.[13]

Young Colonel John Cheves Haskell, of South Carolina, one of the commanders of an artillery battalion attached to Major General John Bell Hood's Division, summed up Lee's predicament. "For months," he wrote, "our men had been on rations such as no troops ever campaigned on and did a tithe of the work ours were called on to do. Corn meal and damaged bacon were the staples, often so damaged that to live on them insured disease." Regarding the decision to invade Pennsylvania, Haskell commented: "It looked easier to go to the enemy's homes to get [food], and leave our poor people a chance to rest and to gather together the fragments left them." Another veteran, a young cavalryman, put it simply: "For the same reason that the children of Israel went down to Egypt. There was famine in the land, and [Lee's army] went [to Pennsylvania] for corn."[14]

Resupplying his army in Pennsylvania presented a strategic benefit, Lee believed. Northern newspapers had been reporting the rise of Copperhead or peace party sentiment in the North. In the face of growing antiwar feelings, President Abraham Lincoln was vacillating over enforcement of the Conscript Act enacted in March 1863. The presence of Lee's army north of the Mason-Dixon Line could crystallize peace party sentiment.[15]

Although Lee undoubtedly visualized a peace dividend, his objectives for the invasion of Pennsylvania appear to have been nothing more complicated than to feed and equip his army and to keep it intact, although he communicated those objectives to no one. Nevertheless, Lee's officers quickly surmised his intentions. "If we could live on the supplies we hoped to find north of the Potomac," recalled Colonel Sorrel, "the already serious question of food and forage for our men and animals would lighten up temporarily, at least." On 21 June 1863 Lieutenant Henry A. Figures of the Forty-eighth Alabama, Hood's Division, wrote to his mother: "[Our brigade surgeon] told me yesterday that General Lee was going to [Pennsylvania] to subsist his army [and] that he would probably remain there for two months." Such a foraging operation in enemy country was recognized by the great military theorists of the age; unquestionably, it was fundamental to the continued existence of Lee's army.[16]

Lee had tried such a foraging operation once before. In September 1862 he invaded Maryland with the express purpose of feeding and equipping his ragged army north of the Potomac River. His intention then was to eventually move into the Cumberland Valley of Pennsylvania and impress livestock, forage, and other goods in that rich farming region. Yet events dictated otherwise, and Lee wound up withdrawing his troops back toward the Potomac while fighting bloody engagements with General George B. McClellan's fast-marching Army of the Potomac in the passes of the South Mountain range and finally at Sharpsburg. In the end, Lee had little to show for the invasion. He could not afford to let that happen again.[17]

In the early planning for the 1863 invasion of Pennsylvania, Lee determined that Lieutenant General Richard S. Ewell's Corps would not only lead the way into the Shenandoah Valley, Maryland, and Pennsylvania, but that its principal mission would be to obtain food, fodder, and equipment from the civilian population for the army and itself while the remaining two corps of the army covered the Army of the Potomac. The records of the quartermaster stores condemned and issued in units of the Army of Northern Virginia tell the story of Ewell's mission. Those records reveal that as early as mid-May 1863 quartermasters in Longstreet's and Hill's Corps and the cavalry brigades had condemned and then drawn significant amounts of what supplies and equipment were available for their use, while drawing almost nothing for Ewell's Corps. Because Ewell's Corps was directed to supply itself first while in Pennsylvania—and it would precede the rest of the army by almost two weeks—it was not considered by the army quartermaster for the condemnation and reissuance of supplies and equipment prior to the campaign.[18]

Lee began his Pennsylvania campaign on 3 June 1863. To maneuver Hooker's army out of Virginia, he directed the divisions of Generals Hood and Lafayette McLaws of Longstreet's Corps, which were northwest of Fredricksburg, to cross the Rapidan River to Culpeper. The two remaining corps would follow; Ewell also moved north from near Fredricksburg to Culpeper on the third; Hill would wait until Union forces evacuated his front.[19]

On 4 June Lee asked Adjutant and Inspector General Samuel Cooper in Richmond to instruct all convalescents belonging to Hood's and McLaws's Divisions and to Major Generals Jubal A. Early's, Robert E. Rodes's, and Edward "Allegheny" Johnson's Divisions of Ewell's Corps to be forwarded to Culpeper. In one day Lee's supply and communications line shifted from the Richmond, Fredricksburg, and Potomac Railroad to the Orange and Alexandria and the Virginia Central Railroads. By 6 June Dr. Lafayette Guild, medical director of the army, was establishing receiving hospitals for the army along the Orange and Alexandria Railroad from Culpeper to Gordonsville.[20]

To hold at bay a Union force then scattered from Bridgeport, near Clarksburg, to New Creek and Grafton, Virginia, Lee dispatched Imboden's independent cavalry command to Romney, Virginia, and Hancock, Maryland, to disrupt all Union communications along the Baltimore and Ohio Railroad, to tear up the railroad's tracks, and to destroy the locks and aqueducts of the Chesapeake and Ohio (C&O) Canal. In his directive, Lee added: "It is important that you should obtain, for the use of the army, all the cattle that you can."[21]

Ewell's Corps continued moving north, through Gaines's Cross-Roads,

Flint Hill, and Front Royal. On 12 June it arrived at Cedarville, where a pontoon train was added to the force. There Ewell divided his corps, sending Rodes's Division with the pontoon train toward Berryville and Early's and Johnson's Divisions into the Shenandoah Valley and on toward Winchester. Lee's army was now strung out for more than one hundred miles; its leading elements were approaching Winchester, and its rear still remained along the Rappahannock River near Fredericksburg.[22]

Early on, the campaign demonstrated significant military success. On 14 June Early's and Johnson's Divisions routed the Union garrison of Major General Robert H. Milroy at Winchester and Rodes's Division overwhelmed Milroy's forces at Martinsburg. On 15 June Rodes's columns proceeded across the Potomac River ford at Williamsport, Maryland, led by a brigade of cavalry commanded by Brigadier General Albert Gallatin Jenkins. Three miles downstream from Williamsport, at a hairpin bend of the river known as Falling Waters, Rodes's Division left the pontoon bridge and its train, together with a small escort to ensure that the army's communication and supply line would remain open if rains obliterated the river fords. The remaining two divisions, Early's and Johnson's, crossed the Potomac at Boteler's Ford at Shepherdstown. "God has again crowned the valor of our troops with success," Lee telegraphed President Davis on 15 June.[23]

With Jenkins's cavalry brigade in advance, Rodes's and Johnson's Divisions marched north to Chambersburg, Pennsylvania, and then to Carlisle, arriving there on 27 June; Early's Division moved north to Chambersburg and then east through York to Wrightsville, Pennsylvania, on the Susquehanna River, getting there on 28 June accompanied by Colonel Elijah V. White and his Thirty-fifth Battalion of Virginia Cavalry. Once across the Potomac, Ewell's Corps not only could lure Hooker northward but also scour the countryside for quartermaster and subsistence stores for itself and Lee's army for as long as it remained unopposed.[24]

Meanwhile, Hill's Corps crossed the Rapidan River on 14 June and moved north. Five days later, it and Longstreet's Corps rested in front of the mountain passes near Millwood and Berryville, Virginia, while Stuart's remaining five brigades of cavalry screened them from the Army of the Potomac, which had, indeed, moved north to protect Washington, D.C., as Lee had gambled it would do.[25]

The day after Hill's Corps started north toward Culpeper, Lee wrote to Inspector General Cooper in Richmond, directing that "all mail and other communications which may be sent to me, may be forwarded by way of Gordonsville and Staunton; also that instructions may be given to forward all convalescents and other soldiers returning to the army by the same route." The new line of communication and supply through the Shenandoah Valley by way of the Virginia Central Railroad would support a full-scale invasion of south central Pennsylvania.[26]

Through the entire campaign, Lee attempted to draw Hooker's army out of war-torn Virginia so that it would not threaten Richmond. For Longstreet's and Hill's Corps to move farther north, Lee believed that Hooker must first move his army across the Potomac River on the east side of the Blue Ridge Mountains; otherwise, Lee's line of communication and support in the Shenandoah Valley and, particularly, all the food, fodder, and supplies he intended to forward there from Pennsylvania would be threatened if Hooker actually followed any northward advance of his army on the west side of those mountains. With a "suggestion" by General Stuart that he authorize an operation behind Hooker by the mounted arm of the army, Lee determined that the best way to protect his own line of communication and supply—which was growing longer every day—and his rear was to disrupt Hooker's communications and preoccupy the Union cavalry. A diversionary cavalry operation was planned which, at the same time, could scour the countryside behind Hooker for forage.[27]

With the cavalry brigades of Brigadier Generals Wade Hampton and Fitzhugh Lee and Colonel John R. Chambliss, a six-gun battery of artillery, and three days' rations, Stuart started out from Salem Depot on 24 June and rode toward Bristoe Station. After Longstreet's and Hill's Corps vacated their positions and moved north, Stuart left behind the brigades of Generals Jones and Robertson to guard the mountain passes—Snicker's and Ashby's Gaps—leading to the Shenandoah Valley. Lee's army would have cavalry protection for its rear as well as for the approaches to its critical line of communication and supply in the Shenandoah.[28]

Lee quickly moved Longstreet's and Hill's Corps northward. Crossing the Potomac via Boteler's Ford at Shepherdstown in newly formed West Virginia on 24 June, Hill's Corps was spotted by a Union wigwag signal station atop Maryland Heights near Harpers Ferry. It was all the definitive information that Hooker ever received of Lee's movements across the Potomac River. The next day Longstreet's Corps splashed across the Potomac at the ford at Williamsport with Lee himself riding beside his "old war horse." Stuart had bottled up all of the Union cavalry.[29]

By 28 June Longstreet's and Hill's Corps were just north of Chambersburg, near Lee's headquarters. Ewell's three divisions were deeper into Pennsylvania; Rodes's and Johnson's Divisions were at Carlisle, and Early's Division was at York and Wrightsville. Only three days into the undertaking, Stuart was well behind Hooker. Thus far the campaign had been a textbook operation.[30]

Chambersburg stood in the Cumberland Valley. The South Mountain range—the northern extension of the Blue Ridge Mountains—loomed to the east and the Allegheny Mountains to the west. Up and down the valley ran the Cumberland Valley Turnpike, a macadamized road that extended to the Potomac River. From Chambersburg, Lee could rely on macadamized valley roads that ran nearly 170 miles south to Staunton, Virginia, broken only by the Potomac. At Staunton, the Virginia Central Railroad ran directly into Richmond. Lee would communicate with his government and his army would send out and receive regular shipments of mail by means of those roads and the railroad throughout the time they were north of the Potomac River. That system would form Lee's lifeline; once he maneuvered the enemy north of the Potomac, he would never move his army away from the ready access to those turnpikes or allow it to be denied their use. To borrow a term used by one military theorist of the nineteenth century, Lee's army, its base of supply, and its line of communication formed a "unity" that would never be broken.[31]

On the night of 27 June Lee had written to General Ewell from army headquarters at Chambersburg, ordering a concentration of the army at Cashtown, a tiny village in Adams County, Pennsylvania, situated at the base of the eastern slope of the South Mountain range and connected to Chambersburg and the Cumberland Valley by a macadamized turnpike. Lee similarly instructed Longstreet and Hill. Having received intelligence that Hooker's army had crossed the Potomac and was on the National Road as far west as Middletown, Maryland, Lee sought to concentrate his army at the base of the mountains and along his line of communication and supply.[32]

In compliance with Lee's orders, Ewell ordered the withdrawal of Early's Division west from the Susquehanna River and the withdrawal of Rodes's and Johnson's Divisions south from Carlisle on 29 and 30 June. Generals Rodes, Johnson, and Early had their divisions on the move the next day. Johnson was directed to take a route back down the Cumberland Valley, west of the mountains, and then to move through Cashtown Pass, as his division was protecting an immense reserve wagon train of purchased, impressed, and confiscated quartermaster and subsistence stores, the product of two full weeks of foraging by Ewell's Corps.[33]

Stuart, at that time, was four days into his operation and behind Hooker's army. When his weary troopers finally appeared at Dover, Pennsylvania, on 1 July, Early's Division was gone. Stuart would not reach Lee's army until the

Adalbert Volck drawing of General J. E .B. Stuart and his men with captured horses in Pennsylvania. Library of Congress, Washington, D.C.

afternoon of 2 July, hauling behind his columns, aside from his own trains, more than 150 wagons loaded with hay and oats along with 900 mules, all captured from the enemy near Rockville, Maryland, on 28 June.[34]

When Lee ordered the concentration at Cashtown, he was not only aware of the presence of the Union Army of the Potomac near Middletown, Maryland, and the newly constituted Department of West Virginia under Brigadier General Benjamin F. Kelley at Grafton and New Creek astride the Baltimore and Ohio Railroad, but also of an army assembling to his north in response to his invasion of Pennsylvania. Since 10 June emergency troops were being raised in Pennsylvania and neighboring states and sent to Harrisburg, Pennsylvania, forming the new Department of the Susquehanna commanded by the former Army of the Potomac Second Corps commander, Major General Darius Nash Couch. The department had only about 250 men in Harrisburg on 15 June, but the number would rise to over 31,000 in July. Lee used Northern newspapers to obtain intelligence, and news of the gathering of the emergency troops was widely printed. Although these troops were hardly a match for Lee's veterans, they could be a serious threat if combined with the Army of the Potomac and the Department of West Virginia in any coordinated operation.[35]

In addition to Couch's Department of the Susquehanna, Lee also had some information about elements of General Milroy's Union forces that fled north to Harpers Ferry and northwest to Bloody Run in Bedford County, Pennsylvania, after Ewell defeated them at Winchester and Martinsburg on 14 June. Those broken units that fled to Harpers Ferry, often referred to as the "debris of Winchester," were being assimilated into a division commanded by Major General William H. French. The "debris of Winchester" units that wound up at Bloody Run were completely cut off from communication with Union forces east of the Cumberland Valley. All of the remnants of Milroy's commands at Bloody Run and in the Cumberland Valley were ostensibly within General Couch's Department and were close to Lee's rear. Although those troops appeared to be a less-than-effective fighting force, they could prove problematic as there were nearly six thousand of them.[36]

Through the South Mountain range there are six key passes between Cashtown and the Potomac River: Cashtown, Monterey, Raven Rock, Turner's, Fox's, and Crampton's. For Lee's foraging operation to succeed with the enemy nearby, he had to protect the passes at Cashtown and Monterey, about ten miles south of Cashtown. Otherwise, if the enemy seized them, Lee would have no option but to withdraw from the Cumberland Valley altogether, as his ability to gather food, fodder, and supplies there—as well as to defend himself in the area—would be lost. The pass at Raven Rock, between Smithsburg and Thurmont, Maryland, was winding, steep, narrow, and of little use for the movement of an army and its immense trains. Turner's Pass at Boonsboro, more than twenty-five miles due south of Cashtown, and Fox's Pass were occupied by elements of French's Division after 28 June, as was Crampton's Pass, about six miles south of Turner's Pass. Through Turner's Pass in the South Mountain range ran the great National Road connecting Frederick and Hagerstown and crossing Lee's rear in the Cumberland Valley. To address the challenge posed by Turner's Pass, Lee, on 1 July, directed Jones's and Robertson's two cavalry brigades to leave Ashby's and Snicker's Gaps in Virginia and move into the Cumberland Valley to protect his line of communication and supply as well as his rear.[37]

Lee intended to position his army along the base of the South Mountain range covering the passes at Cashtown and Monterey. With the mountains to his rear and the two dominant passes in his control, Lee, even without Stuart's three brigades, would be in an enviable position. It would be suicidal for Hooker to attack him there. While holding the eastern entrances to Cashtown and Monterey Passes Lee could seek food, fodder, and supplies for his army in the Cumberland Valley behind him. The army would screen and protect the foraging parties while occupying a position covering the passes that was virtually impregnable to attack from the east. Because of his superior location as well as his concern for his overextended line of communication and supply, Lee later asserted that he never intended to engage the enemy along the eastern base of the South Mountain range unless attacked.[38]

Joseph B. Polley, a veteran of the Fourth Texas of Hood's Division, recalled the purpose of the Cashtown concentration years after the war. Although he was a lowly private, his words resonate. "The topographic features of the country around Cashtown," he wrote, "were peculiarly favorable for a defensive battle, and for drawing supplies from the fertile Cumberland Valley west of South Mountain. The presence there of the Confederate army threatened not only Washington and Baltimore, but as well, Philadelphia, and so seriously that General Lee could safely count on drawing the enemy to his front and thus relieving his rear from danger. Therefore, he proposed to concentrate his army there."[39]

By 29 June the leading elements of Hill's Corps began arriving at Cashtown. Longstreet was marching toward Cashtown from Chambersburg with two of his divisions, Hood's and McLaws's. Ewell was moving two of his divisions south from Carlisle and one west from Wrightsville to the point of concentration. To protect the tremendous wagon trains of quartermaster and subsistence stores that had been collected from the area during the invasion and to ensure the protection of Ewell's reserve train, which was approaching Chambersburg under the escort of Johnson's Division, Longstreet directed Pickett's Division to remain at Chambersburg. It would be relieved by Imboden's command. Brigadier General Evander McIvor Law's Brigade of Hood's Division was ordered to remain at New Guilford, Pennsylvania, to protect the trains of quartermaster and subsistence stores collected by Longstreet's Corps in the area. Lee was obsessed with the protection of those stores.[40]

Imboden's cavalry command was moving rapidly to relieve Pickett's Division, but it was still two days away. Lee ordered Imboden not only to protect the trains when he arrived at Chambersburg but also to continue to forage. He wrote to Imboden: "It will be necessary for you to have your men well together and always on alert and to pay strict attention to the safety of the trains which are for the present placed under your charge, and upon the safety of which the operations of this army depend."[41]

Until 28 June Lee must have been satisfied; he had maneuvered the Army of the Potomac out of war-ravaged Virginia; his army was moving toward the eastern base of the South Mountain range, and it was collecting the supplies it desperately needed to prolong its life. The Cumberland and Shenandoah

Valleys were free of the enemy. To date, Lee had shown total self-confidence in his ability to accomplish his mission.

From the moment the first Confederate soldiers reached the Maryland side of the Potomac River, west central Maryland and south central Pennsylvania were scoured by Confederate quartermasters and commissaries of subsistence for food, fodder, and supplies. Indeed, two days after his corps crossed the Potomac Lee instructed Ewell in writing: "Take what is necessary for the army and give the citizens . . . Confederate money or certificates."[42]

Back on 20 June Lee had congratulated Imboden on the number of cattle and horses he had "captured for the use of the army" and hoped that Imboden's "expectations of obtaining similar supplies [in Maryland and Pennsylvania would] be realized." Imboden did not let his commander down. Civilians living in the Potomac River Valley later observed Imboden's mounted troops, accompanied by large numbers of African American slaves, herding thousands of head of cattle, sheep, and hogs and hundreds of horses and mules from the area onto the Cumberland Valley Turnpike to be driven to Winchester, Virginia, Lee's base of supply. Imboden's veterans remembered impressing horses by the hundreds. Beyond horses, mules, cattle, sheep, and hogs, Imboden secured thousands of barrels of bacon and flour.[43]

The next day Lee issued General Order No. 72, directing the chiefs of the quartermaster, subsistence, ordnance, and medical departments of his army to "make requisitions upon the local authorities or inhabitants for the necessary supplies for their respective departments." Citizens who complied would be paid "the market price" by certificates of payment. If "the authorities or inhabitants neglected or refused to comply" with a requisition, their property would be "taken." If a person declined to receive payment, a receipt was nevertheless required to be completed for the property taken. Anyone removing or concealing property needed by the army, or attempting to do so, would see their property "seized." Lee did enjoin the soldiers in the ranks from taking or molesting private property, and, although much has been made of the injunction, that was all the protection afforded the citizens. As Major General William Dorsey Pender wrote his wife: "Our troops are sending [a] good deal of stock out of Penna. [to Winchester] and General Lee has issued [an] order which alto' [it] prevents plundering, at the same [time] makes arrangements for the bountiful supplying of our people."[44]

On 22 June Lee informed Ewell, who was then below Chambersburg: "It will depend upon the quantity of supplies obtained in [south central Pennsylvania] whether the rest of the army can follow. There may be enough for your command, but none for the others. Every exertion should, therefore, be made to locate and secure them. Beef we can drive with us, but bread we cannot carry, and must secure it in the country."[45]

No sooner had Ewell's Corps crossed the Potomac River than it began to take every usable item in sight. Major Charles C. Blacknall of the Twenty-third North Carolina was named provost marshal of the town of Williamsport as Rodes's Division occupied its environs on 15 June 1863. "Such a scramble for goods [by the soldiers]," he wrote, "was never before seen. I immediately took possession of all stores, hotels, bar rooms and selected through the quartermaster such articles as were needed by the Government." We "impress[ed] all the stores and government goods in town; all of which was done under my instructions; we got an immense deal of goods of all descriptions."

At Greencastle, Pennsylvania, on 23 June, Blacknall declared: "We are now in the most splendid country I ever saw, everything in the way of subsistence being in the most profuse abundance. Our army [is] being amply and abundantly supplied from this country and we cannot consume one tenth of the supplies before or around us, wheat, corn, oats, clover, beef, bacon, butter, etc. being in waste on all sides. We have secured thousands of horses and beef cattle, sending out parties in every direction to bring them in."[46]

Major John Alexander Harman, chief quartermaster of Ewell's Corps, demanded from the citizens of tiny Greencastle "100 saddles and bridles and 12 pistols." That was followed by a call for "two thousand pounds of lead, 1,000 pounds of leather, 100 pistols, 12 boxes of tin and 200 curry combs and brushes." The commissary of subsistence of the corps, through Major A. M. Mitchell, ordered town residents to bring him all the "onions, sauerkraut, potatoes, radishes, etc." that they could locate. That requisition represented precisely what Dr. Lafayette Guild directed the commissaries of subsistence to find in order to cure and ward off scurvy. Diseases of all kinds, including scurvy, seriously affected Ewell's Corps. On the march, one private recalled, the ambulances of every regiment of the corps "were filled with fever cases."[47]

Also on 23 June Lee wrote to President Davis, telling him for the first time about the foraging under way.

> In addition to the supplies that we have been able to gather in Fauquier and Loudoun Counties, in the Shenandoah Valley, and west of the Allegheny, we have collected sufficient [supplies] north of the Potomac for the support of Ewell's corps to the Thirtieth instant, and 1,700 barrels of flour are on hand in Maryland for the rest of the army. I hope we shall get enough for the subsistence of our men. Forage is very scarce, and

we have mainly to rely on grass for the animals. From the reports I receive, I believe we shall obtain enough salt for our purposes while north of the Potomac. . . . I shall continue to purchase all the supplies that are furnished me while north of the Potomac, impressing only when necessary.[48]

Ewell did not disappoint his commander. He reported to Lee that he had stopped at Chambersburg for one day to "secure supplies." "At Carlisle," he continued,

General George H. Steuart, who had been detached to McConnellsburg from Greencastle, rejoined the corps, bringing some cattle and horses. At Carlisle, Chambersburg and Shippensburg requisitions were made for supplies and the shops were searched, many valuable stores being secured. At Chambersburg, a [wagon] train was loaded with ordnance and medical stores and sent back [to Winchester]. Near 3,000 head of cattle were collected and sent back [to Winchester] by my corps, and my chief commissary of subsistence . . . notified [the army's commissary of subsistence] of the location of 5,000 barrels of flour along the route traveled by the command.[49]

On 24 June Ewell's chief quartermaster laid before Chambersburg city officials a requisition for "5,000 suits of clothing, including hats, boots and shoes; 100 good saddles; 100 good bridles; 5,000 bushels of grain (corn and oats); 10,000 lbs sole leather; 10,000 lbs horse-shoes; 400 lbs horse-shoe nails; also, the use of printing office and two printers to report at once." Later that day Ewell called for "6,000 lbs lead; 10,000 lbs harness leather; 50 boxes of tin; 1,000 curry combs and brushes; 2,000 lbs picket rope; 400 pistols; all the caps and powder in town; also, all the Neat's foot oil." Still later on the twenty-fourth Ewell's chief commissary of subsistence, Major Wells J. Hawks, demanded from Chambersburg "50,000 lbs bread; 100 sacks salt; 30 barrels molasses; 500 barrels flour; 25 barrels vinegar; 25 barrels beans; 25 barrels dried fruit; 25 barrels sauerkraut; 25 barrels potatoes; 11,000 lbs coffee; 10,000 lbs sugar; 100,000 lbs hard bread."[50]

When Judge F. M. Kimmell, on behalf of the citizenry, claimed that the town was unable to obtain the supplies Ewell demanded, Ewell's quartermasters and commissary of subsistence officers opened every store, warehouse, and barn in Chambersburg, seizing everything they could find, including all the horses, mules, cattle, sheep, and hogs, along with saddles, wagons, and harnesses, for miles around. Afterward one resident wrote that the townspeople "are at a stand-still in everything. No horses are about except blind ones, and they are scarce and at a premium."[51]

Generally, Lee's men did not destroy private property. There were exceptions, however. Ewell's soldiers burned the furnace, sawmill, two forges, rolling mill, office, and storeroom of the ironworks complex of "notorious" radical Republican Thaddeus Stevens at Caledonia, east of Chambersburg. But before they torched the buildings they seized every horse, mule, and harness, "four thousand pounds of bacon," molasses, "one thousand dollars worth of corn," and "huge heaps of pig iron, bar iron, rod iron in almost every form" worth at least "four thousand dollars," as well as "all the bellows and bellow-houses and run-out establishments." Congressman Stevens's iron business would keep some of Lee's horses and mules in shoes for a considerable period.[52]

Reviewing General Early's operations in York and Wrightsville, Ewell reported that Early "levied a contribution on the citizens of York, obtaining, among other things, $28,600 in United States currency . . . 1,000 hats, 1,200 pairs of shoes, and 1,000 pairs of socks." Colonel Fremantle recorded that while Longstreet's Corps was marching toward Chambersburg, he observed "great quantities of horses, mules, wagons, beef and other necessities" being sent back down the roads to Winchester by Ewell's quartermasters and commissaries of subsistence. Dr. Charles E. Lippitt, surgeon of the Fifty-seventh Virginia, recorded on 24 June that Jenkins's cavalry brigade alone had already sent back to Winchester 2,400 horses and 1,700 cattle. Three days later Lippitt saw "several droves of horses going south" as Longstreet's Corps approached Chambersburg. Indeed, a soldier in the Fifth Alabama in Rodes's Division wrote: "We are taking all the horses & cattle that can be found, & have already got hundreds of horses & droves of beeves."[53]

A diarist in Winchester, Miss Laura Lee, wrote on 24 June that "large herds of cattle are passing through [Winchester] every day, sent back from Pennsylvania. Our army is to be subsisting entirely in the enemy's country." Again on the twenty-ninth she noted: "[Our] cavalry [is] flying around [Pennsylvania] in every direction, bringing in horses, cattle, sheep, etc. [to Winchester]." Dr. Spencer Glasgow Welch, surgeon of the Thirteenth South Carolina in Pender's Division, in a letter of 28 June from near Chambersburg, told his wife: "We are taking everything we need—horses, cattle, sheep, flour, groceries and goods of all kinds, and making as clean a sweep as possible."[54]

On 30 June Colonel Bradley T. Johnson, commander of the garrison at Winchester and Martinsburg until he returned to the army on 2 July, informed Secretary of War Seddon of his "cleanup" efforts in the lower Shenandoah Valley. In the report he noted that Captain John H. McNeill of Imboden's command that day "passed down the Valley road with 740 head of sheep, 160 head of cattle, 40 horses from Pennsylvania." By then, the farmlands around Winchester must have been overwhelmed with impressed and confiscated herds of cattle, sheep, hogs, horses, and mules as well as wagons loaded with quartermaster and subsistence stores.[55]

Although no accounting was ever made, it is reasonable to conclude that while in Pennsylvania Lee's army seized between 45,000 and 50,000 head of cattle, about 35,000 head of sheep, and thousands of hogs. More than half of the cattle, sheep, and hogs were driven back to Lee's supply base at Winchester. There is no way of knowing how many horses and mules were taken; many were immediately taken up by mounted commands, artillery batteries, and ordnance, quartermaster, and subsistence trains. Large numbers, though, were driven to Winchester for the army's future use. Diarists recorded that hundreds of horses and mules were sent to Winchester every day during the first two weeks of the invasion. That, coupled with the thousands known to have been put into service while the army was in Pennsylvania and Maryland, would indicate that Lee's troops seized more than 20,000 horses and mules.[56]

No records exist of Ewell's foraging, though the testimony of one of his brigade quartermasters does survive. Major James C. Bryan was the quartermaster of Colonel Edward O'Neal's Brigade of Rodes's Division. In the two weeks prior to the fighting at Gettysburg, Bryan recalled impressing some of the 219 horses and mules pulling his trains. To feed those animals alone, he impressed more than 42,000 pounds of corn and 49,000 pounds of hay. He also seized other quartermaster stores and the wagons necessary to haul his acquisitions back to Virginia. O'Neal's Brigade was only one of thirteen in Ewell's Corps.[57]

In addition, Captain Charles Frederic Bahnson, assistant quartermaster of the Second North Carolina Battalion in Brigadier General Junius Daniel's Brigade, Rodes's Division, wrote to his father about the foraging by Ewell's Corps. "We have pressed a good many things into service," he wrote:

> I think there is a scarcity of the following articles in that portion of the Keystone State which had the honor of receiving a visit from us, viz. — horses, mules, cattle, sheep, hogs, chickens, turkeys, onions & all kinds of garden truck, wagons, carriages, harness & everything in fact that could be used by us. Fences are rather scarce, & the crops in the fields in many places have been used to feed our horses, but the crops are just as safe without fences as they would be with them, for we left but little stock to run around & destroy crops.[58]

Longstreet's Corps arrived in Chambersburg on 28 June. That day General Longstreet, in Lee's presence, demanded of the Chambersburg mayor that the town deliver to him 60,000 rations; if it failed to do so, Longstreet warned, the quartermasters of his corps would seize everything. Of course, the town was unable to comply. Longstreet undoubtedly knew that it could never meet his demands; the order seems to have been made as an excuse to take whatever Ewell's quartermasters had missed. Longstreet's officers went to work in earnest. As Adjutant Alexander McNeill of the Second South Carolina wrote, the quartermasters "impress horses, cattle and everything else that can be of use to the army and offer in payment Confederate money which, when this is refused, they then leave with the parties a receipt stating the articles and quantity impressed together with the market prices. The stores are opened and all goods needed for the use of the army seized." Colonel Fremantle recorded that quartermaster and commissary of subsistence officers had orders to "open the stores" of towns "by force" and "seize all that [was] wanted for the army."[59]

What quartermaster records from the invasion of Pennsylvania still exist reveal a systematic effort on the part of Lee's army to purchase, impress, or confiscate all the food, fodder, and supplies required to keep the army in the field. The reports consist of manually prepared charts showing the items secured, the parties from whom they were secured, and the amounts paid, if anything. All report forms were prepared in blank in advance and listed, with some variations, virtually identical items to be secured: corn, oats, bran, wheat, rye, hay, letters and envelopes, blank books, pencils, horses, mules, four-horse wagons, two-horse wagons, collars, hames, harness, smith tools, scythes, planks, salt, boots, sledgehammers, and curry combs. Some forms also listed chain halters, hatchets, files, chisels, screwdrivers, vices, hats, socks, nails, rawhide, sheet iron, wagon bows, buckets, forge equipment, bellows, anvils, and even needles. In sum, they obtained all the food, fodder, and equipment the army needed along with horses, mules, and wagons to haul the provisions back to Virginia.[60]

Between 25 and 30 June Major John Denis Keiley Jr., chief quartermaster of Longstreet's Corps, recorded purchasing large quantities of fodder and supplies, including 7,112 pounds of corn, 2,000 pounds of hay, 50 buckets, 50 curry combs, 59 halters, 20 horses, 12 wagons, 4 wagon bows, 12 horse carts, 1 anvil, 3 augers, 18 bits, 21 files, 28 hatchets, 2 sledgehammers, 4 chisels, 11 scythes, 3 vices, 300 hats, 500 nails, 72 pieces of rawhide, 14 bars of steel, 8 slabs of sheet iron, along with shovels, screwdrivers, chains, needles, lead pencils, inkstands, and rubber.[61]

During the same period the quartermaster of Pickett's Division, Major

Robert Taylor Scott, purchased or confiscated 32,500 pounds of hay, 711 bushels of corn, 352 bushels of oats, 36 bushels of bran, 80 horses, 625 pieces of stationery and envelopes, and innumerable small items. One of Pickett's soldiers, Private Jimmie Booker of the Thirty-eighth Virginia, wrote to his cousin, summarizing the foraging efforts of the division: "Our quartermasters and commissaries has goten a great many necessarys for our army since we have bin in this state."[62]

From 24 June to month's end, Major Moses B. George, quartermaster of Hood's Division, bought 36 horses, 2 wagons, 964 bushels of corn, and numerous other articles. For that same six-day period the First Corps Reserve Artillery quartermaster reported purchasing 554 bushels of corn, 568 bushels of oats, 38 bushels of wheat, 7,100 pounds of hay, 5 horses, and countless small items.[63]

Brigade and regimental quartermasters were busy as well. The quartermaster of Brigadier General Paul Jones Semmes's Brigade confiscated three forges, three blacksmith hammers, a bellows, and an anvil; he bought the steel to be used in the forges and a one-horse wagon to haul much of it back to Virginia on 29 and 30 June. Between 26 and 28 June Brigadier General Henry L. Benning's quartermaster contented himself with finding forage; he purchased 1,750 pounds of hay and impressed 150 bushels of corn. To use with the forges confiscated by Semmes's quartermaster, Benning's quartermaster also impressed 10 bushels of coal. Brigadier General George T. Anderson's quartermaster confiscated 2,128 pounds of corn and 384 pounds of oats. On 27 June Brigadier General Evander McIvor Law's Brigade purchased 120 bushels of oats, while the Texas Brigade quartermaster bought 155 bushels of corn and 46 bushels of oats. Brigadier General William Barksdale's quartermaster bought 180 bushels of corn, 2 horses, and 3 ambulance springs. Regimental and artillery battalion quartermasters were similarly busy. Captain William Thomas Hardy, assistant quartermaster of Cabell's Artillery Battalion, reported purchasing 395 bushels of corn and 80 bushels of oats between 26 and 29 June.[64]

While near Leitersburg, Maryland, on 26 June, Brigadier General Alfred Moore Scales's quartermaster impressed slightly over 186 pounds of corn for the brigade's 33 mules and 40 horses. The next day the brigade quartermaster impressed 650 pounds of hay for the animals acquired from one farmer in southern Franklin County, Pennsylvania.[65]

Quartermaster and commissary of subsistence officers in all three corps were ordered to confiscate private property; to do so, they used large numbers of slaves who were traveling with the army as well as soldiers from the ranks.

Thousands of slaves accompanied their Confederate masters to battle; thousands were in the army under lease arrangements with their masters and the quartermaster service. According to Winchester diarist Laura Lee, a sizable number of slaves from Winchester and Frederick County, Virginia, accompanied Imboden's, Jenkins's, and Ewell's troops into Pennsylvania to assist in the foraging effort; many of them had labored for Milroy's forces up until the Confederates forced the surrender of the Union garrisons at Winchester and Martinsburg. Regarding his slave Joe, General Pender wrote his wife on 28 June: "Joe enters into the invasion with much gusto and is quite active in looking up hidden property. In fact the negroes seem to have more feeling in the matter than white men and have come to the conclusion that they will [im]press horses, etc., etc., to any amount."[66]

Some free African Americans were seized by Lee's troops during their foraging operations in Pennsylvania. Rachel Cormany, a resident of Chambersburg, wrote in her diary on 16 June that General Jenkins's leading Confederate cavalry brigade was "hunting up the contrabands and driving them off by droves. . . . Some of the colored people who were raised here were taken along—I sat on the front step as they were driven by just like we would drive cattle. Some laughed and seemed not to care—but nearly all hung their heads." Cormany and other civilians such as the Reverend Dr. Henry Reeves, also of Chambersburg, claimed that women and children were among those taken by the Confederates. The diaries of Cormany and Philip Schaff suggest that most such incidents were associated either with the advance of Jenkins's Brigade or the foraging by Imboden's Brigade. The account of the campaign by Jacob Hoke, a Chambersburg merchant, intimates that partisans operating on the fringes of Lee's army were responsible for most of the seizures of African Americans.[67]

When Lee transferred his army's military operations to the once peaceful southern Pennsylvania, the war's brutal aspects suddenly descended on the region's civilian population. The Army of Northern Virginia foraged in the area on a massive scale and utilized thousands of African American slaves traveling in its trains to assist in the effort. As well, elements of the army used almost every other means at their disposal, including seizing free African Americans, it appears, to locate and gather stores and livestock. Although there is only scant evidence of civilians being physically harmed, the seizures of free African Americans undoubtedly occasioned much grief and heartache among those who lost loved ones or who were separated from their families. The unfortunate captives became, in effect, runaway slaves returned to Confederate control.[68]

The correspondence of some Confederates during the campaign betrays a desire on their part to seize African Americans and return them to slavery. Major Charles Blacknall of the Twenty-third North Carolina, for example, wrote home on 18 June stating that he hoped to procure blacks in Pennsylvania "for southern exportation." Blacknall never found an opportunity, however; he was badly wounded on 1 July and captured by Union soldiers four days later. In a similar vein, Colonel William Christian of the Fifty-fifth Virginia wrote his wife on 28 June that his men "took a lot of negroes yesterday. I was offered my choices but as I could not get them back home I would not take them." "In fact," added Christian, "my humanity revolted at taking the poor devils away from their homes." Many historians have quoted Christian's letter, but the original unfortunately was lost, rendering the Virginian's testimony somewhat problematical.[69]

The extent of the seizures of free African Americans and their ultimate disposition are simply unknown. Whether the blacks who were sighted being herded along by Confederates, riding in their trains, or foraging were slaves laboring in Lee's army or local residents who had been captured were, in most instances, impossible for civilian observers to discern. It appears that some African Americans "captured" by Lee's men were actually runaways from their own trains. As one Chambersburg resident exclaimed to a Confederate quartermaster, "Your negroes run to us a little more willingly than our horses run to you." How many slaves fled Lee's army before the fighting erupted at Gettysburg, of course, is also unknown. Furthermore, it was impossible for civilians to determine whether the free African Americans seized were actually transported to Virginia. Only one Confederate record indicates that Lee's army held "captured contrabands" during the invasion—a 1 July order from General Longstreet directing General Pickett and his division to march from Chambersburg to Gettysburg and bring those captives with them "for further disposition." There is no record that any prominent army commander ordered the seizure of African Americans, and there is no reference that the contrabands were captured by any command other than Jenkins's and Imboden's Brigades. Likewise, no record exists indicating the ultimate disposition of the captured contrabands referred to by Longstreet.[70]

A few accounts of seizures of free African Americans in Pennsylvania by Confederate partisan bands operating forty to fifty miles behind Lee's lines record their captives being taken to Virginia. In addition, some historians have claimed that two Confederate records indicate that blacks were delivered to Virginia from Pennsylvania and were held in Confederate prisons, although it is unknown why they were prisoners of war. In fact, it is unclear from the records that those prisoners were seized in Pennsylvania by any of Lee's men.[71]

The invasion of southern Pennsylvania caused many inhabitants, black as well as white, to go into hiding or flee their homes. Many left in panic, taking with them whatever they could carry. The roads leading to Harrisburg, Baltimore, and the Allegheny Mountains were jammed at times with terrified refugees. Some never returned. In most cases, of those free African Americans whom residents claimed never returned it could not be said whether they were actually seized and taken back to Virginia by Lee's men or fled from them.[72]

In sum, it is accurate to conclude that, apart from terrifying many civilians and causing large numbers of them to refugee from their homes, elements of Lee's invading army seized free blacks in Pennsylvania, most likely for use in locating and collecting quartermaster and subsistence stores, including horses, mules, cattle, sheep, and hogs. Many of those captured accompanied the army as far as Gettysburg. Some free African Americans who were seized by partisan commands operating on the fringes of the army were taken to Virginia. Little else is known for certain.

Irrespective of how stores were seized, or by whom, Lee enforced a system of payment to property owners. Whatever was impressed or purchased by quartermasters and commissary of subsistence officers was paid for with Confederate money or, more often, with certificates redeemable in Confederate currency—all absolutely valueless to the property owners. In many cases, the items were simply taken. Often entries in the quartermaster records show the property owner "not found" and the articles "confiscated." If anyone attempted to hide property, Confederate quartermasters and commissary of subsistence officers were under orders to confiscate it. Private John O. Casler of the Thirty-third Virginia wrote: "Our quartermasters managed to gobble up everything they came to. They would take citizens' horses and wagons and load them with provisions and goods from the stores."[73]

The quartermasters and commissary of subsistence officers of Lee's army did not limit their foraging to the locality where their units bivouacked. The reports reveal that quartermaster parties purchased or confiscated property from farms and towns within a ten-mile radius of wherever their units were camped. Commissary of subsistence parties did likewise, ravaging Washington County, Maryland, and Franklin County, Pennsylvania, and the rich farming regions from Carlisle all the way to the Susquehanna River. Sergeant John S. Tucker of the Fifth Alabama in Rodes's Division recalled on 23 June going all the way "to the foot of the Allegany Mountains with a squad of cavalry after Beef cattle" and having "a lively time." That day he and the mounted squad drove back one hundred head of cattle.[74]

The extent of Lee's foraging was not lost on his enemy. The headquarters of the Army of the Potomac was flooded with intelligence about it. From the day he assumed command of the Army of the Potomac—28 June—Major General George Gordon Meade was informed about the enormous "amount of transportation" accompanying Lee's army and how the Confederates were "helping themselves to everything they needed." He received reports that Lee's men were driving large numbers of cattle and horses toward Williamsport and that they were "pressing all the mills to grind flour, which they would haul away as fast as ground." Accounts from Chambersburg all the way to the Susquehanna River brought the same news about Lee's systematic efforts.[75]

The effort to obtain food, fodder, and equipment would never stop; even three days of battle at Gettysburg did not interfere with it. While the fighting raged, foraging parties were busy as far as forty-five miles away from the army collecting quartermaster and subsistence stores. Corps, division, and brigade quartermasters made sure that a sufficient number of empty wagons accompanied the troops as they marched toward Gettysburg so that the foraging could continue there. While their units were engaged in battle, quartermasters and commissary of subsistence officers scoured the area behind the lines for food, fodder, and supplies. By 1 July the reserve wagon train carrying impressed stores for the army obtained in the two weeks that Ewell's Corps traveled north of the Potomac River was more than fourteen miles long; the trains of Ewell's three divisions, as well, were together nearly twenty miles long, and Longstreet's and Hill's trains were growing by the hour.[76]

While quartermaster and commissary of subsistence teams were busy obtaining stores, the army's horses and mules were given as much grazing time as possible; this was one of Lee's principal objectives of the invasion. Recorded William S. White of the Third Company of the Richmond Howitzers on 25 June: "Our horses are faring much better than when we were in Virginia; we give them corn, oats and clover hay in abundance [in Pennsylvania]."[77]

Beyond the organized activities of the quartermasters and commissaries of subsistence, there was another kind of foraging. Private soldiers took extraordinary liberties with Lee's 21 June injunction. Hardly a man who kept a diary or wrote a letter home did not comment about taking all the food and supplies he could find from houses or shops in Pennsylvania. In almost every instance, the soldiers justified their actions by claiming that their enemy had ravaged and pillaged their own homeland. Although order was generally maintained and citizens, for the most part, were unharmed, the Confederates helped themselves to everything they could find. Foraging was carried out by day and night shifts.

Private Joseph B. Polley of the Fourth Texas recalled awaking on the morning of 30 June north of Chambersburg after a night of foraging. "Every square foot of an acre of ground not occupied by a sleeping or standing soldier, was covered with choice food for the hungry," he wrote:

> Chickens, turkeys, ducks and geese squawked, gobbled, quacked, cackled and hissed in harmonious unison as deft and energetic hands seized them for slaughter, and scarcely waiting for them to die, sent their feathers flying in all directions; and scattered around in bewildering confusion and gratifying profusion appeared immense loaves of bread and chunks of corned beef, hams, and sides of bacon, cheeses, crocks of apple-butter, jelly, jam, pickles, and preserves, bowls of yellow butter, demijohns of buttermilk, and other eatables too numerous to mention. . . . The scene [was] utterly indescribable.[78]

Although General Lee enjoined his soldiers from plundering, it is known that he observed wanton breaches of his order and did nothing to stop them. Private Tally Simpson of the Third South Carolina watched as thirty or forty soldiers seized every guinea fowl, turkey, and chicken in one Pennsylvania farmyard. Lee happened to ride by as a frightened and angry woman who lived in the nearby farmhouse ran outside yelling for him to stop them. Lee merely touched the brim of his hat and said, "Good morning madam"; he rode on down the road to the complete amusement of the men.[79]

A critical part of Lee's operation involved strikes against the logistical support systems that could be used by the enemy. Elements of Ewell's Corps marched as far east as the Susquehanna River and as far north as Carlisle. While their foraging was progressing at a feverish pace, pioneer teams were directed to cut telegraph wires and tear up railroad tracks, burn railroad bridges, and destroy rolling stock along the Northern Central Railroad from below Harrisburg to Hanover Junction and along the York and Cumberland Railroad and the Hanover Railroad, west to Gettysburg, and the spur line to Littlestown. In the end, Ewell's Corps destroyed nineteen bridges of the Northern Central and Hanover Railroads between Harrisburg, York, and Hanover Junction and three more between Hanover Junction and Gettysburg. If Lee was to position his army at the base of the South Mountain range near Cashtown, he had to ensure that the Army of the Potomac could not use the railroads from Baltimore or Washington to provide it with supplies in his front. The tracks of the Cumberland Valley Railroad between Chambersburg and Carlisle were ripped up and the bridges burned for nearly twenty miles to blunt any effort by Couch's Department of the Susquehanna to approach Lee from Harrisburg and rely on that railroad as its means of supply.[80]

Lee, it appears, intended to remain on the eastern base of the South Mountain range at Cashtown in order to forage his army in the Cumberland Valley for a considerable period, as it would take anywhere from five to ten days for those railroads his men wrecked east of Gettysburg to reopen. Lee knew that the Army of the Potomac could not reach his front at Cashtown and remain there without having a rail line from Baltimore to a railhead in its immediate rear to keep it supplied. Lee eliminated Gettysburg as a possible supply base.

On 30 June Pettigrew's Brigade of Major General Henry Heth's Division was ordered to advance from Cashtown eight miles east to Gettysburg. Heth claimed that the purpose of the movement was to obtain more forage and supplies from that rich farming country. Combat troops always accompanied quartermaster and subsistence teams to provide protection. Pettigrew found enemy troops present west of Gettysburg and withdrew to Cashtown. When General Hill arrived at Cashtown, Heth informed him of Pettigrew's discovery. Heth later reported that Hill then ordered him to proceed to Gettysburg with his whole division and a battalion of artillery in order to, among other things, protect the foraging parties of his corps that would be working in the area.[81]

Until 1 July, Lee labored to concentrate his army at Cashtown. If he had intentions beyond foraging and concentrating the army in a good defensive position, he never communicated them to anyone. Only three days before the battle at Gettysburg began, General Pender wrote his wife: "Gen. Lee intimates to no one what he is up to, and we can only surmise." That day the reserve quartermaster and subsistence train was arriving at Chambersburg and being directed toward Cashtown, and Lee himself was engaged in moving his own headquarters from Greenwood—about fifteen miles west of Gettysburg—to Cashtown.[82]

Heth's advance fell upon two brigades of dismounted Union cavalry and, by midmorning, the left wing of the Army of the Potomac. A desperate and

MAP 1.1   29–30 June 1863.
Lee having destroyed bridges along the Northern Central and Hanover Railroads, Meade selects a defense line along Pipe Creek using Westminster as his supply base and the Western Maryland Railroad, with its spur to Union Bridge, as his supply line.

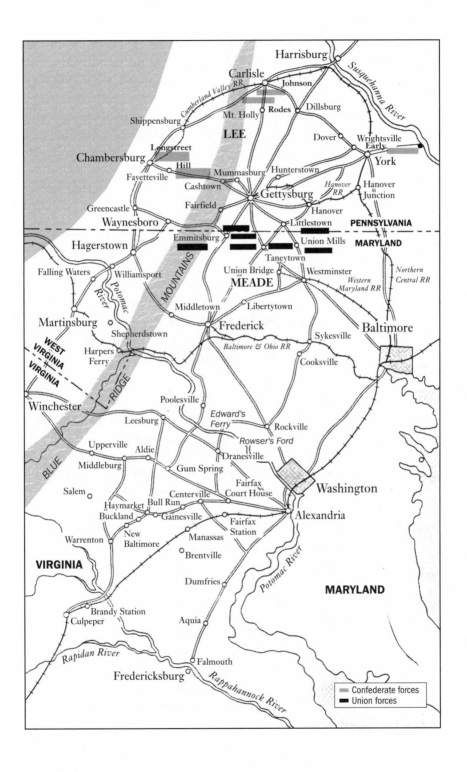

Harrisburg

Susquehanna River

Carlisle
Johnson

Cumberland Valley RR

Shippensburg
Mt. Holly
Rodes
Dillsburg

LEE
Dover
Wrightsville
Early

Longstreet

Chambersburg
Hill
Fayetteville
Mummasburg
Hunterstown
York

Cashtown
Hanover RR
Hanover Junction

Greencastle
Fairfield
Gettysburg

Waynesboro
Hanover

Littlestown
PENNSYLVANIA

Hagerstown
Emmitsburg
Union Mills
MARYLAND

Falling Waters
Williamsport
Taneytown

Potomac River
Union Bridge
Westminster
Northern Central RR

MEADE
Western Maryland RR

Middletown
Libertytown

Martinsburg
Shepherdstown
Frederick
Sykesville
Baltimore

Harpers Ferry
Baltimore & Ohio RR
Cooksville

Poolesville

Winchester
Leesburg
Edward's Ferry
Rockville

Upperville
Aldie
Rowser's Ford

Middleburg
Gum Spring
Dranesville

Salem
Fairfax
Court House
Washington

Centerville
Haymarket
Bull Run
Buckland
Gainesville
Fairfax Station
Alexandria

Warrenton
New Baltimore
Manassas

VIRGINIA
Brentville
Potomac River
MARYLAND

Dumfries

Brandy Station
Culpeper
Aquia

Rapidan River
Falmouth

Fredericksburg
Rappahannock River

	Confederate forces
	Union forces

bloody fight ensued that ultimately brought Pender's Division and two divisions—Rodes's and Early's—of Ewell's Corps into the fray. By the end of the first day, Lee had crushed the Union forces west and north of Gettysburg, taking more than four thousand prisoners. Disorganized Union soldiers were rallied on heights that bore such names as Culp's Hill, Cemetery Hill, and Cemetery Ridge. Hurrying to reinforce the shattered Union forces at Gettysburg under General Meade's urgent orders were five more Union corps and the Artillery Reserve.[83]

Lee determined to continue the fight the next day even though he then occupied a disadvantageous position. Lee later wrote:

> It had not been intended to deliver a general battle so far from our base unless attacked, but coming unexpectedly upon the whole Federal Army, to withdraw through the mountains with our extensive trains would have been difficult and dangerous. At the same time we were unable to await an attack, as the country was unfavorable for collecting supplies in the presence of the enemy, who could restrain our foraging parties by holding the mountain passes with local and other troops. A battle had, therefore, become in a measure unavoidable, and the success already gained gave hope of favorable issue.

Lee had abandoned his own purely defensive plans to forage and reequip his army after he had tasted victory on enemy soil. In the process, he had allowed himself to be lured away from the safety of the mountains.[84]

The audacity of Lee's decision to continue the battle at Gettysburg may be found in an examination of the "Report of Ordnance Stores on Hand in the Reserve Ordnance Train" of the Army of Northern Virginia at Chambersburg on 29 June. That report, a copy of which was delivered to Lieutenant Colonel Briscoe G. Baldwin, Lee's chief of ordnance, reveals only enough reserve artillery ammunition to supply a single small battalion. There were fewer musket caps in the train than there were fighting men in the army and not enough rounds of ammunition for muskets to supply a brigade. Lee had ordered another train of ordnance from Richmond on the eve of the campaign, but he had heard nothing of its whereabouts by 1 July.[85]

Among the problems resulting from Lee's decision to continue the fighting near Gettysburg on 1 July were the confusion and delays in moving troops, especially Longstreet's Corps and Johnson's Division of Ewell's Corps, to the front due to Lee's overriding concern for the safety of the reserve quartermaster and subsistence train and stores being collected between Chambersburg and Cashtown. The impending arrival of that reserve train on 1 July became particularly vexing according to Longstreet's chief commissary of subsistence, Major Raphael Moses. A number of Longstreet's commands, including Law's Brigade of Hood's Division and Pickett's Division, Moses remembered, were held up in order to protect the collected stores and await the arrival of the reserve train until relieved by Imboden's cavalry command. General Johnson complained that his division's march to Gettysburg on 1 July had been delayed by the quartermaster and subsistence trains of Longstreet's Corps. The sudden change from what had been a defensive, foraging expedition to a full-scale offensive engagement thirty miles east of Chambersburg caused marked confusion and delays, notably on 1 July.[86]

Lee, nevertheless, determined to strike Meade's left and center on 2 July using two of Longstreet's Divisions and elements of Hill's Corps. When Longstreet got his two divisions—Hood's and McLaws's—in place and launched his attack on 2 July, it was pursued with a vengeance. By evening the attack was spent, leaving in its wake horrific losses. On Lee's left, bloody assaults by Johnson's and Early's Divisions of Ewell's Corps against Culp's Hill and Cemetery Hill met with only limited success.[87]

Lee again sought to deliver a blow against Meade's army on 3 July. He seemed desperate and agitated; it was as though he were trying to force the result. The battle—and the campaign for that matter—had gone awry. The ground gained along Culp's Hill was given up after bitter fighting in the wee hours. Lee determined to send Pickett's Division, which had arrived from Chambersburg the evening before, along with the remnants of two of Hill's Divisions—Heth's and Pender's—across one mile of open fields against the Union center. The attack was to be preceded by a massive artillery bombardment by nearly 150 guns.[88]

Like the assaults on the previous day, the attack on 3 July lacked planning and coordination. It was a disaster; the losses were appalling. To make matters worse, J. E. B. Stuart's horsemen had been badly handled that same afternoon, and, at the same time, enemy cavalry were now eight miles behind Lee and on his line of communication and supply at Fairfield, where it threatened the reserve quartermaster and subsistence train parked nearby and where foraging parties were actually gathering stores at the time. Given the purpose of the campaign and the desperate need of those stores by the army, nothing, short of the destruction of the army on the battlefield, could have been more alarming to Lee than the loss of that reserve train.[89]

In the end, Dr. Lafayette Guild reported nearly 20,500 Confederate casualties in the three days of bitter fighting. Of that number, Guild claimed that more than 15,000 had been killed or wounded. In actuality, the number of killed or wounded was probably well over 20,000. The command structure of Lee's army had been shattered. Large numbers of wounded were in enemy hands. The wounded and dying within Lee's lines were in hospitals scattered for miles north, west, and south of Gettysburg. They and the enormous trains of quartermaster and subsistence stores and herds of livestock were a serious concern to Lee, as he was forced to give up the field and begin a retreat that would cover forty-five difficult miles to the Potomac River and include traversing a 700-foot mountain range.[90]

Two

The flies and vermin of the dog days

What Lee observed in the pastures ahead of him on the late afternoon of 3 July was a scene of misery and death. A Union soldier recalled the fields in front of Cemetery Ridge after the battle:

> Like sheaves bound by the reaper, in crevices of the rocks, behind fences, trees and buildings; in thickets, where they had crept for safety only to die in agony; by stream or wall or hedge, wherever the battle had raged or their weakening steps could carry them, lay the dead. Some, with faces bloated and blackened beyond recognition, lay with glassy eyes staring up at the blazing summer sun; others, with faces downward and clenched hands filled with grass or earth, which told of the agony of the last moments, here a headless trunk, there a severed limb; in all the grotesque positions that unbearable pain and intense suffering contorts the human form, they lay. All around was the wreck the battlestorm leaves in its wake—broken caissons, dismounted guns, small arms bent and twisted by the storm or dropped and scattered by disabled hands; dead and bloated horses, torn and ragged equipments, and all the sorrowful wreck that the waves of battle leave at their ebb; and over all, hugging the earth like a fog, poisoning every breath, the pestilential stench of decaying humanity.

The whole battlefield was, wrote another observer, "one trodden, miry waste with corpses at every step." All the fences had been destroyed, and the country was so open that citizens of Gettysburg remarked that roads were no longer necessary for travel anywhere in the twenty-five-square-mile vicinity![1]

The town of Gettysburg was in shambles. Buildings, houses, and walls were pocked and riddled by shell and small arms fire. Windows were smashed,

The dead along the fields south of Gettysburg and east of the Emmitsburg Road. Library of Congress, Washington, D.C.

· gardens were trampled, and the streets were littered with debris and dead men and animals. "Stores were ransacked and emptied of their contents," wrote a reporter for a Lancaster, Pennsylvania, newspaper, "but in many such articles as could not be used were destroyed [by the Confederates] and the buildings abused and defiled. Dwellings too were entered and where men's clothing could not be procured, that of women and children was taken into the streets and roads, torn into fragments and cast aside. The houses of some of the professors in the educational institutions hereabouts shared the same fate; and from one store here even the clocks were taken out and destroyed."[2]

Lee's officers and men had marched long distances through soaring heat, dust, rain, and mud; they had fought for three furious days. Some who still manned the front lines were ragged, and many were barefoot. They were filthy. Like their commander, most were diarrheic. Many of those soldiers had not had a change of clothes in more than a month. Some had not bathed since they left Virginia. Civilians wrote of the "stench" of Lee's army. The foul body odors, coupled with the smell of offal and rotting human and animal flesh, must have been indescribable.[3]

The positions of the two armies at Gettysburg remained static in the late afternoon of 3 July. Lee's far right flank was still held by Hood's Division.

Commanded by General Law, Hood having been wounded the day before, the division held a line along the high ground known locally as Houck's Ridge, from Devil's Den down to just west of Round Top, overlooking the meandering Plum Run. Benning's Georgia Brigade held the left flank of the division at Devil's Den, and to its immediate right was the wounded Brigadier General Jerome B. Robertson's Texas Brigade, with Law's own Alabamians, commanded by Colonel James L. Sheffield, anchoring the right. To prevent an enemy approach from the south and into Lee's rear, Law refused the extreme right flank of the division by positioning Anderson's Georgia Brigade, then commanded by Colonel William W. White of the Seventh Georgia after General Anderson, Colonel F. H. Little, and Lieutenant Colonel William Luffman of the Eleventh Georgia were all badly wounded, along a thin line, facing due south, extending from Colonel Sheffield's right flank, west, all the way across the Emmitsburg Road, where it aided in the repulse of General Farnsworth's attack.[4]

McLaws's Division extended Lee's lines north of Law's positions. Its right flank, anchored by Semmes's Georgia Brigade, commanded by Colonel Goode Bryan of the Sixteenth Georgia after General Semmes had been wounded on 2 July, held high ground known as Stony Hill in the Rose Woods some three hundred yards behind Benning's left flank. Brigadier General William T. Wofford's Brigade of Georgians continued the line along that rocky ledge on Semmes's left, overlooking the bloody Wheatfield. What was left of Brigadier General William Barksdale's Mississippi Brigade, commanded by Colonel Benjamin G. Humphreys of the Twenty-first Mississippi after Barksdale had been mortally wounded and left in enemy hands on 2 July, held little more than a skirmish line that extended all the way to a position west of Abraham Trostle's white frame house and brick bank barn. Behind those three brigades, the remnants of Brigadier General Joseph B. Kershaw's Brigade of South Carolinians formed a reserve in the fields just below the battered peach orchard.[5]

Anderson's Division of Hill's Corps extended Lee's lines northward from the area defended by McLaws's Division. The brigades of Generals Wilcox, Wright, Posey, and Mahone and Colonel Lang—Alabamians, Georgians, Mississippians, Virginians, and Floridians—held that part of the line along Seminary Ridge occupied earlier in the day by Pickett's and much of Pettigrew's (Heth's) Divisions. Although what was left of Pettigrew's Division remained along Seminary Ridge, Pickett's Division was sent to its wagon park three miles to the rear. In front of Anderson's lines, many batteries of Longstreet's three divisions along with his reserve battalion grimly remained in their positions along the Emmitsburg Road from below the peach orchard almost all the way to the smoky William Bliss farmyard.[6]

In the Long Lane, north of the Bliss farmyard, the South Carolina and Georgia Brigades of Colonel Abner Perrin and Brigadier General Edward L. Thomas of Pender's Division, Hill's Corps, and the Georgia and North Carolina Brigades of Brigadier Generals George Doles, Alfred Iverson Jr., and Stephen D. Ramseur of Rodes's Division, Ewell's Corps, all thinned by battle losses on 1 July, faced the Union right center, not more than three hundred yards away. About five hundred yards behind those five brigades, extending along Seminary Ridge north of the left flank of Anderson's Division, were the guns of Hill's artillery batteries and some of Ewell's.[7]

Lee's lines extended through the town of Gettysburg, where Colonel Isaac E. Avery's North Carolinians, commanded by Colonel Archibald C. Godwin of the Fifty-seventh North Carolina after Colonel Avery had been mortally wounded on 2 July and Brigadier General Harry T. Hays's Louisianans stood behind barricades or in positions inside houses and buildings. Below Cemetery Hill and near Henry Culp's handsome brick dwelling stood the brigade of Georgians led by General Gordon.[8]

Lee's far left flank, composed of Johnson's Division of Ewell's Corps and General Daniel's and Colonel Edward A. O'Neal's North Carolina and Alabama Brigades of Rodes's Division, held positions near the base of Culp's Hill, west of Rock Creek facing south, not far from the well-entrenched enemy on the summit of the hill. On Lee's far left were Stuart's horse brigades that had arrived on 2 July but had been roughly handled by Union cavalry on the third. Lee's nearly six-mile lines still followed the contour of the "fishhook" defense lines first formed by the Army of the Potomac on the evening of 1 July and early morning of 2 July.[9]

Where Lee had been forced to command his army along exterior lines, his counterpart, General Meade, had benefited from interior lines. Meade's far left flank, not more than seven hundred yards from Lee's right flank, was held by four brigades of Major General George Sykes's Fifth Corps and extended from Round Top to the foot of the northern slope of Little Round Top. Elements of Major General John Sedgwick's Sixth Corps not only extended that line northward, but also two of its brigades held a refused line in the rear of the Round Tops on either side of the Taneytown Road, facing south, to protect the army from any attempt by Lee to reach its rear. Brigades from both the Fifth and Sixth Corps occupied Meade's lines from the northern base of Little Round Top to the stone George Weikert house, and the remnants of Brigadier General John C. Caldwell's Second Corps division continued the line north, up Cemetery Ridge, together with the tattered fragments of Major General David Bell Birney's and Brigadier General Andrew A. Humphreys's Third Corps Divisions.[10]

To the right of Birney and Humphreys, Major General Abner Doubleday's First Corps division and the remaining two divisions of the Second Corps, those of Brigadier Generals John Gibbon and Alexander Hays, held Meade's center all the way to Ziegler's Grove and the western base of Cemetery Hill. Virtually all of the batteries in the reserve artillery brigades of the Army of the Potomac and those of the Second Corps, along with batteries from the First, Third, and Sixth Corps, occupied a line extending from just north of the George Weikert house to Ziegler's Grove, altogether more than one hundred guns.[11]

Brigadier General John C. Robinson's First Corps division, along with the divisions of Brigadier General Adolph von Steinwehr, the wounded Brigadier General Francis C. Barlow, and Major General Carl Schurz of the Eleventh Corps, held the Union lines along Cemetery Hill just southeast of the southern suburbs of Gettysburg and eastward, where they nearly touched the remaining First Corps division under Brigadier General James S. Wadsworth along the western summit of Culp's Hill. To Wadsworth's right, Major General Henry W. Slocum's Twelfth Corps held the northern and eastern summit of Culp's Hill, supported by Brigadier Generals Alexander Shaler's and Thomas H. Neill's Sixth Corps brigades.[12]

The losses in the Army of the Potomac, like those in Lee's army, had been staggering. An appalling 3,155 Union soldiers had been killed and 14,500 had been wounded; 5,365 were missing or in enemy hands. The losses of horses and mules were equally horrendous: 3,183 horses had been killed or wounded and abandoned on the field, and 370 mules had been killed or lost.[13]

Beyond the loss of officers and men, Meade's army was suffering from severe shortages of quartermaster and subsistence stores on the battlefield. Most of the quartermaster and subsistence trains were at or near Westminster, Maryland, nearly twenty-five miles to Meade's rear. They had been ordered there on 1 July as Meade hurried his infantry columns toward Gettysburg from the Pipe Creek line he had just established.[14]

It was Lee's destruction of the Northern Central and Hanover Railroads that caused Meade's supply problems; Meade had been unable to establish a supply base close enough to the Gettysburg area with those rail lines shut down. He had chosen a defense line along Pipe Creek with Westminster in his immediate rear on 1 July. The fighting at Gettysburg, though, had drawn him into battle twenty-five miles northwest of Westminster. Meade had been

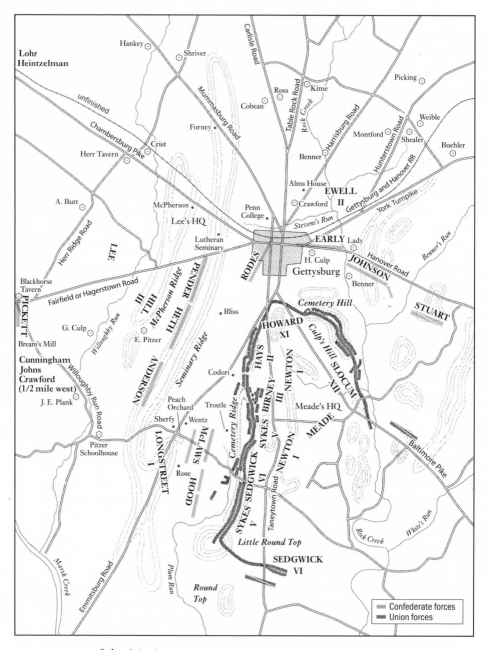

MAP 2.1   3 July 1863, 6:00 P.M.

The positions of Lee's and Meade's armies at the end of the fighting at Gettysburg.

using the Western Maryland Railroad from Baltimore to Westminster when the battle began, and he had been forced to rely on that long line of supply and supply base ever since. From Westminster, quartermaster and subsistence trains had been moving up the Baltimore Pike to Gettysburg to feed and equip the army only since the evening of 2 July; the chaotic situation caused them to start too late, and what they were able to bring had not been enough.[15]

At the end of the fighting, Meade's men were suffering from hunger and the lack of all kinds of equipment, particularly shoes. Some corps commanders reported that as many as half of their men were barefoot. Horses and mules had not been fed, and they had been subsisting, if at all, on grasses and grains seized by Meade's quartermasters from the Gettysburg area. With thousands of wounded on his hands, both his own and Confederate prisoners, his troops facing acute hunger and shortages of necessary equipment, Meade worried over his most pressing military problem—his line of supply to Westminster was so long that it took most of his cavalry brigades to protect it. If Lee retreated, Meade would have to rely on those very cavalry units, the horses of some of which had not been fed or shod in days, to pursue the enemy. Some of his infantrymen, consequently, would have to move to the rear to protect the supply line to Westminster until it was safe enough to send them in pursuit of the enemy.[16]

Lee probably had a good idea of the condition of the enemy; after all, he had planned and ordered the destruction of those railroads. The logistical problems that Lee faced, though, were equally acute. His battle lines were more than six miles long, and the transportation and support systems behind them extended for more than eight miles in his rear. Quartermaster, subsistence, ordnance, and ambulance trains supporting each division, generally mule drawn and anywhere from four to seven miles in length when on the road, were positioned in wagon parks near the division hospitals, two to three miles behind the battle lines. Near the wagon parks, commissary of subsistence teams kept herds of cattle, sheep, hogs, and other seized farm animals in temporary pens for the use of the troops. From those wagon parks, quartermasters and subsistence and ordnance officers moved elements of those trains, including some of the farm animals, closer to the scene of action to keep the commands to which they were attached supplied with food, equipment, and ammunition. Unlike Meade, Lee brought most of the quartermaster and subsistence stores he had obtained during the invasion to the front, although he was careful to ensure that most of it was conserved for the future use of the army. The ambulances, anywhere from fifty to one hundred in each division, operated between ambulance depots in the forward areas and the division hospitals.[17]

The division trains grew larger even while the fighting raged at Gettysburg. While Pender's Division marched toward the battlefield on 1 July, its quartermasters scoured the countryside for stores and supplies. Captain Charles D. Hall, the chief quartermaster of Scales's Brigade, reported impressing corn and hay east of Cashtown only hours before being called into the fighting west of Gettysburg.[18]

That same day, while Hood's and McLaws's Divisions marched toward the sound of gunfire, their quartermasters continued to forage. The quartermaster of Longstreet's Corps recorded purchasing 3,024 pounds of corn, 2,000 pounds of hay, and 5 horses on 1 July. Hood's Division obtained 394 bushels of corn while on the march to Gettysburg. The quartermasters of Hood's Brigades continued their foraging while on the march. Anderson's Brigade bought 840 pounds of corn; the Texas Brigade, 10 bushels; and Law's Brigade, 25 bushels. The Fifteenth Alabama of Law's Brigade purchased 10 bushels of oats. Barksdale's brigade quartermaster picked up 2 barrels of tar. Pickett's Division, while still in Chambersburg, bought 25½ bushels of corn, 12½ bushels of oats, 15 pair of boots, and 75 combs. The records reveal that on 1 July corps, division, brigade, regimental, and artillery battalion quartermasters purchased and seized fodder and other quartermaster stores from farms and shops from Chambersburg and Fayetteville all the way to Gettysburg and as far north as Mummasburg. Because of the need for the quartermasters to support the troops on the battlefield on 2 and 3 July, the foraging in some units of Longstreet's Corps apparently ceased, as some records for those two days show no entries. In others, though, foraging continued on the afternoon of 3 July. In Cabell's Artillery Battalion, for instance, quartermasters recorded purchasing 3,000 pounds of hay.[19]

During the three days of battle, Gettysburg citizens reported that Lee's men had seized in and around the town 800 horses, a dozen mules, 1,000 head of cattle, 200 hogs, and 400 sheep. They also reported the loss of an immense quantity of grains and flour as well as 100 wagons, 9 wagon beds, 50 buggies or carriages, and loads of wagon harness and gear.[20]

Farther behind Lee's lines was Major John Alexander Harman's reserve quartermaster and subsistence train. From all accounts, including Union intelligence reports, that train, on the afternoon of 3 July, was situated eight miles in Lee's rear along the road between Cashtown and Fairfield.[21]

Few Confederate combatants observed the reserve train. Situated far behind the lines, it began moving toward the Potomac River long before the soldiers in the ranks ever took to the road. Private Joseph B. Polley of the Fourth Texas recalled that that train, which he actually observed on 1 July, was fourteen miles long. That day the same estimate was given by a resident of Chambersburg.[22]

By 3 July the reserve train was probably between fifteen and twenty miles long. Quartermaster and commissary of subsistence teams from the reserve train had been foraging in the area between Chambersburg and Fairfield around the clock ever since the fighting began. Mostly mule drawn, the wagons varied from those pulled by two-mule teams to those pulled by four-mule and six-mule teams. In addition, a large number of heavy dray horses pulled the wagons. Many of those wagons and the horses and mules pulling them had been seized in Maryland and Pennsylvania; some had been taken from Milroy's surrendered garrisons at Winchester and Martinsburg. Brought to Cashtown with the reserve train were more than five thousand head of cattle and nearly that number of sheep, along with thousands of hogs held in nearby fields.[23]

Regimental baggage wagons and ambulances were often driven, loaded, and unloaded by detailed soldiers, but the reserve train and the regimental, brigade, and division quartermaster, subsistence, ambulance, and even ordnance trains were driven and maintained, for the most part, by African American slaves who went into the army either by voluntary lease arrangements between their owners and army quartermasters or by impressment. Few quartermaster records of persons employed or hired for service as wagoners have survived. The few such records that do exist, though, illustrate that most wagoners and laborers in the trains were slaves; some were free blacks. Anecdotal evidence from diaries and reminiscences reveals as well that large numbers of wagoners in Lee's army were African Americans. One resident of Chambersburg, Jacob Hoke, claimed that Lee's reserve, corps, and division trains were altogether more than fifty miles in length, an estimate corroborated by Confederate diaries, letters, and memoirs. Trains that long would have consisted of between 5,000 and 6,000 wagons. If most wagoners were African Americans and the reserve, corps, and division trains were more than fifty miles long, it is reasonable to conclude that there were anywhere from 6,000 to 10,000 African Americans attached to those trains, the vast majority of whom were slaves.[24]

The slaves accompanying the troops were also highly visible. "In the rear of each regiment," Colonel Fremantle wrote, "were from twenty to thirty negro slaves." Private John Taylor Smith of the Thirteenth Alabama claimed that there were twenty-five to thirty slaves in his regiment. Those were the slaves of the officers and enlisted men who performed the manual labor necessary to set up, take down, and maintain camps and cook meals. While being marched back toward Marsh Creek as a prisoner of war on the morning of 3 July, Private Dyer B. Pettijohn of the First Minnesota recalled passing "long lines of negro cooks baking corn pone for rebel soldiers at the front" about two miles behind Lee's battle lines. Other Union prisoners were struck by the same spectacle.[25]

If Fremantle's and Smith's accounts of the numbers of slaves accompanying each regiment do, indeed, reflect the number in each of Lee's 198 infantry and cavalry regiments and battalions and 69 artillery batteries, there must have been anywhere from 6,000 to 10,000 slaves laboring for Lee's troops. While on the march, they customarily rode in the army trains.[26]

Closer to the battlefield, the slaves were particularly noticeable. Colonel E. Porter Alexander, who had two slaves accompanying him at Gettysburg, recalled the battlefield after the fighting subsided on 2 July. "Negro servants hunting for their masters," he wrote, "were a feature of the landscape that night." Large numbers of slaves must have been in the fields again on the late afternoon of 3 July.[27]

Although the scenes of the battlefield on 3 July were terrible, those at the hospitals and ambulance depots behind Lee's lines were absolutely heart wrenching and sickening. Division hospitals, ambulance depots, aid stations, and all of the ambulances were always under the command of the Quartermaster Department in the Confederate army. Division hospitals were established by the chief quartermaster of the army, Lieutenant Colonel James L. Corley, and the division quartermasters. Red or yellow flags marked the sites of hospitals, ambulance depots, and aid stations. The chief surgeon of each division, after consulting with the chief quartermaster of the army, actually distributed all medical officers and hospital attendants and oversaw the provision of ambulances, medicines, and stores. Division quartermasters made all arrangements for transporting the sick and wounded of their divisions; they established all the ambulance depots near the battlefield and behind the aid stations. The division quartermasters and their huge trains of stores as well as the subsistence and ordnance trains were always located near the division hospitals, making hospital sites the center of what otherwise were wagon parks containing hundreds upon hundreds of wagons and their horse and mule teams. Because of the proximity of the quartermaster and subsistence trains to the division hospitals, assistant quartermasters and commissary of subsistence officers and their men often served as hospital attendants.[28]

From east of Rock Creek below Culp's Hill, out the Hunterstown Road,

A Confederate soldier and his slave. Thousands of slaves accompanied their masters in Lee's army at Gettysburg. Private collection print courtesy of the Museum of the Confederacy, Richmond, Virginia. Photography by Katherine Wetzel.

north of Gettysburg along the Carlisle Road, northwest on the Mummasburg Road, west of Gettysburg on the Chambersburg Pike and Fairfield Road, and southwest of town along Marsh Creek and Willoughby Run, the properties of local farmers and townspeople were filled with the sick, wounded, dying, and dead of Lee's army. In all, there were nearly forty Confederate hospital and ambulance depot sites in or near Gettysburg caring for more than 15,000 wounded and nearly 5,000 sick officers and men.[29]

Farmhouses and barns were used by surgeons and surgical teams, but all hospital complexes behind Lee's lines were tented. To ward off disease, the surgeons in Lee's army uniformly believed that the casualties should be sheltered in the fresh air during the summer. One observer noted that "the wounds [of the hospitalized Confederates] were in a large proportion of the cases very severe; amputations and resections were frequent. The corps of [Confederate] surgeons are as a body intelligent and attentive. The hospitals are in barns, outbuildings and dilapidated tents. Some few are in dwellings. I cannot speak favorably of the camp police. Often there is a deplorable want of cleanliness, especially in barns and outbuildings; vermin and putrid matter are disgustingly offensive." With all the death, wounds, and stench, the battlefields and all hospitals, ambulance depots, and aid stations were literally covered with dense swarms of flies, a problem everyone was powerless to remedy.[30]

Hood's Division's hospital at the John Edward Plank farm along the Willoughby Run Road, one mile south of the Fairfield Road, made use of the large, two and one-half story brick dwelling and its brick bank barn and frame outbuildings nearby. The Plank farm hospital was established by Major George, the division quartermaster, and Dr. John Thompson Darby, chief surgeon of Hood's Division, in consultation with Lieutenant Colonel Corley, as the division marched toward what was believed to be the Union left flank on 2 July. The next day it was almost two miles behind Hood's battle lines. There, nearly 1,500 sick, wounded, and dying officers and men of Hood's four brigades were hospitalized, mostly in shelter halves. When Hood was badly wounded by shell fragments that ripped through his left hand, forearm, elbow, and biceps on the afternoon of 2 July, he was brought back to the Plank farmhouse where Darby attended to him. Assisting Darby were between ten and fifteen regimental surgeons and assistant surgeons, more than fifty nurses, and several stewards.[31]

One woman in the Plank family recorded that "it was not long before all the beds [in the house] were filled with wounded, and the floor [was] covered with straw carried from the barn, all over the floors in the halls on the porches in the outbuildings, on the barn floor and every place where [there were] wounded men—hauled there in ambulances, on wagons, gun [carriages] and every possible way. . . . [They were] using the Garner Organ room for a surgical or operating room. Many limbs and arms were amputated and their wounds dressed [there], while the battle raged." The horses that drew the ambulances to the Plank homestead from the battlefield were eventually turned out into the fields near the house to eat wheat and oats, but some were so weakened that they collapsed and died in the back yard. "Every morning," she noted, "[the Confederates] buried their dead in shallow graves in the orchard. . . . The yard and garden fences were gone, the flower and garden beds were as the mud roads, the poultry, hogs and cattle were consumed for food . . . part of the buildings were burned for campfires, the floors of the house were strewn with blood, straw [was caked with blood], also the flies and vermin [were so thick it reminded one of] the dog days." Most of the furniture, she recalled, had been taken out of the house and thrown into the fields. In all, almost thirty-five soldiers from Georgia, Alabama, Arkansas, and Texas would be buried in the Plank orchard near the house.[32]

Major Edgeworth Bird, assistant quartermaster of Benning's Brigade, and Major Walter S. Ballard, the brigade's chief commissary of subsistence, were among many officers and enlisted men who left the division trains that were parked all around the Plank farmhouse and along the Willoughby Run Road to assist the surgeons. Ballard's wounded brother, Captain C. M. Ballard of the Eighth Georgia, was brought in on a litter. "He was in great distress," remembered Major Bird. "I assisted as best I could. Held legs while they were taken off."[33]

Treated at the Plank farm on the afternoon of 3 July, near General Hood, were General Anderson, Colonel Little, and Lieutenant Colonel Luffman of the Eleventh Georgia. Also among the wounded there were General Robertson, of the Texas Brigade, who had sustained a leg injury; Colonels Robert M. Powell of the Fifth Texas, John C. G. Key of the Fourth Texas, and Van H. Manning of the Third Arkansas; Lieutenant Colonel Isaac B. Feagin of the Fifteenth Alabama; Lieutenant Colonel W. M. Hardwick and Major C. B. St. John of the Forty-eighth Alabama; Lieutenant Colonel King Bryan of the Fifth Texas; and Captain John R. Woodward, acting major of the First Texas.[34]

Another casualty was Lieutenant Colonel Benjamin F. Carter, of the Fourth Texas, the antebellum mayor of Austin. Badly wounded in the legs and face during the attack against Devil's Den and Little Round Top on the evening of 2 July, Carter was carried from the battlefield to the Plank farm, where he and his slave, Henry Johnson, remained on 3 July.[35]

Accounts of slaves assisting their wounded masters after the fighting at Gettysburg have survived. As the men in Lee's army, black as well as white, began to realize they had suffered a tactical defeat, however, some of those slaves as well as white soldiers left the army. Slaves in the quartermaster service appear to have represented the largest number of African Americans who ran away, and such departures seem to have increased while the army was in motion. After the battle one regimental quartermaster in Anderson's Brigade of Hood's Division wrote his wife that "a great many Negroes have gone to the Yankees."[36]

The hospital of McLaws's Division actually consisted of four brigade hospitals. The complex was established in the early afternoon of 2 July under the direction of Major Abram Huguenin McLaws, division quartermaster and brother of General McLaws, and Lieutenant Colonel Corley, as the division moved toward the battlefield. It was located along Marsh Creek, three miles behind McLaws's lines of battle on 3 July and about one mile northwest of the Plank house. The trains of McLaws's Division were parked in the fields near Marsh Creek.[37]

Francis Bream's Blackhorse Tavern on the north side of the Fairfield Road served as the hospital of Kershaw's Brigade. The two and one-half story stone house and its massive bank barn close to the road were filled with sick and wounded. A surgeon there, Dr. Simon Baruch of Camden, South Carolina, was one of the most interesting men in Lee's army. Only twenty-three years old, Baruch, a Sephardic Jew from Schwerenz, Poland, was with the Third South Carolina Battalion. "We had scarcely opened our battlefield supplies and hurriedly set up operating tables, constructed of doors laid upon dry goods boxes and barrels," Baruch remembered of the afternoon of 2 July, "when the ambulances began to bring their sad load, the result of the charge on the [batteries] in the peach orchard. . . . All day and all night the work continued at the field hospital, and throughout [3 July] also the wounded came pouring in, many on foot, among them several captured Union soldiers, on two of whom I operated [on], attending them like our own."[38]

Kershaw's South Carolinians had suffered intensely on 2 July. Most of the brigade's command structure had been shattered. The wounded transported to the Blackhorse Tavern included Colonels William Davie DeSaussure of the Fifteenth South Carolina and John D. Kennedy of the Second South Carolina, Lieutenant Colonel Elbert Bland of the Seventh South Carolina, and Major Daniel B. Miller of the Third South Carolina Battalion, along with hundreds of others. Colonel DeSaussure died at the tavern and was buried in the Bream family burial ground behind it. Most other Confederates who died there were buried on a hill near the house, in the orchard, or beside DeSaussure's grave.[39]

Major Donald McDairmed McLeod of the Eighth South Carolina had been mangled by artillery fire while in the attack of Kershaw's Brigade across the Rose Farm on the afternoon of 2 July. He was carried to the brigade ambulance depot and then to the Blackhorse Tavern. Also taken to the tavern was Captain John Kalb McIver of McLeod's regiment. Both of McIver's eyes were shot out.[40]

The remaining hospitals of McLaws's Brigades were south of the Fairfield Road, along Marsh Creek. Barksdale's Brigade of Mississippians took over the John S. Crawford farm and its small stone house on the east bank of Marsh Creek. Brought there, among hundreds of other wounded, were Colonels William Dunbar Holder of the Seventeenth Mississippi and Thomas M. Griffin of the Eighteenth Mississippi. John Crawford remembered that the brigade's wounded occupied "the house, barn, sheds and outbuildings and adjacent grounds" were used. The "hospital had tents and buildings," and the surgeons "used the dining room as an amputation room."[41]

Between the Crawford farm and the Plank farm was the Samuel Johns farm and its stone tenant house, the principal hospital site and wagon park of Semmes's Georgia Brigade. The brigades of Semmes and Barksdale established their hospitals and wagon parks on adjoining farms, forming in essence one complex, while across Marsh Creek was the hospital of Wofford's Brigade. The tented facility and wagon park were so immense that, Crawford reported, it destroyed more than nine acres of corn, nearly ten acres of oats, and twenty-two acres of wheat, plus all the fences.[42]

General Semmes, it is believed, was taken to the stone Crawford house after suffering a life-threatening shrapnel injury to the leg. One of his aides, Corporal Thomas Cleveland of the Tenth Georgia, helped tie off the general's wound on the battlefield, then he and two other aides, Captains B. H. Cody and Abner Lewis, along with Private William Ross Stillwell of the Fifty-third Georgia, carried Semmes to the ambulance depot and from there accompanied him in an ambulance to the Crawford house. Semmes remained there on 3 July. Many of the wounded of Semmes's Brigade were carried on litters from aid stations on the battlefield to the brigade ambulance depot, the large stone barn of the Rose farm on the battlefield. There Dr. James B. Clifton, surgeon of the Fifty-third Georgia, worked all day and all night securing their passage by ambulance to the brigade hospital.[43]

The hospital of Pickett's Division was located at Francis Bream's Mineral and Flour Mill, the nearby farmhouse of William E. Myers, and the John F. Currens farm along Marsh Creek, south of the Fairfield Road, sites established by quartermaster Major Scott and chief surgeon Dr. Magnua Lewis of Pickett's Division, along with Lieutenant Colonel Corley. The complex, three miles west of Pickett's front line, was used by all three brigades of the division. The division's trains were parked in nearby fields.[44]

By midnight, 3 July, there were about a thousand sick and wounded from Pickett's three brigades, as well as a few from Hood's and McLaws's Divisions, hospitalized in and around Myers's two-story log house and blacksmith and cooper's sheds, the two and one-half story frame mill, and the Currens's farmyard. The wounded carried to the Myers farm included General Kemper; Colonels William R. Aylett of the Fifty-third Virginia, William Dabney Stuart of the Fifty-sixth Virginia, and Kirkwood Otey of the Eleventh Virginia; Colonel Henry Gantt and Lieutenant Colonel John T. Ellis of the Nineteenth Virginia; Colonel Eppa Hunton and Major Edmund Berkeley of the Eighth Virginia; Majors John C. Owens of the Ninth Virginia and Nathaniel C. Wilson of the Twenty-eighth Virginia; and others. Ellis and Wilson died shortly after their arrival and were buried in the Currens farmyard. A large number of Pickett's wounded remained in Union hands or lay in the no-man's-land between the two armies where neither side could go to their aid for fear of drawing enemy fire.[45]

Surgeons and assistant surgeons from regiments in Pickett's three brigades, including the chief surgeon of the division, Dr. Lewis, served at Pickett's Division hospital at various times on 3 July. Many tended to the wounded at aid stations on the battlefield until well into the night. Also employed at the division hospital complex were several hospital stewards and chaplains, including the Reverend Dr. Peter Tinsley of the Twenty-eighth Virginia, and nearly seventy-five nurses—all soldiers detailed from regiments in Pickett's brigades.[46]

Sergeant Major David E. Johnston of the Seventh Virginia was taken to the Myers house after the bombardment, suffering from a shrapnel wound to his left side and arm. "The shed in which I was placed," he recalled, "was filled with the wounded and dying. . . . I spoke to no one, and no one to me, never closed my eyes to sleep; the surgeons close by being engaged in removing the limbs of those necessary to be amputated. . . . I heard nothing but the cries of the wounded and the groans of the dying, the agonies of General Kemper, who lay nearby, being frequently heard."[47]

Through the afternoon and night of 3 July and over the next few days surgeons performed thirty-four amputations at Pickett's Division hospital. They were unable to save the lives of thirty-six patients, whose remains were buried alongside a fence near the Myers house, on the Currens property near the mill dam, or in the garden nearby.[48]

The two-story Adam Butt farmhouse, bank barn, and yard had been used by Anderson's Division of Hill's Corps as its hospital site and wagon park since 1 July; it was established by Anderson's chief quartermaster, Major James Arthur Johnston, and chief surgeon, Dr. Henry DeSaussure Fraser, together with Lieutenant Colonel Corley. Located along Herr Ridge Road north of the Fairfield Road, about three miles west of the battle positions of Anderson's Division, it was where the casualties of all five Anderson brigades—a total of nearly one thousand men—received medical and surgical care. There would be twenty-one burials in the Butts yard, all from Anderson's Division.[49]

Northwest of the Butt farm were the hospitals of Heth's and Pender's Divisions. The Samuel Lohr farm, on the south side of the Chambersburg Pike slightly more than two miles to the rear of Heth's 1 July battle lines, was the hospital site and wagon park for Heth's Division. That site was selected by Major Alexander W. Vick, Heth's chief quartermaster, and Dr. Henry H.

Hubbard, his chief surgeon, on the morning of 1 July. It was located about four miles west of Gettysburg near the village of Seven Stars. There and on nearby farms more than 1,500 casualties from Heth's Division alone were hospitalized.[50]

The hospital sites and wagon park of Pender's Division were located at the Andrew Heintzelman Tavern and farm at Seven Stars, the Lohr farm, and the David Whisler farm. They were established by Pender's chief quartermaster, Major Scales, and his chief surgeon, Dr. Pleasant A. Holt, along with Lieutenant Colonel Corley, on 1 July. Apparently the Lohr and Heintzelman farms became one enormous complex for Heth's and Pender's Divisions, although all twenty-eight recorded burials on the Lohr farm were of Heth's soldiers, and there seems to have been no burials on the Heintzelman farm. Although no records to date identify the site of the army's reserve ordnance train during the battle, it is likely that it was located beside the Chambersburg Pike near Heth's and Pender's Division hospitals because of the proximity of those sites to army headquarters and their distance from the effective range of enemy artillery.[51]

Lieutenant David Augustus Dickert of the Third South Carolina recalled bivouacking near the Lohr and Heintzelman farms hospital sites on the evening of 1 July. There was "a great sea of white tents, silent and still, with here and there a groan, or a surgeon passing from one tent to another relieving the pain of some poor mortal who had fallen in battle." Surgeon Spencer Glasgow Welch of the Thirteenth South Carolina related to his wife that whenever he approached the site, his "ears were greeted as usual with the moans and cries of the wounded." Almost 1,300 sick and wounded of Pender's Division were cared for at the Lohr and Heintzelman farms and at sites in and around Seven Stars.[52]

It was to the Lohr farm, the Heintzelman Tavern, or the nearby David Whisler farm that General Pender was transported in an ambulance, accompanied by his slave Joe and his brother Captain David Pender, on the evening of 2 July after he was struck in the left thigh by a two-inch piece of shrapnel. To Dr. Holt, it looked as though Pender would survive the wound. General Scales soon arrived after falling in the same attack as his division commander. Scales's shrapnel wound appeared to be mortal. On 3 July the wounded General Trimble was taken to the Whisler house.[53]

Among those hospitalized at the Lohr farm on 3 July were English-born Colonel Collett Leventhorpe, of the Eleventh North Carolina, whose left arm had been shattered and his hip ripped open by a shell fragment on the first, and his young adjutant, nineteen-year-old Lieutenant Henderson B.

Lucas, who had been thrice shot down carrying the regimental colors that same day. The Eleventh North Carolina had lost more than 500 of its 580 men. Near Leventhorpe was the wounded Captain Robert H. Archer, brother and assistant adjutant general to Brigadier General James J. Archer, who had been captured on 1 July. Near Captain Archer lay his brother's acting inspector general, Captain George A. Williams. General Pettigrew's assistant adjutant general, twenty-three-year-old Captain Nicholas Collin Hughes, arrived after being wounded in the hip and spine on 3 July. There were many others, including Colonel William J. Hoke of the Thirty-eighth North Carolina and twenty-six-year-old Lieutenant Colonel James R. Lane, who had been shot through the back of the head, mouth, and face after assuming command of the Twenty-sixth North Carolina when its brave "boy colonel," Henry King Burgwyn Jr., was killed on 1 July. Lane's wounds appeared to be mortal, and his regiment had lost more than 700 men. Colonel John Kerr Connally of the Fifty-fifth North Carolina and Colonel John M. Stone of the Second Mississippi, Major Alfred Horatio Belo of the Fifty-fifth North Carolina, and Major R. O. Reynolds of the Eleventh Mississippi—all casualties of the fighting on 1 July—were also being treated at the Lohr farm.[54]

Musicians were almost always detailed to assist at division hospitals. At the Lohr farm were the regimental bands of both the Eleventh and Twenty-sixth North Carolina. Julius Lineback, a member of the Moravian band of the Twenty-sixth North Carolina, had worked at Heth's Division's hospital on 1 July until late in the day, when the band was sent to cheer up the troops. When he departed, so did elements of the division quartermaster and subsistence trains that had been parked nearby. "As we went to the regiment," Lineback recalled, "we were in the midst of an immense train of wagons, cattle, etc. pushing forward to feed the exhausted and hungry army in front." He returned to the hospital to work through the night and ensuing two days. Of the Lohr farm on the afternoon of 3 July, he wrote: "The yard, road and field were full of men, some who had been wounded in the first day's fight and had received no attention. A good majority had died here, and were still unburied. One man I particularly remember, was horrible to look at, having become bloated out of all human shape."[55]

Working at Heth's Division hospital with Lineback on 3 July was Captain George P. Erwin, quartermaster of the Eleventh North Carolina, whose regimental quartermaster and subsistence trains were parked in the adjoining fields. "I have not been in the fight," he wrote his father that evening, "I have been looking after our wounded and a more sorrowful thing I never saw. Poor fellows lying wounded in every conceivable place and little or no

The Salem "Moravian" Band of the Twenty-sixth North Carolina. Julius Lineback is the third bandsman from the right. Collection of Old Salem, Inc., Winston-Salem, North Carolina.

attention paid them. The doctors don't examine a wound unless amputation is necessary or it is extraordinarily dangerous. In fact, [the wounded] come in so fast that this is necessary. Some of our boys wounded in the first evening have never been looked at by a Doctor yet."[56]

About one mile west of Oak Ridge, along the Mummasburg Road, stood the two-story frame house of Jacob Hankey, now the site of the hospitals and trains of Iverson's and Daniel's Brigades of Rodes's Division, Ewell's Corps. Among the casualties there on 3 July were the mortally wounded Colonel Daniel Harvey Christie, Lieutenant Colonel Robert Daniel Johnston, and Major Blacknall, who had been shot through the mouth and neck, all of the Twenty-third North Carolina of Iverson's Brigade who fell in the attack across the Forney farm on 1 July. In that attack their regiment lost more than seven hundred men.[57]

At the Hankey farmhouse, Dr. Simon Branch of the Twenty-third North Carolina and chief surgeon of Iverson's Brigade and Frank Patterson of the Second North Carolina Battalion and chief surgeon of Daniel's Brigade, among others, attended to the sick and wounded, most of whom were sheltered by tents pitched throughout the farmyards. Nearby lay Lieutenant

Colonel Samuel H. Boyd of the Forty-fifth North Carolina, Major Henry G. Lewis of the Thirty-second North Carolina, Major John M. Hancock of the Second North Carolina Battalion, and two of General Rodes's staff officers, Lieutenant Colonel Wharton J. Green and Lieutenant William R. Bond, among many others, all wounded during the three days of fighting.[58]

A local African American woman recalled the Hankey farm. Of a wounded officer, probably Colonel Christie, she remembered Mr. Hankey asking: "Would you see a colored person protected if she was to help with the work here?" The officer said he would. "We stayed up all night doing nothing but cook and bake for the Rebels," she recalled. "By morning we were pretty near dead. There was no chance to sleep, and I couldn't have slept anyway for hearing the miserable wounded men hollering and going on out in the yard and in the barn and other buildings. They moaned and cried and went on terribly. 'Oh! take me home to my parents,' they'd say."[59]

The two-story stone home of David Schriver, across the Mummasburg Road and east of the Hankey farm, was the site of the hospitals and trains of the brigades of Generals Ramseur and Doles and Colonel O'Neal of Rodes's Division. The house, barn, and yard were filled with the sick and wounded.[60]

At the Schriver farm lay thirty-six-year-old Colonel Francis Marion Parker and Captain Charles N. Allen of the Thirtieth North Carolina. The Reverend Dr. Alexander D. Betts, Methodist chaplain of the Thirtieth, visited the hospital and spied Parker and Allen, both old friends. "Parker had been wounded in the face; the ball had entered just below one eye and came out just below the other, cutting the nasal tubes," recalled Betts. "When I knelt by him and prayed for him and his wife and children, he seemed about to strangle with the blood. I stopped praying and held my arm lovingly over him till he was quiet." Allen's right arm had been so splintered that it had to be amputated, but he refused to allow the surgeons to do it. Dr. George W. Briggs, a Virginian, the regimental surgeon of the Thirtieth North Carolina and chief surgeon of Ramseur's Brigade, asked Betts to help him convince the captain otherwise. "Kneeling by [Allen, Betts] said, 'Captain, I long for you to get home and see that lovely young wife, who is praying for you, but you will never see her if you try to keep that arm.' After a few moments, Captain Allen said: 'Mr. Betts, I wish you would call Briggs to me.'"[61]

Among many wounded Georgians at the Schriver farm was Colonel Samuel H. Lumpkin, a physician in Watkinsville before the war, who had raised a company from his home county and rose to become the commander of the Forty-fourth Georgia of Doles's Brigade. On 1 July, north of Gettysburg, his leg had been shattered by artillery fire. He lay at the Schriver farm in agony, his leg having been amputated. "There was no better, braver or cooler officer in the army than Colonel Lumpkin," recalled one of his men. Lumpkin's surgeon, Dr. Abner Embry McGarity, was also suffering. He had just learned that his wife's brother, Lieutenant Barnett Hardeman Cody of the Fifteenth Alabama, had been mortally wounded.[62]

The Hankey and Schriver farms sheltered more than 1,400 casualties under the supervision of Dr. W. S. Mitchell, chief surgeon of Rodes's Division. The sites were established on 1 July by Rodes's chief quartermaster, Major John Dalrymple Rogers, whose extensive trains were gathered in the nearby fields, in consultation with Mitchell and Dr. Hunter McGuire, medical director of Ewell's Corps.[63]

General Early's Division established its hospital sites and wagon parks along the Harrisburg and Carlisle Roads, almost two miles north of Gettysburg. The sites were selected by Major Charles Edward Snodgrass, Early's chief quartermaster, and Dr. Samuel B. Morrison, his chief surgeon. The two-story brick house of John S. Crawford, the large brick house and barn of Josiah Benner, the William Ross house, the Jacob Kime house and farm, and the whitewashed dormitory of Pennsylvania College were among the principal hospitals of the division. Parked around them were the division's extensive trains.[64]

Lovina Witmer lived on a farm northeast of Jacob Kime's house. She recalled the Kime house after the fighting. "Everyone but [Mrs. Kime's] grandfather, who stayed in the cellar, moved out of the house," Witmer wrote. "When they returned to the house they found the floors piled high with arms and legs that had been amputated from the wounded soldiers. Her grandfather (in the cellar) plainly heard the mad cry of the soldiers for morphine when the operations were being performed."[65]

One of the ambulance depots for Early's Division was the Henry Culp farm. The mortally wounded Colonel Isaac E. Avery, of the Sixth North Carolina, who had commanded Brigadier General Robert F. Hoke's fine North Carolina brigade in the attack against East Cemetery Hill, was taken to the Culp farm. Avery had fallen with a bullet wound in the throat. Surgeons Drs. William Lewis Reese and John Geddings Hardy of the Sixth North Carolina could do nothing for him. Avery died at the Culp farm thirty hours later. Instead of burying Avery's remains, his slave Elijah resolved to take them back to his home in western North Carolina. In the heat and rain, what was left of the colonel did not have an easy journey.[66]

The scenes at the hospitals of Johnson's Division at the Henry A. Picking farm and schoolhouse, the Alexander D. Buehler, W. Henry and Catherine

Montford, Martin Shealer, Daniel Lady, and Elizabeth Weible farms along the Hunterstown Road, York Pike, and Hanover Road were distressing. Overseeing the hospitals of Johnson's Division were quartermaster Major George D. Mercer and chief surgeon Dr. Robert T. Coleman. Johnson's hospitals were arranged by brigade. In all, those neighboring sites received almost 1,300 sick, wounded, and dying soldiers from Johnson's Division.[67]

The brick Montford farmhouse was badly damaged; it, as well as the barn and outbuildings, was used as a hospital by Brigadier General John M. Jones's Brigade. Martin Shealer's thatched-roof barn was also filled with sick and wounded, mostly from Brigadier General George H. Steuart's Brigade; its "mows, stables and floor being filled with wounded . . . while [the] timbers [were] stained with human blood." In all, forty-four wounded Confederates died in that barn alone, and their bodies were buried within a hundred feet of it.[68]

To those brigade hospitals the casualties from Johnson's assaults against Culp's Hill were taken from ambulance depots at the foot of the hill for surgical treatment. Surgeons at the Montford farmhouse on the Hunterstown Road stopped the hemorrhaging of General Jones's thigh wound received at Culp's Hill. He lay there on the afternoon of 3 July under the care of his brigade surgeon, Dr. Bushrod Taylor.[69]

Major Henry Kyd Douglas, Johnson's assistant adjutant general, was wounded on 3 July. He remembered being taken to the Picking farmhouse, "which seemed to be vacated [by the family]. I was laid on the floor of the parlor and during the day not less than half a dozen surgeons came to see and examine [me] . . . among them . . . [my old] friend, Dr. Hunter McGuire." McGuire seemed omnipresent at Ewell's hospitals.[70]

Artillery battalions in all of Lee's three corps established their own hospitals near the hospital sites of the divisions to which they were attached. The Daniel Lady farm and farmhouse on the north side of the Hanover Road was apparently used by the artillery battalion attached to Johnson's Division. Major Joseph W. Latimer, the twenty-year-old commander of Andrew's Artillery Battalion in the division, was probably taken to the Lady farmhouse. Latimer had entered the Virginia Military Institute in 1859 but left for military service at the outbreak of war. A shell fragment had nearly severed his right arm. At the Lady farmhouse, his brother, Dr. Edwin Latimer, amputated the arm just below the shoulder.[71]

One of the ambulance depots of Johnson's Division was at the stone house and farmyard of Christian and Susan Benner along Rock Creek, just below the eastern slopes of Culp's Hill. A son of the Benners recalled the wounded being carried into the house:

They laid them on the floor of our kitchen, and up in the barn and out in the yard. Some were groaning and others would swear. . . . In a little while I could see a man's leg sawed off . . . without being disturbed. After a while the firing ceased and then ambulances came to get the wounded at our place [and take them farther to the rear to the division's hospitals]. A little major came into the house and asked for some red cloth to make a hospital flag . . . and had a soldier climb up a ladder and nail it to the roof.[72]

Twenty-three-year-old Dr. Thomas Fanning Wood of the Third North Carolina was in charge of the ambulance depot at the Benners. Assisting Wood was the almost wholly untrained surgeon, Dr. Augustus B. Scholars of the Second Louisiana, and Dr. Dabney Herndon of the Fifteenth Louisiana, both of Colonel Jesse Milton Williams's (formerly Brigadier General Francis R. T. Nicholls's) Brigade. Wood cared for hundreds of wounded as they were dragged or carried from the fighting along Culp's Hill, including General Jones and the two wounded commanders of the First Maryland Battalion, Lieutenant Colonel James R. Herbert and Major William W. Goldsborough. Wood and his fellow surgeons and assistants at the Benner house worked day and night trying to move as many wounded back to the division hospitals as possible. Exhausted, they finally retired on the night of 3 July, leaving behind a house splattered with blood and completely sacked.[73]

Colonel Thomas S. Kenan of the Forty-third North Carolina was taken to a blacksmith's shop east of Gettysburg near the Culp farm after his men had dragged him from the Union works on Culp's Hill; he had a nasty wound in his thigh. The crude site along the Hanover Road was the ambulance depot of Daniel's Brigade. Kenan was then moved to his brigade hospital at the Hankey farm on the Mummasburg Road to be cared for by his own surgeon, Dr. William T. Brewer. Joining him there on 3 July were Lieutenant Henry E. Shepherd and Lieutenant Thomas A. Baker of the Forty-third, among hundreds of other wounded Confederates.[74]

Some of the wounded of Ewell's Corps were taken to what was called the "Second Corps Field Hospital" located at the Samuel Cobean farm west of the Carlisle Road and north of the Mummasburg Road. There Dr. McGuire employed reserve surgeons from all three divisions of the corps to assist in treating battle casualties. The Second Corps Field Hospital was commanded by Dr. Harvey Black, formerly surgeon of the Fourth Virginia. At the Cobean farm Black was assisted at times by Dr. J. William Walls of the Fifth Virginia, Dr. William Riddick Whitehead of the Forty-fourth Virginia, Dr. Frank L. Taney of the Tenth Louisiana, and Dr. John A. Straight, and others. The hospital consisted of two wall tents, a large hospital tent, and numerous shelter halves. The large two-story brick house of Samuel Cobean and his niece, as well as their brick bank barn, were also used. Because of its position on the battlefield, the Second Corps Field Hospital took care of a disproportionately large number of wounded from Early's Division. As a result, Dr. Morrison was frequently there as well.[75]

Out along the Hunterstown Road, some four miles east of Gettysburg, were the tented hospitals of J. E. B. Stuart's horse brigades established and equipped by Major Norman R. Fitzhugh, chief quartermaster of the cavalry division. Nearby were the division trains, including 150 wagons and 900 mules captured by Stuart on 28 June. There on 3 July lay General Jenkins, who had been wounded in the head the day before, and General Hampton, who had weighed in to the cavalry clash on the afternoon of 3 July but had been carried out with a fractured skull and blood gushing from his head, the result of sabre blows.[76]

At those Hunterstown Road hospitals was another casualty from Hampton's Brigade, Colonel William G. Delony of Cobb's Georgia Legion. Delony and his command had been engaged in the cavalry fighting near Hunterstown on 2 July. Shot and then knocked senseless by sabre blows to the head, Delony fell from his horse. His men fought off attempts by Union cavalrymen to finish him, and he was taken to the rear. On 3 July he lay near Hunterstown with a horrible laceration across his forehead, just over the right eye.[77]

Cobb's Legion had joined Hampton's Brigade in the fighting on 3 July, only to suffer additional losses. More than one hundred troopers from four of Stuart's horse brigades—Jenkins's, Hampton's, Fitzhugh Lee's, and Chambliss's—lay bleeding in those cavalry hospitals east of Gettysburg.[78]

The number of hospitals and sick and wounded men behind Lee's lines on the afternoon of 3 July was staggering. But his hospitals were not confined to the Gettysburg area. Ewell's Corps, much to Dr. Guild's—and Lee's—dissatisfaction, had left its casualties behind at places as far north as Carlisle, Pennsylvania, and as far south as Hagerstown, Maryland. It had even left a sizable hospital in Chambersburg, as well as facilities in Martinsburg, West Virginia, and Winchester, Virginia. Those hospitals remained on 3 July where they had been first established, filled mostly with victims of typhoid, scurvy, diarrhea, and related diseases.[79]

All of the quartermaster, subsistence, and ordnance trains, together with thousands of sick and wounded, posed a tremendous burden to the movement of Lee's army across the mountains. By the morning of 3 July Lee also had on his hands nearly 5,500 Union prisoners of war captured during the three days of fighting at Gettysburg. The prisoners taken on 1 July were still held by Hill's Corps and were probably located near the wagon parks and division hospitals of Heth's and Pender's Divisions. Most of those captured on 2 and 3 July were corralled in a wheat field three miles behind Longstreet's lines, near the hospitals and wagon parks of Pickett's and McLaws's Divisions along Marsh Creek, south of the Fairfield Road, under what one prisoner recalled was a "strong guard." All of them had been collected there during the early morning hours of 3 July by Major John Fairfax, adjutant general of Longstreet's Corps, and his staff.[80]

Among the prisoners behind Longstreet's lines were some civilians from Gettysburg, including George Codori, George Arendt, and Emanuel G. Trostle. They had been seized after being found trying to pass out from behind Lee's lines. Trostle, whose house was located along the Emmitsburg Road, had actually been guided to the rear of Longstreet's lines by a Confederate colonel prior to the fighting on 2 July. Worried about his property, he tried to pass back through the lines to his home on 3 July, when he was apprehended. Lee could ill afford to release anyone with information about his army such as Trostle possessed.[81]

Union officers and enlisted men alike milled about the guarded area. Many lay in the trampled wheat fields. Most of them begged for food, as few had eaten anything of substance during the past three days. Adding to their discomfort was the fact that nearby were those "long lines of negro cooks" preparing heavy corn cakes for Longstreet's and Hill's frontline troops.[82]

Lee bristled at the burden presented by the hungry Union prisoners. He did not collect all of the subsistence stores in Pennsylvania to feed them; in fact, even with the immense stores he had, his own men were hungry. Signaling his intention to try rid the army of those prisoners, he directed Longstreet to collect all of their names for the purpose of presenting an offer to General Meade for an exchange of prisoners at an appropriate time or of simply unilaterally issuing paroles. From the early morning of 3 July, Major Fairfax and his staff had been gathering the prisoners' names. The wounded Brigadier General Charles Kinnaird Graham, who had been captured near the Peach Orchard on 2 July, informed Fairfax that no paroles could be accepted by him or the other Union prisoners based on an order by General Henry W. Halleck and the U.S. War Department at the commencement of the campaign. Fairfax politely listened to Graham, then replied that he would still be glad to take the paroles of the Union prisoners before Lee's army reached Richmond.[83]

Paroles were actually offered to the Union prisoners that morning, but General Graham warned the men of the consequences. Because the Union army could not recognize the paroles, those who accepted them would be re-turned to duty. If paroled Union soldiers were captured again, the Confeder-ates could execute them. Some Union prisoners decided to take their chances; they were too hungry and unwilling to face the long march south to some Confederate prison. On the morning of 3 July almost 1,500 Union soldiers were paroled and marched out the Carlisle Road. Left behind were nearly 4,000. Lee would have to arrange some exchange of prisoners with General Meade if he was ever to relieve his army of the burden they presented.[84]

On the afternoon of 3 July Lee viewed the ghastly sights around him. Simply collecting the sick and wounded who could bear the journey to Vir-ginia would be difficult enough. Finding them transportation and actually moving them would be a monumental effort. All of that, plus the problems attending the withdrawal of the enormous trains along with 4,000 prisoners, not to mention the army itself, may have presented him with one of the great-est challenges of his military career.

Three

We must now return to Virginia

Lee remained out in the fields until he was satisfied that all of the survivors of Pickett's, Pettigrew's, and Trimble's commands who were able had made their way back to Seminary Ridge and that an adequate defense line was being established to resist any counterattack. After stopping briefly at his own head-quarters along the Chambersburg Pike, it was to General Hill's headquarters in the farmyard of Emanuel Pitzer west of Seminary Ridge, about one mile south of the Fairfield Road, that Lee rode with many of his staff officers, de-partment chiefs, and couriers to discuss the details of returning the army to its base in the Shenandoah Valley of Virginia.[1]

Lee had concluded hours before that any withdrawal of the army must be led by Hill's Corps. Longstreet's Corps was too far from the obvious routes of retreat, the Fairfield Road and Chambersburg Pike, and Ewell's Corps would have to execute the longest and most complex movement away from its battle positions in front of Cemetery Hill and Culp's Hill in order to get into posi-tion to embark on a full-scale retreat. Hill's Corps, on the other hand, would not have to reposition itself. Its left flank straddled the Fairfield Road, the thoroughfare that Lee knew all along would be the one on which the vanguard of his army would withdraw from Pennsylvania should it become necessary because it was the shortest route to the Potomac River. Furthermore, Hill's Corps formed the center of the army, and the safest way to get the army on the road south, given the size and configuration of the defense lines, was to start with the corps occupying the center, while keeping the flanks protected. The flanks would be withdrawn simultaneously after the center commands were on the road. Consequently, the planning for the retreat started with General Hill alone at his headquarters.

In the early evening, with maps spread across their knees, Lee and Hill discussed arrangements for the retreat. They sat on camp stools in a "common wall tent," aided only by a single, flickering candle. In a short time they were joined by Generals Longstreet and Ewell and their staffs, department chiefs, couriers, and some division commanders.[2]

If Lee was anything, he was a student of war. As a professional soldier and one-time superintendent of the U.S. Military Academy, he undoubtedly knew of the text of military theorist Baron Antoine Henri de Jomini. Lee probably never read Carl von Clausewitz, but he was keenly aware of the practical concepts about which Clausewitz wrote. Jomini and Clausewitz compiled military axioms for a "retreat after a lost battle." Those axioms were not devised by them; rather, they evolved over the ages and represented the collective experience of armies and commanders in war.[3]

"In order to keep morale as high as possible," Clausewitz wrote of a retreat after a lost battle, "it is absolutely necessary to make a slow fighting retreat, boldly confronting the pursuer whenever he tries to make too much of his advantage. The retreats of great commanders and experienced armies are always like the retreat of a wounded lion." Clausewitz continued:

> Anyone who believes that a few forced marches will give him a good start and help him make a stand is dangerously wrong. The first movements have to be almost imperceptibly short, and it must be a general principle not to let the enemy impose his will. This principle cannot be put into practice without fighting fierce engagements with the pursuing enemy, but it is a principle worth the cost. Otherwise the pace is bound to increase till withdrawal turns to rout. More men will be lost as stragglers than would have been lost in rear guard actions. And the last vestiges of courage will have disappeared.[4]

A slow, fighting retreat sounds simple in theory, but it is extraordinarily difficult in practice, particularly with a large army burdened by enormous trains. Clausewitz noted a few practices a commander must employ, including "a strong rear guard, led by the most courageous general, and support at crucial moments by the rest of the army; skillful use of the terrain; strong ambushes whenever the daring of the enemy's vanguard and the terrain permit. In short, [a slow, fighting retreat] consists of planning and initiating regular small-scale engagements." Finally, Clausewitz warned against separating the retreating forces by using divergent routes. Any separation except "simply for convenience of march" is "extremely dangerous," he wrote. "It goes against the grain, and would be a great mistake. A lost battle always tends to have an enfeebling, disintegrating effect; the immediate need is to reassemble, and to recover order, courage and confidence in the concentration of troops."[5]

In the end, Clausewitz asserted, the object of any retreat is the reestablishment by the retreating army of the "balance of power" between the contending forces. "The magnitude of the losses," he wrote, "the extent of the defeat, and, what is even more important, the nature of the enemy, will determine how soon the moment of equilibrium will return." Although Lee probably never studied Clausewitz, he fully understood these axioms and would apply them to the letter over the ensuing week.[6]

Throughout the fighting at Gettysburg Lee protected two roads and two key passes through the South Mountain range: the Chambersburg Pike through Cashtown Pass and the Fairfield Road through Monterey Pass. Both roads led from Gettysburg to the Cumberland Valley; the Chambersburg Pike led to Chambersburg, thirty miles due west of Gettysburg and thirty-five miles north of Williamsport; the Fairfield Road led to Hagerstown, forty miles southwest of Gettysburg and five miles northeast of Williamsport.

The shortest route to Williamsport was by way of the Fairfield Road. That road left Gettysburg just south of the Lutheran Theological Seminary grounds and headed eight miles west to Fairfield. Southwest of Fairfield, the road forked around Jack's Mountain, a sugarloaf eminence that rises not quite six hundred feet east of the looming South Mountain range. The western fork, known as the Maria Furnace Road, meandered west of Jack's Mountain and up the steep eastern side of the South Mountain range, crossing the mountains at a summer resort known as "Monterey House." The eastern fork, known as the Jack's Mountain Road, ran east of Jack's Mountain and terminated at the east-west toll road connecting Emmitsburg, Maryland, with Monterey and Waynesboro, Pennsylvania, not far from the village of Fountaindale. The Emmitsburg-Waynesboro Turnpike led west directly to Monterey House and the summit of South Mountain and connected there with the Maria Furnace Road near a tollhouse; it then led down the western slope of South Mountain to Waterloo and Waynesboro. At Waynesboro, a turnpike ran due south to Leitersburg and Hagerstown.[7]

Both roads leading to Monterey were steep. There the South Mountain range was nearly 700 feet; the two roads on the summit of Monterey Pass cut a path less than 300 feet below the highest peaks of the mountain range. The Maria Furnace Road rose somewhat gradually at places, but the Emmitsburg-Waynesboro Turnpike climbed over 200 feet at Monterey in less than half a mile. The Maria Furnace Road was dirt, whereas the Emmitsburg-Waynesboro Turnpike was macadamized all the way to Waynesboro. The turnpike down the western side of South Mountain was just as steep as it was up the eastern side.[8]

The Chambersburg Pike, also macadamized, ran through a magnificent pass at Cashtown. Like the pass at Monterey, the mountains rose almost 700 feet behind Cashtown. At its highest point, the road cut a path some 300 feet below the highest mountain peaks. However, at Cashtown Pass, unlike the pass at Monterey, the road took more than three miles to reach its highest level before gradually descending to the floor of the Cumberland Valley.[9]

To reach Williamsport by the shortest route from Cashtown Pass, one had to use a "near road" along the western face of the South Mountain range, known as the Walnut Bottom Road, and then a road that ran southwest, known as the Pine Stump Road, to New Franklin and on to Marion, Pennsylvania. Often the two roads were both known as the Pine Stump Road. Neither road was macadamized. At Marion, one reached Williamsport by means of the Cumberland Valley Turnpike.[10]

Although the Chambersburg Pike through Cashtown Pass provided the best route across the mountains, it was the longest of the two routes to the Potomac River at Williamsport. The Fairfield Road was about twenty miles shorter. Lee had decided to withdraw his entire army by way of the Fairfield Road and Monterey Pass. Although the pass was steep, the distance to the Potomac was shorter, and there the defiles of the South Mountain range could be used to keep the enemy at bay.

To remove all the wounded required more vehicles than the Quartermaster Department had at its disposal. There was a shortage of ambulances as well as wagons in the trains to convey all the thousands of sick and wounded who could bear the journey back to Virginia. Lee would have to find a solution. In the meantime, he instructed Dr. Guild, his medical director, to forward the necessary orders to all army corps medical directors to prepare to move those casualties who could endure the journey and to provide for those who could not.

Guild then dictated a simple set of instructions to the medical directors of the three corps and the chief surgeon of the cavalry division. All sick and wounded soldiers "who can accompany or closely follow" their respective commands must do so "at the earliest moment possible." To transport those who could make the journey, Guild ordered that use be made of "every available means—embracing ambulances, empty wagons of the various trains, and such other transportation as may be furnished by the Quartermaster Department." A sufficient number of ambulances would be held in reserve for those who might become ill during the march and in the event of another battle.

Dr. Lafayette Guild, medical director of the Army of Northern Virginia. The photograph was taken just before the war. The Museum of the Confederacy, Richmond, Virginia. Photography by Katherine Wetzel.

Those wounded left behind "owing to the danger of removal or failure of transportation" would be under the guidance of a sufficient number of medical officers of the respective commands who would be "especially charged with their care and comfort." Guild then directed the chief surgeons of each corps to requisition the commissary department for "abundant supplies for the wounded and sick who would be left behind" and to see that those medical officers detailed to remain with them received ample medical and hospital supplies. Finally, Guild instructed the medical directors and chief surgeon, after they determined who would be able to make the journey on foot or in ambulances, to concentrate, as soon as possible, all the casualties to be left behind at a few hospitals "so as to diminish the number of infirmaries and increase the efficiency of the medical attendants."[11]

To address the serious deficiency in the numbers of ambulances and spring wagons available for the evacuation of the sick and wounded, Guild ordered Dr. Joseph E. Claggett, medical director of the hospitals in and near Winchester, Virginia, and director of receiving and forwarding of ambulance trains, to assemble all ambulances, wagons, carriages, and buggies at his disposal and forward them to the army immediately. Guild handed the order to a courier, who then galloped west toward Monterey Pass so that he could deliver it to Claggett at Winchester before the end of the next day. Guild soon departed the council at Hill's headquarters and rode out to the hospitals to personally supervise the removal of the sick and wounded.[12]

BEFORE LEE COULD BEGIN the retreat, his army had to reposition itself so it would be near the lines of retreat and operating on interior lines. To accomplish that, Lee had to contract his lines back to Seminary and Oak Ridges, away from the heights east of Gettysburg on his left flank and away from the advanced positions east of the Emmitsburg Road on his right flank. He also had to prepare his army for a counterattack, should Meade prove bold, and facilitate communications with all officers and commands.

Lee gave Longstreet oral instructions to return Hood's and McLaws's Divisions from the bases of the Round Tops, along Devil's Den and the ridges overlooking Plum Run, to the densely wooded Seminary Ridge and then refuse his right flank in order to protect the army from attack from the south. Lee reiterated his concern that the enemy might counterattack; he directed Longstreet to instruct his division commanders, once their forces reached their positions along Seminary Ridge, to construct heavy breastworks and prepare for an attack. Longstreet immediately told Generals Law and McLaws to begin their withdrawal to Seminary Ridge. Lieutenant Colonel William Proctor Smith, Lee's chief engineer, directed Colonel Alexander to assist in the construction of the defense line that Longstreet's Divisions would occupy along Seminary Ridge.[13]

Lee gave Ewell the most detailed instructions of all. Ewell's veterans were to abandon their hard-fought positions at the base of Cemetery and Culp's Hills and inside the town, withdraw through the streets of Gettysburg, and form a defensive line along Seminary Ridge, from the Fairfield Road, through the grounds of the Lutheran Theological Seminary, across the Chambersburg Pike and along Oak Ridge, all the way to the densely wooded Oak Hill. Lee's left flank would be anchored on Oak Hill. Lee also directed Ewell to construct heavy breastworks and prepare for a counterattack.[14]

Lee was especially concerned about the enormous reserve quartermaster and subsistence trains situated eight miles to the rear near Fairfield. Those trains contained the stores that Ewell's quartermasters and commissaries of subsistence had collected for use by their own corps and the army in general during the coming season. More than five thousand cattle and nearly an equal number of sheep and thousands of hogs were held alongside the wagons. Lee wanted the stores and animals returned to Virginia intact, but he did not want them to hold up the movement of the army unnecessarily. Consequently, he instructed Ewell to have his chief quartermaster, Major Harman, move the trains and animals onto the road toward the Potomac River immediately and to protect them at all costs. The trains were so long that in his planning for the retreat Lee allowed more than fifteen hours for them to clear Fairfield before the division trains of Ewell's Corps started moving.[15]

Ewell stepped out of the tent and called for Harman. After giving him Lee's instructions, Ewell remarked, echoing Lee's concerns: "Get that train safely across the Potomac or [I] want to see [your] face no more!" Harman returned to the reserve trains. To Major Jedediah Hotchkiss, the topographical engineer, Ewell gave directions to prepare maps for Harman and the division commanders of the route through Monterey Pass to Williamsport. Hotchkiss returned to his own engineer trains parked on the ridge overlooking Blackhorse Tavern. There he and his topographical assistant, an Englishman named Sampson B. Robinson of the Seventh Louisiana, prepared the necessary maps, which would be copied for every army commander. Ewell then dictated orders to all of his division commanders for the realignment of the corps and sent his couriers off into the night to deliver them.[16]

Lee informed Hill that his corps must hold its line on Seminary Ridge from the Fairfield Road all the way south to the left flank of Longstreet's Corps. Ever since 2 July, Hill's Corps had, for the most part, rested behind modest breastworks. Lee ordered them strengthened.[17]

Lee carefully went over the plan for the retreat itself with his three corps commanders. It was a simple one. Because Hill's Corps was astride the Fairfield Road and formed the center of the army, it would lead the retreat once the reserve trains and the trains of Ewell's three divisions had cleared the road ahead. Hill's Corps would begin the movement by withdrawing from its positions after dark on 4 July and marching all night. On reaching Monterey Pass, it was to select the "strongest ground for defense toward the east" in the event the enemy tried to strike the columns there. Longstreet's Corps would follow Hill's, and Ewell's would bring up the rear. Longstreet's and Ewell's Corps would evacuate the defense lines simultaneously; Ewell's Corps would provide the cover for Longstreet's movement before it actually took up the line of march. Lee envisioned Ewell's Corps leading the retreat on the ensuing day and Hill's bringing up the rear. Like any other march, the rear guard would be relieved regularly so that fresh troops would be available in the event of attack. Pickett's Division, under the command of army headquarters, was directed to guard the nearly four thousand Union prisoners of war; it and Longstreet's remaining divisions were to march between Hill's and Ewell's Corps. Many prisoners were already corralled near the trains of Longstreet's Divisions along Marsh Creek, so it would be easiest for one division of that corps to guard them on the retreat. Lee would maintain his headquarters in the middle of the retreating columns.[18]

The quartermaster, subsistence, and ordnance trains that actually accompanied each corps would move between the leading and rear corps. Lee left it to Lieutenant Colonel Corley, his own chief quartermaster, to determine the arrangement of those trains. Lee only admonished his corps commanders that they make sure that quartermasters and commissary of subsistence and ordnance officers remained with their respective trains, that they moved them "steadily and quietly," and that the "animals [were] properly cared for."[19]

Lee had yet another task for the quartermasters and commissary of subsistence officers; he wanted them not only to continue their foraging during the retreat but also to increase its intensity. If he must leave Pennsylvania and Maryland, he would take with him everything usable by his army. Lee intended not only to embark on a slow, fighting retreat, but also to move deliberately enough to collect all the quartermaster and subsistence stores that he could.[20]

The artillery of each corps would move under the direction of the respective corps artillery chiefs. General William N. Pendleton, the army's chief of artillery, was given the task of overseeing this movement.[21]

Finally, Lee sent a courier to his cavalry chieftain, General J. E. B. Stuart, with instructions to withdraw his commands from their positions on the far left flank—to the left of General Ewell's Corps—and re-form them north of Oak Hill, where they would again protect the army's extreme left flank in anticipation of the retreat. Stuart was to designate "a cavalry command, not exceeding two squadrons, to proceed and follow the army in its line of march." The commander of the advance squadron, Lee wrote, would report to Hill and the commander of the rear squadron to Ewell. Two brigades of cavalry would ride to Cashtown to protect the right flank (as the army moved west and south) of the trains; Stuart and his remaining brigades would proceed south toward Emmitsburg, screening the left flank of the retreating army. Lee exhorted his corps commanders orally and Stuart in writing "to see that every officer exerts the utmost vigilance, steadiness and boldness during the whole march."[22]

The first withdrawal of the Army of Northern Virginia was made by Longstreet's Corps on the far right flank. Sometime after 7:00 P.M. on 3 July, Hood's and McLaws's Divisions began to move to positions where Colonel

Alexander was establishing a defense line forming the right front and flank of the army.[23]

McLaws's four brigades abandoned the Stony Hill ridgeline from the Rose Woods all the way to the Trostle farm and retired about one mile west to positions along Seminary Ridge. The right flank of McLaws's Division was formed by Kershaw's Brigade, with its right flank resting on the west side of the Emmitsburg Road and the brigade facing northeast. The division's remaining brigades withdrew to a defense line that formed on Kershaw's left and somewhat resembled the battle lines they had formed on the afternoon of 2 July: Semmes's Brigade, commanded by Colonel Bryan, to Kershaw's immediate left; Wofford's Brigade to Bryan's left; and Barksdale's Brigade, led by Colonel Humphreys, to Wofford's left. The left flank of McLaws's line touched the right flank of Anderson's Division of Hill's Corps.[24]

Hood's Division, commanded by General Law, abandoned the line along Houck's Ridge it held in front of the Round Tops and moved back nearly a mile to a position refused nearly 130 degrees away from Seminary Ridge, facing almost due south and forming the protective right flank of the army. Benning's Brigade withdrew from its battle line near Devil's Den to a position actually "facing down the Emmitsburg Road," connecting the right flank of Kershaw's Brigade of McLaws's Division on the Emmitsburg Road. The removal of Benning's Brigade from the front was apparently conducted with some confusion. The officers and men of the Fifteenth and Twentieth Georgia misunderstood the orders. The brigades to their left had already withdrawn and the enemy had actually begun to advance toward those abandoned positions when the Twentieth Georgia hastened its movement. The Fifteenth Georgia mistakenly moved north, drew enemy fire, and then fell back to Seminary Ridge. As a consequence, the Georgians suffered considerable disorder in the beginning of the withdrawal as well as some casualties. Order was eventually regained, and the Fifteenth and Twentieth Georgia re-formed west of the Emmitsburg Road.[25]

Anderson's Brigade, commanded by Colonel White, "about faced" and marched back "up" the Emmitsburg Road from its refused line and formed on the right of Benning's Brigade, facing southeast. Robertson's Texas Brigade was ordered to move "by the right flank" and march back across the bloody fields it had won the previous day to Seminary Ridge and form on White's right, also facing southeast. Finally, Colonel Sheffield withdrew his Alabamians to the right flank of the Texas Brigade and formed, as they had throughout the battle, the right flank of Longstreet's Corps and the extreme right flank of the Army of Northern Virginia, facing southeast as well.[26]

Only one regiment in Hood's Division remained in any advanced position that night. Colonel William C. Oates's Fifteenth Alabama failed to receive an order to withdraw. As a result, it stayed in front of the division, utterly exposed, until the morning of 4 July, when it finally fell back to Seminary Ridge.[27]

Most of Longstreet's guns had remained on the west side of the Emmitsburg Road, well in front of Seminary Ridge, in much the same position they had occupied during the attack against the Union center on the afternoon of 3 July. Colonel Henry Coalter Cabell's Battalion stayed in battery along the Emmitsburg Road about four hundred yards in front of Anderson's Division. Battery A, First North Carolina Artillery, under Captain Basil C. Manley, occupied the intersection of the Millerstown and Emmitsburg Roads. Major James Dearing's Battalion remained in an advanced position along the Emmitsburg Road during the evening, as did Colonel Alexander's reserve battalion of artillery. In the night hours of 3 July all of those guns were withdrawn to the line along Seminary Ridge to support the infantry that had fallen back.[28]

Every dwelling and farmyard left behind in the wake of the withdrawal of Longstreet's troops had been ransacked. Notably, farmer Joseph Sherfy's brick house on the Emmitsburg Road was in shambles. According to a civilian visitor to the battlefield who gazed upon Sherfy's property: "The rebels had searched the house thoroughly turning everything in drawers etc. out and clothes, bonnets, towels, linen etc. were found tramped in indistinguishable piles from the house out to the barn-yard. Four feather beds never used were soaked with blood and bloody clothes and filth of every description was strewn over the house."[29]

Hill's Corps reinforced the positions it had occupied on the afternoon of 3 July, stretching from McLaws's left flank on Seminary Ridge to—by the wee hours of 4 July—the newly constituted right flank of the division of General Rodes of Ewell's Corps on the Fairfield Road. Hill's breastworks, once completed, were formidable. Even the skirmishers well out in front of the main lines constructed breastworks "made of fence rails, mud and knapsacks filled with earth."[30]

From its position in front of Culp's Hill, Johnson's Division began preparations for the withdrawal about 10:00 P.M. on 3 July; some brigades, like Williams's Louisianians, would not start until 3:00 A.M. on 4 July. The division would move back down the York Road, through the town of Gettysburg, and out the Mummasburg Road, eventually filling a defense line along Oak Ridge with its left flank on Oak Hill. Its right flank would connect with General Rodes's left along Oak Ridge north of the railroad cut.[31]

Brigadier General John A. Walker's Stonewall Brigade began moving toward Oak Ridge about midnight. The brigade's pioneers somehow never received the order to move, remaining near the smoldering ruins of a large farmhouse they had occupied since 2 July. The family had abandoned the house during the fighting. Hungry, the pioneers had helped themselves to several barrels of flour, a smokehouse full of bacon, a springhouse full of milk and butter, a garret full of crocks of apple butter, and everything else edible in the house. They had built fires in the stoves, baked bread, cooked meat and chickens, and milked the cows. Unfortunately, the house caught fire on 3 July and burned to the ground. Even then, the pioneers had rummaged through partially burned bureau drawers, lifting pictures, clothing, and love letters in their quest for loot. Only the arrival of some cavalrymen in the early hours of 4 July alerted them of the movement of Ewell's Corps back to Oak Ridge. Unable to find their way, they asked for help and the cavalrymen piloted them north of Gettysburg to the Oak Ridge defense lines.[32]

Rodes's Division retired from its positions in and just south of the town of Gettysburg, below Culp's Hill and facing Cemetery Hill, back to Seminary Ridge. It would extend the line from Johnson's right flank, across the railroad cut and through the Lutheran Theological Seminary grounds, to the Fairfield Road. Rodes began the movement between midnight and one o'clock in the morning of 4 July. Doles's Brigade, along with Ramseur's and Iverson's Brigades, remained in the sunken, dirt Long Lane until between one and three A.M. Ordered to fall back to the heights around the theological seminary, the three brigades moved "by the left flank" and marched through the southern and western suburbs of Gettysburg and out Middle Street to their positions in line, completing the movement at around daylight on 4 July. Once it reached Seminary Ridge, Ramseur's Brigade formed the right flank of Rodes's Division, connecting the left flank of Hill's Corps on the Fairfield Road. Iverson's Brigade formed on the left of Ramseur in the seminary grounds. Dole's Brigade was to the left of Iverson's, and O'Neal's was to the left of Dole's—on the north side of the railroad cut—having returned from their positions in the town and below Culp's Hill. Daniel's Brigade also withdrew from its position below Culp's Hill, arrived at Oak Ridge at daybreak, and formed on the left of O'Neal just before dawn on the fourth. Daniel's Brigade became the left flank of Rodes's Division and connected with the right flank of Johnson's Division.[33]

Early's Division evacuated its positions in front of Gettysburg facing Cemetery and Culp's Hills, near the Hanover Railroad, between midnight and two o'clock in the morning of 4 July. The division moved "by the right flank" through the town, up the Chambersburg Pike, and into a line along

McPherson Ridge, west of Gettysburg, behind Rodes's and Johnson's Divisions. Once in place, Gordon's Brigade formed on the right of the Chambersburg Pike and around the farmhouse and bank barn of Edward McPherson; it would hold the right flank of Early's Division. To Gordon's left, across the pike, came the brigade of Brigadier General William "Extra Billy" Smith, while to Smith's left was the Louisiana Brigade of General Hays. The left flank of the division would be held by Avery's North Carolina Brigade commanded by Colonel Godwin. At dawn, Early's Division formed Ewell's reserve.[34]

Two guns of Captain Willis J. Dance's First Virginia Artillery Battalion held a position between the railroad cut and the Chambersburg Pike. The rest of the reserve artillery battalion was sent to the rear out of range of enemy guns. Lieutenant Colonel William Nelson's reserve artillery battalion unlimbered within General Johnson's lines, between the railroad cut and the Mummasburg Road.[35]

In accordance with Lee's orders, all trains of Ewell's three divisions that would not travel with the troops were to be sent out the Fairfield Road to Major Harman so he could supervise their movement. Bringing those trains under Harman's immediate control for the retreat was strictly based on army regulations; as chief quartermaster of Ewell's Corps, Harman was responsible for the movement of every train in his corps. He also was in charge of the immense reserve train that would lead the army on the Fairfield Road; army regulations mandated that the trains of Ewell's three divisions follow it.[36]

Born in Augusta County, Virginia, Major John Alexander Harman was one of five brothers who served in the Confederate army. When Confederates first seized Harpers Ferry on 18 April 1861, Harman was their quartermaster. General Thomas J. Jackson made Harman his quartermaster, and he remained in Jackson's service until the general's death. Major Henry Kyd Douglas wrote: "[Harman] seemed to understand the management of teamsters and wagons as [Jackson] did that of soldiers." It was Harman who engineered Lee's successful withdrawal across the Potomac River after the bloody battle of Sharpsburg in September 1862. He was known to ride among the wagoners, kicking the mules, while "pouring out a volume of oaths that would have excited the admiration of the most scientific mule-driver." The mule drivers would swear as best they could but always, it was said, "far below the major's standard." Ingenious, profane, untiring, and loyal, Harman was the very best at what he did in the army.[37]

Because Harman's reserve quartermaster and subsistence train was so extensive—between fifteen and twenty miles in length—and was farthest ahead

Major John
Alexander Harman,
chief quartermaster
of Ewell's Corps.
Courtesy of Internet
Corporation
(Lynchburg Foundry
Company).

of the army—located between Fairfield and Cashtown—it would lead the withdrawal from Gettysburg. Behind it would come the trains of Ewell's three divisions, altogether nearly twenty miles in length. Harman would command the movement of all those trains on the Fairfield Road to the Potomac River. He had performed brilliantly in the campaign into Pennsylvania, but his real test lay ahead.

In preparation for the withdrawal, J. E. B. Stuart was at the center of one of the army's basic tactical difficulties at Gettysburg. For some reason, the courier sent to Stuart with Lee's instructions for the retreat never reached him. When Ewell's Corps abandoned its positions in front of Cemetery and Culp's Hills between 10:00 P.M. and 2:00 A.M., Stuart's horse brigades remained on the far left flank unaware of the movement. Union troops from the Eleventh and Twelfth Corps crept forward toward the town, interposing themselves between Stuart and the main body of Lee's army. Stuart became alarmed the moment he was informed of the Union advance. Upon inquiry of some of Ewell's officers, he learned about Lee's instructions to Ewell. Having received no orders himself, Stuart galloped to Lee's headquarters with some of his staff.[38]

Finding Lee still at Hill's headquarters, Stuart informed him that he had received no instructions. Lee repeated them orally. He directed that two brigades of cavalry—Hampton's, commanded by Colonel Lawrence S. Baker of the First North Carolina Cavalry after Hampton had been wounded, and Fitzhugh Lee's—be sent to Cashtown to protect the trains of Longstreet's and Hill's Corps and the cavalry division that would congregate there, as well as to protect the army's far right flank (as it moved west and south) during the retreat. The cavalry brigades of General Robertson and General Jones, which were at Fairfield with Captains Roger Preston Chew's and Marcellus N. Moorman's horse batteries after their scrape with the Sixth U.S. Cavalry, were ordered to proceed immediately to the two roads around Jack's Mountain that led to Monterey Pass. Pointing to the map, Lee showed Stuart the two roads, one that ran west of Jack's Mountain—the Maria Furnace Road—and one that ran east—the Jack's Mountain Road—connecting with the turnpike between Emmitsburg and Waynesboro. Those two roads were to be kept open by Robertson's and Jones's troops. Stuart's remaining cavalry brigades would protect the army's left flank as it moved west and south during the retreat, and they would proceed by way of Emmitsburg under Stuart's personal direction, crossing the South Mountain range south of Monterey Pass. Lee told Stuart that written instructions would be sent to him in the morning.[39]

Stuart promptly ordered Major Blackford of his staff to proceed to Fairfield and inform Robertson and Jones of the orders for the general movement of the cavalry. Because the roads around Jack's Mountain were in their immediate front—and possibly occupied by enemy cavalry—they should clear them of the enemy and hold them, as Harman's reserve train would soon begin its movement. Their cooperation was also required because Stuart would be directing his two remaining brigades toward Emmitsburg and then toward the gap at Raven Rock in South Mountain. Blackford galloped off into the darkness. Stuart returned to his command and prepared to shift his cavalry brigades, all of his trains, and most of his sick and wounded at the hospitals, ambulance depots, and wagon parks along the Hunterstown Road back toward Mummasburg to anchor the left flank of Lee's newly formed defense lines.[40]

At about 10:30 P.M. Lee dispatched a horseman to find General Imboden. Imboden and his independent command of cavalry had been operating under

Brigadier General
John Daniel Imboden.
Library of Congress,
Washington, D.C.

direct orders from Lee throughout the campaign. Lee had sent a message to
Imboden earlier in the day directing him to return to the army. Imboden and
his forces arrived at Gettysburg by way of the Chambersburg Pike on the
evening of 3 July after protecting Major Harman's reserve train of quartermaster and subsistence stores that they had brought from Chambersburg and
that was parked between Cashtown and Fairfield. The command bivouacked
for the night along the Chambersburg Pike, two miles west of Gettysburg.
Lee's courier arrived at Imboden's camp at about 11:00 P.M. and passed on the
order to report to the commanding general.[41]

General John Daniel Imboden was forty years old. A native of Staunton,
Virginia, and a graduate of Washington College, he had practiced law in
Staunton and represented his district in the Virginia legislature. After raising
the Staunton Artillery, he had marched his guns into Harpers Ferry less than
thirty hours after Virginia's secession from the Union. Imboden fought at the
first battle of Manassas and in the Shenandoah Valley; most recently he had
served in northwestern Virginia along with Grumble Jones, destroying railroads and rounding up horses, mules, and cattle for the army. After the death

of his first wife, Imboden married Mary Blair McPhail. Already, two children had been born to the couple, and in July 1863 Mary was eight months pregnant with their third child.

Imboden commanded an independent cavalry force that consisted of the Eighteenth Virginia Cavalry, led by his brother, Colonel George William Imboden; the Sixty-second Virginia Mounted Infantry, directed by his first cousin, Colonel George H. Smith of Staunton; Captain John H. McNeill's Partisan Rangers; and Captain John McClanahan's Virginia Battery of six 3-inch ordnance rifles. General Imboden's other brother, Captain Francis Marion "Frank" Imboden, commanded Company H of the Eighteenth Virginia Cavalry. Most of Imboden's men were from Augusta County, Virginia.[42]

Imboden's command was indeed "independent"; it operated directly under orders from army headquarters. Although it would appear that Imboden was favored by the army's commanders, that was not the case. He seems to have been disliked by many of the "old army" types, J. E. B. Stuart particularly. His independence from Stuart did not win him any of Stuart's favors. Apart from the fissures in his relationships with the army brass, Imboden was loyal, trustworthy, patriotic, and hard-fighting.

Imboden and an aide, his brother-in-law Lieutenant George W. McPhail, were guided by the courier to Hill's headquarters, where they found Lee still working on the arrangements for the retreat. Lee courteously greeted Imboden but requested that he return to his own headquarters up Seminary Ridge, where the two would confer later that night. Accordingly, Imboden excused himself and rode with McPhail to Lee's headquarters.[43]

It was past midnight when Lee addressed the shortage of ambulances. Calling ordnance chief Lieutenant Colonel Baldwin, chief commissary of subsistence Lieutenant Colonel Robert G. Cole, and chief quartermaster Lieutenant Colonel Corley into Hill's tent, he ordered them to collect, as early in the morning as possible, all the wagons they could commandeer and to make them available to Dr. Guild. Baldwin, Cole, and Corley quickly dictated instructions to Lee's corps commanders and his cavalry chief to direct all of their respective commands, including artillery battalions and batteries, to relinquish to the chief quartermasters of the three corps and the cavalry division all empty wagons except those needed to accompany the troops.

Lee dictated a note to Guild advising him to see that all casualties in Longstreet's and Hill's Corps and Stuart's cavalry division who could undertake the difficult journey to Virginia were placed in the wagons and ambulances to be assembled at Cashtown. Lee had determined that those trains would be protected by General Imboden and his independent cavalry command.[44]

At 1:00 A.M. on 4 July Lee finally concluded his conference at Hill's head-quarters and returned to his own. It had been a sad day for him. He had been awake for well over twenty hours. Lee was exhausted, and he had not been well.[45]

The commanding general rode Traveller at a slow walk. His head was bowed and he appeared "wrapped in profound thought." He passed the Lutheran Theological Seminary and the professors' houses south of his own headquarters. Artillery shells had perforated the buildings; window frames were shattered, sashes broken, and gardens leveled. Inside the main building more than four hundred desperately wounded soldiers, many from the Union First Corps, were hospitalized. Surgeons worked through the night. Dirty linens and bedding were strewn about. The debris of battle lay everywhere.[46]

At his own headquarters, behind the house of James Henry Thompson and across the Chambersburg Pike from the widow Mary Thompson's small stone house, a half-dozen officers' tents were pitched in a small apple orchard. The fields around and behind Lee's headquarters were grim reminders of the carnage spawned by the fighting, as burial parties had not yet completed their work. Dead men and horses had roasted under the hot summer sun for the past three days. "The sights and smells . . . were simply indescribable," recalled Major Robert Stiles, whose Charlottesville Artillery Battery in Lieutenant Colonel Hilary P. Jones's Battalion returned to the fields behind Lee's tents in the early hours of 4 July. "Corpses [were] swollen to twice their original size. Some of them actually burst asunder with the pressure of foul gases and vapors. . . . The odors were nauseating, and so deadly that in a short time we all sickened and we were lying with our mouths close to the ground, most of us vomiting profusely."[47]

James Henry Thompson's stone house directly in front of Lee's tents was so "filled with wounded and dying men of the [Union First] Corps" that his wife and two children, the youngest only one day old, were forced to flee. Casper Henry Dustman's home and barn across the Chambersburg Pike were also teeming with wounded, as were the houses of Samuel and Hannah Faulk and Elias Sheads just down the pike toward Gettysburg. Mary Thompson, whose little stone house had been Lee's headquarters on 1 July, was tending to the wounded who filled her home to capacity. Throughout the night groans, cries, and shrieks issued from those structures, as well as from the nearby seminary building and the professors' homes.[48]

By the time Lee returned to his headquarters elements of Ewell's Corps were beginning to advance back up Middle Street, the Chambersburg Pike, and the Mummasburg Road to the new defense lines along Seminary and Oak Ridges. Battle-weary infantrymen and artillerymen, together with guns and caissons, moved up those two roads. Less than fifty yards east of Lee's head-quarters, Rodes's Division began to construct breastworks along Seminary Ridge. Pioneers were dismantling all of the post and rail fences along the Chambersburg Pike and Fairfield Road and across fields near and far and were piling them up on the temporary fortifications. Even barns and outbuildings were being razed so the logs could be used for breastworks.

The area around Lee's tents was chaotic. Most of his staff officers and cou-riers returned with him. Sentinels guarded the headquarters. Horses of the staff officers, as well as of couriers, scouts, and guides of the Thirty-ninth Battalion of Virginia Cavalry, were tethered to picket pins in nearby fields, where numerous shelter halves were pitched.[49]

Imboden and McPhail were waiting for Lee, lying in the grass beneath a tree near the headquarters tents. From his horse, Lee greeted the officers and dismounted, showing marked pain. Observing Lee's physical exhaustion, Im-boden rushed to offer assistance. Lee "threw his arm across the saddle" and "fixed his legs upon the ground." He then leaned against his horse in silence, "almost motionless." "The moon [when it appeared through the growing clouds] shown full upon his massive features," Imboden later remembered, "and revealed an expression of sadness that I had never before seen upon his face." Imboden stood speechless, waiting for his commander to speak. The silence continued for some time until Imboden became somewhat embar-rassed. Then in a sympathetic tone, he said, "General, this has been a hard day for you."

Lee looked up and softly replied, "Yes, it has been a sad, sad day to us." He then resumed his silent, thoughtful mood. Imboden dared not interrupt. After a few minutes Lee stood erect and with great emotion spoke of the at-tack of Pickett's, Pettigrew's, and Trimble's commands. Once more he lapsed into silence, which was broken when, in a tone of agony, he uttered: "Too bad! Too bad! Too bad!" He then spoke "feelingly" of General Armistead, General Garnett, and General Kemper.

Although very tired, Lee invited Imboden into his tent. The two sat on simple camp stools. The noxious odors from the surrounding fields and the hideous sounds from nearby hospitals all around them must have been hor-rific.[50]

"We must now return to Virginia; as many of our poor wounded as pos-sible must be taken home," Lee said. "I have sent for you because your men and horses are fresh and in good condition, to guard and conduct our train back to Virginia. The duty will be arduous, responsible and dangerous, for I am afraid you will be harassed by the enemy's cavalry. How many men have you?"

"About two thousand, one hundred . . . and all well mounted, including McClanahan's six-gun battery of horse artillery," Imboden responded.

"I can spare you as much artillery as you require," Lee said,

but no other troops, as I shall need all I have to return safely by a different and shorter route than yours. The batteries are generally short of ammunition, but you will probably meet a supply I have ordered from Winchester to Williamsport. Nearly all of the transportation and care of all the wounded will be entrusted to you. You will cross the mountain by the Chambersburg Road, and then proceed to Williamsport by any route you deem best, and without a halt till you reach the river. Rest there long enough to feed your animals; then ford the river, and do not halt again till you reach Winchester, where I will again communicate with you.[51]

Imboden's assignment was to protect the quartermaster, subsistence, ordnance, and ambulance trains of Longstreet's and Hill's Corps and Stuart's cavalry division. Lee told him that the trains of Ewell's three divisions would follow the army's reserve train on the road to Hagerstown. This arrangement would keep all of Ewell's trains under Major Harman's direction. Because the army trains had become extraordinarily long, it would be better to use two parallel routes for the convenience of the march.

The two looked at maps of the region and considered the roads that might be most advantageous for Imboden's trains. Lee pointed out the "near roads" — the Walnut Bottom Road and the Pine Stump Road — which cut a diagonal route across Franklin County. That would be the shortest route. The Walnut Bottom Road intersected the Chambersburg Pike at Greenwood. They discussed the possible disposition of the forces guarding the trains. Obviously, artillery needed to be placed at regular intervals in the long train along with cavalry support.[52]

Lee then turned to Major Walter Taylor, his aide-de-camp, and instructed him to send a message to General Pendleton to select sufficient batteries of artillery to be sent immediately to Imboden at Cashtown. Lee told Taylor to remind Pendleton that in selecting those batteries, he obtain ones that "can best be spared from the army both as regards their efficiency and the ammunition required." Lee wanted artillery that could effectively protect Imboden's trains throughout their long journey to the Potomac.[53]

Lee informed Imboden that written instructions would be forwarded to him later in the morning. Imboden saluted and slipped out of the tent. Lee followed him, saying: "I will place in your hands by a staff officer tomorrow morning a sealed package for President Davis which you will retain in your possession till you are across the Potomac, when you will detail a reliable commissioned officer to take it into the President's own hands. And I impress it on you that, whatever happens, this package must not fall into the hands of the enemy. If unfortunately you should be captured, destroy it at the first opportunity." Imboden and McPhail then rode back to their command.[54]

Peering out of his tent in the wee morning hours, Lee could see that the clouds had completely covered the sky. The "fast-scudding" clouds of the early evening had given way to clouds that were dense; the full moon, visible earlier, had disappeared. It was very humid and muggy. The heavy clouds and humidity foreshadowed rain. If the rain was heavy, the dirt roads would become quagmires, making the movement of men, guns, wagons, and animals — not to mention the thousands of sick and wounded in ambulances and wagons and miles of quartermaster and subsistence trains — exceedingly slow and difficult. The Potomac River would quickly swell, rendering its fords useless. Lee may have felt comforted that his pontoon bridge, so far as he knew, still spanned the Potomac at Falling Waters, about forty-five miles southwest of Gettysburg. With the heavens growing heavier, though, the safety of that pontoon bridge and its train became more and more important to him.[55]

THE PONTOON TRAIN of the Army of Northern Virginia, which consisted of about sixteen large, flat-bottomed, wooden bateaux or pontoons, each over thirty feet long and weighing more than 1,450 pounds; accompanying trestlework; horse-drawn transport vehicles; and a detachment of teamsters, infantrymen, and engineer officers opened the Gettysburg campaign with an auspicious introduction to the army. It was sent by rail from Orange Courthouse to Culpeper Courthouse pursuant to an 11 April 1863 request of Lee to the chief of the Engineer Bureau, Colonel Jeremy F. Gilmer. The train rendezvoused with Ewell's Corps near the Shenandoah River at Cedarville, not far from Front Royal, on 12 June during the opening movements of the invasion.[56]

When Ewell's Corps resumed its march northward the next day, the pontoon train accompanied Rodes's Division to Berryville, thence to Martinsburg where Rodes crushed the Union garrison, sending the retreating bluecoats streaming toward Harpers Ferry, Williamsport, Berkeley Springs, and beyond. By the evening of 15 June the pontoon bridge had been constructed across the Potomac River about three miles downstream from Williamsport at Falling Waters.[57]

The location of the bridge appears to have been determined well in advance of 15 June. Falling Waters had been the site of a river crossing long before the war. For many years a ferry operated there. Named for a cascading stream on the West Virginia side of the river, the site is relatively remote now, although it was not in 1863. The Potomac River runs due south from Williamsport for just over one and a half miles and then turns abruptly west for about the same distance before making a hairpin curve back in an eastward direction. Falling Waters is situated on the southern shore at the westernmost point of that hairpin bend of the river. The terrain on the south side of the river is rather commanding, but it rises gradually, whereas that on the north side is very hilly. Because the river bends westward to such a degree, Falling Waters is situated close to the Valley Turnpike, and, at that time, a well-used road meandered down from the turnpike to the river, where a tavern and a few brick and frame houses stood. Across from Falling Waters on the Maryland side of the river, beyond a narrow bridge that spanned the Chesapeake and Ohio (C&O) Canal, the winding Falling Waters Road led up the bluffs toward the Williamsport-Downsville Road. Some of the traffic on the northern shore followed the well-worn towpath of the canal to Williamsport. Because a ferry had connected Falling Waters, West Virginia, with the C&O Canal, wharves had been constructed along the river, and a small warehouse had been built between the river and the canal to store goods that were awaiting passage across the Potomac or along the canal. For travelers on the great canal, Falling Waters was located between locks 43 and 44.[58]

On the evening of 15 June the brigades of Generals Ramseur, Dole, and Iverson crossed into Maryland by means of the ford at Williamsport; they did not use the pontoon bridge. The brigades of General Daniel and Colonel O'Neal, which had been left behind to escort the division trains and guard the southern approaches to the pontoon bridge, crossed the river at the Williamsport ford two days later. On 19 June Rodes's Division moved from Williamsport to Hagerstown, and on 22 June it advanced north to Greencastle. The pontoon bridge and train were left behind at Falling Waters, guarded only by the small detachment of teamsters, infantrymen, and engineer officers who had accompanied it from the start of the campaign.[59]

According to army regulations, pontoon trains functioned under the army's engineer department, but the troops attached to them received their orders directly from army headquarters. Although the pontoon train traveled with Rodes's Division, neither General Rodes nor any of his brigade commanders ever mentioned it in their official reports, and none of them made use of it once it spanned the Potomac.[60]

After the defeat of the Union garrisons at Winchester and Martinsburg and Ewell's movement into Maryland and Pennsylvania, the Potomac Valley from Harpers Ferry to Cumberland, Maryland, became a focal point for enemy operations. With Union troops of French's Division nearby and the remnants of Milroy's broken commands still in the area (some assimilated into French's Division)—all within striking distance—the pontoon train and bridge were vulnerable to attack and destruction. Although it was the only such equipment accompanying Lee's army up to that point, there is absolutely no indication that Lee issued any directives to Ewell or Rodes regarding its protection.

Ewell, and more immediately Rodes, understood that the pontoon train was operating under orders from Lee and that its protection was the concern of army headquarters. Neither Ewell nor Rodes received instructions to post troops at Falling Waters. If they gave any thought to the pontoon bridge at all—which they probably did not—they must have assumed that, at the time they left it behind, the rear of Ewell's Corps—and that part of the Potomac Valley where the bridge was situated—was free of the enemy presence. Moreover, with Longstreet's and Hill's Corps soon moving toward the Potomac and several regiments of Ewell's Corps left behind at Winchester, the bridge would be protected from enemy attack. In any event, the bridge and its equipment at Falling Waters might be needed to facilitate Hill's and Longstreet's eventual crossing of the river.

When Hill's Corps traversed the Potomac on 24 June and Longstreet's Corps the next day, neither used the pontoon bridge at Falling Waters. Hill's Corps crossed at Boteler's Ford near Shepherdstown and moved through Sharpsburg, Boonsboro, Funkstown, and Hagerstown, whereas Longstreet's Corps used the ford at Williamsport. Like Ewell, neither Hill nor Longstreet was ever directed to assume responsibility for protecting the pontoon bridge and train after they crossed the river and entered Maryland and Pennsylvania. Lee crossed the Potomac River on 25 June with Longstreet's Corps. He made no special arrangements for safeguarding the pontoon bridge and train.

Lee had left the pontoon bridge and train at Falling Waters to ensure, in the event of rising waters, that communications—the movement of mail and necessary dispatches—and the transportation of ammunition and impressed quartermaster and subsistence stores would flow without interruption during the campaign. If there was ever concern expressed about the safety of the pontoon bridge and train once the army crossed the Potomac and before the fighting erupted at Gettysburg, it was never recorded in the reports of any commanding officer of any corps, division, or brigade or by the commander of the army. It seems as if the regiments assigned to garrison Martinsburg and Winchester and to escort prisoners of war to Staunton were never alerted to protect the pontoon bridge and train before 4 July. The records do not indicate any attempt by those units to do so.

In the early hours of 4 July the pontoon bridge was about forty-five miles behind Lee and vulnerable to enemy forays west from Frederick by General French's commands and east from Cumberland, as General Kelley's Department of West Virginia was marching toward the area and remnants of Milroy's commands were not far away. On numerous occasions spies and civilians in the vicinity had reported the presence of the pontoon bridge at Falling Waters to various Union cavalry detachments operating out of Frederick and to General French. As a result, Colonel Andrew T. McReynolds of the First New York (Lincoln) Cavalry, commander of a newly formed cavalry brigade consisting mostly of remnants of Milroy's commands that had fled toward Harpers Ferry after the disasters at Winchester and Martinsburg and were now attached to French's division, had sent a scouting expedition from Frederick to Falling Waters and Williamsport to find out how Lee might recross the Potomac River, as well as what protection he had provided for the often-sighted pontoon bridge and the fords of the river. On the night of 2 July the scouting party had reported to McReynolds that the bridge was guarded only by a small complement of teamsters, infantrymen, and engineer officers and that the ford at Williamsport was also lightly guarded.[61]

Based on that intelligence, McReynolds penned a hurried dispatch in the early morning hours of 3 July to Lieutenant W. F. A. Torbut, assistant adjutant general to French, requesting permission to send a detachment from his cavalry brigade to destroy the bridge. "I beg to submit for consideration of the Major General commanding," he wrote, "that I have information which I deem reliable, that the rebel force in the vicinity of Williamsport is very small; that a force of cavalry about one hundred and fifty strong, could, in my opinion, successfully approach to that point, and by a prompt movement, at break of day to-morrow, destroy the pontoon bridge at that place, which is the only reliance of the rebels for a retreat of their infantry, artillery and wagons in that direction." The proposed expedition met with French's unqualified approval. On the morning of 3 July he so notified his cavalry brigade commander, commenting, "You will use your discretion in effectuating the purpose [of the plan]."[62]

French sent his 3 July communication to McReynolds via Cadet George Gordon Greenough, an eager young temporary member of his staff. A member of what would become the West Point class of 1865, Greenough was an aide-de-camp at French's headquarters. To command the expedition McReynolds selected Major Shadrack Foley, a native of western Pennsylvania and commander of a detachment of the Fourteenth Pennsylvania Cavalry assigned to French's division (the balance of which regiment was attached to Brigadier General William W. Averell's command in the Department of West Virginia). Foley then assembled a special force composed of his own detachment and detachments from the First New York (Lincoln) Cavalry, Thirteenth Pennsylvania Cavalry, and First West Virginia Cavalry (all of which were formerly part of Milroy's command that had escaped to Harpers Ferry)—about three hundred troops in all. Greenough was to accompany Foley. McReynolds advised Foley that to accomplish his mission, he had to reach and destroy the pontoon bridge before daybreak, 4 July.[63]

When "boots and saddles" sounded in the cavalry brigade camp, the raiders mounted up and galloped out of Frederick on the National Road before nightfall while, back at Gettysburg, Robert E. Lee was planning his army's retreat. Foley's command, following the scouts who had performed the reconnaissance of the previous day, headed due west from Frederick, through Middletown, over Turner's Pass, to Boonsboro, and then south to the Potomac River. At the river, the command followed the towpath of the C&O Canal toward Falling Waters. The moon at first showed through heavy, fast-scudding clouds, lighting the well-worn path.[64]

After a long and difficult ride through the rolling hills cut by the Potomac River, the cavalrymen finally reached their destination. The scouts galloped back to Foley at the head of the column to report their sighting of the bridge. To Foley's astonishment, the scouts had not observed any guards posted along the Maryland shore. No guards appeared on the West Virginia shore, either. The major kept his force at a distance downstream from Falling Waters so the noise of the horses—which would echo through the river gorge—would not broadcast their presence to the unwary Confederate detachment at the bridge.

The pontoon bridge, the scouts explained, was made of trestlework that was attached to the wooden pontoons or bateaux and positioned beneath the center of the span. It was easily dismantled and reconstructed. In protecting the bridge, the small detachment of teamsters, infantrymen, and engineer officers would periodically dismantle it and float the pontoons with the disassembled trestlework to the West Virginia shore for safekeeping. Consequently, they did not have to concern themselves every night with guarding the approaches to the bridge from the Maryland shore. On the night of 3 July the disassembled bridge was on the West Virginia shore.[65]

The Potomac River at Falling Waters was relatively deep. The only way a body of troops could cross the river at that site was by boat. Cadet Greenough and two of the cavalrymen volunteered to swim across and bring back enough pontoons from the West Virginia shore to ferry a sufficient number of men to surprise the enemy soldiers camped near the pontoon train and bridge. Some noise would be drowned out by the sound of the cascading stream near the Confederate detachment. Even so, this, and the fact that the scouts had seen no guards posted with the pontoons, provided only modest reassurance to the three volunteers.[66]

Through the inky, predawn darkness, Greenough and his two companions swam across the black, sluggish water. With great caution, they cut three pontoons from their moorings and quietly guided them across the river to the Maryland shore. About forty troops, mostly from the Fourteenth Pennsylvania Cavalry, clambered into the pontoons just as Greenough and his companions slid the wooden hulks up onto the sandy bank. Silently they poled the pontoons back across the river.[67]

When the Union forces arrived on the southern bank, they quickly moved into positions north and east of the sleeping Confederate detachment. In a moment, they opened fire. Shots rang out, echoing through the river gorge; flames from the carbines and pistols lighted the darkness.

The initial volley was all that it took to overwhelm the unwary Confederates. They were startled and seized with panic; many ran into the neighboring woods. Some thirteen men and one officer of the Confederate command, unable to find a means of escape, surrendered. In an effort to keep those Confederates upstream from interfering with the demolition of the pontoon bridge and train, Foley led a larger, mounted portion of his command up the towpath of the canal to Williamsport, where it attacked and dispersed the small Confederate contingent protecting the ford of the river.[68]

Captured with the surprised Confederates at Falling Waters were all the pontoons and trestlework; four pontoon transport wagons, containing various bridge parts, equipment, and assorted ammunition; and the stores of the engineer detachment. While Foley and his troops kept the enemy occupied at Williamsport, Greenough and his men destroyed the captured transport wagons, equipment, and stores at Falling Waters. All of the pontoons and trestlework of the bridge were floated across to the Maryland shore. Most were burned; some were cut to pieces. The captives were quickly sent ahead under guard so they would not slow down the command in the event of an emergency. With the approach of daylight, Foley deemed it the better part of valor to mount up his entire force and get back to Frederick. As a result, a few pontoons escaped total destruction.[69]

The pontoon bridge of the Army of Northern Virginia had been virtually destroyed. In the process, not one officer or trooper in Foley's command had been injured. The expedition was a success. The destruction of the bridge, coupled with the threatened rain on the morning of 4 July, would present serious logistical problems for Lee.

Back in his headquarters tent along Seminary Ridge in the early hours of 4 July, Lee dictated an order to the new commanding officer of Winchester, Major David B. Bridgeford, and gave it to Imboden for delivery. "I wish you to convey to the commanding officers of the regiments of Ewell's Corps (Thirteenth Virginia, Fifty-eighth Virginia, and Fifty-fourth North Carolina)," he wrote,

> instructions from me to proceed to Falling Waters, where they will take position and guard the pontoon bridge at that place, and also the ford at Williamsport, holding there all persons belonging to this army, and collecting all stragglers from it. Any sick of course will be forwarded into Winchester. The senior officer present will take command. Should it be necessary that a part of that force remain in Winchester, you have my authority for retaining it there. Upon arrival of the sick and wounded at Winchester, they will be forwarded to Staunton as rapidly as possible, as also any surplus articles not needed for the army in the field.

Lee's concern for the safety of the pontoon bridge and train came too late. The "debris of Winchester" had struck.[70]

Four

All that was dear to me is gone

At 3:00 A.M. on 4 July Major Harman ordered his immense reserve quartermaster and subsistence train to move out onto the Fairfield Road. Neighing and snorting mules and horses began pulling the wagons down the road from Cashtown to Fairfield and onto the road to Monterey Pass. In the lead and at intervals beside the train were herds of cattle and sheep. Hogs were tied to wagons or rode in them. So long was the reserve train, it would take ten hours for it just to clear Fairfield. As the leading wagons rolled into Fairfield, the rear wagons were deep in Cashtown Pass. Harman's train was able to move with some speed, as the roads were generally dry for most of the ten hours it took to get past Fairfield.[1]

Because Lee made no arrangements for protecting the reserve train, Ewell directed elements of Major Ridgely Brown's First Maryland Cavalry Battalion that had accompanied Ewell's Corps throughout the invasion, along with the four 12-pound Napoleon guns of Captain William A. Tanner's Courtney Virginia Artillery of Jones's Artillery Battalion, to lead them. Once that train passed the screen of Jones's and Robertson's cavalry brigades and Chew's and Moorman's Batteries guarding the approaches to Fairfield from Emmitsburg, only the mounted Marylanders and Tanner's four guns would provide it protection. Lee counted on the very early start and the darkness to give it cover.[2]

Back on Seminary Ridge, eight miles east of where Harman's reserve train was moving through Fairfield, Lee was still awake, dictating orders to his lieutenants and a letter to President Davis. In front of his headquarters infantrymen and artillerymen of Rodes's Division were building log, stone, and earthen breastworks along the ridge, while the dreadful chorus of the wounded could be heard from the residences and seminary building nearby.[3]

That morning Lee dictated explicit orders to General Imboden: "Take

Three Confederate stragglers captured in the wake of Lee's retreat from Gettysburg seated and standing along the Seminary Ridge breastworks of logs, fence rails, and log beams constructed by Rodes's Division during the early morning of 4 July. Library of Congress, Washington, D.C.

charge of the train belonging to this army which I have directed to be assembled in the vicinity of Cashtown this afternoon." He advised Imboden to start by at least 5:00 P.M. and take the trains through Greencastle by "turning off at Greenwood." Imboden was to move through Williamsport to Falling Waters, "whence [the trains] can proceed more leisurely to Winchester." Lee, of course, had no idea that the bridge at Falling Waters had been destroyed. He directed that artillery be distributed at intervals along the trains and that scouts be well posted. Once across the Potomac River, Imboden was to station artillery at the Williamsport ford. "I need not caution you as to preserving quiet and order in your train, secrecy of your movements, promptness and energy, and increasing vigilance on the part of yourself and your officers," Lee concluded.[4]

Lee then dictated a short note to President Davis. In it he recounted the successes of Hill's and Ewell's Corps on 1 July and noted that the army had taken nearly four thousand prisoners of war. About the fighting on 2 July, he wrote: "We were unable to get possession of [the enemy's] position. The next day (3 July) . . . a more extensive attack was made. The works on the enemy's extreme right and left were taken, but his numbers were so great and his position so commanding, that our troops were compelled to relinquish their advantage and retire." Lee admitted that his losses had "not been light." Generals Barksdale, Garnett, Armistead, Pender, Trimble, Hood, Heth, Kemper, and Hampton all were casualties. The letter was succinct and matter-of-fact. The note to Davis and the orders to Imboden were given to a courier who went galloping out the Chambersburg Pike toward Cashtown to deliver them.[5]

Throughout the early hours of 4 July there was activity at all of the hospital sites and wagon parks of Lee's army. As early as 1:00 A.M., orders had been issued at the headquarters of the three corps directing artillery battalion commanders to have their guns in readiness along Seminary and Oak Ridges once they arrived there in order to resist an attack that Lee believed would occur at daylight. The orders directed battalion chiefs to send all of their ordnance wagons, "except such as were required to accompany the artillery," to the chief quartermaster of each corps, loaded with as many sick and wounded as they could carry. They were then to report to Lee's chief quartermaster, Lieutenant Colonel Corley, for disposition. In addition, battalion chiefs were to tell the occupants of ambulance trains that, to every one they saw along the roads, to say "that they [were] going back with the wounded and for ammunition." Empty quartermaster, subsistence, and ordnance wagons were soon being culled from the trains in the division wagon parks and driven to the hospitals. Those wagons would be used as ambulances, but they would not come close to meeting the transportation needs of the wounded.[6]

Corley and his staff worked out all arrangements for the movement of army trains with the chief quartermasters of each corps and Dr. Guild, medical director of the army. Corley's staff and the corps quartermasters and their staffs served as traffic police, directing the movement of the trains onto and along the designated roads.[7]

At the same time the army began withdrawing to the newly established defense lines along Seminary and Oak Ridges, the sick and wounded capable of being transported were placed in ambulances and empty wagons at division hospitals and readied for the long journey to Virginia. Those who could walk were instructed to do so. The objective was to get the wounded to the medical evacuation network in the Shenandoah Valley and, ultimately, to the

General and Receiving Hospital at Staunton, almost two hundred miles away. Once there, they could be forwarded by train to Richmond. This medical evacuation system had been in place since the summer of 1861. Lee had taken advantage of it throughout his invasion of Pennsylvania, and his retreat was designed to fall back on it.

Surgeons ordered many patients to be kept where they were because of the seriousness of their illness or wounds or the woeful lack of transportation. Some surgeons and assistant surgeons, stewards, and nurses were ordered to remain behind to care for those who were left; others were told to prepare to leave with the ambulance trains, and still others were instructed to return to their regiments. At the center of all this activity was the medical director of the army. Dr. Guild could be seen at every division hospital site, ensuring that his orders were carried out to the letter.[8]

No activity was more feverish than that in the hospitals and wagon parks of Ewell's three divisions. Because Johnson's and Early's Divisions were ordered to abandon the areas north and northeast of Gettysburg—from sites along the Hunterstown Road to the foot of Culp's and Cemetery Hills and in the town—decisions had to be made as early as 10 P.M. on 3 July regarding who would leave and who would remain to become prisoners of war among the sick and wounded, surgeons, assistant surgeons, stewards, nurses, and cooks. Dr. McGuire, in consultation with Dr. Guild and Guild's chief medical inspector, Dr. Robert J. Breckinridge, and the division quartermasters and chief surgeons, made the arrangements at each hospital site.[9]

The casualties of Johnson's Division at the Picking farm and schoolhouse and the Buehler, Montford, Shealer, Lady, and Weible farms who could undertake the long journey to Virginia were loaded in ambulances and spare wagons, brigade by brigade, along with the necessary surgical teams, equipment, and rations, and hauled toward Seminary and Oak Ridges behind the division's columns of infantry and artillery. Among the hundreds of wounded placed in ambulances were General Jones and Major Latimer. Dr. Latimer accompanied his wounded brother. Many of the injured were forced to walk. The Thirty-first Virginia's Corporal James E. Hall, who had been wounded in the knee during the last assaults against Culp's Hill on 3 July, was one of them. Lieutenant Colonel Herbert and Major Goldsborough were among those left behind at the Shealer farm. One of those remaining at the Picking farm was Major Douglas.[10]

Dr. Wood of the Third North Carolina was one of the surgeons directed by Dr. Coleman, chief surgeon of Johnson's Division, to select those who were to be transported. "The scene at the division hospital," Wood recalled, "was very distressing. I was sent to report the number of wounded and indicate all who were able to march or be transported in wagons. The men were not slow to find out that we were preparing to fall back, and leave them as prisoners. I knew the men well by this time, and they greatly desired that I remain with them, but Dr. [Dabney] Herndon of Fredericksburg, surgeon in a [Louisiana] regiment was detailed for the purpose. Every empty wagon was loaded with wounded men."[11]

The trains of Johnson's Division followed its troops toward Seminary and Oak Ridges. Like all of the army's division trains, their assembly was systematic, as it was overseen by the staff of the chief quartermaster of the corps as well as by Dr. McGuire and the department chiefs of the division.[12]

Ambulance trains were assembled by brigades and were overseen by the division's chief surgeon and quartermaster. The systematic arrangement of the ambulances was necessary to maintain continuity of care of the wounded. Surgeons and assistant surgeons always remained with the casualties of their own brigade, as they were in a position to know something about the medical or surgical history of those patients. Ambulances always traveled by brigade in one long division train.

Quartermaster trains were assembled by brigade and then aligned by the division quartermaster. Accompanying them were herds of seized horses and mules. Because the troops needed quartermaster and subsistence stores on the march—and foraging was to continue during the retreat—some quartermaster and subsistence wagons accompanied the infantry and artillery columns. The main division and brigade subsistence trains, however, were assembled by division commissaries of subsistence and moved as a division train. Ordnance trains were assembled by division ordnance officers. Most of the ordnance wagons included in the quartermaster trains carried damaged weapons or other hardware; those carrying live ordnance, led by the ordnance chiefs of each division, traveled with the troops.[13]

In most divisions, the trains leaving Gettysburg were led by several brigade quartermaster trains, followed by the division subsistence train and then more brigade quartermaster trains. Artillery battalion quartermaster trains followed. The ordnance wagons that did not accompany the troops continued the procession. Division quartermasters and commissaries of subsistence accompanied their trains; assistant quartermasters and assistant commissaries of subsistence followed the troops with necessary smaller trains. The rear of the division trains was made up of brigade ambulance trains, one brigade train following the other. Behind or in front of brigade ambulance trains were the trains of the artillery battalions. Walking wounded hobbled beside the ambulances. The chief surgeons of each division rode with the trains; the medical directors of each corps remained with the troops. At intervals of about every half mile along the subsistence trains followed herds of cattle and sheep that had been collected by division commissaries of subsistence. Riding in all of the wagon trains were thousands of slaves, wagoners, and laborers.[14]

For those who remained at the division hospitals, either because of the seriousness of their illnesses or wounds or the lack of transportation, surgical teams were ordered to stay with them; they were given as much food and medical supplies as could be spared in the opinion of Dr. Breckinridge and the department chiefs. Medical supplies had to be husbanded, as they would also be needed by the wounded in the ambulance trains and by the troops as they marched south.

In all, 446 of the 1,300 wounded in Johnson's Division were left behind at the division's hospitals northeast of Gettysburg. Most of the rest were sent to the rear in ambulances and wagons or on foot, accompanied by surgeons, assistant surgeons, stewards, and nurses.[15]

Dr. William Riddick Whitehead of the Forty-fourth Virginia, then attached to the Second Corps Field Hospital, was directed by Dr. McGuire as early as 8:00 P.M. on 3 July to stay behind not only to manage the care of those who remained at the hospitals of Johnson's Division in Gettysburg but also to oversee all of Ewell's wounded who were left in Pennsylvania. He would be joined at Johnson's hospitals by Dr. Dabney Herndon of the Fifteenth Louisiana, Dr. Frank L. Taney of the Tenth Louisiana, Dr. Augustus B. Scholars of the Second Louisiana, and others.[16]

West of the hospitals of Johnson's Division were those of Early's Division. As Johnson's trains rumbled through Gettysburg and out the Mummasburg Road toward Oak Ridge, Early's hospitals along the Harrisburg and Carlisle Roads — the Crawford, Benner, Lott, Ross, Kime, Culp, and Cobean houses and farmyards and the dormitory at Pennsylvania College — were being thinned of their patients. In the early hours of 4 July the body of Colonel Avery was loaded into a quartermaster wagon by his slave Elijah. In the hospital of Gordon's Brigade at the Jacob Kime farm, Lieutenant James Mincey of the Sixty-first Georgia was left behind much to the grief of his men. Rube, his slave, took matters into his own hands. He stole a horse and wagon from a nearby farm and lifted his master into it. He then drove the wagon into the ambulance trains of Early's Division.[17]

Some 259 of more than 800 casualties in Early's Division were selected by Dr. Morrison, its chief surgeon, to be left in Gettysburg. To care for them, Dr. Louis E. Gott of the Forty-ninth Virginia was ordered to stay behind as the chief surgeon. Gott would be joined by Dr. William Lewis Reese of the Sixth North Carolina, Dr. Judson A. Butts of the Thirty-first Georgia, Dr. Brodie Strachan Herndon Jr. of the Rockbridge Artillery, and others.[18]

Cannoneer Edward E. Moore of the Rockbridge Artillery received a message from his commander, Captain Archibald Graham, that some of the wounded at the battery hospital on the Lott farm north of Gettysburg had summoned him. After walking a distance, he found the injured soldiers "occupying a neat brick cottage a mile in the rear from which the owners had fled, leaving a well stocked larder. From that larder," he recalled, "we refreshed ourselves most gratefully." Dr. Herndon, the battery surgeon, was overseeing the care of the men. At midnight orders came to move the hospital. Ambulances were driven to the door of the house; after eight or ten wounded men had been placed in them with Moore's assistance and carried off, Moore ran back into the house and "grabbed a bucket of lard, a crock of butter, a jar of apple butter, a ham, a middling of bacon and a side of sole leather." The foraging by Lee's men continued unabated.[19]

Surgery was performed even while ambulance trains were being assembled. General Trimble had been taken from the Whisler house on the Chambersburg Pike, a hospital of Pender's Division, and driven by ambulance to the Cobean house, the site of Dr. McGuire's Second Corps Field Hospital. As Trimble was assigned to Ewell's Corps, McGuire was responsible for his care. When Trimble arrived, the trains of Johnson's Division were passing behind the columns of troops toward Seminary and Oak Ridges and Early's trains were being formed. After the ambulance corpsmen brought Trimble into the parlor, McGuire determined that the leg had to be removed. Beneath the tall case clock that stood in the corner of the room, McGuire, assisted by Dr. Black and Dr. John M. Hayes of the Twenty-sixth Alabama and chief surgeon of O'Neal's Brigade, took off Trimble's left leg. All three doctors believed that the remaining portion of the leg would become inflamed in an ambulance and erysipelas would ensue. Consequently, they left orders for Trimble, when able, to be moved to a private home in town, where he would become a prisoner of war.[20]

At the hospitals of Rodes's Division housed at the Hankey and Schriver farms along the Mummasburg Road behind the new defense lines, surgeons, assistant surgeons, stewards, nurses, and quartermasters were similarly busy transferring the casualties to ambulances and empty wagons. At the Hankey farm, Colonel Christie and Lieutenant Colonel Johnston of the Twenty-third North Carolina were placed in a light, one-horse hack that had been impressed only about a week before at Carlisle, Pennsylvania, by Captain E. V. Turner, the regiment's assistant quartermaster. Arrangements were made for Major Blacknall to ride in an ambulance, but he desired to travel on horseback, believing that it would be less painful.[21]

Behind Christie, Johnston, and Blacknall, ambulance corpsmen lifted Lieutenant Colonel Green and Captain Bond of Rodes's staff into a one-horse buggy that had recently been impressed. Climbing into the buggy with Green and Bond was Guilford, Green's slave, who would drive the vehicle. Nearby, Colonel Kenan was placed in an ambulance with his surgeon, Dr. William T. Brewer. Behind Kenan, other wounded of Daniel's Brigade, including Lieutenant Shepherd of Kenan's Forty-third North Carolina, Lieutenant Colonel Boyd of the Forty-fifth North Carolina, Major Lewis of the Thirty-second North Carolina, and Major Hancock of the Second North Carolina Battalion, were carried to ambulances and empty wagons. They were joined by Dr. J. Robinson Godwin of the Second North Carolina Battalion. Hundreds more wounded from the division filled ambulances and wagons in the procession.[22]

Captain Charles Frederick Bahnson, assistant quartermaster of the Second North Carolina Battalion, moved his trains out of the wagon park and past the Hankey farm hospitals. He had a glimpse of his brother Henry and a few of his friends, all of whose wounds compelled them to remain behind. Bahnson could not leave his trains, so he made his sad farewells from a distance. Lifted into an ambulance was his friend Captain Henry C. Wheeler, of Company G, who had been seriously wounded in both thighs and the left hand on 1 July. The hand had been amputated and his legs were badly inflamed. His ambulance soon joined the procession.[23]

Captain Samuel H. Early, General Early's brother who had accompanied Rodes's Division in the campaign, was wounded on 3 July, "a ball striking him on the shinbone halfway between the knee and foot." His fifteen-year-old son, John Cabell Early, a courier, saw his father's bandaged leg and inquired about his condition. Captain Early told his son that General Early had instructed him to return home to Lynchburg, Virginia, and that young John was to accompany him. The two had spent the night at the wagon park of Early's Division. In the early morning hours, the son rode his father's horse to the Gettysburg almshouse on the Carlisle Road, north of town, where he had seen a buggy near a corn shed. Finding the buggy still there, he hitched his father's horse to it. He then helped his father inside the buggy, and the two joined the ambulance trains of Rodes's Division.[24]

Private W. J. O'Daniel of Company H, Twenty-third North Carolina,

"Good-bye." A. C. Redwood's drawing of a soldier bidding farewell to a wounded comrade being conveyed to Virginia by ambulance. Robert Underwood Johnson and Clarence Clough Buel, eds., *Battles and Leaders of the Civil War*, 4 vols. (New York: Century Co., 1884–87), 3:423.

was at the hospital of Iverson's Brigade at the Hankey farm that morning. He and his hometown friend, Leonidas "Lon" Torrence, of Gaston County, North Carolina, had promised that each would look after the other if either fell in battle. On 1 July Torrence was hit by rifle fire in the thigh and the head, between his eye and ear. Blood spattered and, lapsing in and out of consciousness, he lay at the hospital under a shelter half resigned to die. O'Daniel looked at his boyhood friends nearby; three of them were amputees and would likely not survive. O'Daniel himself had been hit with buckshot in the left cheek. "I wanted to stay and wait on Lon and [another friend]," he wrote to Torrence's mother, "but the Doc would not let me stay. Lon could not eat anything. He drank water but he throwed it all up. He said he was willing to die." Torrence gave O'Daniel all of his personal effects, except his Bible and handkerchief, to be taken to his mother. The two then parted with sad "good-byes." Lon died within hours of O'Daniel's departure.[25]

At the hospital of Ramseur's Brigade at the Schriver farm, Colonel Parker of the Thirtieth North Carolina was placed on the floor of a buggy that had been seized during the foraging operations preceding the battle. Driving the buggy was no teamster but rather Colonel Risden Tyler Bennett of the Fourteenth North Carolina. Bennett had been shot in the groin on 1 July but claimed that he was still able to sit up and take the reins of the horse. In their one-horse buggy, Parker and Bennett joined the ambulance train of Ramseur's Brigade. At the hospital of Doles's Brigade nearby, Colonel Lumpkin of the Forty-fourth Georgia was loaded into an ambulance. Dr. William H. Philpot and Dr. Abner Embry McGarity were doubtful that Lumpkin would survive, given the recent amputation of his leg.[26]

Private John S. Tucker of Company D of the Fifth Alabama was assigned to the trains of O'Neal's Brigade that were lining up on the Mummasburg Road early that morning. Only thirty-six hours before he had buried his younger brother, Tunie, who had been killed on 1 July. Tucker wrote in his diary: "I feel perfectly indifferent as to the result [of the battle], all that was ever dear to me in this army is gone and I care not what the result is."[27]

Placed in the lead wagon of the ambulance train of O'Neal's Brigade were Captains Robert Emory Park, Poleman D. Ross, and Augustus E. Hewlett, along with Lieutenant G. W. Wright, all of the Twelfth Alabama, who had been wounded on 1 July. Park suffered from a painful bullet wound in the thigh; Wright had been hit in the head by a shell fragment that tore off the bone, exposing his brain. The other two officers suffered from painful flesh wounds. The foursome had spent a hideous two days and two nights sharing a tent with two others. Park had rested beside Lieutenant J. M. Fletcher, of his regiment, who, for forty-eight hours, had moaned and groaned in agony from a wound to the abdomen. On the morning of 3 July Park had awakened to find Fletcher "cold in death." Under the watchful eye of Dr. George Whitfield of the Twelfth Alabama, the four wounded officers were driven off in their ambulance by Sam Slaton, a soldier detailed from the regiment. None were sure how long Wright would last in the journey ahead.[28]

Of the 1,600 sick and wounded at the hospitals of Rodes's Division, 760 were left behind with four surgeons, six assistant surgeons, ninety-seven attendants, and rations for ten days. Remaining in Gettysburg to oversee the hospitals was Dr. John M. Hayes. He was accompanied by, among others, Dr. R. G. Southall of the Sixth Alabama, Dr. John Henry Hicks of the Twentieth North Carolina, Dr. Isaac Pearson of the Fifth North Carolina, Dr. J. H. Purefoy of the Twenty-third North Carolina, and Dr. Anthony Benning Johns Jr. of the Forty-fifth North Carolina. Dr. Simon Branch of the

Chambersburg Pike looking west toward the Frederick Herr Tavern. Note the white fence line marking the Herr Ridge Road in the distance. Imboden's trains stretched all the way from Herr Ridge to Cashtown, eight miles west, as they were being assembled on the Chambersburg Pike on 4 July 1863. All of Ewell's trains and troops used the Herr Ridge Road, moving right to left, to reach the Fairfield Road preparatory to the retreat. National Archives, Washington, D.C.

Twenty-third North Carolina and chief surgeon of Iverson's Brigade would assist Hayes. The division's other surgeons and assistant surgeons were directed to accompany the ambulance trains or the troops.[29]

As Major Harman had directed the trains of Ewell's three divisions, along with the horses, mules, cattle, sheep, and hogs accompanying them, to follow his reserve train from Fairfield to the Potomac River, he and Lieutenant Colonel Corley had selected the route they would take. Once Johnson's and Early's trains reached the summit of Oak Ridge, in back of their columns of infantry and artillery, they were ordered to move behind the defense lines that were being established until they reached the Herr Ridge Road. That road ran along Herr Ridge, parallel to Seminary and Oak Ridges and about one mile to the west. The Herr Ridge Road joined the Mummasburg Road near the Schriver farm, the hospital site of the brigades of Ramseur, Doles, and O'Neal of Rodes's Division. The road then ran south about one mile, where it crossed the Chambersburg Pike and continued south just west of the large two-story brick Frederick Herr Tavern. It proceeded almost two miles farther south of the tavern, where it entered the Fairfield Road not far from the Adam Butt farm, the hospital site of Anderson's Division of Hill's Corps. The Herr Ridge Road formed a convenient connector artery for the trains of Ewell's three divisions to reach the Fairfield Road with little or no interference from the troops who were throwing up breastworks along Seminary and Oak Ridges.[30]

The trains of Johnson's and Early's Divisions rolled down the Herr Ridge Road and onto the Fairfield Road; Johnson's trains probably entered the Herr Ridge Road by way of the Mummasburg Road, while Early's trains likely followed the troops out the Chambersburg Pike to the Herr Ridge Road. Once the leading wagons of those trains reached the Fairfield Road, they turned west and wound their way to Fairfield, about six miles farther. The trains of Rodes's Division followed Johnson's and Early's trains.[31]

It took hours for Johnson's and Early's trains to pass down the Herr Ridge Road. There were frequent stops and starts. In the process, some wounded died; some were unable to go on, as burial sites of the dead from both divisions along the road indicate. At the John Crist farm on the Herr Ridge Road, north of the Chambersburg Pike, five Louisianans were buried, including Major Henry L. N. Williams of the Ninth Louisiana, all from Hays's Brigade of Early's Division. A soldier from the Thirty-third Virginia of Walker's Brigade, Johnson's Division, was buried at the Frederick Herr Tavern on the south side of the Chambersburg Pike.[32]

At about midmorning, 4 July, the head of the trains of Johnson's Division finally came to a halt in the fields alongside the Fairfield Road just east of Fairfield. Ahead of it, the reserve train was still moving onto the Fairfield Road, heading toward Monterey Pass. The trains of Johnson's Division, parked in the fields on both sides of the Fairfield Road, stretched about three miles back to the Lower Marsh Creek Presbyterian Church. Early's trains were parked in the fields north of the Fairfield Road between the Presbyterian Church and Marsh Creek. Rodes's trains moved off the Herr Ridge Road and into the fields south of the Fairfield Road abreast of Early's trains. They too stretched all the way back to Marsh Creek. Roads were always kept clear by the quartermasters while trains waited to move so that army communications would not be interrupted. The Herr Ridge Road was unobstructed for the same rea-

MAP 4.1   Midnight, 3–4 July, to 6:00 A.M., 4 July 1863.
Lee's defense lines re-form and Ewell's trains move toward Fairfield. The Union Eleventh and Twelfth Corps reoccupy Gettysburg.

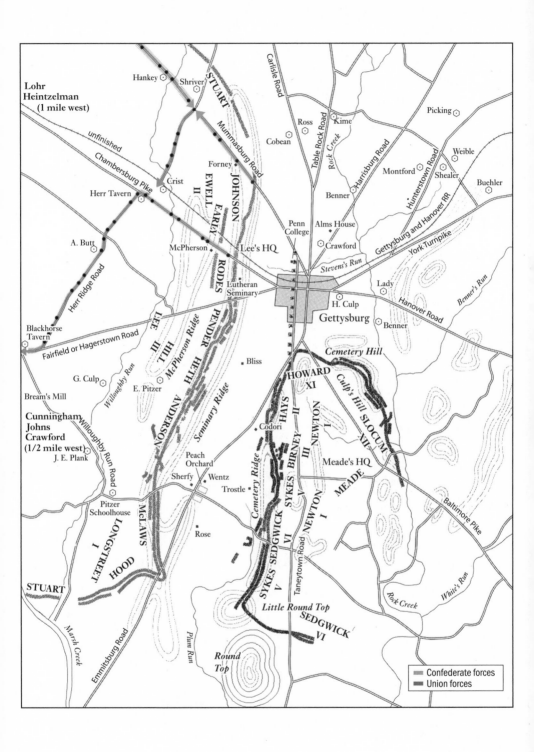

son, as well as to allow other trains to enter the Chambersburg Pike from the southern end of the battle lines.[33]

The trains of Ewell's three divisions extended, when completely stretched out on the Fairfield Road, nearly twenty miles. Their extraordinary length was due in large measure to the size of the quartermaster and subsistence trains. After all, division, brigade, and regimental quartermaster and subsistence teams had been foraging in Pennsylvania for nearly two weeks prior to the fighting at Gettysburg. Like the reserve train, the division trains were filled with purchased, impressed, and confiscated stores, and many of the wagons and teams had been obtained in Pennsylvania, as had all the herds of horses, mules, cattle, sheep, and hogs accompanying them.[34]

A Northern newspaper reporter had occasion to describe a portion of the trains of Ewell's Divisions:

> It is impossible to tell the number of vehicles of all descriptions; there were [wagons] filled with delicacies from stores in Pennsylvania; four and six mule and horse teams; some filled with barrels of molasses, others with flour, hams, meal, clothing, ladies' and children's shoes and underclothing—mainly obtained from the frightened inhabitants of [Pennsylvania]; wagons stolen from Pennsylvania and loyal Maryland farmers; wagons made for the Confederate government (a poor imitation of our own); wagons from North Carolina and wagons from Tennessee—a mongrel train—all stolen, or what is still worse—paid for in Confederate notes, made payable six months after the recognition of the southern Confederacy by the United States Government—or in other words—never.[35]

As the trains of Ewell's Divisions came to a halt beside the Fairfield Road to wait their turn to enter the procession, surgeons, assistant surgeons, stewards, and nurses set up surgical centers in nearby houses and farms to care for the wounded who were in desperate need of treatment. Campfires were started by the side of the road, and soon smoke filled the air all around the parked trains.

The surgeons of Johnson's Division set up hospitals in houses and buildings alongside its ambulance trains at the Lower Marsh Creek Presbyterian Church and at the David Stewart and Joseph Mickley farms about three miles east of Fairfield. Five badly wounded cannoneers of Carpenter's Virginia Battery alone died while being moved from hospitals north of Gettysburg to the Stewart farm; they were buried in one grave on the farm.[36]

Hospitals for Early's Division were established beside the parked ambulance trains at the Andrew Weikert, Christian Byers, William Douglas, and Henry Wintrode farmhouses on the north side of the Fairfield Road, about one mile west of Marsh Creek and four miles west of Gettysburg. In all, at least twenty-eight officers and men from Early's Division died either in transit to their position on the Fairfield Road or after arriving there. All were laid to rest in the Weikert, Byers, Douglas, and Wintrode farmyards.[37]

Rodes's Division's hospitals were located on the south side of the Fairfield Road, mostly in the Jacob Plank farmyard and barn. When Chaplain Alexander D. Betts arrived at the Plank farm, he helped the surgeons and ambulance corps carry the wounded to the barn. But Betts also had other duties; near the barn he buried the remains of Lieutenant Ira T. Connell of his regiment and another soldier of the Fourth North Carolina, both of whom had died in transit. They were among at least twenty-one officers and men of Rodes's Division who would be buried there.[38]

Back along Seminary Ridge, Lee continued to work. At 6:35 A.M. he dictated a note to General Meade: "In order to promote the comfort and convenience of the officers and men captured by the opposing armies in the recent engagements, I respectfully propose that an exchange be made at once." Under a white flag, Lee's couriers galloped across the bloody fields toward the enemy lines with the offer.[39]

There is evidence that Lee sent at least one other request to Meade that morning. He asked if, as a personal favor to himself, Meade would ascertain the condition of fifty-one-year-old Colonel Hugh Reid Miller of the Forty-second Mississippi of Davis's Brigade who had fallen near the stone wall in the Pickett-Pettigrew-Trimble attack the previous afternoon. Why Lee asked about Miller is unknown. It is possible that he also inquired about other officers who had been lost behind Union lines. There is no evidence that the Miller inquiry was ever answered.[40]

Lee had not had any sleep; he probably did not even pause to rest during the early morning hours of 4 July. Instead, he spent the time dictating orders in his headquarters tent near the Chambersburg Pike amid all of the movements of Ewell's Corps around him. Major William Allen, Ewell's chief ordnance officer, was busy overseeing the trains of his corps when he called on Lieutenant Colonel Baldwin, the army's chief of ordnance. Baldwin told him that General Lee was "in the worst possible humor and everybody fears to approach him." At about the same time young Lieutenant Colonel Alexander S. "Sandie" Pendleton, adjutant general of Ewell's staff, rode to Lee's headquarters on the Chambersburg Pike to deliver a report from Ewell on the progress of his corps. He was unaware of Lee's mood. Lee was very fond of Sandie Pendleton, the bright young son of the army's chief of artillery. As Sandie delivered the report to Lee, he remarked: "I hope, General, the other two corps are in as good condition for work as ours is this morning." Lee looked at him coldly and then replied, "What reason have you, young man, to suppose that they are not?" "I never felt so small in my life," Pendleton recalled. He quickly excused himself and returned to Ewell's headquarters.[41]

More than two hours had passed since Lee had dispatched couriers under a white flag carrying his request to General Meade for an exchange of prisoners. He had heard nothing. Finally, just after 9:00 A.M., Union couriers were received by Confederate skirmishers, and Lee's staff officers were handed a handwritten note from Meade. Meade rejected Lee's request, noting only that it was "not in his power to accede to the proposed arrangements." The immense trains would be a burden, indeed. Now Lee had to deal with transporting nearly four thousand prisoners of war south with his army.[42]

Rain was about to fall. Behind the breastworks for nearly a mile to the rear in some places, shelter halves were being pitched in countless encampments. Campfires were started by slaves and soldier details, and the whole defense line, for three miles, became shrouded in smoke that hung close to the ground in the high humidity. Several heavy showers, each lasting about twenty minutes, poured down. Always in the background was the sound of skirmish fire and occasional volleys of musketry as the skirmishers of the two armies continued to spar with one another.[43]

While the trains of Ewell's three divisions moved onto and alongside the Fairfield Road, other trains were being assembled. Imboden's trains were gathering in the fields along the Chambersburg Pike. Like Ewell's trains, Imboden's included large herds of horses, mules, cattle, and sheep driven along at intervals by quartermaster and commissary of subsistence details.[44]

Well before dawn Lieutenant Colonel Corley, Hill's chief quartermaster, Major James Gaven Field, together with Dr. Guild, Dr. Breckinridge, and the chief surgeon of Hill's Corps, Dr. John W. Powell, made the necessary arrangements to move the trains of Hill's Corps. With the hospitals of Pender's Division located at the Lohr and Heintzelman farms on the Chambersburg Pike, midway between Cashtown and Gettysburg, Pender's trains comprised the leading elements of Imboden's column; they formed behind the corps quartermaster train. Dr. Holt, chief surgeon of Pender's Division, directed Dr. John Henry McAden of the Thirteenth North Carolina and chief surgeon of Scales's Brigade, Dr. John Tyler McLean of the Thirty-third North Carolina, Dr. W. M. Scarborough of the Fourteenth South Carolina, and Dr. W. P. Hill of the Thirty-fifth Georgia to remain at Gettysburg. Dr. Spencer Glasgow Welch considered himself "lucky enough" to climb into a medical wagon for the journey with the trains of Colonel Perrin's South Carolina Brigade. Of the nearly 1,300 sick and wounded of Pender's Division at or near the Lohr and Heintzelman farms, 700 would be left behind.[45]

Captain George Henry Mills of the Sixteenth North Carolina had been "struck on the right thigh by a piece of shell" on 1 July. With the aid of a hickory branch, he made his way back to one of Pender's hospitals. Mills hobbled down the ambulance trains until he found "a seat on top of a load of hay" in a quartermaster wagon, where he would spend the next thirty hours.[46]

To permit the other trains to assemble beside the Chambersburg Pike, all of Pender's were ordered to move to Cashtown behind the corps quartermaster train. The wounded General Pender, accompanied by Joe and Captain Pender, was taken to the lead vehicle of his ambulance trains. The twenty-nine-year-old general called for his chief commissary of subsistence, Major D. T. Carraway, and asked about the condition of his men and the supplies on hand. Reassured by Carraway that the men had ample food, Pender was placed in the ambulance beside his old friend, General Scales. In a nearby ambulance was Colonel Hoke of the Thirty-eighth North Carolina. There were hundreds of others. The quartermaster and subsistence trains of Pender's Division moved up the pike to a point about three miles west of Cashtown; they extended back to the village. The division's ambulance trains halted in Cashtown.[47]

At Cashtown, Pender's surgeons established temporary hospitals at the homes of Dr. William Stem, Isaac Rife, and Elizabeth Mickley, among many others, along the Chambersburg Pike, as it would be hours before the sick and wounded could start moving south. Stem actually opened his medical office to assist the Confederate surgeons in caring for those in the trains who were in need of surgical attention. Both Pender and Scales were undoubtedly moved indoors until just past noon, when they were returned to their ambulance in anticipation of movement.[48]

The trains of Heth's Division were readied for the journey before dawn. They were lined up along the Chambersburg Pike from behind Pender's trains to the division hospital and wagon park at Seven Stars, a distance of at least three miles. The ambulance trains in the rear of the column were parked near the division hospitals. Joining the surgeons, stewards, and nurses in the ambulance trains were members of the regimental bands, including those of the Eleventh and Twenty-sixth North Carolina.[49]

Among the wounded riding in Heth's ambulance train was Colonel Leventhorpe of the Eleventh North Carolina. Leventhorpe's adjutant, Lieutenant

Lucas, Lucas's slave, and Captain Hughes of Pettigrew's staff were loaded into one ambulance. Captains Archer and Williams of General Archer's staff, Lieutenant Colonel Lane of the Twenty-sixth North Carolina, Colonel Stone of the Second Mississippi, Major Belo of the Fifty-fifth North Carolina, and Major Reynolds of the Eleventh Mississippi were also put in ambulances. There were hundreds more. Of the more than 1,500 sick and wounded in the hospitals of Heth's Division, almost 700 were left behind, including Colonel Connally of the Fifty-fifth North Carolina.[50]

On the morning of 4 July Dr. LeGrand Wilson of the Forty-second Mississippi was busy at the Lohr farm amputating limbs and re-dressing wounds of soldiers in Heth's Division who had fallen on 1 and 3 July. It was still dark when he was summoned by Dr. Hubbard, the division's chief surgeon and a fellow Mississippian. Arriving at Hubbard's tent, Wilson was informed that the army was preparing to move but he had been detailed to remain at the Lohr farm. Stunned by the announcement, Wilson at first could not speak. At last he begged Hubbard not to leave him behind, but to give him duty that was "more dangerous and more arduous" on the retreat. "I don't want to fall into the hands of the enemy," Wilson said, "although I know they will treat me right. I am real cranky on this subject. Please give me something else." Hubbard relented, telling Wilson that the trains of wounded of Heth's Division were forming beside the Chambersburg Pike and that he must be ready to join them within half an hour. "I am ready now," Wilson said, "just as soon as I can get my blankets and a pocket case of instruments, bandages and a bottle of morphine, and I thank you to boot." Wilson walked out to the trains and inspected each ambulance and wagon to determine the nature of the cases he would be treating. He then filled a haversack full of bandages and climbed into an ambulance.[51]

Hubbard ultimately ordered the following surgeons to remain with the casualties who could not be moved: Dr. William Montgomery, chief surgeon of Archer's Brigade; Dr. John Wilson and Dr. James Parks McCombs, Eleventh North Carolina; Dr. William A. Spence Jr., Forty-seventh Virginia; Dr. James H. Southall, Fifty-fifth Virginia; Dr. A. G. Emory, Fourteenth Tennessee; Dr. William G. McCreight, Forty-second Mississippi; Dr. P. Gervias Robinson, Twenty-second North Carolina; Dr. W. S. Parker, Fifty-fifth North Carolina; and others. Dr. Lewellyn P. Warren of the Twenty-sixth North Carolina and chief surgeon of Pettigrew's Brigade asked to stay behind. His brother, Lieutenant John Christian Warren of the Fifty-second North Carolina, had fallen in front of Cemetery Ridge on 3 July. His whereabouts was unknown, and Dr. Warren could not leave the area under such circumstances. The Reverend Dr. Thomas Dwight Witherspoon, chaplain of the Forty-second Mississippi, also remained in Gettysburg.[52]

Amid all the sadness at the hospital and wagon park of Heth's Division was an unforgettable scene. It fell on Captain Joseph J. Young, assistant quartermaster of the Twenty-sixth North Carolina, to bury the remains of his commander, young Colonel Burgwyn, in a gun case on a farm across the Chambersburg Pike from the Frederick Herr Tavern. Unable to accept Burgwyn's death was "poor Kincheon," his slave, who was profoundly disturbed. As the trains of Heth's Division were lining up on the Chambersburg Pike, Young told Kincheon to take Burgwyn's two horses and his clothes back to his parents in Northampton County, North Carolina. He gave Kincheon ninety-five dollars and sent him off into the midst of the trains. Young knew that Kincheon would complete the journey—even with the two horses—for, as he wrote to Burgwyn's parents, "I never saw fidelity stronger in anyone." Indeed, Kincheon made it all the way home on foot and horseback.[53]

The trains of Anderson's Division were assembled at the Butt farm before 6:00 A.M. and directed to fall into line at Cashtown behind Heth's trains. Dr. Fraser, chief surgeon of Anderson's Division, informed everyone at the hospital that the army was falling back and he was ordered to send to Virginia all those who were able to walk; the "badly wounded," however, would have to be left behind because of inadequate transportation. Fraser volunteered to remain with them.[54]

Sergeant James E. Whitehorne of the Twelfth Virginia lay under a shed in the Butt farmyard, having been struck in the right leg by a shell fragment on 3 July that nearly removed the calf and by a bullet that passed through the left leg below the knee. He was helped to the hospital by a "colored friend." Whitehorne was unable to walk. On hearing Fraser's news, Whitehorne sank into despair knowing that he was one of those who would be left behind. Fraser reassured him that Dr. Henry A. Minor of the Eighth Alabama, as well as some assistant surgeons and nurses, would also remain. Canteens were filled with water, and Whitehorne and the others were urged to make themselves as comfortable as possible.[55]

Captain Charles E. Waddell of the Twelfth Virginia was among those who left the Butt farm. It seems that Waddell had been suffering from typhoid fever. Very sick and chilled, he climbed into a wagon with Captain Thomas F. Owens, the acting regimental quartermaster, and Lieutenant Edwin W. Branch. Those three, along with thirty-six men of Mahone's Brigade in other ambulances, were conveyed to Cashtown to join the rest of Anderson's trains that were lining up along a road south of the village. On his arrival at Cashtown, Waddell was removed from the ambulance and taken to a house, where he slept on the floor until orders were given for the trains to move.[56]

Behind the trains of Hill's three divisions moved those of Longstreet's Corps, starting with the corps quartermaster train. The trains of the Longstreet division farthest from the center of the army moved behind the corps quartermaster train. That meant that Hood's trains led all those of Longstreet's Corps. They were followed by the trains of Pickett's Division and finally by McLaws's. The operation was carried out under the direction of Longstreet's chief quartermaster, Major Keiley, and medical director, Dr. John S. D. Cullen, in consultation with Lieutenant Colonel Corley, Dr. Guild, and Dr. Breckinridge.[57]

Dr. John T. Darby oversaw the removal of Hood's casualties from the Plank farm. General Robertson, commander of the Texas Brigade, and Colonel Key of the Fourth Texas were placed in ambulances along with Lieutenant Colonels Bryan of the Fifth Texas and Carter of the Fourth Texas. Helping Carter into the ambulance and then securing a place beside him was his slave, Henry Johnson. Johnson had also served as the regimental barber and was universally liked by the men. Among the wounded, Colonel Powell of the Fifth Texas would remain behind, whereas Colonel Manning of the Third Arkansas chose to accompany his regiment. Placed in ambulances were General Anderson, Colonel Little, and Lieutenant Colonel Luffman of the Eleventh Georgia.[58]

Dr. Darby helped General Hood into an ambulance; he would never leave his side. Darby then directed those surgeons, assistant surgeons, stewards, and nurses who were to accompany the ambulance trains to pack their medical gear and bandages and find places in the ambulances and wagons; others were instructed to either return to their regiments or remain at the Plank farm.[59]

Private J. W. Lokey of the Twentieth Georgia of Benning's Brigade had been wounded in the right thigh on 2 July and was unable to walk. Lying on a bed of straw at the Plank farm, he observed the ambulances and empty wagons being loaded with the wounded on the morning of 4 July. While organizing the last wagon, the ambulance corpsmen called out that there was room for one more if he could ride sitting up. Lokey asserted that he could. The wagon, wrote Lokey, "had four mules hitched to it, and there were four wounded men lying on their backs in the bed. Two planks were across the bed, with the wagon sheet tied up to the bows in the middle. Two men were on the front board and one on the right of the rear board. I took my place on the left. Being shot through the right thigh, I could not stand any pressure on my wound. So I had to hold my right leg with both hands locked below my knee, letting my left leg hang on the outside of the wagon."[60]

Of the 1,500 sick and wounded in Hood's Division, 515 were left at the Plank farm. Dr. Thomas A. Means of the Eleventh Georgia was placed in charge of the surgeons, assistant surgeons, stewards, and nurses who stayed behind. He would be assisted by Dr. Henry W. Waters of the First Texas, Dr. W. H. Cole of the Eighth Georgia, Dr. Thomas C. Pugh of the Ninth Georgia, and others. Among the chaplains who remained was the Reverend Dr. George E. Butler of the Third Arkansas. In the rear of Hood's trains, the ambulance trains moved into line, heading toward the Chambersburg Pike. Along the entire distance of the division's quartermaster and subsistence trains, herds of horses, mules, cattle, and sheep plodded along with their drovers.[61]

At Bream's Mineral and Flour Mill, the Myers farm, and the Currens farm along Marsh Creek, south of the Fairfield Road, the few survivors of the attack of Pickett's Division who could bear the journey back to Virginia were lifted into ambulances and wagons. Colonel Aylett of the Fifty-third Virginia, Colonels Stuart of the Fifty-sixth Virginia, Otey of the Eleventh Virginia, Terry of the Twenty-fourth Virginia, and Gantt of the Nineteenth Virginia were placed in ambulances and wagons. Major Owens of the Ninth Virginia never made it; he died on the morning of 4 July and was buried in the woods across the creek from the mill.[62]

On the morning of 4 July Sergeant Major Johnston of the Seventh Virginia lay in a shed near the Myers house. His brigade surgeon, Dr. Charles B. Morton of the Seventh Virginia, and General Early, whose own trains were then parked along the Fairfield Road nearby, visited the sick and wounded, urging all those who were able to ride in wagons to leave. Those who could not, they said, would fall into enemy hands. Johnston, unable to move due to the shrapnel wounds in his left side and arm, was resigned to his fate. At the time, he could still hear General Kemper moaning in agony from a cot in the Myers house.[63]

With transportation scarce, some of Pickett's wounded officers were provided with vehicles seized from nearby farms. Colonel Hunton and Major Berkeley of the Eighth Virginia obtained a buggy. The two climbed aboard and drove into the procession of ambulances heading toward the Chambersburg Pike. They would ride together all the way to Staunton, Virginia.[64]

Only 246 casualties remained at the hospital of Pickett's Division. One of them was General Kemper. To care for them, Dr. Lewis, chief surgeon of the division, designated three surgeons—Dr. Edward Rives of the Twenty-eighth Virginia, Dr. Thomas P. Mayo of the Third Virginia, and Dr. Alexander Grigsby of the First Virginia—and two assistant surgeons—Dr. B. C. Harrison of the Fifty-sixth Virginia and Dr. William S. Nowlin of the Thirty-eighth Virginia. With them, Lewis left a hospital steward, a chaplain, and fifty nurses.[65]

Dr. Baruch of the Third South Carolina had worked continuously until the late afternoon of 3 July at the Blackhorse Tavern hospital of Kershaw's Brigade, McLaws's Division. "At sundown," he recalled, "I threw myself on the hay and slept until aroused by an orderly who brought a command from General Lee for Drs. [J. F.] Pearce [of the Eighth South Carolina], [Henry Junius] Nott [of the Second South Carolina], and Baruch to remain at the Blackhorse Tavern field hospital 'until further orders.'"[66]

The casualties at the Blackhorse Tavern who were able to endure the journey were loaded in ambulances and empty wagons in the wee hours of 4 July. Among the wounded, Colonel Kennedy of the Second South Carolina was lifted into an ambulance. Kershaw's brigade surgeon, Dr. T. W. Salmond, secured his hometown friend, Captain W. Z. "Zack" Leitner also of the Second South Carolina, in an ambulance; he had rescued him on the battlefield on the night of 2 July. Salmond had later amputated Leitner's leg. Another officer placed in an ambulance was Major McLeod of the Eighth South Carolina; helped by Dr. Pearce, McLeod was accompanied by his slave. From McLeod's shattered regiment, the blinded Captain McIver was carried to an ambulance by his slave. There were many more.[67]

"The morning [of 4 July] found us amid novel surroundings," remembered Dr. Baruch. "The slightly wounded had been removed, most of them being able to march. The field hospital contained now two hundred and twenty-two seriously wounded men, ten orderlies and three surgeons."[68]

Back at the Crawford house along Marsh Creek and the nearby Johns farm, the sick and wounded of Wofford's and Semmes's Brigades were loaded into ambulances and wagons. George, the slave of Sergeant Major C. C. Cumming of the Seventeenth Mississippi, found an ambulance for his master, Colonel Holder, and an officer from the Twenty-first Mississippi. General Semmes was taken out of the Crawford house by aides Captain Cody, Captain Lewis, and Corporal Cleveland and placed in an ambulance; his three aides joined him. At the Cunningham farm across Marsh Creek, the ambulance corps was similarly employed, placing in ambulances and wagons those from Wofford's Brigade and Longstreet's artillery battalions who were considered able to withstand the long journey to Virginia.[69]

Left behind from McLaws's Division were 576 sick and wounded and seventy nurses and cooks to care for them. In charge of all of McLaws's hospitals along Marsh Creek would be Dr. Frank W. Patterson of the Seventeenth Mississippi. He would be aided by Dr. Pearce, Eighth South Carolina; Dr. Nott, Second South Carolina; Dr. Baruch; Dr. D. H. Ramseur, Eighteenth Georgia; Dr. S. P. Hobgood, Fifty-third Georgia; Dr. R. L. Knox, Seventeenth Mississippi; Dr. C. H. Brown, Eighteenth Mississippi; Dr. H. J. Paramore, Fifth Georgia; and Dr. F. H. Sewell, Cabell's Artillery Battalion. Chaplains William Burton Owen of the Seventeenth Mississippi and C. H. Toy of the Fifty-third Georgia stayed with them.[70]

The trains of Hood's Division moved up the Willoughby Run Road until they reached the Fairfield Road. They then rolled up the Herr Ridge Road Pike and turned west onto the Chambersburg Turnpike, falling into line along the fields behind the trains of Hill's Corps. Pickett's trains followed Hood's. The trains of McLaws's Division were the last to leave the southern sector of the battlefield.[71]

The cavalry hospitals near Hunterstown were cleared of wounded very early in the morning. General Jenkins was placed in an ambulance. General Hampton and Colonel Delony along with many others were also carried to the ambulance trains. Some were left at ambulance depots near the John Rummel farm close to the battlefield and at the division hospitals as far to the rear as the stone Great Conewago Presbyterian Church and the J. L. Grass Hotel in Hunterstown. Dr. James Yates, of the First South Carolina Cavalry, among others, was left behind with a staff of stewards, nurses, and cooks.[72]

While in an ambulance, Colonel Delony scribbled a note to his wife Rosa. He told her of his head wound and of General Hampton's "painful and severe" wounds, then recounted with sadness the loss of Lieutenants Nathan S. Pugh, John W. Cheeseborough, Cicero C. Brooks, and James S. House, as well as others from Cobb's Legion over the past two days. All of them except Cheeseborough were buried under a cherry tree beside the road near Delony's ambulance. Cheeseborough would die and be buried there the next day.[73]

Captain W. A. Graham of the Second North Carolina Cavalry had been wounded in the leg during the cavalry fighting east of Gettysburg on 3 July. The ball had been extracted, but he had been so uncomfortable in the barn where he lay that he found a tree branch and, using it as a staff, hobbled to a nearby abandoned house, accompanied by his slave Edmund. When the ambulances came to pick up the wounded, none were from Graham's regiment, so he and Edmund borrowed a horse from a trooper in the Ninth Virginia Cavalry "who was so badly wounded he could not sit up." Graham quickly found out that he could not make the journey on a horse, either. His slave hailed an ambulance nearby, and the two secured seats, Graham next to the driver and Edmund in the flatbed.[74]

Stuart's cavalry brigades, with all their trains, moved toward the newly formed defense lines on a road north of Gettysburg that connected Hunterstown with Mummasburg. With the long column of wagons and ambulances were the 150 wagons pulled by 900 mules captured by Stuart on 28 June. Most of the hay and oats taken with the wagons had been consumed by the horses in Stuart's commands. Now the wagons were mostly filled with sick and wounded; the empty ones would soon be filled.

Two of Stuart's horse brigades—Fitzhugh Lee's and Wade Hampton's—moved into position to protect Lee's extreme left flank, between Oak Hill and Mummasburg, accompanied by the batteries of Captains James Breathed, William McGregor, and James F. Hart. Because of Hampton's wound, his brigade was commanded by Colonel Lawrence Baker of the First North Carolina Cavalry. Stuart's trains crowded in the fields beside the road from Mummasburg to Cashtown to await movement into General Imboden's trains. Once Fitzhugh Lee's and Baker's Brigades and their artillery support were positioned on the far left flank of the army, Stuart, with Chambliss's Brigade and the brigade of General Jenkins, then commanded by Colonel Milton J. Ferguson of the Sixteenth Virginia Cavalry, along with the batteries of Captains Wiley H. Griffin and Thomas J. Jackson, rode south across the fields behind Seminary Ridge to get into position to protect the army's right flank.[75]

While the trains were assembling along the Chambersburg Pike, one general was actually taken from one ambulance and placed in another. Dr. Darby had heard that his old commander, General Hampton, had been injured. He now lay in an ambulance at the end of the trains of Stuart's Division near Mummasburg. Hampton's head was mostly shaved, and a bandage was wrapped around the ugly sabre wound on his forehead. Darby found Hampton and directed that he be moved into the ambulance with General Hood, then parked near the Fairfield Road, so he could care for both of them. Under a heavy cavalry escort, Hampton's ambulance was taken down the Mummasburg Road to the Herr Ridge Road. The two generals were then laid side by side in Hood's ambulance. The ambulance carrying Hood and Hampton would follow those trains of Hood's assigned to travel with the troops, not Imboden's trains.[76]

In accordance with Lee's instructions, General Pendleton provided artillery support for Imboden's trains. It was an odd assortment of artillery that arrived at Cashtown early on the morning of 4 July. From Colonel J. B. Walton's First Corps artillery command came eight guns from the famed Washington Artillery of New Orleans. Major Benjamin F. Eshleman, the battalion commander, brought Imboden a 12-pound Napoleon from Captain Charles W. Squires's First Company, two 12-pound Napoleons and a 3-inch rifled gun from Captain John B. Richardson Jr.'s Second Company, two 12-pound Napoleons from Captain Merritt B. "Buck" Miller's Third Company, and a Howitzer and a 12-pound Napoleon from Captain Joseph Norcom's Fourth Company.[77]

From Lieutenant Colonel John J. Garnett's Battalion of Heth's Division, Hill's Corps, elements of two more batteries entered Cashtown under the command of Major Charles Richardson. Two 3-inch rifled guns from Captain Joseph D. Moore's Huger, Virginia Artillery, and one 10-pound Parrott rifle and two 3-inch rifled guns from Captain Victor Maurin's Donaldsonville, Louisiana Artillery, under Lieutenant R. P. Landry completed Pendleton's artillery support.[78]

From Major David G. McIntosh's Battalion one other gun would appear. Captain W. B. Hurt of the Alabama Battery accompanying the battalion reported that the axle of one of his Whitworth rifles had broken while firing; it had been sent to the rear for repairs. By the time the axle was fixed, it was not practicable for it to rejoin Hill's main column on the Fairfield Road, so Captain Hurt and the Whitworth rifle would follow Imboden's trains; the rifle's limber chest was dangerously short of ammunition and its horses were worn out.[79]

The guns that arrived at Cashtown joined the six 3-inch rifled guns of the battery led by John McClanahan in Imboden's own independent cavalry command and the four 12-pound Napoleons of Captain Hart's South Carolina Battery accompanying Fitzhugh Lee's and Baker's cavalry brigades. In all, Imboden would have three brigades of cavalry and twenty-four pieces of artillery to protect his trains.[80]

Just past noon, recalled Imboden:

The very windows of heaven seemed to have opened. The rain fell in blinding sheets; the meadows were soon overflowed, and fences gave way before the raging streams. During the storm, wagons, ambulances and artillery carriages by hundreds—nay thousands—were assembling in the fields along the road from Gettysburg to Cashtown. . . . Canvas was no protection against its fury, and the wounded men lying upon the naked boards of the wagon-bodies were drenched. Horses and mules were blinded and maddened by the wind and water, and became almost unmanageable. The deafening roar of the mingled sounds of heaven and earth all around us made it almost impossible to communicate orders, and equally difficult to execute them.[81]

Around 1:00 P.M. on 4 July the last wagons of Major Harman's reserve train finally cleared Fairfield. Ewell's casualties who could travel were removed from the hospitals along the Fairfield Road and again placed in the ambulances and empty wagons. As the rear of the reserve train moved through the streets of Fairfield, quartermasters yelled for General Rodes's trains in the rear to move forward and lead all of Ewell's trains. They began to move at about two o'clock. Behind Rodes's trains would come Early's; Johnson's trains would follow in the rear. The rear column was brought to the front first to clear the road for the troops to follow Ewell's trains. Once in line, all the trains of Ewell's Corps would stretch out for nearly forty miles.[82]

Rodes's trains seem to have moved onto the road without a serious incident; however, Captain Early and his son had trouble at the moment of departure. An army wagoner who attempted to drive past Early's buggy struck one of the wheels and bent the axle "almost double." The buggy was dragged off the road in the pouring rain. Fortunately, an army forge was nearby and the blacksmith accompanying it repaired the axle, although it took him almost eight hours.[83]

A caravan of ambulances, mostly from Wilcox's and Mahone's Brigades of Anderson's Division, had tried to reach Cashtown as the trains got under way. In an ordnance wagon "fitted-up like an ambulance," Captain George Clark of the Eleventh Alabama rode with Colonel John C. Saunders and Major R. J. Fletcher of his regiment, both wounded. For some reason, a decision was made late in the day to send some of Anderson's ambulances, including Clark's, back to Gettysburg. These vehicles returned to the Herr Ridge Road and passed the Adam Butt farm hospital site of the division to get onto the Fairfield Road.[84]

At the Butt farm, Sergeant Whitehorne raised himself on one elbow to watch the moving trains of his division as they returned along the Herr Ridge Road. He saw one of his own regimental ambulances accompanied by a hospital steward named Emmitt Roper. Whitehorne called to him. Roper looked in Whitehorne's direction and recognized him. "What in the name of heaven are you doing here?" Roper asked. Whitehorne explained his situation, then begged Roper to take him along. Roper stopped a passing spring wagon filled with hay, and he and the driver lifted Whitehorne up and put him in it.

The Chambersburg Pike looking toward Cashtown and the Cashtown Pass. Here General Imboden assembled the trains of Hill's and Longstreet's Corps and Stuart's cavalry division. The photograph was taken by Gettysburg photographer William Tipton just after the war. National Archives, Washington, D.C.

The procession of ambulances and wagons proceeded onto the Fairfield Road joining the rear of Ewell's trains.[85]

As the trains of Ewell's three divisions were moving through Fairfield toward Monterey Pass, Imboden readied his own trains for the long journey through Cashtown Pass and down the Cumberland Valley. He had "shared a little bread and meat" with Generals Pender and Scales in the lead ambulance of Pender's trains just past noon. At 4:00 P.M. Imboden put his trains in motion. Leading them was Colonel George W. Imboden's Eighteenth Virginia Cavalry with two rifles of McClanahan's Battery. The lead vehicles consisted of Imboden's own quartermaster, subsistence, ordnance, and ambulance trains. As Imboden's trains ascended Cashtown Pass, they were followed by Hill's Corps quartermaster train and the trains of Pender's Division.[86]

At intervals of about every one mile, in accordance with Lee's orders, Imboden directed a section of artillery to travel among the wagons and ambulances along with a detachment of cavalry from one of his regiments. As

Pender's trains passed, the trains of Heth's Division moved behind them. Three sections of McClanahan's Battery and the Eighteenth Virginia Cavalry covered the leading three to four miles of the trains while in front of, and at intervals along, Heth's trains, Imboden ordered the guns of Lieutenant Landry's Donaldsonville Artillery and Captain Moore's Huger, Virginia Artillery, as well as squadrons of the Sixty-second Virginia Mounted Infantry, to join the procession.[87]

Behind Heth's trains came some of Anderson's Division, followed by Hood's, Pickett's, and McLaws's. Spread among the wagons and ambulances of Longstreet's three divisions, at about one-mile intervals, were two gun sections of the four companies of the Washington Artillery. Finally, behind the trains of Longstreet's three divisions came the trains of most of Stuart's six-horse brigades, protected by Hart's South Carolina Battery traveling in sections at half-mile or mile intervals among the cavalry trains.[88]

Bringing up the rear of the huge column were Fitzhugh Lee's and Baker's cavalry brigades and their artillery support. They followed the trains through Cashtown Pass, up the Chambersburg Pike, and onto the Walnut Bottom and Pine Stump Roads; they then operated at the rear and on the right flank of the column, screening it from attack from the north and west.

Imboden's enormous column was seventeen miles long once all the wagons and ambulances were on the road. Illustrating the extent of foraging that Lee's army had accomplished while in Pennsylvania, Imboden's and Harman's trains, together, extended for more than fifty-seven miles. Made up of quartermaster, subsistence, ordnance, and ambulance trains, along with numerous herds of horses, mules, cattle, sheep, and hogs, the two sets of trains presented breathtaking spectacles. One citizen of Chambersburg who observed Lee's wagon trains only days before the retreat wrote: "The great preponderating impression which was made upon the mind by looking upon [them] . . . was [their] *immenseness*. No idea of [their] magnitude can be formed by any description which can be given."[89]

Five

The scene was wild and desolating

Twenty-six-year-old Private Franklin Gardner Walter of Company A, Thirty-ninth Virginia Cavalry Battalion, had been delivering dispatches for Lee's headquarters since very early morning. His odyssey began at 3:00 A.M. on 4 July, when he was ordered to carry a dispatch to Dr. Guild. Once he found Guild, the army medical director instructed him to take a message to Dr. McGuire. Returning to Lee's headquarters, he was sent with yet another message to McGuire, whom he found at Fairfield helping to establish hospitals for the ambulance trains of Johnson's Division of Ewell's Corps. Finally, at 1:00 P.M. Walter rode into Lee's headquarters along the Chambersburg Pike and found his company being issued "long-range rifles." The headquarters was being dismantled and baggage packed. By two o'clock the headquarters baggage train began to move out the Chambersburg Pike and down the Herr Ridge Road toward the Fairfield Road in the drenching rain, escorted by Walter and his company.[1]

Up to this point, Lee's orders were being executed like clockwork. Major Harman's reserve train with all of its cattle and sheep was partly across the South Mountain range, and the rear elements of the trains of Ewell's three divisions with all their livestock were heading up the road toward Fairfield.

Imboden got his trains in motion on the Chambersburg Pike an hour ahead of schedule. As they started rumbling out of Cashtown, orders were being relayed to the troops along Oak and Seminary Ridges to take down their tents, pack their baggage, and be ready to move. Company drummers sounded "the general." For the men in Hill's Corps, that meant departure within an hour; for those in Longstreet's and Ewell's Corps, it meant "hurry up and wait." Rain poured down in sheets.[2]

Around 5:00 P.M. Hill's troops began to march behind Ewell's trains and some of Anderson's ambulances. The first brigade to move was General Wright's of Anderson's Division. With officers, noncommissioned officers, and detachments of sappers running ahead of the infantrymen to provide direction and to clear fences and other obstacles, Wright's Georgians marched in the fields beside the Fairfield Road. Troops always marched in the fields to keep the road clear for trains and for messengers on horseback. Private William P. Garrett of the Third Georgia noted in his pocket diary that the fields and road were "powerful wet and muddy."[3]

At about six o'clock Lee's headquarters baggage train came to a halt near the Blackhorse Tavern on the Fairfield Road not far from the trains of Major Hotchkiss and his topographical engineers, all of whom were still copying maps of the roads on which the army would retreat. From his vantage point on the ridge above the tavern, Lee, who had been there for several hours, observed through the rain and smoke the columns of wagons and ambulances moving down the Fairfield Road; most of those in view were from Anderson's Division. Across the road, the artillery battalions of Hill's Corps had gathered in the fields waiting to be directed into the line of march by shouting quartermasters.[4]

At about the time that Lee's headquarters baggage train reached the Blackhorse Tavern, Colonel Abner Smead, the corps inspector for General Ewell, rode up to General Iverson, whose brigade occupied a portion of the log, stone, and earthen barricades along Seminary Ridge near the Lutheran Theological Seminary. The poor little brigade had suffered terribly at Gettysburg, losing more than half of its men in one hour's fighting on 1 July. Its ambulance train, carrying what sick and wounded could be evacuated, was just then passing Fairfield; it was the leading brigade ambulance train in Rodes's Division.

What Colonel Smead directed Iverson's Brigade to do was almost unbelievable. As Ewell's trains had little protection at Monterey Pass, Smead ordered Iverson to march his brigade fourteen miles up the Fairfield Road to help provide it. Ewell's trains had been moving along the Fairfield Road since about 2:00 P.M. It would take a Herculean effort for Iverson's little brigade to give them any assistance.[5]

Nevertheless, in obedience to orders Iverson took his men out of the defense lines, formed them on either side of the Fairfield Road, and then marched them, on the double-quick, toward their objective. It was "the most fatiguing march ever witnessed," Iverson later wrote. One sight General Lee witnessed from near the Blackhorse Tavern was Iverson's tattered and bloody

The Fairfield Road looking west with the Blackhorse Tavern and barn visible at center below Herr or Haupt's Ridge. Lee viewed his retreating army marching along the Fairfield Road from the right side of the road in the foreground. South Carolina Confederate Relic Room and Museum, Columbia.

brigade hastening alongside the muddy road with muskets, bayonets fixed, at right shoulder shift.[6]

It would take Iverson's Brigade eight hours to reach Monterey Pass. But already the enemy was on the move. Although General Meade had not received any information about Lee's intentions and his own army was crippled by the distance from its supply base, he quickly mounted a pursuit on 4 July after the Union signal corps spotted Lee's trains heading toward Cashtown and Fairfield. Meade directed Colonel J. Irvin Gregg's Brigade of General David McMurtrie Gregg's Second Cavalry Division to travel north and then west to harass Lee's trains, which he understood were moving through Cashtown Pass. Brigadier General John Buford's two brigades—those of Colonels William Gamble and Thomas S. Devin—and two batteries of artillery then at Westminster were ordered to Frederick, where they would be joined by General Wesley Merritt's Reserve Brigade. From Frederick, Buford's First Cavalry Division could then harass Confederate operations in the Cumberland Valley by means of Turner's Pass. General Hugh Judson Kilpatrick's Third Cavalry Division of two brigades—Colonel Nathaniel Richmond's, formerly the brigade of General Farnsworth, and General George Armstrong Custer's—with two batteries of artillery, then covering Meade's Baltimore Pike supply line to Westminster as well as the army's left flank, was directed to Emmitsburg, where it would link up with Colonel Pennock Huey's Brigade of the Second Cavalry Division and a battery of artillery. Kilpatrick was ordered to find and harass Lee's trains that Meade was informed were traversing Monterey Pass.[7]

Lee's trains were vulnerable at Monterey Pass. At the time, only Company B of the First Maryland Cavalry Battalion, commanded by Captain George Malcolm Emack, and one artillery piece held the steep eastern approaches to the pass near the Monterey House, a four-story frame mountain resort hotel that stood in a large clearing near the summit. In happier times, people had flocked there during the hot summer months to take advantage of the cool mountain air, fresh spring water, and peace and quiet. It was very different now. A detachment of Emack's Company, no more than twenty men commanded by Sergeants Samuel Spencer and William A. Wilson, was positioned on either side of the turnpike below the Monterey House with the gun in the middle of the roadway, about fifty feet above where the Emmitsburg-Waynesboro Turnpike began its winding, steep ascent up the eastern face of the mountain.[8]

The one gun was left there by Captain Tanner, commander of the Courtney Virginia Artillery. The battery's remaining guns had continued on toward Hagerstown, protecting Major Harman's reserve train. The lone gun had less than a dozen rounds of ammunition in its limber chest and caisson. The rest of Emack's Company, led by Lieutenant Henry C. Blackistone, held a reserve position about four hundred yards west of the hotel. Company D of the First Maryland Cavalry, commanded by Captain Warner G. Welsh, took up a position on the western slope of the mountain pass above the village of Waterloo to protect the trains from enemy attack from the direction of Waynesboro to the west and Smithsburg to the south.[9]

Although he had only about ninety men and one gun with only about six rounds of ammunition, Captain Emack had as much courage and boldness as General Lee could ever hope to see in an officer. Emack was twenty-one years old. One of seven children of Elbert Grandison Emack and Margaret Turner

A never-before-published photograph of the Monterey House as it looked in July 1863. The photograph was taken by Gettysburg photographer William Tipton just after the war. National Archives, Washington, D.C.

Emack, he was born at Locust Grove, a plantation near Beltsville in Prince George's County, Maryland. The Emacks were staunchly pro-Southern, although they lived only about eight miles from Washington, D.C. Until he assumed command of Company B, Emack had pursued a rather mysterious course in the army. During the campaign of First Manassas in the summer of 1861, he had served as a "civilian agent" in the Confederate secret service; he was commissioned a second lieutenant on 18 October 1861. Ordered to a special school in Richmond by General John H. Winder, Emack became an intelligence officer and was assigned to Libby Prison to interrogate Union officers who were prisoners of war. He was assigned to the First Maryland Cavalry Battalion when it was officially mustered into service in November 1862 and elected captain of Company B. His brothers also served in the Confederate army; brother James William Emack, a lieutenant in the Seventh North Carolina Infantry, had been killed at Chancellorsville, a loss that Captain George Emack deeply grieved.[10]

By 9:00 P.M. on 4 July Major Harman's reserve train had been on the

A never-before-published photograph of Captain George M. Emack, commander of Company B, First Maryland Cavalry. The photograph was taken just after the war, in Versailles, Kentucky, where he lived, died, and was buried. Courtesy of General William A. Tidwell.

road, heading toward Williamsport, for nearly eighteen hours. The rear of the train was just passing through Monterey Pass; the head of it was almost in Hagerstown, more than twenty-five miles away. Behind the reserve train were the quartermaster, subsistence, ordnance, and ambulance trains of Rodes's Division, commanded by Major Rogers, Rodes's chief quartermaster. The quartermaster trains of Daniels's and Doles's Brigades were in the lead, followed by the division ordnance train, the division subsistence train, and then the quartermaster trains of Iverson's, Ramseur's, and O'Neal's Brigades. The quartermaster trains of the artillery battalions of Dance, Nelson, and Carter followed O'Neal's train. Behind them were the long ambulance trains of Rodes's Division, led by the ambulances of Iverson's Brigade, followed by Daniel's, and then by those of the artillery battalions of Dance, Nelson, and Carter. The ambulances of the brigades of O'Neal, Ramseur, and Doles followed. Herds of cattle and sheep plodded beside the division subsistence train. A cannoneer in Chew's Battery observed the procession that evening.

"The road was muddy and slippery," he recalled, "the night dark, rainy, dreary and dismal. The train moved very slowly, with halts and starts all night. Every time an ambulance struck a rock I heard the pitiful groans of the wounded." [11]

Traveling in the ambulance train of Rodes's Division as it entered the mountain defile leading to Monterey was Private Moore of the Rockbridge Artillery of Dance's Artillery Battalion. Back at Fairfield, he had helped remove from his ambulance a member of the Richmond Howitzers who was dying; the unfortunate artilleryman was left at a house beside the road. Moore spotted Joe, the slave and cook from his mess, leading a horse that he had somehow "appropriated." Moore took the horse from Joe and then rode beside his battalion's ambulances. "Our column," Moore recalled, "consisted of ambulances loaded with wounded men, wounded men on foot, cows, bulls, quartermasters, portable forges, surgeons, cooks, and camp-followers in general, all plodding gloomily along through the falling rain." [12]

Alarmed that the trains might be attacked by Union cavalry approaching from the direction of Emmitsburg, Captain Emack ordered them to halt on the Maria Furnace Road, about midway up the mountain. Judging from the size and position of those trains, Emack probably stopped them just before Rodes's ordnance and subsistence trains reached the summit of the mountain. Those trains, the quartermaster trains of Iverson, Ramseur, and O'Neal, the quartermaster trains of three artillery battalions, as well as the division ambulance trains and all of Johnson's and Early's trains—and the entire Army of Northern Virginia for that matter—would have had to wait until young Emack gave the clearance for all of them to proceed. [13]

While at a standstill, many sick and wounded soldiers in the ambulance trains seized the opportunity to leave the putrid vehicles and find more comfortable quarters. Those who were walking used the pause to lie down or sit along the muddy roadside. Colonel Christie and Lieutenant Colonel Johnston were taken out of their hack and, along with Major Blacknall, helped into a large "brick Dutch house" on the left side of the road, out of the pouring rain. There, they managed to get something to eat and to rest. [14]

Earlier that day Grumble Jones, like Emack, had realized that the trains were exposed to attack from the direction of Emmitsburg. He had asked Stuart's permission to take his entire brigade to protect them early in the evening. Stuart had granted him the use of the Sixth and Seventh Virginia Cavalry and a section of Chew's Battery but then recalled the Seventh Virginia, replacing it with the Fourth North Carolina Cavalry of Robertson's Brigade. Slowed by the trains that Emack had halted in the deep mud of the roadway, and recognizing that the two cavalry regiments and Chew's guns would have a difficult time reaching the summit of Monterey Pass in time to make a difference there because of the crowding of wagons and ambulances, General Jones left the two regiments and artillery battery and galloped ahead through the falling rain, accompanied by his staff officers and couriers.[15]

On the way, Jones hurried along stragglers from the trains and exhorted the drivers to move their wagons and ambulances forward, overruling Emack's orders for them to halt. He then galloped ahead to offer whatever support he could to the small contingent of cavalry and artillery holding the pass.[16]

Colonel Christie and Lieutenant Colonel Johnston were taken back to their hack and carefully placed on the floor. Major Blacknall, who was in terrible pain from the bullet that ripped through his cheek and tore out teeth as well as from the surgery, stayed behind. He decided to follow the trains after getting more rest. Behind Christie and Johnston rolled the one-horse hack carrying Lieutenant Colonel Green and Lieutenant Bond, driven by Green's slave Guilford. Farther down the column were the ambulances transporting Colonel Kenan and his surgeon, Dr. Brewer, and Captain Wheeler.[17]

The sad cavalcade was rolling again, but the journey was slow and tedious. The rain poured down and the darkness was intensified by bolts of lightning. "From time to time," recalled Green, "a horse or mule would be knocked down [by the crowding of the wagons and ambulances on the narrow roadway] from the opposite sides of the road, thus occasioning delay by a halt to detach him from the harness and drag him to one side."[18]

Ten miles east of Monterey Pass, at Emmitsburg, Judson Kilpatrick's Union cavalry division had been joined by the brigade of Colonel Huey, together with Lieutenant William D. Fuller's Battery C, Third U.S. Artillery, which had arrived from the supply base at Westminster. Kilpatrick now had over 4,500 troops with three batteries of rifled guns under his command. Some of his men had been able to draw rations and feed their jaded horses before heading to Emmitsburg; Custer's men and horses had been fed at Littlestown, Pennsylvania, while Richmond's had been fed from quartermaster and subsistence trains that reached Gettysburg from Westminster. Huey's Brigade, though, was suffering; its horses had not been fed or reshod, and they and the men were exhausted. The brigade had not been able to stop and resupply itself at Westminster. From Emmitsburg, Kilpatrick's combined force headed west on the Emmitsburg-Waynesboro Turnpike toward Monterey Pass. Custer's Brigade, mostly armed with Spencer repeating rifles and carbines, led the column with Lieutenant Alexander C. M. Pennington's Battery M, Second U.S. Artillery, followed by Richmond's Brigade with Lieu-

General Hugh Judson Kilpatrick (standing at right in doorway) and his staff. Taken after the Gettysburg campaign, the photograph shows Kilpatrick's flag adorned with battle honors for Smithsburg, Hagerstown, Williamsport, Boonsboro, and Falling Waters—all actions fought during Lee's retreat from Gettysburg. Library of Congress, Washington, D.C.

tenant Samuel S. Elder's Battery E, Fourth U.S. Artillery. Huey's command brought up the rear. Emack's scouts, posted well out on the Emmitsburg-Waynesboro Turnpike, kept their captain informed of the movement of the Union column.[19]

Twenty-seven-year-old Judson Kilpatrick and twenty-four-year-old George Armstrong Custer were an interesting pair. Kilpatrick, a native of Deckertown, New Jersey, was a May 1861 graduate of West Point; Custer, a native of Monroe, Michigan, had graduated from the academy only one month later at the bottom of his class, and he was actually under arrest at the time. Both knew how to maneuver themselves into positions of rank and authority. Kilpatrick was commissioned a brigadier general of volunteers on 14 June 1863; Custer was similarly commissioned on 29 June. Both were brave, but immodest, rash, impulsive, and self-congratulatory. Their success rested on their uncanny ability to ingratiate themselves with those who could make a difference in their careers. Thus, approaching Emack's small force at Monterey was a formidable division of Union cavalry and artillery led by two commanders who were looking for glory.[20]

As the head of the Union column on the Emmitsburg-Waynesboro Turnpike reached Jack's Mountain Road, Kilpatrick ordered a halt. The First Michigan Cavalry was leading the column. Kilpatrick directed that regiment, except for the advance squad, to ride down Jack's Mountain Road toward Fairfield in order to protect his right flank and rear from being attacked by any Confederate cavalry posted along the road east of Jack's Mountain.[21]

As the Wolverines galloped up Jack's Mountain Road toward Fairfield, they spotted mounted Confederates of Company F, Fifth North Carolina Cavalry of Robertson's Brigade, and Companies F and G, Eleventh Virginia Cavalry of Jones's Brigade. The balance of those two regiments held a line on the road closer to Fairfield along with Captain Moorman's Battery of horse artillery. Lieutenant Colonel Peter Stagg detached a squadron of the First Michigan and led the men in an attack, driving the Confederates back through a hail of gunfire. The rest of the regiment dismounted and advanced behind Stagg's squadron. The Confederate troops boldly counterattacked several times but each time were repulsed. Stagg's horse was killed, and Stagg himself was seriously injured by the fall. Lieutenant James S. McElhenny of the First Michigan was killed, Captain William R. Elliott was mortally wounded, and seventeen Michigan cavalrymen were killed or wounded in the fighting. Stagg's men finally erected barricades across Jack's Mountain Road, and, leaving behind several companies to hold them, the rest of the First Michigan rode back to rejoin the main column.[22]

Outside the village of Fountaindale, a "farmer's boy" named C. H. Buhrman, who had observed Lee's wagon trains retreating along the Maria Furnace Road, mounted his horse with the intent of locating Union cavalry. The gunfire from Jack's Mountain Road provided the backdrop to Buhrman's mission. Buhrman quickly encountered Kilpatrick's advance squad from the First Michigan and passed on the information that Confederate trains were proceeding across Monterey Pass. He was then sent to the rear to relay his findings to General Custer. Custer, in turn, sent him directly to Kilpatrick. When Buhrman reported what he knew to Kilpatrick, the general ordered his whole force to increase its pace toward Monterey Pass.[23]

About two miles from the eastern slope of Monterey Pass, the leading squad from the First Michigan came upon a local girl named Hetty Zeilinger who lived with her family east of the summit of the mountain near the hotel. She must have been no more than twelve years old and was walking back home along the muddy turnpike. She knew Buhrman but, unlike him, told the troops that the Confederates had covered the road through the pass with artillery and warned them not to proceed. The information was relayed to Kilpatrick, who quickly brushed it aside. Though undoubtedly frightened by what lay ahead, Hetty nevertheless agreed to lead the command up to the pass. One trooper of the First Michigan lifted her into his saddle and the advance squad, with the entire division in column behind it, proceeded through the driving rain and mud, guided by the girl.[24]

When the column reached the gate of Buhrman's farm outside of Fountaindale, Buhrman asked to leave, wanting no part of the fight ahead. But Kilpatrick ordered him to remain with the division so he could "see the fun." Young Hetty Zeilinger stayed with the leading squad. The rain-soaked Union troopers had been on the move for twelve hours; many had fallen asleep in their saddles.[25]

Led by Custer's Michiganders, Kilpatrick's column pushed up the muddy turnpike in the driving rain. One Michigan trooper recalled: "Up this narrow, unknown way, in a drizzling rain, and enveloped in darkness so deep that the riders, though jostling together, could not see each other, the exhausted, sleepy soldiers on their weary animals slowly toiled, the heavy tread of the horses and the jingling of steel scabbards, the only sound that broke the silence." Then, the one piece of artillery and the handful of dismounted cavalrymen under Captain Emack opened fire on the Union column from the eastern entrance of Monterey Pass about fifty feet above Custer's troops. Kilpatrick's troops were taken completely by surprise. Those who had fallen asleep in their saddles were rudely awakened by the blast and the whirring canister. Some of the men actually fell out of their saddles, startled by the loud report of the gun. Three times the cannoneers at the lone Napoleon gun fired canister rounds at Kilpatrick's column. Each time the shot sprayed over the heads of the Union cavalrymen, as visibility was nonexistent and the cannoneers were unable to depress the gun enough to hit their target.[26]

The gun's loud, reverberating reports, though, had an unnerving effect on the Union cavalrymen in the inky darkness and pelting rain. Adding to the shock felt by the startled men, Emack directed eight Marylanders to charge toward the Union columns. The action so surprised the Union cavalrymen that they quickly withdrew in disorder. Emack then ordered his troops to dismount and placed them in position on either side of the road, supporting the lone Napoleon gun, to wait for the enemy's next move. He called for Lieutenant Blackistone to bring up his reserve squadrons.[27]

Buhrman told Kilpatrick that if he would dismount a regiment and send it through the edge of the dense woods, the men could clamber up the steep sides of the pass, flank the Confederates, and capture the artillery piece. Kilpatrick agreed and ordered a squad of the Eighteenth Pennsylvania Cavalry, commanded by Major Henry C. Potter, to dismount and move to the left of the column in an effort to flank the Confederates. The tactic was quickly discovered by Emack, and the cannoneers withdrew their gun about two hundred yards to the rear, although an empty caisson was left behind and seized by the Pennsylvanians.[28]

Kilpatrick asked Buhrman the likely destination of the wagon trains that were moving through Monterey Pass. Buhrman told him that it was either Smithsburg and Boonsboro and then across the Potomac River at Boteler's Ford or Leitersburg and Hagerstown and then southwest to the ford at Williamsport. Kilpatrick then asked if there was a road that one of his regiments could use to cut off the trains. Buhrman knew such a road; he told Kilpatrick that if a regiment followed him, the trains could be flanked either at the western base of the mountains or at Leitersburg. Kilpatrick ordered Lieutenant Colonel Addison W. Preston and his First Vermont Cavalry of Colonel Richmond's Brigade to follow Buhrman.[29]

It took an hour for Kilpatrick and Custer to reorganize the leading Michigan regiments and begin a second advance toward the eastern entrance to Monterey Pass. The advance squad of the First Michigan led the Wolverines; a squadron of the Fifth Michigan was ordered down a narrow byroad to the right to protect the column from being surprised from the north. Three of every four troopers of the First Michigan advanced on foot; the remaining soldiers held the horses. Emack's men, bolstered by the arrival of Lieutenant Blackistone's squadrons, waited until Kilpatrick's troopers were within a dozen paces of them. With bolts of lightning momentarily lighting the landscape and the rain continuing to fall in sheets, Emack yelled to his troopers to open fire. All of them fired their carbines and muskets in near unison. Once again Custer's Michigan troopers stalled, believing the force ahead of them to be much larger than it really was. The lone artillery piece made "the night hideous with [its] bellowings, the echoes of which reverberated [through] the mountain gorges in a most frightful manner," recalled one Union trooper.[30]

In the darkness and rain, unsure of exactly how many Confederates were in their front, Custer's men advanced slowly on foot a third time, firing at every step. Kilpatrick remembered that "on the left was a deep ravine, on the right a steep, rugged mountain, and a road too narrow to reverse even a gun. To add to this unpleasant position, it was raining in torrents." Soon, though, the sheer weight of Custer's columns forced Emack's small band and its lone gun to the rear. The eastern summit of Monterey Pass was finally gained by the Union cavalrymen. Custer's men were now alongside the Monterey House; they had fought their way up to nearly the summit of a pass that was more than four hundred feet above the valley floor. The three attacks through the driving rain and thunderstorm, though, had left the Michigan regiments badly disorganized.[31]

Emack's little force withdrew one hundred yards to a position just east of the Maria Furnace Road and its intersection with the Emmitsburg-Waynesboro Turnpike, not far from the tollhouse. To his chagrin, Emack saw that the head of the subsistence trains of Rodes's Division with their herds of cattle and sheep was passing behind him.[32]

General Jones soon arrived on the scene. Emack rode over to him and pleaded to keep the Maria Furnace Road and the turnpike clear of the wagon trains and ambulances, arguing that if they were clear a Union breakthrough at the summit would not seriously damage the trains. Jones peremptorily replied that the trains must keep moving. Emack then told him that he had only a handful of men and a single artillery piece with only one or two rounds and that he desperately needed reinforcements if he were to hold back the Union force that was approaching. Jones assured Emack that he had already ordered the Sixth Virginia and Fourth North Carolina Cavalry regiments and Chew's Battery to his aid. Emack turned to his little band of Maryland cavalrymen and ordered them to spread out on either side of the turnpike, conserve their ammunition, and "not to yield an inch." "This brave little band of heroes," Jones recalled, "was encouraged with the hope of speedy reinforcement, reminded of the importance of their trust and exhorted to fight to the bitter end rather than yield."[33]

Jones then directed his couriers and staff officers to take up weapons, lie down beside Emack's Marylanders, and add their firepower to the defense of the road crossing. He positioned the single twelve-pound Napoleon in the middle of the turnpike, and its cannoneers stoically awaited the Union advance.[34]

Led by the dismounted Sixth Michigan Cavalry to the right of the road, Kilpatrick's dismounted troopers again moved cautiously forward through the deep brush and thickets in the darkness and driving rain. The Fifth Michigan then moved forward to a position behind the Sixth Michigan, where it was ordered to dismount and be prepared to support the advanced regiment. Unable to see ahead, a Wolverine of the Sixth Michigan stepped on one of Emack's skirmishers, Private Richard H. H. Key. Key immediately raised his pistol and fired, killing the Union trooper on the spot. That gunfire precipitated a blanket of carbine and pistol fire from Emack's men that, once again, confused Custer's men, causing them to halt.[35]

Kilpatrick and Custer could hear the rumble of the wagons along the Maria Furnace Road and the Emmitsburg-Waynesboro Turnpike toward the Cumberland Valley to the west. Kilpatrick called upon Lieutenant Pennington to unlimber a section of his Battery M, Second U.S. Artillery, to support an attack across the summit of Monterey. Two guns of Pennington's Battery quickly responded, unlimbering in the clearing just west of the Monterey House in the pouring rain. Pennington yelled for support, and Kilpatrick responded, "Here is my escort; they will stand by you." He directed Company A of the First Ohio Cavalry to dismount and deploy on either side of the two guns.[36]

To prevent the two guns from hitting Custer's cavalrymen as they advanced, Kilpatrick asked Pennington to elevate his pieces just enough so they could throw their shells over the advancing Union troopers and explode in the midst of the passing wagon trains. Dismounted, the Sixth Michigan formed a skirmish line and moved ahead along the fields to the right of the turnpike. In the darkness, with lightning flashing all around and rain pouring down, the Wolverines quickly engaged Confederate skirmishers. Sergeant James H. Kidd of the Sixth Michigan recalled: "We were deployed as skirmishers through a thick wood, so dark that we could see nothing, seeing the Rebs only by the flash of their guns. This was a night never to be forgotten." Hindered by thick vines and dense undergrowth, the Sixth Michigan advanced slowly. "Imagine it so dark that you can only hear not see, and a heavy rain falling," Kidd wrote. "One had to be guided by sound and not by sight."[37]

Emack soon obtained a few of the reinforcements he had sought. A little more than 100 troopers of the Sixth Virginia and the Fourth North Carolina Cavalry regiments managed to arrive at the summit; Emack's total number of defenders, however, was at most 210. All of the others, including Chew's guns, were still hopelessly entangled among the trains clogging the road. Iverson's Brigade was struggling down the Fairfield Road; it had just reached Fairfield, six difficult miles away.[38]

The troopers of the Sixth Virginia and Fourth North Carolina were ordered to dismount and join the line formed on either side of the turnpike and advance toward the Union lines. "Among the rocks and trees," recalled Private Luther Hopkins of the Sixth Virginia, "[we moved] forward in an effort to drive [Pennington's] battery away from its position." Behind them, the subsistence and ordnance trains of Rodes's Division had just passed over the summit of Monterey Pass and were winding their way down to the village of Waterloo. Passing the summit were the quartermaster trains of Iverson's, Ramseur's, and O'Neal's Brigades and those of the three artillery battalions. To add to the chaos, the large herds of cattle and sheep following Rodes's subsistence trains had gotten loose. Many were in the roadway; others were wandering in the dense woods. All were bellowing and bleating loudly amid the gunfire.[39]

Pennington's guns fired rapidly; along with the darkness and heavy rain, they slowed the Confederate fire. Private Hopkins recalled: "The booming of the guns that hour of night, with the roar of the thunder, was terrifying indeed, and beyond description. We would wait for a lightning flash and then advance a few steps and halt and then [wait] for a light from the batteries and again advance." The "constant bellowing" of the cows and bleating of the sheep only added to the hideousness of the night. Private John Opie of the Sixth Virginia remembered that Pennington's cannoneers "poured an incessant fire of grape and canister in our direction; but as there happened to be a bend in the road where we were halted, we suffered no injury."[40]

Between the skirmishers of the Sixth Michigan and Emack's cavalrymen was a branch of Red Run, a stream that ran west off the mountain range. A bridge on the turnpike spanned "a very deep gorge" cut by the branch that ran in front of the Sixth Michigan. Colonel Russell A. Alger of the Fifth Michigan, whose dismounted squadrons remained behind the skirmishers of the Sixth Michigan, reported that the bridge "was [in] a very exposed place. The night was very dark and in order to take in the situation I ordered my men to lie down." He sent forward a few of his skirmishers to reconnoiter the bridge to determine whether it still remained in place and could support an attacking column of cavalry. In the driving rain, his skirmishers returned and announced that the bridge remained intact. Alger then dispatched a courier back to Kilpatrick asking permission for elements of his regiment to charge across the bridge and into the Confederate positions protecting the wagon and ambulance trains. Just then, one of Alger's men was shot down. Seizing the dead man's carbine, Alger called out to his leading companies to accompany him across the bridge. With a rush, the men followed him through the inky darkness, lighted only by bursts of gunfire and bolts of lightning. Once across the bridge, Alger spread his men out on either side of the turnpike. The troopers formed a line of battle "by the flashes of [their own] guns," Alger recalled. Both the Fifth and Sixth Michigan were within sixty yards of Ewell's trains and their defenders.[41]

Hearing of Alger's success, Kilpatrick directed General Custer to attack with the rest of his Michigan brigade. "Get ready to charge with sabres!" yelled the officers in Custer's mounted commands. John Bigelow, bugler of the Fifth Michigan, still in line near the Monterey House with the balance of his command, remembered thinking: "Charge what? And at this midnight hour? Up we have come, miles high it seems, and what are we to find up here? 'Tis raining so hard that the water makes it appear lighter." As Custer's mounted Wolverines prepared to make the charge, the lone Confederate artillery piece opened up once again. The ground shook as the gun, behind a lurid flash and deafening report, fired a canister round at the Union troopers forming for the attack. It did little damage, however.[42]

Shifting back behind his skirmish line, Alger ordered his remaining men to lead the advance dismounted. Accordingly, the soldiers proceeded to unsling their carbines, dismount, and move forward. The Seventh Michigan Cavalry was directed to dismount and form on the right near the Sixth Michigan. With the summit of Monterey Pass illuminated by lightning flashes and shaken by thunder, the two sides opened fire in earnest. Alger's men were soon halted by another well-aimed canister round from the lone Confederate artillery piece.[43]

While elements of the Michigan Cavalry Brigade fought in the clearings and dense woods east of the Maria Furnace Road, Kilpatrick called upon Major Charles E. Capehart's First West Virginia Cavalry of Colonel Richmond's Brigade to move forward to Monterey House. When it arrived, he ordered Capehart and his men to go to Custer's support. As Capehart rode up to Custer, the vain young commander of the Michigan Cavalry Brigade directed him to charge ahead and take the wagon trains behind the Confederate defenders. Capehart "immediately informed his officers and men of the duty which devolved upon them." On hearing the order, Lieutenant William P. Wilkin of the First West Virginia felt that "it looked like certain death to make a charge at such time." Like all the other officers and men of the regiment, he could only imagine the inferno into which he was about to gallop.[44]

Meanwhile, Kilpatrick told his headquarters escort, Company A of the First Ohio, to vacate its position beside Pennington's guns and move ahead to support the West Virginians. Once the Ohioans formed for their attack, Custer shook hands with their company commander, Captain T. K. Jones, saying, "Do your duty and God bless you." Jones then turned to his men and yelled, "Use [sabres] alone, I will cut down the first man that fires a shot." The Ohioans drew their sabres and, along with the men of the First West Virginia, galloped past Alger's dismounted troopers, "whooping and yelling," and ran headlong into Emack's dismounted cavalrymen. Lieutenant Wilkin recalled that "less than one hundred men" of the First West Virginia actually made the charge, "the timid ones falling out."[45]

The attack was met with a heavy volley of musketry from in front of and among the wagons. Spotting the positions of the enemy by the flashes of their carbines and muskets, the Union troopers surged toward the wagon and ambulance trains. The one Napoleon gun finally ran out of ammunition, and Emack's men had nearly exhausted all of theirs. Soon "a hand-to-hand conflict ensued. The scene was wild and desolating," recalled Major Capehart.[46]

Captain Emack drew his sabre and led his men into the melee. By then he had already been shot through both arms and his right hand. He was then struck on his right knee by shrapnel from an exploding shell from one of Lieutenant Pennington's rifled guns. That, he remembered, "was more painful than either of my arms." Still in the saddle and brandishing his sabre in his left hand, Emack galloped headlong toward the oncoming Union troopers. He remained mounted until struck three or four times across the shoulder and arms by sabre blows. Then his horse fell to the ground, killed by gunfire. He later wrote that the loss of that horse, a gift from a family friend, was more distressing than any of his own wounds. Bloody and writhing in pain, Emack was finally carried off the field by some of his men. He had done his duty.[47]

Overcome by the excitement of the moment, Custer galloped alongside his Wolverines whom he urged forward behind the West Virginians, but he was thrown from his horse and nearly captured. Captain John Selsor of the First West Virginia came upon a squad of Confederate cavalrymen hiding behind an old building and seized them all, as well as their battle flag. Private B. F. Jones of that regiment apprehended two Confederates hiding near a fence in the woods and sent them to the rear.[48]

Emack's little company suffered many casualties. Lieutenant Adolphus Cooke was wounded and captured. One private was killed and two were wounded and captured; twenty-six more were taken prisoner. In the fight, Grumble Jones narrowly avoided being captured himself in the confusion among the wagons and ambulances and their defenders. In the pelting rain and darkness, those attacking the trains quickly became indistinguishable from those defending them. The noise from the gunfire, neighing and snorting horses and mules, bellowing cows, and bleating sheep made the moment absolutely chaotic. Recognizing the danger, Jones yelled to those nearby not to call him "general," but to refer to him only as "Bill"; he did not want the attacking Union troopers to know that a Confederate general was in the midst of the trains and their defenders.[49]

Lieutenant Pennington sent forward one of his guns under Lieutenant Robert Clarke to support the Union charge and "fire down the [Maria Furnace] Road." As soon as it unlimbered, it opened fire on the trains, smashing wagons and ambulance and blocking the road and any line of retreat toward Fairfield. The Ohioans and West Virginians, followed by Custer's Michiganders, galloped among the wagons and ambulances, "yelling like troopers."[50]

One of the wounded cannoneers in the ambulance train of Dance's Artillery Battalion was Berkeley Minor of the Rockbridge Artillery. He had watched the fighting as it got ever closer to his ambulance. There were frequent stops, passing couriers, and the racket of gunfire. As his ambulance moved onto the Emmitsburg-Waynesboro Turnpike, he saw the flashes of Pennington's artillery pieces to his left:

> "Of course, . . . each team and vehicle was most exposed to [the artillery fire] as it approached the turn," Minor remembered. "We did not get far . . . before we heard the gun, and then came the sharp crack of the shell just behind us, or somewhere very near, and the ambulance in front of us stopped—a horse was killed or something broke; but our driver had no notion of stopping. . . . We could not have helped them in such a stampede as filled the road from side to side with vehicles of all sorts and flying cavalrymen. . . . Then for some minutes there was a mad rush along the pike, a *sauve qui peut*, the road being filled . . . with vehicles and horses, their iron hoofs striking sheets of fire from the stony surface of the pike. I realized at what a dangerous speed we were going, and how fatal a collision with one of the heavy wagons would be, and I tried to get our driver, by whom I was sitting in the front seat, to moderate the speed . . . but he had completely lost his head and just swore at me and drove harder than ever. But . . . our driver was made to halt very quickly by a squad of Yankee cavalry which suddenly overtook us, and, with pistols in our faces from both sides, and many oaths, ordered an instant halt."[51]

Behind Minor's ambulance, cannoneer Edward Moore, still mounted on the horse he had "appropriated" from Joe, saw three cavalry horses with empty saddles pass by. "This was rather ominous," he thought:

> The halts in the mixed column [of wagons and ambulances] were now frequent, darkness having set in, and we had little to say. That cannon had moved more to our front, and our road bore still more to where it was thundering . . . nearer our front were scattering musket shots.

Our halts were still short and frequent, and in the deep shadow of the mountain it was pitch dark. All this time I had not a particle of confidence in my horse. I could not tell what was before me in the dense darkness, whether friend or foe, but suddenly after pausing an instant, [my horse] dashed forward. For fifty or seventy-five yards every other sound was drowned by a roaring waterfall on my right; then, emerging from its noise, I was carried at a fearful rate close by dismounted men who were firing from behind trees along the roadside, the flashes of their guns, "whose speedy gleams the darkness swallowed," revealing me on my tall horse with his head up. [My horse] must see safety ahead, and I let him fly. A hundred yards farther on our road joined the main pike at an acute angle, and entering it [my horse] swept on. Then, just behind me, a Federal cannon was discharged. The charge of canister tore through the brush on either side and over and under me, and at the same instant my steed's hind leg gave way, and my heart sank with it. If struck at all, he immediately rallied and outran himself as well as his competitors.[52]

Moore reached the tollgate just beyond the intersection of the Maria Furnace Road and the Emmitsburg-Waynesboro Turnpike. There he saw a fellow cannoneer, Tom Williamson, who had attended Washington College with him. Williamson's foot had nearly been taken off by a bursting shell on 3 July, and he was unable to walk. "His ambulance had broken down," Moore recalled, "and he was being assisted toward the house. I drew rein, but thought, 'How can I help him? This horse must be well-nigh done for,' and rode on. But again the road was full, and approaching clatter, with sharp reports of pistols, brought on another rush, and away we went—wagons, wounded men, negroes, forges, ambulances, cavalry—everything."[53]

As the charging Union cavalrymen galloped through the trains, they turned down the turnpike toward Waynesboro, past the tollhouse, forcing Confederate wagons and ambulances off the road and down the ravines on the west side of the mountain. In one of those ambulances was Lieutenant Henry E. Shepherd of Colonel Kenan's Forty-third North Carolina. He was completely immobile due to a bullet that had passed through his right knee during the last assault against Culp's Hill on the morning of 3 July. "In its desperate attempt to escape, our train drove through the contending lines of cavalry," Shepherd recalled, "the one striving to capture, the other to protect. I was utterly helpless and disabled, and the ghastly recollections of the gloomy, stormy night, when I was driven through the lines of battle—unable to raise my hand, and in momentary peril of my life—can never be dimmed or effaced."[54]

The wounded Lieutenant Colonel Green and Captain Bond also found themselves in a precarious position. A "heavy ordnance wagon loaded with damaged guns" tried to hurry around their hack to avoid capture. In the process the hub of one of its wheels tore off a wheel of Green and Bond's hack, dropping it and them in the middle of the road. Just then, "a score of blue-coated cavalry [men] were upon [us] with their revolvers leveled," recalled Green. Guilford then "spoke with a fluency of tongue rarely, if ever, surpassed by any of his race," Green continued, "'Don't shoot gentlemen, for God's sake, don't shoot. We surrender. We are prisoners.'"[55]

The rainstorm seemed to intensify. The thunder and lightning, coupled with the small arms and artillery fire and the yells and screams of attackers, defenders, and the wounded, as well as the neighing of horses and mules, bellowing of cows, and bleating of sheep added an "inconceivable terror to the scene," wrote one participant.[56]

Kilpatrick's troopers struck the ambulance trains of Rodes's Division on the summit of the mountain. The trains had been suddenly stalled by the breakdown of a quartermaster wagon of the Thirtieth North Carolina in the train of Ramseur's Brigade down near Waterloo. As the Union cavalrymen galloped down the turnpike toward Waterloo, they overwhelmed ambulance after ambulance and wagon after wagon until they hit the very rear of the quartermaster train of O'Neal's Brigade, capturing ten of its wagons, including the brigade headquarters wagon, which had been captured from General Milroy's fleeing troops at Martinsburg two weeks earlier and was being pulled by horses impressed in Pennsylvania until it had broken down in the road; William Potter, chief brigade quartermaster clerk; seven African American teamsters; Captain John White, assistant quartermaster of the Fifth Alabama; John Wiley, quartermaster sergeant of the Third Alabama; the slave of Major James C. Bryan, chief quartermaster of O'Neal's Brigade; and the entire payroll of O'Neal's Brigade. In the confusion, though, Potter managed to escape.[57]

Kilpatrick's cavalrymen overtook and seized all the quartermaster wagons of Dance's, Nelson's, and Carter's Artillery Battalions. All of Kilpatrick's other captures were ambulances, sick and wounded officers and enlisted men, and their medical attendants from the ambulance trains of Iverson's and Daniels's Brigades and the three artillery battalions. "The clothes that I wore," recalled cannoneer Moore, "were all that I now possessed. My blanket, extra wearing apparel, lard, apple-butter, sole-leather, etc. [that he had

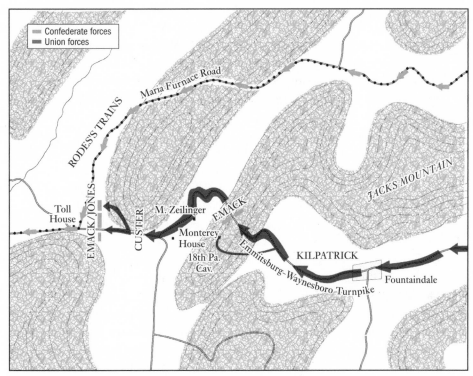

MAP 5.1   4 July 1863, 9:00 P.M., to 5 July 1863, 2:00 A.M.
Kilpatrick's cavalry division attacks Captain Emack's Company B, First Maryland
Battalion, and one gun from the Courtney (Virginia) Artillery east of Monterey
House and then strikes Emack's Company and General Jones's reinforcements
near the tollhouse at the summit of Monterey Pass, seizing a large segment of the
trains of Rodes's Division.

seized at the battery's hospital in Gettysburg], with the wounded, were [now]
in the hands of the Federals."[58]

Narrowly escaping capture was the ambulance carrying Captains Park,
Ross, and Hewlett and the horribly wounded Lieutenant Wright of the
Twelfth Alabama of O'Neal's Brigade. "They were firing uncomfortable
near," Park wrote in his diary. To add to the drama, Park's ambulance broke
down during the height of the chase down the mountain. He and the driver,
Sam Slaton, hobbled over to a farmhouse, took the farmer's small wagon, left
one of their horses with him, and drove the other with the wagon carrying all
four of the wounded on past Waterloo.[59]

The hack carrying the wounded Colonel Christie and Lieutenant Colonel

Johnston at the front of the ambulance train of Iverson's Brigade was over-whelmed by the Union cavalrymen. Behind Christie and Johnston were all of the ambulances from Iverson's and Daniel's Brigades carrying, among others, Lieutenant Colonel Boyd, Major Lewis, Major Hancock, and Dr. Godwin, along with those transporting Colonel Kenan and his surgeon, Dr. Brewer, and Captain Wheeler. All were taken, together with hundreds of other sick and wounded officers and enlisted men, some in ambulances, others on foot, and many slaves.[60]

General Jones reported that "ineffectual efforts were made for a rally and resistance, but without avail, until at the foot of the mountain [just above Waterloo] a few joined" a thin skirmish line held by Welsh's Company of the First Maryland. Major Bryan hastily assembled a command of sixteen team-sters and a lieutenant in the quartermaster service to assist Welsh. The Mary-landers and teamsters stopped the Union charge and briefly drove it back, recapturing two ambulances, including the hack carrying Christie and Johns-ton. In the end, however, Welsh's command was no match for Kilpatrick's Division. A renewed Union thrust dispersed Welsh's defenders by 3:00 A.M., and every quartermaster and ambulance train, from the summit of Monterey Pass all the way to Waterloo, was in the possession of Kilpatrick's Division.[61]

Among the Confederates captured by Kilpatrick's troopers at Monterey Pass in the early morning hours of 5 July were those who were either too weary or in too much pain to go on; some had fallen asleep along the road-side before the attack began. One of these was the slave of Major William H. Chamberlain, who served on the staff of Colonel Reuben L. Walker, artillery chief of Hill's Corps. When the trains of Ewell's Corps had started back to Virginia, Chamberlain's slave went along with them, as it was customary for the slaves of officers and men in Lee's army to accompany the trains, and it seemed to be the safest passage. Chamberlain's slave rode his master's horse and carried most of his equipment; Chamberlain rode a horse he had acquired from Colonel Stapleton Crutchfield about two months before. The slave had been riding at the rear of the column of quartermaster trains of Rodes's Di-vision. When Captain Emack had called a halt to the trains, Chamberlain's slave had tied the horse to a tree and, like many others, fell asleep. By the time he awoke and responded to Kilpatrick's attack, it was too late. He was quickly captured, and Chamberlain "lost servant, horse and equipment."[62]

Major Blacknall of the Twenty-third North Carolina remained on the floor of the "brick Dutch house" with his cousin, an aide, hoping some rest would make the journey more comfortable in the morning. While Blacknall and his cousin slept, Union cavalrymen entered the yard and took their horses. Hearing the enemy all around the house, Blacknall and his cousin got up and ran outside and into a small patch of corn nearby to hide. When all seemed safe, the two tried to catch up to the trains. Within minutes they were captured.[63]

At the western base of the mountain, near Waterloo, Captain Chancellor A. Nelson, Sergeant Charles I. Johnson, and nine of their wounded compatriots from the Forty-ninth Virginia had crawled into a barn not far from the turnpike. Although from Johnson's Division, they had joined Rodes's trains at Fairfield. They subsequently realized what an unwise decision they had made. As Kilpatrick's cavalrymen galloped through and around the trains, forcing wagons and ambulances off the road or to halt, they came upon the barn. Nelson, Johnson, and their men were spotted and quickly taken prisoner.[64]

Equally unlucky was Corporal Hall of the Thirty-first Virginia, also of Johnson's Division. Wounded in the knee, he had hobbled beside the trains of Rodes's Division through the night until his shoes gave out on the rocky, muddy roadway. Once beyond Monterey Pass, he realized that he could not go on. He found a haystack in a barn near the road and fell asleep, only to be awakened by the gunfire, yelling, and shouting outside. Seeing that the trains had been attacked, he limped into the woods and then began to descend the western face of the mountain. Unfortunately, he entered a house that turned out to be in the path of Kilpatrick's charging division and was captured.[65]

In the end, Welsh's Company lost 2 men wounded and 32 taken prisoner. In all, about 250 wagons and ambulances loaded with casualties from Iverson's and Daniel's Brigades and the three artillery battalions were now in enemy hands, as was the rear element of Rodes's quartermaster trains, consisting of 37 wagons, together with those of the three artillery battalions. In all, nearly 1,300 officers, enlisted men, slaves, free blacks, and Maryland, Virginia, and North Carolina cavalrymen were taken in the attack. Among those captured were the African American cooks of the Third Company of the Richmond Howitzers.[66]

During the final attack and chase down the mountain, General Jones became separated from his staff and couriers. He wisely mounted his horse and galloped westward toward Waynesboro, narrowly escaping capture. He would ride across Franklin County, Pennsylvania, and Washington County, Maryland, for hours in the driving rain and darkness, at times not knowing in what direction he was heading.[67]

Kilpatrick's losses were, by contrast, comparatively light. He reported a total of five killed, including a commissioned officer, ten wounded, and twenty-eight missing.[68]

Judson Kilpatrick would boast of his attack and captures. He reported that he had destroyed Ewell's entire train. What he got, of course, was but a small element of the trains stretching forty miles toward Hagerstown. Kilpatrick, though, was now out of touch with his army; he was on the western side of the mountains with the enemy crowding behind him. The captures of which he boasted would quickly become a burden to him and his men.[69]

Six

That vast procession of misery

While Captain Emack boldly defended the steep eastern entrance to Monterey Pass, some of the leading elements of Imboden's trains were passing the stone house of forty-three-year-old Jacob C. Snyder, his wife Martha, and their eight children east of the village of New Franklin, Pennsylvania, and fourteen miles northwest of Monterey Pass in the Cumberland Valley. Snyder recalled hearing the "clattering and tramping" of horses along the road. He surmised that it was another passing detachment of troops heading toward Gettysburg. In a few moments, though, he knew that was not the case. The rumbling of what appeared to be hundreds of wagons and the sound of countless voices through the violent rainstorm prompted him to climb out of bed. He lighted a lamp, walked to his front door, and stepped out onto his porch. There he saw a sight he would never forget. The ambulance trains of Pender's Division were passing down the road toward New Franklin; the quartermaster, subsistence, and ordnance trains of the division had mostly passed his house. Snyder's presence on the front porch attracted many of the walking wounded who were accompanying the trains. "In less than fifteen minutes," he recalled, "the large hall of my house and the yard in front were filled with wounded Confederate soldiers." All feverish and in desperate need of water and fresh bandages, the men begged Snyder and his wife for help. "Water!" they cried, "give us water!"[1]

"Oh, what a sight," remembered Snyder. The rain was falling in torrents. From the ambulance trains were uttered the most mournful "groans of the wounded and shrieks of the dying." Snyder put on his overcoat and walked out to his barnyard, carrying only a walking stick. He found men from Imboden's own Eighteenth Virginia Cavalry driving out some of the young cattle. The foraging continued even in such desperate circumstances. Snyder hurried to

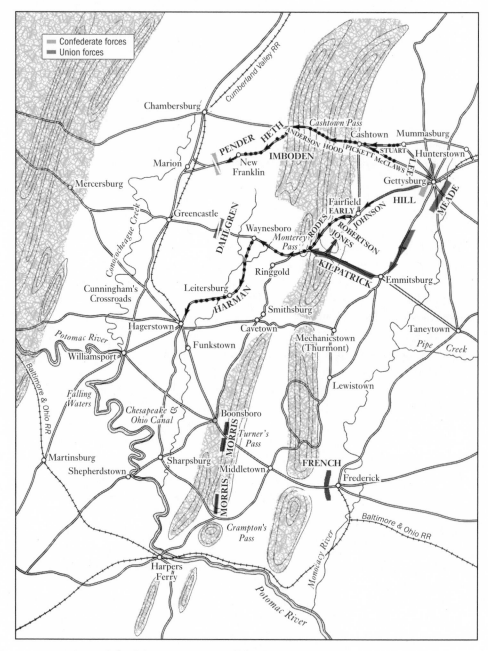

MAP 6.1   4 July 1863, 9:00 P.M., to 5 July 1863, 3:00 A.M.
Harman's reserve train reaches Hagerstown, Rodes's trains are attacked by
Kilpatrick's Division at Monterey Pass, and Imboden's trains arrive at New
Franklin. Hill's leading corps arrives at Fairfield.

close the gate before any more of his herd was released. The officer in charge of the cavalrymen, noticing Snyder's walking stick and, in the rainy darkness, supposing it was a gun, turned his horse around and rode down the muddy pike toward New Franklin.

On through the late hours, the long trains of ambulances and walking wounded passed Snyder's farm. At about 1:00 A.M., 5 July, a mounted officer rode up to the house. The officer appeared to have had one of his legs amputated and was strapped to his saddle. He asked for a drink of water, and Snyder obliged.[2]

Back at Cashtown, the trains were still filtering onto the Chambersburg Pike. It would take Imboden more than thirteen hours to get all of his trains on the road. The trains of McLaws's Division, the last of Longstreet's transportation to fill the column, would take more than fifteen hours to move eight miles from the Herr Ridge Road to Cashtown. "We moved slower than a funeral train," wrote one wounded soldier.

Just before the trains of Stuart's cavalry brigades got under way, some trains of Anderson's Division entered the long column. The ambulance carrying Captain Waddell of the Twelfth Virginia left a private home in Cashtown before dawn on 5 July. As the ambulance rolled into Cashtown Pass, Waddell became more and more ill; he was burning with fever. "I am so unwell that I feel almost desperate," he wrote in his diary.[3]

By the time Hart's Battery actually started moving behind the trains of Stuart's horse brigades, it was well after dawn. By then, the trains were seventeen miles long. Imboden's column contained about six thousand casualties.[4]

Because so many wounded in the trains of Hood's Division could not go any farther than Cashtown, Dr. William P. Powell of the Fifth Texas agreed to stay there with them; he was probably the last surgeon to voluntarily leave the trains before they reached Williamsport. When McLaws's trains reached Cashtown, many of the wounded were removed. Sergeant Major C. C. Cumming of the Seventeenth Mississippi was one of them; he had lost too much blood. His slave George lifted him from the ambulance and carried him to a barn on the left side of the road where nearly thirty other badly wounded men lay.[5]

In the wee hours of 5 July, an odd contingent of troops entered Cashtown. The battalion of engineers attached to Ewell's Corps, like Stuart's cavalry brigades, did not receive the orders to withdraw to Lee's defense lines west of Gettysburg until after all of Ewell's troops had evacuated their lines east and north of Gettysburg. Instead, some cavalry detachments notified them. The little battalion followed the cavalry columns to Mummasburg and Cashtown, where they stopped to determine how they could reach the main body of the army. While there, they were pressed into service at the makeshift hospitals. One member of the engineer battalion was Lieutenant Henry Herbert Harris of Louisa County, Virginia. He recalled that, while waiting at Cashtown, "we buried two Confederates and ministered as best we could to some 20 too badly wounded to be moved." Harris and his engineer battalion remained at Cashtown until midday, 5 July, when they were marched toward Fairfield on the road through Ortanna. There they joined the marching columns of infantry and artillery.[6]

Imboden's trains continued to move up the Chambersburg Pike and onto the Walnut Bottom and Pine Stump Roads in the pouring rain. The Chambersburg Pike was macadamized, but the Walnut Bottom and Pine Stump Roads were not. In fact, the Pine Stump Road, according to one resident of Marion, Pennsylvania, was "considered to be the oldest road in [Franklin] County" and "among the worst roads in the county." Parts of it were "hilly, very stony and rocky, whilst some of the lower places were muddy if not swampy." The heavy rain reduced the road to "a most deplorable condition, becoming almost impassable." Nevertheless, Imboden's enormous trains moved on.

"The retreating army, which kept passing along [the Pine Stump Road] for fully forty-eight hours," wrote the Marion resident, "cut down or opened fences and passed along in the fields, adjacent and parallel with the road. It was a common thing to see some of their horses sticking in the mud nearly body deep. At numerous places wagons and cannon carriages were left on account of the horses not being able to drag them through the mud. The cries and moanings of the wounded rebels could be heard for more than a mile when they were in wagons and crossing over this muddy and rough road."[7]

At about the time Captain Emack's men were valiantly defending the summit of Monterey Pass, Imboden set out from Cashtown with his staff to reach the head of the long column. "My orders," he recalled,

> had been peremptory that there should be no halt for any cause whatsoever. If an accident should happen to any vehicle, it was immediately to be put out of the road and abandoned. The column moved rapidly, considering the rough roads and darkness, and from almost every wagon for many miles issued heart-rending wails of agony. For four hours I hurried forward on my way to the front, and in all that time I was never out of hearing of the screams and cries of the wounded and dying. Scarcely one in a hundred had received adequate surgical aid, owing to the de-

mands on the hard-working surgeons from still worse cases that had to be left behind. Many of the wounded in the wagons had been without food for thirty-six hours. Their torn and bloody clothing, matted and hardened, was rasping the tender, inflamed, and still oozing wounds. Very few of the wagons had even a layer of straw in them, and all were without springs. The road was rough and rocky from the heavy washings of the preceding day. The jolting was enough to have killed strong men, if long exposed to it. From nearly every wagon as the teams trotted on, urged by whip and shout, came such cries and shrieks as these:

'O God! Why can't I die?'

'My God! Will no one have mercy and kill me?'

'Stop! Oh! For God's sake, stop just for one minute; take me out and leave me to die on the roadside.'

'I am dying! I am dying! My poor wife, my dear children, what will become of you?'

Some were simply moaning; some were praying, and others uttering the most fearful oaths and excretions that despair and agony could wring from them; while a majority, with a stoicism sustained by sublime devotion to the cause they fought for, endured without complaint unspeakable tortures, and even spoke words of cheer and comfort to their unhappy comrades of less will or more acute nerves. Occasionally a wagon would be passed from which only low, deep moans could be heard. No help could be rendered to any of the sufferers. No heed could be given to any of their appeals. Mercy and duty to the many forbade the loss of a moment in the vain effort then and there to comply with the prayers of the few. On! On! We *must* move on. The storm continued, and the darkness was appalling. There was no time even to fill a canteen with water for a dying man; for, except the drivers and the guards, all were wounded and utterly helpless in that vast procession of misery.[8]

Traveling with the wounded of Heth's Division were the regimental bands of the Eleventh and Twenty-sixth North Carolina. Julius Lineback, a musician in the band of the Twenty-sixth, remembered that the trains were "a motley procession of wagons, ambulances, wounded men on foot, straggling soldiers and band boys, splashing along in the mud, weary, sad and discouraged." Some time before midnight, Lineback himself gave in to exhaustion. He and two of his fellow Moravian band members had gotten separated from their comrades. "Very tired," he wrote, "we lay down under a tree, not caring very much whether the Yankees came and picked us up or not." One of the trio

A. C. Redwood's drawing of mule-drawn ambulances and wagons, with walking wounded, making their way toward Williamsport in the driving rain. Robert Underwood Johnson and Clarence Clough Buel, eds., *Battles and Leaders of the Civil War*, 4 vols. (New York: Century Co., 1884–87), 3:426.

"had no shoes, and his feet were tender." The rain fell in sheets. "Heavier rain coming on during the night," Lineback noted, "we sat up, with our blankets over us, meditating on our forlorn condition until daylight."[9]

Protecting the trains was exceedingly difficult; the escorts suffered along with the helpless wounded. Private I. Norval Baker of the Eighteenth Virginia Cavalry could hardly forget that night. "'Twas awful," he wrote, "it rained all night, one thunderstorm after another. The rain fell in sheets and vivid flashes of lightning and so dark we could not see our hand an inch from our eyes when there was no lightning. The roar of the waters and the heavy bursting thunder, the cries of the wounded and dying soldiers made it awful." Private W. A. Popkins, one of Baker's compatriots, recalled: "Of all the nights I spent during the war, I think that this was the saddest. We were already sad and disheartened by our misfortune, and this mental condition was made worse by the thunder and lightning and great torrents of rain which came down, augmented by the horrible groans of the wounded and dying."[10]

Private Napier Bartlett, a cannoneer in Buck Miller's Third Company of the Washington Artillery, walked beside his two-gun section in the midst of Longstreet's trains. He watched men fall out of their saddles due to exhaustion and horses "drop down dead" in the muddy roadway. "Over the rocky [Pine Stump Road] some of us had to march barefooted," he remembered, "our shoes having been destroyed by the rough macadamized [Chambersburg Pike], or the heavy mud; and those were especially sufferers whose feet, my own among the numbers, were inconveniently larger than those of the passing Dutchmen whom we would meet on the road." Lack of rest presented an even more difficult challenge to the soaked and muddy escorts. Bartlett continued: "The men and officers on horseback would go to sleep without knowing it, and at one time there was a halt occasioned by all of the drivers—or at least those whose business was to attend to it—being asleep in their saddles. In fact the whole of the army was dozing while marching and moved as if under enchantment or spell—were asleep and at the same time walking."[11]

The ambulances of Pender's Division reached Greencastle at about 4:00 A.M. on 5 July. The residents were awakened by the rumbling wagons and the clatter of thousands of horses and mules. Like Jacob Snyder at New Franklin, the Reverend Dr. J. C. Smith of Greencastle believed at first that more Confederate troops were heading toward Gettysburg. He hastily dressed and ran to the door to see what was going on. There he observed "the army of wounded from the battlefield hastening on toward the Potomac to cross over to Virginia." Smith watched the endless stream of wagons, ambulances, and walking wounded pass by his house. "No one with any feelings of pity," he wrote, "will ever want to see such a sight even once in a lifetime." The whole train seemed to be in a hurry to get to the river. "A more crestfallen, woebegone mob may never have been seen," Smith recalled. The wounded appeared to be pushing one another forward down the turnpike to Williamsport. When Smith inquired about the outcome at Gettysburg, the passing Confederate officers said that they had given the Yankees a sound thrashing.

"If you have thrashed our army so soundly, why are you leaving us so hurriedly?" Smith asked one officer. "Why not stay and occupy your territory?" The officer replied with the precise words that his commanders had directed him to use: "Oh, we are just taking these home to have them cured up, and with these wagons bring on more ammunition and soldiers and finish the job."

The Confederate then asked Smith if he had heard any news from Vicksburg. Smith said that he had not. The officer then told Smith that he had heard that General Pemberton had captured Grant and his entire army.

From his Greencastle house Smith observed that the common soldiers rarely spoke with anyone, although some African American slaves accompanying the trains boldly declared to the civilians they passed that Lee's army had been badly whipped. Smith noted that as the ambulances passed over any part of the street that caused the vehicles to jolt, the wounded "would yell and groan with pain." He could tell that even though these soldiers had been injured two, three, or four days ago, they had not received medical attention since then. "Those wounded in the arms would tear away the garment and expose the wounded part. Such areas — [were] swollen to twice or thrice their natural size — red and angry."

In Smith's yard, as in many yards in the town, was a water pump. When wounded soldiers who were walking beside the ambulances came to the pump, "one would place his wounded member under the spout while another would pump cold water on the sore. Then he would do a like service to his comrade. Thus, the pumps were going all that day." One soldier from North Carolina who entered Smith's yard had been shot through the arm, between the shoulder and the elbow. "The arm," Smith remembered, "was swollen to the size of a man's thigh, very red and very much inflamed." Apparently, the wound had not been cleaned or dressed, save the placement of wads of cotton on the arm at the points of entry and exit of the projectile, since he was shot on 1 July. "I am going home, and I'll never enter the army again," the soldier said. Smith told him that Union troops had cut off Lee's line of retreat. Ignoring Smith's comment, the man declared that he had never wanted to fight in the first place. "The next time they come they may shoot me down at my door; I will rather die than fight again."[12]

Many teamsters, it seems, did not even attempt to keep to the road but tried to take shortcuts across the fields. So heavy was the rain and so saturated was the ground that many of those wagons and ambulances sank up to their axles and became immobilized. Some cavalrymen guarding the trains became lost in the darkness and rain and were seen "jumping their tired horses over the cattleguards" of the Cumberland Valley Railroad outside of Greencastle. George Myers, whose house stood near the railroad station, recalled that his "pump was in continual use for water to bathe the wounds and quench the thirst of the wretched inmates of the wagons." By dawn, "some of the wagons from which groans were heard to come were closed down by curtains, the poor wretches having died."[13]

Greencastle resident David Z. Zook was also awakened by the noise of the passing trains. As he ran out of his house to see them, he noticed, like Reverend Smith, that they appeared to be in a hurry. When he tried to engage some Confederates in conversation, they would say only that they were returning the wounded to Virginia and they would be back. Zook believed that they all tried to "hide" their defeat. As one ambulance passed, Zook heard a soldier beg to be lifted out and laid on the ground; he could not stand the pain from the jolting wagon any longer. The teamsters took no note of his pleas.

Throughout the night the citizens of Greencastle captured horses and cattle from the passing trains. As droves of cattle passed by, Zook saw townspeople cut many loose and conceal them in alleys. "Horses tied behind wagons had their halters cut, and were led away unobserved," he remembered. "Many horses, too, gave out, and were left. They suffered greatly from not being shod, their hoofs being worn off to the quick." Zook himself captured a "fine bay horse" and hid it in his barn. Several days later a resident of Greencastle identified the horse in Zook's barn as one that the Confederates had confiscated from him during the early days of the invasion.

As the trains passed through town, many townspeople taunted the wounded soldiers and their escorts with such questions as: "How are you at Gettysburg? Have you been to Philadelphia already?" "Did you meet the Pennsylvania Militia down there?" When one Confederate officer asked a resident for a drink of water from his pump, the citizen said, "Did you get enough of Meade over there?" The officer became angry and snapped at his impudence.[14]

Back along the Pine Stump Road the scenes of agony continued. Private J. W. Lokey of the Twentieth Georgia had been jostled around in a water-soaked ambulance in Hood's trains for more than ten hours, all the while lying on his back and holding his bloody right leg with both hands locked below his knee and letting his left leg hang over the outside of the ambulance. With every bump in the road, he groaned with pain. Finally, Lokey had had enough. He told the driver and his wounded comrades that he must stop even if the Yankees captured him. He managed to get out of the vehicle and hobbled over to an old schoolhouse outside of New Franklin and managed to get inside. There, out of the driving rain, he fell asleep. When he awakened at dawn on 5 July, he saw that wagons and ambulances were still passing. It was still raining, and every driver refused his appeals to climb aboard for lack of space. Lokey stumbled along the muddy road for almost three miles before an ambulance from the Eleventh Virginia Cavalry in the rear of the column finally picked him up.[15]

Over and over since the hideous journey began, wagons and ambulances from one end of the trains to the other broke down or became mired in the deeply rutted road; the horses and mules, frightened by the intense lightning and knee-deep in the pasty loam, stalled. As a vehicle came to a halt, all those behind it would stop until it could be bypassed or freed. The rain came down in sheets, reducing visibility to zero. When the caravan stopped, drivers often were unable to see whether the vehicle immediately ahead had begun to move again.

Longstreet's trains, led by the corps quartermaster train and the trains of Hood's Division, were traveling through the hard-driving rain and deep mud along the Pine Stump Road west of New Franklin just before dawn on 5 July. Because of the constant stalling and restarting of wagons along the way, the trains had been broken up into many small groups of wagons, the lead wagon in each group blindly following only what was left of the road in the horrendous darkness and rainstorm.

One group of about a dozen ambulances filled with nearly forty wounded officers and enlisted men from Hood's trains approached the fork of the road east of Marion. The Pine Stump Road did not run directly into the town; rather, about a mile east of Marion the road divided. One fork ran northwest, connecting with the Cumberland Valley Turnpike at White Church north of Marion; the other ran southwest, connecting with the turnpike south of town. Chambersburg was almost five miles north of the point where the northwest fork of the Pine Stump Road intersected the Cumberland Valley Turnpike. The ambulance train in front of the little group had vanished in the heavy rain and inky darkness.

The driver in the lead ambulance, unable to see where he was going, cautiously guided his team ahead onto the north fork of the Pine Stump Road, unaware that it would lead him away from the rest of the trains and into Chambersburg. The remaining ambulances in the caravan, each with its driver straining to observe the wagon ahead, followed. The little group of ambulances came to a halt near White Church, where the Pine Stump Road turned north onto the valley turnpike, about one mile north of Marion. The driver of the lead ambulance stepped down and walked over to a house to inquire about the direction to Williamsport. A woman, looking out of the window, waved her hand in the direction of Chambersburg, saying, "You had better go that way."

Accordingly, the small caravan went north along the Cumberland Valley Turnpike. Entering the south ward of Chambersburg, it proceeded about five blocks. The lead driver remembered what Williamsport looked like, and this town did not seem familiar. John A. Lemaster, whose home was situated at the corner of Front and German Streets, heard unusual noises in front of his house. Opening his window curtain, he observed the line of ambulances standing along Front Street, with the lead vehicle stopped at German Street.

Cries and groans came from the ambulances, Lemaster recalled. The rain fell in torrents.

In a few minutes a man on horseback galloped up to the teamster driving the lead ambulance, exhorting, "Why don't you drive on?"

"We are on the wrong road; this is not Williamsport," the teamster replied.

"'Tis Williamsport," the rider said, "only drive on, the Yankees are just behind us."

The teamster looked across the dark intersection at the German Reformed church. It was unfamiliar.

"Williamsport," he said, "has no church steeple like that."

"I tell you," retorted the horseman, "this is Williamsport. Don't you know that just down there in that hollow is the canal and river. Drive on as fast you can, and after you are across the river you can take all the time you want."

Suddenly, another rider raced up to the lead wagon. "That looks more like the right way," he said, quickly perceiving the stalemate, "down there in that hollow are the canal and river."

The lead driver observed more men riding up Front Street toward the ambulances. He knew now that he was not at Williamsport but realized that there was no way to turn back. He thus ordered his team to move ahead. The little caravan rolled up Front Street three more blocks and stopped in the town square. There some citizens informed the ambulance drivers that they were in Chambersburg and that they were prisoners.

From the ambulances issued forth the most hideous cries and groans of the wounded. One desperate soldier from Texas, unable to bear the ambulance any longer, climbed out. He was dirty beyond description. His arm had been amputated at the shoulder, and clearly his filthy, matted bandage had not been changed for quite a while. Jacob S. Brand, a Chambersburg resident who had just arrived at the scene, asked the bloodied Texan, "What does this mean?" The soldier replied, "It means that Uncle Robert has got a hell of a whipping."[16]

The band of citizens led the approximately twelve ambulances through the town square and one block north to King Street. On King Street, just east of Front Street, the caravan stopped at the public schoolhouse next to the county jail. The schoolhouse had served as a hospital for about ten sick Confederate soldiers. Half of them were from the Thirty-third Virginia; the rest were from other regiments of Ewell's Corps. They suffered from diarrhea, dysentery, debilitus, and typhoid. The hospital had been established by Dr. McGuire during Ewell's occupation of the town in June, and its patients had been left behind when Ewell's divisions moved east to York and north to Carlisle. Dr. J. William Walls, of the Fifth Virginia, whom McGuire had directed to oversee the makeshift facility, had departed with Ewell. The sick Confederates had been left in the care of a youthful "doctor" named Hamilton M. Gamble, formerly of the Twentieth Virginia, who, in reality, had never studied medicine and had served only as a hospital steward. At the urgent appeal of Gamble, Dr. John Curtis Richards and Dr. Abraham H. Senseny, both of whom resided on Front Street, had assisted him at the schoolhouse. The fifty-one-year-old Richards had attended Yale College and the University of Maryland Medical School; Senseny, also fifty-one, was a graduate of Jefferson Medical College.[17]

Thirty-eight-year-old Jacob Hoke of Chambersburg observed the wounded Confederates as they were taken from the ambulances. "Bloody wounds undressed, almost famished for water and food, these men presented a sight such as I never wish to see again," he later wrote. One by one, the men were carried into the improvised hospital. For the first time in over eighteen hours they were sheltered from the driving rain. Nearly all of those who had the strength to speak expressed profound relief that their hideous journey was over. They were tired, worn, and filthy. All were feverish, and all were soaked from the heavy rains. The caravan that had been diverted to Chambersburg contained wounded from no less than five brigades and from Hood's and McLaws's Divisions of Longstreet's Corps, including soldiers from the Texas Brigade and Benning's, Kershaw's, Semmes's, and Barksdale's Brigades. They apparently had been mixed together as the trains were loaded at Gettysburg, and all had been transported in Hood's trains.[18]

Imboden's long train of wagons and ambulances continued down the Pine Stump Road and the Cumberland Valley Turnpike. Bandsman Julius Lineback recalled that by the early morning of 5 July the march had become "very fatiguing. We kept moving, with frequent short rests. The roads were deep with a gritty mud that wore the feet of our barefooted boys badly, and getting into the shoes of those who possessed such articles was almost as bad for them." Beyond the rain, mud, and pain of the march, hunger was the soldiers' constant complaint. "We had scarcely anything to eat." Lineback also related:

> Amongst us we had a few small pieces of silver money. We had poor success in begging or buying anything along the road. We came to one house where, for our money, the woman gave us a couple pieces of bread, not nearly its value. This kind of aroused our 'dander,' and some of the boys, going around the house, found the cellar door not

locked. We went in and appropriated what we could find. Our stomachs and canteens relieved the milk crocks of their contents. A dish of
cold meat was transferred to haversacks, other potable edibles, while
[another bandsman] walked off with a ham bone which he and I divided
when we got back to the barn.[19]

With dawn the heavy rains came to an end, but the light brought to full
view the tragedy before Jacob Snyder's eyes back along the Pine Stump Road
near New Franklin. All of the fences had been torn down along the roadway.
Because the road was so deep in mud and so cut up, ambulances and wagons,
together with their cavalry and artillery escorts, were making their way across
the fields, crushing the wheat, corn, and grasslands of the neighboring farms.
All along the route, this great column had left the debris of broken-down
ambulances, wagons, caissons, horses, and mules.

The trains continued to pass Jacob Snyder's house. Those of McLaws's
Division were still making their way in front of Snyder's house well after
midday, 5 July. At about 2:00 P.M. a section of the Washington Artillery of
New Orleans drew up in front of Snyder's barn, accompanied by some of Imboden's cavalry escorts. The cavalrymen dismounted in Snyder's wheat field.
Some ventured back up the road to Jeremiah W. George's farm and began
slaughtering his cattle; thirty-seven-year-old George lived on the farm with
his wife Margaret and their three children. Snyder observed that a number of
ambulances in the immense trains had stopped by the side of the road. There
the remains of those who had died during the journey were removed from the
vehicles and buried in shallow graves beside the roadway and in the barnyards
of Snyder and his neighbors. Many were laid to rest in George's farmyard;
wounded soldiers, too ill to travel any farther, were deposited in his house.[20]

Among the wounded soldiers who had been left in the care of Jeremiah
George on 5 July was Lieutenant Colonel Carter of the Fourth Texas, with
his slave, Henry Johnson, at his side. After falling into Union hands, Carter
was moved to Chambersburg, where he died and was buried.[21]

Among those buried on the afternoon of 5 July was forty-one-year-old
Major McLeod, of the Eighth South Carolina, who had died during the horrible journey. As the trains continued to pass, his slave carried McLeod's remains from the filthy flatbed of the ambulance and buried them near George's
well in what Jacob Snyder described as a "beautiful grove." The grave was
marked by the slave with a crude headboard that bore the major's initials.
Completing his task, the slave climbed back in the ambulance and headed
on down the road to New Franklin. He eventually traveled all the way to

the Great Pee Dee River in the Marlboro District of South Carolina to tell McLeod's family of the major's death. Then he led McLeod's brother-in-law and a close friend back to New Franklin to recover the major's body. The party was taken to George's farmyard, where, on 20 April 1866, they found McLeod's grave. Snyder watched the party exhume the body, carry it to a spring on Snyder's farm, and carefully place it in a wooden box. He learned from the group that McLeod's widow, the former Margaret Alford, who had nearly lost her mind over the loss of her husband, had asked the men to return his remains home for burial.[22]

ALTHOUGH DIFFICULT to imagine, the troubles for the retreating Confederates were just beginning. As the head of Imboden's trains continued south on the Cumberland Valley Turnpike near Greencastle, a Union cavalry detachment of about ten squadrons was bearing down on it from the direction of Waynesboro. On 3 July Captain Ulrich Dahlgren, the son of Rear Admiral John A. Dahlgren of the Southeast Blockading Squadron, had obtained permission from General Alfred Pleasonton, General Meade's cavalry chief, to take a hundred men from the U.S. regular regiments in General Merritt's cavalry brigade, then positioned at Emmitsburg, and move into the Cumberland Valley behind Lee's army.[23]

Dahlgren thus far had had a spectacular career in the Union army. Although he had studied civil engineering and law before the war and was only nineteen years old when hostilities erupted, his rise to military prominence was meteoric. First an aide-de-camp to Major General Franz Sigel, he rose to the post of artillery chief under Sigel at Second Manassas. Dahlgren went on to serve on the staff of General Joseph Hooker during the Chancellorsville campaign and was now attached to the headquarters of General Meade.[24]

Ever since Lee's army had moved east of the South Mountain range, Dahlgren had been operating with only a handful of handpicked cavalrymen behind Lee's lines in and around Greencastle, where he had attacked and harassed the commander's communication route, seizing dispatches, mail, and soldiers returning to the army. One dispatch captured by Dahlgren was to General Lee from President Davis and noted that "he could send no reinforcements."[25]

Leaving Emmitsburg early in the morning of 3 July, Dahlgren's force galloped up the Emmitsburg-Waynesboro Turnpike, across Monterey Pass, to Waynesboro, where the men bivouacked for the night. At 2:00 A.M. on the fourth Dahlgren had his squadrons in the saddle heading toward Greencastle.[26]

Returning to Lee's army by way of the Cumberland Valley Turnpike were large numbers of soldiers and convalescents, together with mail wagons and escorts. One of those soldiers was Lieutenant McHenry Howard, of Maryland, who had served as an aide to General Trimble until the general became ill. Howard had waited in Richmond until 28 June, when he finally left to rejoin the army. He had crossed the Potomac River on 3 July and fell in with a squad of cavalry that had just had a scrape with Dahlgren's troopers that day. Howard had joined the small force and on 4 July rode back up the turnpike toward Greencastle. As Howard reached the town, Dahlgren's troopers came dashing down upon him and his companions. Shots rang out. Howard's small force raced back toward Williamsport, battling its way through squads of Dahlgren's men. Howard reached Williamsport, hoping to fight another day.[27]

On the morning of 5 July Dahlgren realized that the situation in the Cumberland Valley had changed dramatically. Scouts and civilians informed him of the enormous trains and their cavalry and artillery escorts slowly making their way along the Pine Stump Road and onto the Cumberland Valley Turnpike toward Williamsport. By then, those trains stretched out for nearly thirty-one miles. It was taking thirty-six hours for them to pass any given point. Moreover, because of the length of the trains, it was impossible for the cavalry and artillery escorts to cover them adequately. A rapid strike at one of the sections in which there were both cavalry and artillery escorts might overwhelm them before they could effectively resist the attack and before other escorts up and down the trains could reach the point of attack to assist in the defense. General Lee's and Colonel Baker's cavalry brigades were nowhere to be seen, as they were screening the long trains far to the north and to the west. There was no screen east of the trains.[28]

Dahlgren did not need any encouragement. He ordered his squadrons to mount up. Riding to within striking distance of the trains, he waited until the opportunity presented itself, all the time keeping his command out of sight. Then, as the leading elements of the long trains were moving south of Greencastle, Dahlgren, with his sabre flashing, led his squadrons into the very midst of them and their escorts. What they hit was a section of the trains protected by a squadron of the Eighteenth Virginia Cavalry and a two-gun section of McClanahan's Battery under Lieutenant Hugh H. Fultz and Lieutenant F. Carter Berkeley. With the battery section was none other than General Imboden himself. Apparently, Dahlgren's troopers struck Imboden's own command's ambulances and quartermaster and subsistence wagons, as well as the quartermaster train of Hill's Corps and some quartermaster, subsistence, and ordnance trains of Pender's Division. Just behind the point of attack, though, was Captain Frank Imboden, commander of Company H of the Eighteenth Virginia Cavalry, with a squadron of his regiment.[29]

When Dahlgren's blue-coated troopers struck the trains, they stunned and overwhelmed the escorts. They seized 176 wagons and ambulances; 200 prisoners, many of them wounded; 300 horses and mules; and one of McClanahan's rifled guns. They then tried to direct the trains toward Waynesboro.[30]

Hearing the commotion ahead of him, Captain Imboden yelled at his men nearby to gallop forward with him to meet the crisis. It was a most difficult rescue effort; the road was jammed with wagons, ambulances, and cattle, making it impossible for Imboden to use the roadway. He ordered his men to take to the fields beside it. Soon they came upon Dahlgren and his squadrons trying to direct the wagons, ambulances, and an artillery piece off of the roadway. Gunfire rang out. From the head of the trains, other squadrons of the Eighteenth Virginia, including Company F, were also responding, and Dahlgren and his men were suddenly trapped. The Union troopers gave up their captures and sped back toward Waynesboro, leaving behind one of their number dead and eleven prisoners of war. Although Dahlgren never actually seized General Imboden, it had been a close call.[31]

John Hyde Cameron, adjutant of the Eighteenth Virginia, accompanied Captain Imboden. He noted that among those released by the quick response of the escorts were not only Lieutenant Fultz and Lieutenant Berkeley, but also Dr. C. A. Ware, assistant surgeon of McClanahan's Battery, and Dr. Alexander Frederick Wills, assistant surgeon of the Eighteenth Virginia. In his diary Imboden wrote that he "recaptured everything with one Yank captain and ten men." The trains were delayed, though, for more than an hour.[32]

There was damage done to the trains. In the midst of the excitement caused by Dahlgren's attack, citizens became emboldened. Some came out of their houses south of Greencastle and struck the wheels of a number of wagons and ambulances with axes until they collapsed in the road, among them the quartermaster, subsistence, and ordnance wagons and forge of the Donaldsonville, Louisiana, Artillery. Imboden's men dispersed the civilians and even captured some, herding them south with the wagons and ambulances. The trains, though, had been halted again. Imboden's trains, including some damaged wagons of the Donaldsonville Artillery, finally lumbered on toward Williamsport; the escorts, up and down the length of the trains, expected more such attacks as the day wore on.[33]

Captain Waddell finally gave out. Riding in the ambulance only made him more ill. Consequently, he walked, although he was burning with fever and, at times, shivering with chills. Eventually he left the long caravan and found a haystack where he fell asleep. It had been a hideous ordeal for him; there was no comfort anywhere. In fact, he was incensed that the women in the towns and villages he passed "laughed at [the] wounded and sick" in the trains. In all, he "walked nearly 40 miles [on 5 July and] broke down often."[34]

With rain pouring down in sheets, the leading elements of General Gregg's Union cavalry brigade galloped toward the rear of Imboden's trains that had cleared Cashtown at dawn on 5 July; its troopers had picked up stragglers all the way from Gettysburg. "The road," wrote a member of the Tenth New York Cavalry,

> was littered with broken and abandoned wagons, caissons, muskets, clothing, etc. War's devastation was more clearly shown on this route than any upon which the Tenth had ever marched. Squads of Confederate soldiers were met with, plodding dejectedly along toward [Gettysburg] where their valiant conduct had challenged the admiration and respect of their adversaries. Some were under guard, others marched without. They were, generally speaking, a surly, uncommunicative lot. Every building that would afford shelter from the storm or protection from the burning rays of the sun was filled with Confederate wounded and stragglers. The greater part of the [Tenth New York Cavalry] had been sent back to Gettysburg during the day as guards to rebel prisoners.[35]

By the time Gregg's Brigade left Cashtown on the afternoon of 5 July, it had rounded up more than 2,800 Confederate wounded and their attendants as prisoners of war. His five Union regiments continued on up the Chambersburg Pike within eyeshot of Lee's and Baker's rear guard cavalry brigades. Although Gregg's numbers were too few to risk attacking the rear of Imboden's trains and their cavalry escorts, a brief encounter occurred later in the evening at Graefenburg Springs deep in Cashtown Pass. There Gregg's skirmishers made contact with the skirmishers of Lee's and Baker's Brigades. The fight was sharp but very short. Gregg lost only one man.[36]

Gregg's troopers followed the rear of Imboden's trains. Like many of Meade's soldiers, they had not been fed; their horses were in desperate need of forage and shoes. "The suffering from hunger was probably never greater in the regiment than while on this march," wrote one trooper. "Men ate corn from the ear; birchbark, anything that would appease the gnawing of hunger. Taking a few men, the regimental commissary started out in search of food. It was an almost hopeless task, as the rebels had made a pretty clean sweep of everything in the line of grain and provisions." Captain Norman Ball of the Sixteenth Pennsylvania Cavalry summed up the problem: "Our horses are nearly done out and many of them are entirely so as they have been on the constant go for as many days and scarcely any feed."[37]

There were pitiful sights in the wake of Imboden's trains. Private John P. Sheahan of the First Maine Cavalry wrote to his father of the pursuit of the trains on 5 July: "We made them leave their caissons and their ambulances and in many cases their wounded on the road. They all acknowledged that this is the greatest whipping that they ever got and all the prisoners say they hope it will end the war."[38]

Lieutenant Walter Kempster of the Tenth New York Cavalry, like Private Sheahan, recalled capturing "many wagons and ambulances besides prisoners and wounded men and officers" between Cashtown and Graefenburg Springs. "I conversed with many of them," he wrote, "and they expressed a great desire to have the war ended any way they could. . . . One lieutenant had been wounded in the knee; it was giving him great pain and it appeared that it had never been dressed. I examined it and told him he would have to lose his leg. It was a hard thing for him to think of but he soon made up his mind and asked me to do it, but we did not have our amputating case with us, so perhaps he [lost] his life. He was a fine young man and I really pitied him. I consoled him as well as I was able and bade him goodbye. We parted like old friends."[39]

Imboden's trains rumbled on toward Williamsport. Over the past ten hours their length had increased, now stretching out for nearly thirty-one miles. Gregg's hungry troopers and their jaded and famished horses followed them, although they posed little threat because of the presence of Lee's and Baker's Brigades at the rear and on the right flank of the trains. The Union troopers, though, never forgot the spectacle of wreckage and suffering they observed all along the way.

Seven

An awful time crossing South Mountain

General Meade had been trying to follow up his victory. As early as 9:57 P.M. on 3 July he had telegraphed General Couch in Harrisburg, directing him to be prepared to move elements of his Department of the Susquehanna down the Cumberland Valley if Lee retreated to Virginia. Meade said that the Army of the Potomac would pursue Lee down the eastern side of the South Mountain range if he actually retreated. Couch had thereupon ordered General William F. Smith's Division at Carlisle to advance into the Cumberland Valley and directed all the fragmented units with which he had opened communications in Bedford County, Pennsylvania—the "debris of Winchester" —forward to harass the enemy around Chambersburg. Meanwhile, Meade had ordered forward from his supply base at Westminster subsistence and quartermaster trains to feed his men, horses, and mules.[1]

To General French, whose division held Frederick, Maryland, Meade had sent a dispatch early on 4 July instructing him to hold his position, seize and hold the South Mountain passes, harass the enemy's lines of communication in the Cumberland Valley, and reoccupy Maryland Heights—an onerous assignment for one division. French had sent to Turner's Pass, Fox's Pass, and Crampton's Gap a brigade of infantry under Brigadier General William H. Morris, a battery of artillery, and a detachment of cavalry, about four thousand men in all.[2]

Back in Gettysburg, Meade had struggled to overcome significant obstacles in advancing against Lee. To begin with, he had difficulty obtaining any meaningful intelligence of Lee's intentions. At 6:45 A.M. on 4 July, Lieutenant John Calvin Wiggins and Lieutenant Henry N. Camp, signal officers at the Sixth Corps signal station on Little Round Top, had spotted the movement of Lee's trains through their telescope. "The wagon trains of the enemy," they proceeded to write, "are moving toward Millerstown on the road leading from Gettysburg to the Fairfield Road. The enemy show a very heavy line of skirmishers extending from our extreme left to the brick house on our right. Look out for our flag." That message was not received at Meade's newly established headquarters along the Baltimore Pike until 9:00 A.M.[3]

What the Little Round Top signal station observed were Ewell's trains moving down the Herr Ridge Road and onto the Fairfield Road. That intelligence had not come as a surprise to Meade; he had anticipated that Lee might withdraw after the failed attacks on 3 July. But what Meade could not discern was whether Lee was withdrawing to Virginia or to the South Mountain range and "fortifying the mountains." There was significant speculation among Meade's chief lieutenants that Lee was falling back to make another stand along the eastern face of those mountains, but no one could tell for sure. For almost twenty-four hours Meade believed that Lee was, indeed, pursuing the latter course. So convinced was he that Lee was reestablishing a defense line along the base of the South Mountain range on 4 July that he countermanded his earlier orders to General French.[4]

Elements of Meade's army had reoccupied Gettysburg after the Confederates withdrew to their new defense lines on Seminary and Oak Ridges in the very early morning of 4 July. The Signal Corps had taken over the Adams County Courthouse on Baltimore Street and had been using its cupola as an observation post; it had been similarly used when General Reynolds had engaged the enemy west of Gettysburg on 1 July. On 4 July Lieutenant Peter A. Taylor, acting signal officer at the courthouse, sent back only bits and pieces of information from his telescopic observation of enemy lines. He observed bodies of cavalry, ambulances, and wagon trains moving out the Chambersburg Pike and down the Herr Ridge Road, but that was all. The heavy rain and dense smoke from behind Lee's defense lines all the way to Cashtown and Fairfield severely limited visibility.[5]

As darkness fell, the signal station on Little Round Top sent Meade a report of its last sighting of the day. "All quiet in front," it read. "Enemy just relieved their outer pickets. There has been passing for the last twenty-five minutes (and is still passing), along what is called the Fairfield road, a steady stream of heavy wagons, ambulances, cavalry, and what seems to be artillery, or else flying artillery, and no cavalry. They move slowly, and to our left." The intelligence was not conclusive; it mirrored the information Meade had been receiving all day from his corps commanders. The rain fell pitilessly, prohibiting any movement of Meade's army even if plans had been made to advance against Lee's new defenses. Meade had to rely on his available cavalry to gather all other necessary information, but it would take time.[6]

Thousands of Meade's wounded and the wounded of the enemy were being treated or on their way to numerous hospital sites behind his lines. In the fields within and in front of his lines lay thousands of dead soldiers. The stench was horrible. The driving rain only made the situation worse. Pioneer teams were burying the Union dead in the rain-saturated earth. By circular, Meade directed all of his corps commanders to "detail burial parties to bury all the enemy's dead in the vicinity of their lines." It was a grim task, but his men could not remain in line awaiting orders to move in the presence of such sickening sights and odors.[7]

Meade had won a tactical victory at Gettysburg, but his men had fought the battle without food and other necessary stores, his animals had not been fed in days, and his supply line from Westminster to Gettysburg was too long. Brigadier General Rufus Ingalls, Meade's chief quartermaster, telegraphed Quartermaster General Montgomery C. Meigs on the afternoon of 4 July, boasting: "We marched and fought this battle without baggage or wagons." Indeed, as the fighting was about to erupt on 2 July, more than 6,000 wagons, 30,000 horses and mules, and an immense herd of cattle had all finally arrived at Westminster, twenty-five miles away, after having been turned back to that location as the Army of the Potomac advanced toward Gettysburg on 1 July. Meade had even been forced to send nearly all of the army's reserve ammunition trains and his own headquarters baggage train back down the Baltimore Pike to a location near Westminster, fearing for their safety.[8]

Only late on 2 July had subsistence trains of a few of the corps been sent forward to the frontline troops. Because of the distance from Westminster to Gettysburg, none of those trains reached Gettysburg until 3 July. The fighting that day had interrupted the delivery of rations to most of the troops who were supposed to receive them. As a result, many of Meade's men were hungry on 4 July. That day Provost Marshal General Marsena R. Patrick complained in his diary: "Everybody was without anything to eat & waiting for subsistence." Added to the problem was that Meade's horses and mules, like Lee's, had been ill-fed while in Virginia. Few had been given anything to eat since 1 July. If not fed, horses and mules break down within four or five days. An army quickly deteriorates without adequate food and provender. This had left Meade no choice but to impress and confiscate horses, mules, and fodder from the citizenry during the campaign and battle.[9]

Meade had tried to correct his supply problem early on. As the battle raged at Gettysburg, he had directed his chief railroad engineer, Brigadier General Herman Haupt, formerly of Gettysburg, to reopen the rail line between Gettysburg and the Northern Central Railroad. Haupt had supervised gangs of laborers along the Hanover Railroad as they rebuilt bridges and laid tracks for three days; on the afternoon of 4 July, he reported that the line would be open between Gettysburg and the Northern Central by the afternoon of the next day. It had been a Herculean effort. If Lee were "fortifying the mountains," the new supply line would be critical. If Lee were withdrawing back to Virginia, however, Meade would never use it.[10]

With what information he had available, Meade sent a dispatch to General Halleck at noon on 4 July. "The position of affairs," he noted, "is not materially changed from my last dispatch, 7 A.M. The enemy apparently has thrown back his left, and placed guns and troops in position in rear of Gettysburg, which we now hold. The enemy has abandoned large numbers of his killed and wounded on the field." Commenting on his serious supply problem, Meade continued: "I shall require some time to get up supplies, ammunition, & etc., rest the army, worn out by long marches and three days' hard fighting."[11]

The long overland line of supply had necessarily drained Meade of much-needed cavalry during the battle. The Baltimore Pike formed the supply line from Meade's rear at Gettysburg to Westminster. Ewell's Corps, while it was below Culp's and Cemetery Hills, had been dangerously close to it. Stuart's cavalry brigades on Lee's far left flank had formed another threat to it. Consequently, until 4 July Colonel Huey's Brigade of Gregg's Second Cavalry Division had been protecting the approaches to Westminster from Hanover Junction and Manchester. Colonel Gregg's Brigade of that same division had patrolled the Baltimore Pike east of Gettysburg. So long as General Kilpatrick's entire Third Cavalry Division had operated between Gettysburg and Littlestown, it had kept open the long supply line to Westminster while protecting Meade's right flank. At the end of the battle, Kilpatrick's Division had guarded the army's left flank after relieving Buford's two brigades that had been sent back to Westminster to eat, rest, and refit. On 4 July, though, Meade was relying on all of those cavalry units and Buford's Brigades to pursue and strike Lee's trains and send back information that would enable him to determine Lee's intentions.[12]

Meanwhile, Meade had to use his infantry corps to protect the supply line and base as well as the army's flanks. He ordered the battered Second Corps and the Twelfth Corps to pull out of their battle lines and march back to Littlestown and Two Taverns along with the Artillery Reserve. There they would watch over the supply line as well as the army's huge reserve ammunition train. To guard his left flank after the departure of Kilpatrick's cavalry brigades, Meade directed the Fifth Corps toward Marsh Creek.[13]

At 10:00 P.M. on 4 July Meade sent another dispatch to Halleck. "No change of affair since dispatch of 12 noon," he wrote. "I make a reconnaissance to-morrow, to ascertain what the intention of the enemy is. My cavalry are now moving toward South Mountain Pass, and, should the enemy retreat, I shall pursue him on his flanks." [14]

To mount a vigorous pursuit of Lee, if the Confederates retreated to Virginia, Meade would have to overcome serious obstacles. He would need to reconnect all the quartermaster, subsistence, and ordnance trains with each of the seven corps of the army, the Artillery Reserve, and the cavalry divisions, while, at the same time, protecting them. Concurrently, he would have to move his base of supply from Westminster back to the Baltimore and Ohio railhead at Frederick. But Meade could not change his supply base until he had knowledge that Lee was actually retreating to Virginia. Meade planned a reconnaissance of Lee's Gettysburg defense lines in the early morning of 5 July using Sedgwick's Sixth Corps. He had no intention of engaging the enemy; rather, he wanted definitive information about Lee's intentions in order to plan his own operations. [15]

Meanwhile, Lee's army continued to move. At about 11:00 P.M. on 4 July the head of Major Harman's reserve train rumbled into Hagerstown behind a herd of more than five thousand head of cattle and their mounted drovers, escorted by Brown's companies of Maryland cavalry and three of Tanner's twelve-pound Napoleon guns. The train arrived in the vicinity of Williamsport via the Hagerstown-Williamsport Turnpike around midnight, when Captain Emack's Marylanders were battling Kilpatrick's Union cavalry division atop Monterey Pass and the head of Imboden's trains was passing New Franklin. Harman moved as many wagons across the ford at Williamsport as time and the rising river would allow. He may have actually forded elements of the trains for the first ten to twelve hours after reaching Williamsport. [16]

Some of Harman's wagons streamed toward Falling Waters at dawn, where, it was believed, the pontoon bridge still spanned the Potomac River; the main column pressed down Potomac Street in Williamsport, across Conococheague Street, past the Taylor House hotel, the German Lutheran church, and the intersection of Vermont Street, to the Embrey warehouses at the basin of the Chesapeake and Ohio (C&O) Canal. From there, the main column turned up Commerce Street, then down Salisbury Street until it crossed the bridge over the canal. Hundreds of wagons came to a halt in the streets of Williamsport and along the bottomlands of the rising Potomac River. [17]

Williamsport must have been a depressing place to the officers, wagoners, laborers, and slaves accompanying the trains. In the early morning darkness, with rain pelting down, they could see that the river was rising. In fact,

A never-before-published photograph of Williamsport as it looked during the war, taken from the West Virginia shoreline of the Potomac River. Note the aqueduct of the C&O Canal at left and the ferry and cable at right. Author's collection.

where Longstreet's Corps had forded the river less than two weeks before and where wagons had been fording the river, it was almost five feet deep. The river was dangerous. Muddy water swirled, rapidly carrying drifting logs, tree branches, and other debris downstream.

All that was available in Williamsport to transport wagons across the river was Lemen's ferry. One ferryboat, or "flat," was all that was there. A cable strung across the river guided the vessel to the southern shore and back. It was propelled by nothing more than poles. At best, the ferry could take two wagons across the river at one time. Dimly visible through the falling rain along the southern shore were the lights from "Maidstone-on-the-Potomac," the two-and-one-half-story brick house of the ferry's owner, Robert Lemen.[18]

Brown's cavalrymen soon informed Harman that the bridge at Falling Waters had been destroyed; only the partially burned remnants of some of the pontoons remained. The situation appeared desperate. Harman had hundreds of wagons still in Williamsport and lined up all the way to Waynesboro, with another twenty miles of wagons and ambulances behind them. Imboden would arrive with another seventeen miles of wagons and ambulances, although the head of his column was still fifteen hours north of the town. Harman needed help despite his skills as an army quartermaster.[19]

Because of their perishable cargoes, many wagons of Harman's huge train had been stopped from fording the river at Williamsport; they were, instead, placed two at a time on the flat and poled across the swollen river. The procedure was exasperatingly slow. Wagoners fought one another for space on the next trip. The immense wagon train jammed the streets of Williamsport, each wagoner trying desperately to get his vehicle and team to the ferry ahead of the rest. The wagons and their horse and mule teams soon became so snarled that the huge train came to a standstill, leaving thousands of wagons stranded along the turnpike for almost forty miles. If the enemy had been anywhere near Williamsport in force, it would have been impossible to have saved the train from destruction.

To add to the confusion, Harman had difficulty controlling the thousands of wagoners and teamsters accompanying the enormous train. Even with his oaths and kicking of mules and mule drivers, he could maintain little order. But fortune smiled on Harman that morning. After having been separated from his staff and couriers during the fighting at Monterey Pass, Grumble Jones had ridden all night "through fields and byways" toward Williamsport in the hope of avoiding capture and finding himself in a position of being "useful." For the Army of Northern Virginia, the separation of Jones from his brigade was one of the more fortuitous events of the Gettysburg campaign.

Rain-soaked and covered with mud, Jones reached Williamsport just after dawn on 5 July, having groped his way across Franklin County, Pennsylvania, and Washington County, Maryland, in the dark. He found Williamsport in a state of total confusion. He observed only one ferryboat in operation. The ferry, Jones discovered, "could not exceed seventy trips in twenty-four hours" and "everyone was anxious to cross the river." He quickly concluded that "to deprive all of the hope of what but a small fraction could attain was deemed the most expedient means of establishing order." Jones let it be known—as only he could—that he was in command at Williamsport. He ordered the scattered infantrymen in and around the town, many of them returning convalescents, and others, the remnants of the small contingent that had protected the ford during the invasion, to stand guard at the ferry and prevent anyone from crossing the river.[20]

Jones then appealed to all quartermasters, subsistence officers, and wagoners in the wagon train to help bring order out of chaos as well as defend the train if attacked. Soon small contingents of "volunteers" were armed with rifles from the trains and led by shouting quartermasters. Along with Brown's companies of Maryland cavalrymen, they were ordered to take up positions in buildings fronting the Cumberland Valley Turnpike, the Hagerstown-Williamsport Turnpike, and the Williamsport-Boonsboro Road—the three main arteries into the town. Barricades were constructed across each of those roads to aid in the defense while, at the same time, allowing the Confederate trains to enter the town. Jones told the cannoneers of the three guns of Tanner's Battery to remain in readiness near the canal basin in order to respond to any emergency. With such a small force, Jones reasoned, the only way to "buy time," in the event of a Union attack, would be to contest it in the town building by building. "Urban" fighting would increase the odds of the scattered defenders on whom he must depend; they could, at least, hold their own for a short time. Jones was aided by Lieutenant McHenry Howard, who recrossed the Potomac River on 5 July in an attempt to, once again, make himself useful.[21]

Within a few hours Jones had restored sufficient order in Williamsport to resume ferrying wagons across the river. One by one, the wagons were directed to the bottomland between the river and the C&O Canal where they were parked to permit a more orderly crossing. The reserve train was still so large that elements of it extended through the town of Williamsport and out the Hagerstown-Williamsport Turnpike, past Hagerstown, to Leitersburg. Sections of the train, along with herds of horses, mules, cattle, sheep, and hogs, were directed onto the streets and vacant lots of Williamsport and to the river bottomlands east and southeast of town. The heat and humidity and the presence of thousands of farm animals—not to mention the thousands of mules and horses attached to the wagons—would pose an ever-increasing challenge to the defenders of Williamsport. The odor of the offal, together with the flies attracted by it and the animals, would quickly become oppressive.

BEHIND HARMAN'S reserve train were the twenty-mile-long trains of Ewell's three divisions. They were still many hours away because of the delay caused by Kilpatrick's attack at Monterey Pass. Although nearly 250 wagons and ambulances of Rodes's Division had been seized by Kilpatrick's Union troopers at Monterey Pass, its trains still led the long procession. The trains of Early's and Johnson's Divisions followed. Bringing up the rear were elements of the trains of Anderson's Division of Hill's Corps, the only trains in the long caravan not of Ewell's Corps. Rodes's trains had finally descended the western slope of South Mountain. The trains of Early, Johnson, and Anderson were then ascending and on top of the mountain along the Maria Furnace Road.

Among Anderson's trains on the Fairfield Road was the ambulance carrying Sergeant James E. Whitehorne of the Twelfth Virginia. Ever since he had left the Butt farm hospital site, the rain poured down in sheets. Whitehorne's vehicle was probably one of the last to join the long trains on the road to the Potomac River. Close behind, the leading elements of Anderson's infantry brigades marched in the fields beside the roadway.

Whitehorne was in agony from the shrapnel that had nearly removed the calf of his right leg and the bullet that had passed through his left leg below the knee. He could neither sit up nor stretch out without intense pain. He remained flat on his back on a bed of straw while rain poured down on him. "I had an awful time crossing South Mountain," Whitehorne wrote in his journal. "The road was very rough, the night very dark, and the rain came down in torrents. The road must have been very rugged, as at times it seemed to me that the wheels of the wagon passed over rocks of at least two feet high, and I had at such times to hold to the sides of the wagon with both hands to keep from being turned out."[22]

Whitehorne's brigade was not far behind him. Behind Companies A, D, and F of Colonel White's Thirty-fifth Battalion of Virginia Cavalry, also known as the Comanches, Anderson's Division had led Lee's army out of Gettysburg. Wright's Brigade was in advance; the brigades of Mahone, Wilcox, Lang, and Posey, along with the artillery battalions of Colonel John J. Garnett and Major John Lane, followed. Before Hill's troops evacuated their Seminary Ridge lines, they set fire to their log breastworks. The black smoke would help screen them and the army from enemy observation at daylight. Lee often used the cover of heavy smoke to conceal the movements of his army. Once under way, the march was extremely difficult. One of Whitehorne's fellow soldiers in the Twelfth Virginia recorded the journey in his journal. "We were up to our knees in mud and water all night," he wrote. "It was impossible to preserve the company organization in such darkness and difficult marching. The men would halloo out the names of their companies in order to keep together."[23]

So slow was the march through the rain and mud that it took the leading elements of Anderson's Division six hours to reach Fairfield, only eight miles from Gettysburg. After resting at Fairfield for two hours, they began the slow ascent to Monterey.[24]

Once in Fairfield, Wright's Brigade was ordered on the double-quick to the summit of Monterey Pass to aid Iverson's Brigade. The road had been badly cut up by the trains; the mud was deep. It took Wright's Georgians more than six hours to accomplish the task, although they covered only six miles. Once they reached the top of the pass, the soldiers collapsed. Private W. B. Jenkins of the Twenty-second Georgia recalled that the brigade halted at about 9:00 A.M. on 5 July. "All went to sleep," he wrote, "some on the ground in the rain and mud, with just a blanket or oilcloth over them, and some with no cover at all, and went to sleep right where we stopped. I lay down on a bench in a school-house and slept a good nap."[25]

General Wright "found the road so completely blocked up as to prevent any further progress" of the trains. He located Iverson, whose tattered little brigade had reached Monterey Pass shortly before Wright's men, and learned that the danger to the trains there had passed. After allowing his men time to rest, Wright directed them and Iverson's Brigade down the turnpike toward Waynesboro "as rapidly as possible, so as to enable [the] troops [marching up the Maria Furnace Road] to get through the mountain pass."[26]

Behind Anderson's Division marched the remnants of Pender's and Heth's Divisions. Pender's Division remained under the temporary command of General James H. Lane since Pender had been wounded. The Reverend Dr. Francis Milton Kennedy, chaplain of the Twenty-eighth North Carolina, had been detailed to leave Gettysburg with the "medical train" of Hill's Corps, the wagon train carrying the necessary equipment, medicine, and tents to set up hospitals in the event of another engagement. It had been difficult for Kennedy to leave Gettysburg. "I had my feelings sorely tried," he wrote afterward, "when telling the officers and other men good-bye who were so seriously wounded as to disqualify them for traveling. They will necessarily fall into the hands of the enemy and they dreaded it, oh! so much." Yet leave he did, and it proved to be a horrible ordeal. "I was in the saddle all . . . night, in pouring rain, thoroughly wet all night," Kennedy wrote. "Our progress was greatly impeded by the multitude of troops, artillery and wagons along the road . . . I was quite sick. When we started last night, the road was exceedingly rocky and muddy, my horse had one shoe off and everything conspired to render it the most disagreeable night I ever spent." Pender's and Heth's Divisions halted at about 8:00 A.M. on 5 July just as they reached Fairfield. The leading elements of Anderson's Division were then marching toward the summit of Monterey Pass along the Maria Furnace Road; some of the brigades advanced east of Jack's Mountain and approached Monterey on the Emmitsburg-Waynesboro Turnpike so as to cover that entrance to the pass and clear the Maria Furnace Road for Pender's and Heth's Divisions and Longstreet's and Ewell's Corps.[27]

The troops in Hill's three divisions complained of the rain and mud as well as the slowness of the march. Private George Hall of the Fourteenth Georgia "marched all night through mud and water nearly knee deep and rain falling in torrents." To add to his misery, he became desperately ill. "By the help of the Lord," Hall wrote, "I was enabled to keep up." Not far down the line was Private W. R. Tanner of the Thirteenth South Carolina. He had been wounded when a ball struck his cartridge box, then hit two other cartridges, and the three balls penetrated his leg. Tanner nevertheless marched that night through the deep mud. Finally his leg gave out, and "I told the Captain I could not keep up any longer." Tanner then fell out of the ranks and brought up the rear, joining a host of stragglers, most of whom were sick and broken down. File closers, with bayonets fixed, prodded the stragglers onward by jabbing at them. Tanner wanted no part of that. He hobbled about fifty yards from the road to let the file closers pass, then rejoined the long column. "I kept pretty well up," he recalled with satisfaction.[28]

As Lee was in the process of leaving Gettysburg, there were desertions. Darkness, heavy rain, and some confusion in the ranks aided those who sought to leave the army. Some soldiers dropped out of the ranks and simply fled; a few found refuge among civilians. Some slaves ran away. Apparently there were Quakers among the teamsters driving the quartermaster and subsistence wagons of the Fifty-second North Carolina. One of them was twenty-eight-year-old Jacob Hinshaw, from Randolph County, North Carolina, who had been conscripted into service in 1862. With him were four others: his brother Thomas, Nathan and Cyrus Barker, and William Hockett. They never deserted, but they did not leave with the army either.[29]

During the fighting at Gettysburg Hinshaw and the other Quakers had remained behind, near the regimental trains; on the final day of the battle they had been put to use at the hospital of Heth's Division. Their pacifism had been grudgingly honored by the regimental officers. By battle's end, the Fifty-second North Carolina had been demolished: Colonel James Keith Marshall was dead, and most of the officers and men had been either killed or wounded. A lieutenant who was temporarily in command of what was left of the regiment ordered Hinshaw and his Quaker friends to stay in a barn near the hospital. While they were there, Heth's Division moved out behind its trains without telling them. The Quakers had been deliberately left behind. Just before the regiment left Gettysburg, the lieutenant had said to them, "Boys, I do not blame you now for acting or doing as you have, for if everybody had done so there would have been none such [a battle and casualties] as this." The Confederate officer was so moved by the deaths and losses that he decided to abandon the pacifist Quakers. In Hinshaw's words, the lieutenant was a "changed man." Hinshaw happily remembered that his prayers had been answered.[30]

Outside of Gettysburg frustration was rampant. Longstreet's soldiers, who had been directed to follow Hill's in the line of march, were ordered to be ready at sundown, 4 July. While long lines of dirty and bloodied soldiers waited in the pouring rain, the time for their departure was changed to 10:00 P.M. The rain never let up, and Longstreet's soldiers continued to wait through the wee hours of 5 July.[31]

Until midnight, Ewell's Corps remained behind the breastworks overlooking Gettysburg between the Fairfield Road and Oak Hill. Skirmishers had held breastworks well out in front of the defenses. In front of Ewell's Corps, though, infantrymen had been replaced by Captain Frank Bond's dismounted Company A, First Maryland Cavalry Battalion, early on the night of 4 July. Bond's Marylanders had held a mile-long position along the western suburbs of Gettysburg directly in front of Ewell's main defense line. Between Bond's dismounted cavalrymen and the Union skirmish lines in Gettysburg at least twelve houses and outbuildings had been set ablaze in an effort by the skirmishers to prevent Union snipers from using them to fire upon the Confederate lines and to assist in concealing the movement of troops. Even in the pouring rain the buildings still emitted heavy columns of black smoke.[32]

Lee directed Ewell's Corps to abandon its defense line on Seminary and Oak Ridges between midnight and 2:00 A.M. on 5 July, the precise time Longstreet's Corps left its defense works in preparation for the retreat. Under cover of darkness and smoke Ewell withdrew all of his men, guns, and trains back up the Chambersburg Pike and Mummasburg Road to the Herr Ridge Road. Johnson's and Rodes's Divisions left their breastworks first, covered by Early's Division on McPherson Ridge. Ewell then marched his troops south alongside the Herr Ridge Road to the Fairfield Road and to positions east of the ridge beside the Blackhorse Tavern, facing Willoughby Run. Bond's Maryland cavalrymen were relieved as skirmishers and directed by Ewell to "press on to the front, pass all the army, and assist in protecting the trains."[33]

The movement of Ewell's Corps away from Seminary and Oak Ridges was timed to coincide with the lining up of Longstreet's Corps along the Willoughby Run Road preparatory to entering the Fairfield Road at a junction east of the Blackhorse Tavern, about three miles west of Gettysburg. Both corps moved under cover of darkness and heavy smoke. Lee could not leave Ewell's men isolated on Seminary and Oak Ridges, and he needed protection for Longstreet's movement. He thus withdrew Ewell's Corps so that it could occupy a position in front of the intersection of the Willoughby Run and Fairfield Roads. With such an action, Lee was able to protect the approach of Longstreet's columns to the Fairfield Road. It also brought Ewell's Corps back to the rest of the army and put it in position to take up the line of march.

Companies B, C, and E of White's Comanches protected the rear of the army from surprise; they were spread out in the fields two miles ahead of Ewell's position, straddling the Fairfield Road and occupying the smoldering breastworks abandoned by the infantry. The complex movement of the two corps that had occupied the flanks of the army at Gettysburg was accomplished with remarkable precision.[34]

Longstreet's Corps had remained in readiness to move out all through the night. Private John West of the Fourth Texas, Hood's Division, had been miserable. He had been waiting to fall in line for hours. He had had no change of clothes for weeks, and he had been compelled to throw away his undershirt as it had become "a harbor for innumerable body lice." West had lost his socks, and his ankles had been "considerably lacerated by briars in marching across the fields." To add to his embarrassment, his pants had an enormous rent up the back; he believed that he "would be subject to arrest in any well managed city for improper exposure of my person in a public place." He had been unable to stand in line all night. Instead, in the pouring rain, he had fallen asleep "by lying on three [fence] rails, which kept [him] above water."[35]

Already, the wagons that were to accompany Longstreet's troops had left the division hospital sites and lined up beside the Fairfield Road, near its intersection with the Willoughby Run Road, behind the screen formed by Ewell's Corps along Willoughby Run. There, with the corps' artillery battalions parked close by, they awaited the movement of the infantry columns.[36]

Between midnight and 1:00 A.M., 5 July, the baggage trains of Lee's headquarters entered the Fairfield Road from the farm lot of the Blackhorse Tavern in the midst of Hill's Corps. Private Franklin Walter recorded his march with the trains: "[I] Suffered intensely awhile before day for want of sleep; often nodding on my horse and several times coming near falling." Lee was not yet ready to move onto the Fairfield Road and into the long procession, wanting to wait until Ewell's Corps was under way. By then he had not slept for at least forty-two hours.[37]

Colonel Alexander's Artillery Battalion had been directed by Longstreet to move behind the leading infantry brigade of the corps when the march began. Longstreet's Corps was to fall in line behind Heth's Division of Hill's Corps. When Alexander and his battalion had reached the Fairfield Road on the night of 4 July, they found it "full of passing troops and trains." "We parked in a little meadow," Alexander recalled,

> [and] managing to get an old door off some old ruin of a structure near by, we put it on the ground, on a little knoll, some thirty yards from the road, & four of us sat on it, [Major Daniel E.] Hager, [Colonel Raleigh

E.] Colston, the adjutant and myself. Every once in awhile one of us would go to the road & ask, "Is this Heth's division?" It wasn't & nobody knew, either, where Heth's div. was, or when it was coming. After it got to be night we were all so overcome with sleep that we tried to lie down together on the door, & to pull our rubber coats over us, but the hard steady rain soaked through them, & every half hour we took turns going down to the road all that livelong night. It was daylight when Heth's divn. at last came along & sunrise when we got strung out on the road.

It had taken General Hill twelve hours to get his corps up alongside the Fairfield Road far enough to allow Longstreet's Corps to move.[38]

As the sun began to rise, the four infantry brigades and the artillery battalion attached to Hood's Division, along with Alexander's reserve battalion, led Longstreet's Corps out of Gettysburg behind Hill's Corps. According to Longstreet's orders, the leading division of the corps—Hood's Division—detailed a brigade to lead. That brigade was followed by two artillery battalions: the one attached to Hood's Division and Alexander's reserve battalion. Following the two artillery battalions were the remaining brigades of Hood's Division. The trains accompanying Hood's troops followed, along with the trains of the two artillery battalions. With them was the ambulance carrying Generals Hood and Hampton and their surgeon, Dr. Darby. Three brigades of McLaws's Division followed. Next in line came the trains of McLaws's Division and the two remaining artillery battalions of the corps. One brigade of McLaws's Division brought up the rear. In such an order of march, there was ample infantry and artillery support at the front and rear of the corps, and the trains accompanying the troops were protected by moving in between the infantry and artillery columns in accordance with Lee's directions of 4 July for the retreat. This was the order of retreat for all three corps of the Army of Northern Virginia.[39]

Private William A. Fletcher of the Fifth Texas was already in rough shape when Hood's Division began to advance on the Fairfield Road. "My shoes were old and so were my clothes," he later wrote:

My pants were frazzled and split up to the knees so I cut them off just below the knees, and thought if I looked like I felt, I was a fright. Short sleeves worn to near point of the elbow, no socks or drawers, and knee breeches. I was not long after leaving camp, marching in mud about six inches deep I lost the sole of one shoe. I jerked off the upper and tried walking a short distance with one bare foot. It looked like at nearly every step there was a rock to jam between my toes as my foot slipped down and forward. I soon pulled off the other one, thinking that I could walk with less danger to both. This was a mistake, so I soon got out of the road and made my way as best I could through woods and fields, keeping near the road.[40]

Hood's Division was on the march. McLaws's Division was advancing up the Willoughby Run Road and onto the Fairfield Road behind Hood's men. Ewell's Corps still screened the movement from its position along Willoughby Run.

What was left of Pickett's Division was in the fields about a mile west of Marsh Creek protecting the Union prisoners of war who were preparing to take up the line of march. The division, as provost guard, was under the direct command of Lee, not Longstreet. Late at night on 4 July Pickett's men had been ordered to march from Marsh Creek with the prisoners who had been held at that site to the location of the prisoners held by Pender's and Heth's Divisions. The next morning Pickett's Division and its prisoners were waiting alongside the Fairfield Road to fall into line between Hood's and McLaws's Divisions.[41]

The four thousand Union prisoners of war were just as exasperated as Pickett's men. They had waited in the drenching rain all night, and they were hungry. Because of Meade's supply problems, few of them had eaten in days. They were each given a half pint of flour in their tin cups on the night of 4 July, but the ground and wood was so wet that they could not cook it. Most went to sleep hungry. In the early morning, a few prisoners received a small piece of liver that they were able to cook; others obtained small quantities of beef. It was their first meal in three or four days.[42]

The sights around the prisoners left indelible impressions on them. Sergeant R. N. Martin of the Sixty-second Pennsylvania watched Lee's army as it was retreating. To him there appeared to be "confusion among the [Confederate] trains, artillery and ambulances." Indeed, Hill's Corps took an inordinate amount of time getting to Fairfield; there must have been some disorder among his troops. Along the Fairfield Road, Martin noted that "every barn, dwelling and outhouse were filled with wounded and dying, also tents were filled that were pitched along the roadside." These structures held the casualties left by Ewell's Corps. Martin got a glimpse of General Pickett himself. He was a "desperate-looking character [and] wears his hair in long ringlets," he recalled. Most of all, Martin noticed how crippled was Pickett's Division. Brigades numbered only as many soldiers as a regiment did before the battle.

Pickett's men would ask the prisoners: "What you all fighting we'ens for?" All of the Confederate soldiers "talk the Real negro slang," Martin recorded, and the prisoners imitated them "much to [the Confederates'] chagrin." For hours, Martin observed Lee's army pass by; the sights of the endless "trains of wagons, artillery and cattle, stolen horses, hogs, etc." were unforgettable.[43]

Dawn found Meade still trying to obtain definitive information on Lee's intentions. At 5:40 A.M. on 5 July the Union signal station at the courthouse in Gettysburg reported that there were "no indications of the enemy anywhere, only on the Chambersburg Pike and in small force. Their batteries have disappeared from the hills near the Seminary. Prisoners report that the enemy have gone to Hagerstown." Behind Seminary Ridge the air was still thick with smoke, making telescopic observation almost impossible. It was as though Lee's army had vanished behind a curtain of heavy smoke and rain.[44]

By 11:00 A.M. Ewell's Corps finally took up the line of march on the Fairfield Road from its position east of the Willoughby Run Road, three miles west of Gettysburg. At the time the columns began to march, Lee's troops were stretched out for nearly seventeen miles, although only six of his nine divisions were actually under way; the men had been filtering onto and beside the Fairfield Road for almost eighteen hours. Ahead of the troops on the Fairfield Road were wagon and ambulance trains that stretched all the way to the Potomac River, nearly thirty more miles. Iverson's and Wright's Brigades had moved out of Monterey Pass. Anderson's, Pender's, and Heth's Divisions were marching toward the pass from Fairfield, followed by Hood's Division. Pickett's Division and its four thousand Union prisoners had just gotten under way behind Hood's columns. The prisoners had been organized into divisions and entered the Fairfield Road in columns of fours. Pickett's men formed two long files on either side of the road, and the prisoners marched between them. McLaws's Division brought up the rear of Longstreet's Corps. Apart from the delays getting all of Hill's Corps under way, the complex movements had been conducted like clockwork.[45]

Private John King of the Twenty-fifth Virginia, Ewell's Corps, was waiting in the rain to take up the line of march. Not far from him, Lee and Ewell were conferring surrounded by numerous staff officers. "You will march in the rear," Lee said to Ewell, "and if the enemy comes up, give him battle; I will go ahead and open the way." Lee finally moved into line with his staff, heading toward Fairfield.[46]

AS THE COLUMNS filled the Fairfield Road and the fields beside it slightly west of Gettysburg, there was drama building on the western side of the South

Mountain range. The early morning of 5 July found Judson Kilpatrick and his Union cavalry division traveling along the western base of the South Mountain range near Ringgold, Maryland, south of Waterloo. With his three cavalry brigades were the ambulances and wagons captured four hours before at Monterey Pass with over one thousand badly wounded Confederate prisoners. While descending the western face of the South Mountain range, Kilpatrick's troopers had broken the spokes of the wheels of many of Ewell's quartermaster and subsistence wagons that they had seized, opened liquor barrels stored inside some of them, and set them on fire. As the Union column galloped south, the orange glow of some of those fires could still be seen all the way down the turnpike from Monterey Pass.[47]

Kilpatrick called a halt about ten miles south of Monterey Pass. His troopers were "tired, hungry, sleepy, wet and covered with mud," recalled one eyewitness. "Men and animals yielded to the demands of exhausted nature, and the column had not been at a halt many minutes before all fell asleep where they stood." Now west of the South Mountain range and out of touch with the Army of the Potomac, Kilpatrick was in a dangerous position. About seventeen miles due south one brigade of General French's Division held Turner's Pass. Although Kilpatrick had broken a section of the vast Confederate trains, the huge columns of wagons and ambulances of Ewell's Corps were advancing across Monterey Pass behind him. Kilpatrick knew that behind those trains were all the Confederate infantry and artillery. He had to get to Turner's Pass as quickly as possible.[48]

To lighten his load, Kilpatrick ordered all of the captured quartermaster and subsistence wagons still with his columns turned out into a large field and burned. He instructed the men to confiscate what horses were serviceable and to seize any rations and fodder for the troops and horses.[49]

Before the wagons were torched, Kilpatrick's men rummaged through them for plunder. "We found [them] loaded with a promiscuous assortment of goods, as the rebs had gone into stores and dwellings and gathered up whatever was in sight," wrote one Michigan trooper. "Some wagons were loaded with coffee, ladies' shoes, teas, calicos, and all such goods as a country store would have for sale." Charles Blinn, of the First Vermont, who had remained with Kilpatrick's main force, noted in his diary that the trains were "loaded with every kind of plunder from a woman's petticoat to a sewing machine. Many of the boys procured a good suit of new clothes from the train." Another Michigan trooper recalled that the wagons he searched contained "all the little trinkets that you could think of; little babies' playthings not worth three cents."[50]

Once emptied of items coveted by Union troopers, the wagons were set on fire, and Kilpatrick's Division turned south along the western base of the South Mountain range. The Fifth New York was ordered ahead to Smithsburg, the next town on the road to Turner's Pass, to clear it of enemy pickets. Throughout the journey, the wagons and ambulances carrying wounded Confederates from Rodes's Division slowed his march considerably.[51]

After Kilpatrick's attacks atop Monterey Pass had broken through the thin Confederate defenses, civilian C. H. Buhrman had led Lieutenant Colonel Preston and his First Vermont Cavalry down the western slope of South Mountain near Smithsburg and on to Leitersburg, Maryland, where the command intercepted a small segment of the rear of Harman's reserve train just before dawn on 5 July. Preston claimed to have seized "one hundred [Confederates], mostly cavalry and infantry, a drove of cattle and many wagons." Most likely, his captives were teamsters and laborers; many were probably African Americans. He understood that "a large train" had already passed through Leitersburg. Preston had moved on toward Hagerstown but broke off pursuit as he was then too far from the rest of his division and vulnerable to attack from almost any direction. Preston and his Vermonters bivouacked east of Hagerstown. After throwing out strong pickets, they awaited further orders. Thus while Kilpatrick was galloping south toward Smithsburg on the morning of 5 July, Preston's First Vermont was not far away.[52]

Kilpatrick had a very serious problem. The captured wagons and ambulances slowed him down. He knew that the entire Confederate army was crossing the mountains behind him, and that Confederate cavalrymen, also on the move, could appear from any direction. He urgently directed his division to move south toward Boonsboro and Turner's Pass, where he could unload his captures and prisoners and connect with elements of French's Division. Kilpatrick's Division soon neared Smithsburg. The Fifth New York had secured the town, chasing away a small Confederate "picket" on its arrival.[53]

Kilpatrick, his division, and their captured wagons and ambulances arrived at Smithsburg at about 9:00 A.M. on 5 July, just as Longstreet's columns were marching beside the Fairfield Road west of Gettysburg. Kilpatrick's men were met with a reception they never forgot. The rain had stopped, and the sun broke through the clouds and shone brightly. One witness remembered:

> Young misses lined the street sides singing patriotic songs; the General was showered with flowers, and the General and troops were cheered until reechoed by the mountainsides; young ladies and matrons assailed

the column with words of welcome and large plates heaped up with pyramids of white bread spread with jelly and butter, inviting all to partake. While the young sang, the old shed tears and wrung the hands of those nearest to them. The little town was overflowing with patriotism and thankfulness at the arrival of their preservers. While these things were detaining the column, [a regimental] band struck up "Hail Columbia," followed by the "Star-Spangled Banner."[54]

For one of Kilpatrick's wounded captives, Major Blacknall of the Twenty-third North Carolina, it had been a most difficult ride. The show of patriotic fervor in Smithsburg held no interest for him. It seems that Kilpatrick preferred Blacknall's horse to his own. Indeed, Blacknall had always boasted that his mount was the "finest in Lee's army." Kilpatrick had commandeered the horse after his troopers captured Blacknall. Learning that the horse belonged to Blacknall, Kilpatrick assured him that he would return it after the Confederate was exchanged. Blacknall knew better, but, as a prisoner of war, there was nothing he could do. Instead, he had been given Kilpatrick's horse, which he had been riding beside the ambulances from Waterloo to Smithsburg.

When Kilpatrick's column arrived at Smithsburg, Blacknall noticed a rubber coat strapped to the back of the saddle. He put on the coat and rode down the column toward the rear unnoticed. Soon he was free, but, because of the tall stone fences, he could not leave the main road. He dismounted several times and tried to break through or urge the horse over the fences but without success.

Blacknall rode on. Before long the morphine he had been taking to relieve the pain overcame him; he fell into a stupor. Then he was aroused by a loud command to "get up." Three Union troopers who had been separated from their commands at Monterey Pass the night before took Blacknall prisoner and escorted him back to Smithsburg.[55]

THE GALA RECEPTION notwithstanding, Kilpatrick was on a collision course. On the eastern slope of the South Mountain range heading toward Smithsburg were two brigades of Confederate cavalry led by none other than J. E. B. Stuart. General Stuart, with the cavalry brigades of Colonel Ferguson and Colonel Chambliss and the horse batteries of Captain Griffin and Captain Jackson, was riding toward the pass at Raven Rock after screening the movement of Major Harman's reserve trains and Ewell's trains by holding a position along the far right flank of Lee's army outside of Gettysburg and then riding between Lee's army and Emmitsburg.[56]

Stuart had had an interesting ride to the pass at Raven Rock. Early in the morning of 5 July he and his two brigades, after obtaining a guide, had started south from Gettysburg toward Emmitsburg. The columns galloped into Emmitsburg at dawn. Once there, Stuart halted them in order to "procure" rations for the men. In the process, the gray cavalrymen seized a wagon train of hospital stores that was moving from Frederick to Meade's army, along with sixty or seventy prisoners. Also detained at the Farmer's Inn and Hotel outside of Emmitsburg was a cameraman traveling with the famous wartime photographer Alexander Gardner to photograph the sites in and around Gettysburg after the fighting. Gardner himself and another associate had left the hotel to visit Gardner's fifteen-year-old son, Lawrence, who was attending a boarding school near town. The captured cameraman was released when Stuart's two brigades moved south.[57]

While in Emmitsburg that morning, Stuart had had an opportunity to study his maps. In addition, he learned that Kilpatrick's entire cavalry division had passed through Emmitsburg the previous afternoon on its way to intercept the trains moving across Monterey Pass. Believing that there were ample Confederate cavalry brigades to protect the trains at Monterey Pass, Stuart decided to quickly move toward the pass at Raven Rock and Cavetown on the western side of the mountains in order to guard the columns as they passed through Hagerstown toward Falling Waters and Williamsport.

After feeding their horses at Emmitsburg, Stuart and his two brigades took the road toward Frederick until they reached Cooperstown. They then continued galloping through Harbaugh's Valley, by Zion Church, on their way over the Catoctin Mountains. Once across, they began their ascent up the South Mountain range. Stuart was soon informed by his scouts that there was a fork in the road. One fork led to the left, directly to Smithsburg, and the other to the right, "bearing more toward Leitersburg."[58]

Back at Smithsburg, Kilpatrick, fearing a Confederate advance through the pass at Raven Rock, sent scouts into the pass to see if enemy cavalrymen were approaching from the direction of Emmitsburg. The scouts had not gone six miles into the pass when they encountered Confederates. Stuart's vedettes ordered the scouts to surrender. The union scouts turned their horses around and "dashed off down the rocky mountain road at a breakneck speed." For nearly four miles the Confederates were in pursuit, until they saw in front of them that a brigade of Kilpatrick's Division had formed along the road to Smithsburg. There the chase ended, but the brief battle at Smithsburg was about to begin.[59]

Along the road leading to Smithsburg from the mountain pass, Kilpatrick

Farmer's Inn, Emmitsburg, Maryland, where J. E. B. Stuart "captured" a photographer on his way to Gettysburg with Alexander Gardner on 5 July 1863. Library of Congress, Washington, D.C.

placed all three of his cavalry brigades facing east, fearing a Confederate approach from that direction. Huey's Brigade, with Fuller's Battery, occupied the first ridge overlooking the pass, forming the first line of battle and the left flank. Behind and to the right of Huey's force, Kilpatrick placed Richmond's Brigade with Elder's Battery along a second ridge; the third line consisted of Custer's Brigade with Pennington's Battery.[60]

Below an eminence called Raven Rock, Stuart divided his command: Ferguson's Brigade took the left fork of the road, while Chambliss's Brigade took the right. Stuart accompanied Chambliss. When Ferguson's troopers moved through the pass at Raven Rock at about 5:00 P.M., they plainly observed Kilpatrick's troops holding the road between the pass and Smithsburg directly ahead. Chambliss's men continued up the right fork to look for a way to get onto Kilpatrick's left flank.[61]

The skirmish lines of the opposing forces soon came into contact, and shots rang out across the rolling fields east of Smithsburg. Griffin's guns were unlimbered and placed along high ground behind the advancing Confederate cavalry. The fighting became fierce as Ferguson's dismounted graycoats fought "from crag to crag on the mountainside" and in the rough, rocky fields below Raven Rock to dislodge Kilpatrick's skirmishers. Those gray troopers quickly came into contact with Richmond's main line. As they forced their way down the rocky hillside and emerged in the open clearing, Elder's Union cannoneers found them within range of their three-inch rifles and pulled the lanyards. The artillery fire did little damage to the Confederate troopers, though, as the terrain was not conducive to field artillery.[62]

Once in place on the enemy's left, Stuart ordered three of every four of Chambliss's troopers to dismount and advance; the remaining men held the horses. Chambliss's cavalrymen pushed their way south against Kilpatrick's left. Huey's Union brigade could not hold on. Huey was quickly reinforced by the dismounted Fifth New York Cavalry of Richmond's Brigade, but that was not enough. It was now 5:30 P.M. Shells from Griffin's horse battery played upon the Union columns and found their mark as well in buildings and houses in Smithsburg. Kilpatrick's left flank gave way. Stuart quickly sent a courier to Ferguson informing him of his success and directing him to break off the fight and join Chambliss.[63]

It was all over in minutes. As Kilpatrick's troopers were falling back, Stuart increased the pressure against them. Kilpatrick called for a general withdrawal toward Boonsboro. As quickly as they could move, the Union troopers galloped south. Stuart's two brigades then poured into Smithsburg; the celebration of the morning soon gave way to silence as many citizens of the town fled or locked themselves in their houses and root cellars at the Confederate approach.[64]

While in Smithsburg, Stuart learned from a few citizens that the command he had just defeated was Kilpatrick's. The residents claimed that Kilpatrick had captured "several thousand prisoners and 400 or 500 wagons" at Monterey Pass, but Stuart did not believe them. Not long afterward, none other than Captain George M. Emack galloped up to Stuart. His arm was in a sling, and he showed the bruises and cuts of the previous night's desperate fight at Monterey Pass. Reporting on that fight, he confirmed, in part, that Kilpatrick had captured a sizable number of wagons, ambulances, and wounded from Rodes's Division.[65]

Stuart determined that his first duty was to open communications with Lee and the main army. He sent Private Robert W. Goode of the First Virginia Cavalry riding out into the falling darkness along South Mountain to Monterey Pass and on to Lee's headquarters to tell the army commander of Stuart's encounters and present location.

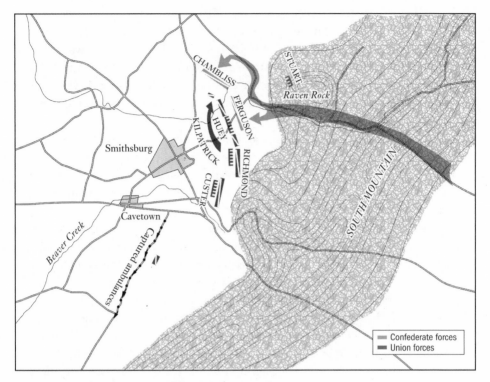

MAP 7.1   Late afternoon, 5 July 1863.
Stuart attacks Kilpatrick's Division at Smithsburg; Chambliss's Brigade overruns
the left flank of Huey's Brigade, causing Kilpatrick to abandon the field. The
ambulances and wounded of Rodes's Division captured at Monterey Pass are
hurried to Boonsboro.

Meanwhile, Stuart ordered his two brigades and artillery batteries forward to Leitersburg. There, by nightfall, they rendezvoused with Jones's and Robertson's Brigades and Chew's and Moorman's Batteries, all of which had groped their way through the mud and mass of wagons and troops from Monterey Pass to Leitersburg to protect the trains. Unbeknownst to Grumble Jones's men at Leitersburg, their commander had escaped capture and found his way to Williamsport.

With his four cavalry brigades and four artillery batteries, Stuart was on the left flank of Lee's army. The trains continued their course toward the Potomac River. The muddy troopers of the commands of Chambliss, Ferguson, Jones, and Robertson watched as the seemingly endless columns of wagons and ambulances rumbled through Leitersburg.[66]

Sergeant Whitehorne noted that the sun had come back out at 10:00 A.M. on 5 July after his ambulance crossed the mountains and entered the Cumberland Valley. "The beautiful landscape," he wrote, "filled my heart with pleasure as we passed over the smooth and easy-graded road." The Emmitsburg-Waynesboro Turnpike and the Hagerstown-Waynesboro Turnpike were a blessing to the wounded; they were macadamized and offered some relief.

As Whitehorne and his companions neared Waynesboro, a straggler acquainted with the ambulance driver approached the vehicle and asked: "Don't you want some whiskey?" He then told the driver that a whiskey distillery was "down the valley about a quarter of a mile" and that the "boys were helping themselves." The driver, recalled Whitehorne, "suddenly had compassion on the poor fellow and said to him, 'Don't you want to ride?'" Obviously the straggler was looking for a ride to the distillery. He climbed aboard. "I noticed," wrote Whitehorne,

> when the driver had given the reins to his acquaintance, he reached over in the ambulance & took with him a quart coffee pot. He returned and resumed his seat in about three quarters of an hour. I heard a few subdued words and smacking of lips, and in a little while he reached over and touched me saying: "Sergeant don't you want a drink?" Well I did not decline, as all soldiers seem to have a perfect [contempt] for any savoring of temperance, so I took a drink and can say with truth it was the vilest whiskey I ever drank.

By the time gunfire was heard from the direction of Smithsburg, Whitehorne could tell that the ambulance driver was drunk. The wounded sergeant would have grabbed the pot and poured it out but he could not reach it. "It had by this time gotten dark," Whitehorne continued, "though the moon gave us some light. We had wagons in front, and wagons in the rear of us. The mules to our ambulance were terribly jaded, and every time the wagon in front stopped, our mules were only too willing to stop, but when the wagon in front moved, our mules would remain still, and as my driver was both asleep and drunk, I had to punch him & make him drive up. This I had to keep up all night, as the train of wagons were stopping every few minutes."[67]

Eight

Use your sabres, don't strike, but thrust

While Lee's army continued to move, Meade continued to try to discern Lee's intentions. On the morning of 5 July the Union general resorted to directly pressuring the enemy; he would maintain that pressure all the way to the base of the South Mountain range. At dawn, Major General Horatio G. Wright's First Division, supported by the remainder of Sedgwick's powerful Sixth Corps, the largest in the Army of the Potomac, advanced across the open fields toward the Fairfield Road from Cemetery Ridge, led by a brigade of cavalry under Colonel John B. McIntosh of Gregg's Division and two rifled guns of Captain Joseph W. Martin's Sixth New York Battery. Just before midmorning, Wright's troops came within two miles of Ewell's lines, which were still aligned in front of the ridge overlooking Willoughby Run, east of Blackhorse Tavern.[1]

Wright ordered one section of Captain William A. Harn's Third New York Battery to the front from the rear of the column. The guns moved forward, unlimbered, and went into position on the Fairfield Road. At a distance of almost two miles, Harn's guns sent shells over Ewell's lines but without serious effect. Wright did not advance any farther. At about eleven o'clock Ewell began to methodically move his infantry, artillery battalions, and trains onto and alongside the Fairfield Road behind McLaws's Division. Rodes's Division, with Daniel's Brigade heading the column, took the lead, followed by Johnson's Division. The flanks moved first, followed by the center. Early brought up the rear, after covering the movement of Rodes's and Johnson's Divisions; Gordon's Brigade and three guns of Captain Charles A. Green's Louisiana Guard Artillery served as the rear guard. Lee had, in the words of Carl von Clausewitz, "a strong rear guard, led by the most courageous general." Companies B, C, and E of Colonel White's Comanches still formed a thin screen ahead of Early's rear guard.[2]

Dr. Baruch and his fellow surgeons of Kershaw's Brigade at the Blackhorse Tavern, just behind the lines of Ewell's rear guard, had killed and roasted a peacock they found "strutting in the meadow." Inside the tavern they had located cold biscuits, coffee, sugar, and dishes. A table had been constructed in the orchard, and the surgeons had "seated themselves to enjoy a feast which the hospital cook had placed steaming on the table." At the time, Baruch thought: "Here was peace at last."

As the surgeons began to carve their "novel roast fowl," the first shell from Harn's guns shrieked over their heads, "its shrill whistling silenced by an explosion in the field nearby." The wounded began to moan, calling for the surgeons. Baruch ordered a yellow cloth quickly fastened to the lightning rod of the bank barn not far from them. As the wounded were being quieted, six more shells exploded, and some of White's cavalrymen, carrying binoculars, dashed down the Fairfield Road.

Later in the morning, after Ewell's Corps had passed Marsh Creek, the surgeons returned to their dinner. It was then that Baruch spotted the Union columns: "As far as the eye could reach, the summit of the ridge was covered by a line of cavalry whose weapons shimmered in the brilliant July sun." Slowly the cavalry advanced down the hill.

Dr. Pearce directed Baruch to meet the pickets and conduct the surrender because, he remarked, "you understand the Yankees." Baruch had been captured during the first invasion of Maryland and knew what was expected. "I hastily donned my gray coat and green sash and sauntered toward the advancing line," Baruch remembered. The leading Union officer was an Irishman, and Baruch distinctly noted his brogue.

"Say cap," the Irishman said to his company commander, "here's a Reb [who] wants to see you."

A Union captain rode up to Baruch's side and saluted. "Are there many Rebels around?" he asked.

"Yes, but they are all wounded," Baruch replied.

As the cavalrymen galloped down the road, the infantry pickets appeared on the hilltop. Soon the entire Sixth Corps mounted the crest of the ridge. In minutes the yard of the tavern was "filled with brilliantly attired officers." Baruch asked to see the medical director of the Sixth Corps and then proceeded to chide the officers for allowing their artillery to open fire "after that hospital flag was hoisted." The officers claimed that they had not seen the flag.

There was some "good-humored chaffing" between the marching soldiers and Baruch's nurses as Sedgwick's columns passed by.

"What command is this?" asked one Confederate soldier.

"We are the chaps that captured Marye's Heights in the battle of Chancellorsville. Who are you?"

"We are the chaps that drove you back afterwards at Salem Church."[3]

The Union infantry continued down the Fairfield Road, overtaking each Confederate hospital along the way and picking up more and more prisoners. Notwithstanding the fire of enemy guns, Early's Division "moved slowly in the rear" of the retreating army. Gordon's Brigade and Green's Battery formed the rear guard. They were followed by the three companies of White's Comanches that screened the retrograde movement.[4]

Confederate infantry and artillery kept marching toward Monterey Pass. Over the past thirty-five hours the Fairfield Road had become a quagmire. The mud was more than twelve inches deep. Some soldiers complained that the mud rose to their knees as they marched. Frustrated, all the troops left the road and resorted to the fields beside it. For close to six miles, the fields were mostly sown in wheat that was almost ripe. By the time Ewell's columns had tramped through them, they were flattened and destroyed.[5]

The Union's Sixth Corps moved deliberately behind Ewell. Spreading out in lines of battle, the three divisions—the First followed by the Second, then the Third—advanced down the Fairfield Road in pursuit. For six miles, Sedgwick's columns followed Early in battle formation, flags flapping in the breeze, with heavy lines of skirmishers and pioneers strung out across the front. As Sedgwick's lines came within range of the rear of Early's columns, a section of Harn's Battery unlimbered and shelled Gordon's Georgians and White's Virginia cavalrymen.[6]

The road ahead of Ewell's Corps was being cleared as Lee, anticipating that Meade would follow closely, directed Longstreet's Corps to take a parallel route to Monterey Pass via the Jack's Mountain Road, east of Jack's Mountain, in the late afternoon. Heth's Division and Lee's own baggage train followed most of Anderson's Division and Pender's Division up the Maria Furnace Road, west of Jack's Mountain. In this way, Ewell was able to direct Rodes's and Johnson's Divisions toward the mountain defiles behind Hill's Corps and the commander's baggage trains with less obstruction. Longstreet's Corps and Pickett's Division with its prisoners of war would follow the Emmitsburg-Waynesboro Turnpike from Fountaindale to Monterey Pass and rejoin the main columns on the summit of South Mountain.[7]

When the head of Early's Division reached Fairfield, the columns came to a halt. The division trains had become bogged down in the mud west of town. Early sent an urgent message to speed them up, but there was no movement. Behind Early's troops, White's vedettes spotted trouble. Sedgwick's heavy blue lines were getting closer. White sent a messenger to Early with the news. Still frustrated over the lack of movement of his trains, Early decided to load some of Colonel Jones's artillery pieces with blank charges and fire them to scare the horses and mules into pulling the vehicles ahead. Just as Early was ordering that the blank rounds be discharged, White's courier arrived to announce that Union troops were approaching. As Early scanned the hillside east of Fairfield, he could see Sedgwick's enormous force appear on the crest of a distant ridge.[8]

Quickly, Early ordered Jones to move some of his guns forward and open fire with shell. At the same time, he sent word to General Gordon to advance one regiment as a skirmish line. Early positioned all the remaining units of the division into battle lines in the fields east of Fairfield. Gordon called upon Colonel Edmund N. Atkinson's Twenty-sixth Georgia to form a line across the Fairfield Road in front of the division battle lines. Jones hurried the three guns of Captain Green's Louisiana Guard Artillery into position in the middle of the road. While Green's guns sent shells across the fields into the blue ranks, the Georgians, with White's cavalrymen as skirmishers, formed a battle line straddling the road in front of a large woodlot, facing Sedgwick's huge force. Their objective was to check the enemy until all the Confederate trains were beyond the reach of Union artillery shells. The main lines of the division, brigade by brigade, methodically withdrew through the town. Colonel Atkinson waited behind the woodlot until elements of the Union's Sixth Corps skirmish lines came within less than one hundred yards. "Charge!" he yelled, and his men, at "charge bayonets," ran toward the oncoming blue ranks and drove them pell-mell back through the woods and into an open field.[9]

Within Wright's lines, which now stretched nearly half a mile from flank to flank, Harn's Third New York Battery and Captain George W. Adams's Battery G, First Rhode Island Light Artillery, unlimbered on a commanding ridge east of Fairfield and began to pound the thin Confederate ranks. The skirmish was spirited, and the fields east of Fairfield became wrapped in smoke. While the Georgians and Virginia horsemen and their scant artillery support fought desperately for time, Early's trains and marching columns moved out of Fairfield and up the Maria Furnace Road toward the South Mountain range.[10]

When the artillery fire erupted, a large group of Confederate officers assembled on a hill near Fairfield. Generals Ewell and Early and "many others of high rank" were there, remembered Major John Warwick Daniel, one of Early's staff officers. Suddenly, someone shouted: "Lookout! Lookout!" A spherical shell, its fuse fizzing, came bounding over the ground nearby and exploded in a nearby woodlot. Soon another shell detonated within "a few feet of the generals." The hill, in Daniel's words, "was soon divested of its visitors."[11]

In fighting that lasted perhaps an hour, Adams's Rhode Island Battery expended 163 rounds of ammunition on Early's rear guard. Within the Twenty-sixth Georgia two enlisted men were killed and eleven were wounded and missing, including two officers. The action of the regiment had been heroic. In the dark afternoon, its battered soldiers crept back through the muddy streets of Fairfield and rejoined Early's Division not far from the base of Jack's Mountain. For all the gunfire, Wright's command suffered only one enlisted man killed and two wounded.[12]

Sedgwick's Sixth Corps held its ground; it had no orders to bring on a general engagement. As the evening wore on, more Union artillerymen moved toward the front and took up positions along the heights east of Fairfield, but the blue columns did not advance. Sedgwick was eight miles ahead of the rest of the Army of the Potomac, and the enemy in his front was withdrawing under cover of darkness into the hills and mountains behind Fairfield. Given Sedgwick's orders and the geography, not to mention the size and potency of Ewell's force, it was hardly the time for a spirited advance. The halting of Sedgwick's Corps, though, was vital to Early's Division west of Fairfield. It safely moved closer to the defiles between Jack's Mountain and the South Mountain range where it could defend itself against any Union assault.[13]

Thirty-seven miles southwest of Fairfield, most of Lee's trains were closing in on their destination on the evening of 5 July. The head of Imboden's trains entered Williamsport, guarded by the leading squadrons of the Eighteenth Virginia Cavalry and a section of McClanahan's Battery, at the same time that Sedgwick's Corps pressed Lee's rear guard along the Fairfield Road east of Fairfield. The wagons and ambulances, including the lead ambulance in the trains of Pender's Division carrying Generals Pender and Scales, proceeded down the Cumberland Valley Turnpike and onto Potomac Street. The town was jammed with the trains that had already come from the direction of Hagerstown. The trains of Ewell's three divisions were just arriving as well. By then there was sufficient order in Williamsport to allow Imboden's trains to roll slowly down Potomac Street; they passed the Catholic church, the Taylor House hotel, and the German Lutheran church, driving all the way to the Chesapeake and Ohio (C&O) Canal basin. The column then crawled up Commerce Street to Salisbury Street, intermingling with the vast number of wagons and ambulances from the trains that had escaped the fighting at Monterey Pass, only to find that the lone ferry was still transporting most of the vehicles across the Potomac.[14]

The magnitude of the problem that faced Imboden's trains may be gleaned from the fact that, after the first elements entered Williamsport, the rest still stretched all the way to New Franklin, Pennsylvania, almost twenty-five miles north. It would take another sixteen hours for all of those wagons, ambulances, and cavalry and artillery escorts to reach the river town.[15]

Imboden, who had been riding at the head of his trains, entered Williamsport just as Pender's trains began to make their way into the town. Imboden desperately needed reinforcements to protect his caravan. He had received reports of the capture of Williamsport. Although they proved to be false, they had been of great concern to him. The news that the river was impassible — which he verified — meant that his trains would probably not reach Williamsport for an even longer time than was otherwise estimated because of the present logjam and backup. After the attack at Greencastle, Imboden had labored under the very real concern that the trains would be bombarded again along the turnpike and that with the thousands of wagons and ambulances jamming the streets of Williamsport — and no more protection than his own cavalry and artillery escorts — the whole column would be stopped; it would then be exposed to destruction by any sizable enemy onslaught.[16]

On entering Williamsport, Imboden received word that two infantry regiments, the Fifty-eighth Virginia and Fifty-fourth North Carolina, were marching toward the Potomac River from Martinsburg, West Virginia, with the army ordnance train that Lee had told him would be on its way north. He must have felt some sense of relief. Although the Fifty-eighth Virginia was somewhat understrength, it and the Fifty-fourth North Carolina could be used to protect the trains at the intersection of the Cumberland Valley Turnpike and the National Road, a most exposed site, and to aid in the establishment of a defensive perimeter north and east of Williamsport, thereby protecting the trains congregating in and around the town from a likely attack from the direction of Hagerstown and Boonsboro.[17]

In the meantime, Imboden directed his brother George to order a company from his regiment to patrol the National Road. Captain Frank Imboden and his company were nearby, and George ordered them back up the turnpike. Members of Company F, Eighteenth Virginia Cavalry, galloped north and took up positions along the National Road east and west of its intersection with the Cumberland Valley Turnpike.[18]

General John Imboden found Grumble Jones still in Williamsport. Anxious to find and return to his own command, Jones gave Imboden a report of all troop dispositions accomplished during the early morning hours and then turned direction of Confederate forces in the town over to him. Jones mounted up and rode back toward Hagerstown to search for his brigade. He rode across Washington County, Maryland, for almost nine hours before finally locating it near Leitersburg.[19]

TO IMBODEN'S GREAT RELIEF, the reinforcements he so desperately needed were just arriving in Williamsport. The ordnance train and its escorts had reached the southern bank of the Potomac River. Close to where the ordnance train stopped was the bivouac site of Captain William Pegram's Company F, Twenty-first Virginia, that had arrived at the Potomac the night before after a long march from Staunton, Virginia. It seems that Captain Pegram, after being left behind with his company at Winchester by Ewell, had been ordered to return to Richmond in order to escort a group of "stragglers" back to the army. Detraining at Staunton on 22 June, the little company and the stragglers had been marching every day since then. From the time of their arrival opposite Williamsport, Pegram's men had been scavenging nearby homes, shops, and mills for all the flour and bacon they could find.[20]

When they reached the south bank of the Potomac with the ordnance train, Colonel Francis Howard Board's Fifty-eighth Virginia and Colonel Kenneth M. Murchison's Fifty-fourth North Carolina had just completed a nearly 400-mile odyssey of their own. Left behind at Winchester by Ewell on 15 June, the two regiments had been directed on 17 and 18 June to march the prisoners of war from Milroy's garrison to Staunton, where they arrived on 22 and 23 June. They had then accompanied the prisoners via the Virginia Central Railroad all the way to Richmond, where they turned them over to the guards at Libby Prison and returned to Staunton on 24 and 25 June, guarding the railroad trains carrying the ordnance Lee had requested earlier in the month. The two regiments had then conducted the ordnance wagon train back to Winchester, arriving on 2 and 3 July while Lee was locked in his desperate struggle at Gettysburg. The next day they traveled from Winchester to the Potomac. The men were dirty and in tatters; most were barefoot due to the long marching on macadamized roads.[21]

The ordnance train and its escorts reached the Potomac River at about 2:00 P.M. on 5 July. The Fifty-eighth Virginia was ferried across to Williamsport under General Imboden's direction; the Fifty-fourth North Carolina remained on the south bank protecting the train. About forty infantrymen at a time stepped aboard the ferryboat as it made its return voyage across the swirling river after releasing cargoes of wagons and ambulances on the West Virginia shore.[22]

In less than an hour, the Virginians marched across the canal, up Salisbury Street, through the town of Williamsport, and out the Cumberland Valley Turnpike on the double-quick. With jingling canteens and tin cups, flapping leather accoutrements, and the splashing of hundreds of feet in the water and deep mud beside the roadway, the soldiers of the Fifty-eighth Virginia made their way to the intersection of the National Road and the Cumberland Valley Turnpike, about four miles north of Williamsport. There they joined Company H of the Eighteenth Virginia Cavalry.[23]

The Fifty-eighth Virginia spread out on either side of the turnpike to protect Imboden's wagon and ambulance trains from an enemy approach on the National Road. The cavalry company, spreading out in the fields east and west of the turnpike, formed advance skirmish lines. However, the protection that the one infantry regiment and cavalry company afforded the trains was of limited value. Any approach by Union raiding parties from Mercersburg toward the intersection of the Hagerstown-Mercersburg Road and the Cumberland Valley Turnpike would be almost unopposed. Likewise, an attack against the trains near Greencastle would be beyond the reach of the infantry.

Back at Williamsport, Colonel Murchison's Fifty-fourth North Carolina remained on the south bank of the river guarding the ordnance train and waiting for orders to move. Those orders were not long in coming. Just before midafternoon, Imboden directed Murchison to ferry his command across the river, leaving only a small force behind to guard the train. Filling up the flat with about forty soldiers at a time, Murchison began to send his men to the other side of the river. The first group of "Tarheels" reached the Maryland shore at about 3:00 P.M. It took approximately one hour to transport the entire regiment across the Potomac.[24]

On the double-quick, the reassembled Fifty-fourth North Carolina was directed up Salisbury Street, through the maze of wagons and ambulances to a position along the high ground about one mile east of town, between the Hagerstown-Williamsport Turnpike and the Williamsport-Boonsboro Road. Acting under Imboden's orders, Colonel George H. Smith, commander of Imboden's own Sixty-second Virginia Mounted Infantry, found Captain Tanner with his three guns parked near the C&O Canal basin. Tanner's guns had been there since early morning; their limber chests and caissons were almost out of ammunition. Smith ordered Tanner to head back up Salisbury Street to the high ground just south of the Hagerstown-Williamsport Turnpike.[25]

Under Imboden's direction, a defense line was being slowly formed east, northeast, and north of Williamsport. In that countryside marked by rolling hills, ridges, and depressions where creekbeds were formed, Smith located a long ridgeline one mile east of Williamsport that ran from south of the Williamsport-Boonsboro Road along the farm of a prominent landowner named Otho Williams, across the road, and between the Williamsport-Boonsboro Road and the Hagerstown-Williamsport Turnpike. The ridge extended west almost to the Cumberland Valley Turnpike. As any sizable threat would have to come from the east or, possibly, northeast, that ridge was critical. There, Williamsport could be defended, and infantry and artillery were directed to occupy the line as soon as they arrived in town.

Having received no instructions for his command and desirous of getting his men and their stragglers back to the army, Captain Pegram ordered his little company across the river on the flat shortly after the Fifty-fourth North Carolina had completed its crossing. On the Maryland side, Pegram's troops, like the other infantrymen, picked their way through the gridlock of wagons, ambulances, and wagoners in Williamsport. Wagons and ambulances jammed the streets and alleys and crowded along the banks of the river. Pegram marched his men up Salisbury Street to a position slightly more than one mile northeast of town, along high ground overlooking both the Hagerstown-Williamsport Turnpike and the Williamsport-Boonsboro Road. At 4:00 P.M. Pegram ordered the troops to fall out, stack arms, and cook what food they had foraged.

One of Imboden's officers, probably Colonel Smith, came across Pegram and his company. He informed Pegram that Imboden was under orders from Lee to stop all troops in Williamsport that were headed north to rejoin the army as a great battle had been fought forty-five miles northeast near Gettysburg, Pennsylvania, and Lee intended to fall back to Virginia by way of Williamsport. Pegram was to keep his company where it was; the trains arriving in Williamsport were extremely vulnerable to enemy attack and every available man would be needed for their defense.[26]

While the defenses of Williamsport were slowly but surely being formed, Imboden directed his attention to the trains gathering in the town. Because so many wounded had arrived in need of medical attention, he converted Williamsport into "a great hospital." He required all the families in town to start cooking for the sick and wounded "on pain of having their kitchens occupied for that purpose by [his] men." The surgeons who had accompanied the trains quickly "pulled off their coats and went to work, and soon a vast amount of suffering was mitigated." Those who had died along the way were buried in the city cemetery overlooking the Potomac River and in churchyards and back lots.[27]

AS THE TRAINS continued to pour into Williamsport, events were developing just to the northwest that would mar the integrity of Imboden's otherwise flawless operation. The First New York (Lincoln) Cavalry and the Twelfth Pennsylvania Cavalry had played rather inauspicious roles in the opening stages of the Gettysburg campaign. Attached to General Milroy's command, they had fought Rodes's advance from Berryville, but at Winchester and Martinsburg a portion of the two regiments managed to avert disaster by escaping all the way to Berkeley Springs and then across the Potomac River to Hancock, Maryland. The remnants of the First New York and Twelfth Pennsylvania halted their flight at a place called "Bloody Run" in distant Bedford County, Pennsylvania. Other remnants of those regiments had fled to Harpers Ferry and wound up in French's command at Frederick. By the end of June, the two regiments, along with the fragments of seven infantry regiments, one Pennsylvania militia regiment, two other cavalry regiments, and one artillery battery, most of which had also fled before Ewell's onslaught in the lower Shenandoah Valley, had been collected into a force that, on paper at least, had been assimilated into Couch's Union Department of the Susquehanna. Leading the odd collection of broken units—among the "debris of Winchester"—was Colonel Lewis B. Pierce of the Twelfth Pennsylvania Cavalry.

For the past eighteen days, Pierce and his command had operated in virtual isolation. The two cavalry regiments had occupied much of that time making forays against Confederate foraging parties along the Potomac River between Williamsport and Hancock. On 2 July a battalion of the First New York had attacked the rear of Imboden's cavalry column as it moved from McConnellsburg toward Chambersburg.[28]

On 3 July Pierce and his troopers left Bloody Run and headed toward McConnellsburg in order to be as close to the two contending armies as possible. Up to that time, his command had no definitive information on the whereabouts of either the Army of the Potomac or the enemy. It had only heard "uncertain rumors" of a bloody engagement at Gettysburg. By nightfall, 4 July, Pierce's column reached McConnellsburg after marching through raging thunderstorms and torrential rains.

Impatient with the near-total lack of information, a company commander in the First New York Cavalry proposed to Pierce that Captain Abram Jones lead a select body of cavalrymen past the rear of Lee's army to hook up with the Army of the Potomac. The purpose of the mission would be to obtain the necessary intelligence as well as direction for the disposition of Pierce's command.

Pierce had been hesitant about authorizing any movement around Lee's army. But apparently even he had grown anxious enough about the situation to give his assent. He insisted, however, that at least half of the force should consist of troopers from his own Twelfth Pennsylvania Cavalry.[29]

The order was given for one hundred men each from the First New York (Lincoln) Cavalry and the Twelfth Pennsylvania Cavalry to form the special command. For some reason, not entirely clear, apparently well over a hundred New Yorkers actually rode in the mission, whereas only about eighty cavalrymen were from the Twelfth Pennsylvania Cavalry. Captain Abram Jones of Company A, First New York, was selected to lead the force. The special force was divided into three detachments commanded respectively by Lieutenant Franz Passegger and Lieutenant Charles Woodruff, both of the First New York, and Lieutenant David A. Irwin of the Twelfth Pennsylvania.

On the morning of 5 July the special force left McConnellsburg in a driving rain and headed southeast toward Mercersburg. By midday the column reached Mercersburg, where it stopped to water and feed the horses and where the troopers were treated to a vast array of pies, cakes, and refreshments from the loyal townspeople. There Captain Jones was informed by refugees from the area just east of Mercersburg that trains of Confederate stores and wounded were slowly moving down the Cumberland Valley Turnpike toward Williamsport.

Jones quickly realized that if the intelligence was accurate, there was no way for his command to travel safely behind Lee's army to the Army of the Potomac. Instead, he decided to move closer and determine if it would be possible for his force to successfully strike the trains. To carry out such an operation, Jones would have to be sure that his force was strong enough to handle any escorts of the trains. Importantly, he needed to find terrain near the Cumberland Valley Turnpike where he could conceal his troopers until they could launch a surprise attack.[30]

Local citizens told Jones that his force could intercept the trains by proceeding down the Hagerstown-Mercersburg Road. Securing a guide, Jones ordered the men to "mount up" and move out. Within a few minutes the column galloped down the muddy road toward Hagerstown. After riding about ten miles and crossing Conococheague Creek, Jones's scouts came within view of the intersection of the Hagerstown-Mercersburg Road and the

Captain Abram
Jones of the First
New York Cavalry.
William H. Beach,
*The First New York
(Lincoln) Cavalry*
(New York:
Lincoln Cavalry
Assoc., 1902),
56–57.

Cumberland Valley Turnpike, known locally as "Cunningham's Crossroads"
or "Cearfoss"—both designations having been derived from the names of
property owners nearby. At the crossroads stood a country store and a small
frame tollgate and house; just up the turnpike was the brick Mount Zion
Evangelical Church.

Cunningham's Crossroads was situated about midway between Greencastle and Williamsport. Jones's vedettes reported the layout of the area. According to them, the west side of the turnpike was dominated by a long ridge
behind which Jones could conceal his men until a coordinated attack could
be launched. The Cumberland Valley Railroad paralleled the turnpike on the

east, and the land there was level enough to prevent the Confederates from finding cover, although there were large woodlots and houses nearby.

Jones halted his column while he and several troopers rode ahead, then walked to the top of the ridge west of the turnpike to get a view of the passing trains. It must have been an awe-inspiring but deeply melancholy sight. Below their vantage point, the trains extended up and down the muddy turnpike for as far as the eye could see. Ambulances and many wagons were filled with wounded men whose piteous cries and moans could be distinctly heard. The wounded who could walk hobbled along in the mud on either side of the trains. Horsemen galloped up and down the line of vehicles and walking wounded.

Jones riveted his attention on the escorts. He noted that the trains apparently were traveling in distinct sections. Cavalry or mounted infantry squads rode beside them while artillery battery sections moved along between sections of the trains at about one-mile intervals. The trains moved very slowly. Judging from the appearance of the turnpike, it seemed to Jones that a significant number of trains had already passed the crossroads and arrived at Williamsport. Was he viewing the rear of the column or was it closer to the head?

The objective of any attack would be to capture as many escorts, wagons, and ambulances as possible and take them back to Mercersburg. Jones needed to select the right moment to strike. He reasoned that if the section of the trains that was passing was near the rear of the column, fewer escorts would answer the attack. But he could not tell. For the attack to succeed, Jones determined, as had Captain Ulrich Dahlgren near Greencastle earlier in the day, that he must strike the column when an artillery section and cavalry escort were actually passing the crossroads. A sudden assault driven home with speed and force would not allow the artillery to get into position to open fire; Jones's troopers would have to overwhelm the artillery support and capture it quickly. If the artillery section were allowed to escape, it would come into battery, open fire, and decimate Jones's command. The next available enemy artillery would be about one mile away. Jones believed that he had enough men to hold at bay the mounted escorts he observed. But his force would have to work fast in order to divert a sufficient number of wagons and ambulances toward Mercersburg before it was in danger of being overwhelmed or checked by artillery brought up from the rear or back from the head of the long column.

The whole command was brought forward under cover of the long ridge. Jones ordered Lieutenant Passegger of the First New York to take his detachment and, on Jones's signal, attack the artillery section and mounted escorts then approaching the crossroads. Passegger's men would have to overwhelm and capture the artillery before it could be unlimbered, then hold at bay any mounted escorts. Lieutenant Woodruff of the First New York was directed to spread his detachment out along the trains and, at gunpoint, order the drivers to steer their vehicles off the Cumberland Valley Turnpike and onto the road to Mercersburg. Lieutenant Irwin's detachment of the Twelfth Pennsylvania Cavalry was held in reserve behind the long ridge; it would be used to take control of the wagons and ambulances as well as any ordnance as they were diverted onto the Mercersburg Road in order to expedite their movement. Irwin's detachment would also serve as a reserve in the event that the mission ran into trouble.[31]

Just passing Cunningham's Crossroads was the ambulance train carrying the wounded of Davis's Brigade, Heth's Division, under the care of, among others, Dr. LeGrand Wilson. Behind it was the ambulance train of Pettigrew's Brigade. Most of the other brigade ambulance trains of Heth's Division had already gone by. The quartermaster, subsistence, and ordnance trains of Heth's Division had passed the crossroads ahead of the ambulances. For Wilson and the wounded under his care, it had been a nightmarish and agonizing twenty-four hours. Though Imboden's own trains had been attacked at Greencastle earlier in the day, most in the caravan were feeling some relief that they were so close to Williamsport. The protection of the trains to Williamsport was left entirely to Imboden's mounted escort, consisting of squadrons from Colonel Smith's Sixty-second Virginia Mounted Infantry and the interspersed artillery battery sections from Hill's Corps.[32]

In the ambulances approaching Cunningham's Crossroads were some of Heth's finest soldiers. Among them were Colonels Leventhorpe and Stone, Captains Archer and Williams, Lieutenant Colonel Lane, Majors R. O. Reynolds and Alfred H. Belo, and Captain T. Edwin Betts of the Fortieth Virginia; Captain C. E. Chambers of the Thirteenth Alabama; Captain J. H. Buchanan of the Second Mississippi; and Captain S. W. Brewer of the Twenty-sixth North Carolina. A host of other wounded were from Davis's and Pettigrew's Brigades and Wright's and Wilcox's Brigades of Anderson's Division; a few were from Fitzhugh Lee's cavalry brigade.[33]

In one ambulance in the train of Pettigrew's Brigade were Lieutenant Lucas, Captain Hughes, and Lucas's slave. Their vehicle was rattling along behind Leventhorpe's leading ambulance in Pettigrew's train. Traveling with the wounded of Pettigrew's Brigade was Dr. Franklin J. White of the Forty-seventh North Carolina.[34]

Also approaching Cunningham's Crossroads were two captured U.S.

3-inch ordnance rifles and one 10-pound Parrott rifle of Captain Victor Maurin's Donaldsonville, Louisiana, Artillery, Garnett's Battalion, led by Lieutenant R. Prosper Landry. The horses drawing the guns, caissons, and battery wagons were jaded and in desperate need of fodder. The trains of that battery had been struck back at Greencastle. Major Charles Richardson, in command of the five artillery pieces of Garnett's Battalion that were attached to Imboden's escort, had been riding hard all night through the driving rain and intense lightning trying to locate Imboden in order to procure fresh horses to draw his artillery. As Jones's New Yorkers and Pennsylvanians prepared to attack, Richardson was galloping down the turnpike just north of Cunningham's Crossroads and moments behind his own three-gun section under Lieutenant Landry.[35]

Darkness was quickly falling; it would be the ally of the attackers, but they had to move swiftly. Jones turned to the two detachments selected to carry out the strike and admonished the men: "If you get into close quarters, use your sabres. Don't strike, but thrust!" Sabres were unsheathed, and pistols were cocked and held at the ready.[36]

Jones gave the signal, and the two columns of Union cavalry galloped over the ridge and into the Confederate wagons, ambulances, and walking wounded above and below Cunningham's Crossroads. Woodruff's detachment, in a flurry of small-arms fire, raced toward the column of ambulances just behind Dr. Wilson's section. From inside his ambulance, Wilson saw Woodruff's column bearing down on the ambulances behind him. Wilson was likely riding with Colonel Stone of Davis's Brigade. Quickly, he jumped out of his vehicle, yelling and waving at the startled and confused walking wounded beside the trains to get out of the road and seek cover in the woods. About one hundred wounded soldiers clambered over the railroad tracks and the tall post and rail fence on the east side of the turnpike and escaped into a large woodlot.[37]

Passegger directed his command to attack the artillery battery section and mounted escorts approaching Cunningham's Crossroads. The suddenness of the thrust, coupled with the desperate condition of the horses drawing the guns, prevented Landry from running all of the guns down the turnpike to avoid their capture. The ten-pound Parrott rifle with its caisson managed to escape, but both ordnance rifles were spiked so they and their caissons were abandoned. Jones, for the moment, had eliminated any threat to his columns from Confederate artillery.[38]

The mounted escort protecting the ambulance trains of Heth's Division, like Landry's Donaldsonville Artillery, was taken by surprise. Passegger's quick action stunned them. The first burst of gunfire from the Union troopers caused the Confederates to recoil. A number of the escorts, all from the Sixty-second Virginia Mounted Infantry, fell from their horses. Within Passegger's command, two privates were killed by Confederate return fire.[39]

Woodruff's detachment, "with uplifted sabres and cocked pistols," galloped up to the wagons and ambulances approaching the crossroads and yelled to the drivers to "turn off there!"—pointing to the road to Mercersburg. What the detachment struck were the ambulance trains of Pettigrew's and Davis's Brigades that included some wounded soldiers from Wright's and Wilcox's Brigades. The wagons and ambulances that were halted north of the crossroads were ordered by Woodruff's troopers to move up the road to Mercersburg. The walking wounded who could not get out of the way were stopped and, at gunpoint, told to get into the wagons and ambulances. Caught in the melee was Major Richardson, who was just riding into Cunningham's Crossroads when the attack began. Overtaken by the Union troopers and ordered to dismount, the frustrated major was hurried toward the muddy Hagerstown-Mercersburg Road at gunpoint to join the growing column of Confederate prisoners.[40]

Colonel Lane was in desperate shape. He had been suffering from wounds to his head, throat, and mouth and had been unable to eat since 1 July. The wounds were terribly inflamed. His surgeons, particularly Dr. Warren, never believed that he could survive. Yet the moment Lane realized that the trains had been struck, he climbed out of the ambulance, mounted his horse, which had been tied to the vehicle, and escaped, riding east to the railroad right-of-way and then south beside the turnpike.[41]

Dr. Wilson's ambulance had just passed the crossroads when the attack began and escaped capture. It continued on toward Williamsport. Seized by Jones's Union troopers were the wounded Colonel Leventhorpe, Captain Archer, and Captain Williams, along with officers and enlisted men from the Eleventh, Twenty-sixth, and Fifty-fifth North Carolina; First and Fourteenth Tennessee; Second, Eleventh, and Forty-second Mississippi; Ninth and Thirteenth Alabama; Third, Twenty-second, and Forty-eighth Georgia; and Fortieth Virginia and Fourth Virginia Cavalry. Also among the captured Confederates were Dr. Franklin J. White and Chaplain M. W. Frierson, a Presbyterian cleric, and his badly wounded brother, Private W. V. Frierson, both of the Second Mississippi. Seized as well was the ambulance carrying Lieutenant Lucas, Captain Hughes, and Lucas's slave. Jones's troopers, at gunpoint, directed the column of wagons, ambulances, and walking wounded up the road to Mercersburg.[42]

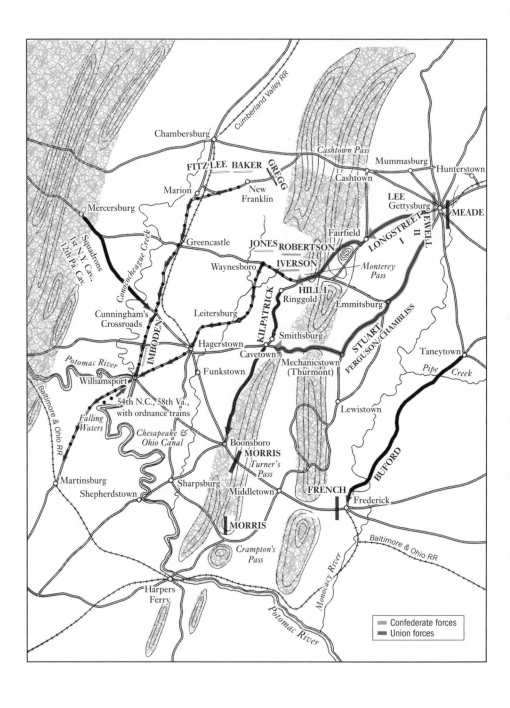

Confederate forces
Union forces

While the wagons and ambulances were moving up the Hagerstown-Mercersburg Road, Captain Jones observed a large covered wagon, drawn by six mules and filled with wounded Confederates, sitting by the side of the road, its driver having escaped. Spotting a young African American—either a wounded soldier's slave or one of the many wagoners who accompanied the trains—standing nearby, Jones asked, "Can you drive that team?"

The man said that he could.

Jumping into the driver's seat, the teamster yelled to his helpless passengers: "By golly, you toted me off, now I tote you off." Laughing, he shouted at the mule team and began to drive the wagon full of wounded into the melancholy procession toward Mercersburg.[43]

After losing his horse in the exchange of gunfire with the escorts guarding the trains, one New York trooper sought safety in an old barn by the side of the road. When he opened the door, he discovered that the barn was filled with wounded Confederates who had left the road seeking to escape capture. The Confederates, obviously more startled than the Union trooper, threw up their hands, crying, "We surrender!"

"All right," said the fast-thinking New Yorker, "just stay right here 'til I can take care of you."

With that, the trooper departed to find another refuge for himself. Another trooper who had lost his horse managed to pick up thirteen wounded Confederates in the fields and along the roadside as he worked his way back to his command on the Mercersburg Road.[44]

What needed to happen for the Union mission to succeed did happen. The Confederate artillery was overwhelmed by the attack; the mounted escorts recoiled and then had to reorganize their ranks before launching a counterattack. It was all the time that the two Union detachments needed to direct the trains off the turnpike and onto the Hagerstown-Mercersburg Road.

The Confederate mounted infantrymen, however, were being reinforced every minute by escort squads from up and down the long line of ambulances and wagons. Major Alexander W. Vick, Heth's chief quartermaster, helped coordinate a response to the Union assault by calling for the mounted escorts to hurry to the point of attack. More assistance was on the way. From

MAP 8.1   5 July 1863, afternoon.
Imboden's trains are attacked at Cunningham's Crossroads; Stuart with Ferguson and Chambliss attack Kilpatrick at Smithsburg, while Hill's Corps reaches Monterey Pass, Longstreet's Corps enters Fairfield, and Ewell's Corps withdraws from Gettysburg. Kilpatrick hurries to Boonsboro.

more than two miles down the trains near Williamsport, Major Nathaniel E. Scales, chief quartermaster of Pender's Division, galloped to the sound of the gunfire, bringing with him elements of Company H, Eighteenth Virginia Cavalry, led by Sergeant Charles Rosebrock.[45]

With a skirmish line spread out in front, the Confederates finally mounted a ferocious counterattack against the rear of Jones's rapidly withdrawing columns. Passegger and Woodruff acted quickly and effectively. Aided by Lieutenant Irwin and some of his Pennsylvanians, they drew up their detachments in the fields behind the captured wagons, ambulances, and artillery pieces. In the closeness and confusion of the brief but fierce contest, Major Richardson was rescued by troopers from the Sixty-second Virginia Mounted Infantry. The thrust of the scattered contingents from the Sixty-second Virginia, though, was not strong enough to recover all that had been lost. Jones's command suffered several casualties, including Irwin who was slightly wounded, but beat back the Confederate attack.[46]

In the confusion and gunfire, the ambulance carrying Lieutenant Lucas and Captain Hughes managed to escape. Its driver turned onto a "byroad" and ran the team of horses pulling the vehicle at breakneck speed hoping to outrun the Union cavalrymen. The road was extraordinarily rough, causing the two wounded officers excruciating pain and anguish. When out of sight of the Union troopers, with darkness falling, the driver continued to urge the horses onward, even though he had no idea of the direction in which they were heading. Lucas's slave had tried to obtain food for the suffering officers but with little success. Over the past two days, he had been able to give them only a single cup of coffee. The lives of the two youthful officers were slowly ebbing away.[47]

Most of Irwin's detachment of Pennsylvanians rode among the captured ambulances and wagons to keep them moving as fast as possible up the muddy Hagerstown-Mercersburg Road. As the Confederate counterthrust died out, Jones's command and its vast prize vanished up the road to Mercersburg and into the darkness.[48]

The alarm had spread up and down the Confederate column. Major Benjamin F. Eshleman, who was with Captain Joe Norcom's forward section of the Washington Artillery two miles back up the turnpike, heard the gunfire. He advanced that section of his artillery down the road to the sound of the guns. By the time Eshleman and his command arrived, however, the fighting had ended, and Jones's command had ridden out of range. Eshleman assumed command of the shattered division trains and their escorts, closed up the column, and got them moving again toward Williamsport.[49]

Young Willis Lea of the Eleventh Mississippi had been accompanying the trains on horseback. Although slightly wounded, he had served the quartermasters of Heth's Division as part of a detail that directed the trains. Exhausted, Lea had stopped at a house to rest. The farmer had kindly taken him inside. He was relaxing in an upstairs bedroom within view of the trains when the Union cavalry attacked. Miraculously, the farmer had taken his horse to the barn, for, when the Irwin's troopers entered the house, they never suspected that an enemy soldier was upstairs. As soon as the Confederate counterattack cleared the area, Lea saddled up his horse and rode back to the trains. Had he not sought refuge in the house, he undoubtedly would have been taken prisoner by Jones's command.[50]

Jones and his command now headed toward Mercersburg hauling a substantial Confederate prize: 100 wagons and ambulances; more than 300 horses and mules; 653 prisoners, 308 of whom were badly wounded; and two 3-inch ordnance rifles and their caissons. Once again, the "debris of Winchester" had struck.[51]

After an eleven-mile journey, the caravan reached Mercersburg at about midnight. "The whole town turned out to see the sight," recalled the Reverend Dr. Philip Schaff, of the German Reformed Theological Seminary, who was startled from his sleep by the noise. Schaff was asked if the seminary building could be used as a hospital for the captured Confederates, as they "were too severely wounded or exhausted to be transported farther that night." He agreed.

Schaff helped unload the wounded. Many were taken to the large brick, four-story seminary building and others to the brick Methodist Episcopal church on Park Street, the barn of a Dr. John King, and the house of a Leonard Leidy. Among those housed in the seminary building were Colonel Leventhorpe, Captain Archer, and Captain Williams; Captain C. E. Chambers of the Thirteenth Alabama; and Captain J. H. Buchanan of the Second Mississippi. With them were Dr. White and Chaplain Frierson, together with Frierson's brother and many others.[52]

In spite of the attack and severe losses, Imboden's trains pushed on toward Williamsport. The general recognized their vulnerability to another attack at Williamsport, for an enemy advance could be easily directed against them from three different roads: the Williamsport-Boonsboro Road, the Hagerstown-Williamsport Turnpike, and the Cumberland Valley Turnpike. Consequently, Imboden ordered the Fifty-fourth North Carolina to hold a position about a mile east of Williamsport along high ground north of the Williamsport-Boonsboro Road. Murchison's Tarheels, once in place, established picket posts well out on the Williamsport-Boonsboro Road and Hagerstown-Williamsport Turnpike. The regiment stacked arms. The soldiers observed the buildup of the defense lines throughout the evening of 5 July.[53]

What must have sorely troubled Imboden was the condition of his men. They were exhausted, and their horses were worn to a frazzle. All were starving. Adjutant John Hyde Cameron of the Eighteenth Virginia Cavalry rode into a field to feed his horse a sheaf of wheat as he entered Williamsport beside the trains. Cameron then "dropped to the wet and muddy ground and went into a deep sleep." Later that night he was awakened by Captain H. K. Cochran, quartermaster of the Fourteenth Virginia Cavalry, as the cavalry trains entered Williamsport. Cochran asked Cameron if he had had anything to eat. Cameron said that he had only had a slice of bread and some apple butter that "a kind little Yankee girl had given [him]." Cochran stopped one of his quartermaster wagons and cut off a "large chunk of fat meat" and "piled [Cameron's] haversack with crackers." He also filled his canteen with whiskey! Cameron quickly hunted up his messmates, Colonel George Imboden, Lieutenant Colonel David E. Beall, and Major Alexander W. Monroe, and they all had a "fine breakfast."[54]

The arrival at Williamsport of David Washington Pipes of Buck Miller's Third Company, Washington Artillery, was much like that of Cameron's. Pipes was near the head of Longstreet's trains. The artillerymen, he recalled, were "dead on their feet"; they had had no sleep and little or no food throughout the horrible journey. He saw an inviting front porch of a nearby house. Dismounting, he walked over to it and laid down. He "was soon asleep, wet and muddy; and there [he] slept until the rear guard came by and woke [him] up." All of Major Eshleman's Washington Artillery, once assembled, went into camp in the fields north of Williamsport.[55]

No sooner had the cannoneers of the Washington Artillery unlimbered their horses than Imboden ordered them to limber up again and occupy positions protecting the eastern approaches to the town on both the Hagerstown-Williamsport Turnpike and the Williamsport-Boonsboro Road. At about 3:00 A.M. on 6 July, Eshleman directed Captain "Buck" Miller, Lieutenant Andrew Hero, and Lieutenant Frank McElroy of the Third Company, with one section of Napoleons, and Captain Joe Norcom, Lieutenant Henry A. Battles, and Lieutenant George E. Apps of the Fourth Company, with one howitzer and one Napoleon, to go into battery along high ground about one mile east of town along the Williamsport-Boonsboro Road. Eshleman then instructed Captain Charles W. Squires of the First Company, with one Napoleon commanded by Lieutenant John M. Galbraith, and Captain John B. Richardson Jr. of the Second Company, with a section of Napoleons under Lieutenant Samuel Hawes and one 3-inch ordnance rifle, into position along the high ground northeast of Williamsport covering the Hagerstown-Williamsport Turnpike.[56]

At dawn on 6 July Imboden ordered Captain Pegram's Company F, Twenty-first Virginia, to move to the right and deploy along the high ground south of the Williamsport-Boonsboro Road and to the right of Buck Miller's and Joe Norcom's Napoleons and howitzer. The Fifty-eighth Virginia, having been relieved of its duty along the Cumberland Valley Turnpike, marched on the double-quick down the turnpike to Williamsport. When the tired infantrymen appeared north of town, Imboden directed them to proceed out Potomac Street to the heights northeast of Williamsport and fill the defense line south of Captain Squires's guns and to the left of Murchison's Tarheels. Once in position, the men in Pegram's Company and the Fifty-eighth Virginia were told to stack arms.[57]

Imboden knew that he was in enemy country and that every civilian was a potential informant. If the Union forces had any indication of the weak state of his command and the size of the trains that it was protecting, they would attack. Captain Pegram was thus ordered to establish a picket guard well out along the Williamsport-Boonsboro Road, relieving Murchison's Tarheels. The Fifty-eighth Virginia, once in line, established picket posts along the Hagerstown-Williamsport Turnpike to prevent anyone from leaving Williamsport.[58]

Pegram ordered Sergeant William S. Archer Jr. to take a picket guard out the Williamsport-Boonsboro Road and establish a post several hundred yards in front of the defense lines. One of those chosen to accompany Archer was Private John Worsham. Archer and his picket guard were to enforce Imboden's strict orders to prevent anyone from leaving the town.

After the picket guard had been established, a young woman and boy, both on horseback, passed the post heading into Williamsport. In less than two hours the woman was observed riding out of Williamsport on the Williamsport-Boonsboro Road. As she reached the picket guard, the sentinel stopped her and called for assistance from other members of the guard. Private Worsham stepped up to the woman and asked the purpose of her visit. She said that she had been in town on business and was simply returning home. Worsham informed her that he was under orders not to allow anyone to leave Williamsport, but that he would accompany her to Pegram so she could discuss her situation with him.

The two walked back to the high ground on the south side of the road, where Worsham related the young woman's explanation to Pegram. Nearby, Private Michael Ward, a straggler from the Third Georgia, turned to Pegram and said, "You ain't going to let that young woman pass are you? She is a spy, come in here to find out all she can, and now she is going back to tell the Yankees." Without a moment's hesitation, Pegram refused the woman permission to pass the picket guard. Satisfied, Worsham returned to his post along the Williamsport-Boonsboro Road. The young woman followed him, demanding to see the senior officer at Williamsport. Worsham told her that he was under orders to serve picket duty. Sergeant Archer stepped in and agreed to escort the lady back to town, where she could speak with General Imboden. Imboden refused her permission to leave, and there the matter ended.[59]

Having finally arrived in Williamsport on foot, Major Charles Richardson reported to Imboden's headquarters and was ordered to ride up to the defense lines that were forming east of town and select positions for his artillery pieces that had accompanied Imboden's trains. Richardson returned to his artillery camp north of town. There he found Captain Joseph D. Moore of the Huger, Virginia, Artillery with his two 3-inch ordnance rifles, the caissons of which had been abandoned during the difficult journey to Williamsport. Richardson ordered Captain Moore's two rifles to follow him. They were hitched to the limbers and quickly moved out the Hagerstown-Williamsport Turnpike and across the heights northeast of Williamsport to a position between the Hagerstown-Williamsport Turnpike and the Williamsport-Boonsboro Road near the right flank of the Fifty-eighth Virginia.

No sooner had Richardson placed Moore's two rifles in position than Lieutenant Landry, under Richardson's orders, arrived along the defense lines with his one remaining ten-pound Parrott rifle of the Donaldsonville, Louisiana, Artillery. Likely showing his deep frustration at all the losses in his batteries, Richardson directed Landry to place his one remaining Parrott rifle in position beside the two ordnance rifles of Captain Moore.[60]

Captain James F. Hart's four-gun South Carolina Battery was the last artillery unit to arrive in Williamsport. Sometime near midmorning, 6 July, Imboden ordered Hart to proceed out the Hagerstown-Williamsport Turnpike. Hart's Battery assumed position along the heights northeast of Williamsport in the midst of the Fifty-eighth Virginia, to the right of Captain Squires's four-gun battery of the Washington Artillery and to the left of Captain Moore's three rifles.[61]

After Moore's and Hart's Batteries fell into line, Colonel Murchison ordered four companies of his Fifty-fourth North Carolina to remain north of the Williamsport-Boonsboro Road to help support those guns, while the rest of the regiment marched into a position south of the Williamsport-Boonsboro Road and to the right of Buck Miller's Washington Artillery guns where there was no infantry other than Pegram's small command.[62]

Imboden had managed to get his trains to Williamsport; he had even established a defensive perimeter east and north of town to protect them. It had been a heroic effort. The stage was set, though, for the ultimate test. Imboden knew that he would be attacked; he also knew that Lee valued those trains in Williamsport as much as the army itself. Without them, the army had no future.

Nine

The cutting and slashing
was beyond description

Early on the morning of 6 July there was action at the rear of Lee's columns of infantry and artillery. Ewell's Corps remained at the rear, although Lee had originally ordered it to take the lead that day. But that was not practicable. The previous night the men had bivouacked about one and one-half miles west of Fairfield. All night long the trains accompanying Ewell's Corps had been escorted through Monterey Pass by the Eleventh Virginia Cavalry. At dawn, Early's Division took up the line of march toward Monterey Pass, followed by Johnson's. Rodes's Division brought up the rear. Early's and Rodes's Divisions switched positions in order to provide "fresher" troops at the rear. A dense mist covered the area, reducing visibility; the morning was very dark. From all appearances it would be another rainy day.[1]

Just behind Rodes's Division was the Union Sixth Corps with all of its artillery batteries in position on a ridgeline facing the Confederate rear guard. The rear guard of Rodes's Division was formed by the battered little brigade of North Carolinians led by Brigadier General Junius Daniel.[2]

In an effort to test the strength of the Confederate rear guard, General Sedgwick moved forward the leading brigade of his First Division, commanded by Brigadier General Thomas H. Neill. Colonel McIntosh's cavalry brigade rode ahead of the infantry, feeling its way through the heavy fog. In a dense wood near the mountain base, Union troops came upon Daniel's skirmishers, who withdrew nearer to the brigade's battle lines. The Forty-fifth North Carolina, formerly Daniel's own regiment, was ordered to occupy a small knoll on the left front of Daniel's Brigade that was covered with tall wheat. That morning the regiment was commanded by Captain James A. Hopkins, a twenty-nine-year-old physician from Rockingham County, North Carolina, who had formerly commanded Company E of the regiment.

Hopkins's colonel, John Henry Morehead, had died of typhoid on 26 June at Martinsburg, West Virginia. Unbeknownst to Hopkins, his wounded lieutenant colonel, Samuel H. Boyd, had been captured at Monterey Pass by Kilpatrick's cavalrymen about thirty hours before. A total of 219 officers and men of the regiment had been killed or wounded at Gettysburg, and Hopkins was now the senior officer of the Forty-fifth.[3]

As Hopkins's regiment approached the knoll, he found it occupied by Union infantry. A Union officer called out, demanding Hopkins's surrender. The Union officer clearly chose the wrong man on whom to make such a demand. Hopkins turned to his gaunt and muddy veterans and yelled: "Fix bayonets!" The men responded with alacrity. Then came the command: "Charge bayonets!" The soldiers' muskets, with bayonets fixed, were brought into position pointing toward the enemy. "Charge!" yelled Hopkins. The little regiment, with drums rolling, sprang forward in battle ranks, driving before them the startled Union infantrymen. Lieutenant James E. Green, of the Fifty-third North Carolina, who was nearby, recalled: "I heard [the enemy officers] give the command—Double quick, & they were going back the way they come from." There was a brisk exchange of gunfire. Daniel's Brigade lost two killed, two wounded, and five missing. General Doles's Georgians were sent forward to the right of Daniels's Brigade to check another advance by the opposite end of Neill's lines. In a short exchange of gunfire, Doles lost none of his men.[4]

Lee's infantry columns, still led by Hill's Corps, extended from near Waynesboro all the way back to within two miles of Fairfield—about twenty miles. Elements of the trains of Johnson's and Anderson's Divisions remained north of Hagerstown just ahead of the infantry columns. Early's trains were approaching Hagerstown while Rodes's trains were close to Williamsport. The cavalry brigades of General Robertson, General Jones, Colonel Ferguson, and Colonel Chambliss, along with J. E. B. Stuart himself, were mostly situated in and near Leitersburg. There Grumble Jones had finally located his brigade merely hours before; the Eleventh Virginia Cavalry rejoined the brigade at 1:00 A.M. after being in the saddle for almost thirty-six hours. Jones had informed Stuart of Imboden's arrival at Williamsport. As the trains of Early's Division moved through Hagerstown, Stuart directed Chambliss to take his brigade ahead on the direct road into town. Robertson, with his two regiments, was ordered to follow Chambliss. Stuart, in the meantime, proceeded with Ferguson's Brigade to Chewsville, east of Hagerstown, while the tired and muddy Grumble Jones and his brigade covered the trains entering Hagerstown from the direction of Funkstown to the southeast.[5]

While the Confederate rear guard stalled Sedgwick's probe at dawn on 6 July near Fairfield and four Confederate cavalry brigades rode toward or to the east of Hagerstown, General John Buford's three Union cavalry brigades were slowly moving toward Turner's Pass from the bivouac site of the previous night west of Frederick. The past two days had been nothing short of hell for many of Buford's troopers. The ordeal began for General Wesley Merritt's Reserve Brigade as the fighting ended at Gettysburg. Merritt's men had "stood to horse" along Meade's left flank south of Gettysburg through the night of 3 July and the wee hours of 4 July. All of Merritt's regiments save one were U.S. regulars. Accompanying them was Captain William M. Graham's Battery K, First U.S. Artillery. The brigade had patrolled the area from Middletown to Frederick to Mechanicstown and Emmitsburg from 28 June to 1 July. Elements of the Sixth U.S. Cavalry of the brigade had galloped to Fairfield on the afternoon of 3 July only to be cut up. That evening, Meade had ordered all of Merritt's weary troopers to retrace their line of march back to Frederick to join Buford's two brigades, which had been ordered to march there from the army's supply depot at Westminster.[6]

At about 5:00 A.M. on 4 July, Merritt had ordered his men to "mount up." The troopers got under way, but it became a terrible ordeal. The horses in the brigade had been without fodder for nearly five days; literally "hundreds of [them] dropped down" while on the march and were left on the roadside with their saddles, blankets, and harness still on them. Horseless troopers, with their carbines slung across their shoulders, trudged along on foot beside the mounted columns, slowing the march to a snail's pace. Because Merritt's Brigade had been separated from its quartermaster and subsistence trains for so long, it was on the brink of collapse.

Just past noon, rain began to fall in sheets and the roads became quagmires. Horses broke down and dropped to the muddy roads at an alarming rate. Finally, a halt was called at Mechanicstown. Merritt's men dismounted and lay down in the wet fields and beside the road with their bridles tied to their wrists. After a four-hour rest, Merritt ordered them to "mount up" again, and the column slowly made its way south through the "merciless storm that beat down upon [them]."[7]

Meanwhile, bugles blew "mount up" in Westminster, twenty-five miles east. There, Buford's two brigades—those of Colonel William Gamble and Colonel Thomas S. Devin—"stood to horse" for nearly three hours. With those two horse brigades was Lieutenant John H. Calef's Battery A, Second U.S. Artillery. Unlike Merritt's men and horses, Buford's had not only rested, they had been able to eat. The horses had even been reshod. At about

4:00 P.M. on 4 July Buford ordered his two brigades to move onto the road to Frederick through the driving rain.[8]

South of Mechanicstown, Merritt's troopers continued their snail's pace down the muddy road toward Frederick through the dark, rainy night. At 3:00 A.M. on 5 July a halt was mercifully called, and the men—without tents, fires, or food—threw themselves on the wet ground to sleep. East of Frederick Buford's two brigades also rested in the darkness.[9]

At 7:00 A.M., 5 July, Merritt's tired and hungry force resumed its journey to Frederick, finally arriving at about noon. Buford's two brigades followed at about 7:00 P.M. The long columns of wet, hungry, and jaded men and horses halted about one mile west of the town in the fields along the National Road.[10]

Frederick was a welcome sight to Buford's men, particularly those in Merritt's Brigade. Private Samuel J. B. V. Gilpin of the Third Indiana, in Gamble's Brigade, recalled girls gathered along the streets singing patriotic songs, including "When This Cruel War Is Over," as the columns moved through town. Gilpin did not even know it was Sunday until he saw people going to church.[11]

Some supplies destined for French's Division had arrived from Baltimore on the Baltimore and Ohio Railroad spur line. Merritt's men at last had something to eat; some of their horses could be fed and some could be reshod. Still, though, the supply system for Meade's army had not shifted to Frederick, so what was available was sparse. Gamble's and Devin's men and their horses could eat and rest, although some of the horses were so worn down that they and their troopers were pulled out of service altogether.[12]

John Buford, the impulsive thirty-seven-year-old commander of the three Union brigades that dismounted west of Frederick, had been a member of the West Point class of 1848. His Woodford County, Kentucky, background placed him in a curious position; a cousin, Abraham Buford, was a Confederate brigadier general fighting under none other than General Nathan Bedford Forrest, and his wife's cousin was Colonel Basil W. Duke, brother-in-law of the noted Kentucky Confederate, General John Hunt Morgan, and commander of the Second Kentucky Cavalry in Morgan's Division. Buford, it seems, was not moved by such relations; family ties apparently did not sway him from what he perceived as his duty to the Union.[13]

On the night of 5 July Buford's pickets reported that numerous civilians were seeking passage through their encampment. Company G of the Sixth Pennsylvania of Merritt's Brigade had been ordered by Buford to serve as provost guard, and during the course of its duties it apprehended numerous persons attempting to pass through the cavalry encampment or linger-

Brigadier General
John Buford.
Library of Congress,
Washington, D.C.

ing just outside of it. Buford was concerned that such persons were enemy informants. Following protocol, those who were apprehended were brought before him for questioning and then routinely sent to Colonel Andrew T. McReynolds's headquarters in Frederick. The cases were ultimately disposed of by the gregarious General French. Buford expressed profound frustration over the situation and declared, after sending several suspicious persons to the rear, that the next one brought before him would not receive such deference. Enemy informants would lurk in his wake with impunity, he believed, unless an example was made of one of them.

Later that night the outer pickets arrested a man who claimed that his name was Richardson. According to the *New York Times*, the pickets, on examination, found notes in the captive's boots from General Ewell, among other Confederates, vouching for him. Whether such notes were actually found is not known, but Richardson allegedly had been seen lurking near Union encampments before; he had all the attributes of an enemy informant. On questioning, he told Buford that he was from Baltimore and that he had several sons in Lee's army and was trying to get back home after attempting to locate them. Buford did not believe the story and was heard to remark: "Hang him, hang him forthwith. If I send him to Washington they'll send him back promoted." He handed the man over to the provost guard with instructions to quietly hang him before morning. The captive pled with his captors and then tried to escape. Apprehended quickly, he was taken to a tree along the National Road. There a rope was thrown over a strong branch and placed around his neck. Three troopers pulled the captive off the ground and the rope was fastened to the tree.[14]

Sergeant William H. Redman of the Twelfth Illinois in Gamble's Brigade, unaware of the problems at division headquarters, tied his horse to a stake that he had made out of a fence rail and hammered into the ground and then fed the mud-splattered animal. It was then about 9:00 P.M. Like the other rain-soaked troopers in Buford's command, he had gathered up hay from the recently cut fields where he camped and made a bed on the wet ground near the stake where his horse was tethered. "Never slept better in my life," Redman wrote to his mother the next day.[15]

Around 9:15 P.M., 5 July, General French's headquarters in Frederick received word that earlier in the day leading elements of the wagon train that had escaped Kilpatrick's midnight attack at Monterey Pass had been sighted in Hagerstown. By that evening Major Harman's reserve trains, followed by Ewell's trains, had been on the road to Hagerstown for more than forty-two hours. Informants told French that nearly 500 Confederate wagons, loaded with sick and wounded as well as military stores, guarded by about 150 infantry, 150 cavalry, and 3 pieces of "inferior-looking artillery," together with from 3,000 to 5,000 head of cattle, passed through Hagerstown between 11:00 P.M., 4 July, and 4:00 A.M., 5 July. The trains were heading toward Williamsport on the Hagerstown-Williamsport Turnpike but were unable to cross the Potomac because of high water. The wagon trains were believed to have been directed to Falling Waters so they could cross the river on the pontoon bridge that, unbeknownst to those leading them, had been destroyed.[16]

French forwarded the information to Buford and then wired it to General Halleck in Washington. He had been under considerable pressure from Halleck and the War Department to strike Lee a serious blow; the destruction of the pontoon bridge had not been enough. When French heard about all the trains traveling to Williamsport—where he knew they could not cross the river—he told Buford he believed that the time was ripe to attack.

Buford saw the opportunity as well. Based on the intelligence received, the trains seemed immense but lightly protected. Buford was confident that his three brigades and two batteries of artillery could attack effectively. But were there other Confederate forces in the vicinity? Neither French nor Buford knew. Under French's urging, Buford decided to move his command down the National Road to Boonsboro. At Boonsboro he would be able to pick up additional information from French's advanced brigade under General Morris at Turner's Pass; by midafternoon he would be in position to attack the trains outside of Williamsport if it seemed prudent to do so. Riders galloped westward to inform Morris and his pickets at Turner's Pass of Buford's operation and deliver the order for them to gather what intelligence they could.

On 6 July reveille sounded in Buford's camp at 3:00 A.M. As the sleepy, rain-soaked troopers arose, noncommissioned officers walked through the camps to make sure that all the men in their companies were awake. The troopers fed and watered their horses and prepared a meager breakfast. At four o'clock the bugle sounded "saddle-up," and soon the three brigades of Union cavalry—nearly 3,500 troopers—and their two 6-gun batteries of artillery were heading west in long columns on the National Road toward Boonsboro at the same time that Sedgwick's Sixth Corps was pressuring the rear guard of Rodes's Division outside of Fairfield. As they rode along the National Road, Buford's men came upon the lifeless body of the man who had called himself "Richardson" dangling from a tree. The sight left an indelible impression on the minds of many troopers; some recalled the scene in memoirs long after the war.[17]

Slightly west of Boonsboro and about seventeen miles west of Frederick, Judson Kilpatrick's Division was aroused at dawn on 6 July after the first real rest they had had in days. They were greeted by none other than Captain Ulrich Dahlgren and his company of regulars, who had just arrived after riding all through the night and wee morning hours across Franklin County, Pennsylvania, and Washington County, Maryland, trying to locate Union cavalry after their unsuccessful attempt to capture a portion of Imboden's trains almost twenty-four hours before. By then, the men and horses must have been in deplorable shape. Kilpatrick learned from scouts and civilian informants that elements of Lee's trains that he had attacked nearly thirty hours earlier were still moving through Hagerstown, protected by some Confederate cavalry and artillery. Dahlgren undoubtedly told Kilpatrick of the trains he had engaged on the Cumberland Valley Turnpike and of those passing through Hagerstown, as he had had to gallop through them to reach Kilpatrick. Couriers from Buford soon notified Kilpatrick that Buford's First Cavalry Division was approaching from Frederick.[18]

Kilpatrick determined to place his division in a position to strike the trains at Hagerstown if he could. By 9:00 A.M. he ordered his men to mount up and ride north along the National Road from Boonsboro to Hagerstown. Richmond's Brigade, along with Lieutenant Elder's Battery and Captain Ulrich Dahlgren's little command, led the advance, followed by Custer's Michigan Brigade and Lieutenant Pennington's Battery. Huey's Brigade followed, although it and Fuller's Battery had almost ceased to be an effective fighting force because of their continuous operations and lack of food, fodder, and horseshoes. Kilpatrick's movement appears to have been rather leisurely; no doubt he preferred to wait for Buford before actually launching an attack in order to confer with him about the appropriateness of the operation as well as enlisting Buford's cooperation. Kilpatrick thus moved his division close to Funkstown, six miles southeast of Hagerstown, but held off engaging the enemy.[19]

By midmorning Buford's column reached Middletown, about nine miles from Boonsboro; from there it began its slow ascent through the rugged Turner's Pass in the South Mountain range where General French had positioned Morris's Brigade and where a signal station had been established atop the ruins of a stone monument erected to the memory of George Washington in 1827 by the local citizenry. That monument overlooked the Cumberland Valley; from it enemy operations westward toward Williamsport could be observed. Passing through the gap made famous the previous autumn by the battles that preceded the desperate engagement at Sharpsburg, Buford's troopers could see the shallow graves of those who had fallen in that fighting. Many graves of the dead soldiers had been eroded by rain, snow, and wind, and their skeletal remains were fully visible.[20]

Buford's Brigades reached Boonsboro shortly after noon. As the column passed through that quaint town at the western foot of the mountains and at the head of Pleasant Valley, it met long lines of Confederate prisoners, mostly wounded, some on foot and others in captured wagons and ambulances, who had been seized by Kilpatrick's Division during the spectacular engagement atop Monterey Pass. In the vans were Lieutenant Colonels Boyd and Green; Colonel Kenan; Majors Blacknall, Lewis, and Hancock; Captains Bond and Wheeler; Drs. Brewer and Godwin; and more than a thousand others, including many African Americans. The prisoners were being led to Frederick by the Tenth Vermont, Morris's Brigade, which had guarded

Turner's Pass since 3 July. Sergeant Redman commented that "[the prisoners] looked as rough as ever." A soldier in the Fourteenth New Jersey nearby recalled that the captured Confederates "were very destitute and ragged [having had] scarcely anything to eat."[21]

West of Boonsboro, Buford's men halted their march in order to rest, water, and feed the horses and to make coffee and eat. The land was rough and undulating; the South Mountain range loomed in their rear, forming a backdrop that extended north as far as the eye could see. Buford's men could see the wigwag signal station atop the Washington Monument near Turner's Pass. What fences still stood in the area were torn down for horse stakes and campfires. Soon coffee pots were boiling on hundreds of campfires on either side of the muddy roadway. For most of the men, the meal consisted of nothing more than hard crackers, fried bacon, and coffee. Preferring to rest after eating his sparse rations, Redman noted that he was "too lazy to go to get more water to make coffee."[22]

Buford's Division occupied the site vacated at 9:00 A.M. by Kilpatrick's three brigades. Buford knew of Kilpatrick's location not only from French's advanced brigade but also from Kilpatrick's couriers. He sent a courier to tell Kilpatrick at Funkstown of his command's arrival in Boonsboro and of his intention to proceed to Williamsport to attack the trains arriving from Hagerstown.[23]

When Kilpatrick received Buford's note, he left his command and rode back to Boonsboro. Escorted to Buford's headquarters, Kilpatrick informed Buford of his intention to strike Hagerstown but said that he would place his force at Buford's disposal if he felt that it was needed. Buford supported Kilpatrick's proposal to attack Hagerstown if the prospects for success appeared to be good. After reviewing their respective tactical plans, the two commanders agreed to cooperate as the two operations unfolded. Kilpatrick quickly departed up the National Road to rejoin his command at Funkstown.[24]

On his return, Kilpatrick ordered Colonel Richmond and Lieutenant Elder's Battery to storm into the streets of Hagerstown. With the leading brigade rode Captain Dahlgren with his U.S. regulars. Custer's Brigade was directed to position itself along the turnpike leading from Hagerstown to Williamsport to cover Richmond's left flank and to be in position to assist Richmond or Buford. Huey's worn-out brigade and Fuller's Battery would remain in reserve. Richmond moved his column ahead four miles to a site just south of A. H. Hager's bone mill, a giant three-story stone structure south of town.[25]

In Hagerstown, a town of over four thousand inhabitants built along hills west of the South Mountain range, the Confederates had been alerted to the approach of Union cavalry. Earlier in the morning Colonel Chambliss had ordered Colonel Richard Turberville Beale's Ninth Virginia Cavalry forward to determine the enemy's whereabouts. Beale's horsemen had galloped all the way to the southern outskirts of the town. They had failed to spot any sign of the enemy then and so informed Chambliss. Beale, nevertheless, set about posting pickets along the roads leading into Hagerstown from the southeast and east. While posting his pickets south of Hager's Mill, Beale spotted Kilpatrick's Division approaching from Funkstown. It was about 1:30 P.M., and rain once again was falling. Riders were sent back to Chambliss with the urgent news.[26]

The National Road becomes Mulberry Street in Hagerstown just beyond Hager's Mill. As Colonel Richmond approached the mill, he ordered the First and Third Squadrons of Company A, Eighteenth Pennsylvania, and one squadron of the First West Virginia to prepare to move west one block below Mulberry Street to the Hagerstown-Sharpsburg Turnpike and attack. The Hagerstown-Sharpsburg Turnpike becomes South Potomac Street in Hagerstown; it is the town's main business street and climbs rather steeply uphill as it proceeds to the north end of town. The glory-hunting Captain Dahlgren requested permission to lead the assault. Kilpatrick agreed.[27]

As the long lines of blue troopers appeared near Hager's Mill, the cry "The Yankees are coming!" swept through the town. Lieutenant Hermann Schuricht of the Fourteenth Virginia had stopped for breakfast in the four-story Washington House hotel on Washington Street west of the city square. For the past two days he had been trying to find the field forges of Jenkins's Brigade so the lame horses could be reshod. Those forges were in Imboden's trains. With him were forty men. They had followed Imboden's trains and then turned toward Hagerstown. Unfortunately, most of their horses were jaded and lame. One of Schuricht's men ran inside, yelling that the Yankees were in town. Schuricht called his men together and marched them to Potomac Street to offer help. W. W. Jacobs, a resident of Franklin County, Pennsylvania, who was visiting Hagerstown that morning with two of his friends, ran to the Eagle Hotel in the center square and climbed to the roof to observe the expected clash of the two contending forces.[28]

Chambliss massed his North Carolinians and Virginians behind hastily constructed barricades in streets and alleys to resist the impending attack. That first line of defense in Potomac Street was established by a fifty-year-old, white-haired, and heavily bearded Virginia colonel named James Lucius Davis, commander of the Tenth Virginia Cavalry. An 1833 graduate of West

Colonel J. Lucius Davis, commander of the Tenth Virginia Cavalry. The Museum of the Confederacy, Richmond, Virginia

Point, Davis was "old army" through and through; he was tough and tough-minded. If he was told to hold a position, he would do so without respect to the odds or cost. Davis's barricades were near St. John's Evangelical Lutheran Church, an edifice that, in part, dated to 1796 and the town's early settlement. Davis positioned the Tenth Virginia and some of the Ninth Virginia along South Potomac Street and in the alleys between Antietam and Church Streets to receive the first onslaught, while other troopers were directed inside buildings and into the cupolas and steeples of nearby churches. The Second North Carolina and Thirteenth Virginia were placed in support well above the public square. Robertson's small brigade of two regiments was just entering the northern edge of town on North Potomac Street and was ordered by Chambliss to remain there in reserve.[29]

The trains of Johnson's and Anderson's Divisions had been stopped north of town. Those of Early already in town were lined up and taken back up the Hagerstown-Waynesboro Turnpike to await the outcome of the clash in the streets below. The wounded Charles Moore Jr. of the Fifth Louisiana remembered his ambulance being turned around north of Hagerstown and driven three miles up the turnpike. There he would wait with all the other trains until 10:00 P.M. Those trains below the town were hurried to Williamsport.[30]

Captain Frank Bond and his company of Marylanders had reached the northern outskirts of Hagerstown after an exhausting ride from Gettysburg when Bond was informed of a looming attack from the south. He had allowed his command to "break ranks" for an hour so the men and horses might have something to eat. He had told them to listen for a bugle call if they were needed. Bond himself was eating breakfast when he was alerted. When his bugler sounded "assembly," 46 of Bond's 109 men reported for duty; the others would eventually gallop toward Hagerstown to rejoin the command. In the meantime, Bond aligned his men in a column of fours and rode south, all the way to the town square behind Colonel Davis's Tenth Virginia. Beside Bond was his friend and compatriot, George W. Booth, adjutant of the First Maryland, who was still recovering from a serious wound but ready to do his duty.[31]

Another friend of Bond's appeared in Hagerstown. A visiting civilian named R. H. Harper Carroll, the brother of former Maryland governor John Lee Carroll, had been warned that an attack was imminent. Although he possessed only a pocket pistol, Carroll hailed Bond and asked if he could join his command. Bond told him to do so immediately. Carroll would not be the only civilian to enter the fight that was about to erupt in the streets of Hagerstown.[32]

Apart from Colonel Beale's men, who were mostly posted far to the front as pickets, the cavalrymen of Colonel Davis and Captain Bond formed the only defense line between the approaching Union forces and Robertson's little brigade and the remaining elements of the trains. Bond grew somewhat nervous about his position. He rode out in front of the barricade and down South Potomac Street to get a view of the approaching enemy. No sooner did he bring his horse to a halt than the blue columns became fully visible less than a mile away.[33]

Chambliss knew that his and Robertson's two small brigades and Bond's Marylanders were no match for a division of Union cavalry and two batteries of rifled guns, but he also had been notified that General Iverson's infantry brigade was marching to his support, although it might take several hours to arrive. Chambliss had already sent riders out the Smithsburg Road to find General Stuart with Jones's and Ferguson's Brigades, which he had been told were on their way from the direction of Smithsburg, to inform them that, because a whole Union cavalry division was fast approaching Hagerstown from the south, reinforcements were desperately needed.

J. E. B. Stuart, then with Colonel Ferguson's Brigade, was near Chewsville. When he learned of the threat to Hagerstown, he ordered Ferguson's Brigade to move toward the town with as much speed as possible. Grumble Jones's Brigade was directed south toward Funkstown. By the time Ferguson reached the hilly eastern end of Hagerstown, Jones's Brigade, if all went well, would be in position to enter the town from behind the Union columns. If Chambliss and Robertson could hold back the Union cavalry in the streets of Hagerstown, Ferguson and Jones could assail it from the flank and rear. The infantry would be arriving in a matter of hours. The Union threat simply had to be stalled until then.[34]

No sooner had Richmond's Union columns exhibited a menacing presence to Chambliss's Brigade south of Hagerstown than Ferguson's hard-riding troopers appeared on the road from Smithsburg accompanied by General Stuart. Spotting their approach, Richmond ordered Lieutenant Elder's Battery to take up a position along the high ground east of town near the impressive brick Hagerstown Female Seminary building to block the advancing Confederates. In minutes, Elder's six Parrott rifles came into battery and opened fire on Ferguson's men. Richmond then directed the Fifth New York to form in the rear of Elder's rifles. The First Battalion of the First Vermont was ordered forward to act as skirmishers in the east end of town in front of Elder's Battery, while the balance of that regiment was held south of town to assist in the operation against the gray cavalrymen barricaded on South Potomac Street.[35]

Responding to the movement of the enemy, Stuart ordered Chew's Battery to unlimber two of its rifled guns that had just arrived on the Smithsburg Road after being detached from Robertson's Brigade north of Hagerstown and to direct their fire at Elder's Union battery. Soon the eastern end of the town was rattled by the thunder of artillery fire. Confederate cannoneer George M. Neese described the artillery fire as "hot and lively." "The range was short," he recalled, "and [Elder's] ten-pound shrapnel whizzed fearfully and exploded all around us." One of Elder's well-aimed shells struck a limber chest in Chew's Battery causing a tremendous explosion.[36]

The artillery fire over the eastern end of Hagerstown terrified the inhabitants. For the past two years they had heard cannonading from distant fields in Washington County and even at Gettysburg, but they had never experienced a bombardment of their own town. From his vantage point atop the Eagle Hotel, W. W. Jacobs observed "the flying shells, which appeared like pigeons sailing in the air, reflecting the golden sun as they whirled and twisted in their angry flight, some bursting high in the air, others falling near the mark."[37]

After about fifteen minutes, the artillery fire slackened. Stuart urged Ferguson to press his brigade forward. The fighting spread through the eastern suburbs of the town. Augmented by squadrons from the First West Virginia, the elements of the Fifth New York and First Vermont and Elder's rifles would hold Ferguson's Brigade at bay for virtually the entire afternoon.[38]

Behind the Confederate barricades in South Potomac Street, Captain Bond galloped up to Colonel Davis. Artillery boomed in the distance and shells burst overhead. It was apparent that the Union cavalry was preparing to charge up South Potomac Street against Davis's barricaded defenders. Bond suggested that, instead of waiting for the attack, the Confederates should strike the mounted enemy on foot. "No body of mounted men in position [could] repel an impetuous assault," Bond argued. Davis listened but gave no orders; he had been directed by Chambliss to hold the barricades and that was what he would do. Bond grew even more nervous; looking at the men in the Tenth Virginia, he observed "that indescribable tremor pervading them." It convinced him that no matter how tough Davis was, his regiment and the Ninth Virginia "would not stand."[39]

Bond galloped back to his little command in the center square. He knew that his men could not hold their position if "a large body of troops in [his] front should retreat precipitately." He determined that he would wheel his command by fours to the right, turn down a side street the full length of his column, then wheel to the front again. If Davis's Virginians were driven back, Bond's force would be able to dash into South Potomac Street between them and the enemy and stop the attack.[40]

At about 2:30 P.M. Richmond ordered his three selected squadrons to charge up South Potomac Street toward the center square. Carbines and pistols were inspected, sabres were drawn from scabbards. Captain Dahlgren, his sabre unsheathed and tightly gripped in his hand, signaled to the nervous but eager troopers to follow him. Then with yells and shouts, Dahlgren's three squadrons galloped up South Potomac Street toward the barricades held by Davis's gray troopers. Gunfire erupted like a volcano. The assault drove Colonel Beale's Virginians up the street toward the barricades.[41]

Davis held his regiment together behind the barricades in the middle of the street. As the mounted troopers of the Ninth Virginia came racing back, closely pursued by Dahlgren's hard-charging squadrons, Davis urged his men to hold fast. He then spurred his horse forward, ordering the Tenth Virginia to charge. But Dahlgren's advance and Beale's retreating Virginians came upon Davis's men so fast that they were caught up in the confusion and overwhelmed.

Bond and all of his Marylanders had just reached a side street when Davis's men were attacked. Brandishing his sabre, Davis tried to steady his troops. It was fruitless. Davis's horse was killed and fell upon the brave colonel, pinning him to the street. He continued to defend himself with his sabre as Dahlgren's troopers passed over and around him. The Confederate force was overwhelmed by the sheer weight and number of the attackers. Davis was finally freed from beneath his dead horse by one of Dahlgren's men and taken prisoner.[42]

The routed Ninth and Tenth Virginia fled up Potomac Street. "Everyone knows the contagion of such a rout," recalled Bond, but his column of forty-six Marylanders withdrew in formation nevertheless. "[I] distinctly remember looking back and scanning the faces of my men and was encouraged to see no sign of excitement, nor do I believe it even occurred to one of them to hasten his movement unless so ordered." Bond intently watched his rear so he could "right-about" the "moment there was nothing between [his men] and the charging Federals." As soon as his rear was cleared, Bond yelled, "By fours, right about, charge!"[43]

It was a "tremendous struggle" for Bond's men, in column-of-fours, "to force their way around, crowded and pressed as they were by largely superior numbers that filled the street from house to house, and swirled around as a mountain torrent around a rock. The sections farthest from the enemy were much longer making the wheel than those who were first released from the pressure, and as each man dashed at full speed at the enemy the moment he could face them, the charge was made nearly in single file."

Dahlgren's troopers suddenly realized in the dense smoke that a body of Confederate cavalry was making the evolutions preparatory to bearing down on them. The Union force halted "in a confused mass in the street." One sergeant mounted on a "bob-tailed horse" boldly rode up to Bond while the Marylanders were getting into line. Bond raised his pistol and shot the sergeant off his horse. Bond remained on his horse in front of his men and ordered them forward. Quickly, he threw up his right hand, halting the Marylanders. "I distinctly remember stopping with a solid wall of blue in a semicircle in front of me," Bond recalled. "I fired several shots very rapidly, and noted a thin curtain of smoke that hung over this circular line, and knew I was under fire from it, but was untouched."

With one shot left in his pistol, Bond looked for an enemy officer: "Aiming to my left . . . [I] slowly swept the circle, and distinctly remember seeing heads inclined to right or left to avoid the expected shot. The last man to my extreme right was on the sidewalk, and endeavored to get his head behind a bow window. I fired at him and the bullet went through his cheeks from side-to-side, and he tumbled off his horse. I do not know whether he could speak English before then or not, but am certain I could not understand him afterwards."[44]

Chambliss's Brigade and Bond's Marylanders, aided by Robertson's undersized command, which was just getting into position, stiffened the resistance. The storm of bullets was almost indescribable. In places, fighting was hand to hand. Captain William C. Lindsey, color-bearer of Company A, Eighteenth Pennsylvania, and a large number of men in the three attacking Union squadrons were killed by the gunfire and the thrusts of sabres.[45]

As Robertson's Brigade was moving into position, Daniel B. Coltrane of the Fifth North Carolina saw a private in his company throw up his arms and fall from his horse. The gunfire was heavy, and Coltrane thought that the soldier had been shot. It was not until the fighting ended that night that Coltrane saw the trooper again and learned that he had become so frightened at the sight of the fighting in the street ahead that he purposefully fell off his horse. The soldier remarked, "I took the blind staggers and fell off my horse and lay there all day."[46]

In the midst of the gunfire, Captain Dahlgren left the remnant of the three squadrons in the town square and rode down South Potomac Street for reinforcements. He called upon Company D of the Eighteenth Pennsylvania to dismount and follow him. Riding up the middle of the street, Dahlgren led the troopers back toward the square. Soon some soldiers from the first three squadrons joined the reserves, tramping on the sidewalks. He ordered the men not to fire until he gave the signal. When they came within about three hundred yards of Chambliss's and Robertson's mounted cavalrymen, who were lined up just above the town square, the Confederates opened fire.

Although still mounted, Dahlgren miraculously was not struck by the small-arms fire. The attack finally reached the square. Dahlgren turned to his men and yelled, "Now boys, give it to them!" A burst of gunfire rang out, and bullets flew across the square. The already depleted Confederate cavalry regiments suffered sizable casualties. Emboldened by the apparent success of the Union effort, one Hagerstown citizen, armed with a musket, scurried out of a nearby house and fell in with Dahlgren's attackers, loading and firing as he ran.[47]

The Confederates grudgingly gave ground until they reached the Zion Reformed Church—the oldest church in the town—at the corner of West Church and North Potomac Streets. The Confederates dismounted and, from behind the churchyard fence and tombstones, poured volley after volley of carbine and pistol fire into the faces of Dahlgren's troopers. Then and there the armed Hagerstown citizen was shot down before he crossed the second block.[48]

W. W. Jacobs and his friends atop the Eagle Hotel had seen John F. Semple, a local artist, enter Marshall and Cranwell's store located across the public square and situate himself in an upper-story window. As the fighting intensified in the streets below, a stray bullet struck Semple in the head, killing him instantly. Private Samuel St. Clair of Company D, Eighteenth Pennsylvania, heard the voice of a woman from the upper-floor window of the store, who apparently saw Semple fall, crying, "Johnny is killed! Johnny is killed!"[49]

In the whir and buzz of the Confederate return fire, Dahlgren, mounted on his horse along the west side of the street and directing a group of his men to proceed toward the Oak Spring near Christ Reformed Church on West Franklin Street—where some Confederates were trying to flank the Union attackers—was wounded in the right leg. He thought that it was a glancing ball but quickly realized that he was losing blood too fast. It was a serious wound.[50]

Dahlgren's forward movement slowed. Then Colonel Richmond launched a third charge. A squadron composed of Companies L and M of the Eighteenth Pennsylvania, led by Captain Charles J. Snyder of the First Michigan, with Captain Enos J. Pennypacker and Captain Henry Clay Potter of Company M of the Eighteenth Pennsylvania, came galloping up South Potomac Street toward the melee in front of Christ Reformed Church. Richmond directed Companies A and D of the First Vermont to follow the attack and, if need be, cover any withdrawal. As Dahlgren observed the squadrons charging up South Potomac Street behind him, he waited for them to pass and then methodically turned his horse around and rode back down the bullet-swept street to report to his commander near Hager's Mill.[51]

This third attack was the most aggressive of the afternoon. W. W. Jacobs watched as the heavy, mounted columns, the troopers brandishing sabres, raced up the street and struck the Confederate defenses. The fighting for possession of the town became close and brutal. "The cutting and slashing," recalled Jacobs,

> was beyond description . . . the deadly conflict was waged in a hand-to-hand combat, with the steel blades circling, waving, parrying, thrusting and cutting—some reflecting the bright sunlight, others crimsoned with human gore—while the discharges of pistols and carbines was ter-

rific and the smoke through which we now gazed down through. On the scene below the screams and yells of the wounded and dying mingled with cheers and commands, the crashing together of the horses and the fiery flashes of small arms presented a scene such as words cannot fully portray.[52]

With his sabre Captain Snyder cut down three Confederate defenders in as many minutes. According to Jacobs, Snyder "struck the first man on his head with his sword, turned and thrust his sword through the body of another, withdrew it and struck another on the head and felled him to the ground." Snyder was then shot in the abdomen and cut down by a sabre blow to the head. At almost the same time, Captain Pennypacker was shot in the leg. His horse reared back and fell on top of him, severely injuring his other leg. Then Captain Potter's horse was killed, and he was wounded and captured along with his lieutenant, William H. Laws.[53]

The Confederate defenders brandished sabres. All joined in the fray. Colonel James B. Gordon's Fifth North Carolina of Robertson's Brigade charged into the bluecoats. Sergeant Hammond Dorsey of the First Maryland, mounted on a white mare, galloped full speed into the blue attackers, flailing his heavy sabre right and left, his head nearly leaning on his horse's neck. Dorsey, with at least twenty blows of his sword, killed five Union troopers, the last of whom was a bugler. Dorsey hacked and hacked at the bugler, who used the bugle to try to ward off the blows. The man's bloody frame fell to the ground, his bugle cut clean through in four or five places. "But for the bugle," Dorsey would later report, "[I] might have gotten two or three more." The Union attack, it seems, went no farther than West Franklin Street.[54]

Twenty-two-year-old Mary Louisa Kealhofer was in the cellar of her home during the fighting. "Lutie," as she was known to her family, was the daughter of George Kealhofer, president of the Hagerstown Gaslight Company, and his wife Mary. The Kealhofers were ardent Southern sympathizers. During Lee's invasion they had entertained Major William W. Blackford of General Stuart's staff with tea and had mingled with General Ramseur and some "old friends" in Lee's army, including Major Henry Kyd Douglas, who hailed from nearby "Ferry Hill Place" in Washington County. Only nine days earlier Lutie had been introduced to Generals Lee, Longstreet, and Pickett. It was different today. She took out her three-by-five-inch cloth-bound diary and nervously made an entry: "Afternoon. At this moment fighting is going on in our very town and balls are whizzing through the streets. I wonder at myself, my composure—oh God of Heaven have mercy upon us and deliver us from this terrible war."[55]

The fighting momentarily died down; skirmishers and snipers took over. Behind the Union lines the streets were cleared of the dead and wounded. The wounded Captain Snyder of the First Michigan and Captain Pennypacker of the Eighteenth Pennsylvania were carried into the Franklin House hotel on Potomac Street just north of the town square.[56]

At the southern edge of town, the Fifth Michigan was dismounted; the men stood beside their horses on the Hagerstown-Williamsport Turnpike. The commander of the first battalion of the regiment, Major Luther S. Trowbridge, was standing in front of his men and beside Kilpatrick when Dahlgren rode up and delivered his report to the division commander. Then, as Kilpatrick was giving instructions to his force, Dahlgren stated matter-of-factly, "General, I am hit." Weakened from loss of blood, Dahlgren dismounted and laid down on the ground to await medical attention. The badly wounded captain was soon placed in an ambulance and taken back to Boonsboro.[57]

All of the Union troopers in and north of the public square had dismounted. Chambliss's and Robertson's men who were still on their horses were ordered to dismount; they fell into line and opened fire. W. W. Jacobs scurried down from the roof of the Eagle Hotel and ran out into the public square to help carry the Union wounded to shelter. He had no sooner offered his aid than the gunfire increased again.[58]

Jacobs saw a Union trooper leading several Confederate prisoners to the rear. As the trooper passed, he handed Jacobs a musket, cartridge box, and cap box taken from one of the captives and told him to lend assistance. Jacobs entered the yard of a house a few doors from Christ Reformed Church on West Franklin Street. There, from behind an iron fence, he, along with troopers of the Eighteenth Pennsylvania and the First West Virginia, exchanged volleys with Chambliss's and Robertson's dismounted commands for nearly an hour. In the fighting three Union cavalrymen fell beside Jacobs.[59]

Chambliss's and Robertson's weary cavalrymen finally saw the approach of infantry reinforcements. On the double-quick, Iverson's hard-luck brigade of North Carolinians was marching down North Potomac Street toward the Confederate lines. The tattered infantrymen soon filled North Potomac Street and spread out into and west of the cemetery of the Zion Reformed Church. With its officers calling out commands above the din, the brigade of Tarheels fired several volleys into the line of the blue cavalrymen.[60]

With the arrival of Iverson's Brigade, the momentum of the fight in the streets of Hagerstown changed for the last time. The Union cavalrymen with-

James E. Taylor's sketch of the center square at Hagerstown, Maryland, looking south on Potomac Street. Washington Street is at right. The steeple of St. John's Evangelical Lutheran Church is visible at right. The Western Reserve Historical Society, Cleveland, Ohio.

drew down Potomac Street. During the withdrawal, Sergeant Joseph Brown, of Company B of the Eighteenth Pennsylvania, a native of nearby Waynesboro, was mortally wounded in the middle of Potomac Street by a young girl—possibly the daughter of Dr. Frederick Dorsey of Hagerstown—who opened fire on the retreating lines from a second-story window of a dwelling on the northeastern corner of the town square. Indeed, the loyalties of the Hagerstown residents were deeply divided. W. W. Jacobs, his ammunition nearly exhausted, ran down the street to a house where he deposited his musket and accoutrements. While running through the public square, he helped the bleeding Sergeant Brown into a nearby house.[61]

Private Samuel St. Clair ran to the corner of Levi's storehouse below the town square. There he ran into a squad from Company A of the First Ohio that had just ridden up the street to assist in covering the withdrawal. The sergeant of the squad dismounted, walked over to St. Clair, and asked him for his carbine. The sergeant got down on one knee and, resting the carbine against the brick corner of the storehouse, fired at the advancing Confederates. St. Clair handed him another cartridge, and the sergeant methodically aimed and fired. "They are coming fast!" the sergeant yelled to his squad. The mounted Ohioans stood still as bullets whizzed by, some hitting their horses. The sergeant continued to load, aim, and fire. Soon all of St. Clair's ammunition had been expended. Iverson's Brigade was now only fifty yards away.

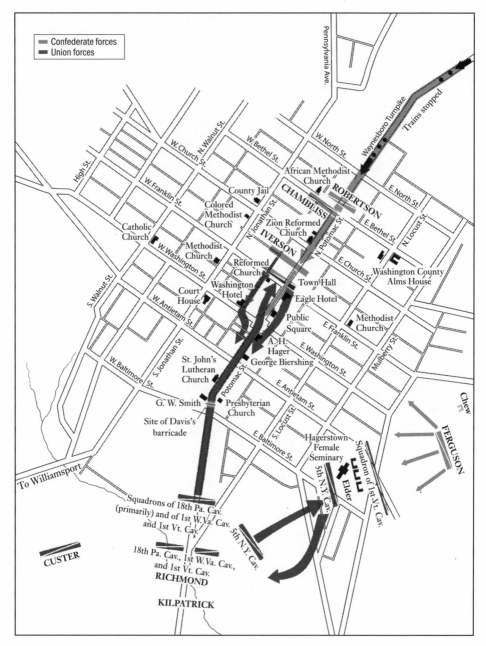

MAP 9.1   6 July 1863, 1:00 to 4:00 P.M.
Kilpatrick attacks Hagerstown.

The sergeant mounted his horse and ordered his men to withdraw down the street.[62]

Meanwhile, St. Clair tried to reach the National Road but became trapped in a yard by a large board fence. Clipping his carbine to his shoulder harness, he climbed two fences and ran down East Antietam Street, where he spotted a young boy trying to hitch a horse to a fence. "Is this your horse?" the boy asked. St. Clair, seeing that it was a horse from Company A of his regiment, replied that he would take him. Sheltered from Confederate bullets by the houses along the street, St. Clair turned south and rode through town until he fell in with the First Vermont on the Hagerstown-Williamsport Turnpike. Large numbers of Iverson's North Carolinians pushed down Potomac Street and the streets west of the Oak Spring and entered the square from the direction of the Washington House hotel and West Washington Street.[63]

Throughout the afternoon, Colonel Ferguson's Brigade had been exchanging fire with Richmond's commands south and east of Hagerstown while trying to advance. Against Ferguson's troopers, Richmond had thrown most of the Fifth New York and squadrons of the First West Virginia and First Vermont as well as Elder's rifles. As the Union troops withdrew down South Potomac Street in response to the advance of the Confederate infantry, Richmond's defense collapsed, and the Union troopers lost control of the high ground southeast of the town. Ferguson's gray cavalry regiments swarmed toward Hagerstown. Kilpatrick was in trouble. His men were rapidly giving up ground, and the Confederates were fast "on their heels!"[64]

Ten

Nowhere is safe

When the First Brigade of Kilpatrick's Division struck Chambliss's troopers in the streets of Hagerstown, General Buford's cavalrymen back near Boonsboro were preparing to remount. While waiting for the bugle call, Sergeant Redman finished a letter home to his mother. "We shall leave here in a few minutes," he wrote, "to go where I cannot tell. I hope to fight the Rebs. I am only satisfied nowadays when I am fighting the enemy. The proper time to fight him is while he is on our northern soil. I shall kill every one of them that I can."[1]

Bugles sounded, and Buford's troopers doused their fires, emptied their coffeepots, and remounted for what promised to be the most trying part of their operation. In the distance they could hear the boom of artillery and the rattle of musketry as Kilpatrick struggled against the Confederate defenders at Hagerstown. Buford's three cavalry brigades and two artillery batteries headed up the muddy, deeply rutted road to Williamsport. The sky was dark and rain was falling. General Merritt's depleted brigade led the advance, followed by Captain Graham's Battery K. Behind Graham's Battery rode Colonel Gamble's Brigade with Lieutenant Calef's Battery. Colonel Thomas S. Devin's Brigade brought up the rear of the column. The blue cavalrymen crossed Antietam Creek over the stone bridge that spans the famous stream at "Devil's Backbone" and then followed the road as it led over ridges and down valleys until they came to a village where the road crossed the Hagerstown-Sharpsburg Turnpike, known as "Jones's Crossroads."[2]

Buford's vedettes at Jones's Crossroads reported that Confederate pickets were posted ahead along the road in a valley near St. James College. From the head of the column all the way to the rear, officers gave the troopers the signal to prepare for action. Pistols and carbines were checked to make sure they were loaded and primed. The gunfire from the direction of Hagerstown, which had intensified all afternoon, formed an ominous backdrop.[3]

All that Buford knew he was facing were the Confederate wagon trains and the small contingent of infantry, cavalry, and artillery escorts reported the night before. Ahead of him, though, was General John Imboden's dismounted brigade, two infantry regiments, assorted infantry and cavalry companies, and twenty-six pieces of artillery! Buford's column steadily moved ahead. Sergeant Redman, whose regiment was riding in the middle of the command, knew that he was about to confront what he told his mother he wanted—a fight. The blue silk eagle on the regimental banner of Redman's Twelfth Illinois flapped nearby. Written across the riband over the eagle was the regiment's motto, "I Like Your Style."[4]

At about 5:00 P.M. Confederate vedettes came riding down the Williamsport-Boonsboro Road toward Williamsport from their advanced positions near St. James College. At that moment, Captain James F. Hart's South Carolina Battery was being unlimbered and rolled into position south of the Hagerstown-Williamsport Turnpike between Captain Squires's four-gun battery of the Washington Artillery and Joseph D. Moore's Battery section. The gunfire from the direction of Hagerstown had brought the Confederate defenders of Williamsport to a high state of alert. Vedettes informed Imboden that Union cavalry and batteries of artillery were approaching from the direction of Boonsboro.[5]

This was what Imboden had feared all along. He needed all the armed men he could find. Alarm spread through the wagon and ambulance trains in Williamsport. Imboden determined to arm teamsters and wagoners as well as all the wounded soldiers who could stand and fight.

Colonel John Logan Black of Hampton's Brigade, who had just arrived in an ambulance accompanied by his slave Howard, though burning with typhoid fever, volunteered his services. Imboden asked him to proceed out the Cumberland Valley Turnpike and stop and organize the teamsters and wagoners, slightly wounded soldiers, and stragglers in the trains that still stretched out along that road. Weapons and ammunition could be obtained from the quartermaster wagons. Although terribly weak and very ill, Black walked from vehicle to vehicle, securing all the men that time and persistence would allow. He managed to arm his little command—teamsters, wagoners, lame cavalrymen, and about 114 wounded infantrymen—and lead them out to the Hagerstown-Williamsport Turnpike, where they were deployed in the fields to the left of Squires's Battery.

Among those in Black's force was a small group of wounded soldiers from

Hood's Division, including some from Robertson's Texas Brigade led by Private Isaac Jackson of Company G of the Fifth Texas who had been badly wounded in the arm at Gettysburg. He quickly became known as "Captain" Jackson. Jackson assured Black that he was willing "to whip off the Yankee cavalry." From the trains in Williamsport, more walking wounded, teamsters, and wagoners poured into the lines directed by shouting quartermasters, commissary of subsistence officers, and bandaged, hobbling line officers. Black discovered that the commissary of subsistence sergeant from his own First South Carolina was already on the battle lines with about fifteen dismounted troopers.[6]

On hearing of the approach of Union cavalry, Colonel Stone of the Second Mississippi, Major Reynolds of the Eleventh Mississippi, and Major Belo of the Fifty-fifth North Carolina—all wounded—got themselves out of their ambulances and began hobbling from vehicle to vehicle calling upon sick and wounded men, teamsters, detailed men, and others to fill the ranks of the defenders outside of Williamsport. Soon a sizable contingent of "recruits" was formed, given arms from the quartermaster wagons, and marched out to the defense lines by the three injured regimental officers from Davis's Brigade.[7]

Also responding to Imboden's desperate call for assistance was the badly wounded Colonel William R. Aylett, of the Fifty-third Virginia, who offered to organize and lead a contingent of walking sick and wounded, teamsters, and wagoners. Aylett had been spitting up blood from the shrapnel wound in his chest, but he was still "game." Imboden directed him to return to the bottomland along the river and in the town and collect as many soldiers as possible from the trains parked there. In a short time, Aylett gathered nearly three hundred men. He then proceeded out the Williamsport-Boonsboro Road and deployed his ragged force in the fields to the right of Captain William Pegram's small company of the Twenty-first Virginia.[8]

Altogether, Black and Aylett managed to assemble nearly seven hundred teamsters, wagoners, and wounded soldiers from the wagon and ambulance trains. The two colonels organized the men into companies of one hundred troopers each, commanded in most instances by wounded foot officers who had also climbed out of ambulances. All of the teamsters, wagoners, and walking wounded were armed with muskets scavenged from the quartermaster wagons in the trains.[9]

Many who otherwise did not have the stomach for battle, but who habitually remained with the quartermaster and commissary teams, found the spirit to fight. Such an odd assortment of men who had never been seen on a battle line appeared in numerous squads all over the field; they were dubbed "Company Q" by the hard-fighting frontline men. To those "recruits" a "wagon seemed better than a prison," and if they were to avoid the latter, they had to fight. Their wagons were "next to home and fireside," and "they decided to fight for their wagons," recalled Captain Hart.[10]

Imboden ordered the Sixty-second Virginia Mounted Infantry and Captain John H. McNeill's Partisan Rangers of his own brigade, then posted north of Williamsport, to proceed east of town, dismount, and take up positions behind Colonel Board's Fifty-eighth Virginia, between the Williamsport-Boonsboro Road and the Hagerstown-Williamsport Turnpike. They were to be ready to respond wherever the need arose. Captain John McClanahan's six-gun Virginia battery was divided into three sections: one section was directed to a location between the Cumberland Valley Turnpike and Conococheague Creek to guard the extreme left flank and the northern approaches to Williamsport, another was posted west of the Williamsport-Downsville Road to protect the extreme right flank and southern approaches to the town, and a third was to unlimber in the center of the defense lines between Squires's guns and Moore's rifles. The Eighteenth Virginia Cavalry remained in position north of town between the Cumberland Valley Turnpike and the Hagerstown-Williamsport Turnpike.[11]

Near St. James College, skirmishers on both sides opened a spattering fire as the Union columns made contact with Imboden's advanced skirmishers. The Confederates withdrew closer to their main lines, and the Union troopers picked up the pace toward Williamsport, their skirmishers firing as they moved forward.[12]

Imboden's position was precarious; his back was to a swollen river, and there was no way his men or the precious quartermaster and subsistence trains they protected could escape from the approaching Union columns if their lines were broken. The Confederates were so close to the trains they protected that any breach of the defenses would allow the Union cavalry to seize the trains in minutes.

As Merritt's leading Union brigade came within two miles of the outskirts of Williamsport, the Confederate defenders grew tense. Captain Squires of the First Company of the Washington Artillery was then at the lovely two-story brick home of Otho Williams, known as "Rose Hill Manor," slightly west of the Williamsport-Downsville Road. That road cut a diagonal course southeast from Williamsport to Downsville, running off of the Williamsport-Boonsboro Road. Williams owned more than 560 acres that extended all the way to the Williamsport-Boonsboro Road. After inspecting the placement of Buck Miller's guns of the Third Company along the Williamsport-

Boonsboro Road, Squires had ridden to Rose Hill Manor to speak with "a party of ladies." Seventy-eight-year-old Otho Williams and his wife Agnes had three daughters, one of whom, Mary Emma, was unmarried and lived at Rose Hill. While on the front porch, Squires noticed in the distance a long column of Imboden's quartermaster wagons rolling up the Williamsport-Downsville Road at "break-neck speed" from the direction of Downsville and Falling Waters. Then someone yelled: "The Yankees are coming!" Sure enough, Squires looked across the fields and saw a large body of Union cavalry "not a quarter of a mile away." [13]

Squires needed to return to his guns. Because the long, tree-lined farm lane led due east from Rose Hill Manor to the Williamsport-Downsville Road, he had to ride toward the advancing Union cavalry before he could get on the road to head northwest back to his lines. "I was well-mounted and reached the turn first," he recalled. "I put my horse at a gentle gait and kept just beyond shot range." The Union columns moved steadily forward. "I first came up with the Third Company, Captain Hero in command," remembered Squires. "He ran out his guns and began firing. I then met Captain Miller of the Third Company [apparently riding back from Squires's guns] and he called out to know if I had opened his guns. I replied 'yes.' He said 'Good, I have just opened yours so we are even!'" Squires made it back to his battery on the Hagerstown-Williamsport Turnpike. Thanks to Buck Miller, his guns were already firing. Squires later acknowledged that "the charming ladies [at Rose Hill Manor] were nearly [his] undoing!" [14]

After Miller's Battery opened fire, he and Captain Hero concluded that their Napoleons and howitzers did not have the range to hit Merritt's troopers. Moore's three rifles then opened up, and the shells from those guns halted the Union advance up the road. Buford ordered Merritt's Brigade and Captain William M. Graham's Battery to move into the fields to the right, north of the Williamsport-Boonsboro Road. He directed Gamble's Brigade along with Calef's Battery to advance across the fields to the left, south of the Williamsport-Boonsboro Road. Devin's Brigade was ordered massed in a large woodlot in reserve behind Gamble. Merritt's troopers and Graham's Battery took up positions along a slight ridge between the Williamsport-Boonsboro Road and the Hagerstown-Williamsport Turnpike. Within minutes, Graham's six 3-inch ordnance rifles began to pound the Confederate positions. [15]

Private I. Norvall Baker and the Eighteenth Virginia Cavalry were in position north of Williamsport, having just returned from protecting Imboden's trains along the National Road. As the regiment was falling into line after grazing its horses, Baker started to "count off" when, to the east of town, he heard the boom of artillery. Then, two or three shells from Graham's Battery "dropped in [the] midst" of his regiment. Baker and his companions waited tensely for orders to direct them to the battlefront.[16]

From the relatively high ground they occupied, Merritt's Union cavalry-men could observe wagons and ambulances massed in and around Williams-port. Ahead of them, though, they could see a line of artillery batteries and what appeared to be infantry holding very favorable positions east of the town. Surprised at the size of the defensive force, Buford nevertheless ordered three of every four troopers in Merritt's Brigade to dismount and advance against Imboden's positions on foot, while the remaining troopers held their horses. Here, unlike on the first day at Gettysburg, the tactic employed by Buford—as it had been by Kilpatrick at Monterey Pass—was an attack against enemy positions along high ground, not in the defense of high ground.

The skirmish line of Merritt's Brigade was formed by the Sixth Penn-sylvania; it became the first Union cavalry regiment to make contact with Imboden's defense lines. Merritt's dismounted troopers struck the line of Confederate skirmishers formed from quickly organized bands of armed teamsters, wagoners, and wounded soldiers, including the little band from Hood's Division. The ragtag Confederate skirmishers fell back as Merritt's troopers advanced.[17]

Once more Miller's and Squires's guns of the Washington Artillery opened fire but halted again until the enemy came within range. Moore's rifles then opened fire on the approaching bluecoats. As the range grew shorter, both batteries of the Washington Artillery and Hart's and Captain William A. Tanner's guns joined Moore's rapidly served rifles. So fast and furious was the artillery fire that Moore's three rifles and Tanner's four guns began to run out of what ammunition they carried. Major Charles Richardson sent urgent appeals into the town for more. To bolster the center of the line where Moore's rifles were about to fall silent, Major Eshleman yelled for Captain J. B. Richardson to bring over his two Napoleons under Lieutenant Samuel Hawes from their position along the Hagerstown-Williamsport Turnpike.[18]

From the rear, Sergeant John Newton of Hart's Battery ran toward the frontlines. He had been detailed to look after the battery's trains but left them on hearing the roar of the guns. After Newton's arrival, another Confederate from the trains in Williamsport appeared in Hart's Battery. This one wore the insignia of a captain on the collar of his coat. Hart immediately put him in command of a squad of volunteers that had just preceded him and was moving into position alongside the guns. Hart was struck by the captain's

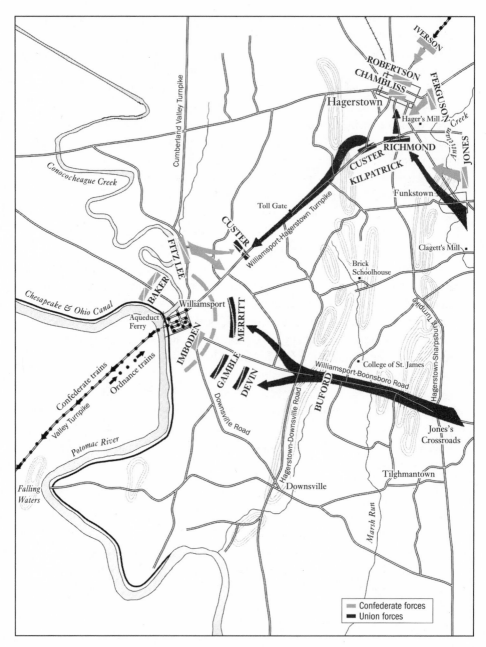

MAP 10.1   6 July 1863, late afternoon and evening.
Kilpatrick attacks Hagerstown and Buford storms Williamsport.

"coolness, self-possession and daring." He would later inquire of his name. He was Manning Brown, chaplain of the Second South Carolina Cavalry and a minister in the Methodist Episcopal Church.[19]

Captain Charles Frederic Bahnson, assistant quartermaster of the Second North Carolina Battalion, wanted to view the fighting, although he had no interest in joining it. He was huddled near the riverbank in Williamsport beside the quartermaster trains of Daniel's Brigade. "[I] slipped away & staid close to one of our batteries while watching the fight," he wrote his father, "but I found it rather unhealthy for six shells fell within 20 feet of me, & accordingly [I] vamosed from that section of the country."[20]

Imboden directed his brother's Eighteenth Virginia from its position between the Cumberland Valley Turnpike and the Hagerstown-Williamsport Turnpike south to support the Sixty-second Virginia Mounted Infantry and McNeill's Partisans. Once fully assembled, Imboden's cavalry and mounted infantry formed behind Moore's and Hart's guns, the Fifty-eighth Virginia, and the four companies of the Fifty-fourth North Carolina.[21]

Hearing the booming of guns east of Williamsport, Colonel William G. Delony, his head wrapped in a dirty, blood-soaked bandage, descended from his ambulance, which was then halted along the Cumberland Valley Turnpike, and called to the wounded soldiers in the ambulances nearby and to teamsters and wagoners to climb down and follow him. About thirteen wounded soldiers, many from Hampton's Brigade, along with some teamsters and wagoners, jumped down and formed a ragged line. Delony saw to it that all of the men were armed with weapons taken from quartermaster wagons. He marched them out toward the sound of the gunfire. The tattered, hobbling little command soon came upon one of Imboden's staff officers. Delony asked where his "company" might be useful, and the officer directed the group to support Captain Hart's Battery south of the Hagerstown-Williamsport Turnpike. By the time Delony reached Hart's guns, he had managed to collect nearly two hundred wounded officers and soldiers as well as teamsters and wagoners![22]

To make the enemy think that he had a large force, Imboden advanced his line of infantry—the four companies of Murchison's Fifty-fourth North Carolina, Board's Fifty-eighth Virginia, and Black's and Delony's battalions of wounded soldiers, teamsters, and wagoners—between the Williamsport-Boonsboro Road and the Hagerstown-Williamsport Turnpike, beyond the artillery, about fifty to one hundred yards toward the advancing Union line, then slowly withdrew them to the high ground behind the guns. In the dense smoke, the maneuver gave General Merritt the impression that he was facing not only a long front of infantry, but also a deep one.[23]

Colonel William G. Delony, commander of Cobb's Legion. Courtesy of Hargrett Rare Book and Manuscript Library, University of Georgia Libraries.

Merritt's assault began to falter; as it neared Imboden's main defense lines, the Confederate infantrymen from Virginia and the Old North State, along with the wounded soldiers, teamsters, and wagoners, poured volleys of rifle fire into the lines of blue troopers. Miller's and Squires's Batteries and Moore's rifles and Tanner's guns—until they finally ran out of ammunition—as well as Hart's South Carolina Battery, fired shell and canister at Merritt's advancing columns. Because of the shortage of ordnance, some of the Confederate batteries actually used railroad iron. The Union cavalrymen watched as the iron bars tumbled toward them end over end, making great arcs through the air.[24]

At the same time that Merritt's Brigade and Graham's rifles exchanged gunfire with Imboden's troops, Gamble's skirmishers were deployed in the fields in front of the long quartermaster train that Squires had spied moving up the Williamsport-Downsville Road toward Williamsport. The wagons were filled with hay and other forage seized from the fields east and south of the town by Imboden's quartermaster for Lee's army. Imboden's men had continued to forage even while preparing for the defense of Williamsport.

Gamble ordered the Third Indiana Cavalry to ride to the left of the brigade and intercept the wagons. The Indiana cavalrymen, whooping and yelling as they fired pistols and carbines, quickly overwhelmed the train. The Union troopers set some of the wagons on fire and, in moments, burning hay wagons and terrified horses and mules, some of the poor brutes in flames, raced across the already smoke-laden fields between the Williamsport-Boonsboro and Williamsport-Downsville Roads. Teamsters, wagoners, and slaves jumped from the burning vehicles and ran for cover; most of them ultimately surrendered to the Hoosier attackers. About twenty-seven wagons and one hundred horses and mules along with forty-six prisoners were taken in the attack.[25]

As the advance of Merritt's Brigade between the Williamsport-Boonsboro Road and the Hagerstown-Williamsport Turnpike stalled in the smoke and racket of gunfire, Buford ordered Gamble's Brigade to proceed along the fields south of the Williamsport-Boonsboro Road toward an apparent gap in Imboden's defenses. Calef's six 3-inch ordnance rifles quickly unlimbered along a ridge east of the Otho Williams house and opened fire while Gamble's horsemen dismounted and formed for the advance. Gamble selected half of the companies of his own Eighth Illinois, all led by Captain Dennis J. Hynes, to comprise the skirmishers. Three of every four troopers in Gamble's regiments, including most of the Third Indiana, followed Hynes's skirmishers on foot.[26]

Calef's cannoneers not only could observe Confederate infantry and artillery in their front, but they also had a glimpse through the smoke from their elevated ground of wagons and ambulances parked in and near Williamsport. They aimed some artillery fire in the direction of the town. As the shells arced across the sky and burst, teamsters and wagoners scurried for cover. After returning to the riverbank near the canal basin, Captain Bahnson recalled shells "dropping amongst the wagons." As he approached his trains, one Confederate quartermaster "was amazed to observe not a single teamster was to be seen." He had no idea where they had gone until he looked toward the river. There he saw "hundreds of black heads just showing above the water. The negro teamsters with one accord had plunged into the river to escape the shells, and were submerged to the neck!" One of those was William, the slave of Major Jedediah Hotchkiss; the next day he told his master that he had been "scared to death" of the exploding shells.[27]

Back along the fields east of the Williams farm, twenty-eight-year-old Major William H. Medill, a native of Massillon, Ohio, who for six years before the war practiced law in Chicago and throughout the war had been a favorite officer in the Eighth Illinois, rode over to his commander, Major

John L. Beveridge. He declared excitedly that "a field officer should command the battalion [of skirmishers]. If you have no objections, I will go." Receiving Beveridge's consent, Medill borrowed a carbine, dug his spurs into his horse, and followed the skirmishers.[28]

Captain Pegram's Company F of the Twenty-first Virginia formed part of the Confederate skirmish line south of the Williamsport-Boonsboro Road, west of the Williamsport-Downsville Road, and just west of the Williams house. The company's advanced pickets had been situated as far out as Rose Hill Manor, but they were quickly withdrawn. When Pegram saw the skirmishers of the Eighth Illinois approach the Williams farm about four hundred yards ahead, he determined that his entire company must occupy the house and outbuildings, as his small number of men could not stand in the open fields and face the oncoming blue regiments. Pegram turned to his odd force of conscripts, substitutes, and stragglers and yelled: "Forward! Double quick!" The little band swept ahead. One soldier fainted at the sight before him, and another fell to the ground. Still another turned around and ran to the rear. As the skulker approached a fence, one of Calef's shells burst in front of him, tearing the fence to pieces. The soldier quickly ran back to catch up with his comrades, exclaiming, "No where is safe!" He remained with the command in the thick of the fighting for the rest of the day; at sundown he was reported to be the only wounded soldier of the company who did not die of his injuries.[29]

Private John Worsham recalled a sunken lane that ran northeast from a barnyard behind Rose Hill Manor to the Williamsport-Downsville Road and the heavy post and rail fences that bordered both sides of the lane. Pegram's "attack" was oblique to the lane; the right flank of the little force crossed the first fence before the left flank. Worsham was on the left. He mounted the first fence, then called for three or four of his men to follow him. Private Michael Ward, donning a red Zouave fez, was among those behind Worsham. They climbed the fence and ran up the lane to a gate in front of the Williams barnyard. Observing the bold move, Major Eshleman ordered Buck Miller to advance his four guns toward the barnyard in support of Pegram.[30]

Gamble's Union command, led by Medill's Illinois skirmishers, were approaching the Williams farm from the east. Medill was the only mounted officer on the field. From the point where he had overtaken the attacking force until his skirmishers reached the Williamsport-Downsville Road, he rode at the head of Gamble's dismounted troops shouting, "Come on, boys!"[31]

At the approach of Pegram's Company and Miller's guns into the fields north of the Williams house, Medill ordered his men to open fire. Brandishing the borrowed carbine, Medill himself fired at the Confederates. The Virginians fired back. In the melee across the Williams fields, Private Michael Ward, the "little Georgian," was killed.[32]

While leading his men through the Williams fields, Medill spurred his horse into the musketry delivered by Pegram's small command and the artillery fire from Miller's Battery. He was soon struck by a ball that passed through the lower edge of his breastbone and slanted downward, tearing through his lung and lodging in his spinal column. He remained in the saddle, but, bending over, with blood fast flowing from the gaping wound, he slowly rode back toward Gamble's reserve lines alongside Calef's booming three-inch rifles. Some mounted troopers rode out to assist the wounded major. They took him off the field and left him in the care of regimental surgeon Dr. Abner Hard in a woodlot behind the lines occupied by Devin's Brigade. Medill's wound was found to be mortal; he was transported by ambulance back to Jones's Crossroads and placed in a nearby church that had been turned into a temporary hospital.[33]

West of the Williamsport-Downsville Road, Pegram's hard-fighting little company managed to occupy some outbuildings of Rose Hill Manor and, in the process, captured five Illinois skirmishers. Buck Miller's guns unlimbered in the fields north of the Williams house and opened fire. In the fighting, four other members of the Eighth Illinois went down, including Captain Darius Sullivan, of Company F, who was badly wounded in the head. As Pegram's men overran the farmyard, the young Virginia captain ordered his force to take up positions along a rail fence north and east of the Williams house, bordering the Williamsport-Downsville Road. The Williams farmyard had thus far cost Company F not only Private Ward but also two others, both of whom had been killed in the action. In Buck Miller's Battery, Mike Keegan, the driver of one of the limbers, had two horses killed under him; incredibly, he also had had two killed beneath him at Gettysburg.[34]

The pressure of the main line of Union dismounted cavalry began to be felt by Pegram's little band. Calef ordered Lieutenant John W. Roder's left section of two rifles to wheel to the left and open fire with canister on Pegram's men. The well-directed artillery fire and the advancing column of dismounted cavalry slowly forced Pegram's infantrymen and Miller's Battery to abandon the fields around Rose Hill Manor. Pegram ordered his men to fall back and brought them to a halt behind a fence line north and west of the Williams house.[35]

Pegram's right flank was slowly being overwhelmed by the force of Gamble's advance. Pegram ordered some of his men to get behind a cross fence and direct their fire south while the main body of his skirmishers fired at the columns approaching from due east. The return fire of the Union lines, though, was more than Pegram's small force could stand. The company started to give way again. Pegram moved back and forth behind his men trying to steady them. Fully exposed to the horrendous gunfire, the brave captain was soon struck by a bullet and killed instantly. He and his courageous men, supported by Miller's four guns, had resisted Gamble's dismounted Union brigade and Calef's six rifles for nearly half an hour. With Miller's artillery support, the little command continued to fight for another half hour after Pegram's death.[36]

Gamble's skirmishers finally pressed into the fields west and north of Rose Hill Manor and took possession of the fence line previously occupied by Pegram's skirmishers. The situation was growing desperate along the Confederate right flank. All but four companies of the Fifty-fourth North Carolina formed the only infantry support remaining south of the Williamsport-Boonsboro Road and west of the Williamsport-Downsville Road.[37]

Two wagonloads of ammunition finally reached the Confederate defense lines after having been ferried across the Potomac River to Williamsport and hauled through town. The ordnance was critically needed by Moore's rifles and Tanner's guns. As the chests were delivered, cannoneers broke them open with axes and ran the rounds forward to the number two cannoneers beside each piece. In minutes, Moore's three-inch ordnance rifles and ten-pound Parrott, along with Tanner's guns, were blazing away at Merritt's approaching column. After losing twelve cannoneers at one piece during the time his two Napoleons occupied the center of the line beside Moore, Lieutenant Hawes finally withdrew the remaining piece and rejoined Squires's Battery along the Hagerstown-Williamsport Turnpike. Because Hawes had lost so many men, Sergeant John Newton of Hart's South Carolina Battery volunteered as a cannoneer for the remaining gun until he was mortally wounded.[38]

Although severely ill, Colonel Black steadied his ragtag command that straddled the Hagerstown-Williamsport Turnpike. Black was very visible along the left flank of Imboden's defense lines. One of those who observed him was his old friend from Camden, Captain Zack Leitner of the Second South Carolina. Leitner's leg had been amputated and he was burning with fever and infection. His ambulance had broken down several miles north of Williamsport, and his driver had been sent back up the turnpike to retrieve some hardware from a disabled ambulance. After his vehicle was repaired, Leitner entered Williamsport via the Cumberland Valley Turnpike "amidst a storm of shells," observing Black "in the line of battle as he passed."[39]

The heavy pressure was felt along the southern lines. Imboden decided to send his entire dismounted brigade to the relief of the lines south of the Williamsport-Boonsboro Road and west of the Williamsport-Downsville Road where it was apparent that the most determined attack was taking place and where his lines were thin. He directed the Sixty-second Virginia Mounted Infantry, Eighteenth Virginia Cavalry, and McNeill's Partisans to vacate their positions behind the center of the lines and move south to meet Gamble's attack. In addition, Imboden ordered Captain Tanner to send two of his guns south to assist in the defense of the right flank. Colonel Black then directed Captain Jackson and his small company of about 114 wounded infantrymen from Hood's Division to the right as well. As these reinforcements approached the fields south of the Williamsport-Boonsboro Road, they came into position alongside Colonel Murchison's North Carolinians and Colonel Aylett's walking wounded, teamsters, and wagoners still "protected" by the remnants of Pegram's battered skirmishers.[40]

A desperate fight soon developed north and west of Rose Hill Manor. For almost two hours Gamble's dismounted troopers, supported by Calef's rifles, kept up the pressure against Imboden's right flank. The fire of Miller's Battery, one section of McClanahan's Battery, two guns of Tanner's Battery, Aylett's wounded, teamsters, and wagoners, and the Fifty-fourth North Carolina, together with Imboden's own brigade, "Captain" Jackson's company of wounded, and the remnants of Pegram's Company, held the Union cavalrymen at bay. But Gamble's troopers gained ground. The Union cavalrymen soon passed Rose Hill Manor and its barn and outbuildings. The fire from Calef's six rifles was incessant.[41]

It was nearly 7:00 P.M. Darkness would be the ally of the Confederates if they could hold on for another hour. Imboden ordered the dismounted Sixty-second Virginia Mounted Infantry and Aylett's wounded, teamsters, and wagoners, supported by the dismounted Eighteenth Virginia Cavalry and Jackson's Company of walking wounded, to attack Gamble's approaching lines in an effort to at least stun the enemy. Major Eshleman, in turn, commanded Captain Norcom to advance one of his Napoleons to shell Rose Hill Manor and its outbuildings, where so many of Gamble's men had secured positions from which they were firing at the Confederate lines, particularly at Miller's and Tanner's cannoneers. Lieutenant Henry A. Battles moved one of the howitzers farther to the right beyond Tanner's guns and opened up on Gamble's troopers. The wounded infantrymen, in an effort reminiscent of the attack of Captain Pegram's company, advanced, yelling, all the way to the Williams house. Nevertheless, the hastily organized assault could not break the blue cavalrymen and their brilliantly served artillery.[42]

Imboden desperately needed a bold movement on his left flank or Gamble would carry the day below the Williamsport-Boonsboro Road. Colonel Black, terribly ill, finally turned command of the left flank over to Captain Hart. Seeing Imboden's daring attack south of the Williamsport-Boonsboro Road, Hart ordered Captain Squires to move his four guns almost four hundred yards ahead and enfilade the right flank of Merritt's columns, which had kept up a continuous fire from the fields ahead of Imboden's center. Hart then directed forward the section of McClanahan's Virginia Battery that had been posted west of the Cumberland Valley Turnpike to join Squires's guns. Cracking their whips, the gunners raced out the Hagerstown-Williamsport Turnpike. As the six guns unlimbered and began pounding the exposed right flank of Merritt's tired troopers, Hart turned to the odd assortment of walking wounded, teamsters, and wagoners, most of whom were following Colonel Delony, fragments of the Fifty-eighth Virginia, and the four companies of the Fifty-fourth North Carolina and ordered them forward against Merritt's Brigade.[43]

No sooner had Hart successfully maneuvered onto Merritt's right flank than columns of gray horsemen were seen riding hard toward the sound of the gunfire from the Cumberland Valley Turnpike. It was General Fitzhugh Lee's Brigade, which had been screening Imboden's trains to the west and rear. Now the brigade was pouring into the fields north of the Hagerstown-Williamsport Turnpike. Fitzhugh Lee sent Colonel Baker's Brigade into Williamsport and then out the road toward Clear Spring to protect the Confederate defenders from an attack from the west. Pushing ahead, elements of Lee's Brigade headed toward Merritt's cavalrymen; others, including the horse artillery battery of Captain James Breathed, pressed up the Hagerstown-Williamsport Turnpike toward the rear of Kilpatrick's Division at Hagerstown.[44]

In the growing darkness and gunfire, Hart's assault and Squires's and McClanahan's guns stunned Merritt's columns. The presence of a large brigade of gray cavalry bearing down on his right flank and rear convinced Merritt that his position was untenable. Fearing that he would be flanked and literally swallowed up in the darkness, he called for his commands to withdraw. The Confederate advance between the Williamsport-Boonsboro Road and the Hagerstown-Williamsport Turnpike extended forward nearly three-quarters of a mile east of the original Confederate defense lines. As Merritt withdrew, Buford urgently ordered Gamble to fall back, alarmed that his division was about to be flanked on its right. Gamble's hard-fighting cavalrymen grudgingly gave way, leaving behind Rose Hill Manor and its farmyards littered with the dead and wounded. Under Buford's direction, Devin brought

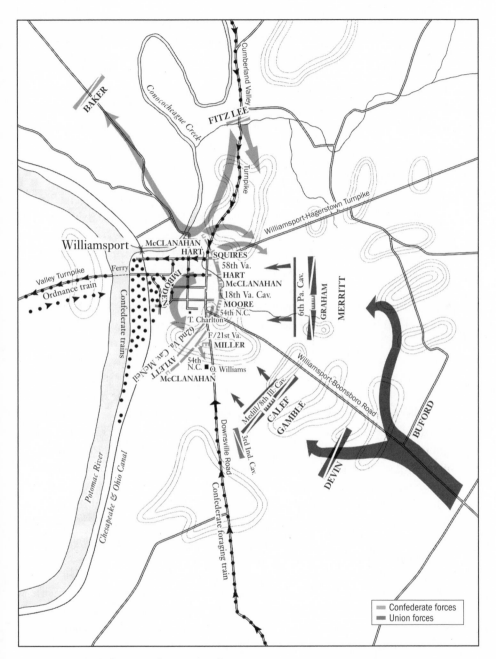

MAP 10.2   6 July 1863, afternoon and evening.
Buford attacks Williamsport.

forward his Second Brigade to cover the retreat. The last Union regiment to leave the battlefield was the Seventeenth Pennsylvania Cavalry of Devin's Brigade.[45]

IT WAS IMPOSSIBLE for Buford's men to accomplish an orderly retreat. As Buford tried to extricate his three brigades from their failed effort at Williamsport, Kilpatrick's troopers were falling back from Hagerstown, largely by way of the Hagerstown-Sharpsburg Turnpike, and were crowding Buford's rear as far south as Jones's Crossroads. Falling darkness made the withdrawal all the more difficult.[46]

As Kilpatrick's battered troopers were withdrawing from Hagerstown, they could hear gunfire from the direction of Williamsport. Anxious that his left flank not be exposed to attack as he retreated south, Kilpatrick ordered General Custer to take his brigade toward Williamsport and cover that flank. Custer's regiments, led by the Fifth Michigan, galloped down the Hagerstown-Williamsport Turnpike.

Nearing Williamsport, Custer sent the Fifth and Seventh Michigan Cavalry regiments to the left of the turnpike and the First and Sixth to the right. The left of the brigade made a desperate attempt to form on the right of Merritt's retreating force. It was hopeless. The artillery fire from Imboden's guns and Captain James Breathed's Battery of Fitzhugh Lee's Brigade tore into Custer's Michiganders. The Sixth Michigan was too exposed. One shell exploded as Adjutant Arron C. Jewett of the Sixth was trying to deliver a message to his regimental commander. Jewett was struck by a shell fragment and fell from his horse; he bled to death in minutes. Another exploding shell tore off the leg of a trooper who had just dismounted. Those nearby observed him "hopping around on his one remaining limb and heard him shriek with pain." Then Lieutenant E. L. Crew of the Sixth Michigan was struck in the throat by a fragment from still another exploding shell; he died instantly.

The Michigan Brigade slowly withdrew back up the Hagerstown-Williamsport Turnpike toward Hagerstown under intense artillery fire. Major Peter A. Weber of the Sixth Michigan helped to steady the brigade. The Michiganders fell back until they were almost "back-to-back" with Colonel Richmond's Brigade as it was withdrawing down the Hagerstown-Sharpsburg Turnpike. Custer's men were in no position to offer Richmond any aid; rather, they moved south toward Jones's Crossroads.[47]

Left with few supports, Richmond called upon the First West Virginia Cavalry and Lieutenant Samuel S. Elder's Battery to cover the withdrawal of the rest of Kilpatrick's force from Hagerstown. They made their first stand south of town between the Hagerstown-Williamsport and Hagerstown-Sharpsburg Turnpikes. Elder's Battery unlimbered on a ridge, and the West Virginia cavalrymen spread out in the fields alongside the guns.[48]

The Confederate cavalry brigades of Colonel Chambliss, Colonel Ferguson, and General Robertson had battled Richmond's Brigade out of Hagerstown. At the same time, Grumble Jones and his brigade were galloping southeast of town in an effort to reach Kilpatrick's rear near Funkstown. Artillery and small-arms fire echoed through the valley. "We were wet to the hide, tired and hungry as hounds and sleepy as owls," recalled one of Jones's troopers. "Many of the boys were sleeping soundly as they rode." Soon there was cheering at the head of the column. Several ladies stood on the porch of a residence near an old stone mill northeast of Funkstown. Among them was a girl no older than fourteen wearing "a white apron which she had fashioned into a Confederate battle flag," remembered Private John Blue of the Eleventh Virginia Cavalry. "It was the sight of this little flag that caused the cheering. The one ray in the land of the foe, which lighted up the gloom."

Major Edward H. McDonald of the Eleventh Virginia stopped in front of the girl and asked her to present him with the apron flag. McDonald and his men were wet, muddy, and bone tired. "Without a word," wrote Private Blue who sat his horse next to McDonald, "she reached with her right hand to her left side. With a single jerk she tore the apron flag from its moorings and threw it over the railing. The major caught it, expressed his thanks and with a lordly bow passed on amid deafening cheers from hundreds of Confederate throats." Private H. Madison Watkins asked to carry the apron flag; he was but a youth in his teens who had enlisted at Winchester at the outset of the invasion of Pennsylvania. McDonald handed the apron flag to Watkins, who tied it to a staff. Beneath its new banner, Jones's Brigade galloped north of Funkstown toward the rear of Kilpatrick's retreating forces with rain continuing to fall.[49]

Pressuring Colonel Richmond's rear guard was the Thirteenth, Ninth, and Tenth Virginia Cavalry, joined by the Fifth North Carolina Cavalry. But the rear guard soon had other worries. Rumbling up the turnpike from Williamsport was a section of Breathed's Battery and elements of Fitzhugh Lee's cavalry. Then, spectacularly, Grumble Jones's Brigade also arrived on the field from north of Funkstown. Out from Jones's ranks Colonel L. Lindsay Lomax led his Eleventh Virginia Cavalry, with sabres drawn, directly into the West Virginians and Elder's guns. It was one of the most awe-inspiring attacks of the day.

Private Blue recalled:

We walked our horses to the top of [a] rise[,] then came the command to charge at a gallop, and away we went straight at [a] stone fence not over two hundred yards away. Not a man could be seen, not a gun was fired, all was silent as the grave. We well knew what this silence meant and what to expect at any moment. It appeared to me that I was riding straight into the mouth of a twelve-pounder which protruded through the stone fence. . . . When we were within a hundred paces of the fence the muzzle of that gun . . . belched forth fire and smoke.

Blue and his horse went down; the horse was killed instantly, and Blue was badly wounded in the foot.

Lomax's line fell back and re-formed for another attack. This time it was followed by Chew's Battery. While Blue remained pinned beneath his dead horse between the two contending lines, frantically waving his sword so his men would not trample him to death, the Eleventh Virginia once again charged the West Virginians and Elder's Battery. Lomax's "charging squadrons" raced toward the enemy with flashing sabres beneath the flapping apron flag. They reached the stone fence and bounded over it, firing pistols and carbines and swinging sabres.[50]

To their credit, the West Virginians and Elder's cannoneers did not run; rather, the guns, after firing a salvo, were limbered up and withdrawn farther down the Hagerstown-Sharpsburg Turnpike under the covering fire of the cavalrymen. The guns were then unlimbered and formed another defense line in front of a woodlot to continue protecting Kilpatrick's fleeing regiments.

The Eleventh Virginia, with "the regular Confederate war whoops," pursued the West Virginians and Elder's cannoneers. It was well after 9:00 P.M. In the meantime, the rest of Jones's Brigade made a circular movement and, under cover of the large woods, came upon the right and rear of the Union cavalrymen and artillerymen. Chew's guns were unlimbered and opened fire. It was not easy firing artillery pieces that night. According to Cannoneer Charles W. McVicar of Chew's Battery, the ground was so saturated with rain that when the guns were fired at Kilpatrick's rear guard, they would recoil and "bury themselves in a field of mud." "I thought we were done for," McVicar wrote in his diary. But the cannoneers ran to a nearby fence, took out the rails, and used them to "[pry] the wheels out."[51]

What Cannoneer George M. Neese of Chew's Battery remembered most was the artillery fighting after dark. "Night fighting," he observed, "is a perilous business and full of guesswork; ofttimes it is difficult to distinguish friend from foe in the darkness. The artillery firing [the night of 6 July] was certainly beautiful and grand. The flash from the gun brilliantly illuminated all its immediate environments and the burning fuses of the shell spun threads of sparkling fire in graceful curves across the somber face of night. The whole scene was a splendid display of dangerous fireworks."

Ahead of Chew's guns there suddenly appeared a frenzied cow running wildly in the farmyard. Then an "old man" and "old lady" came out "trying to drive her to the stable." Elder's guns opened fire, and the shells exploded all around "in showers of whizzing fragments and pinging slugs." Yet the woman chased the cow until another shell exploded and she fell crying, "Oh, God!" With that, the man ran back to the house. All the cannoneers thought that the woman had been killed, but she jumped up and renewed her race after the cow![52]

The Ninth, Tenth, and Thirteenth Virginia, Fifth North Carolina, and Breathed's Battery followed the Union cavalrymen abreast of the Eleventh Virginia. Lieutenant G. H. Beale, the son of the commander of the Ninth Virginia, led the final attack against the Union rear guard. Elder's guns fired one more time, killing a trooper in the Ninth Virginia and wounding others. Colonel Beale thought that his son was the one who had fallen in front of the blasts.

After Elder's guns fired, the charging Confederates immediately called out, "Take the guns, boys!" The Union rear guard realized that it was being assailed in front, rear, and flank. Two Confederate batteries were coming into position. Quickly, Elder limbered up his pieces once again and, covered by a blanket of carbine and pistol fire from the West Virginians, withdrew closer to Jones's Crossroads.

Meanwhile, Colonel Beale dismounted and, discharging his pistol into the Union rear guard ahead, ran over to where he thought he saw his son fall. The smoke was dense and it was dark. What Beale found was Sergeant Richard Washington of the Ninth dead in the arms of his weeping brother. Beale ordered Washington's body taken to the rear so it could be conveyed across the Potomac River.

Behind the Ninth, Tenth, and Thirteenth Virginia, Fifth North Carolina, and Breathed's Battery galloped Colonel Ferguson with his brigade; General Stuart himself was riding alongside them. The chase, though, had ended in the darkness. It was nearly 10:00 P.M. Among the dead was the youthful Private H. Madison Watkins, who had proudly carried the apron flag of the Eleventh Virginia into the fighting along Hagerstown-Sharpsburg Turnpike north of Jones's Crossroads.[53]

Buford's troopers took all night to reach Jones's Crossroads, so jammed were the roads with Kilpatrick's broken commands. The day had been a fiasco. Kilpatrick would later report 15 of his officers and men killed, 52 wounded, and 108 missing. Colonel Huey reported 144 men lost just since his command left Emmitsburg; moreover, during that time he had had to abandon almost 200 horses. Both accounts demonstrated how ineffective cavalry can be when it operates far from its quartermaster trains for more than four or five days.[54]

Buford would report nine killed, twenty wounded, and forty-three missing in his three brigades. Undoubtedly, his figures were understated.[55]

Imboden claimed to have lost about 125, while Chambliss, Robertson, and Jones lost about 200 altogether during the day. Colonel Ferguson failed to report the casualties in Jenkins's Brigade. Iverson noted that his Tarheel brigade suffered 3 killed and 6 wounded in the streets of Hagerstown. Outside of Williamsport, the dead and wounded included a disproportionate number of officers and enlisted men in the quartermaster service, a most unusual phenomenon. One of those killed was Philemon Lineback of the Twenty-first North Carolina, a Moravian from Salem, who had been detailed as a wagoner in Avery's Brigade trains; he was a first cousin of Julius Lineback and a hometown friend of Captain Bahnson.[56]

Darkness blanketed the Potomac River Valley. The Union threat against Lee's trains had been eliminated. Lee's army was moving ever closer to its quartermaster and subsistence trains and, more importantly, to its base of supply in the Shenandoah Valley. By 10:30 P.M., 6 July, Early's, Johnson's, and Anderson's trains began to move through Hagerstown toward Williamsport. Behind them the army itself was closing in on the Potomac River Valley.

Ironically, Meade's army, although it had been defending its own soil, had never been able to keep its supply trains close enough to the troops to maintain their effectiveness. Meade's wide-ranging cavalry probes had been dramatic, but, in the end, they had failed because it had not been possible to keep them supplied. Some of the men and horses had completely broken down. Too, they had faced a vigilant and spirited enemy that had indeed responded like a "wounded lion."

"There had been glory enough won, and neither the wagoners nor Company 'Q' felt any desire to pursue [the enemy] horsemen in search of more," recalled Captain Hart of the Confederate defense of Williamsport. "The wagons were safe, and the teamsters went back to feed their mules and talk over the wonderful victory; Company 'Q' sought shelter from the drizzling rain under the grateful cover of a wagon, where his repose was undisturbed for the remainder of the night." Indeed, even the battle-hardened frontline soldiers of Imboden's slapped-together command breathed a sigh of relief. They had indeed saved the trains of Lee's army.[57]

Lee was rapidly regaining that balance of power with his enemy that Clausewitz claimed was the object of any retreat after a lost battle. In spite of Meade's strenuous efforts, the advantage gained by the tactical victory at Gettysburg was rapidly giving way to a reestablished equilibrium between the two contending armies.

Eleven

By the blessing of providence,
I will do it

As the fighting raged in the streets of Hagerstown and east of Williamsport on the afternoon of 6 July, Lee's main columns stretched on the road from just west of Fairfield all the way to Leitersburg, Maryland. Many soldiers heard the gunfire coming from Hagerstown and Williamsport. The troops had been on the march since dawn; many would not halt until late that night. The entire army would be in Hagerstown by the morning of 7 July.

The movement of Lee's army from the morning of 5 July until the afternoon of 6 July was one of the most critical episodes of the retreat from Gettysburg, although it was far from being filled with battle action. As if he had memorized the words of Clausewitz, Lee moved his forces at a steady but deliberate pace toward Monterey Pass, always posting a strong rear guard, so his adversary was unable to rule out the possibility that he was withdrawing to the mountains in order to fortify them.

While Ewell's rear guard battled elements of the Union Sixth Corps east of Fairfield on the afternoon of 5 July, Hill's Corps continued its slow march up the Maria Furnace Road toward Monterey Pass. Because of the slowness of Hill's Corps and the overarching need to cover the entrance of the Emmitsburg-Waynesboro Turnpike to the pass, Longstreet's columns, including the four thousand prisoners of war guarded by the remnants of Pickett's Division, took the Jack's Mountain Road east of Jack's Mountain and the Emmitsburg-Waynesboro Turnpike through Fountaindale instead of the Maria Furnace Road. They then followed the turnpike west, up the steep eastern entrance to Monterey Pass, using the same approach to the pass employed by Kilpatrick's cavalry division on the stormy night of 4 July. All of Longstreet's Corps reached their positions at Monterey Pass by 1:00 A.M. on 6 July.[1]

At the time Longstreet's Corps reached Monterey Pass, Hill's Corps was stretched out along the Emmitsburg-Waynesboro Turnpike and the Maria Furnace Road, the head of the column well below Waterloo and near Waynesboro. The Maria Furnace Road up the mountain had become deep with mud and horribly rutted after Major Harman's forty-mile-long wagon and ambulance trains passed over it during the previous forty-eight hours. Rodes's and Johnson's Divisions of Ewell's Corps entered the narrow approaches to the pass behind Hill's columns. Early's Division held the rear of Ewell's Corps; it halted along the base of the South Mountain range in late afternoon on 5 July. Although rain had poured down most of the day, it had stopped by then.[2]

Even as Lee's army marched through the rain and mud, foraging was carried out at a feverish pace. Like the foraging during the initial stages of the invasion of Pennsylvania, it was conducted mostly to obtain stores for future use, although the immediate needs of the horses and mules were critical. All along the Fairfield Road, between Gettysburg and Monterey Pass, civilians reported the loss of horses, cows, bulls, wagons, wheat, flour, corn, and hay to the passing Confederate columns. To conduct such foraging while on retreat, the quartermaster of each brigade detailed a company from one of his regiments. The quartermaster and company commander then led the squad on a route parallel to the marching columns. Similarly, corps, division, and artillery battalion details were sent out to forage by quartermasters.[3]

Captain James H. Wood, of Company D, Thirty-seventh Virginia in Steuart's Brigade of Johnson's Division, Ewell's Corps, was one of the many commanders directed by his brigade quartermaster to take his company out of line and forage along a route parallel to the Fairfield Road on the afternoon of 5 July. "I was placed in command of a detail of men and wagons and directed to make a detour to the left of the column to gather food supplies," Wood recalled. "I was provided with Confederate currency with which to pay for such supplies. My route was over a mile out and parallel with the course of the column. The well supplied homes enabled me to soon load the wagons and get them underway on the country road that converged toward the column."

Such foraging details, particularly those from the rear elements of the army, were exposed to attack by Union cavalry. As Ewell's Corps formed the rear of Lee's retreating columns between Gettysburg and Monterey Pass, it was closely pursued by elements of Colonel McIntosh's Union cavalry brigade that was screening Sedgwick's Sixth Corps. Captain Wood's detail was one of those beset along what appears to have been the Jack's Mountain Road south of Fairfield. "I discovered a battalion of Federal cavalry in the distance, bearing down upon us," Wood wrote. "I ordered the teamsters to move forward with all speed. We quickly reached the outer edge of the open lands and entered the thickly wooded course of the narrow road, so closely pursued that I was compelled to give battle. I had time to place my men and deliver fire at close range with signal effect on men and horses."[4]

Wood's detail continued down the Jack's Mountain Road, east of Jack's Mountain, and then onto the Emmitsburg-Waynesboro Turnpike just behind Longstreet's Corps, moving toward a junction with Ewell's columns on the Maria Furnace Road at Monterey Pass. "I saw the wagons some distance to my front, curving to the right, to the road entering the little valley to my right about 300 yards to the front," Wood recounted. "I now started with all possible speed with my little force toward this junction of road and valley, and almost immediately the charge up the valley began as anticipated. It was an exciting struggle." Wood and his forage detail escaped after shooting some of the leading horses of the Union cavalry squadron that blocked the rest of the Union troopers from moving up the road. As the wagons rumbled up the mountainside, the elevated position of Wood's infantrymen made further pursuit by the Union cavalry virtually impossible. Finally, elements of the Eleventh Virginia Cavalry helped cover the foragers return journey to the main columns. The harrowing escape was observed not only by many soldiers in Longstreet's Corps who were also making their way up the mountain, but also by many Union prisoners guarded by Pickett's Division. The chase by Union cavalry gave them fleeting hopes of being rescued.[5]

On the night of 5 July, Lee's army held the South Mountain range at Monterey Pass. Longstreet's Corps covered the Emmitsburg-Waynesboro Turnpike from the base of the mountain all the way to the summit. Hood's Division was in the lead just east of the summit; McLaws's Division held the base of the mountain in the rear. Pickett's Division and the Union prisoners were on the summit. McLaws's and Hood's Divisions were aligned across the turnpike, facing east. Breastworks were constructed of logs, stones, and earth; strong skirmish lines were established well in front of the steep entrance to the pass by McLaws's troops. Hill's Corps was positioned along the Emmitsburg-Waynesboro Turnpike and at the western base of the mountain, covering the western approaches to the pass. Anderson's Division was at the head of the column; Pender's Division followed, and Heth's Division formed the rear. Behind Heth's Division was the head of Ewell's Corps. That night Rodes's Division led Ewell's Corps. Johnson's Division occupied the center, and Early's formed the rear guard. All of those units were aligned on the mountain, facing east. Like McLaws's Division astride the Emmitsburg-

Waynesboro Turnpike on the evening of 5 July, Early's Division and its skirmishers constructed breastworks on either side of the Maria Furnace Road. At dawn, Rodes's Division would form the rear guard and Early's Division would lead Ewell's columns.[6]

Lee wanted Meade to attack him while his army occupied the eastern base of the South Mountain range and the two entrances to Monterey Pass. Isaac Seymour, the adjutant general of Hays's Brigade, recalled that Lee "halted our corps and told General Ewell to try to induce the enemy to fight." Lee remarked to Ewell: "If 'those people' will only come out and give us an open field fight, we will smash them." Seymour was impressed. "I never saw General Lee so anxious for a fight," he recorded in his journal. Yet no serious attack of the Union Sixth Corps materialized on the night of 5 July after its sharp encounter with General Gordon's rear guard east of Fairfield.[7]

General Sedgwick was under orders not to attack Lee's rear, but, rather, to follow him closely and inform Meade of his intentions. Meade had to know with certainty where Lee was going in order to make the critical decisions about moving the Army of the Potomac. But it was impossible for Sedgwick to give Meade a precise answer. Lee's movement toward the South Mountain range was deliberate. In fact, the leading division on the night of 4 July and all of 5 July—Anderson's of Hill's Corps—may have been exasperatingly slow to Lee.[8]

Instead of pushing their way through Monterey Pass on the night of 5 July, Ewell's and Longstreet's forces bivouacked at the base of South Mountain. As a consequence, Sedgwick believed that Lee's army had halted to make a stand there. The "immense number of campfires" that Sedgwick observed that night impressed upon him that "the enemy have a very strong rear guard, and will hold the gaps strongly." He thus reported to Meade the only conclusion that he could reach: Lee appeared to be fortifying the South Mountain range.[9]

Meade had issued orders to the entire Army of the Potomac to march south toward Middletown, Maryland, at midmorning on 5 July. He had also telegraphed the Washington Navy Yard asking that pontoon bridges be sent to Harpers Ferry so the army could cross the Potomac. On receiving messages from General Sedgwick on Lee's slow march and bold rear guard, Meade decided not to forward marching orders to his corps commanders. But Meade's chief of staff, the wounded Major General Daniel Butterfield, sent the orders anyway. By noon, Meade had to rescind the 5 July marching orders. As he could not continue in the field without medical attention, Butterfield was replaced the same day. Brigadier General Gouverneur K. Warren, the army's chief engineer, and Brigadier General Alfred Pleasonton, the chief of cavalry, were temporarily named to alternate as Meade's chief of staff.[10]

Meade ordered Warren to Fairfield to assist Sedgwick in assessing Lee's intentions. Corps commanders were to send couriers to Meade's headquarters so they could speedily receive any marching orders that he might issue. From information Meade had received the day before, it appeared to him that Lee was in full retreat to the Potomac River, but he was unsure. Sedgwick's communications on 5 July came as no surprise. Like many of his corps commanders, Meade had expressed genuine concern over the past twenty-four hours that Lee might be withdrawing to the mountains for the purpose of fortifying them. Sedgwick's messages on the late afternoon of 5 July made Meade even more doubtful of Lee's intentions.[11]

Meade had to be certain about Lee's plan because he needed to know where to move his base of supply at Westminster. If Lee was in full retreat to the Potomac River, that base of supply would have to be reestablished at Frederick, a major town on a spurline of the Baltimore and Ohio Railroad and situated on the National Road, due east of the only other passes in the South Mountain range available to Meade. If, on the other hand, Lee was actually fortifying the mountains west of Fairfield, the base of supply might have to be changed to Gettysburg, in his immediate rear on 5 July, the day that General Haupt's construction crews reopened the Northern Central and Hanover Railroads from Baltimore all the way to Gettysburg.[12]

Meade could not afford to make a mistake. Changing his supply base would involve movement of enormous amounts of men and materiel as well as a shift in the railroads to be used out of Baltimore. Any error would result in the misdirection of all of the army's badly needed shipments of quartermaster, subsistence, and ordnance stores. Once the base was changed, it would take days to reroute them. The army could not go without such necessities any longer. It needed supplies immediately. Horses and mules were on the brink of collapse due to exhaustion and the lack of fodder and shoes. The men were seriously weakened from short rations and the lack of clothing, shoes, and equipment; they would soon be in serious need of ammunition.[13]

MAP II.I　5 July 1863, 9:00 P.M. to midnight.
Hill's Corps reaches the summit of Monterey Pass. Longstreet's Corps follows the road east of Jack's Mountain and entrenches along the entrance to Monterey Pass on the Emmitsburg-Waynesboro Turnpike. Ewell's Corps, following Hill's Corps, entrenches along the entrance to Monterey Pass on the Maria Furnace Road. Sedgwick halts his Sixth Corps, believing that Lee is fortifying the mountains.

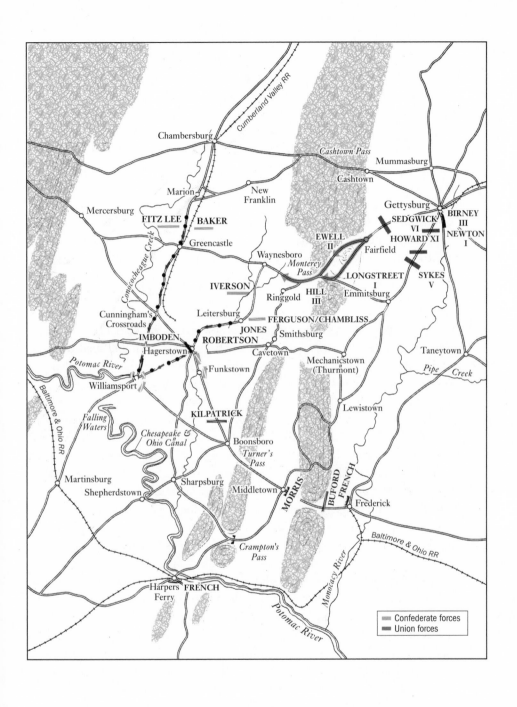

Chambersburg

Cumberland Valley RR

Cashtown Pass

Mummasburg

Cashtown

Marion

New
Franklin

Mercersburg

Gettysburg

FITZ LEE **BAKER**

SEDGWICK
VI

BIRNEY
III

HOWARD XI

NEWTON
I

Greencastle

Waynesboro

EWELL
II

Fairfield

Conococheague Creek

Monterey
Pass

IVERSON

LONGSTREET
I

SYKES
V

Ringgold

HILL
III

Emmitsburg

Cunningham's
Crossroads

Leitersburg

FERGUSON/CHAMBLISS

IMBODEN

JONES
ROBERTSON

Smithsburg

Potomac River

Hagerstown

Cavetown

Taneytown

Pipe   *Creek*

Mechanicstown
(Thurmont)

Funkstown

Lewistown

Baltimore & Ohio RR

Falling
Waters

KILPATRICK

Chesapeake &
Ohio Canal

Boonsboro

Turner's
Pass

Martinsburg

Sharpsburg

Middletown

MORRIS

BUFORD

FRENCH

Shepherdstown

Frederick

Baltimore & Ohio RR

Crampton's
Pass

Monocacy River

Harpers
Ferry

FRENCH

Potomac River

Confederate forces
Union forces

Lee's deliberately slow march and bold rear guard on 5 July had a profound effect on Meade and his lieutenants. Meade halted the movement of the Army of the Potomac altogether for nearly thirty hours. It gave Lee, in the end, almost twelve more hours than Meade to move his army closer to the Potomac River; it gave Lee's trains more than thirty hours to reach Williamsport and cross the river. Sedgwick's Sixth Corps near Fairfield stood still. Newton's First Corps and Birney's Third Corps were at Gettysburg; Major General Oliver Otis Howard's Eleventh Corps held a position along the Emmitsburg Road between Emmitsburg and Gettysburg. All three corps remained within supporting distance of Sedgwick. Sykes's Fifth Corps, bivouacked along the Emmitsburg Road at Marsh Creek south of Gettysburg, also remained within supporting distance. Slocum's Twelfth Corps and the Artillery Reserve were at Littlestown, and Hays's Second Corps was at Two Taverns; both were still protecting the long supply line from Westminster to Gettysburg.[14]

HILL'S AND LONGSTREET'S CORPS remained at Monterey Pass on the night of 5 July. All along the Emmitsburg-Waynesboro Turnpike near the Monterey House, the Union prisoners of war begged for food and medical attention, neither of which their guards or Lee's army were able to give them. They rested that night in ankle-deep mud. Responding to the problems posed by the hungry prisoners, Major Fairfax of Longstreet's staff started to issue paroles to the Union officers and men near the Monterey House early on the morning of 6 July. In spite of the Union War Department injunction against giving paroles, many Union officers and men were glad to oblige.[15]

While elements of Rodes's Division, particularly Captain Hopkins's Forty-fifth North Carolina, fought a sharp rear-guard action at the base of the South Mountain range just west of Fairfield on the foggy morning of 6 July, many Union prisoners were lining up to give their paroles to Major Fairfax. Some of them, like Private Royal N. Joy of the Ninety-fourth New York, used the heavy fog to escape. Small arms and artillery fire from the eastern base of South Mountain echoed through the forests. At about 9:00 A.M. General Longstreet rode up to Major Fairfax. He had received orders from Lee to stop the paroling of prisoners of war. Longstreet ordered Fairfax to cease, gruffly asserting that all of the prisoners would be taken to Richmond, including those who were sick or wounded. Everyone was ordered to form in line to continue the march.[16]

Longstreet's Corps led the march from Monterey Pass to Hagerstown on 6 July. According to Longstreet's orders, McLaws's Division was in front. A brigade of the division was placed at the head of the column, followed by

Colonel Alexander's reserve battalion of artillery, three remaining infantry brigades, the division's trains, and finally Cabell's and Henry's Artillery Battalions. Behind Cabell's and Henry's guns were three brigades of Hood's Division, followed by Hood's trains and those of Cabell's and Henry's Artillery Battalions. With the trains was the ambulance carrying Dr. Darby and Generals Hood and Hampton. One of Hood's brigades formed the rear of Longstreet's Corps.[17]

Hill's Corps followed Longstreet on the morning of 6 July. The order of march was similar to Longstreet's: Heth's Division led the corps, followed by Pender's Division; Anderson's Division brought up the rear. Pickett's Division, Dearing's Artillery Battalion, and all of the Union prisoners of war, under the direction of the army commander, marched with Hill's Corps on 6 July. Pickett's infantrymen, with bayonets attached to their muskets, trudged along in the fields on either side of the roadway where the rainsoaked and muddy Union prisoners were crowded together, proceeding in columns of fours and in distinct divisions. Always separated from the captured enlisted men, the Union officers were marched in a single column by Pickett's men.

Although Lee's 4 July orders for the withdrawal called for army headquarters always to be in the middle of the retreating army and for Longstreet's Corps to remain the center column, it did not work out that way. Lee rode with Longstreet's Corps on 5 July. But after directing Longstreet to take the lead on 6 July, Lee and his staff rode beside Hill's Corps in the middle of the retreating army. That position kept Lee in closer communication with all elements of his force.

Lee's change in plans for the march undoubtedly occurred because it had taken Hill too long to move from Gettysburg to Monterey Pass, and there had been some confusion. Moreover, Hill's troops were tired. Once across the mountains, Lee wanted to pick up the pace of the retreat; he was concerned about the safety of the army's trains at Hagerstown and Williamsport. Longstreet's Corps consequently moved ahead. The Union prisoners were left to follow Hill's Corps; eventually they were even passed on the road by Ewell's Corps.

As Longstreet's Corps cleared the western face of the mountain, Hill's Corps with the Union prisoners at the rear, moved into line. So vast were the columns of troops, artillery, and wagon trains accompanying them that it took nine hours for Longstreet's and Hill's Corps to clear the road so Ewell's troops could begin the march. It was midafternoon before Ewell's men got fully under way. To keep the trains moving at a steady pace and to keep open the lines of communication between Lee and all elements of the army, the infantry marched in the fields on either side of the turnpike once the troops reached the western base of the mountains; the artillery and wagon trains stayed in the middle of the road. Pioneer teams, armed with axes and hatchets, moved ahead of the infantry columns to clear all fences and other obstructions.[18]

Ewell's Corps did not begin to move until between 1:00 and 3:00 P.M. That caused General Sedgwick to remain at Fairfield throughout the day. Sedgwick ordered General Neill and his Sixth Corps brigade and Colonel McIntosh's cavalry forward to follow Lee's rear guard if and when it finally began to march. Neill was accompanied by some staff officers, including a young engineer from General Warren's staff, Lieutenant Ranald MacKenzie. The day was dark and overcast, and the heavy fog that hung close to the ground made visibility very limited. Neill directed McIntosh's troopers forward. Intelligence from Neill soon revealed to Sedgwick that Lee was withdrawing over the mountains toward Waynesboro. It was nearly 4:00 P.M.[19]

On learning from Sedgwick that Lee was moving to Waynesboro, Meade made up his mind to begin the pursuit. Although he had discussed the possibility of following Lee through Monterey Pass to Waynesboro and Hagerstown, it was never a serious option. Such a route would have taken the army far from any base of supply. In fact, it would have cut Meade off altogether from whatever base he chose. Pursuing Lee through the mountain pass would also have exposed Meade's army to attack in the mountains while it was in a most disadvantageous position. Lee clearly wanted Meade to follow him into the mountains. Instead, Meade directed his corps commanders to follow the marching orders to Middletown that he had given almost thirty hours before. He also changed his base of supply from Westminster to Frederick. Meade set his army in motion to intercept Lee through the only other passes available to him — Turner's, Fox's, and Crampton's Passes west of Middletown.[20]

On the morning of 7 July Sedgwick directed his Sixth Corps to move down the Jack's Mountain Road, east of Jack's Mountain, and the Emmitsburg-Waynesboro Turnpike to Emmitsburg, leaving behind Neill's Brigade and McIntosh's Cavalry. Those two brigades, along with a battery of rifled guns, were organized into a "light division" under General Neill and instructed to follow Lee through Monterey Pass and into the Cumberland Valley. Neill's light division was to keep a safe distance from Lee's rear and report enemy movements to Meade. When the Army of the Potomac had crossed the mountains, Neill's command would be reunited with the Sixth Corps.[21]

Meade ordered the First, Third, and Sixth Corps to march at dawn, 7 July, through Emmitsburg to Middletown by a "direct road" through Mechanics-

Edwin Forbes's painting of what appears to be the Third Corps of the Army of the Potomac marching through the rain and mud toward Middletown, Maryland, during Meade's attempt to intercept Lee's army. Library of Congress, Washington, D.C.

town, Lewistown, and Hamburg; and the Fifth and Eleventh Corps, through Emmitsburg, Creagerstown, Utica, and Highknob Pass to Middletown. The Twelfth Corps and the Artillery Reserve at Littlestown and the Second Corps at Two Taverns were to march to Taneytown, then through Middleburg, Woodsborough, and Frederick to Middletown. Meade directed each corps to traverse the South Mountain range to the vicinity of Boonsboro by the evening of 8 July. The pontoon bridges he requested were on the way to Harpers Ferry, one via the Chesapeake and Ohio (C&O) Canal and the other via the Baltimore and Ohio Railroad.[22]

One of Meade's most difficult maneuvers was to realign all of his army's quartermaster and subsistence trains with their respective corps. The trains were ordered to leave Westminster and move to Frederick late on the afternoon of 6 July. There they would be in a position to rejoin their respective corps as they marched from Middletown to the passes in the South Mountain range. General Rufus Ingalls, chief quartermaster of the Army of the Potomac, had issued detailed instructions earlier that day to all corps quartermasters on the most rapid means of getting word to those in charge of the trains at Westminster to rejoin their respective corps when the decision was finally made to change the army's base of supply. Private J. P. Coburn of the 141st Pennsylvania drove a quartermaster wagon in the trains of the First Division, Third Corps. His was one of more than six thousand wagons that started from Westminster on roads that were deep in mud and water. With the trains were thousands upon thousands of cattle. Coburn recalled traveling fourteen miles toward Frederick in a column of wagons and then having to turn back seven miles to Uniontown before finally heading once again to Frederick. Apparently the quartermasters set their trains in motion prematurely on 6 July; they turned back toward Westminster until there was more certainty of Meade's course.[23]

As a result of the difficulty of getting all the trains to Frederick, Meade's troops were required to endure more hard marching without their quartermaster and subsistence stores. Over rough and muddy roads, many of the men became shoeless; all of the men and animals became ravenously hungry, and quartermasters and soldiers had to resort to impressing and confiscating food for themselves and forage for their animals all along the way. The wagon trains did not arrive in Frederick until the afternoon of 7 July; many did not actually reach the troops to which they were attached for days.[24]

A reporter in Meade's army at Frederick on 7 July told of the challenges that the soldiers of the Army of the Potomac faced while being separated from subsistence stores for so long:

> Every hotel, eating house and private house in Frederick, and all the surrounding towns through which the army passed, have been completely eaten out, stripped of everything edible and bibible, and hundreds of hungry officers are turned away from the hotels every hour, disappointed at not being able to get a meal, and as for forage for horses, it is [at] most as scarce as gold dollars. The crops are abundant, but the men can't eat hay, straw and raw corn, and the farmers have exhausted their supplies of bacon, bread and vegetables in supplying the soldiers. If such is our condition, what must that of the rebels be who have no large cities to draw supplies from as we have?[25]

On the western side of the South Mountain range, Lee's army was in the Cumberland Valley on 6 July, only a day's march from the Potomac River. To the sound of gunfire from the direction of Hagerstown and Williamsport, where Kilpatrick's and Buford's cavalry divisions were attacking the defenders of Lee's wagon and ambulance trains, the long lines of Confederate infantrymen and artillery battalions and the trains accompanying them descended the western face of South Mountain and snaked their way toward Waynesboro. Neill's light division pursued Lee's rear guard, although keeping a safe distance from it.[26]

All along the way, foraging parties from every regiment, brigade, division, and corps in Lee's army scoured the countryside for horses, mules, cattle, sheep, hogs, wagons, and quartermaster and subsistence stores. Longstreet's chief quartermaster reported capturing horses on 6 July. That day quartermasters of Hood's Division seized 2 horses, 41 bushels of corn, and 55 bushels of oats. The quartermaster of Law's Brigade reported confiscating more than 100 bushels of corn and 1,700 pounds of hay, while the Texas Brigade appropriated 30 bushels of corn and 27 bushels of oats. Benning's Brigade obtained 51 bushels of oats and 400 pounds of hay; Anderson's Georgia Brigade seized 4,160 pounds of oats, 50 bushels of wheat, and 1 horse. The reserve artillery battalion of Longstreet's Corps brought back numerous bushels of corn and several horses, while the quartermaster of Cabell's Artillery Battalion snapped up 76 bushels of corn and 1 horse. Even the quartermaster of Pickett's Division reported taking sizable amounts of bran and horses.[27]

Less organized foraging was equally effective. Lee's troops had not been fed for days, and marching along roads and fields that were deep in mud and water was most difficult. Although Lee kept good order in the ranks and discouraged depredations, he allowed the hungry soldiers to forage on their own. As during the advance into Pennsylvania, Lee not only accepted foraging by the soldiers but also encouraged it to the extent that it augmented the efforts of the commissaries to supply the men with enough food during the journey.

In a letter home, Lieutenant Alexander McNeill of the Third South Carolina, Kershaw's Brigade, claimed that his men "had not one single full day's rations in nearly a week." They were famished. "We [were] forced to kill sheep, hogs and chickens wherever we could get them to partially allay our hunger." "Our boys are very hungry," wrote Private Eaton of the Fifty-seventh North Carolina, Pettigrew's Brigade, of the march of Hill's Corps along the western base of South Mountain. "[They] shot hogs and sheep down on the way to eat."[28]

Longstreet's leading corps marched down the Emmitsburg-Waynesboro Turnpike to Waynesboro and then turned south, heading toward Leitersburg. So fast was the pace that the troops reached the vicinity of Hagerstown at about 5:00 P.M. on 6 July, not long after the fighting ended in the town's streets. As Hood's and McLaws's Divisions headed down Potomac Street, they were directed onto the Hagerstown-Sharpsburg Turnpike, finally going into bivouac along Antietam Creek just west of Funkstown. The ambulance carrying Generals Hood and Hampton and Dr. Darby proceeded along the Hagerstown-Williamsport Turnpike to Williamsport.[29]

Hill's Corps followed Longstreet. Wright's Brigade began the march on

6 July from well below Waterloo, near Waynesboro. By virtue of its forced march in the wee hours of 5 July to Monterey Pass, Wright's Brigade was ahead of all other brigades in Hill's Corps, although on the sixth its division—Anderson's—formed the rear of Hill's columns. Private W. B. Jenkins of the Twenty-second Georgia, Wright's Brigade, noted in his journal that he and his fellow hungry Georgians, in desperation, resorted to pillaging the burned wagons along the roadside left behind after Kilpatrick's Union cavalry division attacked the trains of Rodes's Division at midnight on 4 July. Jenkins found a quantity of salt in some of the wagons, and he and others in the brigade eagerly divided it up among themselves.[30]

Although the march continued to be deliberately slow, Lee kept the army moving at a steady pace all day and as far into the night and ensuing morning as necessary to reach Hagerstown. With macadamized roads all the way from Monterey Pass, the pace increased. After brief stops at Waynesboro and near Leitersburg, Hill's Corps finally halted just before midnight, 6 July, near the Pennsylvania-Maryland line. The next morning, it marched to Hagerstown and camped due east of the town, covering the Smithsburg Road.[31]

Some of Wright's soldiers decided to forage on nearby farms. Private Jenkins wrote:

> Went to a man's chicken house and brought in five chickens and some of [the men] found a yearling calf, killed it, and brought it in, and [another soldier] found a hog and was after it, and he ran right by Gen'l Wright's headquarters, and the owner of the hog was there talking to General Wright; he asked the General to make the boys let that hog alone, as that was the only one he had left. Gen'l Wright had been drinking [and he] said to him, "The boys must have that spotted hog!" [The soldier] ran it a little way further, shot it and killed it. He skinned it, brought it to the camp, and we had plenty to eat for a day or two.

The foraging continued throughout the early morning of 7 July. "Some of the men," Jenkins recounted,

> went upstairs in a barn, and there they found thirty barrels of brandy hidden there. They knocked the head out of one barrel and by some means they turned it over and poured it out on John Teat of [Company] G, and it made him very drunk. The guard[s] got after them while they were getting the brandy, but they saw [them] in time to get away, for there was wheat all around the barn, as high as a man's head, they got into that and escaped. The guard[s] didn't catch any of them. I don't

supposed they tried very hard for they wanted some of the brandy themselves, and I suppose they got it.[32]

That brandy was the cause of more mischief. Infantrymen from the Sixteenth Mississippi in Posey's Brigade found it, and a "number of the men got drunk," according to Private Franklin Riley. Soon other Mississippians found the brandy. In the midst of it all, a drunken private in the Twelfth Mississippi shot an officer of the Nineteenth Mississippi.[33]

For the Union prisoners, the march was grueling indeed. They were very hungry, but food was scarce for even their captors. There were no more than two stops before evening, one at Waterloo and another at Waynesboro. Each time, the prisoners received only a small amount of flour. After resting at Waynesboro, they were on their feet again at dark. As the march resumed, they heard the clock atop the old town hall strike nine. Guarded by the remnants of Pickett's Division, they moved along until 2:00 A.M., when the column halted south of Leitersburg.[34]

On 7 July the prisoners of war were awakened at dawn. After waiting for Ewell's Corps to pass, they filed onto the turnpike, finally reaching Hagerstown at 10:00 A.M. The prisoners were guided down Potomac Street and out the Hagerstown-Williamsport Turnpike to within one mile of Williamsport. Their spirits were buoyed while passing through largely pro-Union Hagerstown as large numbers of townspeople lined the street to cheer them and deride their captors. But the cheers did not fill their empty stomachs. At Williamsport they each received a half pint of flour and a little beef. It was hardly enough. Many of them tried to barter for food from their captors, offering personal effects like gold watches, hats, shoes, lockets, clothing, and money for the measly Confederate rations.[35]

LIEUTENANT WILLIAM GORDON of the Eighth Virginia never forgot the march of Pickett's Division from Monterey Pass to Williamsport. "During all this time," he wrote,

> the rain continued to fall, the nights were pitchy dark, the roads a sea of mud and congested with men, artillery and wagons; but save for some occasional halts of short duration, the column never ceased to push on until [Hagerstown] was reached. It was a hard experience; fatigue, want of sleep and food, wet to the skin and cold, yet there was scarcely any confusion and but little complaining. For me everything was new, and in one of my letters dated on [July] 6th I gave utterance to my feelings as follows: "Am so tired I can scarcely keep my eyes open. Have

been constantly on the road, the rain falling in torrents. To add to my inconvenience my blankets and clothes have been sent off on another road (they were with Imboden's trains), and I have the prospect ahead of being compelled to live in damp and dirty clothes for many more days. It may appear grand and delightful to talk of soldiering but the reality, sleeping in a mud hole the rain wetting to the skin, with but a filthy saddle blanket to keep out the cold, is exactly the reverse."[36]

Late in the afternoon of 6 July Major John Warwick Daniel rode ahead of Ewell's columns on the Emmitsburg-Waynesboro Turnpike to locate army headquarters. Ewell's Corps continued to be the last column in the march; Rodes's Division brought up the rear, screened by Colonel White's Comanches. Daniel passed Pickett's Division along the way. "It was mournful to see the small squads that represented the full regiments that had so lately been proud of their numbers and their neat soldierly appearance," he wrote in his journal. He found the army's commander beside the turnpike east of Waynesboro, not far from a branch of Little Antietam Creek. Hill's Corps was then moving through Waynesboro. Ewell's Corps followed Hill's. "I saw General Lee," Daniel continued, "who had halted with his staff and pitched his tent by the side of a little brook. He was studying a map intently, seated on a stool, in the open air, and General A. P. Hill, Early and others were near him."

Lee had just received messages from Generals Imboden at Williamsport and Stuart near Hagerstown that the army had repulsed the enemy attacks against its trains and that the long-awaited reserve ordnance train had arrived from Winchester. He had also learned that the pontoon bridge at Falling Waters had been partially destroyed. Although the destruction of the bridge concerned him greatly, the victories at Hagerstown and Williamsport kept his trains safe, and now the army could replenish its ammunition. That was the most important news to Lee. With Longstreet's and Hill's Corps closing in on Hagerstown, Lee knew then that his army was in a position to protect those trains against another enemy strike.

Major Daniel was reassured by Lee's countenance. "It was impossible not to be struck with [Lee's] calm, composed and resolute bearing," he wrote:

He seemed to be entirely undisturbed by the trying scenes which he had so lately passed through, and by the still more trying ordeal through which he was now passing. He had seen the hopes of success blighted in a few hours; he had seen his gallant army twice driven back after hundreds had fallen, and he felt that the responsibility rested on his shoulders. The enemy's cavalry had been in his rear and destroyed a large portion of his trains, and a broad river was still between him and his country. Yet with all these misfortunes weighing upon him he was as calm as on a peaceful summers day.[37]

Major Hotchkiss soon galloped up to Lee, announcing that General Ewell had sent him to get more information about the route ahead. Lee stood up and told Hotchkiss to ride back quickly and inform Ewell that the army had not lost a critical number of wagons along the retreat routes and that the wagoners under General Imboden "had whipped the Yankee cavalry at Williamsport." "Tell General Ewell," Lee said, "if these people keep coming on, turn back and thresh them soundly." On reaching Ewell above Waterloo, Hotchkiss passed on the news and Lee's instructions. "By the blessing of Providence," Ewell remarked, "I will do it."[38]

Following Longstreet's and Hill's Corps, Ewell's men saw their own wagons that had been destroyed by Kilpatrick's army during its 4 July attack atop Monterey Pass. "This was a bitter sight for many as they passed along the road," wrote Daniel, "recognizing the remnants of their own wardrobes, torn garments, and the wrecks of a thousand and one articles that constitute a soldier's outfit strewed the road in profusion."[39]

Because of its late start on 6 July and its deliberate march, Ewell's Corps did not reach Waynesboro until nightfall. All along the way "details" from regiments were sent out "to kill hogs, chickens, etc.," wrote Private Watkins Kearns of the Twenty-seventh Virginia, Stonewall Brigade. Lee directed Ewell's troops to bivouac just east of Waynesboro. Neill's light division made no attempt to engage Ewell's rear guard, and there had been no opportunity for Ewell to "turn back" upon Neill's force, although his rear guard skirmished with Neill's vedettes almost every step of the way. Ewell's men stopped nearly twelve miles back up the road from Longstreet's leading corps. The Union columns following Ewell also halted and reported to Meade that Lee's army had reached Waynesboro.[40]

At Waynesboro, Ewell's men tried to find something to eat. "Our cooking detail with the wagons had only a half day's rations to cook up," noted Private Pickens of the Fifth Alabama Battalion, O'Neal's Brigade, Rodes's Division, "so we sent two or three men from our Co. to forage. They brought in flour only; [one soldier], though, came up with three hens." As Pickens's battalion was camped in a farmyard near a huge barn, the men were determined to provide themselves with as much comfort as possible. They literally stripped the barn of its wooden plank sides, laid them on larger beams, and covered them

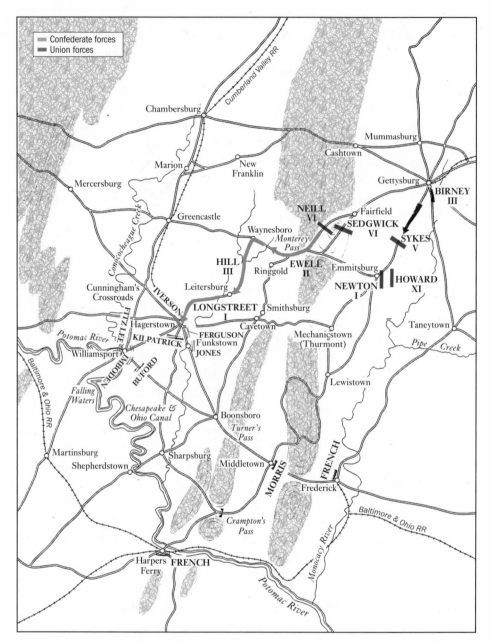

MAP 11.2   6 July 1863, evening.

Longstreet's Corps leads Lee's army, followed by Hill's Corps. Ewell brings up
the rear. Kilpatrick's Division strikes Lee's trains at Hagerstown, while Buford's
Division attacks at Williamsport. Meade gets his army under way in the late
afternoon.

with hay. They then "spread [their] blankets [over the hay]. I had as nice a bed as could be desired."[41]

Apparently the citizens of Waynesboro paid special attention to the large numbers of African Americans accompanying Lee's army. Although most slaves rode in the trains ahead of the marching troops, some of them followed their masters. While Ewell's Corps bivouacked east of Waynesboro, several slaves approached the farm of John Frantz, southeast of town, along Little Antietam Creek, looking for food for their masters. Seeing them, Frantz concealed his horses in a back room of the barn. The black men claimed that they were looking for eggs, but, while scouring the barn and farmyard, they found the horses. Frantz watched from his farmhouse as all of his horses "joined the Confederate army."[42]

Lack of rations was not limited to the soldiers in the ranks. Even General Ewell suffered from the same shortage. He thus sent Lieutenant Elliott Johnston, a volunteer aide on his staff, with a small escort from his courier company and some wagons to forage in the area. Elliott heard of one individual east of Waynesboro with "a good deal of bacon & a strong Radical bias" and called on him. The man was not at home, but his wife was. According to Elliott, she had "the eye of a tigress & a voice full of vinegar." When he asked for provisions, she claimed that there were none. He then demanded the key to her smokehouse, but she refused to let him have it. Elliott ordered the door broken down, but she got in front of it and screamed at him. He finally ordered her removed and the door smashed. The smokehouse was loaded with food. Elliott took bacon, fifty to sixty pounds of sausage, barrels of flour, and more. He brought back "all we needed & more than we expected," recalled Major Campbell Brown of Ewell's staff, though Elliott would forever claim that "he was never so abused in his life as by the old woman."[43]

Ewell's Corps left Waynesboro at daybreak, 7 July, and marched south through pouring rain toward Leitersburg and Hagerstown. Private John L. Hubbard of the First Maryland Battalion, Steuart's Brigade, Johnson's Division, had learned his trade as a buggymaker from a man named Peter Warner in Waynesboro before the war. As a consequence, he knew many people in town. The night before he had obtained permission from his temporary battalion commander to have supper at the home of his uncle and to spend the night at the Warners'. He returned to the ranks as Ewell's columns marched through the town at daybreak. "I was treated with respect by all," he wrote his uncle.[44]

Ewell's Corps marched through Leitersburg at noon, then past Pickett's Division and the Union prisoners to within two miles of Hagerstown. "There was a brass band on the side of the road playing 'Dixie' and 'Maryland' as [the troops] passed. It had the effect of enlivening & cheering us up very much," wrote Private Pickens.[45]

Nearby, Lee and his staff had stopped for a brief rest beside the road. It was hot and very humid; more rain was expected. Approaching on the turnpike were the long columns of Union prisoners with Pickett's infantrymen marching in the fields on either side of the road with bayonets fixed. Lee was sitting on a camp stool in the corner of a fence, "his hat at his feet and handkerchief in hand wiping his sunburned face and his white hair, matted with perspiration, clinging to his temples." Soon the band nearby struck up "Yankee Doodle" to enliven the prisoners as they passed. It then quickly changed to "Bonnie Blue Flag," to the laughter of the large number of Confederate officers and men. Prisoner of war Captain Frank E. Moran of the Seventy-third New York noticed that Lee's manner "was of quiet dignity, strongly at variance with the boisterous mirth of the young men around him, on whose harmless trick with the band he looked as he might on the gambles of so many kittens."[46]

To protect Lee's rear and left flank and the Hagerstown-Waynesboro Turnpike approach to Hagerstown, Ewell was directed to position his corps north and slightly northwest of the town. There it camped for the night and the next two days.[47]

On arrival at Hagerstown, Lee issued general orders to the troops. "The commanding general," they read, "desires that all needful arrangements be promptly made for an engagement which may be expected at any time. Additional ammunition has been received at Williamsport, and all required will be procured in the different commands respectively." Lee then added: "Animals needed in the artillery will be taken wherever found in the hands of officers and men unauthorized to be mounted and by impressment if necessary in the country, the animals to be paid for. The unauthorized practice of taking horses must be stopped." Systematically all soldiers who had seized horses while foraging forfeited their "finds" to the artillery service, where they were desperately needed.[48]

As Lee's columns settled down near Hagerstown, the quartermasters again "went into action." Longstreet's chief quartermaster reported seizing 7 horses, and the quartermaster of Hood's Division impressed 100 bushels of corn and 30 bushels of oats on 7 July. The quartermaster of Pickett's Division appropriated 210 bushels of corn and 6,000 pounds of hay; the quartermaster of the Texas Brigade, nearly 30 bushels of corn and 1,800 pounds of hay. Semmes's Brigade impressed 460 pounds of coal, 560 pounds of corn, and 2 horses; Anderson's Brigade, 3,100 pounds of hay; Benning's Brigade,

52 bushels of corn and 4,000 pounds of hay that day; and the Twenty-first Mississippi, 3 horses. The artillery battalions reported the largest amount of stores seized. Cabell's Battalion took 72 bushels of corn and 2,000 pounds of hay; Alexander's Battalion, 6 horses, 23 bushels of oats, 20 bushels of assorted grains, 55 bushels of corn, and 5,500 pounds of hay on 7 July. Details from Crenshaw's Battery in Major William J. Pegram's Battalion spent 7 and 8 July scouring the countryside for horses. The quartermasters of every regiment, artillery battalion, brigade, division, and corps of the army were similarly employed.[49]

The soldiers foraged all through the day and rainy night of 7 July. Private Jenkins of the Twenty-second Georgia described the day:

[Two soldiers in the regiment] went off somewhere and killed a large sheep, stole it, the lowest down stealing of all, but we did not stand on formalities for a hungered soldier would steal anything that he could eat, for we were nearly all the time hungry, and we were not going to let a sheep bite them anywhere. They brought it in [to camp], and we barbecued it, putting salt, vinegar and red pepper on it; we would get one side cooked, and turn it over to cook the other side, and what was cooked on the top side we would eat to where it was raw while the other side was cooking; eating it without any bread at all, for we had none of that for five days. When the other side was cooked we turned it over and ate that and by the time it was cooked it was all eaten. It did not take 22 men as hungry as we were long to eat a sheep weighing about 75 pounds.[50]

Posey's Mississippi Brigade bivouacked east of Hagerstown. Many of the troops wandered through the town foraging for food on 7 July. One soldier who accompanied a group of Mississippians began to rummage through a store. He suddenly shouted:

"Whiskey! Get a crowbar!" Some members of the Sixteenth Mississippi helped him break open the door. Before them was a cellar full of liquor. "The men flocked in, knocking out the heads of barrels and filling canteens," recalled Private Riley. As fast as one set got out, another took its place. Major [Edward] Counsel went down to try and get the men out, and separate those who were fighting, but they rolled a barrel of whiskey over him. It was impossible to do anything with them, and the whiskey had to give out before the men could be dispersed. Long after daylight the brigade moved out of town and into a field where it could sober up. That was the biggest "drunk" I ever saw.[51]

The ransacking of stores, houses, cellars, and outbuildings by the hungry soldiers occupying Hagerstown was not confined to Posey's Mississippians. Confederates from almost every element of the army milled in the streets searching for stores. Finally, Lee ordered provost guards to stop the plundering. The Reverend Dr. Kennedy of the Twenty-eighth North Carolina rode into Hagerstown on the rainy evening of 7 July. The town "was crowded with soldiers and the stores all guarded by sentinels," he noted in his diary. "I am informed that stores were broken open this morning and robbed. Gen'l Lee is trying hard to prevent incidents of that sort but I am sorry to say he has not been successful."[52]

Kennedy was right. One of the regiments designated to serve as provost guard on 8 July was Colonel Robert M. Mayo's Forty-seventh Virginia of Brockenbrough's Brigade, Heth's Division. Reportedly while serving as provost marshal, Mayo himself became intoxicated, undoubtedly from liquor removed from a cellar or store. He was arrested and, in August, tried and found guilty of violating army regulations. Nevertheless, he was never removed from command.[53]

In Hagerstown, Lee's troops found one of the hospitals that they had left behind on their way to Pennsylvania. A number of private residences had been serving as hospitals since mid-June. Filled mostly with Confederate soldiers who were sick with typhoid, debilitus, diarrhea, and other diseases, they had received a sizable number of wounded from the fighting in and around Hagerstown on 6 July, including Captain Frank Bond. The chief surgeon of the hospital in Hagerstown was Dr. Charles MacGill, a native of Hagerstown, who had practiced medicine there since 1829 and was well known in the area and in the lower Shenandoah Valley of Virginia. An ardent southern sympathizer, MacGill had been arrested and imprisoned by Union authorities in 1862. Released shortly afterward, he and his son, Dr. Charles G. W. MacGill, volunteered to open the hospitals in Hagerstown as Lee's troops moved toward Pennsylvania. Young Dr. MacGill followed the Second Virginia into Pennsylvania but rejoined his father as Lee's men returned to Hagerstown. One of those who was sent to the MacGills' hospitals for about three days was Sergeant James E. Whitehorne, of the Twelfth Virginia, whose ambulance managed to enter the town on 6 July after the fighting had stopped.[54]

Lee and his staff rode through Hagerstown to a location about one and a half miles south of town on the Hagerstown-Sharpsburg Turnpike. There

they established army headquarters west of Antietam Creek, immediately behind the bivouac sites and defensive positions of McLaws's and Hood's Divisions of Longstreet's Corps.[55]

APART FROM MEADE and his lieutenants, the persons most frustrated by
Lee's movements thus far were Southern newspaper reporters. The closest
many got to Lee's operations while in Pennsylvania was Martinsburg, West
Virginia. The reporters relied on the sick and wounded being hauled up
the Shenandoah Valley to explain what had occurred during the Gettysburg
campaign. That information being scant and unreliable, the Southern press
had been publishing Northern accounts of the campaign and battle. When
Lee's army withdrew to Hagerstown, some Southern reporters managed to
cross the Potomac River. Few got farther than Williamsport, though. Lee,
of course, did not want them near the army; he certainly did not tolerate
them anywhere near his headquarters. "We hear as little from the Confederate army [near Hagerstown]," wrote one reporter for the *Richmond Enquirer*,
"as if it were in the middle of Africa." Most Southerners would not learn about
the campaign until its casualties began to pour into Richmond and Lee's army
recrossed the Potomac River.[56]

After the army reached Hagerstown, Lee knew that more Union forces
than just the Army of the Potomac were on the move to confront him. Scouts
and civilians as well as Northern newspapers reported that troops from the
Department of the Susquehanna and the Department of West Virginia were
on their way to Hagerstown from the north and west respectively. Troops
from Major General Samuel Heintzelman's defenses of Washington were
marching toward Frederick, too. From Harrisburg, General Couch sent a division of raw militia under the command of General Smith south to Carlisle. Smith's Division struggled from Carlisle to Cashtown and then moved
south along the western base of the South Mountain range, through Altodale
toward Waynesboro, to report to General Neill.[57]

Smith's march to Waynesboro was a comic spectacle. The raw troops
quickly revealed to their general how little they were worth as a combat force,
although there were more than three thousand of them. "As a pitchy black-
ness rendered everything invisible," wrote Private George W. Wingate of the
Twenty-second New York National Guard,

> a lantern was carried at the head of the column to prevent those behind
> from being lost. Every few minutes we would be plunged into a moun-
> tain stream running across the road, and which could be heard falling

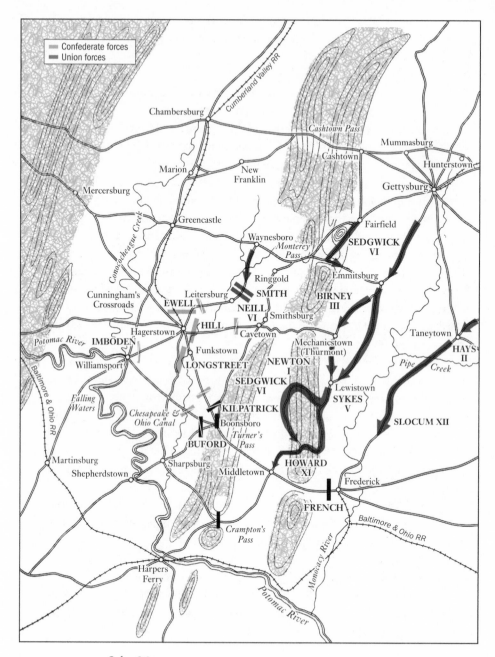

MAP 11.3   7 July 1863.

Lee rests in Hagerstown while Meade rapidly moves toward Middletown to be in position to push the Army of the Potomac through Turner's, Fox's, and Crampton's Passes.

an indefinite distance down the other side, wading across this, in an instant more we would find ourselves struggling knee deep in mud of an unequaled tenacity; and the efforts made to extricate ourselves generally resulted in getting tripped up by projecting roots and stumps. As those in front reached an obstacle, they passed the word down the line, "Stump!" "Ford!" "Stones!" "Mud hole!" Frequently, this latter cry became altered to "Man in a mud hole!" "Two men in a mud hole—look out sharp!"

Thus while Lee was resting his army at Hagerstown, Smith's Division was struggling along the muddy roads, trying to reach Waynesboro. Many of the men became shoeless on the way.[58]

Five miles southwest of Hagerstown, on 7 July, most of the trains brought to Williamsport by Major Harman and General Imboden stood in the streets and along the banks of the Potomac River waiting to cross. The river was swollen, yet only one flat still operated between Williamsport and the West Virginia shore. From the early hours of 5 July until the afternoon of 6 July, a seemingly endless stream of ambulances filled with sick and wounded officers, troops, and quartermaster, subsistence, and ordnance wagons, loaded with all kinds of impressed and confiscated stores, accompanied by herds of horses, mules, cattle, sheep, and hogs, had entered Williamsport both on the Hagerstown-Williamsport Turnpike ahead of Lee's army and on the Cumberland Valley Turnpike.

The remnants of the ambulance trains of Rodes's Division of Ewell's Corps had entered Williamsport by way of the Hagerstown-Williamsport Turnpike around noon, 5 July. Captains Park, Ross, and Hewlett, as well as Lieutenant Wright, all of the Twelfth Alabama, reached Williamsport at about the same time. They had stopped in Hagerstown long enough for some to get sandwiches and a bottle of whiskey at the Washington House hotel before continuing their journey to the Potomac River. The rain was pouring down. As the river was rising but still fordable then, Park and his comrades were driven through the Potomac River ford in a caravan of wagons and ambulances.[59]

As Park and his fellow officers entered Williamsport, the ambulance carrying Colonel Christie and Lieutenant Colonel Johnston of the Twenty-third North Carolina also arrived. Colonel Parker of the Thirtieth North Carolina and his "driver," Colonel Bennett of the Fourteenth North Carolina, maneuvered their two-seat buggy through the crush of men, animals, and wagons. Parker's face was matted with blood and swollen beyond recognition; Bennett's groin wound was inflamed and painful. Nevertheless, they reached the canal basin and, like Park and his officers, secured a place in a caravan of wagons and ambulances to cross the Potomac at the ford.[60]

Hundreds of Confederate casualties reached Williamsport but could go no farther. Colonel Lumpkin of the Forty-fourth Georgia was too sick to proceed, the stump of his amputated leg burning with infection. Unable to stand the journey in the filthy ambulance any longer, he was taken into a house near the Catholic church on Potomac Street.[61]

The ambulance carrying Generals Pender and Scales had reached Williamsport in the early afternoon of 5 July at the head of Imboden's trains. As they were high-ranking officers and were able to continue the journey, they were quickly taken down to the canal basin and piloted across the river by ferry.[62]

More and more critically wounded officers and men entered Williamsport. Probably in the early morning hours of 6 July, the ambulance carrying Lieutenants Hughes and Lucas and Lucas's slave from Imboden's trains entered Williamsport after traveling down muddy and deeply rutted roads south of Cunningham's Crossroads for nearly eight hours. Neither Hughes nor Lucas had had anything to eat before or after their narrow escape from capture at the hands of the "debris of Winchester." Their driver took them down to the riverbank, where they were ferried across the rapidly rising waters to the southern shore.[63]

Private Lineback of the Moravian band of the Twenty-sixth North Carolina arrived at Williamsport via the Cumberland Valley Turnpike at 2:00 A.M. on 6 July in the midst of General Imboden's trains and crossed the river with other wagons and ambulances. Just above Robert Lemen's two-story brick house, Maidstone-on-the-Potomac, he fell asleep beneath his oil cloth in the pouring rain. At daylight, Lineback "washed his feet, shoes and pants which were all equally muddy" and then made the return trip to Williamsport. "I managed to get a day's rations and after a good deal of difficulty, found most of my comrades together, there being an immense concourse of wagons parked in the river bottom."[64]

By the afternoon of 6 July, about 4,000 to 5,000 wagons and ambulances jammed the streets of Williamsport and the bottomland between the C&O Canal and the river. Nearly 30,000 horses and mules pulled them. "Wagons and wounded men on foot were ordered to cross [the river] as fast as possible," wrote Lineback, "as the river was rising slowly from the heavy rains." The river eventually reached a depth of more than thirteen feet due to the heavy rain on 4 and 5 July.[65]

Arriving in Williamsport at about the same time as Private Lineback was

A never-before-published photograph of Williamsport, Maryland, showing the bottomland between the C&O Canal and the Potomac River, where most of the nearly four to five thousand wagons and ambulances of Lee's army were parked waiting to cross the swollen river. The photograph was taken shortly after the war, when the railroad tracks were constructed. Library of Congress, Washington, D.C.

Dr. LeGrand Wilson, of the Forty-second Mississippi, who had narrowly avoided capture at Cunningham's Crossroads. "When I reached Williamsport," he recounted, "I found the streets all barricaded with wagons, and I thought I would never get into town. Had it been light I would have had no trouble, but I had to feel my way, and finally crawled over two or three wagons and reached an open street." Wilson found a house with lights burning and asked if he could have something to eat. He was given a cup of coffee, a meal, and a bed. There he slept through the early morning hours.

Wilson awoke about midmorning, 6 July, and reported to General Imboden, who instructed him to assume command of a train of ambulances that had just been assembled across the Potomac. By then, however, the river had become too deep and treacherous to ford. The one ferryboat was still all that was available. A long train of ambulances and wagons had arrived from Winchester under orders from Dr. Joseph Claggett; they were lined up along the southern shore near Robert Lemen's house waiting to be filled with the sick and wounded who were to be ferried across the river. "You will find it slow and hard work," Imboden told Wilson, "as I have but one ferry boat. There are 50 extra ambulances on the other side and surgeons to accompany them to the hospitals at Jordan Springs and Winchester. When you get them across, report to me."

Wilson found that it was indeed slow, hard work, but he kept the ferry running back and forth; he loaded his last ambulance and group of casualties at about midafternoon and proceeded across the river. He then reported to General Imboden that he had completed his crossings. The general thanked him and asked where he had been ordered to report.

"To the chief surgeon at Winchester," Wilson replied.

"Hurry up," Imboden said, "for the ambulances may leave you."

Wilson saluted and turned away.

"Good-bye," Imboden remarked. "I am very much obliged to you."

Wilson made it across the river and followed his ambulance train along the Valley Turnpike, leaving behind a town teeming with wagons, ambulances, and immense herds of cattle, sheep, hogs, horses, and mules and thousands of sick and wounded soldiers. They all awaited their turn to cross the swollen river on the one flat available. As he departed Williamsport, Wilson heard booming guns as Buford's cavalry division was storming Imboden's defense line east of town and Kilpatrick's Division was attacking Hagerstown.[66]

The ambulances carrying Generals Jenkins, Jones, Anderson, and Semmes and Major Latimer were directed to the canal basin, then ferried across the Potomac on the flat. They were placed in ambulances lined up along the southern bank of the river and driven up the Valley Turnpike toward Martinsburg and Winchester.

After the fighting ended east of Williamsport, General Imboden oversaw the launching of a second ferryboat that had been assembled near the canal basin by the assorted infantrymen and cavalrymen under his command. Stretching another cable across the river and attaching a flat to it, the second ferry began plying its cargo back and forth at a site upstream from the mouth of the Conococheague Creek near another river ford.[67]

Cannoneer Edward Moore of the Rockbridge Artillery arrived in Williamsport after the second ferry was put into operation. Moore's horse was nearly broken down. He saw another horse tied up to a nearby house where the owner, a muddy infantrymen, was fast asleep on the porch. Moore "exchanged" horses before the infantryman awoke and rode the fresh mount down to the canal basin. Virtually all of Moore's companions in the ambulance train of his artillery battalion had been captured at Monterey Pass on the night of 4 July and the early hours of 5 July, save for the badly wounded Tom Williamson, his friend from Washington College. "More of the horses," Moore recalled of the Williamsport ford,

> had to be swum over, as there was little room in the ferry boats for them. The river was so high that [swimming the horses over the river] was very dangerous and only expert swimmers dared to undertake it. Twenty dollars was paid for swimming a horse over, and I saw numbers swept down by the current and landed hundreds of yards below, many on the side from which they had started. I crossed in a ferry boat on my recently acquired horse, having left my faithful old charger, his head encased in mud to the tips of his ears, with mingled feelings of sadness and gratitude.[68]

Like Cannoneer Moore, Major Reynolds of the Eleventh North Carolina and Major Belo of the Fifty-fifth North Carolina sought to cross the river on the night of 6 July. They paid a wagoner to swim their horses across while they, along with their slaves, were transported on one of the flats.[69]

Colonel Black of the First South Carolina Cavalry was taken back to Williamsport just before the end of the fighting on 6 July. Wracked with typhoid fever, he had collapsed on the battle line and was carried to the tent of his regimental surgeon in town. Within a short time he was moved into the Presbyterian church, where he saw his old friend, the blind Captain McIver of the Eighth South Carolina. McIver was soon taken to a private house, where the surgeon believed that he would die quietly. On examining Black, the surgeon concluded that he must get to Winchester as quickly as possible. After saying good-bye to McIver, Black was taken to the canal basin and placed on a flat to cross the river. Late that night he was riding in an ambulance along the Valley Turnpike toward Martinsburg.[70]

After Black was ferried to the southern shore, the ambulance carrying Dr. Darby and Generals Hampton and Hood arrived at the Williamsport crossing. The two generals and their surgeon were quickly transported across the river on one of the flats.[71]

So slow was the movement of trains into Williamsport, due to the backup created by the high water and the limited means of crossing the Potomac, that the ambulance trains of Early's Division, Ewell's Corps, that were held up north of Hagerstown by the fighting on 6 July had to pull off the Hagerstown-

Williamsport Turnpike. Quartermasters and surgeons overseeing those trains established temporary hospitals in houses and barns nearby, as well as in the tollhouse midway between Williamsport and Hagerstown, in order to attend to the growing number of desperate cases under their care. Private Moore of the Fifth Louisiana, who had been wounded along East Cemetery Hill, reached a farmhouse about two miles north of Williamsport when the column of ambulances from Hays's Brigade halted. Rather than leave the sick and wounded men in the ambulances, the quartermasters and surgeons moved them into houses and barns, out of the pouring rain. Moore spent the next two days in a barn.[72]

In Williamsport, the division quartermasters and surgeons in the trains had made a concerted effort to organize hospitals by divisions and even by brigades. Warehouses along the canal basin and the dwellings up Potomac Street, including the German Lutheran church, were turned into hospitals for the sick and wounded of Hill's three divisions. Longstreet's casualties occupied the Presbyterian church on Conococheague Street and the dwellings beside it, across the street, and along Potomac Street nearby. Ewell's sick and wounded filled the Catholic church on Potomac Street and the dwellings on either side of the church and behind it, including "Springfield," the lovely Federal home built by Revolutionary War general Otho Williams on the north side of town. Even in the chaos that attended the arrival of Harman's and Imboden's trains, quartermasters and surgeons attempted to ensure some continuity of care of the sick and wounded. From nearly every church, dwelling, and public building on Potomac, Salisbury, Church, Artisan, Conococheague, Vermont, and Commerce Streets hung red and yellow flags denoting their use as hospitals.[73]

General Iverson's Brigade had entered Williamsport on the evening of 6 July after helping to defeat Kilpatrick's cavalry division at Hagerstown. Imboden designated the little brigade as the provost guard of the town and Iverson as provost marshal. As such, Iverson and his men protected Williamsport from being pillaged, oversaw the preparation and distribution of rations to the wounded and the return of empty ambulances, and organized all ambulance trains that crossed the Potomac River. Iverson's headquarters was established in the Taylor House hotel on Potomac Street, a two-story brick hostelry owned and operated by the pro-Union J. A. Ensminger and his wife. There, as well, were the quarters of Imboden himself as well as those of many of the surgeons attending the sick and wounded in the town.[74]

By the time Lee's army reached Hagerstown, Williamsport and its environs had become foul. With all the horses and mules, accompanied by thousands of cattle, sheep, and hogs, the stench from offal was overpowering. On the evening of 7 July, Private Baker of the Eighteenth Virginia Cavalry, Imboden's Brigade, returned to Williamsport after being on patrol west of town near Clear Spring. "[Williamsport] was an awful place," he recalled, "the dead horses and the offal of the great number of beeves, etc. packed around the little town made it very unpleasant for us when we returned to camp after night. The green flies were around us all the time and orders were not to unsaddle or unbridle our horses [but] be ready for duty all the time. Our blankets were under our saddles and soaked with water and the green flies were working under the rawhide covering our saddles and ulcerated [the backs] of our horses." Lieutenant Gordon of the Eighth Virginia noted the odors that permeated the town and the surrounding countryside while he guarded Union prisoners as they rested under thousands of shelter halves north of town. "We camped amongst dead horses and Union people," he wrote his wife, "who sent forth stench enough to create a plague."[75]

As a result of the fighting east and north of Williamsport on 6 July, the town was inundated with more wounded and dying officers and men. Riverview Cemetery on Commerce Street, overlooking the Potomac River, became the graveyard for many of the dead from the fighting that day as well as some occupants of the ambulance trains who died in the Williamsport hospitals. Buried there on 6 and 7 July were J. T. Hubble, quartermaster of the Fifth Virginia; Private Philemon Lineback of the Twenty-first North Carolina; Private James W. Driskill of the Sixth Alabama; and Sergeant John R. Barnes of the Forty-third North Carolina; and with fifty others—all killed on 6 July while trying to save the trains that had gathered in Williamsport from the attack of Buford's cavalry division. Also buried in that cemetery was Captain Pegram of Company F, Twenty-first Virginia, and three of his men.[76]

There was another burial in Riverview Cemetery. Elijah, the slave of Colonel Avery of the Sixth North Carolina, finally realized that he could not take the remains of his dead master any farther in the heat and rain. He drove his quartermaster wagon to Riverview and buried Avery's remains in the soft earth near the graves of the battle casualties of the "wagoners' fight" and those who had died in Williamsport hospitals.[77]

The dead were laid to rest all over Williamsport; there were burials in a town lot opposite the Presbyterian church, in the Catholic burial ground, in the town's stone quarry, and in a lot beside the Embrey warehouse at the canal basin. Otho Williams's farm on the Williamsport-Downsville Road and "Springfield" on the Hagerstown-Williamsport Turnpike also contained

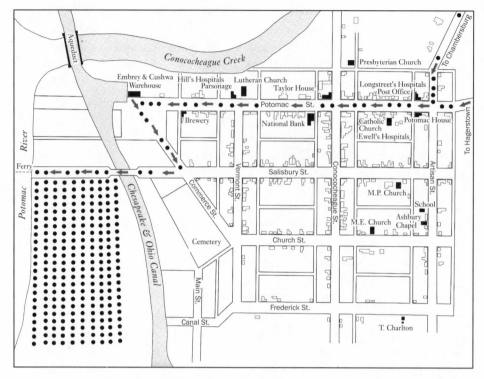

MAP 11.4   6 July 1863, Williamsport, Maryland.
Major Harman's trains reach Williamsport by way of the Hagerstown-
Williamsport Turnpike, and General Imboden's trains are arriving by way of the
Cumberland Valley Turnpike. Both converge on Potomac Street. Most are parked
along the river bottom between the C&O Canal and the Potomac River. Division
and brigade hospitals of Longstreet's, Ewell's, and Hill's Corps are established
along Potomac Street.

a number of Confederate graves, as did the farm lots on either side of the
Hagerstown-Williamsport Turnpike and even the lot behind the tollgate.[78]

Major Bird, quartermaster of Benning's Brigade, wrote to his wife from
his tent in the wagon park beside the Potomac River at Williamsport. He
had arrived in the rear of Imboden's trains on 6 July. "Oh, my darling," Bird
wrote, "these are sad, sad times. I sicken and weary of them, and my heart
turns to you and longs so earnestly for your presence."[79]

Twelve

A strong line of gopher holes

The morning of 8 July was cloudy and dark, but the rain had stopped. The Potomac River was still swollen, and there were no prospects of it falling soon after the heavy rain of the previous day and night. As his army could not cross the river, Lee realized that he must position it in the strongest defenses he could find in the area between Hagerstown and the Potomac as well as reconstruct the pontoon bridge at Falling Waters. The establishment of defenses was the first order of business, as the army's vast trains crowded in Williamsport needed protection. Lee and his personal staff engineers, Lieutenant Colonel William Proctor Smith, Major John J. Clarke, Captain Henry T. Douglas, and Captain S. R. Johnston, met with Generals Longstreet, Ewell, and Hill and their staffs and staff engineers at Lee's headquarters. The entourage then mounted up and reconnoitered the area to determine the contours and makeup of a line of defense from Hagerstown to the Potomac. Lee, accompanied by his corps commanders, was in the saddle until dark.[1]

Meade's army was approaching the mountain passes, only twelve miles away. General Howard's Eleventh Corps and General Sykes's Fifth Corps were both at Middletown. Two or three miles behind the Fifth Corps was Newton's First Corps. The Sixth Corps, under General Sedgwick, and the Third Corps, under newly appointed General French, were farther to the rear. All of those commands, plus the Artillery Reserve, were expected to move through the mountain passes by evening. The Second and Twelfth Corps had just arrived in the vicinity of Frederick because of their late start and duty along the Baltimore Pike near Two Taverns and Littlestown, east of Gettysburg. They had been on the march since 5:00 A.M. The journey of the Army of the Potomac had been incredibly fast. It slowed down only as

James E. Taylor's sketch of Middletown, Maryland, looking east with the tall steeple of the Reformed Church, one of Meade's signal stations, visible in the center. The Western Reserve Historical Society, Cleveland, Ohio.

the troops reached the mountain passes because the rains had made the roads through them "frightful."[2]

The Union soldiers marching up the National Road on 8 July were a sight to behold. They were soaked; many had lost their shoes in the deep mud. "For two days," wrote Captain Charles H. Weygant of the 124th New York, "we had been bespattering each other with mud and slush, and soaked with rain which [fell] in torrents. Our guns and swords were covered with rust; our pockets were filled with dirt; muddy water oozed from the toes of the footmen's government shoes at every step, ran out of the tops of the horsemen's boots and [rain still] dropped from the ends of the fingers, noses and chins of all."[3]

Many soldiers who had lost their shoes "kept their pants rolled above their knees and declared they would 'wade it through bare-footed, sink or swim.'" Half of the men in the Eleventh Corps were said to be shoeless by 8 July. That figure was probably much the same in Meade's other six corps. All were ravenous. To ease the hunger pains, quartermaster and subsistence teams and individual soldiers seized, impressed, and stole all the food they could locate at stores, houses, or farms along the way.[4]

Illustrative of the desperate condition of Meade's army, many artillery batteries could not accompany their corps on the march from Middletown through the mountain passes to Boonsboro. The horses and mules pulling

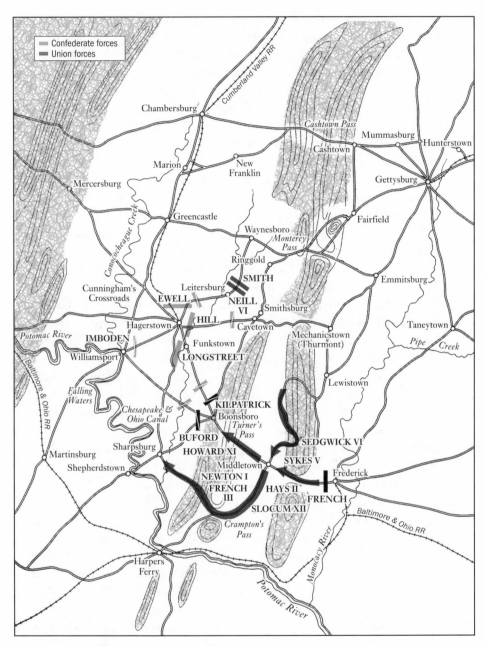

MAP 12.1 8 July 1863.
Meade approaches Lee through Turner's, Fox's, and Crampton's Passes.

many of the guns and caissons were so exhausted and weakened by excessive campaigning and lack of forage that they collapsed in the middle of the National Road. Up to this point in the campaign, nearly 15,000 horses and mules had been abandoned by Meade's troops or had broken down and were unserviceable. Meade had been trying to remedy the problem for days. He had been assured by Quartermaster General of the Army Montgomery C. Meigs that rail shipments of horses were being sent from Washington, D.C., to Frederick. On 7 July Meigs notified him that 4,800 horses would leave Washington the next day.[5]

Buford's and Kilpatrick's cavalry divisions screened Meade's fast-approaching columns from positions along the National Road near Beaver Creek and along the Williamsport-Boonsboro Road west of Boonsboro. But Lee needed time to construct a defense line between Hagerstown and the Potomac River; this meant that Meade's army had to be kept at a distance. Colonel Alexander believed on 8 July that Lee had only about forty-eight hours before all of Meade's army would be in position to strike.[6]

On the morning of 8 July Lee directed the indefatigable J. E. B. Stuart to take five of his brigades and the Stuart Horse Artillery and move as close to Boonsboro as possible, covering the Beaver Creek, National, and Williamsport-Boonsboro Roads. There, Stuart could determine for Lee the whereabouts of Meade's main columns, while, at the same time, scouring the area for more "flour and forage." If Meade's cavalry advanced against him, he could slow its progress there while the engineers and their pioneers and laborers finished laying out the defense line west of Funkstown.[7]

Stuart called upon the brigades of Jones, Fitzhugh Lee, Baker, Chambliss, and Ferguson and the batteries of Breathed, Chew, Griffin, McGregor, and Moorman of the Stuart Horse Artillery to move forward. Led by Grumble Jones and his brigade, most of those brigades and batteries advanced down the National Road from Funkstown to Beaver Creek; Ferguson's Brigade and McGregor's Battery proceeded down the Williamsport-Boonsboro Road from near St. James College to about four miles west of Boonsboro. Robertson's undersized brigade was left to protect the approaches to Hagerstown by way of the Smithsburg Road, and the battalions of cavalry from Maryland were sent out to patrol the Cumberland Valley Turnpike, screening Lee's left flank and rear. Imboden's independent brigade, under Lee's personal orders, patrolled the roads west of Williamsport all the way to Clear Spring.[8]

The movement of Stuart's five brigades was spotted by the Union signal station atop the ruins of the stone, silo-shaped Washington Monument in Turner's Pass. General Buford responded quickly to the signal flags. To screen the movements of Meade's main columns then marching toward the passes through South Mountain, Buford placed Gamble's Brigade to the right of the National Road about one and a half miles from Boonsboro. Lieutenant Calef's six ordnance rifles were unlimbered to the right of the roadway. Merritt's Brigade covered the fields between the National Road and the Williamsport-Boonsboro Road to the left of Gamble. Devin's Brigade held the Williamsport-Boonsboro Road to the left of Merritt, while Lieutenant Graham's six ordnance rifles came into battery in the road supporting Devin. Kilpatrick's Division remained in reserve east of Boonsboro, impressing food and fodder from the civilians in Boonsboro and Pleasant Valley to feed its hungry men and jaded horses.[9]

Jones approached the skirmishers of Buford's Division along the National Road just after midmorning. Because the ground was so soft from heavy rains, a mounted advance was out of the question. Instead, Jones ordered his men to dismount, every fourth trooper holding the horses of the other three. He advanced the men toward Gamble's Union brigade on foot, accompanied by the four guns of Chew's Battery. The brigades of Fitzhugh Lee, Baker, and Chambliss and three artillery batteries remained mounted behind Jones, ready to respond as the action unfolded. In the meantime, quartermasters and subsistence officers from all four brigades, along with forage teams, gathered all the grain and hay they could find from neighboring farms; they even took some of the grain they had seized to mills along Antietam Creek and ground it into flour while Jones's troopers drew enemy fire.[10]

Along the Williamsport-Boonsboro Road, the dismounted brigade of Colonel Ferguson made contact with Devin's Union troopers. Colonel Devin had the Sixth New York and Seventeenth Pennsylvania dismount and advance on foot on either side of the road to contest Ferguson. Captain McGregor then raced his four-gun Virginia Battery forward to an eminence on the left of the road, completely commanding the Union position. The fighting grew intense. Troopers on both sides fired at one another from behind stone fence lines, trees, and underbrush. While Lee's engineers were laying out a defense line for the army and gangs of pioneers and laborers were digging trenches and gun emplacements two miles west of Funkstown, brutal, close-order fighting erupted between cavalry skirmish lines and artillery batteries two miles west and northwest of Boonsboro.[11]

Soon the sheer weight of numbers began to tell. The Confederate brigades and field artillery on the National Road outstripped Buford's men. The Union cavalrymen's ammunition was rapidly being depleted, and their horses were in need of forage and shoes. Devin's Brigade tried desperately to get possession of the eminence along the Williamsport-Boonsboro Road held by McGregor's four guns but could not. The dismounted Sixth New York and Seventeenth Pennsylvania were pushed back to the main lines of Devin's Brigade by heavy Confederate rifle and artillery fire. The Napoleons of McGregor's Battery threw shell and canister at the Union cavalrymen and cannoneers with marked effect. Buford needed help, and he called for Kilpatrick to bring forward his division.[12]

Buglers blew "boots and saddles," and Kilpatrick's troopers mounted their worn-out horses. Soon, the column, led by the Fifth Michigan of Custer's Brigade, galloped through Boonsboro toward the sound of gunfire, accompanied by Pennington's and Fuller's rifled guns. As Gamble's Brigade was pulling back down the National Road, Kilpatrick ordered his leading commands to advance in its place. The Fifth Michigan dismounted and moved up the right side of National Road toward Jones's lines. The Michiganders drove the Confederates back, but then artillery fire from Chew's Battery brought the advance to a halt. To the chagrin of the Michigan troopers, they were called back to their horses. It was difficult "wallowing through the [muddy] fields," Private Henry Gordon Bliss of the Fifth Michigan wrote in his diary. The men remounted their horses, though, and moved to the left, dismounted, and were again led up the National Road.[13]

Buford called up the Eighth Illinois to reenter the fighting, but Colonel Gamble objected unless he could use his entire brigade. Buford agreed. Gamble's full brigade then came up to reinforce the Fifth Michigan along the National Road. Private Bliss always believed that he fired the first shot that led to what he referred to as a victory that day. As the skirmishers moved toward the Confederate lines, they were under instructions to hold their fire. A Confederate officer rode along his lines in the fields ahead of Bliss, giving instructions to his men. "I put my gun through the fence and said, 'Look at that Rebel. I have a notion to shoot,'" Bliss noted. "Several of [Bliss's fellow troopers] said, 'You must not shoot yet.' But my gun went off and the Rebel fell from his horse. Then the Colonel said, 'when you see a good chance, shoot.'"[14]

Several companies of Gamble's regiments dismounted and joined the skirmishers of the Fifth Michigan, driving the Confederates back. Without halting, "but yelling like Indians," they drove the Confederates from a woodlot. Caught up in the fighting, General Buford dismounted and followed the skirmishers as they advanced up the road. Jones's Confederates slowly fell back.[15]

General Stuart observed the action from a position along the National Road. As his cavalry brigades withdrew across Beaver Creek, a squadron of

Union cavalry galloped after them "as if to charge." Elements of the First North Carolina Cavalry of Baker's Brigade waited for the Union cavalrymen to reach "striking distance." Quickly the Union squadron veered off across the fields just as the crew of a Blakely gun in Chew's Battery found them in range. "Never did [a] sportsman bring down his bird with more unerring shot than did that Blakely tell upon that squadron," wrote Stuart. "In vain did [the enemy squadron] turn to the right and left. Each shot seemed drawn to the fly-ing target with fatal accuracy until the enemy, driven by the shots of the Blakely and followed by shouts of derision of our cavalry, escaped at full speed over the plain." By nightfall Stuart withdrew his cavalry about two miles back up the National Road and Beaver Creek Road toward Funkstown.[16]

Although the heavy clouds had cleared and there were rays of sunshine on the morning of 9 July, Buford and Kilpatrick were forced to remain in their positions. Their men were exhausted and hungry, and their horses were in desperate need of fodder and shoes. Far from any base of supply, the two cav-alry divisions, like their opponents, were forced to live off the land; they im-pressed and confiscated all the hay and grain they could find on neighboring farms. While Lee and his corps commanders and their staff engineers con-tinued their work on the defense line, the forward area covered by Stuart's cavalry brigades fell eerily silent, save for occasional skirmish fire and the movement of Union signal stations closer to Buford's front.[17]

West of Funkstown, Lee and his own staff engineers and his three corps commanders and their staff engineers, including Colonel Alexander and Major Hotchkiss, laid out a defense line that would protect the area be-tween Hagerstown and the river as well as Williamsport and the fords of the river. Scouring the terrain south of Hagerstown on 9 July, they "patched together" a defense line using a long and dominant, but very broken, ridge known locally as "Salisbury Ridge," while Stuart kept the Union cavalry at a distance. Lee, Longstreet, Ewell, and Hill rode along the defense line until noon. Lee himself seems to have paid the greatest attention to the center and, particularly, the right flank of the line, believing them to be the most vulnerable. To the left flank of the ridgeline Lee sent his chief engineer, Colonel Smith, along with Major Hotchkiss, to oversee the layout of its de-fenses. Accompanying Smith and Hotchkiss was a volunteer aide, Lieutenant McHenry Howard; it was dark when they returned to Lee's headquarters. There, Hotchkiss, whose topographical engineer train was parked nearby, was instructed to prepare maps of the entire line for Lee and his corps com-manders.[18]

"There was no very well defined & naturally strong line," recalled Colonel

Colonel Edward
Porter Alexander.
Library of Congress,
Washington, D.C.

Alexander, "& we had to pick & choose, & string together in some places by make-shifts & some little work." High, with long, undulating, and rocky slopes, Salisbury Ridge commanded the boggy lowlands drained by Antietam Creek, from Hagerstown to just south of Funkstown, and by a stream known as Marsh Run, from just north of the Williamsport-Boonsboro Road near St. James College to the Potomac River. The ridge rises to nearly 150 feet above Marsh Run, about one mile west of the stream. Any assault against the ridgeline by the Army of the Potomac would require it to crest several small ridges, struggle through muddy bottomlands, and then wade across Marsh Run before ascending forward slopes that extended nearly half a mile ahead of the crest.

Lee exercised considerable direction over the layout of the breastworks and gun emplacements and personally oversaw the work. "On the last day," noted Alexander, "at one point, where we differed [probably over the placement of artillery just west of St. James College], General Lee came out to see the ground, & decided in my favor, of which I was very proud."

Alexander claimed that he rather enjoyed laying out the defense line; he was, after all, a very competent military engineer. He also savored the "ripe cherries & raspberries which grew everywhere." But there was more. "I specially recall one day," he wrote, "when we got at some farm a lot of corn, Irish potatoes & other vegetables, & some fat chickens, & took them by my camp about noon, & late in the afternoon came back to one great big camp kettle, where everything was cooked up together. It was unanimously voted that no one had ever seen that dish equaled before."[19]

In anticipation of the army filling the defense line, Lee ordered Lieutenant Colonel Corley and Dr. Guild, along with the chief quartermasters and medical directors of Longstreet's, Ewell's, and Hill's Corps and the division quartermasters and chief surgeons, to establish division and brigade hospitals in Williamsport, three miles behind the frontline troops. Dr. James B. Clifton of the Sixteenth Georgia noted in his diary that the chief surgeon of Semmes's Brigade told him to organize the brigade hospital in Williamsport on the morning of 9 July. He was not only to set up the hospital in anticipation of receiving wounded from any attack against the defense line south of Hagerstown but also to assist in caring for the sick and wounded already in Williamsport. By all means, Clifton, like every surgeon in Williamsport, had the overarching duty to send to Winchester, as rapidly as possible, as many sick and wounded soldiers as he could. He left the camp near Funkstown and proceeded to Williamsport, arriving there at 10:30 A.M. He stopped first at the Taylor House hotel, where he reported to General Iverson, the provost marshal, and where the Ensmingers provided him with a bed and some food. Clifton then set out to visit the sick and wounded and organize a brigade hospital.[20]

On the morning of 9 July thousands of ambulances and wagons still huddled in the bottomland between Williamsport and the river and in the town streets. Thousands of cattle, sheep, hogs, horses, and mules were corralled among the ambulances and wagons and in the town. The rain that fell on the night of 7 July was so heavy that by 9 July the bottomland had become flooded and "seemed to be in danger of being overflowed," bogging down thousands of ambulances and wagons in a sea of water and soft alluvial mud. The "whole flat on which the wagons are parked," wrote Private Lineback of the Moravian band of the Twenty-sixth North Carolina, "was almost like a pond."[21]

The Eighth Virginia's Lieutenant Shotwell, who guarded the Union prisoners at Williamsport, got a glimpse of the thousands of wagons and ambulances huddled along the bottomland waiting to cross the river. "The spectacle," he wrote, "of our white canvas-covered vehicles, with horses and mules intermingled, is a very novel one, especially at night when campfires are blazing between the wagons. It can only be compared to the scenes of the great Mormon exodus across the prairies to Salt Lake, when 10,000 families, with every description of vehicle, were to be seen encamped."[22]

Jammed in the streets of Williamsport and along the canal basin were thousands of Union prisoners. Pickett's men had been trying to get them across the river for more than twenty-four hours. When they had started passing the prisoners across on 8 July, a rope holding one of the flats broke, forcing them to turn the prisoners around and march them back to camp north of town. Meanwhile, only the captured Union officers were ferried across the river on the remaining flat.[23]

At the time Dr. Clifton arrived in town, all prisoners of war had been moved back into Williamsport in an effort to get them across the river. A rope to guide the disabled ferry had been restrung, and both flats were again in operation. To increase the pace of the crossing, additional ropes were stretched across the river upstream from Williamsport, and canal boats were hauled up the canal to river ford sites upstream. The canal boats were attached to cables with makeshift pulleys and poled across the river with the ambulances, Confederate casualties, and Union prisoners. At least four ferryboats were in use on 9 July, plying their cargoes across the river and back from sites in front of Williamsport and as far as one mile upstream.[24]

Lieutenant Shotwell managed to cross the river with a group of Union prisoners on 9 July. From his vantage point near Maidstone-on-the-Potomac, he penned an unforgettable description of Williamsport that day:

> Once more on "Old Virginia's Shore"—and right glad to arrive! This afternoon all the prisoners and their guards were ferried over the Potomac—about 25 men per boat-load. The river is very full, muddy and swift, making the passage a not entirely safe or pleasant undertaking. I came over in the "first boat," and coming to the crest of a grassy slope, where I am now writing—stretched myself on the sward to rest and watch the ferrying over of the prisoners.
>
> It is novel, and not unpicturesque scene:—the broad rolling river with a creaking craft moving to and fro across it, the dense mass of blue clad prisoners, the innumerable wagons, ambulances, artillery and animals crowding the broad meadows on the suburbs of Williamsport, distant about a mile from where I am now lying, the tall church spires

pointing to the peaceful skies, and beyond them, high in the horizon, the bursting shells of Lee's artillery near Hagerstown!

Yet there is a sombreness about the drizzly atmosphere, and leaden sky that befits the contrast of the scene below—this dribbling return in a crazy craft, with the enemy howling at our heels—with the flaunting, cheering, joyous enthusiasm of our passage of this same stream scarce sixteen days ago. True we are not whipped, and need not return same as we wish. But, for all that may be said and truly said to that effect, the contrast is a sad one.[25]

Since the early morning of 5 July, herds of horses, mules, cattle, and sheep had been periodically driven through the swift moving Potomac River to the West Virginia shore by teams of mounted drovers. Most of the livestock had made it across safely, but some had not. On 7 July more than a thousand sheep and seven hundred cattle had been swept downstream and drowned. Their bloated carcasses, snagged in dams of driftwood and brush, lined the shores downstream as far as Harpers Ferry and Sandy Hook. Some, swept over feeder dams, drifted in midstream. With each effort to swim livestock across the swollen river, more dead and bloated animals had been added to the dreadful scene.[26]

Williamsport was a mess. Crowded into the streets and along the river bottomland were the thousands of horses, mules, cattle, sheep, and hogs; sick and wounded Confederate soldiers; thousands of Union prisoners; and all the personnel attached to the quartermaster, subsistence, ordnance, and ambulance trains. The stench was overpowering; animal and human offal and rotting animal corpses outside of town made the village intolerable. "Williamsport is a one-horse town," wrote Private Florence McCarthy of the Seventh Virginia, Kemper's Brigade. "The houses are riddled and almost all deserted and the country for a mile around is feted with beef offal and dead horses." The horses and mules pulling the trains and the horses of the cavalry were covered with green bottle flies. "Our horses backs were raw with ulcers, one and two inches deep and full of maggots," noted Private Baker of the Eighteenth Virginia Cavalry, Imboden's Brigade. "The green flies had put up a big job on us, our blankets were full of maggots and rotten, our saddles had from a pint to a quart of maggots in them."[27]

Private dwellings and public buildings as well as all the churches—German Lutheran, Catholic, Methodist-Episcopal, and Presbyterian—and warehouses along the canal basin had been used as hospitals ever since Ewell's trains first entered Williamsport in the wee hours of 5 July. As army surgeons and quartermasters followed on the ninth to establish brigade and division hospitals, they found that the town had already been somewhat organized. The newly arrived surgeons engaged in a concerted effort with their quartermasters to consolidate as many of their casualties as possible. Private Moore of the Fifth Louisiana recalled being moved from a barn on the Hagerstown-Williamsport Turnpike to the Catholic church, which had become the hospital for Hays's Brigade and Early's Division.[28]

As the quartermasters and surgeons set up division and brigade hospitals in Williamsport, the hospital in Hagerstown was slowly cleared of sick and wounded in anticipation of Lee's withdrawal. Dr. MacGill and his nurses took with them to Williamsport all of the patients who could be transported by ambulance, leaving behind Dr. John Wroe of Hagerstown to care for those who remained. One of those conveyed to Williamsport was Sergeant James E. Whitehorne of the Twelfth Virginia. He would remain in a shelter half in a hospital of Anderson's Division on Potomac Street until 13 July. Left behind was Captain Frank Bond, of the First Maryland Cavalry, whose leg wound was too serious to allow him to be moved.[29]

By the early morning of 10 July the Williamsport defense line was almost ready to receive the troops. It was none too soon. By then Meade's forces had all pushed west through Turner's, Fox's, and Crampton's Passes. The First, Second, Third, Fifth, Sixth, Eleventh, and Twelfth Corps and Artillery Reserve had passed through and around Boonsboro and were filling a line that extended from just west of Boonsboro to Rohrersville, covering the passes. It had taken hours to get artillery batteries and wagon trains through the deep mud of the roads across the mountain passes. Meade established his headquarters at the Mountain House in Turner's Pass, not far from the Washington Monument signal station, where Meade's telegraph service opened its office using the wires already in place to Middletown and Frederick. Additional signal stations were set up at Crampton's Pass and at Elk Ridge, overlooking Pleasant Valley, Antietam Creek, and Sharpsburg.[30]

At dawn Lee reassigned his own staff engineers to the task of building a bridge across the Potomac; he called upon all of his corps commanders to send their division pioneer teams to Williamsport to assist in the effort. Lee then set about personally inspecting the nine-mile-long defenses. After a while, he dismounted in "a little oak grove, near the line." He was all alone. Colonel Alexander spotted him and rode over to get instructions for some aspect of the works. Lee seemed uneasy; he was evidently concerned about whether his army could defend itself in the defense line. "His greeting," recalled Alexander, "was specially friendly & most affectionate, & after the matter upon which I had come was finished he detained me, & asked many questions about our lines, & seemed to try to draw out my opinion, & to take satisfaction in the confidence I felt that we could hold them."[31]

There was a growing urgency about filling the defense lines. That morning Lee's headquarters had received intelligence of the movement of two more Union armies. Reaching Waynesboro, twelve miles north of Hagerstown, was Smith's Division of Couch's Department of the Susquehanna. On the same day Neill's light division was near Leitersburg, pressuring Lee's left flank.

On 10 July Smith's green troops arrived at Waynesboro soaked to the bone, mostly shoeless, covered with mud, and famished. Rations had given out days before, and what quartermaster and subsistence trains had accompanied the troops were far behind, "broken down [and] stuck all along in the mud." On reaching the town, Smith's soldiers searched for food but found it "so cleaned out by the rebels that you could not even buy a tin cup; and although foraging parties scoured the country both in and outside the pickets with untiring zeal, the results were meagre enough." For operational purposes, Smith's Division was attached to the Sixth Corps behind Neill's light division.[32]

Moving east toward Hancock, Maryland, was Kelley's Army of West Virginia, nearly six thousand strong. With the Army of the Potomac west of Turner's Pass, Lee realized that he had a very narrow window of opportunity—three days at most—to cross the Potomac. But the continuous rain kept the river too high to ford. Meanwhile, Lee had to move his army into positions along the Williamsport defense line before Meade could deny him the opportunity.[33]

On the morning of 10 July most of Stuart's brigades and their artillery batteries had withdrawn up the National Road, across the stone Antietam bridge at Funkstown and onto the flanks of the army. Ferguson's Brigade remained along the Williamsport-Boonsboro Road with McGregor's Battery. Stuart brought Lieutenant Colonel Vincent A. Witcher's Battalion of mostly western Virginia cavalrymen from Ferguson's Brigade onto the National Road southeast of Funkstown; he sent Captain William Beverly Wooldridge and his company of the Fourth Virginia Cavalry from Fitzhugh Lee's Brigade onto the Beaver Creek Road, east of Funkstown.[34]

While Stuart recalled his brigades to positions west of Antietam Creek, General Meade put the Army of the Potomac in motion toward Lee. The Second and Twelfth Corps were ordered to march to Bakersville by way of Keedysville; the Fifth Corps was to move out the Williamsport-Boonsboro Road to the stone bridge over Antietam Creek, at the "Devil's Backbone."

The Third Corps was to follow the Fifth Corps. The Eleventh Corps and the Artillery Reserve were held in position just west and northwest of Boonsboro, while the Sixth Corps, followed by the First, were ordered to head out the National Road toward Beaver Creek, screened by Buford's cavalry division.

Meade kept his headquarters at the Mountain House until late in the day, when he informed his commanders that he would relocate to a position behind the Third Corps on the Williamsport-Boonsboro Road. His telegraph office would move only as far as Boonsboro. Meade admonished all of the commanders to remain in communication with the columns on their right and left and to be prepared to move forward "as the developments of the day should require." He expected a collision of some sort to occur, as he had been informed that Lee was "concentrating" in his front. Where that concentration was, though, he did not know. He had to find out before committing any of his troops to combat. In that rough countryside marked by dominating ridges and hills, Meade could not afford to let any of his corps become isolated and be attacked. Thus, his movement forward was a cautious one, each of his corps commanders seeking information as to the exact location of Lee's main lines.[35]

Lee's foraging continued even as Meade moved forward. Early on the morning of 10 July one company from each brigade was detailed to look for horses, mules, cattle, sheep, hogs, wagons, subsistence stores, and quartermaster supplies. General Mahone sent out his brigade quartermaster and Company A of the Twelfth Virginia. Captain Waddell of the Twelfth Virginia had left his ambulance in Williamsport on 8 July and reported to his regiment, then bivouacked northeast of Hagerstown. He found out that his slave Willis had run away with all of his camp gear. Waddell was still very ill with typhoid fever, but he was willing to do his duty. At 6:00 A.M. on the tenth, while the army waited to fill the trench lines, Waddell took his company, along with twelve empty quartermaster wagons, and scoured the countryside east of St. James College, covering more than eight miles. As the Union infantry columns neared his foraging teams, the brigade quartermaster called for Waddell to return his men to Mahone's camp. They arrived just in time to begin the march toward the defense line, their wagons filled with impressed and confiscated stores.[36]

The morning of 10 July was very warm; everyone knew the day would become intensely hot and humid. J. E. B. Stuart's vedettes on the National Road reported that Buford's columns were moving toward Funkstown, accompanied by an entire infantry corps and artillery. Indeed, Sedgwick's Sixth Corps was on the National Road just behind Buford. With no cavalry brigades left east of Funkstown, Stuart needed infantry and artillery reinforcements to keep Buford and Sedgwick from interfering with the completion of the Williamsport defense line as well as with the numerous foraging teams. What cavalry battalions remained were insufficient.[37]

Just east of Funkstown were fields marked by deep depressions and high, long ridges, broken by dense woodlots and stout post and rail and stone and rider fence lines. Enormous brick and stone bank barns, built by German farmers beside the roads, dominated the landscape.[38]

On the two roads leading into Funkstown from Boonsboro, Stuart deployed the skirmishers who remained. Witcher's Battalion dismounted and spread out behind stone fence lines mostly on the northern side of the National Road, about two miles east of Funkstown. Supporting Witcher's dismounted cavalrymen were the four guns of Chew's Battery that unlimbered in the middle of the road. On either side of the Beaver Creek Road, in Jacob Stover's Woods about one mile east of Funkstown, Wooldridge and his company dismounted and positioned themselves behind stone fence lines.[39]

Stuart had called for artillery to support Wooldridge as early as 6:00 A.M. From Longstreet's Corps came Captain Manley's Battery A, First North Carolina Artillery, around midmorning. The four guns rumbled across the Antietam bridge, down Baltimore Street in Funkstown, and then up a ridge to a position along the Beaver Creek Road in what was known as "Gilbert Field," about one mile east of the town, to assist Wooldridge's dismounted cavalrymen. Once unlimbered, Manley added considerable firepower to Wooldridge's men. Grumble Jones's Brigade formed the extreme left of Stuart's line, occupying the fields north of the Beaver Creek Road.[40]

What Stuart needed, though, were infantry brigades that could fill the huge spaces between his dismounted cavalry battalions and match the firepower of the Union columns approaching on the National Road. In the meantime, the dismounted troopers and their artillery support contested Buford's and Sedgwick's advance up the National Road throughout the morning.

A courier from Stuart arrived at the position of the Georgia Brigade, formerly commanded by General "Tige" Anderson, at about 1:00 P.M. The Georgians were protecting the stone bridge across Antietam Creek west of Funkstown under orders from General Law, temporary commander of Hood's Division. They had been foraging in the vicinity for two days. On 8, 9, and the morning of 10 July the brigade had impressed from the Funkstown area 5,124 pounds of corn, 12,400 pounds of hay, 1,181 pounds of bran, and 1 horse. One of the regiments, the Seventh Georgia, had been detached back on 8 July to help Ferguson's Brigade protect the approaches to the Williamsport defense line by the Williamsport-Boonsboro Road. The Seventh Georgia remained in position along that road on the morning of 10 July.[41]

The courier now informed Colonel William W. White, of the Seventh Georgia, who had been commanding the Georgia Brigade since the evening of 3 July, Anderson having been wounded, that he must take the brigade—without his own Seventh Georgia—and report to General Stuart east of Funkstown. White refused, claiming that he had been stationed at the bridge under orders from his division commander. White then mounted up and rode across the bridge with the courier to find General Stuart. Just east of Funkstown, White and Stuart met. There, Stuart "peremptorily" ordered White to advance his brigade "at once." White tried to explain that he was under orders from General Law. Stuart told him that he was under Stuart's orders and that, "as to this man Law, he knew nothing of him!" White concluded that, given Stuart's superiority in rank, he was bound to obey his orders. He thus returned to his four Georgia regiments and ordered them to cross the bridge, march through Funkstown, and report to Stuart.[42]

As White's Georgians reached the eastern outskirts of Funkstown, one of Stuart's aides conducted White to General Fitzhugh Lee. Lee instructed him to halt along the National Road on the eastern edge of town while he directed the artillery fire against the approaching Union columns.

Indeed, White could see the ominous threat ahead. Up the National Road were dense Union columns. Dismounted cavalry was being deployed in the fields on either side of the road, while what appeared to be infantry was striking out in the direction of the Beaver Creek Road on the far Union right. Witcher's and Wooldridge's cavalrymen kept up a steady fire, although Witcher's troops had already withdrawn nearly a mile from their first position. Chew's Battery had also pulled back but was shelling the Union skirmishers ahead.[43]

Buford's three brigades were coming into position. On the right flank, north of the National Road, Merritt's Brigade was moving into line along a high ridgeline; Gamble's Brigade was deploying to the left of Merritt, its left flank crossing the National Road. Devin's Brigade formed the left flank of Buford's line, establishing a line of battle to the left of Gamble's Brigade, extending almost to the bank of Antietam Creek. Lieutenants Calef's and Graham's Batteries were unlimbering in the fields in the midst of Merritt's troops and in the National Road. Colonel Lewis A. Grant's Vermont Brigade, Sedgwick's Corps, was marching behind Merritt's Brigade and deploying in Stover's Woods between Merritt's right flank and the Smithsburg Road, eight hundred yards ahead of Manley's guns and Wooldridge's dismounted cavalrymen. The Union line soon extended for more than two miles. Union sharpshooters quickly seized Jacob Stover's large bank barn along the Beaver Creek Road and began to fire into Manley's Battery and Wooldridge's cavalrymen, inflicting some damage.[44]

It was not an easy deployment for General Buford. Accompanied by Dr. Abner Hard, surgeon of the Eighth Illinois Cavalry, Buford dismounted and walked up to the ridgeline occupied by Merritt's and Gamble's men so he could "see how the day was going." Within seconds, bullets passed through his sack coat, cutting five holes in the garment but narrowly avoiding Buford. Some of those bullets just missed Dr. Hard, who was standing behind Buford.[45]

What Buford briefly observed was not encouraging. His men were falling rapidly, and the Confederates were cheering the arrival of what appeared to be infantry support. The Confederate line was literally backed up to Funkstown. Even if Buford broke through it, it would mean street fighting against infantry and artillery, the toughest task of all in battle.

Moving up behind White's Georgians was the Georgia Brigade of the wounded General Semmes, commanded by Colonel Goode Bryan. Bryan's brigade, like White's, had been foraging in and around Funkstown for two days, collecting everything from bushels of coal to corn. Couriers from General Stuart called it to the front behind White's men. Kershaw's South Carolinians remained west of Funkstown near the stone bridge, ready to support the Georgians if necessary or to move toward the Williamsport-Boonsboro Road. To the left of the stone bridge was the Pulaski (Georgia) Artillery of Cabell's Battalion, Lieutenant Robert M. Anderson commanding, supporting Kershaw.[46]

East of Funkstown, the fighting intensified. Fitzhugh Lee yelled for White to advance "forward by flank through a narrow lane, *a la cavalry*, to within 150 yards of the enemy, before deploying in line of battle." White again protested, asking Lee that he actually deploy his brigade in line of battle before coming under fire. Fitzhugh Lee overruled him. Thus, the Eighth, Ninth, Eleventh, and Fifty-ninth Georgia Regiments were ordered to bring their muskets to "right-shoulder-shift" and advance to their left front across the undulating fields east of Funkstown.

White's little brigade moved on the double-quick up a long, narrow lane across the fields, oblique to the Union line. Calef's and Graham's rifles blasted the Georgians as they tried to reach the Beaver Creek Road. White's men were stalled by small outbuildings and fence lines that stood in their path. They were exposed to galling artillery and small-arms fire. The Fifty-ninth

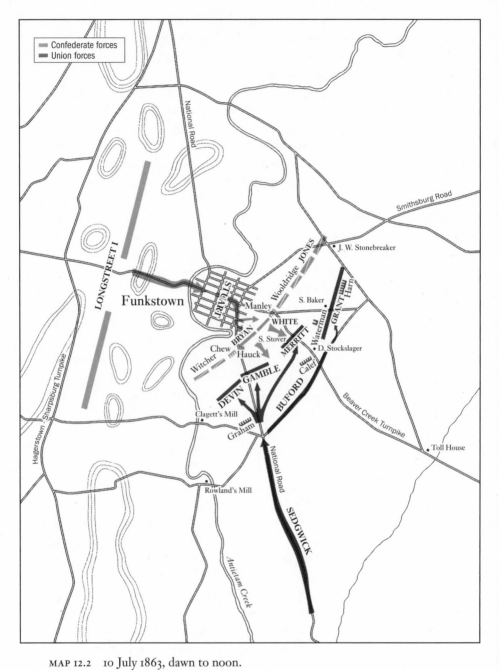

MAP 12.2 10 July 1863, dawn to noon.
East of Funkstown, Stuart, assisted by infantry brigades and artillery from
Longstreet's Corps, holds back Buford's Union cavalry division and Grant's
Brigade of Sedgwick's Sixth Corps.

Georgia formed the rear and right flank of the brigade. As they marched through the fields, the men in the Fifty-ninth were subjected to a "raking fire from the enemy."[47]

The Union line grew more formidable. To the right of Merritt's Brigade, Colonel Grant's Vermont Brigade began forming its battle line. Its left flank occupied a position in Stover's Woods, east of Funkstown along the Beaver Creek Road; its right was being extended to the large bank barn of John W. Stonebraker on the Smithsburg Road. Deploying with Grant's infantrymen were the six guns of Captain William A. Harn's Third New York Battery and a two-gun section of Captain Richard Waterman's Battery C, First Rhode Island Artillery.[48]

In spite of the growing Union firepower, the Georgians pressed forward. Colonel White directed his little brigade toward the junction of Merritt's and Grant's Brigades and their artillery support. All the time, Manley's guns played upon the Union troops from the Beaver Creek Road in front of Funkstown, while a section of Chew's guns supported White's advance from the National Road. As White's Georgians moved over fence lines and through wheat fields, several shells from Chew's Battery prematurely exploded overhead of the Fifty-ninth Georgia, killing and wounding six men in one company and several others. All the while, the Georgians continued to be subjected to a galling fire from Union artillery and small arms in their right and front.[49]

The intense fire was felt by Funkstown residents. Most of the townspeople who remained had taken shelter in their cellars. Young Joseph R. Stonebraker sought refuge in the garret of Solomon Keller's house on Baltimore Street. From the east garret window he watched the events as they unfolded along the Beaver Creak Road. Suddenly a stray bullet smacked into the wood frame of the garret window, nearly killing him.

Stray bullets and exploding Union artillery shells pocked little Funkstown throughout the afternoon. Several houses were struck. A cabin owned by Jacob Bierly on North High Street was hit by Union artillery fire. Nearby, a man and his horse were "blown to pieces" by an exploding shell.[50]

From its position on the National Road, Chew's Battery hammered Buford's cavalrymen until, one by one, the guns ran out of ammunition. In Lieutenant John Shoemaker's gun crew, two of his cannoneers were shot down and the Napoleon gun fell silent. Shoemaker ordered his men to lie down until more ammunition arrived. Amid the storm of shot and shell General Stuart soon rode by and asked Shoemaker why the men were not firing their gun. Shoemaker explained that his men were lying down for their protection while they waited for more ammunition. Stuart responded curtly, "Let them stand up for moral effect." Forever after, Stuart was known to Shoemaker's cannoneers as "Moral Effect" Stuart.[51]

Bryan's Georgia Brigade formed its battle line east of Funkstown, between White's right flank and the large stone barn of Jacob Hauck on the National Road. Chew's Battery was finally withdrawn. Witcher's dismounted cavalry, though, still held the line between Bryan's right and Antietam Creek.[52]

White kept up the pressure against Merritt and Grant while Bryan's brigade exchanged volleys with Gamble's and Devin's Brigades. One Confederate brigade, it seemed, was doing most of the work and taking most of the losses; White's Georgians were suffering terribly. Manley's gun crews got the proper range and directed their fire at Calef's, Harn's, and Waterman's Batteries. The fighting became ferocious in Stover's Woods, south of the Beaver Creek Road, as White's men finally formed a battle line.

White had endured staggering losses from enfilade fire. Many Georgians had fallen from wounds received on their right sides. While approaching Stover's Woods, Major Henry Dickerson McDaniel, commander of the Eleventh Georgia, was hurled to the ground; shrapnel "struck him on the right side of the abdomen, letting out a small portion of the intestines." Beside McDaniel was Private William T. Laseter, who had arrived at Funkstown with the brigade's quartermaster and subsistence trains when the fighting began. He had hurried across the fields to rejoin his company. Seconds before McDaniel was wounded, Laseter was struck between his right hip and cartridge box. Nevertheless, he saw McDaniel fall with a ghastly wound. Although in terrible pain himself, Laseter called for two of McDaniel's cousins; the three men carried the major off the battlefield.[53]

Nightfall was the ally of the Confederates. White fired volley after volley until darkness ended the fighting. More than 127 officers and men in White's Georgia Brigade had fallen. To his right, the two lines had exchanged heavy gunfire, and Bryan's Georgians suffered significant losses, but there had been no attempt to advance on either side. Stuart's dismounted troops lost at least fifty officers and men in the action. Buford's three brigades suffered less than fifty total casualties, while Grant's Vermonters had similar losses. Rain started to fall, causing the heavy smoke to hang close to the ground all around Funkstown. Stover's farm and other farms nearby were soon turned into graveyards.[54]

Funkstown was the site of all the Confederate hospitals after the battle. Dr. Joseph P. Chaney's two-story frame house on the south side of Baltimore Street became the hospital for Stuart's battalions. There the wives of Solomon Keller and Jacob Bierly, prosperous town citizens, aided the wounded, and thirteen-year-old Clara Kauffman offered her services as a nurse, as did Chaney's large number of slaves. Kauffman recalled the "pitiful" sights at the Chaney house. The condition of most of the wounded was desperate. "Many had their legs taken off," she noted, "lots died from neglect." One soldier cried, "Oh God! Please let me die tonight." Another asked her, "Please little women recite the childhood prayer for me like my mother used to do at bedtime, as I think I am dying." As the wounded died, they were placed in wagons and hauled to the Lutheran and Dunker cemeteries in town, while the voices of Chaney's slaves could be heard up and down Baltimore Street singing hymns.[55]

Across from the Chaney house on Baltimore Street was the 1860 German Reformed Church and the two-story frame house of Solomon Keller, now the hospitals for White's and Bryan's brigades. The Reformed church appears to have been their receiving hospital. It was to that building that Major McDaniel was carried by his two cousins and Private Laseter. They first laid him on a mattress near the front steps. Young Joseph Stonebraker stood looking at the major "with pitying eye." Dr. Elisha James Roach, a surgeon of the Eighteenth Georgia, came to examine the wound. Roach was McDaniel's cousin. McDaniel asked if his wound was mortal. Roach did not know, but he thought that it was. McDaniel was then heard to utter: "Dulce et decorum est, pro patria mori." He was taken into the Keller house and placed on a table. There Roach tried to push McDaniel's entrails back into the gaping wound with his fingers, but he experienced difficulty. Dr. George W. Boteler, the town physician, was in the room, although he was completely inebriated. Boteler yelled to Roach: "Damn it, doctor, dilate the wound." This was done, and the wound was dressed.[56]

"As fast as the wounded were dressed," recalled young Stonebraker, "they were carried into the [Keller] home and laid on the floor in rows. The citizens administered to their wants; many died and their cries and suffering were distressing to behold." That night, while standing in front of the Keller house, Stonebraker "could hear the cries of the wounded that had been left on the battlefield to die." In the midst of those cries and the singing of the slaves across the street, Simon Knode, a local Methodist deacon, sang to the dying at the Chaney house himself. The cacophony of groans, shrieks, and hymns would never be forgotten by the local citizens. As fast as they could be moved, the wounded were taken to Hagerstown. Major McDaniel was moved to the home of Dr. Wroe in Hagerstown that night. Through it all Stuart's cavalrymen and their infantry and artillery supports had purchased Lee's army a precious twelve hours that day.[57]

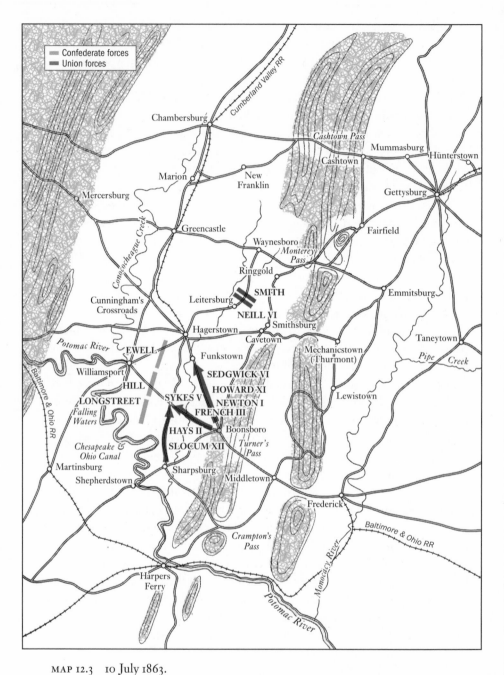

MAP 12.3   10 July 1863.
Lee fills the defense line protecting Williamsport as Meade approaches up the National Road, the Williamsport-Boonsboro Road, and the Hagerstown-Sharpsburg Turnpike.

During the afternoon and night of 10 July and the early hours of 11 July, the Army of Northern Virginia moved into the Williamsport defense line west of Funkstown. The gunfire east of Funkstown formed the backdrop for the operation. First, two of Longstreet's Divisions—Hood's, commanded by General Law, and McLaws's—marched south toward Downsville on the Hagerstown-Downsville Road, filling the right flank of the defense line, with Hood's Division on the extreme right, extending almost to the river, and McLaws's Division extending the line north to the Williamsport-Boonsboro Road. This was accomplished under the personal direction of Robert E. Lee. Pickett's Division of Longstreet's Corps remained at the ford at Williamsport until it had transported all of the Union prisoners across the river. It reassembled on the southern bank of the Potomac and marched the prisoners up the Valley Turnpike toward Martinsburg and Winchester.[58]

Hill's Corps was directed to hold the center of the defense line. Anderson's Division of Hill's Corps was positioned west of St. James College, connecting with the left flank of McLaws's Division. To the left of Anderson's, in front of a brick schoolhouse, was the division of General Heth, and to Heth's left was Pender's Division, still commanded by General Lane.[59]

Within Anderson's Division and the right flank of Heth's Division was one of the army's heaviest concentrations of artillery. On Anderson's right flank, batteries from Longstreet's Corps helped bolster the defense line along the Williamsport-Boonsboro Road. The Pulaski (Georgia) Artillery of Cabell's Battalion took up a position behind St. James College, extending to the road on the right. Placed into line to the right of the Pulaski Artillery, on the Williamsport-Boonsboro Road, was Lieutenant C. W. Mote's Troup Georgia Artillery of Cabell's Battalion, and to the left, the battalions of Major David Gregg McIntosh and Major William J. Pegram, the latter commanded by Captain E. B. Brunson, as well as Major William T. Poague's four batteries. The Pulaski Artillery and Mote's Battery and the battalions of McIntosh, Brunson, and Poague—thirteen batteries in all—were positioned along the broken ridgeline behind St. James College. Within and to the left of the line of Pender's Division were the four batteries of Garnett's Battalion.[60]

On the far right flank near Downsville was another concentration of artillery. There all of Major M. W. Henry's Battalion of four batteries and Colonel Alexander's Battalion of six batteries were brought into position. Those two battalions supported Hood's Division. To the left of Henry's and Alexander's positions were the four batteries of Major James Dearing's Battalion, and to Dearing's left was Colonel Cabell's four batteries. Dearing's guns supported McLaws's Division. Cabell's guns partly supported McLaws's Division of Longstreet's Corps and partly Anderson's Division of Hill's Corps.[61]

The left flank of the defense line was held by Ewell's Corps. Johnson's Division extended the line from Pender's left, northward, across the Hagerstown-Williamsport Turnpike. To Johnson's left was Early's Division, and to Early's left was Rodes's Division, which extended the defense line north of the National Road and west of Hagerstown and formed the extreme left flank of the army. Fitzhugh Lee's and Colonel Chambliss's cavalrymen screened the left flank all the way to the Conococheague Creek. They were joined by Ferguson's and Robertson's Brigades. Jones's Brigade protected the approaches to Hagerstown along the Smithsburg Road, east of the city.[62]

Salisbury Ridge was turned into a long military bastion. Soldiers and laborers, guided by engineers, proceeded to dig entrenchments for the infantry and gun emplacements for artillery. On 10 July and for the next three days the work continued around the clock. The defense works extended north and south more than nine miles, from heights just west of Hagerstown all the way to Downsville on the Potomac River. Period illustrations, together with written accounts by military and civilian observers, reveal that the nine-mile-long defense line was thoroughly engineered if hastily constructed. The gun emplacements were deep, with six-foot-wide parapets made from fence rails and rocks packed with earth. According to one Union artillery officer, any enemy approaching Lee's defense line would have been "swept" by artillery fire during the long advance and caught in a "perfect cross-fire" if it entered the vales where the ridges were broken. At Downsville on the far right flank and west of the site of St. James College, near the Williamsport-Boonsboro Road, Lee and Colonel Alexander directed the heaviest concentrations of artillery. They both believed that if Meade attacked the Confederate defenses, he would do so against the right flank to interpose his forces between Lee's army and the river, or at the center where the ridgeline was broken by the Williamsport-Boonsboro Road and the feeder streams forming Marsh Run.[63]

The infantry works consisted of two parallel lines of entrenchments. The front line, it seems, was relatively weak and was designed only for skirmishers. Positioned along the forward slopes of the broken ridge, the front line consisted of trenches with forward bastions made of packed earth and, at places, wheat sheaves covered with earth, built up behind a long ditch. In the rear, just below the summit of the ridgeline, were stronger earthworks constructed with fence rails, rocks, and packed earth—described by one eyewitness as a "very strong line of gopher holes and rifle pits." On either side of the earthworks were long ditches, making any approach particularly difficult.[64]

An elder of the Pipe Creek Church of the Brethren named D. P. Sayler provided one of the best descriptions of the Williamsport defense line after

Edwin Forbes's painting of Lee's defense line between Hagerstown and Downsville. Note the concentration of artillery emplacements and the broken configuration of ridgeline. In the distance at left is probably Funkstown, Maryland. Library of Congress, Washington, D.C.

he visited the area following the departure of the armies. "They are about 8 or 9 miles long," he wrote, "and are built by first packing what wheat sheaves [the Confederates] could lay hands on (carrying some ¼ mile) in the bottom, the digging up the earth and packing it tight on it. The breast is built up with rails, stone and logs, with a deep ditch on the side occupied, sometimes on each side where wheat could not be got, it required more earth to raise the embankment, and hence a ditch on either side."[65]

Lee's nine-mile defense line had significant military advantages beyond height and construction. Behind it was a network of roads. The National Road extended through the extreme left flank of the defense line and connected it to the Cumberland Valley Turnpike. The Hagerstown-Williamsport Turnpike provided the means by which the troops holding the left flank of the line could be supplied from Williamsport and could be evacuated to the Williamsport ford. The Williamsport-Boonsboro Road enabled the center of the line to be readily supplied and evacuated. Those roads radiated northeast and east from Williamsport to the defense line like the spokes of a wheel from its hub. Another road running north and south from Hagerstown to Downsville and along the western slope of Salisbury Ridge—the Hagerstown-Downsville Road—provided a ready communications linkage between the flanks of the defense line as well as the means by which troops could move from one position to another completely out of view of the enemy. The Hagerstown-

Downsville Road also offered a route by which the center and right flank could be supplied and evacuated.

So well planned and engineered were the defenses in front of Williamsport that Lee could have held them against any attack of the Army of the Potomac. "They were," wrote Colonel Charles Wainwright, commander of the Union First Corps artillery brigade, "by far the strongest I have seen yet; evidently laid out by engineers and built as if they meant to stand a month's siege."[66]

With the extremely heavy rains on 4, 5, and 7 July and the night of 8 July, the lowlands along Marsh Run had turned into lakes. Troops assaulting the ridgeline would be nearly waist deep in Marsh Run and then ankle to knee deep in water and mud much of the way to the ridgeline. "It was difficult even to walk about [the fields in front of Lee's works]," according to Wainwright. No position ever held by Lee's army, save for Marye's Heights at Fredericksburg, was more formidable.[67]

Lee's staff moved the general's headquarters behind the defense line to a site near the tollhouse on the Hagerstown-Williamsport Turnpike, midway between Williamsport and Hagerstown. There, Lee's tents were pitched along with those of his staff and the company of scouts, guides, and couriers of the Thirty-ninth Battalion of Virginia Cavalry.[68]

Even as Lee's army took up positions along the Williamsport defense line, the soldiers seized everything they could find from residences in the area. The home of John S. Rowland, his wife, son, and two daughters was situated northwest of St. James College amid intricate entrenchments and gun emplacements that were occupied by Anderson's and Heth's Divisions of Hill's Corps. "The line of rebel entrenchments pass through [Rowland's] farms," recorded Elder Sayler, "and he estimates 2,000 bushels of his wheat being packed in and destroyed by the rebels. He lost seven of his best horses and all of his cattle. He thought he had 40 head. All his bacon—he knew he had 17 hams, shoulders and sides he did not know the number of pieces. All his corn, and nearly all his hay [were taken]."

The Rowlands were told by the occupying troops to leave; without protest, Rowland's wife and two daughters left with what they could pack in a four-horse wagon. Rowland and his son were determined to remain. "While the family were thus separated," wrote Elder Sayler,

> the rebels led one by one of their [colonels] demanded admittance [into the Rowland house], and after gaining it, they went from cellar to garret and plundered it of everything they could carry away. Even taking the little notions the two daughters yet at home had, letters, dress-patterns

etc., all eatables, clothing, coats, pants, hats and shoes, etc. And they finally divested themselves of their filthy, lousy rags, and clothed themselves in the clean garments [that were] stolen [from] Rowland.

Like so many civilians in the area, the Rowlands were offended by the odor of Lee's men. "The house," they claimed, "was filled with a stench peculiar to the rebels." In fact, after Lee's army evacuated the defense line, the Rowlands claimed that they had to burn tar in their house get rid of the offensive odor.[69]

As Longstreet's men filled the defense line between the Williamsport-Boonsboro Road and Downsville, they seized all of the horses, mules, cattle, sheep, hogs, forage, and equipment they could find. Quartermaster Major Keiley reported impressing on 10 July 11 horses and 2 mules, along with 2,000 pounds of hay and 4,760 pounds of corn. Hood's chief quartermaster snagged 8 horses, 20 bushels of corn, 50 bushels of rye, and 1,500 pounds of hay while moving into the trenches. Brigade quartermasters were busy, too. From farms near their positions in the defense line Anderson's Brigade seized 1,400 pounds of corn and Barksdale's, 120 bushels of corn and 3,500 pounds of hay. Laws's Brigade confiscated 1,800 pounds of hay, 7 bushels of corn, and 31 bushels of oats and the Texas Brigade, 2 horses. While moving into position near Downsville, quartermasters of the First Corps Reserve Artillery Battalion captured 15,000 pounds of hay, 235 bushels of corn, 3 horses, and 21 curry combs. Such seizures were accomplished that day by corps, division, brigade, and regimental quartermasters from one end of the nine-mile defense line to the other.[70]

Once in position, quartermasters spread out behind and in front of the defense line, scouring farms and dwellings for needed stores. On 11 July Major Keiley impressed 7,000 pounds of hay and 20 cords of wood, while the reserve artillery battalion of Longstreet's Corps took 10,600 pounds of hay. Benning's Brigade impressed 1,300 pounds of hay; Anderson's Brigade, 2,016 pounds of corn, 1,600 pounds of hay, and 1 horse; the Texas Brigade, 3,800 pounds of hay; and Laws's Brigade, 60 bushels of corn and 1,500 pounds of hay. Much of that forage came from farms near Downsville. The Thirteenth Mississippi, though, seized from the shot-torn farm of Otho Williams and Rose Hill Manor near the Williamsport-Downsville Road—the site of Captain Pegram's death five days earlier—20 bushels of corn.[71]

At noon on 11 July General A. P. Hill and General Cadmus Wilcox rode over to St. James College, east of the defense line. The small Episcopal school was conducted in a lovely Federal mansion, designed by Benjamin H. Latrobe Jr. and built in 1806, called "Fountain Rock." The college had been a

The Ringgold Mansion at St. James College as it looked during the war. Author's Collection.

gathering place for many of Lee's officers during the Pennsylvania invasion. Captain James Breathed of the Stuart Horse Artillery was a graduate of St. James, and his father and mother lived in a brick home on Salisbury Ridge nearby. Dr. J. S. D. Cullen, whose wife was Captain Breathed's aunt, and Major Osmun Latrobe, a graduate of the school and the son of John H. B. Latrobe, the designer's brother, both of Longstreet's staff, visited the college on 25 June, and Dr. Robert Poole Myers of the Sixteenth Georgia was a dinner guest the night before he accompanied his regiment into the defense line below the Williamsport-Boonsboro Road.[72]

Hill and Wilcox found Dr. John Barrett Kerfoot, rector of St. James College, and Eliza Porter, the mother of none other than cashiered Union major general Fitz John Porter and the school's matron, still in residence along with about twelve students and several professors and their families. At the time, the skirmish lines of Hill's Corps extended north and south of the college and were already exchanging gunfire with Union skirmish lines nearby. Fountain Rock was now being used as a Confederate signal station. General Hill wanted the civilians in the school moved to a safe place. Acting on Hill's advice, Kerfoot ordered the families and students to pack up. In a long procession, they left the institution by way of the Williamsport-Boonsboro and

Hagerstown-Downsville Roads to Hagerstown as small arms and artillery fire echoed up and down the contending lines.[73]

As Lee's army moved into the defense line and started improving the trenchworks and gun emplacements, the Army of the Potomac pressed forward. On 11 July Meade began moving all seven of his corps up to the Hagerstown-Sharpsburg Turnpike, less than two miles east of Lee's defense line. Huey's Brigade of Gregg's Cavalry Division pushed up the Williamsport-Boonsboro Road. Buford's Division entered the rough countryside on the far left flank of Meade's line, searching for signs of the enemy near Downsville. Kilpatrick's Division screened Meade's movement on the right in front of Hagerstown.[74]

Anticipating an attack, Lee issued one of the most remarkable orders of his military career that day. "After long and trying marches, endured with the fortitude that has ever characterized the soldiers of the Army of Northern Virginia," it read:

> You have penetrated to the country of our enemies, and recalled to the defense of their own soil those who were engaged in the invasion of ours. Once more you are called upon to meet the enemy from whom you won, on so many fields, names that will never die. Let every soldier remember that on his courage and fidelity depend all that makes life worth having, the freedom of his country, the honor of his people, and the security of his home. Soldiers, your old enemy is before you. Win from him honor worthy of your right cause, worthy of your comrades dead on so many illustrious fields.

Read before every regiment in the army, the order had a profound effect on the soldiers. Without question, those in the trenches were ready for an attack.[75]

With the mail delivery, news arrived of the fall of Vicksburg. Almost every soldier who wrote a letter or diary entry commented on it. Even with the bad news, though, most of Lee's men were unshaken. They were determined to hold what was becoming known as the "Downsville line." General McLaws, like all division commanders, repeatedly rode up and down his line making sure that the work on the breastworks and gun emplacements was progressing and that his men were steady. On the night of 11 July he approached a group of Mississippians from Barksdale's Brigade. The Mississippians told McLaws that they were all right. When he informed them that the Army of the Potomac was just across the fields, one soldier replied that if the enemy decided to attack, the Union troops would "get their bellies full." When McLaws asked them again what they would do if the enemy attacked, the response was that they would "make the ground blue with them." McLaws was satisfied with the spirit of the troops and bid them goodnight.[76]

After the troops settled in the defense line, quartermasters brought to the front lines quartermaster and subsistence trains from Williamsport. As Lee was conserving food, the subsistence stores were sparse. All of the army's artillery battalions sent empty caissons and limbers to Williamsport, where ammunition was brought to them from the ordnance train still parked across the river.[77]

Meade's army continued to move the next day, 12 July. In the morning General Howard advanced his Eleventh Corps up the National Road from Funkstown to Hagerstown, pushing back enemy skirmishers and cavalrymen. Leading Howard's Corps was the 157th New York of Brigadier General Adelbert Ames's Brigade. Most of the men in the regiment were barefoot; about one hundred of them had just returned from hospitals or other areas in the rear. In the streets ahead of them was the Twenty-fifth Virginia, screening Ewell's Corps as it hastily prepared breastworks and gun emplacements on the heights west of Hagerstown.[78]

Soon the "boys" of the 157th "started on a keen run for the town." Up South Potomac Street they dashed, dodging Confederate bullets along the way. They reached the town square and then, under a hot fire from the Virginians ahead, pressed up West Washington Street, past the Washington House hotel. The Twenty-fifth Virginia slowly gave way until it reached a position in front of the heights west of town. Now that Hagerstown was finally in Union hands, Meade was able to direct Neill's Light Division and Smith's Division of Couch's Department, both still north of town, to join the Army of the Potomac.[79]

Soldiers of the 157th New York mingled in the streets of Hagerstown; some signed their names in the register of the Washington House hotel below signatures of Confederates who had departed minutes ago. General Howard climbed into the tall steeple of St. John's Evangelical Lutheran Church on South Potomac Street to observe the Confederate defense line west of town. As the gunfire died down in Hagerstown, so did the threat of a general assault against Lee's works.[80]

Howard's Eleventh Corps anchored the Union right flank between Hagerstown and Funkstown. To Howard's left was Newton's First Corps and to Newton's left was Sedgwick's Sixth Corps, south of Funkstown, along the Hagerstown-Sharpsburg Turnpike. To Sedgwick's left was Sykes's Fifth Corps and to Sykes's left was Hays's Second Corps, extending down to

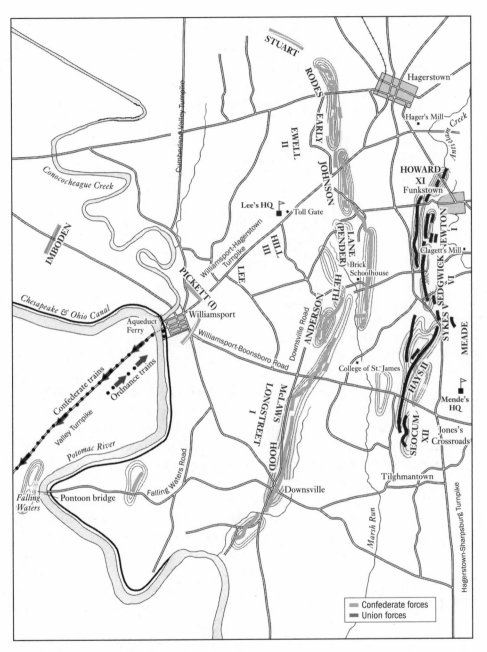

MAP 12.4   11, 12, and 13 July 1863.
Lee's defenses are in place at Williamsport.

Edwin Forbes's drawing of a Union signal station in a house along Marsh Run overlooking the Confederate defense line east of Williamsport, Maryland, 12 July 1863. Note the legs of a signalman who is sitting on the roof waiting for the telescopic observations. From the roof, wigwag signals were sent down the line to Meade's headquarters. Library of Congress, Washington, D.C.

the Williamsport-Boonsboro Road. South of the Williamsport-Boonsboro Road, along a high ridge, was Slocum's Twelfth Corps, forming the left flank of the army. The soldiers constructed modest breastworks up and down the turnpike. The artillery reserve and the Third Corps occupied positions just behind the left and center of the Union line near Jones's Crossroads so they could respond to any crisis.[81]

From a Union treetop signal station located east of St. James College, rooftop signal stations in houses overlooking Marsh Run, and a signal station atop the Dunker Church in Funkstown, Meade was able to obtain information on the enemy's position along Salisbury Ridge, although heavy fog and dense smoke from campfires obscured much of the view. Signal officers close to the front reported on 12 July that Lee's army continued to dig trenches and prepare gun emplacements along Salisbury Ridge and breastworks along the skirmish lines. But the smoke in the area was so dense that communication by flag signals had been suspended. In its place, General Meade had ordered field telegraph wires extended from his headquarters along the Williamsport-Boonsboro Road near Jones's Crossroads to General Sedgwick's headquarters at Funkstown so he could receive the necessary intelligence from the signal stations.[82]

Pressure from Huey's cavalry brigade along the Williamsport-Boonsboro Road west of the Hagerstown-Sharpsburg Turnpike met with stiff resistance on 12 July. On the far Union left, Buford was content to observe the Confederate line from a distance, as the irregular, wild countryside would impede any meaningful offensive effort, and the fog was so dense that he could barely see the way to Downsville.[83]

That afternoon Meade received an ominous message written by Lieutenant Ranald MacKenzie, one of General Warren's engineer officers then at Sandy Hook, Maryland, with one of the newly arrived pontoon trains. "The river," it read, "has fallen [at Sandy Hook] 18 inches in the last twenty-four hours, and is still falling. A citizen states that he is acquainted with the river here, and that he judges from its appearance at this place that the fords near Shepherdstown and Williamsport are now practicable for infantry." If Meade was going to prevent Lee from crossing the Potomac, he would have to risk an attack. Without carefully viewing the ground over which such an assault would be made, Meade forwarded an advisory to General Halleck in Washington by way of his telegraph office at Boonsboro asserting that it was his intention to "attack in the morning." It was a message he would deeply regret having sent.[84]

Thirteen

I would die before
being taken prisoner

Orders from Lee's headquarters to proceed to Williamsport for the purpose of constructing a bridge across the Potomac River were received at the camp of Captain Summerfield Smith's engineer battalion at daybreak on 10 July. Because engineers were under the authority of the army commander, Lee and his staff oversaw the project. Lieutenant Harris was aroused from a fitful sleep northeast of Hagerstown; at 5:00 A.M. he set off on an eight-mile trek to an orchard near Williamsport where he and his battalion established a camp. They got something to eat and were then marched down to the Potomac River at eleven o'clock. Longstreet's, Hill's, and Ewell's Corps were just getting ready to fill their positions in the Williamsport defense line, and the sound of gunfire was intensifying east of Funkstown.[1]

Captain Justus Scheibert, a former engineer in the Prussian army and a recent immigrant to America, was assigned to help build the bridge. Landing at Charleston, South Carolina, he eventually made his way to Lee's army and had been riding with the staff of J. E. B. Stuart ever since. On the morning of 10 July he appeared at Lee's headquarters in response to an order from Lee himself. Scheibert then rode down to the Chesapeake and Ohio (C&O) Canal basin with instructions to assist the engineers.[2]

Pioneer companies from each division had been detailed to the bridge-building effort and were already at work when Harris and Scheibert arrived at the river. According to Scheibert, a "reconnaissance soon showed that the trees standing by the river were mostly oaks, which [were] not suitable for floats and are too hard to work for the quick completion of other structures." However, several sawmills soon discovered in Williamsport contained sufficient "boards and crossbeams." Private Casler of the Thirty-third Virginia was one of the pioneers from Johnson's Division. At the Shoop and Lefever and William Steffey lumberyards along the river and in the east end of Williamsport, he and teams of pioneers removed all the two-inch planks there and carried them to the canal basin. One of the lumbermen protested, calling Casler and his pioneers thieves. Casler yelled back, "Charge it to Jeff Davis and Company." He added that Lee's army was worth more than the man's lumber in gold.[3]

The engineers consumed some time drawing the dimensions of the pontoons necessary to support the bridge. Lieutenant Colonel Smith, Major Clarke, Captain Douglas, and Captain Johnston of Lee's staff were the primary engineers of the project. Using ten of the sixteen pontoons recovered along the riverbank downstream from Falling Waters that had been partially wrecked by the enemy cavalry on the morning of 4 July, the engineers drew up plans for the construction of sixteen new pontoons, together with spans of trestlework. The pontoons were to be three feet deep, with a bottom length of eighteen feet and a top length of thirty feet, and have six- to seven-foot beams. They would be held in the swiftly moving river by multiple anchors made of wooden boxes, each thirty-six inches long and filled with stones. Heavy cables would anchor the bridge on each shore. All of the bridge's components would be assembled beside the canal basin in Williamsport.[4]

The work began in earnest on 11 July. The pioneer teams started at dawn, finishing one pontoon, anchors and all, and most of a second by the end of the day. Tools were so scarce that "each squad had to be content with an ax, a saw and chisel." The whole time the pioneers and engineers were working at the riverbank, the two flats and the two canal boats continued to ferry ambulances and quartermaster, subsistence, and ordnance wagons to the southern shore and bring back ammunition from the ordnance train still parked along the Valley Turnpike near Maidstone-on-the-Potomac. As he had done since the morning of 5 July, Major Harman continued to direct the shipment of wagons and ambulances across the river.[5]

As each pontoon was completed, the pioneers brought tar from the quartermaster wagons and nearby warehouses and lumberyards and boiled it in large kettles "taken from around town." Private Casler recalled that one "old woman wanted to raise a row when we took her kettles, but we promised to bring them back; but we didn't." "Oakam picked from old rope" was forced into all the seams of the pontoons. They were then "caulked and pitched" with the hot tar, making them watertight.[6]

When a pontoon was finished, it was launched at Williamsport and floated downstream to Falling Waters. At 9:00 A.M. on 12 July the first pontoon, loaded with lumber, began its maiden voyage. It took Lieutenant Harris and his crew two and a half hours to reach Falling Waters. "By no means," penned Harris in his diary, "the least pleasant part was half an hour spent in swimming along by the boat." Three more pontoons carrying large amounts of lumber were launched behind Harris's; one of them was floated downstream by Lieutenant David Stewart Hessy, who, along with Smith and Harris, had been one of the first commissioned officers in Lee's engineer battalion. Private Casler piloted more pontoons that afternoon. The work at Williamsport continued around the clock.[7]

WHILE THE PONTOONS were being constructed at Williamsport, pioneers at Falling Waters were building the approaches to the bridge. On the southern bank of the river it was a matter of smoothing out the old road that led to the Valley Turnpike and building the road up to the bridge. On the Maryland side, the job was somewhat more difficult, as a firm roadway needed to be prepared up to and across the C&O Canal and down to the river. The bridge over the canal was strengthened so it could handle all of the army's wagons, artillery, and marching troops.[8]

The engineers had started building the bridge on the Virginia side using three sets of three pontoons strapped together, separated by trestlework. In midstream, they strapped together two sets of four pontoons, again separated by trestlework, then completed the bridge by using three more sets of three pontoons, held together by trestlework, extending to the Maryland shore. "It was after 11:00 P.M.," wrote Harris, "before [the entire span] was connected and covered [with lumber]." In two full days and the better part of two nights, Lee's engineers and pioneer teams had managed to lay an 800-foot bridge supported by twenty-six pontoons across the Potomac River; the project had taken sixty-eight hours. The engineer battalion and its wagon trains, along with the pioneer teams, tested the bridge by moving back and forth across the span for almost two hours.[9]

Lee's army continued to improve the entrenchments and gun emplacements along the defense line between Hagerstown and Downsville on 12 July. With Couch's and Kelley's armies drawing nearer and the Army of the Potomac about two miles away, Lee was anxious to get his army across the Potomac River. The bridge at Falling Waters was ready, but, given the size of the trains still in and along the river bottomland at Williamsport, the entire army could not cross it in time to avoid being attacked. Lee still needed the river to fall so that some of his troops could ford it at Williamsport.

Captain Smith was directed to leave an element of his engineer battalion on the bridge to keep it repaired during the crossing and to take another

A never-before-published photograph of the site of Lee's pontoon bridge at Falling Waters, taken on the Maryland side of the Potomac River. Visible is the bridge over the C&O Canal, the poles for the ferryboat cable, and the Cunningham house and Falling Waters Tavern on the West Virginia side. Author's collection.

group from his battalion, along with some division pioneers, and "reconnoiter for a line of defense for the army" as it crossed the Potomac. Smith and Lieutenant Harris found a high ridge about one and a half miles up the Falling Waters Road on the farm, and near the two-story brick farmhouse of J. M. Downey, where the men from the engineer battalion and pioneers began to construct breastworks and gun emplacements. Because the river made a great hairpin bend at Falling Waters, the defenses were laid out literally from one shoreline of the bend to the other. There, the army would be protected if it was attacked while crossing the river.[10]

On 12 July Lee was informed that the river at the Williamsport ford would still be close to four feet in the morning in the absence of additional heavy rain. Indeed, Lieutenant MacKenzie at Sandy Hook told General Meade the same thing. Thus, at 11:00 P.M. on the twelfth, Lee ordered that all of the quartermaster, subsistence, and ordnance wagons and ambulances waiting to cross the river on the flats and canal boats at Williamsport be directed down the canal towpath to cross at the bridge. There were so many ambulances filled with casualties and wagons carrying quartermaster and subsistence stores, ordnance, thousands of African American slaves, laborers, and wagoners that Lee allowed twenty-six hours for them to cross the bridge at Falling Waters.[11]

To cover all the trains as they crossed the Potomac, as well as to keep open all lines of communication with Winchester, Lee directed Grumble Jones and his brigade to proceed to the other side of the river and patrol the Valley Turnpike. Jones's Twelfth Virginia was detached to cover the trains east of the Valley Turnpike as far as Jefferson County. Lee ordered General Imboden to take his brigade to "the vicinity of Cherry Creek on the [West] Virginia side of the river," as information had been received of the approach of Kelley's Union troops, who were marching beside the Baltimore and Ohio Railroad tracks from Hancock. Imboden's Brigade was to protect the trains moving along the Valley Turnpike to Winchester in concert with Grumble Jones.[12]

While the bridge was being completed, Lee was with Longstreet at Falling Waters. Extraordinarily tired, he asked Longstreet to remain at the bridge and monitor the crossing through the early hours of 13 July so he could get some rest. "Such a night is seldom experienced even in the rough life of the soldier," Longstreet recalled. "The rain fell in showers, sometimes in blinding sheets, during the entire night." Wagons cut deep in the mud and often stalled, as did batteries of artillery. "The best standing points," he noted, "were ankle-deep in mud." The roads, though, were "half-way to the knee."

Throughout this period, only three or four torches remained lighted near the bridge. The heavy rains kept them dim. "Then," Longstreet continued,

> to crown our troubles a load of wounded came down [from Williamsport], missed the end of the bridge, and plunged the wagon in the raging torrent. Right at the end of the bridge the water was three feet deep, and the current swift and surging. It did not seem possible that a man could be saved, but everyone who could get through mud and water rushed to their relief, and Providence was there to bring tears of joy to the sufferers. The wagon was righted and on the bridge and rolled off to Virginia's banks.

Green willow poles were placed at the ends of the bridge to prevent the wheels of the wagons from cutting too deeply into the mud. But the ground beneath the poles was so saturated that by daylight the poles would bend under the wheels of the wagons and the feet of the horses and mules until they could bend no farther. They would then slip from one side to another and "spring up and catch a horse's foot and throw him broadside in the puddled mud." "Needless to say," Longstreet wrote, "everyone was exhausted of patience, the general and staff ready for a family quarrel as the only relief for their pent-up trouble."[13]

On the rainy morning of 13 July the surgeons at brigade and division hospitals in Williamsport heard that the army was crossing the river. The wounded who could bear the journey were placed in ambulances and readied for the ride to the bridge. From his brigade hospital near the Taylor House hotel, Dr. Clifton watched as enormous herds of horses, mules, cattle, and sheep, along with some artillery from the town, were driven across the river.[14]

WHILE LEE WAS at his headquarters drawing plans for the evacuation of his defense lines, rapid artillery fire was heard from the direction of Hagerstown. He hurriedly mounted up with his staff and rode toward the sound of the gunfire. Lee had previously asked a courier to find General Imboden, whose brigade had operated in the area for much of the campaign, and bring him to his headquarters. After recrossing the river, Imboden galloped up to Lee while the commander was observing an artillery duel near Hagerstown. Lee said he had heard that he was familiar with the fords of the Potomac River from Williamsport to Cumberland. Imboden said that he was. Lee then called upon Colonel Armistead L. Long nearby to write down Imboden's answers to his questions. Lee asked Imboden to "name and describe ford after ford, all the way up to Cumberland, and to describe minutely their character, and the roads and surrounding country on both sides of the river." He then told Imboden to send Colonel George Imboden and his Eighteenth Virginia Cavalry to his headquarters to act as guides if he needed them.[15]

General Imboden now believed that his commander's "situation was precarious in the extreme." When Lee was about to dismiss Imboden, he said: "You know this country well enough to tell me whether it ever quits raining about here? If so, I should like to see a clear day soon." The tenseness of the meeting was broken, and the two generals laughed as they parted. Lee returned to his headquarters to finish his plans for evacuation.

Once the arrangements were complete, Lee rode out to the defense lines to personally oversee their implementation. Ewell's Corps, according to Lee's design, would abandon its defense line on the night of 13 July and march the six miles to Williamsport. There, Ewell's infantrymen, followed by all of the army's cavalry brigades, would cross the Potomac by wading the ford. Unfortunately, the shallowest part of the river, so Lee was informed, was off a point on the west bank of Conococheague Creek. To get there, Ewell's men and the cavalry would have to wade through the waters of the aqueduct of the

C&O Canal, which spanned the creek before descending a steep bank into the river. The artillery battalions and those quartermaster, subsistence, and ordnance trains accompanying Ewell's Corps would either cross in the flats and canal boats that had been in use around the clock over the past six days or ford the river. All of Stuart's cavalry brigades would cross the river behind Ewell's Corps.[16]

Longstreet's and Hill's Corps would cross on the night of 13 July and the morning of 14 July using the pontoon bridge at Falling Waters. Longstreet's Corps, on the right flank and nearest to the river, would evacuate the defense lines first. McLaws's Division would lead, followed by Hood's. Again, the rear column would move first. Hill would follow Hood with Anderson's Division in the lead and Pender's Division, commanded by General Lane, next in line. Heth's Division would serve as the rear guard of Hill's Corps and of the army. The artillery battalions and the trains accompanying the two corps would traverse the bridge with their own divisions.[17]

At Jones's Crossroads, a mile east of Lee's defense lines, General Meade was deeply concerned about the possibility that Lee might escape across the river. Nevertheless, the Union commander had not yet carried out his intention—as he had notified Halleck the previous evening—to attack Lee that morning. Under pressure from Abraham Lincoln and the War Department to follow up his "glorious result" at Gettysburg, Meade examined Lee's works and probed for an opening. But Lee's position was simply too formidable. Although he was being severely criticized in Washington and by some in the army for his failure to attack Lee at Williamsport, there was nothing Meade could have done to prevent Lee from winning the race to the Williamsport defense line or holding it. Now he faced the very real prospect of Lee escaping altogether.[18]

Meade had called a council of war at his tented headquarters near Jones's Crossroads on the warm and smoky 12 July. In attendance were six commanders of Meade's Corps, his new chief of staff, Major General Andrew A. Humphreys, chief engineer General Warren, and commander of the cavalry General Pleasonton. Meade expressed his desire to attack Lee frontally the next morning. At first, four of his chief lieutenants were in agreement. General Sedgwick, however, and four others emphatically rejected his proposal. After considering Lee's defense works and the condition of the fields over which an attack would be launched, the group ultimately voted seven to two against an assault. Meade finally stated that he would not assume responsibility for provoking an engagement against the advice of so many of his commanders. That decision—a correct one given the circumstances—was all Lee needed to make his escape.[19]

General George Gordon Meade and some of his lieutenants after Gettysburg. Left to right: General Gouverneur K. Warren, General William H. French, General Meade, General Henry Hunt, Major General Andrew A. Humphreys, and General John Sedgwick. Library of Congress, Washington, D.C.

Hill's rain-soaked soldiers, who had been sleeping on beds of cut wheat, were aroused early on 13 July. Rain fell steadily. Soon the men began to work, improving the trenches and nearby gun emplacements. In want of adequate rations, they also began searching for ways to alleviate the pangs of hunger. Orders to "fall-in" and prepare for the march would not come until almost nightfall. Meanwhile, the hospitals in Williamsport were cleared of all casualties who could possibly be moved. The Fifth Louisiana's Private Charles Moore, for example, was carried from the Catholic church and placed in an ambulance. The trains rumbled down the canal towpath from Williamsport and crossed the pontoon bridge at Falling Waters in a seemingly endless procession. Immense herds of horses, mules, cattle, and sheep continued to be driven across the Potomac River.[20]

Near the trench line of Mahone's Brigade overlooking St. James College, a flock of sheep still grazed even though an army of hungry men was entrenched nearby. As one soldier recalled with sarcasm, the men "were guilty of casting sheepish eyes at the field." Rumors spread quickly that Mahone had given the order to slaughter the herd. A report then traveled through the ranks that one of Mahone's orderlies was seen with a "sheep bleating from behind his horse on his way to headquarters." The story was likely false, but it had the desired effect. In minutes, the entire flock of sheep disappeared among the soldiers in the defense line. "Sheep meat," wrote one veteran, "was now the fashion of the campfires. All hands, officers as well as men, were eating sheep, without bread or salt, roasted and barbecued, which was better than anything we could get from our quartermasters." The absent farmer had been stripped of his wheat, hay, fences, and livestock.[21]

Throughout 13 July sporadic gunfire between the contending armies could be heard all along the skirmish lines. Yet Meade made no serious move against the Confederate lines. Lee's men prepared for the withdrawal.

In anticipation of moving out, quartermasters scoured the countryside behind the lines, confiscating everything they could find. The quartermaster of the First Corps Reserve Artillery Battalion near Downsville reported seizing a whopping 18,500 pounds of hay on 13 July alone. In addition, his battalion impressed an amazing 25 horses from nineteen different owners. Also that day Cabell's Artillery Battalion carried off 19,900 pounds of hay and Longstreet's quartermaster, 3,932 pounds of corn and 1,680 pounds of hay. Brigade and regimental quartermasters were equally busy, hauling in everything available in anticipation of leaving Maryland.[22]

As afternoon turned into evening, Ewell's Corps began its evacuation of the defense line on the left flank behind Hagerstown and its march toward Williamsport via the Hagerstown-Williamsport Turnpike. Rodes's Division, on the left flank, moved first; Johnson's Division, on the right, followed. Early's Division, in the center, covered Rodes's and Johnson's until those divisions cleared the roads behind Early. Early then moved his division out of the trenches and onto the turnpike, forming the rear guard of Ewell's Corps. With the infantry regiments and artillery battalions were the trains that had been providing food, stores, and ammunition to the troops along the defense line. Those trains followed their respective divisions.[23]

As each division evacuated the defenses, one regiment from each brigade remained holding the brigade's position in the trenches to cover the withdrawal. The regiments detailed to stay behind assigned companies to occupy the forward rifle pits as skirmishers. From the artillery battalions of each division, individual guns and gun crews were ordered to support the rear guard infantry regiments. The rear guard infantry and artillery of Ewell's Corps were relieved by Chambliss's and Robertson's cavalry brigades later in the evening. When relieved, the rear guard units withdrew to join their command. All eight of Lee's divisions withdrew from the Williamsport defenses using that systematic method.[24]

In the empty gun emplacements up and down the nine-mile-long defense line, Lee's men had placed logs cut to resemble artillery barrels. Over those "Quaker guns" flapped flags made of large square cloth painted red. At dawn, Union observers would see what appeared to be Confederate flags flying over occupied gun emplacements.[25]

Left behind along the abandoned defenses were thousands of burning campfires. Lee would withdraw under cover of darkness, rain, and heavy smoke just as he had done at Gettysburg on the night of 4 July and in the wee hours of 5 July. Rodes's Division led Ewell's columns to Williamsport, followed by Johnson's Division. Early's Division brought up the rear.[26]

It was a difficult evacuation. The diary of Private Samuel Pickens of the Fifth Alabama, Rodes's Division, tells us that his regiment "had very rough, muddy and bad marching before reaching the [Hagerstown-Williamsport] Pike, which was itself perfectly sloppy; and to make it still more disagreeable there was a light rain falling for a while." The turnpike "was so blocked up with troops that we did not get on very fast, and when we got to Williamsport we found it crowded with soldiers."[27]

On entering the town, Ewell's artillery battalions were directed through the thousands of infantrymen and wagon trains to the ferry. Controlling the traffic into Williamsport were Colonel Long, Major Charles S. Venable, and Lieutenant Colonel Corley of Lee's staff, along with the indefatigable Major Harman and his staff of assistant quartermasters. Confusion reigned, as delay after delay indicated to Corley and Ewell's department chiefs that the artillery would be unable to cross the river in time. Then Corley took it upon himself to direct Ewell's artillery battalions toward Falling Waters through the canal towpath, following the long trains of the army, where they would cross on the pontoon bridge. An infantry escort made up of the five Louisiana regiments of Hays's Brigade accompanied the artillery battalions.[28]

Corley ordered the quartermaster and subsistence trains traveling with Ewell's three divisions to ford the river using all four ford sites in front of and upstream from Williamsport under the direction of Major Harman, assisted by Colonel Long and Major Venable. Meanwhile, the infantry marked time in the rain and mud. "We had to stand and wait an hour or more," wrote Private Pickens, "for there was no place to sit down as the streets [in Williamsport] were ankle deep with mud and water. Finally we moved on down towards the river, but every few yards the column would halt—so that we were just creeping along at a most fatiguing pace."[29]

Ewell's infantrymen were told to hold their cartridge boxes above their heads as they passed the canal basin and waded through the aqueduct of the canal over Conococheague Creek because the corps' trains occupied the towpath of the canal as they were being directed to fords upstream from Williamsport. The infantrymen then would descend the riverbank into the water. Both the Maryland and the southern shores were ablaze with bonfires to provide light in the otherwise pitch-black, rainy night.[30]

The weary, muddy soldiers waded through the aqueduct over the mouth of Conococheague Creek. The water, which had been standing in the canal for some time, was filled with refuse and offal. Private Pickens noted that it "smelt very offensively." When the men reached the river, they were ordered to descend the steep riverbank and step into the water by twos, each holding the hand of the soldier alongside him to "resist the current better and be more steady." Loud "yelling and hallooing" was heard all night as the men stepped into the cool waters of the Potomac.[31]

According to General Rodes, the soldiers of his division descended the "steep bank of soft and slippery mud, in which numbers lost their shoes and down which many fell. The water was cold, deep and rising; the lights on either side of the river were dim, just affording enough light to mark the places of entrance and exit; the cartridge-boxes of the men had to be placed around their necks; some small men had to be carried over on the shoulders of their comrades; the water [was] up to the armpits of a full-sized man." Rodes's Division made the perilous crossing without losing a single soldier, although 25,000 to 30,000 rounds of ammunition were "wetted and spoiled."[32]

"Our clothes, blankets (partly) and haversacks all got wet," wrote Pickens, "which increased our load and made it very disagreeable marching after crossing. The banks [on the southern shore] were muddy and so steep and slippery that it was difficult to scuffle up it [*sic*]."[33]

Major Blackford of Stuart's staff observed Rodes's, Johnson's, and Early's troops wading the river from a position near the canal basin. "It was a strange and interesting sight," he recalled:

On either bank fires illuminated the scene, the water was very swift. By the bright lurid light the long line of heads and shoulders and the dim sparkling of their musket barrels could be traced across the watery space, dwindling away almost to a thread before it reached the further shore. The passage of the wagon trains was attended with some loss, for the current in some places swept them down past the ford into deep water. It was curious to watch the behavior of the mules in the teams. As the water rose over their backs they began rearing and springing vertically upward, and as they went deep and deeper the less would be seen of them before they made the spring which would bring their bodies half out of the water; then nothing would be seen but their ears above the water; until by violent effort the poor brutes moved again springing aloft; and indeed after the waters had closed over them, occasionally one would appear in one last plunge high above the surface.[34]

As soldiers often do, Ewell's men punctuated the crossing with humor. A tall soldier shouted to a shorter one ahead of him who was "struggling to hold his feet under him, with the water up to his armpits. 'Pull ahead, Johnny; General Meade will help you along directly by turning loose a battery of Parrott guns on you.'" Another soldier called out to a shorter one: "Run here, little boy, and get on my back, and I'll carry you over safely." Still another soldier observed that wading the Potomac gave the men their first bath in weeks. "General Lee," he said, "knows we need it." One trooper commented in midstream that Ewell's Corps should change its name to "Lee's Waders."[35]

The sight of Ewell's quartermaster and subsistence trains crossing the river left an indelible impression on a reporter for the *Daily Richmond Examiner* who had reached the southern bank of the river after an exhausting journey from Martinsburg. "It was quite a sight at the river, and on either side, to witness the falling back," he wrote:

The roads were muddy, the rain falling, the river was barely fordable, and teamsters, quartermasters and commissaries vied with each other in their efforts to get across, some of the more wicked mingling horrid oaths, with other more potent spurs, to the slowly gaited beasts, already much fatigued by excessive marching. Once on this side, the next things to be attained were the most desirable stands for the teams; and, in this, as in other things, human nature developed his well known qualities. On an occasion of this sort, it is astonishing what an immense crowd of men manage to keep with the trains. Those thus accompanying, with the servants of the officers, make up in themselves quite a respectable show for an army—certainly in numbers. Besides these, each wagon train seemed to have along with it quite large droves of beef cattle, which, we suppose, guarantees the subsistence question for a while at least, in the way of meat.[36]

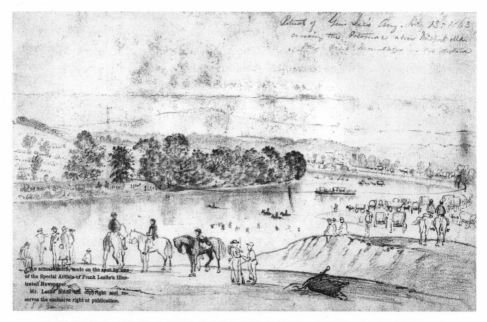

C. E. H. Bonwill's illustration for *Frank Leslie's Illustrated Newspaper* of the crossing of Lee's army above Williamsport, Maryland, on 13 July 1863. Note the canal boat being used as a ferry, the long line of wagons moving along the towpath of the C&O Canal upstream from Williamsport, and the wagons fording the river. Fords and makeshift ferries were used by Lee's trains for well over a mile west of Williamsport. Print Collection, Miriam and Ira D. Wallach, Division of Art, Prints and Photographs, The New York Public Library, Astor, Lenox and Tilden Foundations.

The movement of Ewell's artillery on the canal towpath was slow. Ahead were all of the army's trains. Horses and mules would break down and have to be dragged to the side of the towpath; wagons and ambulances would become mired in the mud and have to be pried loose. The stops and starts were nerve-racking to those in the long column. Cannoneer Henry Robinson Berkeley of the Amherst-Nelson Battery was worn out. The rain poured down. Once, when the column stopped, he sat down on a box of store goods that he took from a quartermaster wagon and fell asleep. An infantryman walked by and awakened Berkeley, telling him to "move on if he did not wish to be captured."[37]

At the same time Ewell's Corps began moving toward the river, Longstreet's Corps withdrew from its defense line and marched along the Hagerstown-Downsville and Falling Waters Roads toward the pontoon bridge. Replacing skirmishers and artillery pieces and crews along the trenches were regiments from Fitzhugh Lee's cavalry brigade. Unlike at Gettysburg, at Williamsport Lee withdrew his two flanks first, leaving the center of the army—Hill's Corps—to cover the retreat. Such a movement was necessitated by the strength of the center and by the length of the defense line, which extended over nine miles.[38]

Some of Longstreet's men found time to forage even during the evacuation of the trenches. Apparently Company D of the Fourth Texas was one of the companies sent out to occupy the skirmish lines as the rest of Hood's Division lined up on the Hagerstown-Downsville Road to march to the pontoon bridge at Falling Waters. No sooner had the skirmishers established their position than several of them "detailed themselves into a foraging party" to secure something to satisfy their hunger. Combing the countryside near Downsville, they found a "big, heavy bee gum" and carried it back to their position and filled their canteens with honey just before their skirmish line was filled by dismounted cavalrymen.[39]

The movement of Longstreet's Corps was marked by some confusion and countless halts. The men were directed to proceed down the Hagerstown-Downsville Road and onto the Falling Waters Road. McLaws's Division, the farthest from the river crossing, moved first, followed by Hood's Division. Torches and burning piles of fence rails lighted the Hagerstown-Downsville and Falling Waters Roads all the way to the river. At the junction of those two roads were large bonfires. There, Lee sat on Traveller, observing the march and giving encouragement to the endless columns of tired, muddy soldiers as they passed by.[40]

Private Simpson of the Third South Carolina, McLaws's Division, recalled the night as "the worst [he] ever saw." "The mud," he wrote, "was almost knee deep and about as thick as corn meal batter. We waded through it like horses, and such a squashing you never heard. I believe I had over fifteen or twenty pounds of mud clinging to my shoes and pants." McLaws's Division reached the pontoon bridge first but had to wait until all the remaining wagons and ambulances and all of Ewell's artillery battalions had crossed. It would be nearly daylight, 14 July, before Hood's Division arrived.[41]

Private Val C. Giles of the Fourth Texas provided a vivid description of the march to the bridge: "All night long the rain descended piteously on Longstreet's devoted corps as it moved slowly on through the dense night and yellow mud. We could hear the distant rumbling of an electric storm far away to our left and see the incessant glimmering of the lightning as it played along the lofty summit of old South Mountain. Now and then a pent up bolt of electricity would burst asunder the murky clouds above us, splitting the black night with a brilliant flash and terrific roar followed by utter darkness." Giles recalled the comment of one soldier, "as he measured his full length in the soft mud," that "hell is not half a mile from here."[42]

Anderson's Division of Hill's Corps evacuated its trenches overlooking St. James College on the evening of 13 July and headed down the Downsville Road, then west on the Williamsport-Boonsboro Road. East of Williamsport, the division was directed onto the Falling Waters Road. Pender's Division followed. Again, like Ewell's Corps and the army itself, the two flanks of Hill's Corps evacuated the defense line first, leaving the command holding the center—Heth's Division—to cover the withdrawal. The trains accompanying each division moved along with the infantry and artillery columns to which they were attached. Baker's cavalry brigade positioned itself to fill the trenches and skirmish lines of Hill's Corps on the withdrawal of the infantry skirmishers and their artillery support.[43]

Private Riley of the Sixteenth Mississippi remembered not only that the road was knee-deep in water, but also that "underneath sometimes the surface [was] slippery, sometimes sharp with rocks." Most of the men in his regiment who wore shoes before the withdrawal that night left Maryland without them. Beyond the bonfires that lighted the roads, the columns carried torches to light their way. The rain doused many of them. Riley claimed that his regiment could keep only "3 or 4 torches burning at [one] time."[44]

The sight of the marching troops in the daylight was something the survivors never forgot. "Mud reigned supreme," recalled a soldier in Hill's Corps, "not one but who had his share. The unfortunate men were covered with mud from head to foot." Having wrestled through so much rain and mud, fewer than half of the muskets of the soldiers in the ranks could be fired. For almost ten hours the army was virtually unable to defend itself. Most men believed that if the enemy attacked, their only means of defense would be their bayonets.

The march was frightful. The rain fell in sheets by late evening, and it became so dark that the men could not see their file leaders. "Every step we made," wrote a soldier in the Forty-first Virginia, "was ankle deep or knee-deep in mud." The men were "falling down continually, sometimes head and ears in mud and water, losing their muskets, sometimes five minutes would elapse before they could be recovered in the darkness." The shoes of those who still had them were literally sucked off their feet. It took Anderson's Division the entire night to march eight miles from its defense line to about three miles from Falling Waters. Waiting for Longstreet's Corps to clear the junction where the road from Hagerstown to Downsville entered the Falling Waters Road was particularly vexing. Anderson's men halted at daylight behind the muddy columns of Hood's Division.[45]

Heth's Division was ordered to abandon the defense line north of St. James College and in front of the brick schoolhouse late at night on 13 July after Anderson's and Pender's Divisions had cleared the Hagerstown-Downsville Road. Heth's was the last division to leave the trenches and served as the rear guard for the army. The column took the Hagerstown-Downsville Road to the Williamsport-Boonsboro Road, marched west to Williamsport, then followed the Falling Waters Road to the river. According to the procedure of all the army's divisions, details of one regiment from each brigade were left behind in the trenches and outer rifle pits; their officers told them that they would be relieved by cavalry later that night. Once relieved, they would follow the division to the river. Left behind in the rain were thousands of smoldering campfires.[46]

At the time of Heth's evacuation of the Williamsport defenses, the night had become black and the rain now fell in sheets. Dr. Welch of the Thirteenth South Carolina, Pender's Division, just ahead recalled: "It appeared to me that at least half of the road was a quagmire, coming in places nearly up to the knees." The Falling Waters Road had indeed become knee-deep in mud and water because of the incessant movement of Anderson's and Pender's Divisions and, below the junction with the road from Hagerstown to Downsville, the movement of Longstreet's Corps. The roads were getting even worse as more and more trains, artillery, and marching infantry columns passed and more rain fell. Heth's men made very slow progress. The infantrymen halted every few minutes to allow artillery and wagons to pass ahead to the pontoon bridge. One stop lasted nearly two hours. In all, it took twelve hours for the division to march the seven miles to the bridge at Falling Waters.[47]

So deep was the mud and so worn out were the horses and mules pulling the artillery that two rifled guns in Captain John W. Lewis's Virginia Battery had to be abandoned. Lieutenant Colonel Garnett tried everything to retrieve them from the mud, but the horses and mules collapsed. Later in the morning a relief effort with spare horses was blocked after Union cavalry closed the Falling Waters Road.[48]

Lee crossed the bridge to the southern shore, and there he sat on his horse. His anxiety was palpable to all around him; he expected to be attacked during the river crossing. At the time, Longstreet's Corps was still traversing the bridge. Lee turned to Colonel Sorrel of Longstreet's staff and asked him to recross the bridge, find General Hill, and urge him to speed up the withdrawal.

"I immediately pushed back, finding the road deep in mud but clear of any

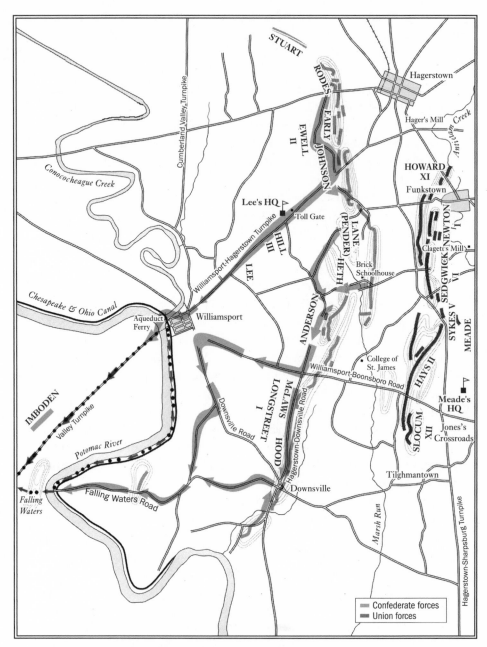

MAP 13.1   Darkness, 13 July 1863, to dawn, 14 July 1863.
Lee evacuates Williamsport. Ewell's Corps and Stuart's cavalry brigades cross the
Potomac River at Williamsport Ford. Longstreet's and Hill's Corps follow the
trains of the army and Ewell's artillery across the pontoon bridge at Falling Waters.

impediment to the men," Sorrel recalled. "Broken wagons or a dismounted gun or two had been cleared away and thrown [to] one side. General Lee's message was given and Hill asked me to assure the commander that he should safely get across." Sorrel returned to the southern shore, picking his way through the columns of troops and their artillery batteries and wagons. He rode up to Lee and reported that "all was clear, Hill was about three quarters of a mile from the bridge and marching rapidly to it."

"What was the leading division?" Lee asked.

"General Anderson," Sorrel replied.

"I'm sorry, Colonel; my friend Dick is quick enough pursuing, but in retreat I fear he will not be as sharp as I should like." Lee was probably recalling Anderson's slow march on 4 and 5 July.

But Anderson's Division did make the march in time. His men were ready to fall in line to cross the bridge as soon as Hood's Division cleared the way. Pender's Division was close behind.[49]

Early on the morning of 14 July Heth's Division reached an elevated ridge about one and a half miles in front of the river crossing. Lieutenant William Frierson Fulton of the Fifth Alabama Battalion recalled the scene at Falling Waters. "Tired, foot-sore, wet, hungry, and literally frazzled out," he wrote, "our division lay down in the old field in the edge of which was an apple orchard." General Hill, who had been overseeing his corps as it approached the pontoon bridge, rode up the hill to locate General Heth. On finding Heth, Hill directed him to place his division in a line of battle on either side of the road extending across the ridge, where Lieutenant Harris's engineers and pioneers had completed the breastworks and gun emplacements. But Hill could not afford to give Heth the guns to fill the gun emplacements; all of the corps artillery had to get across the Potomac as rapidly as possible. Heth expressed regret that there was no artillery support. General Pettigrew turned to Heth and asked, "Did you ever hear of a rear guard of a retreating army without artillery?"[50]

Heth ordered his brigade commanders to form a line of battle. On the left of the road, Pettigrew, then in command of his own brigade of North Carolinians and the remnants of Archer's Brigade of Tennesseans and Alabamians, placed his commands in the defense line. The right flank of Pettigrew's line was held by the Tennesseans and Alabamians, who took up positions in an apple orchard just north of the red brick two-story Downey farmhouse, facing north. The right was held by the First Tennessee, its front extending from the slab fence corner of farmer Downey's vegetable garden along the road and just behind the house to the right of the Thirteenth Alabama. The Seventh and Fourteenth Tennessee and the Fifth Alabama Battalion extended

Edwin Forbes's painting of Lee's army crossing the pontoon bridge at Falling Waters in the early morning of 14 July 1863. Visible are the C&O Canal and bridge, the ferryboat poles, wagons, and innumerable fires lighting the shorelines. Library of Congress, Washington, D.C.

the line in front of Downey's apple orchard to the left. To the left of the Tennesseans and Alabamians was Pettigrew's own brigade, which formed the left flank of the rear guard, extending the line all the way to the C&O Canal.

To the right of the road was positioned Brockenbrough's Virginia brigade and to Brockenbrough's right, Davis's Brigade, which held the right flank all the way to the C&O Canal. Heth directed General Lane to form Pender's Division in reserve along the low-lying ground on either side of the road about

two hundred or more yards behind and below Heth's Division. Along the road between Pettigrew's right (the First Tennessee) and Brockenbrough's left, seemingly endless streams of the division's artillery and quartermaster, subsistence, and ordnance wagons and stragglers continued to move toward the pontoon bridge below.[51]

Although informed that his division was to serve as the rear guard of the army, Heth seemed unconcerned about any immediate confrontation with the enemy. The long lines of artillery, wagons, and stragglers moving down the road gave him every indication that his men were not, in fact, the last Confederates to leave the Williamsport defense line. Furthermore, his own skirmishers were in front of him, and, he hoped, heading toward him after having been replaced in the Williamsport defense line by cavalry.[52]

One of those in front of Heth's line was Lieutenant Fulton. His horse was in desperate need of fodder, and he walked it out into the fields in front of Heth's line. There he lay down in the tall grass, watching his horse "nibbling his grass for dear life." Soon, a large contingent of Fitzhugh Lee's cavalry passed back up the road toward Downsville to screen the continued withdrawal. Thus, it was not without thought that Heth ordered his exhausted and hungry men to "lie down and take all the sleep possible." Muskets were stacked behind the lines, and the weary men fell to the ground. "Everybody," recalled Fulton, "stretched out under the trees fast asleep, their guns and clothing wet, muddy and dirty, they presented a pitiable spectacle indeed."[53]

Pettigrew was somewhat disturbed by the position of the division and its lack of pickets. Because Heth seemed unconcerned, Pettigrew took it upon himself to order pickets advanced along the left and front of his own brigade and that of the Tennesseans and Alabamians.[54]

JAMES J. PETTIGREW was one of the notable figures in Lee's army. Thirty-five years old, he hailed from North Carolina and was an honors' graduate of the University of North Carolina; when the war broke out he was practicing law in Charleston, South Carolina. His first post was captain of the First South Carolina Rifles. Elevated to brigade command, he led a force of North Carolina regiments that had suffered terribly at Gettysburg. He had been placed in charge of Heth's Division during the last great frontal assault on 3 July. His own brigade had been reduced to the size of a regiment; some companies in his regiments had vanished altogether. During the campaign Pettigrew rode his favorite horse, Zaida, that he had brought from Charleston. In addition to enjoying a very loyal staff, Pettigrew had a slave named Peter from his youth on the North Carolina family estate, "Bonarva," who had served him throughout the war. Peter rode beside Pettigrew that morning.[55]

Rain had fallen all night, and the early morning of 14 July was very foggy. Yet through the fog, Heth's line had an unobstructed field of fire extending over a mile to their front. About one mile back up the Falling Waters Road a heavy belt of woods could be seen dimly through the heavy mist.[56]

Behind Heth's and Pender's Divisions, the last of Longstreet's Corps—Hood's Division—was crossing the pontoon bridge. Like all elements of

Brigadier General James J. Pettigrew as a captain in the First South Carolina Rifles. Ruffin-Roulhac-Hamilton Papers, Southern Historical Collection, Wilson Library, University of North Carolina at Chapel Hill.

Longstreet's and Hill's Corps, Hood's artillery and wagon trains were moving up the middle of the bridge with infantrymen marching in single file on either side of the long line of vehicles. Anderson's Division was waiting to cross. The river was blanketed in fog. General Lee had crossed to the Maryland side; he and a host of officers and couriers were on horseback near the bridge.[57]

It was daylight when the head of the Texas Brigade reached the river. "The rain had ceased," recalled Private Giles,

> and a heavy mist hung over the valley, which is all on the Maryland side at Falling Waters. General Lee, mounted on old Traveller, sat calmly in the saddle near the river. He had always appeared to me before that morning as a model of elegance. On that gloomy occasion he looked pale, haggard, and old, but sat old Traveller as knightly as a Chevalier Bayard. He was bespattered with mud from the spurs on his boots to the gold cord on his black Kossuth hat. Old Traveller, whose original color was a light iron gray, on that memorable morning was a veritable

claybank. General Lee was calm but wore an anxious look as he spoke in a low, pleasant tone, telling the men to fall in two ranks and keep [open] the middle of the bridge.[58]

Anderson's men had been standing along the road waiting for Hood's Division to pass so they could fall in line to cross the bridge. One soldier in Mahone's Brigade probably epitomized Lee's once-proud invading army. Undoubtedly, Lee observed him. The soldier stood beside the road about a mile from the river with an expression of total dejection, "besmeared with mud from head to foot, with a mutton round in his hand, which was like himself coated well with mud, having been submerged times without number on the memorable night's march to the river. He was hatless as well as shoeless." Noticed by his command as it passed, the regimental major walked over to him and asked why he felt so pensive. "His reply," recalled an onlooker, "was merriment to all." The forlorn soldier remarked that he went into Maryland determined to "change his old ragged suit for a fine one, but he beheld himself coming without [a] suit, even shoeless and hatless, [and] was minus all save his mutton round."[59]

While Heth's troops were dozing near their stacked arms back up the road and Longstreet's Corps continued to cross the river, General Kilpatrick's Union Third Cavalry Division was galloping toward the Confederate river crossing, undetected by Lee's men. The division had been aroused at 3:00 A.M. at its campsite south of Hagerstown with orders to attack at seven o'clock. The enemy was reported falling back after Meade had ordered a reconnaissance of the abandoned Williamsport defense line. Captain George A. Drew of Custer's staff had ridden over to Colonel Trowbridge of the Fifth Michigan Cavalry and exclaimed: "Make no noise about it—no bugle calls—but 'boots and saddles' right away. The enemy has fallen back, and we are ordered to find out where he has gone." In less than five minutes the Fifth Michigan had formed in columns of fours. Drew rode up to Trowbridge again. "Are you ready?" he asked.

"Yes, sir," replied Trowbridge.

"Move out," Drew said, "and take the road to Williamsport."[60]

Led by the Fifth Michigan, Custer's cavalry brigade galloped down the road toward Williamsport. As they cautiously rode up to the smoky Confederate defense line with their frowning "Quaker guns," they saw that Lee had escaped. So many of the fences along the way had been removed for breastworks and firewood that the "whole country was an open common," remembered one trooper. Alongside the flank of the column as it galloped down to Williamsport rode Kilpatrick and Custer.

The Michiganders entered Williamsport on Potomac Street. The streets of the town were largely empty. The blue troopers could see Ewell's infantry and artillery drawn up in line of battle across the river, while below, in the river, the last squadron of Confederate cavalry had nearly completed its crossing. "I cannot describe my feelings of disappointment and discouragement," wrote Colonel Trowbridge. His men were angry. Trowbridge and his regiment were ordered to round up stragglers.

While in Williamsport, Kilpatrick received word that at Falling Waters, three miles below Williamsport, Confederate troops were still crossing the river. He immediately directed his command, in columns of fours, down the Williamsport-Downsville Road and then off onto the Falling Waters Road toward the river crossing. In advance were Companies B and F, Sixth Michigan Cavalry, led by Major Weber. Kilpatrick and Custer followed. The Fifth Michigan was left behind to round up stragglers in and around Williamsport before joining the command.[61]

Sergeant Kidd of the Sixth Michigan remembered the early morning hours of 14 July as "a wild night." "For the whole distance," he wrote, "the horses were spurred at a gallop. Kilpatrick was afraid he would not get there in time to overtake the enemy, so he spared neither man nor beast. The road was soft and miry, and the horses sank to their knees in the sticky mud." The column straggled badly; it was impossible to keep the troops closed up in columns of fours. At around 11:20 A.M. the two lead companies of the Sixth Michigan emerged from the heavy woods nearly a mile across the clearing from Heth's defense line.[62]

The rear guard of Lee's army was unaware of Kilpatrick's approach. Heth's men were lying on wet blankets with their arms stacked. In spite of the heavy mist, Heth observed through his binoculars the two companies of Michigan cavalry. He was perplexed. The pickets were not far enough ahead to be of any help to him. Heth remembered Fitzhugh Lee's cavalry passing up the road just a short time ago. Were these Fitzhugh Lee's horsemen? He conferred with Pettigrew. The two agreed that they must be Confederate cavalry. A private in the Seventh Tennessee then called to his lieutenant that a troop of cavalry in blue uniforms was advancing toward them.[63]

Back up the road, Major Weber, in the lead, turned to Kilpatrick and Custer for instructions. All of the Michiganders could see that Confederate infantry held the ridge a mile ahead. It appeared to them as though the Confederates had gone into bivouac. Custer ordered Companies B and F of the Sixth Michigan to dismount and advance on foot to determine the enemy's strength. Kilpatrick countermanded the orders of the young brigadier and, instead, ordered Weber to charge the Confederates on horseback. Hearing the order, Weber turned to the two companies and yelled "Forward!" They emerged from the woods at a gallop, their Union colors unfurled.[64]

Through their binoculars Heth and Pettigrew could dimly see the Union horsemen in the fog. Heth remarked that they must be Confederates, that the flag had been captured, and some officer was simply displaying some "culpable braggadocio" by unfurling it. The two Michigan companies rode closer to the Confederate line. Weber turned to his Union troopers and called out, "Wheel into line and damn them, split their heads open!"[65]

Heth reached for his field glasses again. Why would so small a band of cavalry show such a bold front in the face of an infantry division if they were unfriendly? Pettigrew and the staff officers gathered around Heth agreed. Some of the pickets opened fire; they then ran toward their main lines on the far left flank of the division. Still, in front of Heth there was no indication that the riders were enemy cavalry. On the Union horsemen came; now they were nearly 175 yards in front of the Confederate line. Nervous infantry officers called for their men to open fire. Heth yelled down the line countermanding the orders. Lieutenant Fulton got up, grabbed the reins of his horse, and, with all his strength, ran toward his sleeping comrades, yelling, "The Yankees, the Yankees!" Fulton stopped to join his men, but his old horse continued to run; he never saw it again. Pettigrew mounted his own horse and, with Lieutenant William Blount Shepard, Captain Louis G. Young, and his slave Peter, rode up to the regimental commanders in both of his small brigades, telling them to be ready but to hold their fire until ordered to open up. Heth peered through his field glasses. Intermittent shots rang out. Heth became alarmed. These were Union cavalrymen![66]

The color-bearer of the Forty-seventh Virginia, Brockenbrough's Brigade, carried his flag to the front, yelling: "Come on, boys, it's nothing but cavalry." The color-bearers of the other Virginia regiments did likewise. Colonel John M. Brockenbrough then ordered all of his regiments forward to join the color-bearers, although he remained behind. Brockenbrough would live to regret that order.[67]

Through the mist, Weber's Michigan companies, with sabres drawn, dashed toward the Confederates, yelling "Surrender! Surrender!" Heth exhorted, "It's the enemy cavalry." He turned to Pettigrew and ordered him to open fire while he and his staff retired to a position below the Downey farm. From there, Heth rode back and forth, behind his division, shouting "Keep cool, men, keep cool."[68]

Mounted when the first shots rang out, Pettigrew had trouble steadying his horse. His right hand was still somewhat immobile from his wound at Seven

Pines, and his left arm was in a sling as a result of an injury received at Gettysburg on 3 July. With the loud reports from the first volley, Pettigrew's horse reared back and fell to the ground, the general momentarily pinned beneath the saddle. Pettigrew managed to get up and ran to a position behind the First Tennessee at the fence corner of the garden near the roadside. From there he directed the fire of his men.[69]

The Michigan cavalrymen galloped ahead; some guided their snorting mounts around the gun emplacements to the left of the Tennesseans and Alabamans, but most pressed down the road past the right of the First Tennessee and obliquely through Brockenbrough's and Davis's Brigades, capturing large numbers of infantrymen and their colors. Weber's men sped through the Confederate line "yelling, cutting right and left, and riding over [some of Heth's] men while asleep, breaking arms and legs and tramping some to death." In a moment the two Michigan companies had galloped past the Confederate defense line and were firing at Pettigrew's, Brockenbrough's, and Davis's men from the rear and at Pender's Division ahead.[70]

At the time of the attack, Lee was observing the bridge crossing, anxiously waiting for Anderson's Division to reach the riverbank. The gunfire from the hills back up the Falling Waters Road suddenly filled "the gorge of the river with most threatening echoes," recalled Colonel Sorrel.

"There," said Lee, "I was expecting it, the beginning of the attack."[71]

At the onset of the assault, many of Heth's men, who had just awakened to empty muskets, fled. Some left their muskets still stacked. Seeing an old barn in farmer Downey's field about one hundred yards away, a dozen or so Confederates ran inside. Six Michiganders rode up through the gunfire swearing that they would cut off the Confederates' heads if they did not surrender!

When the mounted Michiganders swung their sabres, the fleeing Confederates in the fields would "fall flat on the ground, and before [the mounted troopers] could check their horses' speed, the Confederates would [get up] and [run] some distance from them." Private John McCall of the Seventh Tennessee and a comrade ran to an old fence. Two Michigan troopers saw them and came at them at "full speed." The Confederates jumped the fence and ran as fast as their legs could carry them. They came to another fence, and, looking back, saw the two troopers bearing down upon them, yelling as they came. McCall's comrade suddenly spotted a musket on the ground that happened to be loaded. When the troopers were within a few yards of him he fired the musket, killing one of the Michiganders. The other trooper turned around and galloped back into a squad of Confederates and was taken prisoner.[72]

Edwin Forbes's drawing of the attack of Major Peter Weber's companies of the Sixth Michigan Cavalry at Falling Waters, showing the Downey house and barn near where General Pettigrew was mortally wounded on the late morning of 14 July 1863. Library of Congress, Washington, D.C.

Recovering their composure, Pettigrew's, Brockenbrough's, and Davis's soldiers retrieved their muskets, loaded them, and formed a line of battle. Pettigrew actually had to order his troops to "about face" and open fire. Under General Lane's direction, Pender's men retrieved their stacked muskets and fired volleys into the mounted Michiganders. Colonel Perrin, whose brigade held the right flank of Pender's Division, extended his line toward the canal to keep Weber's cavalrymen from getting behind the Confederate line and menacing the bridge crossing. Scales's Brigade, commanded by Colonel William Lee J. Lowrance, followed Perrin, extending the right flank of the division. Volleys resounded across the hills and fields above Falling Waters, dismounting a large number of blue cavalrymen. Return fire found their mark in a number of Pender's troops, particularly in Perrin's Brigade.[73]

Undaunted, Major Weber ordered what men were left in his command to turn around and charge directly into Heth's men, slashing and cutting with their sabres. The brunt of Weber's attack was probably directed at

Brockenbrough's and Davis's troops, for they suffered the greatest number of killed and wounded in Heth's Division. The Eleventh and Forty-second Mississippi, Eleventh and Fifty-fifth North Carolina, and Fortieth and Fifty-fifth Virginia also experienced significant losses. With no time to reload, the North Carolinians, Tennesseans, Alabamians, Virginians, and Mississippians used bayonets and clubbed muskets. One North Carolinian wrote: "The men clubbed their guns and knocked the Yankees off of their horses. One man knocked one off with a fence rail and another killed a Yankee with an ax." Close-order fighting and confusion reigned all along Heth's line.[74]

Observing a Michigan corporal shooting from behind Downey's barn, Pettigrew directed some nearby Tennesseans to aim in that direction. Muskets were loaded and fired. Bullets chipped and splintered the barn but did not hit the blue corporal. Pettigrew reached for his own pistol, a small police revolver, and foolishly walked through the garden toward the barn to get a closer shot. But the corporal opened fire first. A bullet hit Pettigrew in the lower abdomen just to the left of the naval and passed out through the base of the spine. The general crumpled to the ground. Seeing Pettigrew fall, Peter and the general's staff officers, including Lieutenant Shepard and Captain Young, carried him back to the main line. Peter sat beside Pettigrew as nearby surgeons ran to help him. The physicians believed that Pettigrew's only hope was to lay perfectly still. They proposed to take him into farmer Downey's barn when the fighting subsided and leave him in the enemy's care. The general "obstinately declined." "I would die before I would again be taken a prisoner," he declared.[75]

Seeing his commander fall, Private N. B. Staton of the Twenty-sixth North Carolina tried to shoot the blue corporal but his musket misfired. Determined to kill the trooper who had shot Pettigrew, Staton grabbed a big stone, ran up to the corporal and knocked him to the ground, then hurled the stone at him. Repeated blows ultimately killed him.[76]

THE FIGHTING CONTINUED. Some files in Brockenbrough's and Davis's brigades let loose several volleys at the now-scattered enemy cavalrymen while Pettigrew's men used clubbed muskets and fence rails to brain Union horsemen. Major Weber was shot through the head and killed. In the melee the Michiganders lost a staggering forty killed and eighty-five wounded. Within minutes the remnants of the Michigan troopers began to find ways to get out of the Confederate line.[77]

As the fighting ended, it was clear where the brunt of the attack had been directed. Pettigrew's and Archer's Brigades suffered only three known casu-

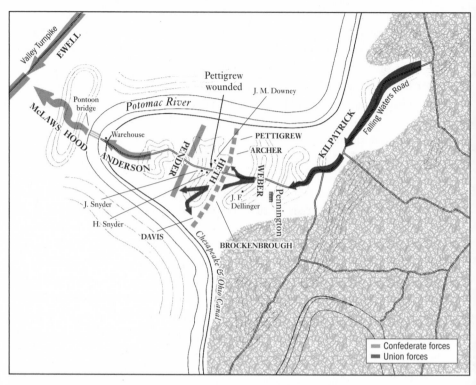

MAP 13.2   14 July 1863, 11:30 to noon.
Major Weber's companies of the Sixth Michigan Cavalry attack Heth's Division at
Falling Waters. General Pettigrew is mortally wounded.

alties: one killed and two wounded. Davis's Brigade, though, lost fifteen to wounds and an undetermined number killed. Brockenbrough's Brigade lost seven to wounds and an unknown number of dead and captured. Colonel William S. Christian of the Fifty-fifth Virginia, Brockenbrough's Brigade, and Christian's second in command, Lieutenant Colonel Evan Rice, were both captured, as was the regiment's battle flag. Suffering rather heavy casualties as well was the Forty-seventh Virginia, whose battle flag was also taken. Captured, too, was the battle flag of the Fortieth Virginia. Even the brigades of Colonel Perrin and General Scales and Lane's own brigade of Pender's Division lost a significant number of men in the attack. Perrin's South Carolinians lost five men to wounds and thirty captured; Lane's North Carolinians lost one man killed and twenty-seven skirmishers captured.[78]

Weber's offensive had been directed obliquely across the Falling Waters Road toward Brockenbrough's and Davis's Brigades. Although some Michigan cavalrymen mounted the gun emplacements in front of Pettigrew's two brigades, that was not the direction of the rash attack. Ironically, General Pettigrew was lost in a fight that merely skirted his own two brigades and cost them only three casualties, apart from their lamented commander.

Pennington's six rifles were unlimbered behind the cavalry columns of Kilpatrick's Division that remained in the fields in front of Heth's line. Soon they began to fire shells that exploded over the heads of Heth's road- and battle-weary soldiers.[79]

While Heth's Division battled Kilpatrick's cavalry, Hood's Division continued crossing the pontoon bridge one and a half miles below. Private Giles well remembered the scene. "The thunder of artillery from the hills," he wrote,

the rattle of musketry on Pettigrew's skirmish line, the long, gray columns of infantry standing there in the misty dawn, patiently waiting their turn to cross the bridge was a gloomy picture, but a grand one. As the [Fourth Texas] Regiment struck the bridge, I looked back and that scene was photographed on my memory. The band of my regiment was in front, and as they reached the Virginia side old Collins, the bugler, ordered his men to play "Dixie." The glorious tune rang out merrily, blending its melody with the hoarse roar of Federal artillery and greeting the weary infantry who answered back with a cheer that went echoing over the hills. The bridge began to sway as the men picked up the step to the tune. Officers admonished the men to stop, and keep moving. But we plodded on in rags and hope, believing we were right and would finally win.[80]

The fighting along Heth's Falling Waters defense line was finally ending. Pennington's Battery fell silent. As the last few musket shots rang out, Kilpatrick's cavalry and artillery re-formed along the Falling Waters Road to await infantry support.

Pettigrew lay on the ground near his aides. He knew his wound was mortal. While waiting for a stretcher to be brought from the rear, he spoke to those around him. He told Lieutenant Shepard and Captain Young to take his horses. To Shepard he also gave one of his swords. Finally the stretcher arrived. Pettigrew was placed on it and carried one and a half miles to the bridge, then over the bridge and up to the Valley Turnpike.[81]

The Confederate retreat continued. Anderson's Division crossed the Falling Waters bridge behind Hood's. With little further harassment, Pender's and Heth's Divisions moved down to the river. Pender's troops crossed the bridge first, followed by Heth's. To protect the rear guard as it traversed the bridge, Lee ordered Lieutenant Colonel Lawrence H. Scruggs to take his Fourth Alabama from Hood's Division to the right and into position in rifle pits on the eastern side of the bridge along the southern shore. Skirmishers of the regiment were sent out to the Maryland side along a ridge just ahead of the bridge. Lee directed Scruggs's regiment to help the engineers take up the bridge as soon as the crossing was completed.[82]

DR. CLIFTON may have been one of the last men in Lee's army to leave Williamsport and cross the pontoon bridge at Falling Waters. When he awoke at the Taylor House hotel on the morning of 14 July, he found that General Iverson, the provost marshal of Williamsport, had left, as well as most of the sick and wounded and their surgical attendants. "Unless I made my escape immediately," he wrote, "I should be captured, as the Yankees were advancing on the town, and having sold my horse [the day before], I started on foot for the ferry, with my saddle, etc. on my back." Unable to cross on the ferry, Clifton walked all the way to Falling Waters on the canal towpath. He crossed the pontoon bridge in the midst of Hill's troops, carrying his saddle, saddle blanket, and bridle on his back.[83]

Confederate artillery came into battery along the bluffs overlooking the southern shore. Lieutenant Colonel Thomas Carter's entire battalion was placed "just below [downstream] the bridge," while six of Lieutenant Colonel Garnett's guns, "two Napoleons and four rifled guns, took up position above the bridge." The twenty-pound Parrott rifles of Major John Lane's Sumter (Georgia) Artillery were posted farther downstream and the two Whitworth rifles of Captain W. B. Hurt's Alabama Battery, farther upstream. That vast array of guns and rifles "kept the enemy at a distance."[84]

Colonel Long and Major Venable returned to Lee after overseeing Ewell's crossing at Williamsport. They were exhausted. Lee continued observing the bridge crossings from the southern bank of the river. Venable dismounted not far from Lee and laid down on the rain-soaked grass. Lee walked Traveller over to Venable and saw that he was sleeping. He took off his overcoat and covered the major, then rode back to watch the last units cross the bridge. Handed a cup of coffee, Lee sipped it and pronounced it the best he had ever tasted.[85]

Pettigrew's tattered little brigade was the last to cross the bridge; the Twenty-sixth North Carolina brought up the rear. It was only fitting, given the sacrifices the Twenty-sixth had made since the opening of the campaign. Just ahead of Pettigrew's infantrymen, Major William T. Poague was moving his artillery battalion across the pontoon bridge under cracking whips. It was said that the last man in Heth's Division to cross the bridge was Captain Thomas J. Cureton of the Twenty-sixth North Carolina.[86]

The bridge was cut loose on the Maryland side, then pulled by cables out into the swirling river and onto the southern shore by the soldiers of the Fourth Alabama and the engineer battalion. The skirmishers of the Fourth Alabama soon appeared on the Maryland side, yelling for help across the river. Someone had forgotten that they were there. Quickly, their comrades grabbed some pontoons, poled them across, and retrieved the skirmishers. Those skirmishers of the Fourth Alabama were, in fact, the last Confederates to cross the Potomac River.[87]

Within the artillery batteries of Lee's army there had been losses on the march to Falling Waters, but they were hardly significant given the conditions. Owing to the rain and deep mud, the field artillery lost, altogether, ten forges, two caissons, two guns, and a sizable number of battery wagons and horses. Given that the army had captured seven Union field pieces at Gettysburg and that the artillery battalions had moved through mud that, at times, reached the axles of the guns, limbers, and caissons, the result was not unsatisfactory.[88]

General Lee reported that nearly five hundred men were lost or captured during the march to the Williamsport ford and the bridge at Falling Waters. There are no definitive records of all of those captured that dark and rainy night and morning. Some, of course, were taken prisoner by Kilpatrick's troopers during the morning attack; others were good soldiers who were simply too sick or exhausted to continue. One record tells part of the story. A roll of prisoners of war at Point Lookout, Maryland, shows seventeen names of soldiers captured on 14 July. Thirteen of them were taken at Falling Waters. In every instance, the captive was a conscript, not a volunteer. One of them was born in Ohio, another in Pennsylvania. Three were born in Ireland, two in England, and two in Germany. They were from a host of regiments: the Twelfth, Fifty-third, and Fifty-fifth Virginia; the Second, Twenty-first, and Forty-eighth Mississippi; the Eleventh, Thirtieth, and Thirty-seventh North Carolina; and the Third and Thirteenth Virginia Cavalry and the Madison, Louisiana, Artillery. Although the roll of prisoners is hardly definitive, it does seem to illustrate that some of those Confederates captured during the horrific march to the Potomac River were soldiers who had not entered the army of their own free will and, consequently, had little desire to continue in military service. Conscription helped fill the ranks, but it often did not give the army soldiers who were dedicated to the cause.[89]

As the last soldiers were retrieved from the Maryland shore, the pontoon bridge was systematically dismantled by the engineer battalion and the soldiers in the Fourth Alabama. Pontoons and trestlework were placed atop and in wagons and hauled off with the army. Lee would use them again.[90]

Once all of the army had reached the southern shore, Longstreet's and Hill's Corps halted while Ewell's Corps moved up the Valley Turnpike toward Martinsburg behind the long quartermaster, subsistence, ordnance, and ambulance trains. "It was one of the hottest of July days," recalled Colonel Sorrel. The troops were "suffering from the heat." Sorrel saw one soldier leave the ranks and approach General Lee, who was seated on Traveller not far from the James L. Cunningham house and the Falling Waters Tavern. An officer tried to stop him, but Lee "kindly encouraged his coming forward." The soldier was a "stout, well-built" man and was "sweating awfully."

"What is it you want?" Lee asked him.

"Please, General, I don't want much, but its powerful wet marching in this weather. I can't see for the water in my eyes. I came aside to this hill to get a rag or something to wipe the sweat out of my eyes," he replied.

"Will this do?" Lee handed him one of his red bandanas.

"Yes, my Lordy, that indeed!"

"Well, then take it with you, and back quick to ranks; no straggling this march, you know, my man," Lee said.[91]

In the words of Clausewitz, Lee had at last restored "the balance of power" in his theater of operations. It had taken him only ten days.[92]

Fourteen

It is heart-rending
to live among such scenes

Meade's tattered and muddy troops had been poised on 12 and 13 July to engage Lee's Army of Northern Virginia in what they thought would be the climactic struggle along the Williamsport defense line. With the dawn of 14 July, the Union soldiers could tell that the final battle was not going to happen north of the Potomac River. In the wake of the advance of Kilpatrick's cavalry division toward Williamsport, news spread rapidly among the Union troops that Lee had escaped.

Meade pushed Newton's First Corps, Sykes's Fifth Corps, Sedgwick's Sixth Corps, and Howard's Eleventh Corps from their positions along the Hagerstown-Sharpsburg Turnpike to Williamsport behind Kilpatrick's cavalry. Hays's Second Corps and Slocum's Twelfth Corps, screened by Buford's cavalry brigades, marched to Falling Waters, arriving just in time to see the last remnants of Heth's Division cross the Potomac.

Many Union soldiers were angry, giving vent to their feelings in letters home that General Meade and the high command had allowed Lee to escape. Already Gregg's cavalry division was galloping down the Pleasant Valley to Harpers Ferry to screen the movement of the Army of the Potomac toward the two pontoon bridges that had been constructed over the Potomac at Sandy Hook and Berlin, Maryland, and to scout Lee's movement into northern Virginia.[1]

For General Meade, Lee's escape proved to be a bitter episode in his career. When he had been forced to halt his army on 5 and 6 July to determine whether Lee was fortifying the mountains at the Monterey Pass, the delay irritated President Lincoln and General Halleck. To them, it appeared that Meade was content to allow Lee's army to leave Pennsylvania and Maryland.[2]

The problem intensified as Meade's troops struggled across the South

Meade's wagon trains arriving at the pontoon bridges at Berlin, Maryland.
Library of Congress, Washington, D.C.

Mountain range and approached Lee's defense line at Williamsport. Lincoln and Halleck's desired attack never materialized. Meade's reconnaissance revealed the impossibility of a direct assault. But once again, it seemed to Washington that Meade had no intention of trying to destroy Lee.[3]

After reading Meade's dispatch recounting Lee's escape, Halleck wrote the Union commander that the "enemy should be pursued and cut up, wherever he may have gone." He added: "I cannot advise details, as I do not know where Lee's army is, nor where your pontoon bridges are. I need hardly say to you that the escape of Lee's army without another battle has created great dissatisfaction in the mind of the President, and it will require an active and energetic pursuit on your part to remove the impression that it has not been sufficiently active heretofore."[4]

Meade shot back a response, asserting that he had performed his duty "conscientiously" and to the best of his ability, and that the "censure of the President" was "undeserved." He asked that he be relieved of his command "immediately." Halleck tried to repair the damage by claiming that the president did not intend to censure Meade but only provide "a stimulus to an active pursuit." That angered Meade even more.[5]

Meade had already ordered the construction of pontoon bridges across the

Potomac on the eastern side of the South Mountain range. If he had to re-cross the river, he needed his line of supply clear and the supply base close to his rear, especially given the depleted state of his army. If Lee withdrew to Virginia, Meade knew that he would have to confront him again east of the Blue Ridge Mountains. On 15 July Meade ordered the First, Fifth, Sixth, and Eleventh Corps, the Artillery Reserve, and Kilpatrick's and Buford's cav-alry divisions to cross the Potomac at Berlin; the Second, Third, and Twelfth Corps and Gregg's cavalry division were directed to cross at Sandy Hook near Harpers Ferry. Meade moved his own headquarters to Berlin.[6]

Once across the Potomac, Lee's troops moved up the Valley Turnpike toward Martinsburg, West Virginia. Ewell's Corps led the march on 14 July, followed by Hill's Corps, with Longstreet's Corps bringing up the rear. Bands played "Dixie" and "Bonnie Blue Flag." The Confederate soldiers were uni-versally pleased about being in the Old Dominion again. Lee was justifiably relieved.

Left behind at Williamsport were hospitals filled with sick and wounded officers and men who were unable to continue the journey back to Virginia. Those, combined with the casualties who fell into Union hands at the hospi-tals in Hagerstown, numbered 214. Among them were Colonel Lumpkin of the Forty-fourth Georgia, Major McDaniel of the Eleventh Georgia, Cap-tain Bond of the First Maryland Cavalry, the blind Captain McIver of the Eighth South Carolina, and Major J. M. Bradley of the Thirteenth Missis-sippi. To oversee the wounded at Williamsport, Dr. Guild chose Dr. John Mutius Gaines, surgeon of the Eighteenth Virginia; Dr. W. D. Bringle, chief surgeon of Wofford's Brigade; and Dr. E. F. DeGraffenreidt, surgeon of the Fourth Alabama. They were accompanied by a host of convalescent soldiers who would serve as nurses and stewards.[7]

While Lee's army marched up the Valley Turnpike, organized foraging by quartermasters ceased, although it would resume when the troops reached Darkesville and Bunker Hill, West Virginia. The foraging by individual sol-diers and soldier details, however, continued. Their hunt for chickens, hogs, sheep, honey, berries, eggs, and flour and meal never stopped.

Remarkably, during the entire Gettysburg campaign the only known inci-dent involving the loss of life at the hands of Confederate foragers occurred near Hedgesville in Berkeley County, West Virginia. On the other hand, civilians shot and killed a foraging quartermaster of the Thirty-third Virginia in Franklin County, Pennsylvania.[8]

The incident near Hedgesville took place on 16 July, when two Confeder-ate soldiers were foraging around a stone farmhouse built in 1772 by Samuel

Hedges, a Revolutionary War veteran. It was for Hedges and his family that the village along the Valley Turnpike north of Martinsburg got its name. In 1863 the house and farm were owned by Thomas Newton Lemen and his wife Margaret. Lemen was sixty years old and was the kin of Robert Lemen, owner of the Williamsport ferry. The Lemens were well known in the lower Shenandoah Valley.

The two Confederates appear to have been stragglers. As they approached Lemen's corncrib, Lemen told them to leave. But the hungry soldiers refused to go empty-handed. There was an altercation, and one of the foragers shot and killed Lemen. The incident was reported as far away as Winchester, Virginia, within days of its occurrence.[9]

FOR THE BETTER PART of nine days before Lee's army recrossed the Potomac River, ambulance trains had been transporting casualties from the Williamsport ford and ferry up the Valley Turnpike to Martinsburg, West Virginia, and Winchester. As soon as those trains were organized at the river crossing, they were sent on their way. They continued moving up the Valley Turnpike day and night until they reached Winchester. The sick and wounded soldiers who were able to walk were required to do so, leaving the ambulances to the critical cases.

The Shenandoah Valley had served as the corridor for the supply of Lee's army and the evacuation of its casualties since 14 June, the day Ewell's Corps took Winchester and Martinsburg from Milroy's Union forces. It was to that corridor that Lee had sent much of the impressed quartermaster and subsistence stores and animals along with mail and military communications while north of the Potomac River. And it was that corridor that Lee had relied on to receive soldiers returning to the army after their convalescence as well as military communications, mail, supplies, and ammunition from Richmond.

The Valley Turnpike made that corridor so important. The road was twenty-two feet wide, eighteen feet of which were macadamized using twelve-inch-thick crushed rock that formed a hard surface. The turnpike was almost impervious to rain; it stretched all the way from the Potomac River to Staunton, Virginia. Along the Valley Turnpike were key supply and hospital centers.[10]

Martinsburg was the first sizable town in the lower Shenandoah Valley through which Lee's army would pass on its return to Virginia. Because a hospital had been established there after Ewell captured Milroy's Union garrison on 14 June, it became a wayside for those returning to Virginia in ambulance trains who were in need of immediate medical attention.

James E. Taylor's sketch of Queen Street, Martinsburg, West Virginia, looking north. The Berkeley County Courthouse is shown at left; to the left of the courthouse stood the United States Hotel. The Western Reserve Historical Society, Cleveland, Ohio.

The sick and wounded from Lee's army began entering Martinsburg as early as Sunday, 5 July. That morning Susan Nourse Riddle, a resident of the town, attended the Presbyterian church on Queen Street to hear the sermon of the Reverend Dr. William J. Hoge, an evangelist in the Army of Northern Virginia who had remained in Martinsburg in the wake of Lee's invasion. From inside the church Susan Riddle heard the rumble of wagons and ambulances and the chatter of sick and wounded soldiers and their mounted escorts as they came up Queen Street. She ran home to make bandages. Hotels and churches were hurriedly prepared to receive the casualties.[11]

Ambulance trains, along with quartermaster and subsistence trains, moved through Martinsburg for days. "Wounded, mangled men still coming through," Riddle noted in her diary on 8 July. "The streets nearly all the time lined with wagons and ambulances. Those that are able are sent on. Terrible sights. Yet the poor fellows are generally cheerful and ready to go back as soon as they are able."[12]

Churches, homes, public buildings, and hotels in Martinsburg became hospitals. The Presbyterian church, the German Reformed church, the Lutheran church, George Swinley's Eagle Hotel, George Ramer's Everett House,

James Meade's Valley House, all on Queen Street, and Henry Staub's well-known United States Hotel on King Street were overwhelmed with soldiers, many of them with hemorrhaging wounds and burning infections who could no longer endure the journey. The Depot House over the Baltimore and Ohio Railroad passenger station was in shambles, having been partially destroyed by Stonewall Jackson's troops in the spring of 1862, but the office of the Southern Telegraph Company located there was in operation. For days it was jammed with soldiers seeking to notify loved ones of their whereabouts and condition.[13]

On King Street, next to the Berkeley County Courthouse, the United States Hotel became the receiving hospital in Martinsburg. There, Colonel Morehead of the Forty-fifth North Carolina had died of typhoid fever on 26 June. Ambulances brought their sick and wounded passengers to the hotel only if they needed immediate medical attention. After being examined by the chief surgeon or one of his staff, the soldiers in ambulance trains were either directed up the Valley Turnpike to Winchester or, if absolutely necessary, to one of the hotels, residences, or churches in town that had been converted into a hospital. Local doctors volunteered as surgeons, and some regimental surgeons traveling in the ambulance trains were assigned to duty there. The Confederate casualties were to leave Martinsburg as soon as possible; if they were not moved up the valley quickly, they would be captured, as Lee intended to abandon the town; his army would occupy the area around Darkesville and Bunker Hill, ten miles south.[14]

Placed in charge of Ewell's sick and wounded in Martinsburg by Dr. McGuire on 15 June was twenty-eight-year-old Dr. Jacob M. Hadley, a North Carolinian. Hadley had three brothers who served in the Confederate army; two had died and one had been severely wounded. In the fall of 1862 Hadley had been commissioned surgeon of the Fourth North Carolina, a hard-fighting regiment with which he had served through the battles of Fredericksburg and Chancellorsville. He was aided by some assistant surgeons and stewards. His nurses were all convalescent soldiers or local residents.[15]

Generals Pender, Scales, Jenkins, Jones, Anderson, Hood, and Hampton and Major Latimer passed through Martinsburg on 6 and 7 July. All stopped long enough for Dr. Hadley to examine and re-dress their wounds and provide them with food for the journey ahead.

Captain Hughes, Pettigrew's adjutant general, and Lieutenant Lucas of the Eleventh North Carolina, with Lucas's slave, were finally removed from their dirty ambulance after they arrived in Martinsburg on 6 July and were assigned to one of the hotels. Hughes died on 15 July, the day after his commander, General Pettigrew, was mortally wounded and while Lee's army was marching through Martinsburg on its way to Darkesville and Bunker Hill. Lucas died nine days later. Both were buried in Green Hill Cemetery, Martinsburg.[16]

Colonel Parker of the Thirtieth North Carolina and Colonel Bennett of the Fourteenth North Carolina were removed from their one-horse buggy and taken to the farmhouse most likely of Colbert Anderson, his wife Isabella, and their three children, just outside of Martinsburg. Parker and Bennett would survive their wounds and return to the army. Entering town with Parker and Bennett was the wounded Lieutenant William J. Broadfoot of the First Maryland Battalion. He died in Martinsburg shortly after his arrival.[17]

At 11:00 A.M. on 7 July, the ambulance carrying General Semmes reached the town square of Martinsburg. Like Captain Hughes and Lieutenant Lucas, Semmes had taken a turn for the worse when his leg wound became inflamed. The four-day journey along rough roads had taken its toll. Soaked with rain and mud, Semmes was feverish, his leg oozing with infection. Captains Cody and Lewis and Corporal Cleveland still accompanied him. The ambulance came to a halt in front of the United States Hotel and Semmes was taken inside. At the time, the hotel was managed by a woman named Mary Oden and other members of her family.[18]

Although buoyed by signs that the general was beginning to recover, all soon recognized that his condition was deteriorating. While Semmes was in the United States Hotel, ambulance trains brought two visitors to his bedside: Captain Edward Foster Hoge, of the Ninth Georgia, the son-in-law of the general's sister Caroline, who had been wounded on 2 July at Gettysburg, and the wounded William Hemphill of Carlton's Georgia Battery, the nephew of Semmes's wife. Both left their ambulances when they were told Semmes was in the hotel.[19]

Dr. Hadley examined the wound on 10 July and proclaimed Semmes's condition to be hopeless. In the evening the Reverend Dr. Theodore Pryor, Presbyterian missionary chaplain of Longstreet's Corps, arrived. Pryor observed that the general was near death. No sooner had he begun reading a passage from the New Testament than Semmes died. At that very moment, Semmes's old brigade was battling Buford's Union cavalry and Grant's Sixth Corps infantry east of Funkstown. Semmes was buried in Green Hill Cemetery.[20]

One of Semmes's young officers from the Second Georgia, Lieutenant Elisha Sapp, was brought into Martinsburg shortly after Semmes arrived. Surgeons initially thought that Sapp's abdominal wound was not serious. By the time he reached Martinsburg, however, it was badly infected. Susan Riddle helped nurse him. He died on 20 July and was buried at Green Hill Cemetery, the ladies of town "covering his coffin and grave with flowers."[21]

Sergeant Whitehorne was driven to the United States Hotel on the morning of 14 July. He had spent the night before on the side of the road, his driver letting the "tired and jaded" mules rest. "Driving up to a large building, now a hospital," wrote Whitehorne, "a surgeon came out and examined my wound, but finding that I was doing well, he only had my canteen filled with water and said 'keep the wound wet' [and] left me. We were given something to eat here much to my satisfaction. We found on our arrival here a great many ambulances already loaded with wounded men ready to start to Winchester."[22]

All of the trains of Lee's army were directed to Winchester as fast as they could get there. Winchester had changed hands several times since the outbreak of war. Situated at the foot of the valley, about thirty-five miles south of the Potomac River, it was inhabited by nearly 4,500 people. Over the past two years, though, some had refugeed up the valley.

Located in the midst of one of Virginia's most fertile plains, Winchester was the market town for the lower valley. What had contributed the most to its growth was the Valley Turnpike. That road gave Winchester ready access to the Baltimore and Ohio Railroad and the Chesapeake and Ohio (C&O) Canal in the Potomac River Valley. Winchester was also the terminus of the Winchester and Potomac Railroad, a single line of "strap rails" that ran northeast, connecting the town with the Baltimore and Ohio Railroad at Harpers Ferry by way of Stephenson's Depot and Charles Town; nearly all of the railroad had been destroyed by Lee's army in October 1862.[23]

Almost 500 Union soldiers and between 700 and 800 Confederate troops had been hospitalized in Winchester after Milroy's defeat by Ewell's Corps back on 14 June. All of them had been treated by Dr. McGuire and his staff and regimental surgeons. After Longstreet's Corps rested in the mountains near Millwood and Berryville during its northward movement in June—only one day before the arrival of Hill's Corps—Lee moved to secure Winchester, then less than twenty miles to his rear, as the receiving hospital for the Army of Northern Virginia. Because Lee had shifted his line of supply to the Shenandoah Valley by way of the Virginia Central Railroad only four days earlier, he chose to make Winchester his supply base for the invasion of Pennsylvania as well.

Lee sent his medical director, Dr. Guild, to Winchester on 18 June. On arriving with his staff, Guild found the town in such a "filthy condition" and "low forms of fever so rife" that he decided to move the Union and Confederate sick and wounded out of the town. Indeed, typhoid fever was spreading

James E. Taylor's sketch of Winchester, Virginia, looking south on Loudoun Street (the Valley Turnpike). The Western Reserve Historical Society, Cleveland, Ohio.

through the town at an alarming rate as a result of the fecal contamination of the water supply.[24]

Occupied and fought over for two years, Winchester had indeed become foul. Streets and public buildings were littered with debris. Uncontaminated water was nonexistent. Until Guild's arrival, all Union casualties were hospitalized in the Taylor Hotel on Loudoun Street and in and around the courthouse; Dr. McGuire hospitalized the Confederate sick in the old, rather dilapidated Union Hotel, while the Confederate wounded were taken to the nearby York Hotel.[25]

Guild directed McGuire and his staff and regimental surgeons to correct the problem. The Union sick and wounded were moved to a hospital camp established southeast of town at a site east of the Valley Turnpike along Abraham's Run known as Shawnee or Garden Springs, where there was ample spring water. By the time Lee's army recrossed the Potomac River, most Union soldiers had been transferred to Staunton and Richmond.[26]

On 18 June McGuire ordered Dr. Black to organize a hospital at Jordan White Sulphur Springs, Virginia, six miles northeast of Winchester, near Stephenson's Depot. On the twenty-fourth Black directed that all patients at the Union and York Hotels be moved there. Once the hospital was in full operation, Black returned to duty with Ewell's Corps and Guild's own staff physicians assumed responsibility for the hospitals in and around Winchester. Dr. George W. Heagy, a surgeon who had been mustered into service with the Eighty-ninth Virginia Militia less than one month before, was left in charge of the hospital at Jordan White Sulphur Springs. Guild noted that the site was "a very suitable place for a hospital; the patients are well cared for and are comfortable."[27]

Even though many of its patients had already been sent to Staunton and on to Richmond by the time Lee's army began its retreat from Gettysburg, the Jordan White Sulphur Springs hospital was a rather large operation. It had four wardmasters, twenty-six nurses, three matrons, and two cooks. Nearly all were soldiers detailed from Ewell's Corps. Joseph Neil, a local justice of the peace, served as a steward and Mary Kurtz and Mary Anne Slagle, both local citizens, were matrons. A young woman named "Jam" Brown of Winchester was listed as a "colored girl" who volunteered as a cook to assist another civilian named J. W. Hamilton. The wardmasters and nurses were a collection of convalescents from a host of regiments in Ewell's Corps.[28]

The physicians serving in the Winchester hospitals when Lee's casualties returned to Virginia were all regimental surgeons from Ewell's Corps who had remained there under orders from Dr. McGuire. Among them were Dr. Samuel Meeker of the Seventh Louisiana, Dr. W. C. Dixon of the Fourteenth Louisiana, and Dr. William Shepherd Grymes of the Thirteenth Virginia.[29]

Left behind by Guild on 18 June to oversee all of the receiving hospitals in the lower Shenandoah Valley was thirty-three-year-old Dr. Joseph Edward Claggett, director of receiving and forwarding of the ambulance trains of the Army of Northern Virginia, from Guild's staff, and Claggett's assistant, Dr. Samuel H. Moffitt. Claggett was born and raised in Pleasant Valley, not far from Boonsboro, Maryland, and was very familiar with the region. His duties included supervising hospital administration in Winchester, Shawnee Springs, and Jordan White Sulphur Springs as well as the transportation of casualties from Lee's army to the valley hospitals and, ultimately, to the general hospitals in Richmond. He was also responsible for resupplying Lee's army with ambulances when the need arose. Claggett reestablished the York

Hotel as the receiving hospital in Winchester. There he and Moffitt set up their headquarters and created and managed a system for receiving and forwarding Lee's sick and wounded returning to Virginia.[30]

Claggett purchased and impressed two- and four-horse wagons from residents of the town and the surrounding countryside; together with the army ambulances at his disposal, he organized and directed the ambulance trains that regularly left the hospitals at Winchester, Shawnee Springs, and Jordan White Sulphur Springs bound for Staunton. Under directions from Guild and pressure from some of Longstreet's Brigade commanders back in mid-June, Claggett, through the quartermaster department, even chartered the stagecoach lines—including the line owned by Major John Alexander Harman—that ran between Winchester and Staunton to remove the sick and wounded brought to Winchester as quickly as possible. Those ambulance trains with the chartered stagecoaches continued to operate between Winchester and Staunton as Lee's casualties returned from Gettysburg.[31]

Claggett's assistant, Dr. Moffitt, was a seventy-three-year-old physician from New Market, Virginia. Mrs. Hugh Holmes Lee noted in her diary that Claggett and Moffitt "[were] plain men, they will do anything I ask." Dr. W. H. Geddings of Guild's staff was assigned to establish a medical purveying depot at Winchester.[32]

AT THE TIME of Lee's withdrawal to Virginia there were two infantry units in Winchester. Bivouacked near the Northwestern Turnpike were Colonel James Barbour Terrill's Thirteenth Virginia and Major David B. Bridgeford's First Battalion (Irish) of Virginia Infantry. Bridgeford, a native of Richmond, who had served as provost marshal on Stonewall Jackson's staff, had been named provost marshal of Winchester by Ewell in mid-June. By virtue of his staff position, he was commander of the post after the departure of Colonel Bradley T. Johnson, a duty Bridgeford had performed there at least three times before. Bridgeford's First Battalion was the provost guard of the garrison.

Terrill's and Bridgeford's commands had been keeping the peace and guarding Winchester's hospitals and supply depots, including all the captured stores, equipment, and clothing in Milroy's earthen forts as well as the quartermaster and subsistence stores and horses, mules, cattle, sheep, and hogs sent to Winchester by Lee's army while it was in Pennsylvania and Maryland. All of those stores and animals were kept south of Winchester in large open fields awaiting the army's return.[33]

A war correspondent for the *Richmond Daily Dispatch* presented a dour portrait of Winchester on 4 July. "Whatever Winchester may have been in different times," he wrote,

> it certainly now presents a picture of sad coloring. Not a cart, wagon or drag is to be seen. Save the army wagon, not a carriage enlivens the streets. The thoroughfares are miry with filth, and the general impression upon entering the town is that you have driven into a huge livery stable, not particularly well kept. Nearly every door is closed and few persons are seen save soldiers and a few refugees, just returned from nine months banishment, looking with anxious and careful scrutiny to discover amidst the general desolation a few faces of well remembered scenes and localities.

In two days, Winchester would become chaotic.[34]

The townspeople got their first news of the result of the fighting at Gettysburg on the night of 5 July, when Dr. Claggett, in response to Guild's order, began rounding up "every ambulance and spring wagon in town" to send to Williamsport. That night Mrs. Hugh Holmes Lee wrote that she had a "presentiment" that many of her friends were among the casualties. Indeed, they were.[35]

Mrs. Lee left her home in the evening to visit the wife of the Reverend Dr. Andrew Hunter Holmes Boyd of the Loudoun Street Presbyterian Church; she then walked to the old York Hotel near her residence "to make arrangements for the reception of the wounded." After helping to notify all the churches in town to be prepared to receive the wounded, she returned home in order to make "every arrangement to give up our rooms to any of our men who may require them."[36]

On Monday night, 6 July, Major Bridgeford informed the citizenry of the magnitude of what was to descend upon them. He had received a dispatch stating that 5,000 sick and wounded were on their way to Winchester. In fact, there were over 8,500. At daylight, 7 July, the casualties began pouring into the town. Laura Lee, Mrs. Hugh Holmes Lee's sister-in-law, described their arrival in her journal: "From daylight, crowds, hundreds, of wounded men have been trooping by, all wounded in the hand, arm or head but able to walk. The commissary furnishes rations for the citizens to cook, and the poor fellows had a good meal as soon as they arrived, some at the hospital, but hundreds at the doors as they pass[ed] through the streets."[37]

As there had been at Martinsburg, Claggett established a system to receive the sick and wounded at Winchester. All of them were first directed to the

York Hotel. Claggett and his staff would examine each case and determine the disposition to be made. For those who needed to remain in Winchester, there was a procedure for hospital assignment. Cases of sickness went to the hospital at Jordan White Sulphur Springs, the Union Hotel, or private residences where only the sick were received. The York Hotel was the surgical center, as it had been after Ewell's capture of Milroy's garrison. There were specific residences and churches in town where postsurgical cases or soldiers suffering from wounds were conveyed.[38]

The four wardmasters and twenty-six nurses at Jordan White Sulphur Springs were quickly overwhelmed by the sick—over one thousand soldiers— arriving from Pennsylvania in the wake of Lee's return to Virginia. Nine surgeons—among them, Dr. Abner Embry McGarity of the Forty-fourth Georgia—were in attendance. Dr. Harvey Black briefly returned to oversee the hospital. But if Jordan White Sulphur Springs was inundated by the sick from Lee's army, the town of Winchester was taxed to the limit by the casualties. With a polluted water supply and rampant typhoid fever, it was in no position to receive thousands of sick and badly wounded soldiers who were burning with fever and in desperate need of being washed and of receiving clean dressings, clothes, and food.[39]

Claggett and Moffet organized the townspeople to help. They called meetings with all the men and women whose houses were pressed into service. Captain Charles W. Coontz, a local industrialist and the chief commissary, met with them as well. The townspeople were directed to prepare food for the general use of the sick and wounded. If their houses were to be used as adjunct hospitals, they received instruction on how to requisition rations from the commissary for the patients under their care. Major Bridgeford required local citizens to bring to his depot extra bedding, sheets, medicines, and clothing. Women were organized into teams to attend to patients at the York, Union, and Taylor House hotels and eleven churches. When not on duty, they cared for the sick or wounded in their own homes.[40]

As surgeons arrived at Winchester with ambulance trains, Dr. Claggett assigned them to specific hospitals. Dr. LeGrand Wilson, who arrived in the wee hours of 8 July, was detailed to supervise the hospital at the Market Street Methodist Church and obtained living quarters at Mrs. Lee's residence across the street.

"I was placed in charge of a large new church," Wilson later wrote,

which was being used as a hospital. Here I went into the wholesale receiving and forwarding business. For three long weeks I suppose I dressed wounds of from thirty to fifty men every day, and shipped them up the valley to Staunton. Many of these wounds had not been dressed since the battle, and were in a terrible condition. I don't know how the poor fellows stood it, but I never heard a murmur. Their wounds were very offensive, and 90 percent were infested with vermin. It would frequently require a half an hour or longer to get the maggots out of a wound, and when you remember that we had no disinfectants, you can understand why it was so tedious, why it was so disagreeable. It was certainly the most disagreeable duty I ever performed. I was engaged at it from morning till night, taking time at noon to go to dinner. In a few days I began to lose my appetite, simply because I could never remove the offensive odor from my hands, and of course I began to lose flesh. In a short time I began to have fever. I could see no place to stop and rest. The poor men must be attended to, and there was no one else, it seemed, to do the work.

Wilson asked Claggett for an assistant, but none was sent to him. "If it had not been for the good ladies of Winchester who came to the rescue and helped me in every way possible," he declared, "I don't know what I would have done. They made and brought me bandages, soft cloths, soap and everything they could furnish, and one dear mother brought me every morning a basketful of a strong decoction of elder, which helped me very much in getting rid of the vermin [t]o say nothing of the good edibles and rich soups furnished the poor fellows."[41]

To move the sick and wounded to Staunton, Claggett and his staff assembled ambulances, spring wagons, and stagecoaches along Loudoun Street in front of the Taylor House hotel as the availability of the vehicles and the number of patients able to travel warranted. Because of the need for vehicles, drivers of ambulances entering Winchester were instructed to turn them over to Major Bridgeford so they would be available for the ambulance trains. The departure of these trains was announced by Claggett's staff at all hospitals, churches, and private residences so that doctors could clear the beds of those able to make the journey. Usually two or three ambulance trains left for Staunton every day. Like the trains leaving Gettysburg, Claggett's ambulance trains were accompanied by sick and wounded soldiers who could walk. Ambulances were always reserved for men whose illness or wounds required them to ride in vehicles.[42]

A seemingly endless stream of casualties poured into Winchester. Generals Pender and Scales arrived on the afternoon of 7 July and were taken to a private residence for rest and medical attention. General Anderson was brought into Winchester later that evening and assigned to the home of Robert Sherrard on South Loudoun Street. Joining Anderson was Captain Zack Leitner of the Second South Carolina. General Jenkins, General Jones, and Major Latimer soon entered the town and were conveyed to private residences, as were Generals Hood and Hampton. Mrs. Lee fed some of the wounded soldiers on her front porch; she also sent food and supplies to the York Hotel and the nearby Market Street Methodist Church, where many injured troops were crowding into the sanctuary.[43]

On the night of 7 July, Mrs. Lee and her sister-in-law Laura heard from the soldiers streaming into Winchester of the death of old friends at Gettysburg. Mrs. Lee's house was filled with wounded and dying men. Then Claggett sent more. Two lieutenants from Georgia, each with a leg amputated, were brought to her home. "We could not send the poor fellows wandering about the town at such a time to seek lodging, and hastily prepared a bed in the back parlor and had them brought there," Laura Lee recorded in her diary. "It is heart rending to live among such scenes."[44]

Captain Park and his three companions of the Twelfth Alabama reached Winchester at 4:00 P.M., 7 July. Their wounds had been dressed in Martinsburg the previous day, and they had spent the rainy night beside the turnpike. Miraculously, Lieutenant Wright was still alive despite his open head wound. On Park's arrival, he turned his ambulance over to Major Bridgeford once his companions were assigned to a medical facility. Park then left Winchester for Staunton aboard a chartered mail coach in a train of ambulances that Claggett had just assembled on Loudoun Street.[45]

Arriving at Winchester at about the same time as Park were Colonel Christie and Lieutenant Colonel Johnston of the Twenty-third North Carolina. Christie's injured spine appeared to be mortal; Johnston's wounds in the face, jaw, and clavicle looked awful but did not seem life threatening. Christie was carried to the home of Dr. J. Philip Smith near Christ Episcopal Church on the corner of Boscawen and Washington Streets; Smith was professor of medicine at the Winchester Medical College. Johnston was probably sent to the Smith home as well.

The surgeons could do nothing for Christie. He died on 17 July while calling for "darling Lizzie," his wife. His remains were buried in the Episcopal burying ground on the nineteenth. As a group of officer friends were returning from his interment, they met Christie's wife and three children at the front gate of the Smith home. She had driven all the way from Suffolk, Virginia, but had arrived too late.[46]

Still burning with typhoid fever, Colonel Black also arrived in Winchester on 7 July; he had spent the rainy night in his ambulance along the turnpike with the wounded General Jones. Black was taken to the York Hotel, where Dr. Claggett examined him. He was then ordered to the residence of a widow named O'Bannon at the corner of Kent and Philpott Streets. In that household was O'Bannon's niece, Emma Cassandra Reily, whose parents had died of scarlet fever before the war. Black was carried inside. A week later, Brigadier General Junius Daniel was brought into the house from his brigade's Darkesville bivouac site. He had become seriously ill with typhoid fever during the closing days of the campaign. Daniel and Black, it seems, were friends from their days at West Point.[47]

Private Charles Moore of the Fifth Louisiana reached Winchester at about noon on 13 July. Like Colonel Black, he had spent the previous night sleeping in his ambulance along the Valley Turnpike south of Martinsburg. On his arrival he was received at the York Hotel, then sent to the Market Street Methodist Church. Soon he was transferred a few blocks west to the Loudoun Street Presbyterian Church and later was taken to the home of a John Campbell.[48]

Sergeant Whitehorne finally arrived late on the afternoon of 15 July. He first stopped at the York Hotel. "[I] didn't like the looks of things," he confided to his diary, "too many wounded men in the house, the oder [*sic*] was distressingly bad." Whitehorne was placed on a cot near the door, for which he was very thankful. The wounded soldier beside him was from Bertie County, North Carolina. The two began talking and soon became friends.

By the next day Whitehorne and his Tarheel friend were sent to the home of Kate Sperry. Kate's mother was dead, and her father was in the Confederate service. She and her sister were living with their grandfather, Peter Graves Sperry. At the time Kate, a vivacious, high-spirited young woman, was engaged to Dr. Enoch Newton Hunt, surgeon of the Second Mississippi. The lower floor of the Sperry house was a store; the upper floor was the residence. Whitehorne and his friend were taken to the front room of the second floor, which they occupied with three other wounded soldiers. "Every day," Whitehorne wrote, people "bring us berries, milk, cake for which we are very grateful. We are as comfortable as can be expected."

Whitehorne remained in Winchester until 19 July. He and his Tarheel friend were told that "a train of empty wagons would leave for Staunton at 8 o'clk, and all of the wounded able to take care of themselves would be allowed to go with it." Whitehorne was determined to leave:

I got down [and] sat in the front door, here [I] waited till the wagons drove up, and as it happened one wagon stopped directly in front
of the door and not over eight feet off. [Whitehorne's friend] put his
arms around me and almost lifted me across the pavement to the front
wheel of the wagon. . . . I climbed into the wagon and sat down on the
straw before any of the wounded got out of the house, and unnoticed
by any of the nurses. Before making a start, a surgeon came up and got
on the wheel of the wagon and inspected us, asking each man "Are you
able to stand the trip?" Every solitary man said "Oh yes." The surgeon
then gave every man a drink of whiskey and bade us goodbye, and we
started.[49]

MEANWHILE, the Union prisoners of war had made their way to Winchester
six days ahead of Lee's army. They had started the march after crossing the
Potomac River on 9 July. Under guard of Pickett's Division, they arrived on
10 July.[50]

While all the Union prisoners were gathered along the Valley Turnpike
north of Winchester preparatory to renewing the march up the Shenandoah
Valley, Captain Henry T. Owen of the Eighteenth Virginia noticed that a
"fine-looking" Union officer was trying to get some bread from a few guards.
He seemed to be offering the guards a silver-mounted pocket flask for a "half
cake of bread," and the guards were "trying to see how small a piece he would
agree to take."

Owen walked over to the Union officer and told him that he would soon
have some beef and flour and that he should wait for it. But the officer claimed
that he had never been given any beef and flour and was very hungry. Soon
Owen was informed by one of his men about a house nearby where he could
get breakfast. Owen approached the Union officer and said that if he promised not to try to escape, he would take him there for a meal. The officer agreed, and the two walked over to a house where an "old lady and her
three daughters" treated them to "lightbread, fried ham, coffee (genuine) and
honey." She refused Owen's Confederate money, but the Union officer insisted that she accept his greenbacks. The officers purchased three dozen biscuits from her and then "jogged back to camp." The officer told Owen that
his name was Captain F. R. Josselyn of the Eleventh Massachusetts and that
he was from Boston. The two men then parted.[51]

The Union prisoners were marched along Loudoun Street through Winchester on 12 July. South of town, they were turned over to Imboden's cavalry brigade and proceeded up the Shenandoah Valley to Strasburg the next day. On 14 July they passed through Woodstock and Edinburgh and camped about seven miles north of Mount Jackson. The prisoners passed through Mount Jackson the next day and reached Harrisonburg on 16 July. Finally, on 18 July they entered Staunton, completing on foot a journey of two hundred miles in fourteen days. At Staunton the prisoners were loaded on cars of the Virginia Central Railroad and taken to Richmond.[52]

Led by Ewell's Corps, Lee's army entered Martinsburg on the afternoon of 14 July. The "Union people [were] jubilant," wrote Susan Riddle, "Southern hearts sad. Went up the street in the evening. Saw the Stonewall Brigade pass through town." Riddle prepared meals for countless soldiers, particularly those in Martinsburg's Second Virginia, including Colonel John Q. A. Nadenbousch, her cousin Sergeant Major John H. Leathers, and Dr. MacGill and his son from Hagerstown. Hill's Corps marched behind Ewell; Longstreet's Corps brought up the rear.[53]

Lee's immediate destination was Darkesville and Bunker Hill, midway between Martinsburg and Winchester. Although all of the sick and wounded and most of the seized quartermaster and subsistence stores, including animals, were being conveyed to Winchester, Lee did not want his army near the town because of the putrid water and the typhoid fever epidemic.

Darkesville and Bunker Hill were ideal locations to bivouac the army. Darkesville, about ten miles south of Martinsburg, had been laid out in the late eighteenth century and named for Revolutionary War general William Darke, one of the first magistrates of Berkeley County. The village grew up where the Valley Turnpike crossed Middle Creek. When the war began, Bunker Hill was a sleepy village inhabited by about two hundred people. In two years of war, however, it had been the site of numerous campgrounds of both Confederate and Union armies; its churches, public houses, private dwellings, and other structures had all been repeatedly used as barracks, stables, and hospitals, and they showed the effects of it.[54]

Named for the 1775 Revolutionary War engagement, Bunker Hill grew up where Mill Creek crossed the Valley Turnpike. A stone tavern built in the late eighteenth century stood on the east side of the turnpike; in July 1863 it was still in business, operated by Henry and Sarah Bowers. The brick 1853 Bunker Hill Presbyterian Church stood along the west side of the Valley Turnpike, and a one-story, brick Methodist-Episcopal church was located behind the Presbyterian church. Alfred Ross's brick residence was near his large mill on Mill Creek.[55]

James E. Taylor's sketch of Bunker Hill, West Virginia, looking north and showing the Bowers hotel on the right and the Presbyterian church on the left. The Western Reserve Historical Society, Cleveland, Ohio.

In nearby Gerrardstown, Sarah Morgan McKown had been feeding passing sick and wounded soldiers on their way to Winchester since 6 July; some spent the night in her home to get out of the driving rain. She observed large herds of livestock being driven past her residence on the way to Winchester.

On 15 July McKown provided dinner for "eight soldiers, one of them black." From them she learned that Lee's army was falling back to Darkesville and Bunker Hill. Although unwell, McKown fed nineteen soldiers the next day as Lee's whole army began pouring into the vicinity of Mill Creek. "They are camped near [S. P.] Henshaw's Mill; some of them are in one of uncle George [McKown's] fields," she wrote in her diary. "They are scouring the country for provisions of every kind, for man and beast." For the next ten days McKown constantly prepared food for soldiers. She even helped some of them mend their tattered garments.[56]

Hill's and Longstreet's Corps arrived at Bunker Hill at night on 15 July. Hill's Corps halted west of Bunker Hill and Longstreet's, east of the village. Both camped along Mill Creek. Ewell's Corps went into bivouac along Middle Creek.[57]

The ambulance carrying General Pettigrew, traveling with Hill's Corps, stopped at "Edgewood," the 1839 two-story brick home of John E. Boyd, located along the Valley Turnpike south of Bunker Hill not far from Mill

Creek. The house stood within the bivouac sites of Heth's Division of Hill's Corps. Pettigrew was carried into the house, up the stairs, and into the southeast bedroom. Boyd was not present when the general arrived, but the Reverend Dr. Joseph P. B. Wilmer was there on a visit. Wilmer, an Episcopal priest, had been an army chaplain as well as rector of St. Mark's Church in Philadelphia before the war. Southern in sympathies, he had been arrested at Fort Monroe in January 1862 after contraband goods had been found in his baggage; he was incarcerated in the Old Capitol Prison in Washington. Released in March 1863, he settled in Albermarle County, Virginia. In June he and his son Skipwith had arrived in Winchester, where he had agreed to serve as the interim rector of Christ Church. Since then, he had been tirelessly serving sick and wounded troops as well as the famished people of Winchester.[58]

Pettigrew said very little; he suffered greatly from nausea and was seriously weakened by the loss of blood. Dr. George Trescott of the First South Carolina Rifles was called from his regiment to treat him. Trescott had been Pettigrew's surgeon in the First South Carolina when the war began; the general had requested that Trescott attend to him after he was wounded.

A constant stream of high-ranking officers entered Edgewood to see Pettigrew. Lee called upon the dying general, expressing his profound sorrow. Pettigrew quietly replied that having joined the army, his condition was no worse than he might expect; that he was prepared for it; and that he was willing to die for his country. Generals Longstreet and Hill also sadly visited with Pettigrew. It was said that Lee's aides had never observed such gloom at the commanding general's headquarters as they did during the days Pettigrew lay dying at the Boyd house.

Reverend Wilmer informed Pettigrew that there was no probability of his recovery. As the day wore on, Pettigrew's nausea increased and the fluid became darker. Captain Young and the general's slave Peter tried to comfort him.

Pettigrew became noticeably weaker on the night of 16 July, and at 6:25 A.M. the next morning "he died without a groan or a struggle." After a casket was secured, his remains were conveyed in an ambulance train from Winchester to Staunton on 19 July, accompanied by Captain Young, Lieutenant Shepard, and Peter; the remains were then transported to Richmond and finally to eastern North Carolina, where they were interred at Bonarva.[59]

FOR MORE THAN two weeks after 6 July, Lee's sick and wounded were carried or walked from Winchester to the General and Receiving Hospital for the

Shenandoah Valley at Staunton, one hundred miles south. The journey took them through Strasburg, Edinburgh, Woodstock, Mount Jackson, New Market, and Harrisonburg. It was a difficult trek, even in the best of circumstances, as the farther one traveled up the valley, the rougher the land and the road became. Mount Jackson was the site of the first wayside hospital south of Winchester.

North of Mount Jackson, on the east side of the Valley Turnpike, the Confederate Medical Department had constructed a large hospital in September 1861. It consisted of three large, two-story frame buildings, each 150 feet in length and built perpendicular to the turnpike and the Manassas Gap Railroad tracks. One of the buildings had a large cupola adorning its roof. The hospital could accommodate more than five hundred patients. An observer described the buildings as "admirably contrived and constructed" as well as "perfectly ventilated, and yet warm."[60]

It was to this hospital that many casualties from the battles of First and Second Manassas were first sent by way of the Manassas Gap Railroad from Manassas Junction. The sick and wounded from the early valley campaigns and the 1862 invasion of Maryland were brought there via the Valley Turnpike. The hospital at Mount Jackson had been a receiving facility then; it cared for those who could not make the fifty-mile trip to the General and Receiving Hospital at Staunton. Almost every month for nearly two years of war at least one hundred beds were constantly occupied.[61]

Until 1 July 1863, the medical director at Mount Jackson was Dr. Andrew Russell Meem, a thirty-nine-year-old lifelong resident of the town. He and his wife, Anne Jordan, resided in a lovely two-story stone house known as "Mt. Airy," situated on a bluff east of the Valley Turnpike south of town. They were arguably the best-known and most-liked couple in the valley. Meem had practiced medicine in Shenandoah County for slightly under ten years by the time the war began. He offered his services as a surgeon when the Confederate Medical Department first opened the hospital at Mount Jackson in September 1861 and had served as medical director ever since.[62]

The Mount Jackson Hospital required the assistance of local charities to stay open because, for more than ten months before Lee's invasion of Pennsylvania, no commissary or subsistence officer had been assigned to the valley. Led by Meem's wife, along with many supporters of the local Soldiers Relief and Aid Association, the hospital received some perishables. Apart from what was issued by the commissary department, Meem had to buy or impress large amounts from the local citizenry.[63]

The medical director had previously brought to the attention of the Confederate Medical Department in Richmond his anxiety over the high mortality rate at Mount Jackson. Incredibly, the hospital had been ignored by the department ever since the end of Lee's invasion of Maryland in the fall of 1862, even though the facility continued to care for Confederate soldiers. In fact, the Medical Department did not even know that Meem was still serving there in July 1863; it believed that he was with Lee's army. Only four nurses—all convalescent soldiers, including George Washington Miley of the Tenth Virginia who had been wounded at First Manassas—were present to assist Meem as late as 30 June 1863. On 6 July eighty-four Confederate troops from Winchester and Jordan White Sulphur Springs were taken to Mount Jackson, only to be directed on to Staunton because of the hospital's lack of supplies and personnel.[64]

On 22 June Dr. Guild notified Dr. Samuel P. Moore, the surgeon general of the Confederacy, of the need to "reopen" the wayside hospitals at Mount Jackson and Harrisonburg. After Ewell's Corps seized Winchester, the number of sick and wounded grew significantly, and they needed to be removed to Staunton and on to Richmond. Guild told Surgeon General Moore that Mount Jackson and Harrisonburg "would make good by-road hospitals, temporarily, in which the sick and wounded who could not bear a long journey in ambulance wagons [to Staunton] might be accommodated."[65]

Finally recognizing the necessity of using the hospital at Mount Jackson in the wake of Lee's campaign into Pennsylvania and on Guild's request, the Confederate Medical Department, on 1 July 1863, ordered that a receiving hospital be "reestablished" at Mount Jackson "immediately to receive the sick and wounded back from the Army of [Northern] Virginia" because of the "exigencies of the service." Ordered that same day to assume the position of medical director at Mount Jackson was thirty-four-year-old Dr. Robert F. Baldwin, of Winchester, a surgeon at the General and Receiving Hospital at Staunton. Dr. Meem, whose whereabouts were still unknown by the Medical Department, was "ordered" to "report to Mt. Jackson" to serve as one of Baldwin's surgeons. Meem, of course, had never left Mount Jackson.[66]

Notified of his assignment to Mount Jackson, Baldwin set to work assembling assistant surgeons, wardmasters, nurses, stewards, and cooks from the General and Receiving Hospital. He put together a sizable staff to care for the wounded of Lee's army returning from Gettysburg. Assistant surgeons William Wilson S. Butler and James B. McCarty were ordered to accompany Baldwin to Mount Jackson. Eleven convalescent soldiers at Staunton were directed to join him. All of them had been ill with dysentery, hepatitis, debilitus, typhoid, or other maladies. Two of the convalescents were assigned to serve as wardmasters. J. L. Costner of the Twenty-eighth North Carolina, a hepatitis victim, was detailed as the cook, and A. W. Gillespie of the Twelfth Georgia, a victim of ascites, was ordered to serve as the baker. Nine soldiers from Staunton were assigned as nurses. In addition, "Rebecca," a "free woman of color" from the General and Receiving Hospital, volunteered to accompany Baldwin's contingent to serve as the hospital laundress.[67]

The Confederate Medical Department directed Baldwin to "provide accommodation for 300 men." Because of the summer heat, the department wanted the casualties under Baldwin's care to be sheltered in tents, not in the hospital buildings. Accordingly, the Medical Department ordered twenty-five hospital tents to be forwarded to Mount Jackson from Gordonsville. "You will pitch them near to the hospital building as required," Baldwin was instructed. The department also informed Baldwin that hospital supplies for four hundred men for one month were being sent to Mount Jackson with a steward under the direction of the quartermaster at Staunton. As soon as his facility was ready to receive sick and wounded, Baldwin communicated with Dr. Claggett in Winchester.[68]

In the wake of the retreat from Gettysburg, Mount Jackson was taxed to the limit. Nearly 8,500 Confederate soldiers, plus 4,000 Union prisoners, passed through. A total of 667 wounded were hospitalized during the month of July; 215 suffered from gunshot wounds, whereas the rest were victims of typhoid, diarrhea, dysentery, pneumonia, debilitus, and rheumatism. Thirteen patients died in July. One of them was Dr. John H. G. Tuskett, assistant surgeon of the Seventh Tennessee, who succumbed to pneumonia on 24 July. Doctors were not immune to the diseases that wracked Lee's army.[69]

The object of all hospitals in the Shenandoah Valley was to forward the sick and wounded to Staunton for rail transport to Richmond. The fifty-mile journey from Mount Jackson to Staunton was a difficult one. The Valley Turnpike led from Mount Jackson to Harrisonburg, twenty-five miles south. The endless ambulance trains, accompanied by hobbling sick and wounded soldiers, began streaming into Harrisonburg on 9 July. "Nothing but poor distressed soldiers," wrote one citizen, "passed through the town for nearly two full weeks." From Harrisonburg, the turnpike extended twenty-five more miles to Staunton. In all, it took more than two full days to reach Staunton from Mount Jackson.[70]

The people living along the turnpike in the upper valley tried to alleviate the suffering as much as they could. A reporter for the *Richmond Sentinel* wrote: "At Harrisonburg and New Market, systematic arrangements were made for feeding the hungry; men being stationed near the road to hail them as they passed and supply them, without charge, with what they needed, while volunteer physicians and kindhearted ladies were at hand to give such relief to their wounds as a mere passing attention would secure." As in the lower valley, private homes and taverns were opened to the sick and wounded soldiers who passed by.[71]

One of those left in Harrisonburg was Major Latimer, who arrived there on 22 July, his amputation badly infected. He died on 1 August, claiming that he was not afraid because "my trust is in God," and was buried in Harrisonburg. Nicknamed the "boy major," for he was only twenty years old, it was written after the war that "no more brilliant name illumines the annals of Virginia Military Institute" than Latimer's.[72]

STAUNTON WAS the site of the General and Receiving Hospital for the Shenandoah Valley and the commercial and transportation center of the upper Shenandoah Valley. Running through the southern suburbs of Staunton was the Virginia Central Railroad. In 1863 twenty-five steam locomotives of the Virginia Central ran over more than two hundred miles of track—from Richmond all the way to Jackson River near Clifton Forge, thirty miles west of Staunton. About four thousand people lived there.[73]

To and from Staunton and Richmond, passenger and freight trains of the Virginia Central ran daily. Leaving Staunton at 7:00 A.M., one passenger train would arrive in Richmond ten hours later, at 5:00 P.M. Another passenger train left Staunton for Richmond at 2:30 P.M. The eastbound trains would travel across a single track for much of the way to Waynesboro, through a tunnel in the Blue Ridge Mountains at Rockfish Gap to Charlottesville, then reach double tracks for two miles at Gordonsville, the site of the junction of the Virginia Central and the Orange and Alexandria Railroads. Here the westbound trains, which left Richmond at the same time the eastbound trains departed Staunton, would pass on the alternate track bound for Staunton. Gordonsville was also the site of a receiving hospital. The eastbound trains continued to Hanover Junction, the site of the intersection of the Virginia Central with the Richmond, Fredericksburg, and Potomac Railroad and another receiving hospital. From Hanover Junction, the Virginia Central trains ran south to the heart of Richmond, entering the capital city on tracks along Broad Street.[74]

The Virginia Central provided the Shenandoah Valley with the only direct rail link with Richmond, which housed the Confederacy's vast general hospitals and prisons as well as the supply center for the Army of Northern Virginia. All Confederate sick and wounded and all Union prisoners of war were transported to Richmond by train. Returning on trains were soldiers who had completed their convalescence, bound for Lee's army.[75]

Staunton boasted a large number of hotels and inns, the most prominent being the American Hotel, a three-story building that could accommodate nearly 150 guests, situated alongside the Virginia Central Railroad near the passenger station at the southern end of Augusta and New Streets. The stage-coach office was located at the American Hotel. Inside the hotel, the telegraph operator for the Southern Telegraph Company, known as "Stump," had become the town's most popular person during Lee's invasion of Pennsylvania, as he was the first to receive the latest news from the front. East of the American Hotel, on Market Street, was a hostelry known as the "Kalorama Boarding House," formerly a female school opened in 1831. Located near the railroad, it held fifty guests and was one of Staunton's noted hostelries in 1863.[76]

In the fall of 1861 the three-story, Greek Revival residence hall and dependencies of the Virginia School for the Deaf, Dumb, and Blind east of Staunton became the Confederate General Hospital for the Shenandoah Valley. The children were relocated in the town, and the residence hall was converted into a large hospital with two divisions, one for the sick and the other for the wounded.[77]

The American Hotel became the receiving hospital. There, all sick and wounded were "received" and then moved to appropriate quarters in the General Hospital or to rooms in the hotel or transported to Richmond. As the need arose, private homes and buildings, such as the Kalorama Boarding House, were used to hospitalize the overflow.[78]

Serving in Staunton as chief quartermaster for the Shenandoah Valley was thirty-seven-year-old Major Henderson Moffett Bell, a graduate of Washington College and a well-respected lawyer in the town before the war. It was Major Bell who supplied not only the General and Receiving Hospital at Staunton but also the receiving hospital at Mount Jackson, the wayside hospitals at Harrisonburg and Woodstock, and the receiving hospitals at Winchester and Jordan White Sulphur Springs.[79]

Dr. William Hay became medical director of the General and Receiving Hospital on 2 June 1862 and remained in that capacity during Lee's invasion of Pennsylvania. A thirty-year-old surgeon from Clarke County, Virginia, Hay had been with the Thirty-third Virginia in Stonewall Jackson's winter campaign to Romney and Bath before he was assigned to the General and Receiving Hospital. Reportedly, he was one of the best operating surgeons in the army; he was equally adept in administrative matters.[80]

By July 1863 Hay had an enviable staff of surgeons and assistant surgeons

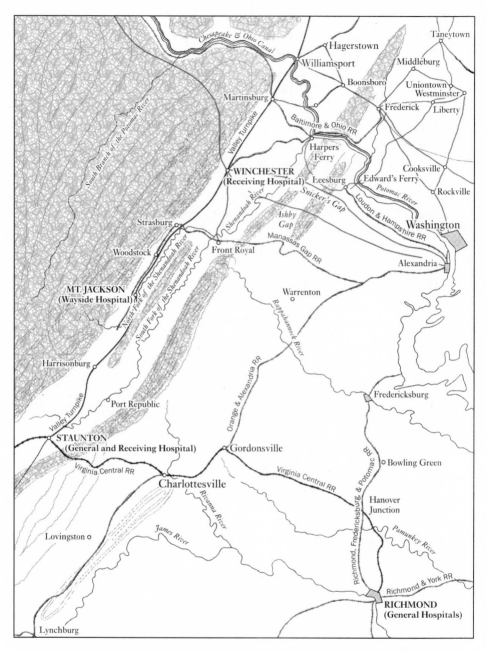

MAP 14.1   Lee's medical evacuation system: the Valley Turnpike from Winchester through Mount Jackson to Staunton and the Virginia Central Railroad from Staunton to Richmond.

Ed Beyer's painting of Staunton, Virginia, just before the war. The Virginia
School for the Deaf, Dumb, and Blind can be seen at right, and the American
Hotel is visible along the tracks of the Virginia Central Railroad in the center of
the picture. Library of Congress, Washington, D.C.

to treat the wounded returning from Gettysburg. His assistant surgeon in
charge was a Virginian named J. C. M. Merillat, who had first been assigned to Staunton on 19 July 1861. Another surgeon was Dr. John Lewis,
a local physician and a former surgeon in Staunton's own Fifty-second Virginia who was sent to the General and Receiving Hospital on 20 June 1863.
Among the assistant surgeons at Staunton were nine Virginians: Dr. C. W. J.
Davidson; Dr. Newton Wayt, a local Staunton contract surgeon; Dr. W. W.
Douglass, formerly an assistant surgeon with the Tenth Virginia Cavalry; Dr.
William Wilson S. Butler; Dr. Richard H. Woodward; Dr. F. L. Bronaugh;
Dr. Robert Hayne Bush; Dr. Thomas Opie, formerly an assistant surgeon
with the Twenty-fifth Virginia; and Dr. William Hamilton Dulaney, for-
merly an assistant surgeon with the Thirteenth Battalion, Virginia Artillery.
Assistant surgeons also included Dr. J. O. Harris, Dr. Richard H. Woodward,
Dr. Thomas J. Michie, and Dr. D. M. Clark. Since April 1863 Hay also had
four acting assistant surgeons: James B. McCarty, N. B. Tatom, P. W. Anderson, and Isham Talbot. Tatom, Anderson, and Talbot were local contract surgeons from Staunton and Augusta County.[81]

Convalescent soldiers formed the core of Hay's nursing staff. By the time
the wounded began to arrive in Staunton, thirty-seven convalescents were

serving as nurses. Four stewards assisted the surgical staff. The nurses were aided by dozens of male and female volunteers from Staunton and elsewhere. Among the more notable matrons was Kate Korff, a girl barely fourteen years of age, from Georgetown, Washington, D.C.[82]

As a result of Ewell's operations in the lower Shenandoah Valley and Lee's movement north, the hospitalizations at Staunton rose to 1,542 in June 1863. There were 14 deaths that month. Diarrhea and dysentery accounted for nearly half of the hospitalizations in June, but typhoid fever and pneumonia caused virtually all of the deaths.[83]

For days after the fighting had ended at Gettysburg, Staunton residents struggled to get information. Heavy rain fell in the upper valley as well as in Pennsylvania and Maryland. Many of Augusta County's sons had been in the fight. Naturally, the key figure in town was Stump, the telegraph operator at the American Hotel. It was first reported that he had received news of "a glorious victory; some forty thousand to sixty thousand of the enemy laying down their arms." But later he indicated that that news "must have come by some other line." Major Bell told those milling around the hotel that Stump never authorized any news story. Thus, as late as 8 July no one in Staunton knew the truth of what had happened in Pennsylvania.

The next day Stump heard that Vicksburg had surrendered; reports circulated in Staunton by passengers of the westbound Virginia Central trains were mostly about that event. Still, nothing definitive came from Lee's army.

Finally, on 10 July, a clear and warm day, the sick and wounded from Lee's army began to stream into Staunton. News of the fighting and casualties stunned those who greeted the long lines of soldiers entering the town. The wounded gave "fearful accounts of the slaughter"; they spoke of Pickett's Division having been "annihilated." The names of many casualties were well known to the citizens of Staunton.[84]

The Valley Turnpike on 10 July, wrote one resident, was "lined with wounded soldiers coming up from the battlefield. It is a sad sight to see so many poor fellows dragging themselves along to get nearer home." The next day it was the same. "Wounded soldiers," according to the same resident, "have come into town today in a constant stream; some of them in vehicles and some on horseback, but most on foot. Many of them are without shoes." The casualties arrived daily for almost twenty days. In all, nearly 8,500 made their way to Staunton.[85]

As quickly as they rode or hobbled down New and Augusta Streets to the receiving hospital at the American Hotel, they were assigned to one of two wards in the General Hospital at the School for the Deaf, Dumb, and Blind residence hall and outbuildings, the American Hotel, the Kalorama Boarding House, or one of many private residences. Staunton was soon overrun with sick and wounded soldiers.

One of the most prominent wounded soldiers to appear was General Pender. Badly injured by a shell fragment in the left thigh on the evening of 2 July, he had made the 200-mile journey from Gettysburg in a filthy ambulance accompanied by his brother Captain Pender, his slave Joe, and General Scales. Although the journey was agonizing, he had actually shown some improvement when he arrived at the American Hotel on 17 July and was carried into the General Hospital; the weather had been clear and warm for the past three days. It seemed as though his remarkable recovery from serious battle wounds was going to continue.

That night, however, the large artery in Pender's left thigh began hemorrhaging. With incredible presence of mind, the general reached for a towel and began wrapping it around his thigh, then tightening it with a hairbrush, staunching the blood flow. Surgeons and a chaplain were summoned in the early hours of 18 July.

There was chatter in the room as the surgeons, probably Hay and Merillat, examined Pender's wound. When some aides told Pender that Lee's army had returned to Virginia, he seemed pleased to hear it. Then came the news of the wounding of fellow North Carolinian, General Pettigrew. It visibly saddened Pender. The chaplain asked him about the state of his soul. "Tell my wife," said the twenty-nine-year-old major general, "that I do not fear to die. . . . My only regret is to leave her and our two children. I have always tried to do my duty in every sphere in which Providence has placed me."

First, the surgeons attempted to repair the artery and save the leg. The surgery was no sooner concluded than the artery broke again. The decision was quickly made to remove the leg. In a lengthy and trying procedure, the general's left leg was taken off just below the hip. Within a few hours Pender was dead.

A coffin was procured, and the remains of General Pender left Staunton for Richmond by train on 19 July, the same day Pettigrew's remains departed Winchester for Staunton. Captain Pender and Joe accompanied the Pender's remains to Tarboro, North Carolina, where they were buried. General Scales was eventually moved to Richmond, where he miraculously recovered.[86]

Generals Hood and Hampton, along with Dr. Darby, made the 100-mile journey from Winchester to Staunton in the same ambulance. Hood recalled that he "suffered very much." Hampton could not sit up and Hood could not lie down. "Along the pike," Hood wrote, "were seen our wounded, making their way to the rear, the noble women of Virginia standing by the wayside to supply them with food and otherwise administer to their wants." After a brief stay in Staunton, Hood and Hampton were taken by rail as far as Charlottesville and hospitalized.[87]

The wounded Colonel Stuart of the Fifty-sixth Virginia arrived at Staunton at about the same time as Pender and Scales. Stuart was taken to the home of his mother; his father, Thomas J. Stuart, had died several years before. Stuart had fallen near Colonel Alexander's guns on 3 July as Pickett's Division was advancing toward the Emmitsburg Road. He was apparently wounded in the abdomen by shrapnel; there was little the surgeons could do for such cases. On 29 July Stuart, an honors' graduate of the Virginia Military Institute and nephew of the distinguished political figure, Honorable Alexander H. H. Stuart of Staunton, died at his home. He was buried in Thorn Rose Cemetery, Staunton.[88]

Private Moore of the Fifth Louisiana left Winchester in an ambulance train on 16 July. Four days later he entered Staunton after "suffering a great deal" during the arduous trip up the turnpike. At 6:00 A.M. on the twentieth he reported to the American Hotel. After being examined by a surgeon, he was assigned to the General Hospital. He remained there only until 22 July, when he was conveyed to Richmond via the Virginia Central Railroad and admitted to Seabrook Hospital.[89]

Sergeant Whitehorne and his Tarheel friend arrived in Staunton after a four-day journey up the valley. "We reached the end of our journey, Staunton, about sundown [22 July]," wrote Whitehorne, "and we were carried into the American Hotel, which had been converted into a hospital. From what we can see of Staunton we are impressed with its beauty & situation. The Institute for Deaf and Dumb is a beautiful brick building in the distance, situated on an elevated and picturesque site. The Western Lunatic Asylum and several college buildings can also be seen." On 26 July Whitehorne and his friend were loaded onto a car on the Virginia Central Railroad bound for Richmond, where, like Private Moore, they entered Seabrook Hospital.[90]

In July the number of admissions at the General and Receiving Hospital in Staunton was staggering; 8,428 hospitalizations were recorded. All were from Lee's army and the result of the Gettysburg campaign. Of the hospitalizations, 4,855 were for gunshot wounds. Diseases—debilitus, diarrhea, typhoid, rheumatism, and a host of others—made up the rest.[91]

If a sick or wounded soldier got as far as Staunton, he actually had a good chance of surviving. The records indicate that in July there were only thirty-five deaths. As the objective was to transport the sick and wounded to

Richmond's general hospitals, Dr. Hays and his staff moved patients out of Staunton with remarkable efficiency. By August, only 1,209 patients remained at the General and Receiving Hospital in Staunton. Of that number, most suffered from debilitus and typhoid, not gunshot wounds. In all, 37 of them died there that month.[92]

THE SHENANDOAH VALLEY was not only a corridor for the evacuation of Lee's sick and wounded, it also served as a holding area for much of his immense quartermaster and subsistence stores. As the Army of Northern Virginia left Darkesville and Bunker Hill, Lee directed its reserve quartermaster and subsistence train carrying the stores impressed in Pennsylvania and Maryland up the Valley Turnpike to Mount Jackson and New Market, guarded by elements of Ewell's Corps. With that vast train, Lee sent more than 26,000 head of cattle and 22,000 head of sheep, all obtained north of the Potomac River. To protect them from enemy attack and to prevent them from slowing down the army—as well as for political reasons—Lee did not want that ponderous train and the immense herds of livestock following the army. Instead, they were to be taken up the valley and, eventually, over the Massanutten and Blue Ridge Mountains by way of Luray and Thornton Gaps to join the rest of the army in central Virginia. In the meantime, the livestock would be kept in the Shenandoah Valley and the mountain foothills to graze until needed, as central Virginia was barren of pastureland. At last Lee's hungry soldiers would be able to eat for the foreseeable future.[93]

The army achieved a general success

What Lee lost during the Gettysburg campaign was going to be difficult to replace. His horses and mules were in desperate need of shoes, and few horseshoes or muleshoes were found in Pennsylvania and Maryland. The clothes of his men were in tatters; most of his soldiers had not had a change of clothing in more than three months. Long marches along macadamized roads and the retreat through deep mud and water left many of Lee's men without shoes; indeed, more than half of the army was barefoot. So serious was the problem that many soldiers wrote home begging their families and friends for shoes.[1]

The Confederate casualties in the three days of battle at Gettysburg had been staggering. Nearly 4,500 had been killed or mortally wounded. Lee left a total of 6,739 sick and wounded soldiers in his own hospitals and in Union medical facilities at Gettysburg; ahead of his marching troops, he safely conveyed up the Shenandoah Valley more than 8,500 more.[2]

To Lee it was critical to return to the army as many of the casualties transported to Virginia as possible. To do that, he relied on the hospital and evacuation system in the Shenandoah Valley to care for them and move them up the valley so they could be moved to the hospitals in Richmond by rail. Lee counted on many of them recuperating and returning to the ranks. In mid-1863 replacements for lost officers and men were very difficult to find.

Many of the sick and wounded Confederates left at Gettysburg died there. Colonel Waller Tazewell Patton of the Seventh Virginia was one of them. After his jaw was ripped away by artillery fire at the culmination of the assault on the afternoon of 3 July, Patton lingered at the hospital in the dormitory of Pennsylvania College for more than two weeks. With the chaplain of the Thirty-third Virginia singing "Rock of Ages Cleft for Me," the twenty-eight-

year-old colonel, one of eighteen field-grade officers in Pickett's Division—
all of them graduates of the Virginia Military Institute—who fell at Gettysburg, died on 21 July.[3]

The sights all around Gettysburg were grim. Added to the enormous number of sick and wounded Confederates were 13,603 Union casualties. After
the Hanover Railroad was opened, Union medical teams and provost mar-
shals began to move as many of them as possible to hospitals, and in the
case of Confederates to prison camps, along the eastern seaboard. Between
11 and 22 July eighteen trains left Gettysburg filled with Confederate sick and
wounded, bound for prison hospitals in Baltimore, Maryland; Chester, York,
and Harrisburg, Pennsylvania; and David's Island, New York.[4]

From the Fairfield Road and the Chambersburg Pike, almost five thousand
Confederate prisoners of war were herded through the streets of Gettysburg
for transport to Union prisons. Most had been captured during the fighting;
others were deserters or stragglers who had been picked up along Lee's retreat routes by trailing Union cavalry. Some were African American slaves
who had run away or had become separated from the army's trains or their
masters.[5]

The Confederate sick and wounded from the retreat routes were eventually sent to Northern hospitals and prisons. Colonel Leventhorpe, Captain
Archer, and the other injured Confederates at Mercersburg were taken to
Chambersburg, where they and the officers and men left behind in a hospital—ninety-two altogether—were moved out for rail transport east. One of
them, Lieutenant Colonel Carter of the Fourth Texas, could not be shifted;
he died in Chambersburg on 26 July and was buried in the Methodist cemetery.[6]

The hospitals in Williamsport were emptied, and the sick and wounded
Confederates were taken to the Hagerstown Female Seminary to be hospitalized with those left behind in Hagerstown's private residences. Colonel
Lumpkin, Major McDaniel, Captain Frank Bond, and Captain McIver, along
with 210 more, were placed together until they could be moved. Lumpkin
never left Hagerstown; he died there on 11 September and was buried in
the town's Presbyterian graveyard. McIver was transferred to Point Lookout
Prison, in Maryland, where he died on 15 October.[7]

Those in Hagerstown who could be moved were taken to Frederick. There,
men like Lieutenant Colonels Green and Boyd, Colonel Kenan, Majors
Lewis, Hancock, and Blacknall, and Captains Bond and Wheeler, along with
nearly 1,300 other Confederates who were captured at Monterey Pass, were
transported from Frederick to Northern hospitals and prisons via the Balti-

Confederate prisoners of war being marched toward Westminster after the fighting at Gettysburg. Note the barn at right center, which was used as a Union division or corps hospital, with the flag flying overhead and the quartermaster, subsistence, ordnance, and ambulance trains parked nearby. Library of Congress, Washington, D.C.

more and Ohio Railroad. Some of them recuperated, were exchanged, and returned to the army.[8]

The Union quartermasters at Gettysburg tried desperately to clean up the town and battlefields. Local citizens in both the town and the surrounding countryside systematically pilfered the battlefield, appropriating countless horses, weapons, and other government property. By 9 July civilians and the Thirty-sixth Pennsylvania militia assigned to Gettysburg by General Smith had buried more than 3,500 Confederate dead and were still looking for more. They buried nearly 3,000 Union dead there as well. The heavy rains, though, unearthed many graves, necessitating reburial. "You could smell [the dead for] five miles," said one Pennsylvania soldier. "It was a nasty job." Gettysburg, to one eyewitness, was "a sight filled with gloom and horror, [where] rider and horse, friend and foe [were mingled] in one red burial blend." Dead horses and mules were mostly dragged into piles and burned. It was no easy task, as more than four thousand of them were spread over the battlefields. The stench was intolerable.[9]

BY 21 JULY the Richmond newspapers, although more tame than the *Charleston Mercury*, were blaming Robert E. Lee for the loss at Gettysburg and labeling the invasion of Pennsylvania a failure. The *Richmond Enquirer* claimed that Lee had failed to press his advantage at the close of the first day's fighting and thus failed to seize "the wooded heights beyond Gettysburg." His direct assault against the Union center on 3 July was, it asserted, a "great mistake" and "cannot well be justified." The *Daily Richmond Examiner* referred to the attack as a "blunder." Cropping up in the press was the assertion that the army "felt most keenly the loss of our [Stonewall] Jackson."[10]

"Many other causes are said to have operated," noted a correspondent for the *Richmond Enquirer*. "Among them it is affirmed that Gen. Lee had too much transportation, and that he was cramped in the handling of his troops in order to guard the trains." In a note of optimism, however, the reporter went on to say that "the army is to-day fully fifteen thousand men weaker than when it entered Pennsylvania, but in its confidence in final success, and in the courage and capacity of its Generals and especially its great Captain, nothing has been abated by the recent reverse."[11]

The comments in the *Richmond Enquirer* were perceptive. The reporter bristled about the fact that he had not been allowed near Lee's headquarters and had not been given access to any after-action reports. What he wrote came from interviews with officers and enlisted men, most of them sick or wounded. His claim that Lee had "too much transportation" and was "cramped in the handling of his troops in order to guard the trains" reflected the central purpose for the invasion of Pennsylvania, which the writer clearly did not know.

Although the battle of Gettysburg was indeed a Confederate loss, the invasion of Pennsylvania may not have been. In fact, Lee successfully brought his army and all its trains across the Potomac River. In the process, he managed to get out of Pennsylvania and Maryland more than forty-five miles of quartermaster and subsistence trains filled with impressed stores. Ten to twelve miles of his trains consisted of ambulances and ordnance wagons. The trains altogether included nearly 6,000 vehicles and anywhere from 30,000 to 40,000 horses and mules that pulled them. In all, Lee probably delivered more than 20,000 horses and mules seized in Pennsylvania and Maryland. He had to leave about 12,000 head of cattle and 8,000 head of sheep along the muddy roads between Gettysburg and the Potomac River. Some were lost crossing the river. Yet Lee was able to save nearly 30,000 head of cattle, almost 25,000 head of sheep, and thousands of hogs. For the first time during the war, Lee's army had fresh meat available for the foreseeable future.[12]

North of the Potomac River some of Lee's artillery batteries had been able to exchange their worn-out and sick horses and mules for fresh ones. There were significant numbers of horses and mules to restock some batteries and to replenish some of the trains whose horses and mules had broken down. Most Confederates believed that the horses seized in Pennsylvania and Maryland were of an inferior quality, but, nevertheless, they welcomed them.[13]

Apart from the livestock transported across the Potomac, Lee returned with thousands of tons of hay and grains of all kinds, as well as thousands of barrels of flour for the soldiers. Because of the tremendous amount of fodder required to feed the army's thousands of horses and mules, what was seized in Pennsylvania and Maryland would not last long. The fodder obtained, though, was needed to keep the army in the field at that time. Lee would call for more by the end of August, but the amount acquired north of the Potomac River meant the difference between the army staying intact and falling apart. In addition, Lee brought home large quantities of leather harnesses, saddles, bits, bridles, iron bars, sheets of steel, bellows, forges, coal, hammers, screwdrivers, wagon parts, tar, coal oil, pencils, pens, paper, blank books, and a wide variety of cloth materials, hats, and medicinal items—all required to keep the army operating. Only an examination of the retreat from Gettysburg could reveal such results.[14]

Although Lee never called attention to what his army seized in Pennsylvania and Maryland, probably for fear of not getting more supplies from his government, he did remind Jefferson Davis on 31 July 1863 that the army "achieved a general success, though it did not win a victory." Lee did not elaborate, but he was undoubtedly referring to the quartermaster and subsistence stores and livestock the army obtained as well as some of its tactical successes at Gettysburg and the losses it inflicted on the enemy.[15]

Lee's army left Darkesville and Bunker Hill, West Virginia, on 20 July after only a five-day encampment. Before its departure, though, it systematically destroyed the Baltimore and Ohio Railroad between Martinsburg and Harpers Ferry. Lee thereby denied Kelley's Department of West Virginia and any other Union army the use of the Shenandoah Valley as a supply depot until that railroad was reopened. The hospital at Jordan White Sulphur Springs was closed, and the critical cases were taken to Winchester. As Lee and his men cleared Loudoun Street in Winchester, they left behind 123 sick and wounded officers and men unable to be moved from its hospitals. Dr. Willis W. Dickie, formerly of the Tenth Alabama, and Dr. Alexander Bear from South Carolina who had served in the Fourth Virginia, were left behind to care for them. Once again, the citizens of Winchester were left to the mercy of Union troops, whom most of them had grown to despise over the past two years.[16]

Some Winchester residents, like Cornelia McDonald, went south with the ambulance trains and hobbling soldiers, never to return. McDonald and her children rode along the Valley Turnpike with Lee's army in front of and behind them. "Many wounded men were among them making their way to a place of safety," she wrote, "while fugitives of every grade and degree of misery were toiling on, on foot, or in any kind of broken-down vehicle. Sick men, hungry men, and women with crowds of children, all hurrying on." Most of Lee's army proceeded toward Front Royal and the Luray and Page Valleys; Early's Division marched up the Shenandoah Valley behind the reserve train of quartermaster and subsistence stores and vast herds of livestock.[17]

Meade's Army of the Potomac was also on the move. After crossing the Potomac River at Berlin and Sandy Hook, the Federal troops marched up the Loudoun Valley, seizing key passes in the Blue Ridge Mountains, including Manassas Gap, where Buford's cavalry division and French's Third Corps positioned themselves to block Lee's passage. A sharp action at Wapping Heights on 23 July forced Buford and French to withdraw. Lee's army marched toward its destination, Orange Courthouse, where a new line of communication and supply would be opened to Richmond by means of the Orange and Alexandria and Virginia Central Railroads. At Orange Courthouse, the vast herds of cattle and sheep and the extensive reserve quartermaster and subsistence train that were routed up the Shenandoah Valley and through Luray and Thornton Gaps in the Massanutten and Blue Ridge Mountains would eventually meet the rest of the army.[18]

That Lee's campaign into Pennsylvania was a foraging expedition carried out on an immense scale, and that it succeeded in bringing back to Virginia the enormous stores and herds of livestock that it did, was never understood by Southern civilians or newspaper reporters. In fact, few soldiers ever observed all of what had been seized. Yet the campaign may well have furnished enough meat, fodder, and stores to extend the life of the Army of Northern Virginia until the harvests in the Southern seaboard states could be used. For certain, it guaranteed that Lee's men had flour and fresh meat for several months, and the horses and mules had fodder through the rest of the summer. All of that was totally unavailable in Virginia at the time. Only two months before, Lee's army had been on the brink of collapse.

With morale still high among Lee's officers and men, and with stores available to take them through the balance of the summer and early fall, it can be argued that the retreat from Gettysburg, at a minimum, turned a tactical defeat—and a potential strategic disaster—into a kind of victory for Lee and the Army of Northern Virginia. It restored the balance of power between the two great, contending armies in the eastern theater of war. Although a costly tactical defeat for the Army of Northern Virginia, Gettysburg cannot be viewed as the turning point of the Civil War or even a turning point of the eastern theater of war after Lee's remarkable retreat.[19]

Order of Battle

Army of the Potomac and Army of Northern Virginia, 1–3 July 1863

The Order of Battle is reproduced from U.S. War Department, *The War of the Rebellion: A Compilation of the Official Records of the Union and Confederate Armies*, 128 vols. (Washington, D.C.: U.S. Government Printing Office, 1880–1901), ser. 1, 27 (1):155-68, and (2):283-91.

No. 9.

Organization of the Army of the Potomac, Maj. Gen. George G. Meade, U. S. Army, commanding, at the battle of Gettysburg, July 1–3, 1863.

GENERAL HEADQUARTERS.

COMMAND OF THE PROVOST-MARSHAL-GENERAL.

Brig. Gen. MARSENA R. PATRICK.

93d New York,* Col. John S. Crocker.
8th United States (eight companies),* Capt. Edwin W. H. Read.
2d Pennsylvania Cavalry, Col. R. Butler Price.
6th Pennsylvania Cavalry, Companies E and I, Capt. James Starr.
Regular cavalry (detachments from 1st, 2d, 5th, and 6th Regiments).

SIGNAL CORPS.

Capt. LEMUEL B. NORTON.

GUARDS AND ORDERLIES.

Oneida (New York) Cavalry, Capt. Daniel P. Mann.

ARTILLERY.†

Brig. Gen. HENRY J. HUNT.

ENGINEER BRIGADE.‡

Brig. Gen. HENRY W. BENHAM.

15th New York (three companies), Maj. Walter L. Cassin.
50th New York, Col. William H. Pettes.
United States Battalion, Capt. George H. Mendell.

FIRST ARMY CORPS.§

Maj. Gen. ABNER DOUBLEDAY.
Maj. Gen. JOHN NEWTON.

GENERAL HEADQUARTERS.

1st Maine Cavalry, Company L, Capt. Constantine Taylor.

FIRST DIVISION.

Brig. Gen. JAMES S. WADSWORTH.

First Brigade.	*Second Brigade.*
Brig. Gen. SOLOMON MEREDITH. Col. WILLIAM W. ROBINSON.	Brig. Gen. LYSANDER CUTLER.

19th Indiana, Col. Samuel J. Williams.
24th Michigan:
    Col. Henry A. Morrow.
    Capt. Albert M. Edwards.
2d Wisconsin:
    Col. Lucius Fairchild.
    Maj. John Mansfield.
    Capt. George H. Otis.
6th Wisconsin, Lieut. Col. Rufus R. Dawes.
7th Wisconsin:
    Col. William W. Robinson.
    Maj. Mark Finnicum.
	7th Indiana, Col. Ira G. Grover.
	76th New York:
	    Maj. Andrew J. Grover.
	    Capt. John E. Cook.
	84th New York (14th Militia), Col. Edward B. Fowler.
	95th New York:
	    Col. George H. Biddle.
	    Maj. Edward Pye.
	147th New York:
	    Lieut. Col. Francis C. Miller.
	    Maj. George Harney.
	56th Pennsylvania (nine companies), Col. J. William Hofmann.

---

* Not engaged.
† See artillery brigades attached to army corps and the reserve.
‡ Not engaged. With exception of the regular battalion, it was, July 1, and while at Beaver Dam Creek, Md., ordered to Washington, D. C., where it arrived July 3.
§ Maj. Gen. John F. Reynolds, of this corps, was killed July 1, while in command of the left wing of the army; General Doubleday commanded the corps July 1, and General Newton, who was assigned to that command on the 1st, superseded him July 2.

SECOND DIVISION.

Brig. Gen. JOHN C. ROBINSON.

First Brigade.	*Second Brigade.*
Brig. Gen. GABRIEL R. PAUL.	Brig. Gen. HENRY BAXTER.
Col. SAMUEL H. LEONARD.	
Col. ADRIAN R. ROOT.	12th Massachusetts:
Col. RICHARD COULTER.	Col. James L. Bates.
Col. PETER LYLE.	Lieut. Col. David Allen, jr.
Col. RICHARD COULTER.	83d New York (9th Militia), Lieut. Col.
	Joseph A. Moesch.
16th Maine:	97th New York:
Col. Charles W. Tilden.	Col. Charles Wheelock.
Maj. Archibald D. Leavitt.	Maj. Charles Northrup.
13th Massachusetts:	11th Pennsylvania:*
Col. Samuel H. Leonard.	Col. Richard Coulter.
Lieut. Col. N. Walter Batchel-	Capt. Benjamin F. Haines.
der.	Capt. John B. Overmyer.
94th New York:	88th Pennsylvania:
Col. Adrian R. Root.	Maj. Benezet F. Foust.
Maj. Samuel A. Moffett.	Capt. Henry Whiteside.
104th New York, Col. Gilbert G. Prey.	90th Pennsylvania:
107th Pennsylvania:	Col. Peter Lyle.
Lieut. Col. James MacThomson.	Maj. Alfred J. Sellers.
Capt. Emanuel D. Roath.	Col. Peter Lyle.

THIRD DIVISION.

Brig. Gen. THOMAS A. ROWLEY.
Maj. Gen. ABNER DOUBLEDAY.

First Brigade.	*Second Brigade.*
Col. CHAPMAN BIDDLE.	Col. ROY STONE.
Brig. Gen. THOMAS A. ROWLEY.	Col. LANGHORNE WISTER.
Col. CHAPMAN BIDDLE.	Col. EDMUND L. DANA.
80th New York (20th Militia), Col. Theo-	143d Pennsylvania:
dore B. Gates.	Col. Edmund L. Dana.
121st Pennsylvania:	Lieut. Col. John D. Musser.
Maj. Alexander Biddle.	149th Pennsylvania:
Col. Chapman Biddle.	Lieut. Col. Walton Dwight
Maj. Alexander Biddle.	Capt. James Glenn.
142d Pennsylvania:	150th Pennsylvania:
Col. Robert P. Cummins.	Col. Langhorne Wister.
Lieut. Col. A. B. McCalmont.	Lieut. Col. H. S. Huidekoper.
151st Pennsylvania:	Capt. Cornelius C. Widdis.
Lieut. Col. George F. McFarland.	
Capt. Walter L. Owens.	
Col. Harrison Allen.	

Third Brigade.

Brig. Gen. GEORGE J. STANNARD.
Col. FRANCIS V. RANDALL.

12th Vermont,† Col. Asa P. Blunt.
13th Vermont:
    Col. Francis V. Randall,
    Maj. Joseph J. Boynton.
    Lieut. Col. William D. Munson.
14th Vermont, Col. William T. Nichols.
15th Vermont,† Col. Redfield Proctor.
16th Vermont, Col. Wheelock G. Veazey.

---

* Transferred, in afternoon of July 1, to the First Brigade.
† Guarding trains, and not engaged in the battle.

ARTILLERY BRIGADE.

Col. CHARLES S. WAINWRIGHT.

Maine Light, 2d Battery (B), Capt. James A. Hall.
Maine Light, 5th Battery (E):
 Capt. Greenleaf T. Stevens.
 Lieut. Edward N. Whittier.
1st New York Light, Battery L:*
 Capt. Gilbert H. Reynolds.
 Lieut. George Breck.
1st Pennsylvania Light, Battery B, Capt. James H. Cooper.
4th United States, Battery B, Lieut. James Stewart.

SECOND ARMY CORPS.†

Maj. Gen. WINFIELD S. HANCOCK.
Brig. Gen. JOHN GIBBON.

GENERAL HEADQUARTERS.

6th New York Cavalry, Companies D and K, Capt. Riley Johnson.

FIRST DIVISION.

Brig. Gen. JOHN C. CALDWELL.

First Brigade.

Col. EDWARD E. CROSS.
Col. H. BOYD McKEEN.

5th New Hampshire,Lieut. Col. Charles
 E. Hapgood.
61st New York, Lieut. Col. K. Oscar
 Broady.
81st Pennsylvania :
 Col. H. Boyd McKeen.
 Lieut. Col. Amos Stroh.
148th Pennsylvania, Lieut. Col. Robert
 McFarlane.

Second Brigade.

Col. PATRICK KELLY.

28th Massachusetts, Col. R. Byrnes.
63d New York (two companies) :
 Lieut.Col. Richard C. Bentley.
 Capt. Thomas Touhy.
69th New York (two companies) :
 Capt. Richard Moroney.
 Lieut. James J. Smith.
88th New York (two companies), Capt.
 Denis F. Burke.
116th Pennsylvania (four companies),
 Maj. St. Clair A. Mulholland.

Third Brigade.

Brig. Gen. SAMUEL K. ZOOK.
Lieut. Col. JOHN FRASER.

52d New York:
 Lieut. Col. C. G. Freudenberg.
 Capt. William Scherrer.
57th New York, Lieut. Col. Alford B.
 Chapman.
66th New York:
 Col. Orlando H. Morris.
 Lieut. Col. John S. Hammell.
 Maj. Peter Nelson.
140th Pennsylvania:
 Col. Richard P. Roberts.
 Lieut. Col. John Fraser.

Fourth Brigade.

Col. JOHN R. BROOKE.

27th Connecticut (two companies) :
 Lieut. Col. Henry C. Merwin.
 Maj. James H. Coburn.
2d Delaware:
 Col. William P. Baily.
 Capt. Charles H. Christman.
64th New York:
 Col. Daniel G. Bingham.
 Maj. Leman W. Bradley.
53d Pennsylvania, Lieut. Col. Richards
 McMichael.
145th Pennsylvania (seven companies) :
 Col. Hiram L. Brown.
 Capt. John W. Reynolds.
 Capt. Moses W. Oliver.

* Battery E, 1st New York Light Artillery, attached.
† After the death of General Reynolds, General Hancock was assigned to the command of all the troops on the field of battle, relieving General Howard, who had succeeded General Reynolds. General Gibbon, of the Second Division, assumed command of the corps. These assignments terminated on the evening of July 1. Similar changes in commanders occurred during the battle of the 2d, when General Hancock was put in command of the Third Corps, in addition to that of his own. He was wounded on the 3d, and Brig. Gen. William Hays was assigned to the command of the corps.

SECOND DIVISION.

Brig. Gen. JOHN GIBBON,
Brig. Gen. WILLIAM HARROW.

First Brigade.

Brig. Gen. WILLIAM HARROW.
Col. FRANCIS E. HEATH.

19th Maine:
  Col. Francis E. Heath.
  Lieut. Col. Henry W. Cunningham.
15th Massachusetts:
  Col. George H. Ward.
  Lieut. Col. George C. Joslin.
1st Minnesota:*
  Col. William Colvill, jr.
  Capt. Nathan S. Messick.
  Capt. Henry C. Coates.
82d New York (2d Militia):
  Lieut. Col. James Huston.
  Capt. John Darrow.

Second Brigade.

Brig. Gen. ALEXANDER S. WEBB.

69th Pennsylvania:
  Col. Dennis O'Kane.
  Capt. William Davis.
71st Pennsylvania, Col. Richard Penn Smith.
72d Pennsylvania:
  Col. De Witt C. Baxter.
  Lieut. Col. Theodore Hesser.
106th Pennsylvania, Lieut. Col. William L. Curry.

Third Brigade.

Col. NORMAN J. HALL.

19th Massachusetts, Col. Arthur F. Devereux.
20th Massachusetts:
  Col. Paul J. Revere.
  Lieut. Col. George N. Macy.
  Capt. Henry L. Abbott.
7th Michigan:
  Lieut. Col. Amos E. Steele, jr.
  Maj. Sylvanus W. Curtis.
42d New York, Col. James E. Mallon.
59th New York (four companies):
  Lieut. Col. Max A. Thoman.
  Capt. William McFadden.

Unattached.

Massachusetts Sharpshooters, 1st Company:
  Capt. William Plumer.
  Lieut. Emerson L. Bicknell.

THIRD DIVISION.

Brig. Gen. ALEXANDER HAYS.

First Brigade.

Col. SAMUEL S. CARROLL.

14th Indiana, Col. John Coons.
4th Ohio, Lieut. Col. Leonard W. Carpenter.
8th Ohio, Lieut. Col. Franklin Sawyer.
7th West Virginia, Lieut. Col. Jonathan H. Lockwood.

Second Brigade.

Col. THOMAS A. SMYTH.
Lieut. Col. FRANCIS E. PIERCE.

14th Connecticut, Maj. Theodore G. Ellis.
1st Delaware:
  Lieut. Col. Edward P. Harris.
  Capt. Thomas B. Hizar.
  Lieut. William Smith.
  Lieut. John T. Dent.
12th New Jersey, Maj. John T. Hill.
10th New York (battalion), Maj. George F. Hopper.
108th New York, Lieut. Col. Francis E. Pierce.

---

* 2d Company Minnesota Sharpshooters attached.

Third Brigade.

Col. GEORGE L. WILLARD.
Col. ELIAKIM SHERRILL.
Lieut. Col. JAMES M. BULL.

39th New York (four companies), Maj. Hugo Hildebrandt.
111th New York:
    Col. Clinton D. MacDougall.
    Lieut. Col. Isaac M. Lusk.
    Capt. Aaron P. Seeley.
125th New York, Lieut. Col. Levin Crandell.
126th New York:
    Col. Eliakim Sherrill.
    Lieut. Col. James M. Bull.

ARTILLERY BRIGADE.

Capt. JOHN G. HAZARD.

1st New York Light, Battery B:*
    Lieut. Albert S. Sheldon.
    Capt. James McKay Rorty.
    Lieut. Robert E. Rogers.
1st Rhode Island Light, Battery A, Capt. William A. Arnold.
1st Rhode Island Light, Battery B:
    *Lieut. T. Fred. Brown.
    Lieut. Walter S. Perrin.
1st United States, Battery I:
    Lieut. George A. Woodruff.
    Lieut. Tully McCrea.
4th United States, Battery A:
    Lieut. Alonzo H. Cushing.
    Sergt. Frederick Fuger.

THIRD ARMY CORPS.

Maj. Gen. DANIEL E. SICKLES.
Maj. Gen. DAVID B. BIRNEY.

FIRST DIVISION.

Maj. Gen. DAVID B. BIRNEY.
Brig. Gen. J. H. HOBART WARD.

First Brigade.

Brig. Gen. CHARLES K. GRAHAM.
Col. ANDREW H. TIPPIN.

57th Pennsylvania (eight companies):
    Col. Peter Sides.
    Capt. Alanson H. Nelson.
63d Pennsylvania, Maj. John A. Danks.
68th Pennsylvania:
    Col. Andrew H. Tippin.
    Capt. Milton S. Davis.[?]
105th Pennsylvania, Col. Calvin A. Craig.
114th Pennsylvania:
    Lieut. Col. Frederick F. Cavada.
    Capt. Edward R. Bowen.
141st Pennsylvania, Col. Henry J. Madill.

Second Brigade.

Brig. Gen. J. H. HOBART WARD.
Col. HIRAM BERDAN.

20th Indiana:
    Col. John Wheeler.
    Lieut. Col. William C. L. Taylor.
3d Maine, Col. Moses B. Lakeman.
4th Maine:
    Col. Elijah Walker.
    Capt. Edwin Libby.
86th New York, Lieut. Col. Benjamin L.
    Higgins.
124th New York:
    Col. A. Van Horne Ellis.
    Lieut. Col. Francis M. Cummins.
99th Pennsylvania, Maj. John W.
    Moore.
1st United States Sharpshooters:
    Col. Hiram Berdan.
    Lieut. Col. Casper Trepp.
2d United States Sharpshooters (eight
    companies), Maj. Homer R.
    Stoughton.

*Transferred from Artillery Reserve, July 1; 14th New York Battery attached.

Third Brigade.

Col. P. Regis de Trobriand.

17th Maine, Lieut. Col. Charles B. Merrill.
3d Michigan:
    Col. Byron R. Pierce.
    Lieut. Col. Edwin S. Pierce.
5th Michigan, Lieut. Col. John Pulford.
40th New York, Col. Thomas W. Egan.
110th Pennsylvania (six companies):
    Lieut. Col. David M. Jones.
    Maj. Isaac Rogers.

SECOND DIVISION.

Brig. Gen. Andrew A. Humphreys.

First Brigade.

Brig. Gen. Joseph B. Carr.

1st Massachusetts, Lieut. Col. Clark B.
    Baldwin.
11th Massachusetts, Lieut. Col. Porter D.
    Tripp.
16th Massachusetts:
    Lieut. Col. Waldo Merriam.
    Capt. Matthew Donovan.
12th New Hampshire, Capt. John F.
    Langley.
11th New Jersey:
    Col. Robert McAllister.
    Capt. Luther Martin.
    Lieut. John Schoonover.
    Capt. William H. Lloyd.
    Capt. Samuel T. Sleeper.
    Lieut. John Schoonover.
26th Pennsylvania, Maj. Robert L. Bo-
    dine.
84th Pennsylvania,* Lieut. Col. Milton
    Opp.

Second Brigade.

Col. William R. Brewster.

70th New York, Col. J. Egbert Farnum.
71st New York, Col. Henry L. Potter.
72d New York:
    Col. John S. Austin.
    Lieut. Col. John Leonard.
73d New York, Maj. Michael W. Burns.
74th New York, Lieut. Col. Thomas
    Holt.
120th New York:
    Lieut. Col. Cornelius D. West-
    brook.
    Maj. John R. Tappen.

Third Brigade.

Col. George C. Burling.

2d New Hampshire, Col. Edward L. Bailey.
5th New Jersey:
    Col. William J. Sewell.
    Capt. Thomas C. Godfrey.
    Capt. Henry H. Woolsey.
6th New Jersey, Lieut. Col. Stephen R. Gilkyson.
7th New Jersey:
    Col. Louis R. Francine.
    Maj. Frederick Cooper.
8th New Jersey:
    Col. John Ramsey.
    Capt. John G. Langston.
115th Pennsylvania, Maj. John P. Dunne.

---

*Guarding corps trains, and not engaged in the battle.

ARTILLERY BRIGADE.

Capt. GEORGE E. RANDOLPH.
Capt. A. JUDSON CLARK.

New Jersey Light, 2d Battery:
Capt. A. Judson Clark.
Lieut. Robert Sims.
1st New York Light, Battery D, Capt. George B. Winslow.
New York Light, 4th Battery, Capt. James E. Smith.
1st Rhode Island Light, Battery E:
Lieut. John K. Bucklyn.
Lieut. Benjamin Freeborn.
4th United States, Battery K:
Lieut. Francis W. Seeley.
Lieut. Robert James.

FIFTH ARMY CORPS.

Maj. Gen. GEORGE SYKES.

GENERAL HEADQUARTERS.

12th New York Infantry, Companies D and E, Capt. Henry W. Rider.
17th Pennsylvania Cavalry, Companies D and H, Capt. William Thompson.

FIRST DIVISION.

Brig. Gen. JAMES BARNES.

First Brigade.	*Second Brigade.*
Col. WILLIAM S. TILTON.	Col. JACOB B. SWEITZER.
18th Massachusetts, Col. Joseph Hayes.	9th Massachusetts, Col. Patrick R.
22d Massachusetts, Lieut. Col. Thomas	Guiney.
Sherwin, jr.	32d Massachusetts, Col. G. L. Prescott.
1st Michigan:	4th Michigan :
Col. Ira C. Abbott.	Col. Harrison H. Jeffords.
Lieut. Col. William A. Throop.	Lieut. Col. George W. Lumbard.
118th Pennsylvania, Lieut. Col. James	62d Pennsylvania, Lieut. Col. James C.
Gwyn.	Hull.

Third Brigade.

Col. STRONG VINCENT.
Col. JAMES C. RICE.

20th Maine, Col. Joshua L. Chamberlain.
16th Michigan, Lieut. Col. Norval E. Welch.
44th New York :
Col. James C. Rice.
Lieut. Col. Freeman Conner.
83d Pennsylvania, Capt. Orpheus S. Woodward.

SECOND DIVISION.

Brig. Gen. ROMEYN B. AYRES.

First Brigade.	*Second Brigade.*
Col. HANNIBAL DAY.	Col. SIDNEY BURBANK.
3d United States (six companies):	2d United States (six companies):
Capt. Henry W. Freedley.	Maj. Arthur T. Lee.
Capt. Richard G. Lay.	Capt. Samuel A. McKee.
4th United States (four companies),	7th United States (four companies),
Capt. Julius W. Adams, jr.	Capt. David P. Hancock.
6th United States (five companies),	10th United States (three companies),
Capt. Levi C. Bootes.	Capt. William Clinton.
12th United States (eight companies),	11th United States (six companies), Maj.
Capt. Thomas S. Dunn.	De Lancey Floyd-Jones.
14th United States (eight companies),	17th United States (seven companies),
Maj. Grotius R. Giddings.	Lieut. Col. J. Durell Greene.

Third Brigade.

Brig. Gen. STEPHEN H. WEED.
Col. KENNER GARRARD.

140th New York:
Col. Patrick H. O'Rorke.
Lieut. Col. Louis Ernst.
146th New York:
Col. Kenner Garrard.
Lieut. Col. David T. Jenkins.
91st Pennsylvania, Lieut. Col. Joseph H. Sinex.
155th Pennsylvania, Lieut. Col. John H. Cain.

THIRD DIVISION.*

Brig. Gen. SAMUEL W. CRAWFORD.

First Brigade.	*Third Brigade.*
Col. WILLIAM MCCANDLESS.	Col. JOSEPH W. FISHER.
1st Pennsylvania Reserves (nine companies), Col. William C. Talley. 2d Pennsylvania Reserves, Lieut. Col. George A. Woodward. 6th Pennsylvania Reserves, Lieut. Col. Wellington H. Ent. 13th Pennsylvania Reserves: Col. Charles F. Taylor. Maj. William R. Hartshorne.	5th Pennsylvania Reserves, Lieut. Col. George Dare. 9th Pennsylvania Reserves, Lieut. Col. James McK. Snodgrass. 10th Pennsylvania Reserves, Col. Adoniram J. Warner. 11th Pennsylvania Reserves, Col. Samuel M. Jackson. 12th Pennsylvania Reserves (nine companies), Col. Martin D. Hardin.

ARTILLERY BRIGADE.

Capt. AUGUSTUS P. MARTIN.

Massachusetts Light, 3d Battery (C), Lieut. Aaron F. Walcott.
1st New York Light, Battery C, Capt. Almont Barnes.
1st Ohio Light, Battery L, Capt. Frank C. Gibbs.
5th United States, Battery D:
Lieut. Charles E. Hazlett.
Lieut. Benjamin F. Rittenhouse.
5th United States, Battery I:
Lieut. Malbone F. Watson.
Lieut. Charles C. MacConnell.

SIXTH ARMY CORPS.

Maj. Gen. JOHN SEDGWICK.

GENERAL HEADQUARTERS.

1st New Jersey Cavalry, Company L, } Capt. William S. Craft.
1st Pennsylvania Cavalry, Company H, }

FIRST DIVISION.
Brig. Gen. HORATIO G. WRIGHT.

Provost Guard.

4th New Jersey (three companies), Capt. William R. Maxwell.

First Brigade.	*Second Brigade.*
Brig. Gen. A. T. A. TORBERT.	Brig. Gen. JOSEPH J. BARTLETT.†
1st New Jersey, Lieut. Col. William Henry, jr. 2d New Jersey, Lieut. Col. Charles Wiebecke. 3d New Jersey, Lieut. Col. Edward L. Campbell. 15th New Jersey, Col. William H. Penrose.	5th Maine, Col. Clark S. Edwards. 121st New York, Col. Emory Upton. 95th Pennsylvania, Lieut. Col. Edward Carroll. 96th Pennsylvania, Maj. William H. Lessig.

---

* Joined corps June 28. The Second Brigade left in the Department of Washington.
† Also in command of the Third Brigade, Third Division, on July 3.

Third Brigade.

Brig. Gen. DAVID A. RUSSELL.

6th Maine, Col. Hiram Burnham.
49th Pennsylvania (four companies), Lieut. Col. Thomas M. Hulings.
119th Pennsylvania, Col. Peter C. Ellmaker.
5th Wisconsin, Col. Thomas S. Allen.

SECOND DIVISION.*

Brig. Gen. ALBION P. HOWE.

Second Brigade.	*Third Brigade.*
Col. LEWIS A. GRANT.	Brig. Gen. THOMAS H. NEILL.
2d Vermont, Col. James H. Walbridge.	7th Maine (six companies), Lieut. Col. Selden Connor.
3d Vermont, Col. Thomas O. Seaver.	
4th Vermont, Col. Charles B. Stoughton.	33d New York (detachment), Capt. Henry J. Gifford.
5th Vermont, Lieut. Col. John R. Lewis.	43d New York, Lieut. Col. John Wilson.
6th Vermont, Col. Elisha L. Barney.	49th New York, Col. Daniel D. Bidwell.
	77th New York, Lieut. Col. Winsor B. French.
	61st Pennsylvania, Lieut. Col. George F. Smith.

THIRD DIVISION.

Maj. Gen. JOHN NEWTON.†
Brig. Gen. FRANK WHEATON.

First Brigade.	*Second Brigade.*
Brig. Gen. ALEXANDER SHALER.	Col. HENRY L. EUSTIS.
65th New York, Col. Joseph E. Hamblin.	7th Massachusetts, Lieut. Col. Franklin P. Harlow.
67th New York, Col. Nelson Cross.	10th Massachusetts, Lieut. Col. Joseph B. Parsons.
122d New York, Col. Silas Titus.	
23d Pennsylvania, Lieut. Col. John F. Glenn.	37th Massachusetts, Col. Oliver Edwards.
82d Pennsylvania, Col. Isaac C. Bassett.	2d Rhode Island, Col. Horatio Rogers, jr.

Third Brigade.

Brig. Gen. FRANK WHEATON.
Col. DAVID J. NEVIN.

62d New York:
    Col. David J. Nevin.
    Lieut. Col. Theodore B. Hamilton.
93d Pennsylvania, Maj. John I. Nevin.
98th Pennsylvania, Maj. John B. Kohler.
102d Pennsylvania,‡ Col. John W. Patterson.
139th Pennsylvania:
    Col. Frederick H. Collier.
    Lieut. Col. William H. Moody.

ARTILLERY BRIGADE.

Col. CHARLES H. TOMPKINS.

Massachusetts Light, 1st Battery (A), Capt. William H. McCartney.
New York Light, 1st Battery, Capt. Andrew Cowan.
New York Light, 3d Battery, Capt. William A. Harn.
1st Rhode Island Light, Battery C, Capt. Richard Waterman.
1st Rhode Island Light, Battery G, Capt. George W. Adams.
2d United States, Battery D, Lieut. Edward B. Williston,
2d United States, Battery G, Lieut. John H. Butler.
5th United States, Battery F, Lieut. Leonard Martin.

---

* No First Brigade in division.
† See foot note (§), p. 155.
‡ Guarding wagon train at Westminster, and not engaged in the battle.

ELEVENTH ARMY CORPS.*

Maj. Gen. OLIVER O. HOWARD.

GENERAL HEADQUARTERS.

1st Indiana Cavalry, Companies I and K, Capt. Abram Sharra.
8th New York Infantry (one company), Lieut. Hermann Foerster.

FIRST DIVISION.

Brig. Gen. FRANCIS C. BARLOW.
Brig. Gen. ADELBERT AMES.

First Brigade.

Col. LEOPOLD VON GILSA.

41st New York (nine companies), Lieut.
    Col. Detleo von Einsiedel.
54th New York:
    Maj. Stephen Kovacs.
    Lieut. Ernst Both [?].
68th New York, Col. Gotthilf Bourry.
153d Pennsylvania, Maj. John F. Frue-
    auff.

Second Brigade.

Brig. Gen. ADELBERT AMES.
Col. ANDREW L. HARRIS.

17th Connecticut:
    Lieut. Col. Douglas Fowler.
    Maj. Allen G. Brady.
25th Ohio:
    Lieut. Col. Jeremiah Williams.
    Capt. Nathaniel J. Manning.
    Lieut. William Maloney.
    Lieut. Israel White.
75th Ohio:
    Col. Andrew L. Harris.
    Capt. George B. Fox.
107th Ohio:
    Col. Seraphim Meyer.
    Capt. John M. Lutz.

SECOND DIVISION.

Brig. Gen. ADOLPH VON STEINWEHR.

First Brigade.

Col. CHARLES R. COSTER.

134th New York, Lieut. Col. Allan H.
    Jackson.
154th New York, Lieut. Col. D. B. Allen.
27th Pennsylvania, Lieut. Col. Lorenz
    Cantador.
73d Pennsylvania, Capt. D. F. Kelley.

Second Brigade.

Col. ORLAND SMITH.

33d Massachusetts, Col. Adin B. Un-
    derwood.
136th New York, Col. James Wood, jr.
55th Ohio, Col. Charles B. Gambee.
73d Ohio, Lieut. Col. Richard Long.

THIRD DIVISION.

Maj. Gen. CARL SCHURZ.

First Brigade.

Brig. Gen. ALEX. SCHIMMELFENNIG.
Col. GEORGE VON AMSBERG.

82d Illinois, Lieut. Col. Edward S. Sal-
    omon.
45th New York :
    Col. George von Amsberg.
    Lieut. Col. Adolphus Dobke.
157th New York, Col. Philip P. Brown, jr.
61st Ohio, Col. Stephen J. McGroarty.
74th Pennsylvania:
    Col. Adolph von Hartung.
    Lieut. Col. Alexander von Mitzel.
    Capt. Gustav Schleiter.
    Capt. Henry Krauseneck.

Second Brigade.

Col. W. KRZYZANOWSKI.

58th New York:
    Lieut. Col. August Otto.
    Capt. Emil Koenig.
119th New York:
    Col. John T. Lockman.
    Lieut. Col. Edward F. Lloyd.
82d Ohio:
    Col. James S. Robinson.
    Lieut. Col. David Thomson.
75th Pennsylvania:
    Col. Francis Mahler.
    Maj. August Ledig.
26th Wisconsin:
    Lieut. Col. Hans Boebel.
    Capt. John W. Fuchs.

---

* During the interval between the death of General Reynolds and the arrival of General Hancock, on the afternoon of July 1, all the troops on the field of battle were commanded by General Howard, General Schurz taking command of the Eleventh Corps, and General Schimmelfennig of the Third Division.

ARTILLERY BRIGADE.

Maj. THOMAS W. OSBORN.

1st New York Light, Battery I, Capt. Michael Wiedrich.
New York Light, 13th Battery, Lieut. William Wheeler.
1st Ohio Light, Battery I, Capt. Hubert Dilger.
1st Ohio Light, Battery K, Capt. Lewis Heckman.
4th United States, Battery G:
Lieut. Bayard Wilkeson.
Lieut. Eugene A. Bancroft.

TWELFTH ARMY CORPS.

Maj. Gen. HENRY W. SLOCUM.*
Brig. Gen. ALPHEUS S. WILLIAMS.

PROVOST GUARD.

10th Maine (four companies), Capt John D. Beardsley.

FIRST DIVISION.

Brig. Gen. ALPHEUS S. WILLIAMS.
Brig. Gen. THOMAS H. RUGER.

First Brigade.

Col. ARCHIBALD L. McDOUGALL.

5th Connecticut, Col. W. W. Packer.
20th Connecticut, Lieut. Col. William B. Wooster.
3d Maryland, Col. Jos. M. Sudsburg.
123d New York:
Lieut. Col. James C. Rogers.
Capt. Adolphus H. Tanner.
145th New York, Col. E. L. Price.
46th Pennsylvania, Col. James L. Selfridge.

Second Brigade.†

Brig. Gen. HENRY H. LOCKWOOD.

1st Maryland, Potomac Home Brigade, Col. William P. Maulsby.
1st Maryland, Eastern Shore, C . James Wallace.
150th New York, Col. John H. Ketcham.

Third Brigade.

Brig. Gen. THOMAS H. RUGER.
Col. SILAS COLGROVE.

27th Indiana:
Col. Silas Colgrove.
Lieut. Col. John R. Fesler.
2d Massachusetts:
Lieut. Col. Charles R. Mudge.
Maj. Charles F. Morse.
13th New Jersey, Col. Ezra A. Carman.
107th New York, Col. Nirom M. Crane.
3d Wisconsin, Col. William Hawley.

SECOND DIVISION.

Brig. Gen. JOHN W. GEARY.

First Brigade.

Col. CHARLES CANDY.

5th Ohio, Col. John H. Patrick.
7th Ohio, Col. William R. Creighton.
29th Ohio:
Capt. Wilbur F. Stevens.
Capt. Edward Hayes.
66th Ohio, Lieut. Col. Eugene Powell.
28th Pennsylvania, Capt. John Flynn.
147th Pennsylvania (eight companies), Lieut. Col. Ario Pardee, jr.

Second Brigade.

Col. GEORGE A. COBHAM, Jr.
Brig. GEN. THOMAS L. KANE.
Col. GEORGE A. COBHAM, Jr.

29th Pennsylvania, Col. William Rickards, jr.
109th Pennsylvania, Capt. F. L. Gimber.
111th Pennsylvania:
Lieut. Col. Thomas M. Walker.
Col. George A. Cobham, jr.
Lieut. Col. Thomas M. Walker.

* Exercised command of the right wing of the army during a part of the battle. But see Slocum to Meade, December 30, 1863, p. 763, and Meade to Slocum, February 25, 1864, p. 769.
† Unassigned during progress of battle; afterward attached to First Division, as Second Brigade. The command theretofore known as the Second (or Jackson's) Brigade had previously been consolidated with the First Brigade.

Third Brigade.

Brig. Gen. GEORGE S. GREENE.

60th New York, Col. Abel Godard.
78th New York, Lieut. Col. Herbert von Hammerstein.
102d New York:
    Col. James C. Lane.
    Capt. Lewis R. Stegman.
137th New York, Col. David Ireland.
149th New York:
    Col. Henry A. Barnum.
    Lieut. Col. Charles B. Randall.

ARTILLERY BRIGADE.

Lieut. EDWARD D. MUHLENBERG.

1st New York Light, Battery M, Lieut. Charles E. Winegar.
Pennsylvania Light, Battery E, Lieut. Charles A. Atwell.
4th United States, Battery F, Lieut. Sylvanus T. Rugg.
5th United States, Battery K, Lieut. David H. Kinzie.

CAVALRY CORPS.

Maj. Gen. ALFRED PLEASONTON.

FIRST DIVISION.

Brig. Gen. JOHN BUFORD.

First Brigade.	*Second Brigade.*
Col. WILLIAM GAMBLE.	Col. THOMAS C. DEVIN.
8th Illinois, Maj. John L. Beveridge. 12th Illinois (four cos.), } Col. George H. 3d Indiana (six cos.), } Chapman. 8th New York, Lieut. Col. William L. Markell.	6th New York, Maj. Wm. E. Beardsley. 9th New York, Col. William Sackett. 17th Pennsylvania, Col. J. H. Kellogg. 3d West Virginia (two companies), Capt. Seymour B. Conger.

Reserve Brigade.

Brig. Gen. WESLEY MERRITT.

6th Pennsylvania, Maj. James H. Haseltine.
1st United States, Capt. Richard S. C. Lord.
2d United States, Capt. T. F. Rodenbough.
5th United States, Capt. Julius W. Mason.
6th United States:
    Maj. Samuel H. Starr.
    Lieut. Louis H. Carpenter.
    Lieut. Nicholas Nolan.
    Capt. Ira W. Claflin.

SECOND DIVISION.

Brig. Gen. DAVID McM. GREGG.

Headquarters Guard.

1st Ohio, Company A, Capt. Noah Jones.

First Brigade.	*Second Brigade.‡*
Col. JOHN B. McINTOSH.	Col. PENNOCK HUEY.
1st Maryland (eleven companies), Lieut. Col. James M. Deems. Purnell (Maryland) Legion, Company A, Capt. Robert E. Duvall. 1st Massachusetts,* Lieut. Col. Greely S. Curtis. 1st New Jersey, Maj. M. H. Beaumont. 1st Pennsylvania, Col. John P. Taylor. 3d Pennsylvania, Lieut. Col. E. S. Jones. 3d Pennsylvania Heavy Artillery, Section Battery H,† Capt. W. D. Rank.	2d New York, Lieut. Col. Otto Harhaus. 4th New York, Lieut. Col. Augustus Pruyn. 6th Ohio (ten companies), Maj. William Stedman. 8th Pennsylvania, Capt. William A. Corrie.

*Served with the Sixth Army Corps, and on the right flank.
†Serving as light artillery.
‡At Westminster, etc., and not engaged in the battle.

Third Brigade.

Col. J. IRVIN GREGG.

1st Maine (ten companies), Lieut. Col. Charles H. Smith.
10th New York, Maj. M. Henry Avery.
4th Pennsylvania, Lieut. Col. William E. Doster.
16th Pennsylvania, Lieut. Col. John K. Robison.

THIRD DIVISION.

Brig. Gen. JUDSON KILPATRICK.

Headquarters Guard.

1st Ohio, Company C, Capt. Samuel N. Stanford.

First Brigade.	*Second Brigade.*
Brig. Gen. ELON J. FARNSWORTH. Col. NATHANIEL P. RICHMOND.	Brig. Gen. GEORGE A. CUSTER.
5th New York, Maj. John Hammond. 18th Pennsylvania, Lieut. Col. William P. Brinton. 1st Vermont, Lieut. Col. Addison W. Preston. 1st West Virginia (ten companies): Col. Nathaniel P. Richmond. Maj. Charles E. Capehart.	1st Michigan, Col. Charles H. Town. 5th Michigan, Col. Russell A. Alger. 6th Michigan, Col. George Gray. 7th Michigan (ten companies), Col. William D. Mann.

HORSE ARTILLERY.

First Brigade.	*Second Brigade.*
Capt. JAMES M. ROBERTSON.	Capt. JOHN C. TIDBALL.
9th Michigan Battery, Capt. Jabez J. Daniels. 6th New York Battery, Capt. Joseph W. Martin. 2d United States, Batteries B and L, Lieut. Edward Heaton. 2d United States, Battery M, Lieut. A. C. M. Pennington, jr. 4th United States, Battery E, Lieut. Samuel S. Elder.	1st United States, Batteries E and G, Capt. Alanson M. Randol. 1st United States, Battery K, Capt. William M. Graham. 2d United States, Battery A, Lieut. John H. Calef. 3d United States, Battery C, Lieut. William D. Fuller.*

ARTILLERY RESERVE.

Brig. Gen. ROBERT O. TYLER.
Capt. JAMES M. ROBERTSON.

Headquarters Guard.

32d Massachusetts Infantry, Company C, Capt. Josiah C. Fuller.

First Regular Brigade.	*First Volunteer Brigade.*
Capt. DUNBAR R. RANSOM.	Lieut. Col. FREEMAN MCGILVERY.
1st United States, Battery H: Lieut. Chandler P. Eakin. Lieut. Philip D. Mason. 3d United States, Batteries F and K, Lieut. John G. Turnbull. 4th United States, Battery C, Lieut. Evan Thomas. 5th United States, Battery C, Lieut. Gulian V. Weir.	Massachusetts Light, 5th Battery (E),† Capt. Charles A. Phillips. Massachusetts Light, 9th Battery: Capt. John Bigelow. Lieut. Richard S. Milton. New York Light, 15th Battery, Capt. Patrick Hart. Pennsylvania Light, Batteries C and F, Capt. James Thompson.

---

* With Huey's Cavalry Brigade, and not engaged in the battle.
† 10th New York Battery attached.

Second Volunteer Brigade.

Capt. Elijah D. Taft.

1st Connecticut Heavy, Battery B,* Capt. Albert F. Brooker.

1st Connecticut Heavy, Battery M,* Capt. Franklin A. Pratt.

Connecticut Light, 2d Battery, Capt. John W. Sterling.

New York Light, 5th Battery, Capt. Elijah D. Taft.

Third Volunteer Brigade.

Capt. James F. Huntington.

New Hampshire Light, 1st Battery, Capt. Frederick M. Edgell.

1st Ohio Light, Battery H, Lieut. George W. Norton.

1st Pennsylvania Light, Batteries F and G, Capt. R. Bruce Ricketts.

West Virginia Light, Battery C, Capt. Wallace Hill.

Fourth Volunteer Brigade.

Capt. Robert H. Fitzhugh.

Maine Light, 6th Battery (F), Lieut. Edwin B. Dow.
Maryland Light, Battery A, Capt. James H. Rigby.
New Jersey Light, 1st Battery, Lieut. Augustin N. Parsons.
1st New York Light, Battery G, Capt. Nelson Ames.
1st New York Light, Battery K,† Capt. Robert H. Fitzhugh.

Train Guard.

4th New Jersey Infantry (seven companies), Maj. Charles Ewing.

No. 124.

Organization of the Army of Northern Virginia at the battle of Gettysburg, July 1–3.*

FIRST ARMY CORPS.

Lieut. Gen. JAMES LONGSTREET.

M'LAWS' DIVISION.

Maj. Gen. LAFAYETTE McLAWS.

Kershaw's Brigade.

Brig. Gen. J. B. KERSHAW.

2d South Carolina :
    Col. J. D. Kennedy.
    Lieut. Col. F. Gaillard.
3d South Carolina :
    Maj. R. C. Maffett.
    Col. J. D. Nance.
7th South Carolina, Col. D. Wyatt Aiken.
8th South Carolina, Col. J. W. Henagan.
15th South Carolina :
    Col. W. D. De Saussure.
    Maj. William M. Gist.
3d South Carolina Battalion, Lieut. Col. W. G. Rice.

Semmes' Brigade.†

Brig. Gen. P. J. SEMMES.
Col. GOODE BRYAN.

10th Georgia, Col. John B. Weems.
50th Georgia, Col. W. R. Manning.
51st Georgia, Col. E. Ball.
53d Georgia, Col. James P. Simms.

Barksdale's Brigade.

Brig. Gen. WILLIAM BARKSDALE.
Col. B. G. HUMPHREYS.

13th Mississippi, Col. J. W. Carter.
17th Mississippi :
    Col. W. D. Holder.
    Lieut. Col. John C. Fiser.
18th Mississippi :
    Col. T. M. Griffin.
    Lieut. Col. W. H. Luse.
21st Mississippi, Col. B. G. Humphreys.

Wofford's Brigade.

Brig. Gen. W. T. WOFFORD.

16th Georgia, Col. Goode Bryan.
18th Georgia, Lieut. Col. S. Z. Ruff.
24th Georgia, Col. Robert McMillan.
Cobb's (Georgia) Legion, Lieut. Col. Luther J. Glenn.
Phillips (Georgia) Legion, Lieut. Col. E. S. Barclay.

Artillery.

Col. H. G. CABELL.

1st North Carolina Artillery, Battery A, Capt. B. C. Manly.
Pulaski (Georgia) Artillery :
    Capt. J. C. Fraser.
    Lieut. W. J. Furlong.
1st Richmond Howitzers, Capt. E. S. McCarthy.
Troup (Georgia) Artillery :
    Capt. H. H. Carlton.
    Lieut. C. W. Motes.

---

*The actual commanders are indicated as far as practicable.
†No reports on file for this brigade. Bryan was in command July 7, and was probably Semmes' immediate successor. The commanders of the Tenth, Fifty-first, and Fifty-third Georgia are given as reported for June 22 and July 31. Manning reported in command of Fiftieth Georgia, June 22. No commander reported on return for July 31.

PICKETT'S DIVISION.

Maj. Gen. GEORGE E. PICKETT.

Garnett's Brigade.

Brig. Gen. R. B. GARNETT.
Maj. C. S. PEYTON.

8th Virginia, Col. Eppa Hunton.
18th Virginia, Lieut. Col. H. A. Carrington.
19th Virginia :
    Col. Henry Gantt.
    Lieut. Col. John T. Ellis.
28th Virginia :
    Col. R. C. Allen.
    Lieut. Col. William Watts.
56th Virginia :
    Col. W. D. Stuart.
    Lieut. Col. P. P. Slaughter.

Kemper's Brigade.

Brig. Gen. J. L. KEMPER.
Col. JOSEPH MAYO, Jr.

1st Virginia :
    Col. Lewis B. Williams.
    Lieut. Col. F. G. Skinner.
3d Virginia :
    Col. Joseph Mayo, jr.
    Lieut. Col. A. D. Callcote.
7th Virginia :
    Col. W. T. Patton.
    Lieut. Col. C. C. Flowerree.
11th Virginia, Maj. Kirkwood Otey.
24th Virginia, Col. William R. Terry.

Armistead's Brigade.

Brig. Gen. L. A. ARMISTEAD.
Col. W. R. AYLETT.

9th Virginia, Maj. John C. Owens.
14th Virginia :
    Col. James G. Hodges.
    Lieut. Col. William White.
38th Virginia :
    Col. E. C. Edmonds.
    Lieut. Col. P. B. Whittle.
53d Virginia, Col. W. R. Aylett.
57th Virginia, Col. John Bowie Magruder.

Artillery.

Maj. JAMES DEARING.

Fauquier (Virginia) Artillery, Capt. R. M. Stribling.
Hampden ((Virginia) Artillery,Capt. W. H. Caskie.
Richmond Fayette Artillery, Capt. M. C. Macon.
Virginia Battery, Capt. Joseph G. Blount.

HOOD'S DIVISION

Maj. Gen. JOHN B. HOOD.
Brig. Gen. E. M. LAW.

Law's Brigade.

Brig.Gen. E. M. LAW.
Col. JAMES L. SHEFFIELD.

4th Alabama,Lieut. Col. L. H. Scruggs.
15th Alabama :
    Col. William C. Oates.
    Capt. B. A. Hill.
44th Alabama, Col. William F. Perry.
47th Alabama :
    Col. James W. Jackson.
    Lieut. Col. M. J. Bulger.
    Maj. J. M. Campbell.
48th Alabama :
    Col. James L. Sheffield.
    Capt. T. J. Eubanks.

Robertson's Brigade.

Brig. Gen. J. B. ROBERTSON.

3d Arkansas :
    Col. Van H. Manning.
    Lieut. Col. R. S. Taylor.
1st Texas, Lieut. Col. P. A. Work.
4th Texas :
    Col. J. C. G. Key.
    Maj. J. P. Bane.
5th Texas :
    Col. R. M. Powell.
    Lieut. Col. K. Bryan.
    Maj. J. C. Rogers.

Anderson's Brigade.

Brig. Gen. GEORGE T. ANDERSON.
Lieut. Col. WILLIAM LUFFMAN.

7th Georgia, Col. W. W. White.
8th Georgia, Col. John R. Towers.
9th Georgia :
    Lieut. Col. John C. Mounger.
    Maj. W. M. Jones.
    Capt. George Hillyer.
11th Georgia :
    Col. F. H. Little.
    Lieut. Col. William Luffman.
    Maj. Henry D. McDaniel.
    Capt. William H. Mitchell.
59th Georgia :
    Col. Jack Brown.
    Capt. M. G. Bass.

Benning's Brigade.

Brig. Gen. HENRY L. BENNING.

2d Georgia :
    Lieut. Col. William T. Harris.
    Maj. W. S. Shepherd.
15th Georgia, Col. D. M. DuBose.
17th Georgia, Col. W. C. Hodges.
20th Georgia :
    Col. John A. Jones.
    Lieut. Col. J. D. Waddell.

Artillery.

Maj. M. W. HENRY.

Branch (North Carolina) Artillery, Capt. A. C. Latham
German (South Carolina) Artillery, Capt. William K. Bachman.
Palmetto (South Carolina) Light Artillery, Capt. Hugh R. Garden.
Rowan (North Carolina) Artillery, Capt. James Reilly.

ARTILLERY RESERVE.

Col. J. B. WALTON.

Alexander's Battalion.

Col. E. P. ALEXANDER.

Ashland (Virginia) Artillery :
    Capt. P. Woolfolk, jr.
    Lieut. James Woolfolk.
Bedford (Virginia) Artillery, Capt. T. C.
    Jordan.
Brooks (South Carolina) Artillery, Lieut.
    S. C. Gilbert.
Madison (Louisiana) Light Artillery, Capt.
    George V. Moody.
Virginia Battery, Capt. W. W. Parker.
Virginia Battery, Capt. O. B. Taylor.

Washington (Louisiana) Artillery.

Maj. B. F. ESHLEMAN.

First Company, Capt. C. W. Squires.
Second Company, Capt. J. B. Richardson.
Third Company, Capt. M. B. Miller.
Fourth Company :
    Capt. Joe Norcom.
    Lieut. H. A. Battles.

SECOND ARMY CORPS.

Lieut. Gen. RICHARD S. EWELL.

Escort.

Randolph's Company Virginia Cavalry, Capt. William F. Randolph.

EARLY'S DIVISION.

Maj. Gen. JUBAL A. EARLY.

Hays' Brigade.

Brig. Gen. HARRY T. HAYS.

5th Louisiana :
    Maj. Alexander Hart.
    Capt. T. H. Biscoe.
6th Louisiana, Lieut. Col. Joseph Hanlon.
7th Louisiana, Col. D. B. Penn.
8th Louisiana :
    Col. T. D. Lewis.
    Lieut. Col. A. de Blanc.
    Maj. G. A. Lester.
9th Louisiana, Col. Leroy A. Stafford.

Smith's Brigade.

Brig. Gen. WILLIAM SMITH.

31st Virginia, Col. John S. Hoffman.
49th Virginia, Lieut. Col. J. Catlett Gibson.
52d Virginia, Lieut. Col. James H. Skinner.

Hoke's Brigade.

Col. ISAAC E. AVERY.
Col. A. C. GODWIN.

6th North Carolina, Maj. S. McD. Tate.
21st North Carolina, Col. W. W. Kirkland.
57th North Carolina, Col. A. C. Godwin.

Gordon's Brigade.

Brig. Gen. J. B. GORDON.

13th Georgia, Col. James M. Smith.
26th Georgia, Col. E. N. Atkinson.
31st Georgia, Col. Clement A. Evans.
38th Georgia, Capt. William L. McLeod.
60th Georgia, Capt. W. B. Jones.
61st Georgia, Col. John H. Lamar.

Artillery.

Lieut. Col. H. P. JONES.

Charlottesville (Virginia) Artillery, Capt. James McD. Carrington.
Courtney (Virginia) Artillery, Capt. W. A. Tanner.
Louisiana Guard Artillery, Capt. C. A. Green.
Staunton (Virginia) Artillery, Capt. A. W. Garber.

JOHNSON'S DIVISION.

Maj. Gen. EDWARD JOHNSON.

Steuart's Brigade.

Brig. Gen. GEORGE H. STEUART.

1st Maryland Battalion Infantry :
   Lieut. Col. J. R. Herbert.
   Maj. W. W. Goldsborough.
   Capt. J. P. Crane.
1st North Carolina, Lieut. Col. H. A.
   Brown.
3d North Carolina, Maj. W. M. Parsley.
10th Virginia, Col. E. T. H. Warren.
23d Virginia, Lieut. Col. S. T. Walton.
37th Virginia, Maj. H. C. Wood.

Stonewall Brigade.

Brig. Gen. JAMES A. WALKER.

2d Virginia, Col. J. Q. A. Nadenbousch.
4th Virginia, Maj. William Terry.
5th Virginia, Col. J. H. S. Funk.
27th Virginia, Lieut. Col. D. M. Shriver.
33d Virginia, Capt. J. B. Golladay.

*Nicholls' Brigade.**

Col. J. M. WILLIAMS.

1st Louisiana, Capt. E. D. Willett.
2d Louisiana, Lieut. Col. R. E. Burke.
10th Louisiana, Maj. T. N. Powell.
14th Louisiana, Lieut. Col. David Zable.
15th Louisiana, Maj. Andrew Brady.

Jones' Brigade.

Brig. Gen. JOHN M. JONES.
Lieut. Col. R. H. DUNGAN.

21st Virginia, Capt. W. P. Moseley.
25th Virginia :
   Col. J. C. Higginbotham.
   Lieut. Col. J. A. Robinson.
42d Virginia :
   Lieut. Col. R. W. Withers.
   Capt. S. H. Saunders.
44th Virginia :
   Maj. N. Cobb.
   Capt. T. R. Buckner.
48th Virginia :
   Lieut. Col. R. H. Dungan.
   Maj. Oscar White.
50th Virginia, Lieut. Col. L. H. N. Salyer.

Artillery.

Maj. J. W. LATIMER.
Capt. C. I. RAINE.

1st Maryland Battery, Capt. William F. Dement.
Alleghany (Virginia) Artillery, Capt. J. C. Carpenter.
Chesapeake (Maryland) Artillery, Capt. William D. Brown.
Lee (Virginia) Battery :
   Capt. C. I. Raine.
   Lieut. William W. Hardwicke.

---

* The regimental commanders are given as reported for June 14,

RODES' DIVISION.

Maj. Gen. R. E. RODES.

Daniel's Brigade.

Brig. Gen. JUNIUS DANIEL.

32d North Carolina, Col. E. C. Brabble.
43d North Carolina :
    Col. T. S. Kenan.
    Lieut. Col. W. G. Lewis.
45th North Carolina :
    Lieut. Col. S. H. Boyd.
    Maj. John R. Winston.
    Capt. A. H. Gallaway.
    Capt. J. A. Hopkins.
53d North Carolina. Col. W. A. Owens.
2d North Carolina Battalion :
    Lieut. Col. H. L. Andrews.
    Capt. Van Brown.

Iverson's Brigade.

Brig. Gen. ALFRED IVERSON.

5th North Carolina :*
    Capt. Speight B. West.
    Capt. Benjamin Robinson.
12th North Carolina, Lieut. Col. W. S.
    Davis.
20th North Carolina :†
    Lieut. Col. Nelson Slough.
    Capt. Lewis T. Hicks.
23d North Carolina :‡
    Col. D. H. Christie.
    Capt. William H. Johnston.

Doles' Brigade.

Brig. Gen. GEORGE DOLES.

4th Georgia :
    Lieut. Col. D. R. E. Winn.
    . Maj. W. H. Willis.
12th Georgia, Col. Edward Willis.
21st Georgia, Col. John T. Mercer.
44th Georgia :
    Col. S. P. Lumpkin.
    Maj. W. H. Peebles.

Ramseur's Brigade.

Brig. Gen. S. D. RAMSEUR.

2d North Carolina :
    Maj. D. W. Hurtt.
    Capt. James T. Scales.
4th North Carolina, Col. Bryan Grimes.
14th North Carolina :
    Col. R. Tyler Bennett.
    Maj. Joseph H. Lambeth.
30th North Carolina :
    Col. Francis M. Parker.
    Maj. W. W. Sillers.

O'Neal's Brigade.

Col. E. A. O'NEAL.

3d Alabama, Col. C. A. Battle.
5th Alabama, Col. J. M. Hall.
6th Alabama :
    Col. J. N. Lightfoot.
    Capt. M. L. Bowie.
12th Alabama, Col. S. B. Pickens.
26th Alabama, Lieut. Col. John C. Goodgame.

Artillery.

Lieut. Col. THOMAS H. CARTER.

Jeff. Davis (Alabama) Artillery, Capt. W. J. Reese.
King William (Virginia) Artillery, Capt. W. P. Carter.
Morris (Virginia) Artillery, Capt. R. C. M. Page.
Orange (Virginia) Artillery, Capt. C. W. Fry.

---

* The four captains present (West, Robinson, James M. Taylor, Thomas N. Jordan), were reported as wounded July 1 ; Robinson and Taylor as having rejoined July 2, but it does not appear who commanded during Robinson's absence.

† Lieutenant-Colonel Slough and Maj. John S. Brooks reported as wounded at 4 p. m. July 1.

‡ Colonel Christie, Lieut. Col. R. D. Johnston, Maj. C. C. Blacknall, and the senior captain (Abner D. Peace), reported as wounded early in the fight, July 1,

ARTILLERY RESERVE.

Col. J. THOMPSON BROWN.

First Virginia Artillery.

Capt. WILLIS J. DANCE.

2d Richmond (Virginia) Howitzers, Capt. David Watson.
3d Richmond (Virginia) Howitzers, Capt. B. H. Smith, jr.
Powhatan (Virginia) Artillery, Lieut. John M. Cunningham.
Rockbridge (Virginia) Artillery, Capt. A. Graham.
Salem (Virginia) Artillery, Lieut. C. B. Griffin.

Nelson's Battalion.

Lieut. Col. WILLIAM NELSON.

Amherst (Virginia) Artillery,. Capt. T. J. Kirkpatrick.
Fluvanna (Virginia) Artillery, Capt. J. L. Massie.
Georgia Battery, Capt. John Milledge, jr.

THIRD ARMY CORPS.

Lieut. Gen. AMBROSE P. HILL.

ANDERSON'S DIVISION.

Maj. Gen. R. H. ANDERSON.

Wilcox's Brigade.

Brig. Gen. CADMUS M. WILCOX.

8th Alabama, Lieut. Col. Hilary A. Herbert.
9th Alabama, Capt. J. H. King.
10th Alabama:
  Col. William H. Forney.
  Lieut. Col. James E. Shelley.
11th Alabama:
  Col. J. C. C. Sanders.
  Lieut.' Col. George E. Tayloe.
14th Alabama:
  Col. L. Pinckard.
  Lieut. Col. James A. Broome.

Wright's Brigade.

Brig. Gen. A. R. WRIGHT.
Col. WILLIAM GIBSON.
Brig. Gen. A. R. WRIGHT.

3d Georgia, Col. E. J. Walker.
22d Georgia:
  Col. Joseph Wasden.
  Capt. B. C. McCurry.
48th Georgia:
  Col. William Gibson.
  Capt. M. R. Hall.
  Col. William Gibson.
2d Georgia Battalion:
  Maj. George W. Ross.
  Capt. Charles J. Moffett.

Mahone's Brigade.

Brig. Gen. WILLIAM MAHONE.

6th Virginia, Col. George T. Rogers.
12th Virginia, Col. D. A. Weisiger.
16th Virginia, Col. Joseph H. Ham.
41st Virginia, Col. William A. Parham.
61st Virginia, Col. V. D. Groner.

Perry's Brigade.

Col. DAVID LANG.

2d Florida, Maj. W. R. Moore.
5th Florida, Capt. R. N. Gardner.
8th Florida, Col. David Lang.

Posey's Brigade.

Brig. Gen. CARNOT POSEY.

12th Mississippi, Col. W. H. Taylor.
16th Mississippi, Col. Samuel E. Baker.
19th Mississippi, Col. N. H. Harris.
48th Mississippi, Col. Joseph M. Jayne.

Artillery (Sumter Battalion).

Maj. JOHN LANE.

Company A, Capt. Hugh M. Ross.
Company B, Capt. George M. Patterson.
Company C, Capt. John T. Wingfield.

HETH'S DIVISION.

Maj. Gen. HENRY HETH.
Brig. Gen. J. J. PETTIGREW.

First Brigade.

Brig. Gen. J. J. PETTIGREW.
Col. J. K. MARSHALL.

11th North Carolina, Col. Collett Leventhorpe.
26th North Carolina:
    Col. Henry K. Burgwyn, jr.
    Capt. H. C. Albright.
47th North Carolina, Col. G. H. Faribault.
52d North Carolina:
    Col. J. K. Marshall.
    Lieut. Col. Marcus A. Parks.

Second Brigade.

Col. J. M. BROCKENBROUGH.

40th Virginia:
    Capt. T. E. Betts.
    Capt. R. B. Davis.
47th Virginia, Col. Robert M. Mayo.
55th Virginia, Col. W. S. Christian.
22d Virginia Battalion, Maj. John S. Bowles.

Third Brigade.

Brig. Gen. JAMES J. ARCHER.
Col. B. D. FRY.
Lieut. Col. S. G. SHEPARD.

13th Alabama, Col. B. D. Fry.
5th Alabama Battalion, Maj. A. S. Van de Graaff.
1st Tennessee (Provisional Army), Maj. Felix G. Buchanan.
7th Tennessee, Lieut. Col. S. G. Shepard.
14th Tennessee, Capt. B. L. Phillips.

Fourth Brigade.

Brig. Gen. JOSEPH R. DAVIS.

2d Mississippi, Col. J. M. Stone.
11th Mississippi, Col. F. M. Green.
42d Mississippi, Col. H. R. Miller.
55th North Carolina, Col. J. K. Connally.

Artillery.

Lieut. Col. JOHN J. GARNETT.

Donaldsonville (Louisiana) Artillery, Capt. V. Maurin.
Huger (Virginia) Artillery, Capt. Joseph D. Moore.
Lewis (Virginia) Artillery, Capt. John W. Lewis.
Norfolk Light Artillery Blues, Capt. C. R. Grandy.

PENDER'S DIVISION.

Maj. Gen. WILLIAM D. PENDER.
Brig. Gen. JAMES H. LANE.
Maj. Gen. I. R. TRIMBLE.
Brig. Gen. JAMES H. LANE.

First Brigade.

Col. ABNER PERRIN.

1st South Carolina (Provisional Army), Maj. C. W. McCreary.
1st South Carolina Rifles, Capt. William M. Hadden.
12th South Carolina, Col. John L. Miller.
13th South Carolina, Lieut. Col. B. T. Brockman.
14th South Carolina, Lieut. Col. Joseph N. Brown.

Second Brigade.

Brig. Gen. JAMES H. LANE.
Col. C. M. AVERY.
Brig. Gen. JAMES H. LANE.
Col. C. M. AVERY.

7th North Carolina:
    Capt. J. McLeod Turner.
    Capt. James G. Harris.
18th North Carolina, Col. John D. Barry.
28th North Carolina:
    Col. S. D. Lowe.
    Lieut. Col. W. H. A. Speer.
33d North Carolina, Col. C. M. Avery.
37th North Carolina, Col. W. M. Barbour.

Third Brigade.

Brig. Gen. EDWARD L. THOMAS.

14th Georgia.
35th Georgia.
45th Georgia.
49th Georgia, Col. S. T. Player.

Fourth Brigade.

Brig. Gen. A. M. SCALES.
Lieut. Col. G. T. GORDON.
Col. W. LEE J. LOWRANCE.

13th North Carolina :
    Col. J. H. Hyman.
    Lieut. Col. H. A. Rogers.
16th North Carolina, Capt. L. W. Stowe.
22d North Carolina, Col. James Conner.
34th North Carolina :
    Col. William Lee J. Lowrance.
    Lieut. Col. G. T. Gordon.
38th North Carolina :
    Col. W. J. Hoke.
    Lieut. Col. John Ashford.

Artillery.

Maj. WILLIAM T. POAGUE.

Albemarle (Virginia) Artillery, Capt. James W. Wyatt.
Charlotte (North Carolina) Artillery, Capt. Joseph Graham.
Madison (Mississippi) Light Artillery, Capt. George Ward.
Virginia Battery, Capt. J. V. Brooke.

ARTILLERY RESERVE.

Col. R. LINDSAY WALKER.

McIntosh's Battalion.

Maj. D. G. McINTOSH.

Danville (Virginia) Artillery, Capt. R. S. Rice.
Hardaway (Alabama) Artillery, Capt. W. B. Hurt.
2d Rockbridge (Virginia) Artillery, Lieut. Samuel Wallace.
Virginia Battery, Capt. M. Johnson.

Pegram's Battalion.

Maj. W. J. PEGRAM.
Capt. E. B. BRUNSON.

Crenshaw (Virginia) Battery.
Fredericksburg (Virginia) Artillery, Capt. E. A. Marye.
Letcher (Virginia) Artillery, Capt. T. A. Brander.
Pee Dee (South Carolina) Artillery, Lieut. William E. Zimmerman.
Purcell (Virginia) Artillery, Capt. Joseph McGraw.

CAVALRY.

STUART'S DIVISION.

Maj. Gen. J. E. B. STUART.

Hampton's Brigade.

Brig. Gen. WADE HAMPTON.
Col. L. S. BAKER.

1st North Carolina, Col. L. S. Baker.
1st South Carolina.
2d South Carolina.
Cobb's (Georgia) Legion.
Jeff. Davis Legion.
Phillips (Georgia) Legion.

Robertson's Brigade.

Br'g. Gen. BEVERLY H. ROBERTSON.*

4th North Carolina, Col. D. D. Ferebee.
5th North Carolina.

Fitz. Lee's Brigade.

Brig. Gen. FITZ. LEE.

1st Maryland Battalion : †
    Maj. Harry Gilmor.
    Maj. Ridgely Brown.
1st Virginia, Col. James H. Drake.
2d Virginia, Col. T. T. Munford.
3d Virginia, Col. Thomas H. Owen.
4th Virginia, Col. Williams C. Wickham.
5th Virginia, Col. T. L. Rosser.

Jenkins' Brigade.

Brig. Gen. A. G. JENKINS.
Col. M. J. FERGUSON.

14th Virginia.
16th Virginia.
17th Virginia.
34th Virginia Battalion, Lieut. Col. V. A. Witcher.
36th Virginia Battalion.
Jackson's (Virginia) Battery, Capt. Thomas E. Jackson.

---

* Commanded his own and W. E. Jones' brigade.   † Serving with Ewell's corps.

Jones' Brigade.	*W. H. F. Lee's Brigade.*
Brig. Gen. WILLIAM E. JONES.	Col. J. R. CHAMBLISS, Jr.
6th Virginia, Maj. C. E. Flournoy.	2d North Carolina.
7th Virginia, Lieut. Col. Thomas Marshall.	9th Virginia, Col. R. L. T. Beale.
	10th Virginia, Col. J. Lucius Davis.
11th Virginia, Col. L. L. Lomax.	13th Virginia.

Stuart Horse Artillery.

Maj. R. F. BECKHAM.

Breathed's (Virginia) Battery, Capt. James Breathed.
Chew's (Virginia) Battery, Capt. R. P. Chew.
Griffin's (Maryland) Battery, Capt. W. H. Griffin.
Hart's (South Carolina) Battery, Capt. J. F. Hart.
McGregor's (Virginia) Battery, Capt. W. M. McGregor.
Moorman's (Virginia) Battery, Capt. M. N. Moorman.

IMBODEN'S COMMAND.

Brig. Gen. J. D. IMBODEN.

18th Virginia Cavalry, Col. George W. Imboden.
62d Virginia Infantry,* Col. George H. Smith.
Virginia Partisan Rangers, Capt. John H. McNeill.
Virginia Battery, Capt. J. H. McClanahan.

ARTILLERY.†

Brig. Gen. W. N. PENDLETON.

Notes

ABBREVIATIONS

ANMP	Antietam National Military Park, Sharpsburg, Md.
ANV	Army of Northern Virginia
BFM	B. F. Moore Collection, Cincinnati, Ohio
BU	Brown University Special Collection, Providence, R.I.
CHS	Connecticut Historical Society, Hartford
CSHS	Clear Spring Historical Society, Md.
CWM	College of William and Mary Special Collection, Williamsburg
DPL	Detroit Public Library Collection, Detroit, Mich.
DU	Duke University Special Collection, Durham, N.C.
EU	Emory University Special Collection, Atlanta, Ga.
FLE	Fletcher L. Elmore Jr. Collection, Louisville, Ky.
GC	Gettysburg College Special Collection, Gettysburg, Pa.
GNMP	Gettysburg National Military Park Collection, Gettysburg, Pa.
HS	Horse Soldier, Sam and Wes Small Collection, Gettysburg, Pa.
HWCHS	Hagerstown–Washington County Historical Society, Hagerstown, Md.
ISL	Indiana State Library, Indianapolis
JHK	John H. Krohn Jr. Collection, Wilmington, N.C.
JJF	J. J. Fraboni Collection, Myrtle Beach, S.C.
JLH	Jane L. Hershey Collection, Williamsport, Md.
KL	Dr. Ken Lawrence Collection, Orwell, Ohio
KMB	Kent Masterson Brown Collection, Lexington, Ky.
LC	Library of Congress, Washington, D.C.
LL	Lewis Leigh Jr. Collection, Leesburg, Va.
LSU	Louisiana State University Special Collection, Baton Rouge
MAG	Michael A. Gureasko, M.D., Collection, Cincinnati, Ohio
MBCPL	Martinsburg–Berkeley County Public Library, Martinsburg, W.Va.
MHS	Maine Historical Society Collection, Portland
MOC	Museum of the Confederacy, Richmond, Va.
MSS	Michael S. Saks Collection, Providence, R.I.
MSU	Michigan State University Special Collection, Lansing
NA	National Archives and Records Administration, Washington, D.C.
NCDAH	North Carolina Division of Archives and History, Raleigh

NYPL	New York Public Library
OR	U.S. War Department, *The War of the Rebellion: A Compilation of the Official Records of the Union and Confederate Armies*. 128 vols. Washington, D.C.: U.S. Government Printing Office, 1880–1901. *OR* citations take the following form: volume number: page number. Unless otherwise indicated, all references are to series I.
OS/MESDA	Old Salem/Salem Museum of Early Southern Decorative Arts, Winston-Salem, N.C.
PHMC	Pennsylvania Historical and Museum Commission, Harrisburg
RKI	Richard Keith Irish Collection, Marshall, Va.
RPL	Rochester Public Library Collection, N.Y.
TU	Tulane University Special Collection, New Orleans
UA	University of Alabama Special Collection, Tuscaloosa
UGA	University of Georgia Special Collection, Athens
UK	University of Kentucky Special Collection, Lexington
UM-MHC	University of Michigan, Michigan Historical Collection, Ann Arbor
UNC-SHC	University of North Carolina, Southern Historical Collection, Chapel Hill
USAMHI	U.S. Army Military History Institute Collection, Carlisle Barracks, Pa.
USC-SCL	University of South Carolina, South Caroliniana Library, Columbia
UVA	University of Virginia Special Collection, Charlottesville
VHS	Virginia Historical Society, Richmond
VMI	Virginia Military Institute Special Collection, Lexington
VSL	Virginia State Library Special Collection, Richmond
WAT	General William A. Tidwell Collection, Fairfax, Va.
WFCHS	Winchester–Frederick County Historical Society, Winchester, Va.
WFCHS-BR	Winchester–Frederick County Historical Society, Ben Ritter Collection, Winchester, Va.
WLU	Washington and Lee University Special Collection, Lexington, Va.
WMU	Western Michigan University Special Collection, Kalamazoo
WT	William Turner Collection, Lanham, Md.

PROLOGUE

1. Byrne and Weaver, *Haskell of Gettysburg*, 156; Owen, *In Camp and Battle*, 248–49; Edward Porter Alexander, *Fighting for the Confederacy*, 257–61; Porter, "The Confederate Soldier," 460.

2. Frederick M. Colston Memoir, 14, Campbell-Colston Papers, UNC-SHC.

3. George R. Stewart, *Pickett's Charge*, 263; *New York Times*, 6 July 1863 (quotation); Homer Baldwin to Father, 7 July 1863, GNMP. For the casualty figures of Pickett's Division, see Georg and Busey, *Nothing but Glory*, 226–31; *OR* 27(2):338–46; Krick, *Gettysburg Death Roster*, 3–18; and General Order No. 63, Medical Director's Office, 14 May 1863, Letters and Orders Issued and Received, NA.

4. Poindexter, "General Armistead's Portrait Presented," 147–51; Peters, "Lost Sword of General Richard B. Garnett," 27–30; Bright, "Pickett's Charge," 234; "Opposing Forces at Gettysburg"; *OR* 27(2):385–87.

5. Trimble, "Civil War Diary," 12; "Opposing Forces at Gettysburg," 439; George R. Stewart, *Pickett's Charge*, 263; *OR* 27(2):333–34. The figures quoted include the casualties for 1 July as well as 3 July.

6. George R. Stewart, *Pickett's Charge*, 264; "Col. J. K. Marshall," unknown newspaper, n.d., Scrapbook, Pettigrew Family Papers, P.C. 13. 25, NCDAH (Colonel Marshall was the grandson of Chief Justice John Marshall); Stubbs, *Duty, Honor, Valor*, 435–37; Maud Morrow Brown, *University Greys*, 46; Flowers, "Thirty-eighth Regiment," 693; Martin and Outlaw, "Eleventh Regiment," 590.

7. Trimble, "Civil War Diary," 12.

8. *OR* 27(1):377; *John Reed et al. v. Gettysburg Battlefield Mem. Ass'n.*, 235, GC.

9. *Richmond Enquirer*, 21 July 1863.

10. Emory M. Thomas, *Robert E. Lee*, 45, 225–26, 291. Lee's three sons were Colonel George Washington Custis Lee, age 31; Brigadier General William Henry Fitzhugh Lee, age 26; and Robert E. Lee Jr., age 20. Lee's daughters were Mary, age 28; Eleanor Agnes, age 22; and Mildred Childe, age 17.

11. Robert E. Lee to Mary Lee, 6 (pp. 427–29), 12 (p. 432), 19 (pp. 437–38), 24 April 1863 (pp. 439–40), and Robert E. Lee to Agnes Lee, 11 April 1863 (431–32), Dowdey and Manarin, *Wartime Papers*.

12. W. W. Blackford, *War Years with JEB Stuart*, 230; Sorrel, *Recollections*, 164.

13. Fremantle, *Diary*, 197–98.

14. Edward Porter Alexander, *Fighting for the Confederacy*, 265.

15. Shotwell, *Papers*, 2:23–24.

16. Morgan, *Reminiscences*, 167.

17. William R. Aylett to Brother, MSS.

18. Dooley, *Confederate Soldier*, 106–9; Walker, *Memorial*, 26–29, 425–27, 535–36; Kemp, *Alumni Directory*, 440; Charles Minor Blackford, *Letters*, 2:60.

19. *Philadelphia Weekly Times*, 26 March 1881, Gettysburg Clippings, GNMP.

20. Special Order, Medical Director's Office, 17 April 1863, Letters and Orders Issued and Received, NA; William H. Taylor, "Experiences as a Confederate Assistant Surgeon," 94, 117 (quotation).

21. Francis Milton Kennedy Diary, 3 July 1863, Kennedy Papers, UNC-SHC.

22. Fremantle, *Diary*, 212.

23. Ibid.; Frederick M. Colston Memoir, 13, Campbell-Colston Papers, UNC-SHC.

24. *OR* 27(2):614–15 (quotation), 625; Westwood A. Todd Memoir, 132, Todd Papers, UNC-SHC; Jenkins Journal, 64, GNMP.

25. Fleming, *Memoir*, 79–80.

26. Fremantle, *Diary*, 214.

27. Shotwell, *Papers*, 2:24–25. See also Shotwell, "Virginia and North Carolina in the Battle of Gettysburg," 95.

28. Shotwell, *Papers*, 2:25.

29. Edmund Berkeley to John W. Daniel, 26 September 18[?], Daniel Papers, box 23, UVA.

30. Bright, "Pickett's Charge," 234.

31. Ibid. (quotation); Erasmus Williams, "A Private's Experience in the 14th Virginia Infantry," Daniel Papers, box 23, UVA.

32. Edward Porter Alexander, *Fighting for the Confederacy*, 266; Fremantle, *Diary*, 215 (quotation).

33. *OR* 27(1):993.

34. Edward Porter Alexander, *Fighting for the Confederacy*, 266.

35. *OR* 27(2):352-53, 697-98, 724-25, 752, 756.

CHAPTER ONE

1. Goff, *Confederate Supply*, 67-68; Trimble, "Civil War Diary," 8; Robert E. Lee to Jefferson Davis, 16 April 1863, *OR* 25(2):724-25.

2. Goff, *Confederate Supply*, 79-80; James Seddon to William M. Wadley, 25 March 1863, *OR* IV, 2:457.

3. Circular, 23 March 1863, Letters and Orders Issued and Received, NA.

4. Robert E. Lee to James Longstreet, 18 February 1863, *OR* 25(2):632-33; Sorrel, *Recollections*, 144. The number of horses and mules in Lee's army can only be approximated. The cavalry had nearly 11,000 horses, the artillery almost 6,000 horses and mules, and the officers more than 1,000 mounts. If there were 3,000 wagons in Lee's trains—and that figure would appear to be fairly accurate in early June 1863—then anywhere from 12,000 to 18,000 horses and mules were pulling them.

5. Archer Jones, "Gettysburg Decision," 331.

6. Jefferson Davis to Robert E. Lee, 10 March 1863, *OR* 51(2):683; Lee to J. E. B. Stuart, 12 March 1863, *OR* 25(2):664; Lee to Davis, 20 April 1863, *OR* 25(2):740-41; Lee to Davis, 4 April 1863, *OR* 25(2):702-3; Samuel Cooper to Lee, 14 April 1863, *OR* 25(2):720; Lee to Davis, 16 April 1863, *OR* 25(2):724-25; Lee to Cooper, 16 April 1863, *OR* 25(2):725-26.

7. *OR* 25(1):794-805.

8. Longstreet, "Lee in Pennsylvania," 415-16, and *Manassas to Appomattox*, 326-28; Archer Jones, "Gettysburg Decision," 37-38; Robert E. Lee to James Seddon and endorsement of Jefferson Davis, 10 May 1863, *OR* 25(2):790; Davis, *Jefferson Davis*, 499, 506; Lee to Jefferson, 11 May 1863, *OR* 25(2):791-92; John B. Jones, *Diary*, 209-10.

9. William Alexander Gordon Memoirs, 135-36, Gordon Papers, WLU; Fremantle, *Diary*, 178; Robert E. Lee to James Longstreet, 18 February 1863, *OR* 25(2):632; Freeman, "Confederate Congress," 12-17.

10. John B. Jones, *Diary*, 222; Fremantle, *Diary*, 180; Rozier, *Granite Farm Letters*, 115; William S. White, "Diary," 198. Union quartermasters also knew that it was the perfect time of year for harvesting animal forage and for using the grazing grasses in southern Pennsylvania. The assistant quartermaster general of the U.S. Army acknowledged that the horses and mules in the Army of the Potomac were also in des-

perate shape in central Virginia due to the serious lack of forage and grazing grasses. T. Rue to D. H. Rucker, 28 December 1868, Records of the Quartermaster General, Consolidated Correspondence File, NA.

11. Fremantle, *Diary*, 180; Charles Minor Blackford, *Letters*, 194–95.

12. Gordon, *Reminiscences*, 138–39; Robert E. Lee to Samuel Jones, 1 June 1863, *OR* 25(2):846–47; Chapman, *Bright and Gloomy Days*, 63.

13. Robert E. Lee to Samuel Jones and to James Seddon, 1 June 1863, *OR* 25(2): 846–47.

14. Haskell, *Memoirs*, 54; Luther W. Hopkins, *From Bull Run to Appomattox*, 110.

15. Robert E. Lee to Jefferson Davis, 10 June 1863, *OR* 27(3):880–82.

16. Oeffinger, *A Soldier's General*, 185; Sorrel, *Recollections*, 150; Henry S. Figures to Ma, KMB; Jedediah Hotchkiss to Sara, 25, 28 June 1863, Hotchkiss Papers, LC; Jomini, *Art of War*, 141–46; Clausewitz, *On War*, 330–40.

17. Robert E. Lee to Jefferson Davis, 4 September 1862, *OR* 19(2):591–92; Lee to Davis, 5 September 1862, ibid., 593–94; Lee to Davis, 7 September 1862, ibid., 596–97; Lee to Davis, 9 September 1862, ibid., 602–3; Lee to Davis, 12 September 1862, ibid., 604–5. Lee informed Davis not only that his primary purpose for the invasion of Maryland in September 1862 was to forage for his army, but also that he intended to advance to Hagerstown, Maryland, and then to Chambersburg, Pennsylvania, to accomplish his foraging mission.

18. Quartermaster Department, Records of Quartermaster Stores Issued to and Condemned in Units of the ANV, NA; Robert E. Lee to Jefferson Davis, 23 June 1863, *OR* 27(2):297–98; Lafayette Guild to Hunter McGuire, 27 June 1863, Records of Medical Department, ANV, Letters Sent, NA.

19. Robert E. Lee to Jefferson Davis, 7 June 1863, *OR* 27(2):293–94; Lee to James A. Seddon, 8 June 1863, *OR* 27(3):868–69. Lee's 8 June letter to Secretary of War Seddon illustrates an absence of a "meeting of the minds" between Lee and his president and secretary of war over details. In that letter Lee argues the merits of his operation even though his army was already five days into it. This has caused one distinguished historian to contend that Lee intentionally withheld information from Davis and Seddon to forestall any objections to his plan. Archer Jones, "Gettysburg Decision" and "Gettysburg Decision Reassessed."

20. Robert E. Lee to Samuel Cooper, 4 June 1863, *OR* 27(3):858–59; Lafayette Guild to Samuel P. Moore, 6 June 1863, *OR* 27(3):863–64.

21. Robert E. Lee to John D. Imboden, 7 June 1863, *OR* 27(3):865.

22. *OR* 27(2):439–40; James E. Green Diary, 9, Green Papers, NCDAH.

23. *OR* 27(2):439–42; Robert E. Lee to Jefferson Davis, 15 June 1863, in Freeman and McWhiney, *Lee's Dispatches*, 102.

24. *OR* 27(2):443–44.

25. *OR* 27(2):306; Robert E. Lee to A. P. Hill, 16 June 1863, *OR* 27(3):896.

26. Robert E. Lee to Samuel Cooper, 15 June 1863, *OR* 27(3):890.

27. *OR* 27(2):305–7; Robert E. Lee to Richard S. Ewell, 19 June 1863, *OR* 27(3):905; Lee to J. E. B. Stuart, 22 June 1863, *OR* 27(3):913.

28. *OR* 27(2):692-93.

29. *OR* 27(2):306-7, 316-17. Lee accompanied Longstreet throughout the Gettysburg campaign. *OR* 27(1):200-201.

30. *OR* 27(2):307, 316-17.

31. *Greencastle Echo-Pilot*, 23 March 1905. "Army and base [of operations]," wrote Clausewitz, "must be conceived as a single whole . . . the lines of communication link the army to its base, and must be considered as its arteries." They are part of the "unity of an army and its operational base." Clausewitz, *On War*, 341, 345.

32. *OR* 27(2):443-44; Robert E. Lee to Richard S. Ewell, 28 June 1863, *OR* 27(3): 943-44; Lee to John D. Imboden, 1 July 1863, *OR* 27(3):947-48. Whether or not Lee ordered the concentration of 27 or 28 June remains a matter of contention. In their reports, both Lee and Longstreet referred to 28 June as the date intelligence was received that the enemy was at Frederick and the order for a concentration was issued. An advance against Harrisburg, Lee claimed, was arrested by the news. *OR* 27(2):307, 316. Prominent historians have accepted this. Coddington, *Gettysburg Campaign*, 189; Sears, *Gettysburg*, 132-33. The best evidence, of course, is the contemporaneous letter of Lee's to Ewell, dated 28 June, which states that the concentration was ordered "last night." A spy named Harrison undoubtedly reported his findings to Lee and Longstreet on 28 June, but Lee's letter that day indicates that he had already determined to concentrate his army and not advance deeper into Pennsylvania. *OR* 27(3):943-44.

33. *OR* 27(2):444, 468, 504, 552.

34. *OR* 27(1):63, 27(2):694-97, 27(3):378-80, 381-82; W. W. Blackford, *War Years with JEB Stuart*, 224-25.

35. *OR* 27(3):205, 211-19, 811-14. New Jersey sent 1 regiment; New York sent 19 regiments and 1 artillery battery; and Pennsylvania sent 8 regiments of six months' militia, 22 regiments of three months' militia, 5 artillery batteries, 1 battalion of six months' cavalry, and 1 battalion of three months' cavalry. Billett, "Department of the Susquehanna," 1-14. The Department of West Virginia was created on 24 June 1863 by severing from the Middle Department the region west of Hancock, Maryland. General Kelley was named commander of the new department on the same day. *OR* 27(3): 299.

36. *OR* 27(2):182-83, 27(3):445; Major General William H. French coined the phrase "the debris of Winchester." *OR* 27(1):488.

37. *OR* 27(1):488-89, 27(2):751-52. General Stuart referred to the pass at Raven Rock as "Eyler's Gap." *OR* 27(2):700.

38. *OR* 27(2):308, 318. In both of his post-Gettysburg reports, Lee wrote: "It had not been intended to deliver a general battle so far from our base unless attacked."

39. Polley, *Hood's Texas Brigade*, 149.

40. Robert E. Lee to John D. Imboden, 1 July 1863, *OR* 27(3):947-48, 51(2):731.

41. *OR* 27(2):317, 358, 391; Robert E. Lee to John D. Imboden, 1 July 1863, *OR* 27(3): 947-48.

42. Robert E. Lee to Richard S. Ewell, 17 June 1863, *OR* 27(3):900-901.

43. Robert E. Lee to John D. Imboden, 20 June 1863, *OR* 27(3):905-6; Frank M. Imboden Diary, 7-8, Imboden Family Papers, UVA; Baker, "Diary and Recollections,"

97. Imboden and Baker wrote of the use of large numbers of slaves to forage. Otto Nesbitt and Philip Schaff both observed large numbers of African Americans accompanying Imboden's foragers. Nesbitt Diary, 17, CSHS; Schaff, "Gettysburg Week," 168–69. Rachel Bowman of Chambersburg noted the "darkies" accompanying Lee's troops. Mohr, *Cormany Diaries*, 328–41.

44. *OR* 27(3):912–13; Hassler, *The General to His Lady*, 252.

45. Robert E. Lee to Richard S. Ewell, 22 June 1863, *OR* 27(3):914.

46. Charles C. Blacknall to G. W. Blacknall, 18, 23 June 1863, Oscar W. Blacknall Papers, NCDAH.

47. Hoke, *Great Invasion*, 134; Circular, 23 March 1863, Letters and Orders Issued and Received, NA; Samuel Pickens Diary, 14 June 1863, Pickens Papers, UA.

48. Robert E. Lee to Jefferson Davis, 23 June 1863, *OR* 27(2):297–98.

49. *OR* 27(2):443.

50. Hoke, *Great Invasion*, 139.

51. Warner, Beers and Co., *Franklin County*, 369, 657; Rev. Dr. Henry Reeves to My Dear Lizzie, KMB.

52. Nye, *Here Come the Rebels*, 270, quoting Thaddeus Stevens Papers, vol. 2, LC; Benjamin W. Justice to My Precious, Sweetie Darling Wife, 12 August 1863, Justice Papers, EU. Other properties were burned. Buildings in Wrightsville, Pa., for instance, accidentally caught fire after Union militia torched the bridge over the Susquehanna River. *OR* 27(2):466–67.

53. *OR* 27(2):443; Fremantle, *Diary*, 186; Charles Edward Lippitt Diary, 7, 9, Lippitt Papers, UNC-SHC; Samuel Pickens Diary, 22 June 1863, Pickens Papers, UA.

54. Laura Lee Diary, 126–27, Lee Papers, CWM; Welch, *Letters to His Wife*, 57–58; see also Robert Thurston Hubbard Jr. Reminiscences, 80, Hubbard Papers, UVA. For similar statements, see David Wyatt Aiken to Wife, 28 June 1863, Aiken Papers, folder 7, USC-SCL; James B. Clifton Diary, 29 June–1 July 1863, Clifton Papers, NCDAH; Alexander McNeill to Wife, June 28, 1863, McNeill Papers, SLC-USC; Westwood A. Todd Memoirs, 125–26, Todd Papers, UNC-SHC; J. Warren Jackson to R. Stark Jackson, 20 July 1863, Boyd Papers, LSU; and J. S. Hard to Emma, 28 June 1863, Hard Papers, JHK.

55. Bradley T. Johnson to James Seddon, 30 June 1863, *OR* 51(2):731.

56. Laura Lee Diary, 126–27, Lee Papers, CWM; Chase Diary, 7, WFCHS; *OR* 27(2):443, 550, 27(3):546, 905–6; Fremantle, *Diary*, 186; Hassler, *The General to His Lady*, 254; Otho Nesbitt Diary, 17, CSHS; Chapman, *Bright and Gloomy Days*, 70; Welch, *Letters to His Wife*, 57–58; Samuel Pickens Diary, 22 June 1863, Pickens Papers, UA; Charles Edward Lippitt Diary, 7, 9, Lippitt Papers, UNC-SHC; James B. Clifton Diary, 29 June–1 July 1863, Clifton Papers, NCDAH; Alexander McNeill to Wife, 28 June 1863, McNeill Papers, USC-SCL; Westwood A. Todd Memoirs, 125–26, Todd Papers, UNC-SHC; Tucker, "Diary," 24; J. S. Hard to Emma, 28 June 1863, Hard Papers, JHK; William O. Johnson, "49th Virginia Infantry at Gettysburg," Daniel Papers, box 23, UVA. According to Private G. W. Nichols of the Sixty-first Georgia, "About twenty-six thousand head of cattle and twenty-two thousand head of sheep" were herded up the Shenandoah Valley in the wake of Lee's retreat from Penn-

sylvania to join the army by a route through Luray and Thornton Gaps. Large herds of cattle and sheep also accompanied Lee's troops back through Virginia east of the Blue Ridge Mountains. General John Sedgwick wrote that the Army of the Potomac "captured twelve thousand head of cattle and eight thousand head of sheep that [Lee] had driven from Pennsylvania." Sizable numbers of cattle and sheep were consumed by the troops while in Pennsylvania, and on 7 July alone some 700 cattle and 100 sheep were lost in the swollen Potomac River during the crossing. Undoubtedly more were lost on the previous and ensuing days while crossing the river. G. W. Nichols, *A Soldier's Story*, 123; Stoeckel and Battelle, *Correspondence of John Sedgwick*, 2:138; *Philadelphia Inquirer*, 11 July 1863.

57. Report of Court of Inquiry of Major James C. Bryan, Testimony of Bryan, 29 August 1863, Compiled Service Records, NA.

58. Chapman, *Bright and Gloomy Days*, 70.

59. Edward Owen Diary, 28 June 1863, CSA "Core Collection": Regiments and Soldiers, MOC; Alexander McNeill to Wife, 28 June 1863, McNeill Papers, USC-SCL; Paul Turner Vaughan Diary, 28 June 1863, Vaughan Papers, UA; Fremantle, *Diary*, 192. See also Parker, *Touched by Fire*, 61–62, and David Wyatt Aiken to Wife, 28 June 1863, Aiken Papers, folder 7, USC-SCL.

60. Quartermaster Records, Articles Purchased, Impressed and Confiscated, Longstreet's Corps, Pickett's Division, Hood's Division, Law's Brigade, Semmes's Brigade, Benning's Brigade, Barksdale's Brigade, Anderson's Brigade, Texas Brigade, Cabell's Artillery Battalion, First Corps Reserve Artillery Battalion, ANV Collection, MOC.

61. Quartermaster Records, Articles Purchased, Impressed and Confiscated, Longstreet's Corps, ANV Collection, MOC; Krick, *Staff Officers*, 192.

62. Quartermaster Records, Articles Purchased, Impressed and Confiscated, Pickett's Division, ANV Collection, MOC; Krick, *Staff Officers*, 261; Jimmie Booker to Cousin, 30 June 1863, Booker Family Papers, UVA.

63. Quartermaster Records, Articles Purchased, Impressed and Confiscated, Hood's Division and First Corps Reserve Artillery, ANV Collection, MOC; Krick, *Staff Officers*, 137.

64. Quartermaster Records, Articles Purchased, Impressed and Confiscated, Semmes's Brigade, Benning's Brigade, Barksdale's Brigade, Anderson's Brigade, Law's Brigade, Texas Brigade, Cabell's Artillery Battalion, ANV Collection, MOC.

65. Quartermaster Records, Statements of Property Impressed, 26, 27 June 1863, and Statement of Forage, ANV Collection, MOC.

66. Laura Lee Diary, Lee Papers 126, CWM; *OR* 51(2):732–33; Hassler, *The General to His Lady*, 254. Diaries and letters of eyewitnesses, as well as the few quartermaster records on persons hired for service that still exist, reveal that large numbers of slaves were attached to the quartermaster service and assisted in the foraging effort. Frank M. Imboden Diary, 7–8, Imboden Family Papers, UVA; Baker, "Diary and Recollections," 97; Otho Nesbitt Diary, 17, CSHS; Schaff, "Gettysburg Week," 168–69; Mohr, *Cormany Diaries*, 329–30; *Mercersburg Journal*, 17 July 1863; Rev. Dr. Henry Reeves to My Dear Lizzie, KMB; Frank Moore, *Rebellion Record*, 7:325; Hoke, *Great Invasion*, 108; McKim, *Recollections*, 189–90; Rozier, *Granite Farm Letters*, 119; Shotwell, *Papers*, 2:

35; Report of Persons and Articles Employed and Hired at Fairfield and Blakely's Mill during the Month of June 1862 by R. L. Christian, Capt. and A. Q., and Report of Persons and Articles Employed and Hired by First Va. Arty. during the Month of July 1863 by R. L. Christian, Capt. and A.Q., R. L. Christian and First Regiment Virginia Artillery Papers, box 5, folder 206, Hill Collection, MOC.

67. Mohr, *Cormany Diaries*, 329–30; Rev. Dr. Henry Reeves to My Dear Lizzie, KMB; Schaff, "Gettysburg Week," 168–70; Hoke, *Great Invasion*, 108. Reeves provided evidence that the young son of a woman with whom he was acquainted was among those African Americans seized by the Confederates.

68. Nye, *Here Come the Rebels*, 144–46; Sears, *Gettysburg*, 111–12; Coddington, *Gettysburg Campaign*, 161; Ayers, *In the Presence of Mine Enemies*, 390–415. Ayers provides an eloquent discussion of Lee's invasion of Pennsylvania and its effects on the people of Franklin County. Ted Alexander, "Regular Slave Hunt."

69. Charles C. Blacknall to G. W. Blacknall, 18 June 1863, Oscar W. Blacknall Papers, NCDAH; William Christian to Wife, 28 June 1863, printed in Frank Moore, *Rebellion Record*, 7:325. The *Rebellion Record* stated that the letter had been "found on the Gettysburg battlefield."

70. Rev. Dr. Henry Reeves to My Dear Lizzie, KMB; *OR* 51(2):732–33.

71. Williamson, *Mosby's Rangers*, 80; *Mercersburg Journal*, 17 July 1863; *OR* II, 6: 704–5, 7:1145. The order in the last citation refers to "negroes confined at Salisbury [Prison]." It does not state that those confined were ever "free" or that they were even captured in Pennsylvania. An editor's note at the bottom of the page reads: "Brought from Pennsylvania by the C.S. Army." How the editor knew that to be true is unknown.

72. Vermilyea, "Effect of the Confederate Invasion"; Rev. Dr. Henry Reeves to My Dear Lizzie, KMB.

73. Quartermaster Records, Articles Purchased, Impressed and Confiscated, Longstreet's Corps, Hood's Division, Pickett's Division, McLaws's Division, First Corps Reserve Artillery Battalion, Cabell's Artillery Battalion, Semmes's Brigade, Law's Brigade, Benning's Brigade, Barksdale's Brigade, Anderson's Brigade, Texas Brigade, ANV Collection, MOC; Apperson, *Repairing the "March of Mars,"* 473; Casler, *Four Years*, 168.

74. Quartermaster Records, Articles Purchased, Impressed and Confiscated, Longstreet's Corps, Hood's Division, Pickett's Division, McLaws's Division, First Corps Reserve Artillery Battalion, Cabell's Artillery Battalion, Semmes's Brigade, Law's Brigade, Benning's Brigade, Barksdale's Brigade, Anderson's Brigade, Texas Brigade, ANV Collection, MOC; Tucker, "Diary," 24.

75. *OR* 27(1):65, 27(3):371–72, 377.

76. Quartermaster Records, Articles Purchased, Impressed and Confiscated, Longstreet's Corps, Hood's Division, Pickett's Division, McLaws's Division, Cabell's Artillery Battalion, First Corps Reserve Artillery Battalion, Semmes's Brigade, Law's Brigade, Benning's Brigade, Barksdale's Brigade, Anderson's Brigade, Texas Brigade, ANV Collection, MOC. Ewell's reserve train was fourteen miles long. Longstreet, "Lee in Pennsylvania," 440; Hoke, *Great Invasion*, 228; Polley, *Hood's Texas Brigade*, 150 (Confederates spoke of Ewell's trains totaling forty miles in length); Chapman, *Bright and*

Gloomy Days, 70–71; Bradwell, *Under the Southern Cross*, 132; Jedediah Hotchkiss to My Darling, 14 July 1863, Hotchkiss Papers, LC. Jacob Hoke of Chambersburg recalled Ewell's reserve train as fourteen miles long and the division trains of Ewell's Corps as twenty-five miles long. Hoke, *Great Invasion*, 216. Those were accurate assessments.

77. William S. White, "Diary," 198.

78. Samuel Pickens Diary, 22–28 June 1863, Pickens Papers, UA; Robert A. Moore, *A Life for the Confederacy*, 152; Polley, *Hood's Texas Brigade*, 148.

79. Everson and Simpson, *Far, Far from Home*, 262.

80. *OR* 27(2):466–67; Herman W. Haupt to Henry W. Halleck, 3 July 1863, and Haupt to Montgomery C. Meigs, 9 July 1863, Records of the Quartermaster General, Consolidated Correspondence File, NA; *OR* 51(2):729; Haupt, *Reminiscences*, 206, 236, 239–40; Turner, *Victory Rode the Rails*, 278–79.

81. *OR* 27(2):606–7. Heth reported that he sent Pettigrew's Brigade forward to Gettysburg to "search the town for army supplies (shoes especially) and return the same day." *OR* 27(2):637; Leinbach, "Scenes at the Battle of Gettysburg," 75–76, OS/MESDA.

82. Miller Memoir, 3 July 1863, KMB; Robert E. Lee to John D. Imboden, 1 July 1863, *OR* 27(3):947–48, 51(2):732–33; Hassler, *The General to His Lady*, 253–54.

83. *OR* 27(2):317, 27(1):114–16.

84. *OR* 27(2):318. The same statement appears in Lee's 31 July 1863 report. *OR* 27(2):308.

85. Recently discovered by Wes and Sam Small of Gettysburg, the "The Report of Ordnance Stores on Hand" reveals that the following ordnance was all that was available in the reserve train: "12 pdr. Gun (Napoleon)," 528 rounds of shell, 1,152 rounds of case, 168 rounds of shot, and 58 rounds of canister; "10 pdr Parrott," 448 rounds of shell, 512 rounds of case, and 36 rounds of canister; "20 pdr Parrott," 152 rounds of shell; "3 inch Rifle," 32 rounds of shell; "12 pdr. Howitzer," 230 rounds of shell, 210 rounds of case, and 40 rounds of canister; "24 pdr. Howitzer," 48 rounds of shell and 16 rounds of canister; "Whitworth," 70 rounds of shot (72 charges); and "12 pdr. Blakeley," 12 rounds of shell and 96 rounds of case. The report listed only 70,250 musket caps, 22,000 rounds of .54 caliber ammunition, and 40,000 rounds of .69 caliber ammunition on hand. There were also 640 artillery fuses, 1,432 fuse igniters, and 2,720 artillery friction primers, along with drills, sledgehammers, turpentine, and two barrels of cannon powder. "Report of Ordnance Stores on Hand," HS.

86. Young, *Last Order of the Lost Cause*, 187–88; *OR* 27(2):358, 504.

87. *OR* 27(2):358–59, 446–47.

88. *OR* 27(2):320–21, 359–60, 447–48, 608.

89. *OR* 27(2):320–21, 352–53, 359–60, 608, 697–98.

90. *OR* 27(2):338–46; Edward Perry Vollum to Montgomery C. Meigs, 7 August 1863, Records of the Quartermaster General, Consolidated Correspondence File, NA.

CHAPTER TWO

1. Marbaker, *Eleventh New Jersey Volunteers*, 109–10 (long quotation); Robert Goldthwaite Carter, *Four Brothers in Blue*, 322; Skelly, *A Boy's Experiences*, 21.

2. *Lancaster Daily Express*, 10 July 1863.

3. Many of Lee's commanders wrote of the need for shoes and clothes and that many of the men were barefoot. *OR* 27(2):443, 466, 550–51, 637; Gordon, *Reminiscences*, 142; Michael W. Taylor, *To Drive the Enemy*, 288. Soldiers wrote of or recalled their destitute condition, their scant rations, and their lack of shoes and clothes. Edward E. Moore, *Story of a Cannoneer*, 193; Casler, *Four Years*, 173; Riley, *Grandfather's Journal*, 147; Chapman, *Bright and Gloomy Days*, 66; Shotwell, *Papers*, 1:487–96. Probably the best description of a Confederate soldier on the eve of the retreat was left by William Andrew Fletcher of the Fifth Texas on the night of 3 July. Fletcher, *Rebel Private*, 65. That many of Lee's men were filthy and crawling with lice has been well documented. Frederick M. Colston Memoir, 8, Campbell-Colston Papers, UNC-SHC; Riley, *Grandfather's Journal*, 147–48; Mohr, *Cormany Diaries*, 336, 339; Hoke, *Great Invasion*, 208; West, *A Texan in Search of a Fight*, 99. Sickness, particularly diarrhea, plagued Lee's troops during the invasion of Pennsylvania. Samuel Pickens Diary, 14 June 1863, Pickens Papers, UA. Sickness was widespread in the army. Of the thirteen soldiers who died at Mount Jackson Hospital, Virginia, in July 1863 after seeing action in Gettysburg, twelve succumbed to disease. Of those, three died of diarrhea and nine of typhoid fever. Report of Sick and Wounded, July 1863, Records of Hospitals in Virginia, Mount Jackson, NA. At the General Hospital in Staunton during July, nearly 8,500 of Lee's sick and wounded from the Pennsylvania campaign were hospitalized. Of that number, there were almost 3,000 cases of diarrhea, dysentery, and debilitus and 300 cases of typhoid fever. Report of Sick and Wounded, July 1863, Records of Hospitals in Virginia, Staunton, NA. "In passing over the field and woods where they encamped," wrote William Heyser of Chambersburg on 2 July, "there is already a great stench." Heyser, "Diary."

4. *OR* 27(2):391–92, 396, 400, 406, 411, 423; Bachelder, *Battle of Gettysburg*, 646, 648, 653.

5. *OR* 27(2):369–70; Bachelder, *Battle of Gettysburg*, 653–54.

6. *OR* 27(2):376, 380–81, 384–85, 389, 430, 615, 625, 633; Bachelder, *Battle of Gettysburg*, 655–56.

7. *OR* 27(2):556–57, 580, 582, 587–88, 604, 663–64, 668–69, 676. With the wounding of General Pender, the command of his division was given to Brigadier General James H. Lane. Lane had led Pender's Division on the afternoon of 2 July but was replaced by General Trimble the next day. After Trimble was wounded, Lane, once again, became commander of Pender's Division. The command of Lane's Brigade was given to Colonel C. M. Avery. For clarity and consistency, the division is referred to herein as Pender's Division. *OR* 27(2):665–67.

8. *OR* 27(2):481, 485.

9. *OR* 27(2):568–69, 572–74, 577, 699.

10. *OR* 27(1):380, 485, 536, 593, 608, 613, 618, 626, 663, 665, 674, 678.

11. *OR* 27(1):238–40, 262–63, 369–77.

12. *OR* 27(1):266, 290, 663, 704–5, 730–31, 758–61.

13. *OR* 27(1):187; Edward Perry Vollum to Montgomery C. Meigs, 17 August 1863, and Otto Louis Hein to Meigs, 11 September 1863, Records of the Quartermaster General, Consolidated Correspondence File, NA.

14. *OR* 27(1):72, 27(3):462, 465, 467, 471–72, 520.

15. *OR* 27(1):66–72, 27(3):520–21, 584, 604; Coburn Diary, 2 July 1863, Archives Collection, USAMHI; Tilney, *My Life in the Army*, 47.

16. *OR* 27(1):970, 993–94, 27(3):604; T. Rue to Daniel Henry Rucker, 28 December 1868, Records of the Quartermaster General, Consolidated Correspondence File, NA. The assistant quartermaster general of the U.S. Army acknowledged that the Army of the Potomac was forced to seize forage and stores from civilians to keep its horses and mules alive in Pennsylvania.

17. War Department, *Regulations*, §§ 713–18. There were somewhat more than fifty ambulances in each division of the Army of the Potomac. Lee's divisions, although fewer in number than their opponents', each contained more men than an average Union division. Lee's ambulances were equal to or greater in number in each division than in the divisions of the Army of the Potomac. Livermore, *Days and Events*, 239–40. One reason there were often delays in moving large bodies of troops into position to attack an enemy was the establishment by the chief quartermaster of the logistical support systems required to respond to the troops' medical and surgical needs as well as their needs for nourishment and equipment once the troops were committed to combat. For evidence that most of the trains in Lee's army were mule drawn, see Quartermaster Records, Certificates of Property Given to Jacob Deardorff, Henry Deardorff, and John A. Scholl, ANV Collection, MOC, and Consolidated Report of Means of Transportation, Pettigrew's Brigade, 12 June 1863, Pettigrew Family Papers, P.C. 13–17, 93, NCDAH. The foregoing documents illustrate that the brigade trains of Scales and Pettigrew were mostly mule driven.

18. Quartermaster Records, Certificates of Purchased Property Given to Jacob Deardorff, Henry Deardorff, and John A. Scholl, ANV Collection, MOC.

19. Quartermaster Records, Articles Purchased, Impressed and Confiscated, Longstreet's Corps, Hood's Division, Pickett's Division, McLaws's Division, First Corps Reserve Artillery Battalion, Cabell's Artillery Battalion, Semmes's Brigade, Law's Brigade, Benning's Brigade, Barksdale's Brigade, Anderson's Brigade, Texas Brigade, ANV Collection, MOC.

20. Damage Claim Applications, PHMC. Kathy Georg Harris, Senior Historian, GNMP, compiled all of the damage claims for Adams County for me on 15 January 2003.

21. Darius N. Couch to George G. Meade, 3 July 1863, and Lorenzo Thomas to Edwin M. Stanton, 3 July 1863, *OR* 27(3):501, 509, 51(2):732–33; Krepps, "Regular Cavalry at Gettysburg."

22. Soldiers who observed Ewell's reserve and division trains on 4 July agreed that they were, altogether, forty miles long when stretched out on the road. Jedediah Hotchkiss to My Darling, 14 July 1863, Hotchkiss Papers, LC; Chapman, *Bright and Gloomy Days*, 70–71; Bradwell, *Under the Southern Cross*, 132. If that was so, the reserve train had to have been at least twenty miles long by the fourth, as the trains of Ewell's divisions were, altogether, about twenty miles long. Polley, *Hood's Texas Brigade*, 150; Neese, *Three Years*, 189; Casler, *Four Years*, 168; Hoke, *Reminiscences*, 95.

23. Hoke, *Reminiscences*, 95; Polley, *Hood's Texas Brigade*, 150; Quartermaster Rec-

ords, Articles Purchased, Impressed and Confiscated, Longstreet's Corps, Hood's Division, Pickett's Division, McLaws's Division, First Corps Reserve Artillery Battalion, Semmes's Brigade, Law's Brigade, Benning's Brigade, Barksdale's Brigade, Anderson's Brigade, Texas Brigade, ANV Collection, MOC; *OR* 27(3):546; Vaughan, "Battle of Fairfield, Pa."

24. Hoke, *Great Invasion*, 215–16. Army regulations contemplated African American slaves driving, loading, and unloading the trains. War Department, *Regulations*, §§ 754, 756. Major Hotchkiss, Captain Bahnson, and Private Isaac Gordon Bradwell of the Thirty-first Georgia recalled that the trains of Ewell's Corps were forty miles long and contained more than 4,000 wagons. Jedediah Hotchkiss to My Darling, 14 July 1863, Hotchkiss Papers, LC; Chapman, *Bright and Gloomy Days*, 70–71; Bradwell, *Under the Southern Cross*, 132. General Imboden claimed that the trains of Longstreet's and Hill's Corps and the cavalry division were seventeen miles long. Imboden, "Confederate Retreat," 423. The report of persons hired by the quartermaster service for the First Virginia Artillery may be one of the few such records in existence. Virtually all of the wagoners and laborers in the First Virginia Artillery were African Americans. Most were slaves; some were free blacks. Report of Persons and Articles Employed and Hired at Fairfield and Blakey's Mill during the Month of June 1862 by R. L. Christian, Capt. and A.Q., and Report of Persons and Articles Employed and Hired by First Va. Arty. during the Month of July 1863 by R. L. Christian, Capt. and A.Q., R. L. Christian and First Regiment Virginia Artillery Papers, box 5, folder 206, Hill Collection, MOC. Christian's report illustrates that quartermasters obtained the slaves by means of the 26 March 1863 Impressment Act; most, though, had been brought into the army months before by lease arrangements between their owners and the Quartermaster Department. Freeman, "Confederate Congress," 10–17. Of course, a myriad of letters, diaries, reports, and memoirs of soldiers and civilians discuss the African Americans in the wagon trains. Frank M. Imboden Diary, 7–8, Imboden Family Papers, UVA; Baker, "Diary and Recollections," 97; Otho Nesbitt Diary, 17, CSHS; Schaff, "Gettysburg Week," 168–69; Mohr, *Cormany Diaries*, 328–41; Jedediah Hotchkiss to My Darling, 14 July 1863, Hotchkiss Papers, LC; Edward E. Moore, *Story of a Cannoneer*, 203; McKim, *Recollections*, 189–90; Rozier, *Granite Farm Letters*, 119; Shotwell, *Papers*, 2: 35; Hoke, *Reminiscences*, 89; Beach, *First New York (Lincoln) Cavalry*, 264; Chamberlaine, *Memoirs*, 73; Report of Court of Inquiry of Major James C. Bryan, Testimony of Bryan, 29 August 1863, Compiled Service Records, NA. Bryan's testimony illustrates that most of the wagoners and laborers in the trains of Rodes's Division were slaves.

25. Fremantle, *Diary*, 186. Private Smith wrote home that "there are twenty-five or thirty [African Americans] in the regiment"; John Taylor Smith to Narcissa Heath, 8 March 1863, Smith-Johnson Family Collection, CSA "Core Collection": Soldiers Letters, MOC; Pettijohn, *Gettysburg and Libby Prison*, 6–7. See also William S. White, "Diary," 213; R. N. Martin to My Dear Aunt and Cousin, HS; and Caffey, *Battlefields of the South*, 278. Caffey, one of Lee's soldiers, wrote that in 1862 "in our whole army there must be at least 30,000 colored servants who do nothing but cook and wash."

26. Chamberlaine, *Memoirs*, 73.

27. Edward Porter Alexander, "Artillery Fighting at Gettysburg," 360; *OR* 51(2): 732–33.

28. War Department, *Regulations*, §§ 713–18; Rozier, *Granite Farm Letters*, 116; George Phifer Erwin to Father, 3 July 1863, Erwin Papers, UNC-SHC.

29. Report of Sick and Wounded, July 1863, Records of Hospitals in Virginia, Staunton, NA. According to the report, nearly 4,000 sick Confederates had been returned to Staunton. Although not recorded, probably 1,000 sick men were left in Gettysburg and elsewhere in Pennsylvania.

30. Duncan, *Medical Department*, 256; Campbell, "Sights at Gettysburg." A general review of the backgrounds of the surgeons in Lee's army reveals that nearly 80 percent of them were graduates of either the University of Pennsylvania Medical School or Jefferson Medical College in Philadelphia.

31. Quartermaster Records, Articles Purchased, Impressed and Confiscated, Hood's Division, ANV Collection, MOC; Duncan, *Medical Department*, 258; Crute, *Confederate Staff Officers*, 18, 112; Record of Confederate Burials, "Plank Farm," O'Neal Journal, GNMP; Coco, *Vast Sea of Misery*, 141–43; McMurry, *John Bell Hood*, 75. Among the surgeons known to have served at the Plank house were Dr. Thomas A. Means of the Eleventh Georgia, Dr. Thomas C. Pugh of the Ninth Georgia, Dr. Henry W. Waters of the First Texas, Dr. John Curtis Jones of the Fourth Texas, Dr. William P. Powell of the Fifth Texas, Dr. Carl H. A. Kleinschmidt of the Third Arkansas, Dr. E. F. DeGraffenreidt of the Fourth Alabama, Dr. W. H. Cole of the Eighth Georgia, Dr. Thomas A. Rains, chief surgeon of Benning's Brigade, and Dr. William O. Hudson, chief surgeon of Law's Brigade. Simpson, *Hood's Texas Brigade*, 11, 169; Frank Moore, *Rebellion Record*, 7:127; Duncan, *Medical Department*, 258; Lillian Henderson, *Roster . . . Georgia*, 1:914; Joseph Jones, "Medical Officers . . . of Tennessee," 186, 194, 234, 249, 268. The Plank house still stands; it is one of the most remarkable sites on or near the Gettysburg battlefield.

32. Elizabeth Plank Memoir, GNMP; Record of Confederate Burials, "Plank Farm," O'Neal Journal, GNMP.

33. Rozier, *Granite Farm Letters*, 116.

34. *OR* 27(2):404–17.

35. *OR* 27(2):405–6, 411; Simpson, *Hood's Texas Brigade: Lee's Grenadier Guard*, 29, and *Hood's Texas Brigade: A Compendium*, 548.

36. Rozier, *Granite Farm Letters*, 119 (quotation); Waddell Diary, 8 July 1863, CSA "Core Collection": Regiments and Soldiers, MOC.

37. *OR* 27(2):364; Krick, *Staff Officers*, 210; Coco, *Vast Sea of Misery*, 150–52.

38. Patricia Spain Ward, *Simon Baruch*, 1–25; Baruch, "A Surgeon's Story of Battle and Capture," 545. Dr. Baruch's son was Bernard Baruch, one of the great financiers of the twentieth century. The Blackhorse Tavern is still standing. The chief surgeon of Kershaw's Brigade was Dr. T. W. Salmond of the Second South Carolina. Salmond served at the brigade ambulance depot at the Pitzer schoolhouse before returning to the Blackhorse Tavern. Among those assisting the wounded at the tavern were Dr. J. F. Pearce of the Eighth South Carolina and Dr. Henry Junius Nott of the Second South Carolina. *OR* 27(2):364.

39. *OR* 27(2):369; Record of Confederate Burials, "Frank Bream's Farm," O'Neal Journal, GNMP.

40. Dickert, *Kershaw's Brigade*, 251–54; Hoke, *Great Invasion*, 495; Black, *Crumbling Defenses*, 51–53; Kirkland, *Broken Fortunes*, 250.

41. Record of Confederate Burials, "Crawford's Farm," "J. Cunningham's Farm," and "Georgia (at John's Farm)," O'Neal Journal, GNMP; Coco, *Vast Sea of Misery*, 150–52; Frassanito, *Early Photography*, 388–89; Damage Claim Applications, "John S. Crawford," PHMC. The Crawford house still stands. Serving at the Crawford farm were Dr. Taylor Gilmer, Barksdale's chief surgeon, and Dr. Frank W. Patterson of the Seventeenth Mississippi and his acting assistant surgeon, Dr. R. L. Knox; Dr. C. H. Brown, acting assistant surgeon of the Eighteenth Mississippi; and the surgeons of the Washington Artillery of New Orleans, the artillery battalions of Colonel E. Porter Alexander, Colonel Henry Coalter Cabell, and Major M. W. Henry, including Dr. Aristides Montiero, Dr. John Somers Buist, and Dr. F. H. Sewell. The Rev. Dr. William Burton Owen of the Seventeenth Mississippi was chaplain. *OR* 27(2):364; Jones, "Medical Officers . . . of Tennessee," 22:245.

42. Coco, *Vast Sea of Misery*, 151; Damage Claim Applications, "John S. Crawford," PHMC. The Johns house no longer stands. Among the surgeons present at Semmes's Brigade hospital were Dr. S. P. Hobgood and Dr. James B. Clifton of the Fifty-third Georgia and Dr. H. J. Paramore of the Fifth Georgia. Ministering to its wounded was Rev. Dr. C. H. Toy, chaplain of the Fifty-third Georgia. *OR* 27(2):364.

43. Paul Jones Semmes to Wife, 9 July 1863, WT; Mary Oden to Mrs. Paul Jones Semmes, 10 July 1863, WT; W. R. Stillwell to Mollie, 10 July 1863, GNMP; James B. Clifton Diary, 4, James B. Clifton Papers, NCDAH. It has always been said in and around Gettysburg that Semmes was taken to the Crawford house after being wounded, but there is no record that he actually was. Record of Confederate Burials, "J. Cunningham Farm," O'Neal Journal, GNMP. Among the ten or more surgeons there were Dr. W. D. Bringle, chief surgeon of Wofford's Brigade, Dr. Robert P. Myers and Dr. Erwin J. Eldridge of the Sixteenth Georgia; and Dr. James Broyles Brown, Dr. Elisha James Roach, and Dr. D. H. Ramsaur of the Eighteenth Georgia. *OR* 27(2): 364; Simpson, *Hood's Texas Brigade: A Compendium*, 326; Myers Diary, 1–4 July 1863, CSA "Core Collection": Regiments and Soldiers, MOC; Lillian Henderson, *Roster . . . Georgia*, 2:615; Sams, *With Unabated Trust*, 177–78; Joseph Jones, "Medical Officers . . . of Tennessee," 176. The Crawford house and farm are still intact.

44. Record of Confederate Burials, "Frank Bream's Mill," "Bream's Mill Dam," "John Currens, Bream's Mill," and "Virginia," O'Neal Journal, GNMP; Quartermaster Records, Articles Purchased, Impressed and Confiscated, Pickett's Division, ANV Collection, MOC; Coco, *Vast Sea of Misery*, 147–49; Krick, *Staff Officers*, 261.

45. Frey, *Longstreet's Assault*, 159–89. The original record of the hospital of Pickett's Division published in Frey's book contains only the names of those left behind after Lee's army withdrew from Pennsylvania. Duncan, *Medical Department*, 258. Duncan records that the hospital eventually cared for 1,200 wounded Confederates of Pickett's Division. Bream's Mineral and Flour Mill and the Myers house no longer stand.

46. Among the surgeons known to have served at the hospital of Pickett's Di-

vision were Dr. Thomas P. Mayo of the Third Virginia; Dr. James W. Oliver and Dr. Robert H. Worthington of the Seventh Virginia, assistant surgeons; Dr. Charles E. Lippitt of the Fifty-seventh Virginia; Dr. John Mutius Gaines of the Eighteenth Virginia; Dr. John R. Ward of the Eleventh Virginia; Dr. William H. Taylor of the Nineteenth Virginia, assistant surgeon; Dr. Alexander Grigsby of the First Virginia; Dr. B. C. Harrison of the Fifty-sixth Virginia, assistant surgeon; Dr. William S. Nowlan of the Thirty-eighth Virginia, assistant surgeon; and Dr. Charles B. Morton, chief surgeon of Kemper's Brigade. Duncan, *Medical Department*, 176–78; Georg and Busey, *Nothing but Glory*, 320–456; Charles Edward Lippitt Diary, 13, Lippitt Papers, SHC-UNC; Johnston, *Confederate Boy*, 218–19; Riggs, *7th Virginia Infantry*, 88, 100; Frey, *Longstreet's Assault*, 159–89.

47. Johnston, *Confederate Boy*, 217–19.

48. Frey, *Longstreet's Assault*, 175; Record of Confederate Burials, "Frank Bream's Mill," "Bream's Mill Dam," "John Currens, Bream's Mill" and "Virginia," O'Neal Journal, GNMP; Coco, *Vast Sea of Misery*, 140–41.

49. Coco, *Vast Sea of Misery*, 140–41. Assisting Dr. Fraser were Dr. Henry A. Minor of the Eighth Alabama, Dr. J. R. Woods of the Second Georgia Battalion, Dr. W. F. Nance of the Second Florida, Dr. James W. Claiborne and Dr. Samuel Dickinson of the Twelfth Virginia, and Dr. W. F. Richardson of the Ninth Alabama, as well as at least ten others and Rev. Dr. J. O. A. Cook, chaplain of the Third Georgia. Record of Confederate Burials, "Adam Butt Farm," O'Neal Journal, GNMP; Krick, *Staff Officers*, 173; Crute, *Confederate Staff Officers*, 5; "Tribute to Henry DeSaussure Fraser"; Duncan, *Medical Department*, 260; Hooker, *Mississippi*, 424–25; *OR* 27(2):343; Roll of Prisoners of War, Gettysburg Hospitals, Wounded Transferred, 21 July 1863, Papers Relating to Union Hospitals, NA; Waddell Diary, 3 July 1863, CSA "Core Collection": Regiments and Soldiers, MOC; William D. Henderson, *12th Virginia Infantry*, 116, 121. The Butt farmhouse, although altered, still stands.

50. Coco, *Vast Sea of Misery*, 134–37; LeGrand Wilson Jr., *Confederate Soldier*, 15–20, 116–17; Roll of Prisoners of War, Gettysburg Hospitals, List of Confederate Officers Sent to Baltimore, 19 July 1863, Wounded transferred, 21 July 1863, Papers Relating to Union Hospitals, NA; Maud Morrow Brown, *University Greys*, 47; Record of Confederate Burials, "Major Lohr Farm," O'Neal Journal, GNMP; Krick, *Staff Officers*, 293; *OR* 27(2):333, 639; Duncan, *Medical Department*, 259.

51. Coco, *Wasted Valor*, 64–65, and *Vast Sea of Misery*, 135–38. No burial records illustrate the Lohr farm's use as a hospital for Pender's Division, but there are none at any of the nearby farms or tavern at Seven Stars either. Mills, "Supplemental Sketch," 182; Krick, *Staff Officers*, 260; Welch, *Letters to His Wife*, 3, 58, 67–68; Dickert, *Kershaw's Brigade*, 231. Welch and Dickert both say that Pender's hospital was about midway between Gettysburg and Cashtown. The Heintzelman Tavern still stands; the Lohr house is in ruins.

52. Dickert, *Kershaw's Brigade*, 231; Welch, *Letters to His Wife*, 67; *OR* 27(2):334; Duncan, *Medical Department*, 259–60.

53. Coco, *Vast Sea of Misery*, 135–38; Imboden, "Confederate Retreat," 424; Quartermaster Records, ANV Collection, Statements of Property Impressed, Scales's Bri-

gade, ANV Collection, MOC; Duncan, *Medical Department*, 259–60; Hassler, *The General to His Lady*, 259–60.

54. Roll of Prisoners of War, Chambersburg Hospital, 31 July 1863, Papers Relating to Union Hospitals, NA; Manarin and Jordan, *North Carolina Troops*, 3:462, 5:6; Collett Leventhorpe to General Marcus J. Wright, 30 May 1888, Wright Papers, DU; Bennett H. Young, "Lane and His Regiment"; Underwood, "Twenty-sixth Regiment," 354–61. Known to have served at Heth's and Pender's division hospitals were Dr. William Montgomery, chief surgeon of Archer's Brigade; Dr. John Henry McAden, Thirteenth North Carolina, chief surgeon of Scales's Brigade; Dr. Lewellyn P. Warren, Twenty-sixth North Carolina, chief surgeon of Pettigrew's Brigade; Dr. William A. Spence, Forty-seventh Virginia; James H. Southall, Fifty-fifth Virginia; Dr. A. G. Emory, Fourteenth Tennessee; Dr. Benjamin T. Green and Dr. W. S. Parker, Fifty-fifth North Carolina; Dr. John Wilson Jr. and Dr. James Parks McCombs, Eleventh North Carolina; Dr. William G. McCreight, Forty-second Mississippi; Dr. Franklin J. White, Forty-seventh North Carolina; Dr. Enoch Newton Hunt, Second Mississippi; Dr. John H. G. Turkett, Seventh Tennessee; Dr. Benjamin Ward, Dr. William B. Shields, and Dr. Joseph Holt, Eleventh Mississippi; Dr. P. Gervais Robinson, Twenty-second North Carolina; Dr. William H. Green, Lane's artillery battalion; Dr. Robert Gibbon, Twenty-eighth North Carolina; Dr. John Tyler McLean, Thirty-third North Carolina; Dr. R. S. Baldwin, Sixteenth North Carolina; Dr. George Trescott, First South Carolina Rifles; Dr. Francis LeJau Frost, First South Carolina; Dr. Spencer Glasgow Welch, Thirteenth South Carolina; Dr. William H. Scarborough, Fourteenth South Carolina; and Dr. W. P. Hill, Thirty-fifth Georgia. Roll of Prisoners of War, Gettysburg Hospitals, List of Confederate Officers Sent to New York, 18 July 1863, and to Baltimore, 19 July 1863, and Wounded Transferred, 21 July 1863, Papers Relating to Union Hospitals, NA; Manarin and Jordan, *North Carolina Troops*, 5:7; "John W. C. O'Neal Memoir," *Gettysburg Compiler*, 5 July 1905; Blanton, *Medicine in Virginia*, 416; Hartzler, *Medical Doctors*, 60; Archie K. Davis, *Boy Colonel*, 334; Galloway, "Gettysburg," 389; Rosen, Jordan, and Moomaw, *Our Soldiers Cemetery*, 15; Côté, *Mary's World*, 293–95; Stubbs, *Duty, Honor, Valor*, 659; "Surrender! Never Surrender!," 429–33, WFCHS; "Life of Gen. James Johnston Pettigrew," holographic memoir, 32, Pettigrew Family Papers, SHC-UNC.

55. Julius Lineback Diary, 1, 3 July 1863, Lineback Papers, vol. 2, SHC-UNC.

56. George P. Erwin to Father, 3 July 1863, Erwin Papers, SHC-UNC.

57. Record of Confederate Burials, "Hankey Farm," O'Neal Journal, GNMP; Coco, *Vast Sea of Misery*, 128–31; E. V. Turner, "Twenty-third Regiment," 236–37; Manarin and Jordan, *North Carolina Troops*, 4:10, 128, 6:433, 7:142–45; *OR* 27(2):562–63. The Hankey farmhouse and farm site are intact.

58. Green, *Recollections*, 176; E. V. Turner, "Twenty-third Regiment," 236–37. Dr. David Russell and Dr. J. H. Purefoy, along with Dr. Isaac F. Pearson of the Fifth North Carolina, Dr. John Henry Hicks of the Twentieth North Carolina, Dr. J. Robinson Godwin of the Second North Carolina Battalion, and Dr. William T. Brewer of the Forty-third North Carolina, are known to have served at the Hankey farm. Manarin and Jordan, *North Carolina Troops*, 3:265, 4:10, 128, 6:433, 7:142–45.

59. Coco, *Vast Sea of Misery*, 131.

60. Ibid., 129–30.

61. Betts, *Experiences*, 38–39. Parker had been wounded in the head at Sharpsburg; he survived his injury at Gettysburg only to be wounded in the head a third time at Spottsylvania Courthouse on 19 May 1864. His three head wounds prompted Robert E. Lee to jokingly assert in a letter to Parker that his head was too big. Hill, *North Carolina*, 684–85; Manarin and Jordan, *North Carolina Troops*, 8:322. Parker outlived the war and returned to his wife Sally. He died in 1905; his remains and those of Sally, who died three years later, were buried in the cemetery of Calvary Episcopal Church, Tarboro, N.C., a few paces from the grave of General William Dorsey Pender. The Schriver farm remains intact.

62. Thomas, *Doles-Cook Brigade*, 485; Coco, *Vast Sea of Misery*, 129–30. Assisting Dr. Briggs at the Shriver farm were Dr. John M. Hayes of the Twenty-sixth Alabama, chief surgeon of O'Neal's Brigade, and Dr. William H. Philpot, chief surgeon of Doles's Brigade. Also known to have served at the Hankey farm were Dr. R. G. Southall, Sixth Alabama, and Dr. George Whitfield, Twelfth Alabama, of O'Neal's Brigade; Dr. William Proby Young, Fourth Georgia; Dr. James A. Etheridge, Twelfth Georgia; Dr. Abner Embry McGarity, Forty-fourth Georgia; Dr. John F. Shaffner, Fourth North Carolina; and Dr. Leonidas Kirby, Second North Carolina. *OR* 27(2): 342, 550; Crute, *Confederate Staff Officers*, 167; Roll of Prisoners of War, Seminary Hospital, 10 August 1863, Papers Relating to Union Hospitals, NA; "Whitfield," 416; Park, *Twelfth Alabama Infantry*, 54; Duncan, *Medical Department*, 259; Thomas, *Doles-Cook Brigade*, 80, 82–83, 231; Burnett, "Letters of a Confederate Surgeon," 161.

63. *OR* 27(2):560; Duncan, *Medical Department*, 259; Krick, *Staff Officers*, 257.

64. Coco, *Vast Sea of Misery*, 123–27. Among the more notable surgeons at the hospitals of Early's Division were Dr. Judson A. Butts, Thirty-first Georgia; Dr. Louis E. Gott, Forty-ninth Virginia; and Dr. William Lewis Reese and Dr. John Geddings Hardy, Sixth North Carolina. Record of Confederate Burials, "Jacob Keims" and "Josiah Benners Farm," O'Neal Journal, GNMP; Coco, *Wasted Valor*, 66–69; Hale and Phillips, *Forty-ninth Virginia Infantry*, 220; Thomas, *Doles-Cook Brigade*, 345–47; *OR* 27(2):466; Lillian Henderson, *Roster . . . Georgia*, 3:645; Manarin and Jordan, *North Carolina Troops*, 4:268; Apperson, *Repairing the "March of Mars,"* 483–86; Krick, *Staff Officers*, 271. The Crawford, Benner, Cobean, Ross, and Kime houses still stand.

65. Coco, *Vast Sea of Misery*, 121–27; *Gettysburg Times*, 9 August 1937.

66. Coco, *Vast Sea of Misery*, 115; Iobst and Manarin, *Bloody Sixth*, 138–39. A note from Avery to Major Samuel McDowell Tate, written while he lay wounded on the battlefield, is in the collection of the NCDAH. It reads: "Tell father I died with my face to the enemy." *Raleigh News-Observer-Chronicle*, 11 May 1894. The Culp farm has been fully restored.

67. Coco, *Vast Sea of Misery*, 116–23; Duncan, *Medical Department*, 259.

68. *OR* 27(2):341; Record of Confederate Burials, "H. A. Picking's Farm," "Montford's Farm," "Mrs. Wible," "M. Shalers," "Mrs. Wibles Place above Barn along the fence," "Field opposite Mrs. Wibles, near Shealer Place," O'Neal Journal, GNMP; Article, Newspaper Clipping File, No. 5, GNMP; Coco, *Vast Sea of Misery*, 116–20. The Picking, Buehler, Montford, Lady, and Weible houses still stand.

69. Coco, *Vast Sea of Misery*, 116-17. Serving the wounded at the hospitals of Johnson's Division were, among others, Dr. Benjamin M. Cromwell and Dr. Lucius C. Coke, First North Carolina; Dr. Walker Washington and Dr. Thomas Fanning Wood, Third North Carolina; Dr. DeWilton Snowden, First Maryland Battalion; Dr. Casper C. Henkel, Tenth Virginia; Dr. Charles W. MacGill and Dr. Robert A. D. Munson, Second Virginia; Dr. John A. Hunter, Twenty-seventh Virginia; Dr. Edwin Latimer, Latimer's (Andrews's) Battalion; and Dr. Bushrod Taylor, chief surgeon of Jones's Brigade. Duncan, *Medical Department*, 258-59; Manarin and Jordan, *North Carolina Troops*, 3:142, 488; Coco, *Wasted Valor*, 74; Dr. Casper C. Henkel to Cousin, 12 July 1863, Heth Papers, MC-3, file 4-474, Confederate Military Leaders Collection, MOC; *OR* 27(2):510; Hartzler, *Medical Doctors*, 57, 74, 76; Apperson, *Repairing the "March of Mars,"* 486; Frye, *2nd Virginia Infantry*, 120; Blanton, *Medicine in Virginia*, 406.

70. Douglas, *I Rode With Stonewall*, 252-53; Record of Confederate Burials, "H. A. Picking's Farm," O'Neal Journal, GNMP.

71. Coco, *Vast Sea of Misery*, 115; Walker, *Memorial, Virginia Military Institute*, 332-33; Wise, *Virginia Military Institute*, 249.

72. Coco, *Vast Sea of Misery*, 115; Wood, *Doctor to the Front*, 105-7.

73. Wood, *Doctor to the Front*, xi-xvi, 105-7; Roll of Prisoners of War, Gettysburg Hospitals, List of Confederate Officers Sent to New York, 23 July 1863, Papers Relating to Union Hospitals, NA.

74. Kenan, "Forty-third Regiment," 6; Manarin and Jordan, *North Carolina Troops*, 10:293; Hill, *North Carolina*, 584-85; Wellman, *Rebel Boast*, 129-33; Shepherd, "Wounded and Captured," 76; *OR* 27(2):570, 573-74.

75. Apperson, *Repairing the "March of Mars,"* 483-86; Whitehead, "July 1st, July 3rd," *Adventures*; Blanton, *Medicine in Virginia*, 416; Booth, *Louisiana Confederate Soldiers*, 3:765. Dr. Whitehead claimed that his hospital was located "northwest of Gettysburg" on the "west side of the Mummasburg Road." Hospital steward John Samuel Apperson places the Second Corps Field Hospital first along the Mummasburg Road and then the Carlisle Road. Whitehead's claims are only from memory, but his description of the hospital makes it clear that the field hospital was located on the Cobean farm, west of the Carlisle Road. He mistakenly remembered the hospital being west of the Mummasburg Road. Because General Trimble's leg was actually amputated by Dr. McGuire at the Cobean house is confirmation of the use of that house and farm as the Second Corps Field Hospital. Georg, McIlhenny Memoir, GNMP; Coco, *Vast Sea of Misery*, 125-26; Trimble, "Civil War Diary," 12. It is noteworthy that Whitehead, a Virginia Military Institute graduate, and Dr. Taney had been acquaintances in Paris, France, where they both studied medicine before the war.

76. Coco, *Vast Sea of Misery*, 108-10; *OR* 27(2):710; Wellman, *Giant in Gray*, 120-21.

77. Stegman, *These Men She Gave*, 26, 46, 87, 95-96; Mitchell, "A Georgia Henry of Navarre"; William G. Delony to Rosa, 4 July 1863, Delony Papers, UGA; Galloway, *Dear Old Roswell*, 28-30.

78. *OR* 27(2):345-46, 741; Roll of Prisoners of War, Gettysburg Hospitals, Wounded Transferred, 21 July 1863, Papers Relating to Union Hospitals, NA; Black, *Crumbling Defenses*, 29, 43. The surgeons included Dr. Talcott Eliason, chief surgeon

of the cavalry division; Dr. James Yates and Dr. Horace Drennan, First South Carolina Cavalry; Dr. Walter Taylor, Hampton's Brigade; Dr. J. B. Fontaine, Fitzhugh Lee's Brigade; and others.

79. Coco, *Vast Sea of Misery*, 165–66; Hartzler, *Medical Doctors*, 56.

80. R. N. Martin to My Dear Aunt and Cousin, HS; Pettijohn, *Gettysburg and Libby Prison*, 6–7.

81. *OR* II, 8:426; Warner, Beers and Co., *Adams County*, 454.

82. R. N. Martin to My Dear Aunt and Cousin, HS; Pettijohn, *Gettysburg and Libby Prison*, 6–7.

83. Gantt, "The Gettysburg Prisoners," KMB.

84. Harris Diary, 5 July 1863, GNMP; *OR* 27(3):518.

CHAPTER THREE

1. Georg, "Confederate and Union Field Hospitals," 9, GNMP; Imboden, "Confederate Retreat," 420.

2. Imboden, "Confederate Retreat," 420.

3. Jomini, *Art of War*, 230–46; Clausewitz, *On War*, 271–72.

4. Clausewitz, *On War*, 271.

5. Ibid., 271–72.

6. Ibid., 271.

7. Lake, "Outline Map," "Hamiltonban," *Atlas of Adams Co.*; Beers, "Franklin County," "Washington," *Atlas of Franklin County*; Lake, Griffing, and Stevenson, "Outline Plan," *Illustrated Atlas*. What remains of the old Maria Furnace Road is now called the Jacks Mountain Road; the old Jacks Mountain Road is now called the Fairfield Road. The Emmitsburg-Waynesboro Turnpike is now Route 16.

8. TopoZone.com UTM Zone 18, N 4401854, E 291097, N 4401855, E 289065, N 4401855, E 287032; N 4401856, E 284999; Lake, *Atlas of Adams Co.*, 35; dePeyster, *Gettysburg and After*, 87.

9. TopoZone.com UTM Zone 18, N 4417155, E 297137, N 4418676, E 297143, N 4418675, E 295115, N 4418674, E 293087, N 4420196, E 291058, N 4420185, E 289030; N 4420175, E 287002, N 4420165, E 284974. That the Chambersburg Pike was macadamized, see Lake, *Atlas of Adams Co.*, 30–31, 42. The Chambersburg Pike is now U.S. 30, the Lincoln Highway.

10. Imboden, "Confederate Retreat," 422; Hoke, *Great Invasion*, 477–78. The Walnut Bottom Road is now Route 997. The Pine Stump Road runs west from Route 997 at Pond Bank; it is now Duffield Road and becomes New Franklin Road. Just before Marion, New Franklin Road runs into Alleman Road. The Cumberland Valley Turnpike is now Route 63.

11. Lafayette Guild to Dr. John S. D. Cullen, Dr. Hunter McGuire, and Dr. J. W. Powell, 3 July 1863, Records of Medical Department, ANV, Letters Sent, NA. Guild's 3 July 1863 correspondence with the medical directors of the three army corps does not appear in the *Official Records*; rather, the compilers were unable to locate it, noting that it was "not found." *OR* 27(2):328. It was misfiled, but I found it in Guild's corre-

spondence book between two letters dated 10 July 1863. Its contents are related here for the first time.

12. Mrs. Hugh Holmes Lee Diary, 429, WFCHS. Mrs. Lee reported that the ambulances, wagons, buggies, and carriages were collected and left Winchester on 5 July.

13. OR 27(2):360; Edward Porter Alexander, *Fighting for the Confederacy*, 267.

14. *OR* 27(2):448.

15. Hotchkiss, *Make Me a Map*, 158; Edward Porter Alexander, *Fighting for the Confederacy*, 267.

16. Hotchkiss, *Make Me a Map*, 158, 303 n. 19; Andrew B. Booth, *Records of Louisiana Confederate Soldiers*, 3:358.

17. *OR* 27(2):360.

18. *OR* 27(2):311.

19. Ibid.

20. Quartermaster Records, Articles Purchased, Impressed and Confiscated, Longstreet's Corps, Hood's Division, Pickett's Division, McLaws's Division, First Corps Reserve Artillery Battalion, Semmes's Brigade, Law's Brigade, Benning's Brigade, Barksdale's Brigade, Anderson's Brigade, Texas Brigade, ANV Collection, MOC. What quartermaster records still exist reveal a systematic collection of stores on each and every day of the retreat.

21. *OR* 27(2):311.

22. Ibid.

23. Edward Porter Alexander, *Fighting for the Confederacy*, 267.

24. *OR* 27(2):370, 372.

25. *OR* 27(2):416–17, 421, 423–24, 426–27.

26. *OR* 27(2):392, 396, 398, 406, 411, 413.

27. *OR* 27(2):392; Coles, *From Huntsville to Appomattox*, 112; Oates, *War*, 238–39.

28. *OR* 27(2):376, 381, 384, 389, 430, 432.

29. Linn, "Journal of My Trip," Archives Collection, USAMHI.

30. *OR* 27(2):608; Skelly, *A Boy's Experiences*, 20; James E. Green Diary, 9, Green Papers, NCDAH; Linn, "Journal of My Trip," Archives Collection, USAMHI.

31. *OR* 27(2):448, 471, 505, 513, 519, 557, 569.

32. *OR* 27(2):519; Casler, *Four Years*, 176–77.

33. *OR* 27(2):557, 569, 580, 582, 588, 590, 593.

34. *OR* 27(2):471, 481, 485, 490.

35. *OR* 27(2):604, 606.

36. The division quartermaster, subsistence, ordnance, and ambulance trains of Ewell's Corps followed the reserve train for the journey back to Virginia; they did not accompany the main body of the corps.

37. Bean, "John A. Harman"; Douglas, *I Rode with Stonewall*, 71–72; Imboden, "Incidents of the First Bull Run," 238; Harman and Cameron Family Papers, James and Judy Philpot, Lexington, Ky.

38. *OR* 27(2):699.

39. *OR* 27(2):311, 699.

40. *OR* 27(2):699.

41. Imboden, "Confederate Retreat," 420.

42. "Imboden Family Genealogy," Imboden Family Papers, UVA.

43. Ibid. McPhail was the brother of Imboden's wife. Imboden, "Confederate Retreat," 420.

44. Imboden, "Confederate Retreat," 422; Osmun Latrobe to J. B. Walton, 4 July 1863, 1:00 A.M., Order Book, Col. J. B. Walton, Chief of Artillery, First Army Corps, ANV, Walton Collection, TU.

45. Imboden, "Confederate Retreat," 420.

46. Ibid.; Pennsylvania Hospital Registers, Seminary Hospital, NA; Foster, "Story of the Battle."

47. Stiles, *Four Years*, 219–20.

48. Foster, "Story of the Battle"; Timothy H. Smith, *Story of Lee's Headquarters*, 38.

49. Franklin Gardner Walter Diary, 1–9, Walter Papers, VSL.

50. Imboden, "Confederate Retreat," 420–21.

51. Ibid., 422.

52. Ibid.; Hoke, *Great Invasion*, 477–78.

53. Walter Taylor to William N. Pendleton, 4 July 1863, Taylor Papers, VHS.

54. Imboden, "Confederate Retreat," 422.

55. Oates, *War*, 237.

56. OR 25(2):715, 735; Nichols, *Confederate Engineers*, 99; Hotchkiss, *Make Me a Map*, 151; Lord, *Collector's Encyclopedia*, 93.

57. James E. Green Diary, 9, Green Papers, NCDAH; Hotchkiss, *Make Me a Map*, 150–51.

58. Hahn, *Towpath Guide*, 142–46; York, "The Falling Waters Mill," 43–44.

59. James E. Green Diary, 9, Green Papers, NCDAH; OR 27(2):550.

60. War Department, *Regulations*, §§ 478, 1366, art. 63.

61. Beach, *First New York*, 268.

62. Ibid., 268–69; OR 27(1):489.

63. Beach, *First New York*, 269; OR 27(1):489, 491; Heitman, *Historical Register*, 1: 476.

64. As Foley's force could not approach the pontoon bridge from the Falling Waters Road for fear of being detected, it would have had to follow the towpath of the canal westward from one of the roads west of Boonsboro, probably the Hagerstown-Downsville Road.

65. *New York Times*, 13 July 1863.

66. Ibid. The *New York Times* erroneously refers to Cadet Greenough as Leonard Greewald. Beach, *First New York*, 269.

67. *New York Times*, 13 July 1863.

68. Ibid.; Beach, *First New York*, 269–70.

69. *New York Times*, 13 July 1863; OR 27(3):524.

70. OR 27(3):967.

CHAPTER FOUR

1. Hotchkiss, *Make Me a Map*, 158.

2. The First Maryland Cavalry Battalion, temporarily commanded by Major Harry Gilmore, had accompanied Ewell's Corps throughout the campaign. Gilmore and one of his company commanders, Captain Warner G. Welsh, claimed to have been the first Confederates to enter the town of Gettysburg. Major Ridgely Brown, after recovering from a wound, arrived to assume command of the battalion; Gilmore became a company commander in the battalion after 5 July. *OR* 27(2):290; Gilmore, *Four Years in the Saddle*, 92–100.

3. Imboden, "Confederate Retreat," 421–22; Franklin Gardner Walter Diary, 9, Walter Papers, VSL.

4. Robert E. Lee to John D. Imboden, 4 July 1863, *OR* 27(3):966–67.

5. Robert E. Lee to Jefferson Davis, 4 July 1863, *OR* 27(2):298.

6. Osmun Latrobe to J. B. Walton, 4 July 1863, 1:00 A.M., Order Book, First Army Corps, ANV, Col. J. B. Walton, Chief of Artillery, Walton Collection, TU.

7. Ibid.; War Department, *Regulations*, § 751. Army regulations required the chief quartermaster of the army to oversee trains put together from different divisions or corps.

8. Franklin Gardner Walter Diary, 9, Walter Papers, VSL.

9. War Department, *Regulations*, §§ 716–18, 758.

10. Record of Confederate Burials, "H. A. Picking's Farm," "Montfort's Farm," "Mrs. Wible," "M. Shalers," "Mrs. Wibles Place above Barn along the Fence," and "Field opposite Mrs. Wibles, near Shealer Place," O'Neal Journal, GNMP; Coco, *Vast Sea of Misery*, 116–20; Thomas Fanning Wood, *Doctor to the Front*, 107; Hall, *Diary*, 83; Goldsborough, *The Maryland Line*, 159; Douglas, *I Rode with Stonewall*, 252–53. When in column with marching troops, the trains followed the infantry and artillery. War Department, *Regulations*, § 755.

11. *OR* 27(2):502; Thomas Fanning Wood, *Doctor to the Front*, 108.

12. A U.S. Sanitary Commission map of Confederate hospital sites prepared in July 1863 shows that the hospitals of Johnson's Division were located at and near Fairfield, the farthest west of all hospital sites of Ewell's Divisions. Unquestionably, the trains of Johnson's Division led Ewell's trains during the movement to Fairfield. Coco, *Vast Sea of Misery*, 175.

13. War Department, *Regulations*, §§ 752, 755.

14. Report of Court of Inquiry of Major James C. Bryan, Testimony of William T. Potter, Captain John M. Jones, and Major John D. Rogers, 29 August 1863, Compiled Service Records, NA. The testimony in Bryan's case provides the only known evidence of the arrangement of a division train during the retreat. Herds of cattle and sheep were placed about every one-half mile to one mile in the subsistence trains. William O. Johnson, "The 49th Virginia Infantry at Gettysburg," Daniel Papers, box 23, UVA; Bradwell, *Under the Southern Cross*, 132.

15. Duncan, *Medical Department*, 259; *OR* 27(2):341. According to Dr. Guild, Johnson's Division suffered 1,269 wounded at Gettysburg. Estimating the number of deaths

due to wounds, coupled with the number of wounded known to have been left behind, somewhere between 500 and 700 wounded were removed.

16. Whitehead, "July 3rd," *Adventures of an American Surgeon*; Duncan, *Medical Department*, 259; Roll of Prisoners of War, Gettysburg Hospitals, List of Confederate Officers Sent to New York, 23 July 1863, Papers Relating to Union Hospitals, NA.

17. *Raleigh News-Observer-Chronicle*, 11 May 1894; G. W. Nichols, *A Soldier's Story*, 120; Coco, *Vast Sea of Misery*, 126. At the Kime farm there were burials from the Thirty-eighth and Sixty-first Georgia of Gordon's Brigade; Record of Confederate Burials, "Jacob Keims," O'Neal Journal, GNMP.

18. Record of Confederate Burials, "Jacob Keims" and "Josiah Benners Farm," O'Neal Journal, GNMP; Coco, *Vast Sea of Misery*, 121–27; Storrick, *Gettysburg*, 61–62; Duncan, *Medical Department*, 258–59; Hale and Phillips, *Forty-ninth Virginia Infantry*, 220; Lillian Henderson, *Roster . . . of Georgia*, 3:645; Driver, *1st and 2nd Rockbridge Artillery*, 67.

19. Edward E. Moore, *Story of a Cannoneer*, 200.

20. Trimble, "Civil War Diary," 12; Memoir of Mrs. Hugh McIlhenny Sr., GNMP; Apperson, *Repairing the "March of Mars*," 483–86; Coco, *Vast Sea of Misery*, 125–26.

21. Record of Confederate Burials, "Hankey Farm," O'Neal Journal, GNMP; Coco, *Vast Sea of Misery*, 128–30; Memoirs of Oscar W. Blacknall, 15, Blacknall Papers, NCDAH.

22. Green, *Recollections*, 177–78; Wellman, *Rebel Boast*, 133; Manarin and Jordan, *North Carolina Troops*, 3:264–65, 9:5–6, 10:382, 11:7.

23. Chapman, *Bright and Gloomy Days*, 70; Manarin and Jordan, *North Carolina Troops*, 3:319.

24. John Cabell Early, "Southern Boy," 40–41.

25. Torrence, "Road to Gettysburg," 514–15.

26. Michael W. Taylor, *To Drive the Enemy*, 295; Henry W. Thomas, *Doles-Cook Brigade*, 80, 475–76, 485; Coco, *Vast Sea of Misery*, 121–30.

27. Tucker, "Diary," 24–25.

28. Park, *Twelfth Alabama Infantry*, 53–55.

29. *OR* 27(2):557; Duncan, *Medical Department*, 259; Roll of Prisoners of War, Seminary Hospital, 10 August 1863, Papers Relating to Union Hospitals, NA; Manarin and Jordan, *North Carolina Troops*, 4:128, 6:433, 7:144, 11:9.

30. The U.S. Sanitary Commission map of July 1863 pinpointing Confederate hospital sites shows that the hospitals of Ewell's three divisions along the Fairfield Road stretched from Fairfield east to near Marsh Creek, just west of where the Herr Ridge Road enters the Fairfield Road. The only way the ambulance trains could have reached those sites was via the Herr Ridge Road. Too, burial records indicate that soldiers from Ewell's Corps were laid to rest along the Herr Ridge Road. U.S. Sanitary Commission map, dated July 1863, in Coco, *Vast Sea of Misery*, 175. Eyewitnesses wrote of the use of the Herr Ridge Road. Betts, *Experiences*, 40; Whitehorne Diary, 34, FLE. The Union signal station cited wagons moving to the Fairfield Road by means of the Herr Ridge Road. *OR* 27(1):514.

31. Coco, *Vast Sea of Misery*, 175; Betts, *Experiences*, 40; *OR* 27(1):514.

32. Record of Confederate Burials, "On Crist's Farm under Gum Tree" and "John

Crists Farm," O'Neal Journal, GNMP; Coco, *Vast Sea of Misery*, 134. The Crist house and the Frederick Herr Tavern still stand.

33. U.S. Sanitary Commission map, dated July 1863, in Coco, *Vast Sea of Misery*, 175.

34. Green, *Recollections*, 177. Green recalled, with understatement, that the trains of Ewell's divisions were eleven miles long. William O. Johnson, "The 49th Virginia Infantry at Gettysburg," Daniel Papers, box 23, UVA.

35. Frank Moore, *Rebellion Record*, 7:188.

36. Record of Confederate Burials, "David Stewart's Farm," O'Neal Journal, GNMP; Coco, *Vast Sea of Misery*, 154–56, 170; Fonderen, *Carpenter's Battery*, 43. Burials at the Lower Marsh Creek Presbyterian Church and the Stewart and Mickley farms were of soldiers from the First Maryland Battalion and Carpenter's Battery, all of Johnson's Division. The Presbyterian Church and Stewart and Mickley houses still stand.

37. Record of Confederate Burials, "Andrew Weikert, Millerstown Road," "Chris Byers Farm, Millerstown Road," and "Wm Douglas, Millerstown Road," O'Neal Journal, GNMP; Coco, *Vast Sea of Misery*, 152–56. Buried on the Weikert, Byers, Douglas, and Wintrode farms were soldiers from the Sixtieth and Thirteenth Georgia, Sixth North Carolina, and Eighth and Ninth Louisiana, all of Early's Division. The Weikert, Byers, and Wintrode houses are still standing.

38. Record of Confederate Burials, "At Jacob Planks, Millerstown Road, Left Side above Breams, Buried in Back of Barn," O'Neal Journal, GNMP; Coco, *Vast Sea of Misery*, 153; Betts, *Experiences*, 40. Those buried were from the Second North Carolina Battalion and the Thirty-second, Forty-fifth, and Fiftieth North Carolina, all of Rodes's Division. The Plank farmhouse still stands.

39. *OR* 27(3):514.

40. I examined the original handwritten message to Meade, signed by Lee, when it was in the possession of Ted Sutfin of Gettysburg. Colonel Miller died on 19 July 1863.

41. Bean, *Stonewall's Man*, 140–41.

42. *OR* 27(3):514.

43. Samuel Pickens Diary, 4 July 1863, Pickens Papers, UA; James E. Green Diary, 4 July 1863, Green Papers, NCDAH; Peter A. Taylor to George G. Meade, 4 July 1863, 5:15 P.M., *OR* 27(3):516; Daniel, "Gettysburg Campaign," Daniel Papers, box 23, UVA.

44. Rozier, *Granite Farm Letters*, 115; Imboden, "Confederate Retreat," 426; Francis Milton Kennedy Diary, 4 July 1863, Kennedy Papers, UNC-SHC; Hoke, *Reminiscences*, 89.

45. Roll of Prisoners of War, Gettysburg Hospitals, List of Confederate Officers Sent to New York, 18 July 1863, List of Confederate Officers Sent to Baltimore, 19 July 1863, and Wounded Transferred, 21 July 1863, Papers Relating to Union Hospitals, NA; Manarin and Jordan, *North Carolina Troops*, 5:285, 9:120; Welch, *Letters to His Wife*, 69; Duncan, *Medical Department*, 259–60; Krick, *Staff Officers*, 127.

46. Mills, "Supplemental Sketch," 181.

47. Rosborough to Pender, 5 September 1904, D. T. Carraway MS, n.d., p. 5, and J. G. Field to D. Gilliam, n.d., p. 3, all in Pender Papers, UNC-SHC; Hassler, *The General to His Lady*, 254, 260; Imboden, "Confederate Retreat," 423–24.

48. Record of Confederate Burials, "[I.] Rife's Cashtown," O'Neal Journal,

GNMP; Coco, *Vast Sea of Misery*, 138–40, and *Gettysburg's Confederate Dead*, 121; Warner, Beers and Co., *Adams County*, 413.

49. LeGrand Wilson Jr., *Confederate Soldier*, 125–26; Julius Lineback Diary, 4 July 1863, Lineback Papers, vol. 2, UNC-SHC.

50. Manarin and Jordan, *North Carolina Troops*, 5:6, 7:463; Louis G. Young, "Pettigrew's Brigade," 557; Duncan, *Medical Department*, 259; *Charlotte Daily Bulletin*, 28 August 1863; Belo, *Memoirs*, 22; Cooke, "Fifty-fifth Regiment," 302.

51. LeGrand Wilson Jr., *Confederate Soldier*, 125. Hubbard was the surgeon of the Second Mississippi.

52. Roll of Prisoners of War, Gettysburg Hospitals, List of Confederate Officers Sent to New York, 18 July 1863, List of Confederate Officers Sent to Baltimore, 19 July 1863, and Wounded Transferred, 21 July 1863, Papers Relating to Union Hospitals, NA; *Raleigh Daily Progress*, 14 July 1863.

53. Capt. J. J. Young to H. K. Burgwyn, 11 July 1863, Burgwyn Family Papers, UNC-SHC; Archie K. Davis, *Boy Colonel*, 337. Burgwyn's remains were later exhumed and reburied in Oakwood Cemetery, Raleigh, N.C.

54. Record of Confederate Burials, "Adam Butt Farm," O'Neal Journal, GNMP; Coco, *Vast Sea of Misery*, 140–41; Whitehorne Diary, 33–34, FLE; "Tribute to Henry DeSaussure Fraser."

55. Whitehorne Diary, 30–34, FLE.

56. Waddell Diary, 3, 4 July 1863, CSA "Core Collection": Regiments and Soldiers, MOC.

57. Civilian accounts of Imboden's trains clearly indicate that Hood's trains led those of Longstreet's Corps, as Hood's trains reached Marion before daylight, 5 July. Hoke, *Great Invasion*, 503–4; Quartermaster Records, Articles Purchased, Impressed and Confiscated, Longstreet's Corps, ANV Collection, MOC. The records list Major John D. Keiley as chief quartermaster of Longstreet's Corps.

58. Record of Confederate Burials, "Plank Farm," O'Neal Journal, GNMP; Coco, *Vast Sea of Misery*, 141–43; Simpson, *Hood's Texas Brigade: A Compendium*, 4, 90, 167, 253, and *Hood's Texas Brigade: Lee's Grenadier Guard*, 275 n. 64.

59. Hood, *Advance and Retreat*, 60.

60. Lokey, "Wounded at Gettysburg."

61. Duncan, *Medical Department*, 258; Lillian Henderson, *Roster . . . Georgia*, 1:914, 2:74; Simpson, *Hood's Texas Brigade: A Compendium*, 11, 255; Joseph Jones, "Medical Officers . . . of Tennessee," 249.

62. Record of Confederate Burials, "Frank Bream's Farm," O'Neal Journal, GNMP; Coco, *Vast Sea of Misery*, 147–49; Georg and Busey, *Nothing but Glory*, 275, 308, 339, 372, 389, 437.

63. Georg and Busey, *Nothing but Glory*, 263; Johnston, *Story of a Confederate Boy*, 218–20.

64. Hunton, *Autobiography*, 101.

65. Duncan, *Medical Department*, 258; Frey, *Longstreet's Assault*, 163–89. Duncan claims that 279 soldiers from Pickett's Division were left behind; the list of Dr. Edward Rives shows 246.

66. Baruch, "A Surgeon's Story," 545.

67. Record of Confederate Burials, "Frank Bream Farm," O'Neal Journal, GNMP; Coco, *Vast Sea of Misery*, 144–47; Dickert, *Kershaw's Brigade*, 251–54; Hoke, *Great Invasion*, 495–96; Black, *Crumbling Defenses*, 51–53; Kirkland, *Broken Fortunes*, 250.

68. Baruch, "A Surgeon's Story," 545.

69. Cumming, "Tribute to the Man in Black"; Paul Jones Semmes to Wife, WT; Mary Oden to Mrs. Paul Jones Semmes, 10 July 1863, WT; Record of Confederate Burials, "Crawford's Farm," "J. Cunningham's Farm," and "Georgia (at John's Farm)," O'Neal Journal, GNMP; Coco, *Vast Sea of Misery*, 150–52.

70. *OR* 27(2):364–66; Duncan, *Medical Department*, 257–58.

71. Imboden, "Confederate Retreat," 420–24; Hoke, *Reminiscences*, 88–92; Roll of Prisoners of War, Chambersburg Hospital, 30 July 1863, Papers Relating to Union Hospitals, NA. Considering the times when it was reported the trains left Cashtown and when some individuals in those trains were spotted by civilians, it is clear that Hood's trains were followed by Pickett's and then McLaws's. Hoke, *Great Invasion*, 495–504.

72. William G. Deloney to Rosa, 4 July 1863, Delony Papers, UGA; Coco, *Vast Sea of Misery*, 108–11; Wounded Transferred, 21 July 1863, Papers Relating to Union Hospitals, NA.

73. Record of Confederate Burials, "Hunterstown Road under Cherry Tree near Hunterstown," O'Neal Journal, GNMP; William G. Delony to Rosa, 4 July 1863, Delony Papers, UGA; Hewett, *Roster of Confederate Soldiers*, 2:392, 3:364, 8:176, 12:511.

74. *Raleigh News and Observer*, 7 February 1907.

75. Black, *Crumbling Defenses*, 45–46; *OR* 27(2):699–700; Dickinson, *Jenkins of Greenbottom*, 64–65.

76. Hood, *Advance and Retreat*, 60; Wade Hampton to Sister, 18 July 1863, Hampton Family Papers, folder 80, USC-SCL; *OR* 27(3):516.

77. Imboden, "Confederate Retreat," 422–23; *OR* 27(2):436–37.

78. Imboden, "Confederate Retreat," 422–23; *OR* 27(2):437, 653–56; Landry Diary, 4 July 1863, Harrisburg Civil War Roundtable Papers, USAMHI.

79. *OR* 27(2):675.

80. Imboden, "Confederate Retreat," 422–23; Driver, *Staunton Artillery—McClanahan's Battery*, 76–78; Brooks, *Stories*, 261–62.

81. Imboden, "Confederate Retreat," 423.

82. Park, *Twelfth Alabama Infantry*, 55. Park notes that the trains of Rodes's Division, after a long halt, began to move toward Hagerstown at 1:00 o'clock. Although it reads "1:00 o'clock A.M.," this must have been a misprint because none of Ewell's trains started that late. Report of Court of Inquiry of Major James C. Bryan, Testimony of Major John D. Rogers and Captain John M. Jones, 29 August 1863. Compiled Service Records, NA. Jones was the acting quartermaster of Iverson's Brigade. He testified that Rodes's trains actually started moving at 2:00 P.M. Rogers, chief quartermaster of Rodes's Division, testified that Rodes's trains were ordered by Major Harman to "move to the rear of the corps train." The immense reserve train was also

known as the corps train. Chapman, *Bright and Gloomy Days*, 70–71; Bradwell, *Under the Southern Cross*, 132; Jedediah Hotchkiss to My Darling, 14 July 1863, Hotchkiss Papers, LC.

83. John Cabell Early, "Southern Boy," 40–41.

84. George Clark, *A Glance Backward*, 41.

85. Whitehorne Diary, 33–34, FLE.

86. Imboden, "Confederate Retreat," 423–24; Frank W. Imboden Diary, 9, Imboden Family Papers, UVA.

87. Alumni Records, "John Hyde Cameron in the War between the States," 19, VMI; Landry Diary, 5 July 1863, Harrisburg Civil War Roundtable Papers, USAMHI; *OR* 27(2):654–55.

88. Imboden, "Confederate Retreat," 423–24; *OR* 27(2):436–39.

89. The length of Harman's reserve train, the trains of Ewell's three divisions, and Imboden's trains together equals fifty-seven miles of trains. Imboden, "Confederate Retreat," 423–24; Jedediah Hotchkiss to My Darling, 14 July 1863, Hotchkiss Papers, LC. Hotchkiss recorded that there were forty miles of wagons in Ewell's trains. He was corroborated by others. Chapman, *Bright and Gloomy Days*, 70–71; Bradwell, *Under the Southern Cross*, 132; Hoke, *Great Invasion*, 215–16.

CHAPTER FIVE

1. Franklin Gardner Walter Diary, 9, Walter Papers, VSL.

2. War Department, *Regulations*, § 669.

3. *OR* 27(2):625; Owen, *In Camp and Battle*, 257; James E. Green Diary, 5 July 1863, Green Papers, NCDAH; W. P. Garrett Diary, 4 July 1863, KMB. Pickens wrote: "The wagon trains kept [to] the roads & a column of troops marched thro' the fields on each side." Samuel Pickens Diary, 5 July 1863, Pickens Papers, UA.

4. Franklin Gardner Walter Diary, 9, Walter Papers, VSL; *OR* 27(2):676. Major David G. McIntosh reported that the artillery waited to get into line on the Fairfield Road at the "Stone Bridge." The only stone bridge on that road was the one across Marsh Creek at the Blackhorse Tavern.

5. *OR* 27(2):581.

6. Ibid.

7. *OR* 27(1):928, 939, 943, 970, 977, 993–94.

8. McClellan, *Campaigns of . . . J. E. B. Stuart*, 353.

9. Ibid., 353–55; *OR* 27(2):498–99.

10. The Emack Family, 1–15; *Baltimore Sun*, 13 May 1886; L. Dale to Madam (Captain G. M. Emack's mother), 24 July 1863, George M. Emack Letters, WAT. After the war Emack moved to Versailles, Ky.; he died there and was buried in the City Cemetery.

11. Report of Court of Inquiry of Major James C. Bryan, Testimony of William T. Potter, Captain John M. Jones, and Major John D. Rogers, 29 August 1863, Compiled Service Records, NA. The order of the quartermaster, subsistence, ordnance, and ambulance trains is gleaned from the evidence of the three officers who testified at Major

Bryan's Court of Inquiry. Clearly O'Neal's was the last quartermaster train of Rodes's Brigade in the column. It followed Iverson's and Ramseur's. Neese, *Three Years*, 190 (quotation).

12. Edward E. Moore, *Story of a Cannoneer*, 201.

13. McClellan, *Campaigns of . . . J. E. B. Stuart*, 354.

14. Oscar W. Blacknall Memoirs, 15, Blacknall Papers, NCDAH.

15. *OR* 27(2):752–53.

16. Ibid.

17. Oscar W. Blacknall Memoirs, 15, Blacknall Papers, NCDAH; Green, *Recollections*, 177; Wellman, *Rebel Boast*, 133.

18. Green, *Recollections*, 177.

19. *OR* 27(1):154, 970, 988, 991, 993–94, 1035; Busey and Martin, *Regimental Strengths*, 99–100.

20. Warner, *Generals in Blue*, 108–9, 266.

21. *OR* 27(1):994, 998.

22. *OR* 27(1):998, 27(2):764; *Supplement to OR* 1(5):258.

23. Warner, Beers and Co., *Franklin County*, 376–77; *OR* 27(1):994. General Kilpatrick referred to Buhrman as a "farmer's boy."

24. Warner, Beers and Co., *Franklin County*, 376–77; Matthews to Zeilinger and Huff to Zeilinger, ANMP. Lieutenant Matthews and Private Huff of the First Michigan wrote to Zeilinger thanking her for her assistance.

25. Matthews to Zeilinger and Huff to Zeilinger, ANMP.

26. Boon, "Charge at Monterey"; McClellan, *Campaigns of . . . J. E. B. Stuart*, 353–54; Kidd, *Personal Recollections*, 168; Potter, *Memoirs*, 10–11; Bliss Diary, 4 July 1863, KL.

27. McClellan, *Campaigns of . . . J. E. B. Stuart*, 354.

28. Warner, Beers and Co., *Franklin County*, 376–77; Potter, *Memoirs*, 10–11.

29. Warner, Beers and Co., *Franklin County*, 376–77; *OR* 27(1):1014.

30. Glazier, *Three Years*, 268; Luther S. Trowbridge to J. Allen Bigelow, GNMP.

31. *OR* 27(1):994; Kidd, *Personal Recollections*, 168.

32. McClellan, *Campaigns of . . . J. E. B. Stuart*, 354.

33. Ibid.; *OR* 27(2):753.

34. *OR* 27(2):753.

35. *OR* 27(1):994; *Supplement to OR* 1(5):254; Edwin Bigelow, "A Michigan Sergeant," 222; McClellan, *Campaigns of . . . J. E. B. Stuart*, 355; Driver, *First and Second Maryland Cavalry*, 250.

36. Capehart, "Fighting His Way"; *OR* 27(1):994, 1019; *Supplement to OR* 1(5):285–86; Gillespie, *Company A, First Ohio Cavalry*, 155–56.

37. James Harvey Kidd to Father and Mother, 9 July 1863, Kidd Papers, UM-MHC; Kidd, *Personal Recollections*, 169.

38. McClellan, *Campaigns of . . . J. E. B. Stuart*, 355; Opie, *Rebel Cavalryman*, 173; Hopkins, *From Bull Run to Appomattox*, 105–6; *OR* 27(2):753.

39. Hopkins, *From Bull Run to Appomattox*, 105.

40. Ibid., 105–6; Opie, *Rebel Cavalryman*, 173.

41. Russell A. Alger to S. L. Gillespie, 27 April 1899, and Alger to Gen. L. G. Esten, 12 February 1897, Alger Papers, UM-MHC; *Supplement to OR* 1(5):273.

42. John A. Bigelow, "Draw Saber, Charge!"

43. Russell A. Alger to Gen. L. G. Esten, 12 February 1897, Alger Papers, UM-MHC; *Supplement to OR* 1(5):267–68.

44. *OR* 27(1):994, 1019; William Porter Wilkin to Dear Wife, 31 July 1863, Wilkin Papers, RKI.

45. Gillespie, *Company A, First Ohio Cavalry*, 157–58; James Harvey Kidd to Father and Mother, 9 July 1863, Kidd Papers, UM-MHC; Kidd, *Personal Recollections*, 170; William Porter Wilkin to Dear Wife, 31 July 1863, Wilkin Papers, RKI.

46. *OR* 27(1):1019.

47. L. Dale to Madam (Mother of Captain George M. Emack), 24 July 1863; George M. Emack to Dora, 27 July 1863, WAT.

48. B. F. Jones, "No Terrors There."

49. Driver, *First and Second Maryland Cavalry*, 59; Hopkins, *From Bull Run to Appomattox*, 107.

50. *Supplement to the OR* 1(5):286; Kidd, *Personal Recollections*, 170.

51. Minor, "Night after Gettysburg," 140.

52. Edward E. Moore, *Story of a Cannoneer*, 202–3.

53. Ibid., 203; Driver, *1st and 2nd Rockbridge Artillery*, 81.

54. Shepherd, "Wounded and Captured," 76.

55. Green, *Recollections*, 177–78.

56. Boon, "Charge at Monterey."

57. Report of Court of Inquiry of Major James C. Bryan, Testimony of William T. Potter, 28 August 1862, Compiled Service Records, NA.

58. Edward E. Moore, *Story of a Cannoneer*, 208.

59. Park, *Twelfth Alabama Infantry*, 55.

60. Turner, "Twenty-third Regiment," 238; Manarin and Jordan, *North Carolina Troops*, 3:264–65, 319, 9:5–6, 10:293; 11:7; Chapman, *Bright and Gloomy Days*, 70.

61. *OR* 27(2):753; McClellan, *Campaigns of . . . J. E. B. Stuart*, 355.

62. Chamberlaine, *Memoirs*, 73–74.

63. Oscar W. Blacknall Memoirs, 15, Blacknall Papers, NCDAH.

64. William O. Johnson, "The 49th Virginia Infantry at Gettysburg," Daniel Papers, box 23, UVA.

65. Hall, *Diary*, 83.

66. Driver, *First and Second Maryland Cavalry*, 59; Edward E. Moore, *Story of a Cannoneer*, 205; William S. White, "Diary," 211–12. Most observers put the number of captured wagons and ambulances at between 250 and 300 and the number of prisoners at about 1,300. Allen Price to Abram Wear, ANMP; B. F. Jones, "No Terrors There"; Lovejoy, "Charge at Monterey"; Bliss Diary, 4 July 1863, KL; Edwin P. Havens to Nell, 6 July 1863, Havens Papers, MSU; William V. Stuart to Friend, 9 July 1863, William W. Stewart Papers, DPL; William Ball to Father and Mother, 8 July 1863, Mr. and Mrs. Ed Ridgeway Collection, WMU; *OR* 27(1):1019.

67. *OR* 27(2):753.

68. *OR* 27(1):994. The burial of two soldiers from the Fourth North Carolina Cavalry near the gatehouse at Monterey Springs was noted in the Record of Confederate Burials, "At Gatehouse near Monterey Springs," O'Neal Journal, GNMP.

69. Kilpatrick completely overstated his captures in claiming that "Ewell's large train was entirely destroyed." *OR* 27(1):994.

CHAPTER SIX

1. Warner, Beers and Co., *Franklin County*, 801; Hoke, *Great Invasion*, 493–94. Snyder was the assessor and collector of taxes, school director, auditor, and justice of the peace in Franklin County. His lovely stone house still stands on the New Franklin Road east of New Franklin.

2. Hoke, *Great Invasion*, 493–94.

3. Waddell Diary, 5 July 1863, CSA "Core Collection": Regiments and Soldiers, MOC. Waddell was the "wounded soldier" quoted in the previous paragraph.

4. Imboden, "Confederate Retreat," 423.

5. Ibid.; Cumming, "Tribute to the Man in Black."

6. Harris, "Civil War Diary," 1772.

7. Hege, *Marion and Environments*, 56–57.

8. Imboden, "Confederate Retreat," 424–25.

9. Julius Lineback Diary, 4 July 1863, Lineback Papers, vol. 2, UNC-SHC.

10. Baker, "Diary and Recollections," 98; Popkins, "Imboden's Brigade," 552.

11. Bartlett, *Military Record of Louisiana*, 195.

12. Hoke, *Reminiscences*, 89.

13. Ibid., 88.

14. Ibid., 89–90.

15. Lokey, "Wounded at Gettysburg."

16. Hoke, *Reminiscences*, 90–91.

17. Ibid.; Warner, Beers and Co., *Franklin County*, 283, 684–95; Apperson, *Repairing the "March of Mars,"* 477.

18. Hoke, *Reminiscences*, 90; Roll of Prisoners of War, U.S. General Hospital, Chambersburg, 31 July 1863, Papers Relating to Union Hospitals, NA.

19. Julius Lineback Diary, 5 July 1863, Lineback Papers, vol. 2, UNC-SHC.

20. Hoke, *Great Invasion*, 495–96; Warner, Beers and Co., *Franklin County*, 798–99.

21. Hoke, *Great Invasion*, 495–96; Coco, *Wasted Valor*, 30. Carter was buried in the Methodist Cemetery, Chambersburg.

22. Hoke, *Great Invasion*, 495–96; Dickert, *Kershaw's Brigade*, 251. The McLeod's remains were finally buried in the Parnassus Methodist Church graveyard in Marlboro County, S.C. Coco, *Gettysburg's Confederate Dead*, 32.

23. Boatner, *Civil War Dictionary*, 218; Ulrich Dahlgren Notebook, 261, Adm. John A. Dahlgren Papers, LC; Dahlgren, *Memoir*, 157–58.

24. Dahlgren, *Memoir*, 158–63; Boatner, *Civil War Dictionary*, 218.

25. Ulrich Dahlgren Notebook, 260, Adm. John A. Dahlgren Papers, LC; Dahlgren, *Memoir*, 162–63.

26. Ulrich Dahlgren Notebook, 260, Adm. John A. Dahlgren Papers, LC; Dahlgren, *Memoir*, 163–67.

27. Ulrich Dahlgren Notebook, 261–62, Adm. John A. Dahlgren Papers, LC; Dahlgren, *Memoir*, 158–67; McHenry Howard, *Recollections*, 207–13.

28. Ulrich Dahlgren Notebook, 261–62, Adm. John A. Dahlgren Papers, LC; Dahlgren, *Memoir*, 158–67.

29. Frank M. Imboden Diary, 9, Imboden Family Papers, UVA; Alumni Records, "John Hyde Cameron in the War between the States," 19, VMI; Driver, *Staunton Artillery—McClanahan's Battery*, 110, 113; Landry Diary, 15, Harrisburg Civil War Roundtable Papers, USAMHI; Popkins, "Imboden's Brigade," 552; Imboden, "Confederate Retreat," 425.

30. Ulrich Dahlgren Notebook, 261, Adm. John A. Dahlgren Papers, LC; Dahlgren, *Memoir*, 167.

31. Popkins, "Imboden's Brigade," 552; Frank M. Imboden Diary, 9, Imboden Family Papers, UVA; Imboden, "Confederate Retreat," 425.

32. Alumni Records, "John Hyde Cameron in the War between the States," 19, VMI; Driver, *Staunton Artillery—McClanahan's Battery*, 110, 113, 118; Delauter, *18th Virginia Cavalry*, 99; Frank M. Imboden Diary, 9, Imboden Family Papers, UVA.

33. Imboden, "Confederate Retreat," 425; Landry Diary, 15, Harrisburg Civil War Roundtable Papers, USAMHI.

34. Waddell Diary, 5 July 1863, CSA "Core Collection": Regiments and Soldiers, MOC.

35. Preston, *Tenth Regiment of Cavalry*, 129.

36. Gregg, Manuscript, 218, Gregg Papers, LC; Norman Ball Journal, 5 July 1863, Ball Papers, CHS; Resser Diary, 5 July 1863, and Robinson Diary, 5 July 1863, *Civil War Times Illustrated* Collection, USAMHI. Tobie, *First Maine Cavalry*, 180; OR 27(1): 977. Resser, Robinson, and Tobie all agree that the number of prisoners exceeded 2,000.

37. Preston, *Tenth Regiment of Cavalry*, 129–30; Norman Ball Journal, 1863, Ball Papers, CHS.

38. John Parris Sheahan to Father, 6 July 1863, Sheahan Papers, MHS.

39. Walter Kempster to My Dearest Best-Beloved One, LLC.

CHAPTER SEVEN

1. OR 27(3):499, 502, 506.

2. OR 27(3):501–2, 517–18, 27(1):489.

3. OR 27(3):514.

4. OR 27(3):517–18, 27(1):78; Hyde, *Union Generals Speak*, 111–14. Meade reiterated his uncertainty regarding Lee's intentions on 4, 5, and 6 July at the hearings before the Joint Committee on the Conduct of the War in 1864.

5. OR 27(3):516. Taylor's sightings were recorded at 5:15 P.M. and 7:15 P.M., 4 July.

6. Ibid. Signal officers William H. Hill and Isaac Slayton Lyon on Little Round Top recorded their last sighting at 7:40 P.M., 4 July. Hyde, *Union Generals Speak*, 315.

7. *OR* 27(3):519-20.

8. Rufus Ingalls to Montgomery C. Meigs, 4 July 1863, Records of the Quarter-master General, Consolidated Correspondence File, NA; *OR* 27(3):520; Tilney, *My Life in the Army*, 47; Hering, "Dr. Hering Describes Wagon Trains and Prisoners"; Miss S. C. Shriver to My Dear Lizzie, 29 June 1863, William H. Shriver Papers, LC.

9. Coburn Diary, 2 July 1863, Archives Collection, USAMHI; Rhodes, *Battery B, First Regiment Rhode Island Light Artillery*, 208; *OR* 27(1):761, 27(3):472, 520, 601, 604-6; Patrick, *Inside Lincoln's Army*, 268.

10. *OR* 27(3):472, 494-95, 521-24; Haupt, *Reminiscences*, 208-22; Ward, *That Man Haupt*, 159-62.

11. *OR* 27(1):78.

12. *OR* 27(1):939, 956, 970, 977, 987-88, 993.

13. *OR* 27(1):429, 455, 771, 791, 795, 834, 27(3):530, 537, 540.

14. *OR* 27(1):78.

15. *OR* 27(3):517, 530-31.

16. *OR* 27(3):546. On 5 July General French received word that "five hundred wagons (rebel), guarded by about 150 infantry, 150 cavalry, three pieces of inferior-looking artillery, and from 3,000 to 5,000 head of cattle passed through Hagerstown last night after 11 o'clock to about 4 o'clock." Undoubtedly obtained from civilian informants, this dispatch is the only information known to exist of the time Harman's trains reached Hagerstown. Williams, *Washington County, Maryland*, 1:348. Williams recorded that the "supply train" of Lee's army "was heard in the streets" of Hagerstown "before the dawn on July 5" and continued "all day long." McCall, "7th Tennessee—Battle of Falling Waters." Private McCall remembered that "most of our wagons had passed over [to Virginia] before the rise in the river."

17. *OR* 27(3):517, 530-31. The Taylor House (though significantly altered) and the Embrey warehouses at the canal basin still stand. Much of Williamsport is still intact. The Embrey warehouses were operated by Embrey and Company, a business owned by Theodore Embrey of Williamsport. Williamsport Chamber of Commerce, *Williamsport and Vicinity*, 85.

18. Mish, "Maidstone-on-the-Potomac," 41. Also known as "Watkins Ferry," it was created by an act of the Virginia House of Burgesses and extended "from the mouth of Canagoshego (Conococheague) Creek in Maryland across the Potowmack to the Evan Watkins Landing, about 250 yards southeast." Thompson, "Data on Watkins Ferry," 8, Watkins Ferry File, MBCPL; *OR* 27(2):753. "Maidstone-on-the-Potomac" still stands along Route 11 near the Potomac River. The ferry operated between "Maidstone-on-the-Potomac" and the canal basin, following, roughly, the course of the present-day bridge over the river for U.S. 11.

19. *OR* 27(3):546.

20. *OR* 27(2):753.

21. Ibid.; McHenry Howard, *Recollections*, 213.

22. Whitehorne Diary, 31, 35, FLE.

23. *OR* 27(2):615, 625; Myers, *The Comanches*, 204; Tanner, *Reminiscences*, 11; Westwood A. Todd Memoirs, 135, Todd Papers, UNC-SHC.

24. *OR* 27(2):625.

25. Ibid.; Jenkins Journal, 65, GNMP.

26. *OR* 27(2):625.

27. Francis Milton Kennedy Diary, 4, 5 July 1863, Kennedy Papers, UNC-SHC; Henry Clay Albright Diary, 4, 5 July 1863, Albright Papers, NCDAH. According to his after-action report, General Lane assumed command of Pender's Division after the wounding of General Trimble on 3 July and led the division during the march to Hagerstown. *OR* 27(2):667.

28. George Washington Hall Diary, 4, 5 July 1863, Hall Papers, LC; Tanner, *Reminiscences*, 10–11.

29. Hinshaw, "Society of Friends during the Late Rebellion," 8–10, BFM. Gettysburg resident William Hamilton Bayly recalled that a young Confederate—also from North Carolina—knocked on his door and asked if he could hide in Bayly's home. After 1 July, the soldier had seen enough of death and destruction. The Bayly family concealed him. Miers and Brown, *Gettysburg*, 89–90, citing the William Hamilton Bayly Diary, GNMP.

30. Hinshaw, "The Society of Friends during the Late Rebellion," 8–10, BFM.

31. Charles Edward Lippitt Diary, 4, 5 July 1863, Lippitt Papers, UNC-SHC.

32. Bond Memoir, 180–81, CSA "Core Collection": Bound Volumes, MOC; Berkeley, *Four Years*, 52. Cannoneer Henry Robinson Berkeley of the Amherst-Nelson Battery counted "ten or a dozen dwelling houses on fire between our line and the town."

33. John Warwick Daniel Journal, 20, and William O. Johnson, "The 49th Virginia Infantry at Gettysburg," Daniel Papers, box 23, UVA; Samuel W. Eaton Diary, 4, 5 July 1863, Eaton Papers, UNC-SHC; James E. Green Diary, 9, Green Papers, NCDAH; Bond Memoir," 180–81, CSA "Core Collection": Bound Volumes, MOC.

34. Myers, *The Comanches*, 204.

35. West, *A Texan in Search of a Fight*, 99.

36. Edward Porter Alexander, *Fighting for the Confederacy*, 267. The road Colonel Alexander discussed using to reach the Fairfield Road was the Willoughby Run Road.

37. Franklin Gardner Walter Diary, 9, Walter Papers, VSL.

38. Edward Porter Alexander, *Fighting for the Confederacy*, 267.

39. *OR* 51(2):734–35; Circular, 6 July 1863, 5:30 A.M., Order Book, Col. J. B. Walton, Chief of Artillery, First Army Corps, ANV, Walton Collection, TU. Although the order cited is dated 6 July, it provides the general pattern for the arrangement of Longstreet's troops on 5 July.

40. Fletcher, *Rebel Private*, 65.

41. *OR* 51(2):734–35. The orders of march for Longstreet's Corps of 6 July 1863 do not mention Pickett's Division. As provost guard for the prisoners of war, the division was transferred, for operational purposes during the retreat, from Longstreet's Corps to the headquarters of the army. Gantt, "The Gettysburg Prisoners," 4 July 1863, KMB; R. N. Martin to My Dear Aunt and Cousin, HS; Newell Burch Diary, 4, 5 July 1863, Winey Collection, USAMHI.

42. R. N. Martin to My Dear Aunt and Cousin, HS; Gantt, "The Gettysburg Prisoners," 4, 5 July 1863, KMB.

43. R. N. Martin to My Dear Aunt and Cousin, HS.

44. *OR* 27(3):532.

45. Brown, *Brown's Civil War*, 226; Edward Porter Alexander, *Fighting for the Confederacy*, 267. Colonel Alexander, whose battalions led Longstreet's Corps with Hood's Division, fell into line behind Heth's Division of Hill's Corps. Major G. Campbell Brown commented that the head of Ewell's Corps fell into line behind McLaws's Division of Longstreet's Corps. Pickett's Division had to have marched between Hood's and McLaws's Divisions. Collins, "A Prisoner's March," 3:432.

46. King, *My Experience*, 14.

47. John R. Morey Diary, 4 July 1863, Morey Papers, UM-MHC; Allen Price to Abram Wear, ANMP.

48. Frank Moore, *Rebellion Record*, 7:188.

49. Ibid.; John R. Morey Diary, 5 July 1863, Morey Papers, UM-MHC; Blinn Diary, 5 July 1863, GNMP; Bliss Diary, 5 July 1863, KL.

50. John A. Bigelow, "Flashing Sabers"; Blinn Diary, 5 July 1863, GNMP; Allen Price to Abram Wear, ANMP.

51. John A. Bigelow, "Flashing Sabers"; Frank Moore, *Rebellion Record*, 7:188; Beaudry, *Fifth New York Cavalry*, 68.

52. *OR* 27(1):1014; Frank Moore, *Rebellion Record*, 7:188.

53. Frank Moore, *Rebellion Record*, 7:188.

54. Ibid., 188-89.

55. Oscar W. Blacknall Memoirs, 6-7, Blacknall Papers, NCDAH.

56. *OR* 27(2):699.

57. Ibid., 700; Frassanito, *Gettysburg*, 26-27.

58. *OR* 27(2):700.

59. Frank Moore, *Rebellion Record*, 7:189.

60. *OR* 27(1):994.

61. Ibid.; 27(2):700.

62. *OR* 27(2):700; R. T. L. Beale, *Ninth Virginia Cavalry*, 90-91.

63. *OR* 27(1):994, 1009, 1035-36, 27(2):700; Frank Moore, *Rebellion Record*, 7:189.

64. *OR* 27(2):700.

65. *OR* 27(2):700-701.

66. *OR* 27(2):701.

67. Whitehorne Diary, 35-36, FLE.

CHAPTER EIGHT

1. *OR* 27(1):663, 666, 678-79; Hyde, *Union Generals Speak*, 112-13.

2. *OR* 27(1):692, 27(2):448, 471, 493, 558; Brown, *Brown's Civil War*, 226; John Warwick Daniel Journal, 20, Daniel Papers, box 23, VHS; W. B. Bailey Diary, 5 July 1863, Bailey Papers, TU. Over the past two days Green's force had seen service with the cavalry at Gettysburg and was seriously short of ammunition. One of its guns and the gun crew were riding with Colonel Baker's cavalry brigade. *OR* 27(2):497-98.

3. Baruch, "A Surgeon's Story," 545-46.

4. *OR* 27(2):471; Myers, *The Comanches*, 204.

5. James E. Green Diary, 5 July 1863, Green Papers, NCDAH.

6. *OR* 27(1):663, 666, 692, 695, 27(2):471.

7. Charles Edward Lippitt Diary, 5 July 1863, Lippitt Papers, UNC-SHC.

8. *OR* 27(2):471-72.

9. Ibid., 493; W. B. Bailey Diary, 5 July 1863, Bailey Papers, TU; Murray, *South Georgia Rebels*, 139-40; Lillian Henderson, *Roster . . . of Georgia*, 3:183-84.

10. *OR* 27(1):692, 695.

11. Major John Warwick Daniel Journal, 21, Daniel Papers, box 23, VHS.

12. *OR* 27(1):692, 695, 27(2):493.

13. *OR* 27(3):530-31. Meade made it clear to Sedgwick that he had "[no] intention to bring on an engagement" with the enemy. Sedgwick's only purpose in advancing on 5 July was to ascertain the "position and movement of the enemy."

14. Imboden, "Confederate Retreat," 425.

15. Ibid.; Edward Owen Diary, 127, CSA "Core Collection": Regiments and Soldiers, MOC; Brooks, *Stories*, 110. Private I. Norval Baker of Company F, Eighteenth Virginia Cavalry, was stationed at the intersection of the National Road and the Cumberland Valley Turnpike when the last wagon passed him on its way to Williamsport "several hours after sunrise on the 6th of July." Baker, "Diary and Recollections," 96.

16. Imboden, "Confederate Retreat," 425.

17. Ibid.; *OR* 27(2):488; Williams, "Fifty-fourth Regiment," 270-71; Wingfield, "Diary," 27.

18. Baker, "Diary and Recollections," 98; *OR* 27(2):753.

19. *OR* 27(2):753.

20. *OR* 27(2):488; Worsham, *One of Jackson's Foot Cavalry*, 104.

21. *OR* 27(2):488; Williams, "Fifty-fourth Regiment," 270-71; Wingfield, "Diary," 27; John Paris Diary, 15 June to 5 July 1863, Paris Papers, UNC-SHC; Waddell, *Annals*, 310.

22. John Paris Diary, 5 July 1863, Paris Papers, UNC-SHC.

23. Wingfield, "Diary," 27; Baker, "Diary and Recollections," 98.

24. John Paris Diary, 5 July 1863, Paris Papers, UNC-SHC.

25. Ibid.; *OR* 27(2):488, 498.

26. Worsham, *One of Jackson's Foot Cavalry*, 104.

27. Imboden, "Confederate Retreat," 425.

28. Beach, *First New York*, 254-63.

29. Ibid., 263.

30. Ibid., 263-64; Schaff, "Gettysburg Week," 174.

31. Beach, *First New York*, 264. The Mount Zion Evangelical Church still stands on the west side of Route 63 just north of Cearfoss.

32. LeGrand Wilson Jr., *Confederate Soldier*, 126; *Richmond Enquirer*, 14 August 1863. The *Enquirer* listed the wounded who were taken to Mercersburg. Most of them were from Davis's and Pettigrew's Brigades; a few were from Wright's and Wilcox's Brigades.

33. *Richmond Enquirer*, 14 August 1863; Belo, *Memoirs*, 22; Collette Leventhorpe to Marcus J. Wright, May 30, 1888, Wright Papers, DU; Schaff, "Gettysburg Week," 173, 175.

34. *Charlotte Daily Bulletin*, 23 August 1863; Unknown newspaper, n.d., Scrapbook, P.C. 13. 25, Pettigrew Family Papers, NCDAH; Manarin and Jordan, *North Carolina Troops*, 11:245.

35. *OR* 27(2):652–56.

36. Beach, *First New York*, 264.

37. LeGrand Wilson Jr., *Confederate Soldier*, 126.

38. Beach, *First New York*, 264–65; *OR* 27(2):654–56. Both Lieutenant Colonel John J. Garnett and Major Richardson claimed that Lieutenant Landry "turned over to Captain Hart his two three-inch United States rifles because he was unable to move them due to the jaded condition of the horses." It is clear, though, that they were abandoned. In fact, Richardson concludes his after-action report by stating: "From the reports of Captain Moore and Lieutenant Landry, I believe that the abandonment of the pieces and caissons of their batteries was unavoidable." Colonel Pierce reported to Couch: "Two pieces of artillery swamped and spiked; one here, in good trim." *OR* 27(3):577, 580. Obviously Landry left the guns behind because of his inability to pull them out of harm's way.

39. Gaines, "Sick and Wounded." Dr. John Mutius Gaines reported the names, regiments, and dates of wounding of all the injured left behind at Williamsport after Lee recrossed the river. He also noted that all of those at Williamsport who were wounded on 5 July were from the Sixty-second Virginia Mounted Infantry.

40. Beach, *First New York*, 265; *OR* 27(2):655; Lake, Griffing, and Stevenson, *Illustrated Atlas*, 15.

41. Underwood, "Twenty-sixth Regiment," 370; Hill, *North Carolina*, 591.

42. LeGrand Wilson Jr., *Confederate Soldier*, 126; *Richmond Enquirer*, 14 August 1863; Schaff, "Gettysburg Week," 173, 175; Manarin and Jordan, *North Carolina Troops*, 11:245; Beach, *First New York*, 264–65.

43. Beach, *First New York*, 265.

44. Ibid., 266.

45. Mills, "Supplemental Sketch," 182; Frank M. Imboden Diary, 9, Imboden Family Papers, UVA.

46. Beach, *First New York*, 265; Mills, "Supplemental Sketch," 182; Frank M. Imboden Diary, 9, Imboden Family Papers, UVA; Gaines, "Sick and Wounded."

47. *Charlotte Daily Bulletin*, 23 August 1863.

48. Beach, *First New York*, 265.

49. *OR* 27(2):437; Wingfield, "Diary," 27.

50. Maud Morrow Brown, *University Greys*, 49.

51. *OR* 27(3):580; Beach, *First New York*, 265–66.

52. Schaff, "Gettysburg Week," 173. The seminary building still stands on the present-day Mercersburg Academy campus.

53. *OR* 27(2):488.

54. Alumni Records, "John Hyde Cameron in the War between the States," VMI.

55. Pipes, "The First Twenty-three Years," 30, David Washington Pipes Papers, VHS.

56. *OR* 27(2):437.

57. *OR* 27(3):488; Worsham, *One of Jackson's Foot Cavalry*, 104; Wingfield, "Diary," 27–28.

58. Worsham, *One of Jackson's Foot Cavalry*, 104.

59. Ibid., 104–5.

60. *OR* 27(2):655.

61. *OR* 27(2):437, 655; Imboden, "Confederate Retreat," 426–27.

62. *OR* 27(2):488.

CHAPTER NINE

1. *OR* 27(1):672, 27(2):472, 558, 764.

2. *OR* 27(2):558, 570.

3. *OR* 27(2):570, 574–76; Manarin and Jordan, *North Carolina Troops*, 11:7, 56.

4. *OR* 27(1):680, 27(2):570, 576; James E. Green Diary, 6 July 1863, Green Papers, NCDAH.

5. *OR* 27(2):701; Charles Moore Jr. Diary, 6 July 1863, Moore Papers, TU.

6. *OR* 27(1):943; Gracey, *Sixth Pennsylvania Cavalry*, 181–82.

7. Gracey, *Sixth Pennsylvania Cavalry*, 181–82.

8. *OR* 27(1):928, 939; Cheney, *Ninth Regiment, New York Volunteer Cavalry*, 117.

9. Gracey, *Sixth Pennsylvania Cavalry*, 182.

10. Ibid.; Cheney, *Ninth Regiment, New York Volunteer Cavalry*, 117; Hard, *Eighth Cavalry Regiment, Illinois Volunteers*, 260.

11. Samuel J. B. V. Gilpin Diaries, 5 July 1863, Gilpin Papers, LC.

12. Cheney, *Ninth Regiment, New York Volunteer Cavalry*, 117.

13. Borries, "General John Buford," 4–5.

14. Gracey, *Sixth Pennsylvania Cavalry*, 183; Hard, *Eighth Cavalry Regiment, Illinois Volunteers*, 260–61; *New York Times*, 13 July 1863 (quotation); Hart, "Hanged at Frederick City"; Kelly, "The Spy at Frederick, Md."; Risch, "The Federick Spy Again."

15. William Henry Redman to Mother, 6 July 1863, Redman Papers, UVA.

16. *OR* 27(3):546

17. Ibid., 928; William Henry Redman to Mother, 6 July 1863, Redman Papers, UVA; John B. McIntosh to Wife, 6 July 1863, McIntosh Papers, BU; Gracey, *Sixth Pennsylvania Cavalry*, 183; Hard, *Eighth Cavalry Regiment, Illinois Volunteers*, 261; Hart, "Hanged at Frederick City"; Kelly, "The Spy at Frederick, Md."; Risch, "The Frederick Spy Again"; Busey and Martin, *Regimental Strengths*, 101–3.

18. John R. Morey Diary, 6 July 1863, Morey Papers, UM-MHC; *OR* 27(1):971, 995.

19. *OR* 27(1):995, 1006, 1036; Dahlgren, *Memoir*, 168.

20. Terrill, *Fourteenth Regiment, New Jersey Volunteers*, 18–19; Haynes, *Tenth Regiment, Vermont Volunteers*, 35–36; Williams, *Washington County, Maryland*, 1:173–74.

21. William Henry Redman to Mother, 6 July 1863, Redman Papers, UVA; Haynes, *Tenth Regiment, Vermont Volunteers*, 35-36; Terrill, *Fourteenth Regiment, New Jersey Volunteers*, 21.

22. William Henry Redman to Mother, 6 July 1863, Redman Papers, UVA.

23. Ibid.; *OR* 27(1):995.

24. *OR* 27(1):995.

25. Ibid., 995, 1006; Dahlgren, *Memoir*, 168.

26. R. T. L. Beale, *Ninth Virginia Cavalry*, 92; Williams, *Washington County, Maryland*, 1:450.

27. *OR* 27(1):1006; Rodenbough, "Historical Sketch," 17-18; St. Clair, "The Fight at Hagerstown," 94.

28. Schuricht, "Jenkins's Brigade," 346-47; Jacobs, "Custer's Charge."

29. *OR* 27(1):1006; R. T. L. Beale, *Ninth Virginia Cavalry*, 92; Krick, *Lee's Colonels*, 101; Williams, *Washington County, Maryland*, 1:396. St. John's Lutheran Church, although altered, is still standing.

30. Charles Moore Jr. Diary, 6 July 1863, Moore Papers, TU.

31. Bond Memoir, 183, CSA "Core Collection": Bound Volumes, MOC; George Wilson Booth, *Personal Reminiscences*, 193.

32. Bond Memoir, 183, CSA "Core Collection": Bound Volumes, MOC.

33. Ibid., 184; R. T. L. Beale, *Ninth Virginia Cavalry*, 92.

34. *OR* 27(2):702.

35. *OR* 27(1):1006, 1009-10, 1014; Beaudry, *Fifth New York Cavalry*, 68-69. The Hagerstown Female Seminary was located at the present site of the Hagerstown Hospital. Williams, *Washington County, Maryland*, 1:259.

36. Neese, *Three Years*, 193-94; Charles William McVicar Diary, 19, McVicar Papers, VSL.

37. Jacobs, "Custer's Charge."

38. *OR* 27(1):1006, 27(2):702.

39. Bond Memoir, 183-84, CSA "Core Collection": Bound Volumes, MOC.

40. Ibid., 184.

41. *OR* 27(1):1006; R. T. L. Beale, *Ninth Virginia Cavalry*, 92; Ulrich Dahlgren Notebook, 261, Adm. John A. Dahlgren Papers, LC.

42. R. T. L. Beale, *Ninth Virginia Cavalry*, 92; Bond Memoir, 184, CSA "Core Collection": Bound Volumes, MOC; Ulrich Dahlgren Notebook, 261, Adm. John A. Dahlgren Papers, LC.

43. George Wilson Booth, *Personal Reminiscences*, 93-94; Bond Memoir, 184, CSA "Core Collection": Bound Volumes, MOC.

44. Bond Memoir, 185, CSA "Core Collection": Bound Volumes, MOC.

45. Phillips, "Hanover, Gettysburg and Hagerstown," 85; St. Clair, "The Fight at Hagerstown," 94.

46. Coltrane, *Memoirs*, 17.

47. St. Clair, "The Fight at Hagerstown," 94-95.

48. Ibid.; Williams, *Washington County, Maryland*, 1:394, 485. Zion Reformed Church is still standing.

49. Jacobs, "Custer's Charge"; St. Clair, "The Fight at Hagerstown," 96–97.

50. St. Clair, "The Fight at Hagerstown," 95; Ulrich Dahlgren Notebook, 261–62, Adm. John A. Dahlgren Papers, LC; Dahlgren, *Memoir*, 169–70.

51. St. Clair, "The Fight at Hagerstown," 95–96; *OR* 27(1):1006, 1014; Potter, *Memoirs*, 11–12.

52. Jacobs, "Custer's Charge."

53. Ibid.; Rodenbough, "Historical Sketch," 18; Phillips, "Hanover, Gettysburg and Hagerstown," 85.

54. Bond Memoir, 186, CSA "Core Collection": Bound Volumes, MOC; George Wilson Booth, *Personal Reminiscences*, 94.

55. Green, "A People at War," 254–58.

56. Jacobs, "Custer's Charge."

57. Luther S. Trowbridge to J. Allen Bigelow, n.d., GNMP; Ulrich Dahlgren Notebook, 262, Adm. John A. Dahlgren Papers, LC.

58. R. T. L. Beale, *Ninth Virginia Cavalry*, 92; Jacobs, "Custer's Charge."

59. R. T. L. Beale, *Ninth Virginia Cavalry*, 93; Jacobs, "Custer's Charge."

60. *OR* 27(2):58.

61. Rodenbough, "Historical Sketch," 18; St. Clair, "Hanover, Gettysburg and Hagerstown," 95–96; Jacobs, "Custer's Charge."

62. St. Clair, "Hanover, Gettysburg and Hagerstown," 96.

63. Ibid., 96–97.

64. *OR* 27(1):1006; William Wells to Parents, 7 July 1863, Wells Papers, UVA; Beaudry, *Fifth New York Cavalry*, 68–69.

CHAPTER TEN

1. William Henry Redman to Mother, 6 July 1863, Redman Papers, UVA.

2. *OR* 27(1):928; Gracey, *Sixth Pennsylvania Cavalry*, 183.

3. *OR* 27(1):928.

4. Hendershott, "The Civil War," 32, Gary Hendershott, Little Rock, Ark. The Hendershott sale catalog of September 2000 pictured the blue regimental flag of the Twelfth Illinois. "I Like Your Style" was hand painted on the riband above the eagle; "12th Regt. Ill. Cavalry" was painted on the riband below the eagle. The flag was the one carried by the regiment at Gettysburg.

5. Imboden, "Confederate Retreat," 426–27; *OR* 27(2):437.

6. Black, *Crumbling Defenses*, 46–47, 50; Shotwell, *Papers*, 2:35.

7. Belo, *Memoirs*, 22.

8. Imboden, "Confederate Retreat," 426; Black, *Crumbling Defenses*, 46–47; William R. Aylett to Brother, MSS. The battle of Williamsport has always been known as the "Wagoners' Fight." Shotwell, *Papers*, 2:35; Worsham, *One of Jackson's Foot Cavalry*, 104–5.

9. Imboden, "Confederate Retreat," 426–27.

10. Hart et al., "Hart's Battery," 52–56, Hart Papers, USC-SCL.

11. Imboden, "Confederate Retreat," 427.

12. *OR* 27(1):928.

13. Squires, "The Last of Lee's Battle Line," chap. VI, Squires Papers, LC; Last Will and Testament of Otho Williams, JLH. Rose Hill Manor was designed by Benjamin H. Latrobe Jr. and built in 1803, when Otho Williams acquired his lands east of Williamsport. The house is of classic Federal design with a beautiful fan window over the front door. Williams and his second wife, the former Agnes McDowell, had six daughters, three of whom died in infancy. Of the three survivors—Mary Emma, Virginia, and Louisa Jane—Mary Emma and one other may have been at Rose Hill on 6 July with their father and mother. Williams was apparently a collateral relation to General Otho Williams, the Revolutionary War hero who settled at Williamsport and for whom the town was named. Rose Hill Manor and most of Otho Williams's farm are still intact. At the time of this writing, the house and farm were owned by Jane L. Hershey, of Williamsport, who materially assisted me by sharing her manuscripts and knowledge of the Williams family and her photographs of the manor.

14. Squires, "The Last of Lee's Battle Line," chap. VI, Squires Papers, LC.

15. *OR* 27(1):928, 27(2):437, 655.

16. Popkins, "Imboden's Brigade," 552; Baker, "Diary and Recollections," 98.

17. Gracey, *Sixth Pennsylvania Cavalry*, 183-84.

18. *OR* 27(2):437, 499, 655.

19. Hart et al., "Hart's Battery," 52-56, Hart Papers, USC-SCL.

20. Chapman, *Bright and Gloomy Days*, 71.

21. Imboden, "Confederate Retreat," 427.

22. William G. Delony to Rosa, 7 July 1863, Delony Papers, UGA.

23. Imboden, "Confederate Retreat," 427.

24. Ibid.; *OR* 27(2):437, 499, 655; Gillespie, *Company A, First Ohio Cavalry*, 161-62.

25. *OR* 27(1):935; Samuel J. B. V. Gilpin Diaries, 6 July 1863, Gilpin Papers, LC; Flavius Josephus Bellamy to Parents, 9 July 1863, and Bellamy Diary, 6 July 1863, Bellamy Papers, ISL; Worsham, *One of Jackson's Foot Cavalry*, 105; Cheney, *Ninth Regiment, New York Volunteer Cavalry*, 118. Cheney reported the capture of twenty-seven wagons and forty-six prisoners by the Third Indiana. Bellamy reported similar numbers.

26. *OR* 27(1):935, 1032; Hard, *Eighth Cavalry Regiment, Illinois Volunteers*, 261.

27. Chapman, *Bright and Gloomy Days*, 71; McKim, *Recollections*, 189-90; Jedediah Hotchkiss to My Darling, 7 July 1863, Hotchkiss Papers, LC.

28. Barnet, *Martyrs and Heroes*, 74.

29. Worsham, *One of Jackson's Foot Cavalry*, 106-8.

30. Ibid., 106; *OR* 27(2):437.

31. Barnet, *Martyrs and Heroes*, 74-75.

32. Ibid.; Worsham, *One of Jackson's Foot Cavalry*, 106.

33. Barnet, *Martyrs and Heroes*, 75.

34. Worsham, *One of Jackson's Foot Cavalry*, 107; Hard, *Eighth Cavalry Regiment, Illinois Volunteers*, 261; David Washington Pipes Memoirs, 30, Pipes Papers, VHS.

35. *OR* 27(1):1032; Worsham, *One of Jackson's Foot Cavalry*, 107.

36. *OR* 27(1):1032, 27(2):437-38, 655; Worsham, *One of Jackson's Foot Cavalry*, 107.

37. *OR* 27(1):1032; Worsham, *One of Jackson's Foot Cavalry*, 107-8; Williams, "Fifty-Fourth Regiment," 271.

38. Imboden, "Confederate Retreat," 427; Brooks, *Stories*, 261–62.

39. Brooks, *Stories*, 261–62.

40. Imboden, "Confederate Retreat," 427; Black, *Crumbling Defenses*, 47.

41. Ibid.; *OR* 27(2):437, 655; Worsham, *One of Jackson's Foot Cavalry*, 107–8.

42. Imboden, "Confederate Retreat," 427; Black, *Crumbling Defenses*, 47.

43. Black, *Crumbling Defenses*, 47; William G. Delony to Rosa, 7 July 1863, Delony Papers, UGA.

44. *OR* 27(2):702–3; Morrissett Diary, 6 July 1863, CSA "Core Collection": Regiments and Soldiers, MOC.

45. *OR* 27(1):928, 935, 940; Gracey, *Sixth Pennsylvania Cavalry*, 185; Moyer, *Seventeenth Regiment Pennsylvania Volunteer Cavalry*, 67.

46. *OR* 27(1):928; Gracey, *Sixth Pennsylvania Cavalry*, 184; Hard, *Eighth Cavalry Regiment, Illinois Volunteers*, 262; Flavius Josephus Bellamy to Parents, 9 July 1863, and Bellamy Diary, 6 July 1863, Bellamy Papers, ISL. Gracey characterized Kilpatrick's men as "demoralized." Hard maintained that Kilpatrick, "falling in our rear, blocked up the only road by which we could retreat, and thus left us to receive and resist the entire force of the enemy."

47. Kidd, *Personal Recollections*, 174–77.

48. Ibid., 1020.

49. Blue Reminiscence, 91, *Civil War Times Illustrated* Collection, USAMHI; McDonald, *Diary*, 177. Cornelia McDonald mistakenly refers to the events surrounding the apron flag as taking place on 13 July 1863 instead of 6 July.

50. *OR* 27(1):702, 27(2):764; R. T. L. Beale, *Ninth Virginia Cavalry*, 93–94; Blue Reminiscence, 91–92, *Civil War Times Illustrated* Collection, USAMHI; *St. Mary's Beacon*, 27 April 1905.

51. *OR* 27(1):1020; Blue Reminiscence, 91–92, *Civil War Times Illustrated* Collection, USAMHI; Charles William McVicar Diary, 19, McVicar Papers, VSL; Bond Memoir, 187–88, CSA "Core Collection": Regiments and Soldiers, MOC.

52. Neese, *Three Years*, 194.

53. R. T. L. Beale, *Ninth Virginia Cavalry*, 93–94; *St. Mary's Beacon*, 27 April 1905; Bond Memoir, 188, CSA "Core Collection": Regiments and Soldiers, MOC.

54. *OR* 27(1):971, 995.

55. *OR* 27(1):931.

56. Imboden, "Confederate Retreat," 428; *OR* 27(2):715; Chapman, *Bright and Gloomy Days*, 71; Julius Lineback Diary, 6 July 1863, Lineback Papers, vol. 2, UNC-SHC.

57. Hart et al., "Hart's Battery," 52–56, Hart Papers, USC-SCL.

CHAPTER ELEVEN

1. Charles Edward Lippitt Diary, 5 July 1863, Lippitt Papers, UNC-SHC.

2. Ibid.; Samuel Pickens Diary, 5 July 1863, Pickens Papers, UA; W. B. Bailey Diary, 5 July 1863, Bailey Papers, TU; Henry Clay Albright Diary, 5 July 1863, Albright Papers, NCDAH; Paul Turner Vaughan Diary, 5 July 1863, Vaughan Papers, UA; James B. Clifton Diary, 5 July 1863, Clifton Papers, NCDAH; Garrett Diary, 5 July

1863, KMB; Francis Milton Kennedy Diary, 5 July 1863, Kennedy Papers, UNC-SHC; *OR* 27(2):448, 471-72, 558.

3. Kathy Georg Harrison to Author, January 15, 2003, citing Damage Claim Applications, PHMC; James H. Wood, *The War*, 154.

4. James H. Wood, *The War*, 154-56.

5. Ibid.; *OR* 27(2):764.

6. *OR* 27(2):448, 471-72, 558.

7. *OR* 27(1):663, 27(2):558; Seymour Journal, 5 July 1863, GNMP.

8. *OR* 27(3):554-55, 558, 561; Hyde, *Union Generals Speak*, 113.

9. *OR* 27(3):555.

10. *OR* 27(1):80-81, 27(3):532-33, 547; Meade, *Life and Letters*, 2:125-26; Butterfield, *Biographical Memorial*, 125-27; Hyde, *Union Generals Speak*, 113-14.

11. *OR* 27(3):533-35, 537, 554-55, 558.

12. Ibid., 523.

13. *OR* 27(1):84, 86, 27(3):568-69, 601.

14. *OR* 27(3):535, 537, 540, 557-58.

15. R. N. Martin to My Dear Aunt and Cousin, HS; Gantt, "The Gettysburg Prisoners," 6 July 1863, KMB; Burch Diary, 6 July 1863, Michael Winey Collection, USAMHI; Paxton Diary, 6 July 1863, Civil War Miscellaneous Collection, USAMHI; *Philadelphia Weekly Times*, 22 April 1882.

16. Gantt, "The Gettysburg Prisoners," 6 July 1863, KMB; R. N. Martin to My Dear Aunt and Cousin, HS; *Philadelphia Weekly Times*, 22 April 1882; Royal N. Joy to Wife, n.d., Joy Papers, JJF.

17. Circular, 6 July 1863, Order Book, Col. J. B. Walton, Chief of Artillery, First Army Corps, ANV, Walton Collection, TU.

18. W. B. Bailey Diary, 6 July 1863, Bailey Papers, TU; Samuel Pickens Diary, 5, 6 July 1863, Pickens Papers, UA.

19. *OR* 27(3):555, 560-61; Samuel Angus Firebaugh Diary, 6 July 1863, Firebaugh Papers, UNC-SHC; Samuel Pickens Diary, 6 July 1863, Pickens Papers, UA; Francis Milton Kennedy Diary, 6 July 1863, Kennedy Papers, UNC-SHC.

20. *OR* 27(3):532-33, 554; Hyde, *Union Generals Speak*, 114.

21. *OR* 27(3):561-62.

22. *OR* 27(3):523-33, 564-65.

23. Coburn Diary, 6 July 1863, and Circular from Brigadier General Rufus Ingalls, Archives Collection, USAMHI.

24. *OR* 27(3):606; Coburn Diary, 7, 8, 9 July 1863, Archives Collection, USAMHI.

25. *Daily Richmond Examiner*, 14 July 1863.

26. *OR* 27(2):322.

27. Quartermaster Records, Articles Purchased, Impressed and Confiscated, Longstreet's Corps, Pickett's Division, Hood's Division, Benning's Brigade, Law's Brigade, Anderson's Brigade, Texas Brigade, Cabell's Artillery Battalion, First Corps Reserve Artillery Battalion, ANV Collection, MOC.

28. Alexander McNeill to Wife, 15 July 1863, McNeill Papers, USC-SCL; Samuel W. Eaton Diary, 6 July 1863, Eaton Papers, UNC-SHC.

29. *OR* 27(2):361; Hood, *Advance and Retreat*, 60.

30. Jenkins Journal, 65, GNMP.

31. *OR* 27(2):609-10, 615.

32. Jenkins Journal, 65-67, GNMP.

33. Riley, *Grandfather's Journal*, 150.

34. R. N. Martin to My Dear Aunt and Cousin, HS; Gantt, "The Gettysburg Prisoners," 6 July 1863, KMB; Whipple Diary, 17, JJF; Charles Edward Lippitt Diary, 6 July 1863, Lippitt Papers, UNC-SHC; Stoner, *Fifteen Days*, cover.

35. R. N. Martin to My Dear Aunt and Cousin, HS; Gantt, "The Gettysburg Prisoners," 6, 7 July 1863, KMB; William Porter Wilkin Diary, 7, 8 July 1863, Wilkin Papers, RKI.

36. William Alexander Gordon Memoirs, 142-43, Gordon Papers, WLU.

37. John Warwick Daniel Journal, "The Rear Guard," Daniel Papers, box 23, UVA.

38. Hotchkiss, *Make Me a Map*, 159.

39. John Warwick Daniel Journal, "The Rear Guard," Daniel Papers, box 23, UVA.

40. *OR* 27(2):448, 472, 558; Watkins Kearns Diary, 6 July 1863, Kearns Papers, VHS.

41. Samuel Pickens Diary, 6 July 1863, Pickens Papers, UA.

42. Stoner, *Fifteen Days*, 23.

43. Brown, *Brown's Civil War*, 226.

44. J. L. Hubbard to Uncle, KMB.

45. Samuel Pickens Diary, 7 July 1863, Pickens Papers, UA.

46. *Philadelphia Weekly Times*, 22 April 1882.

47. *OR* 27(2):448, 472, 558.

48. Robert H. Chilton to Robert E. Rodes, 7 July 1863, Rodes Papers, Vol. 51, ANV Collection, MOC.

49. Quartermaster Records, Articles Purchased, Impressed and Confiscated, Longstreet's Corps, Hood's Division, Pickett's Division, Texas Brigade, Semmes's Brigade, Benning's Brigade, Anderson's Brigade, Texas Brigade, Twenty-first Mississippi, Cabell's Artillery Battalion, First Corps Reserve Artillery Battalion, ANV Collection, MOC.

50. O'Farrell Diary, 8 July 1863, CSA "Core Collection": Regiments and Soldiers, MOC; Jenkins Journal, 68, GNMP.

51. Holt, *Mississippi Rebel*, 207.

52. Francis Milton Kennedy Diary, 7 July 1863, Kennedy Papers, UNC-SHC.

53. General Orders No. 156, Adjutant and Inspector Generals Office, KMB; McMurry, *Virginia Military Institute Alumni*, 171.

54. Hartzler, *Medical*, 56; Whitehorne Diary, 36, FLE.

55. Franklin Gardner Walter Diary, 6, 7 July 1863, Walter Papers, VSL.

56. *Richmond Enquirer*, 21 July 1863.

57. *OR* 27(3):579-80, 593.

58. Wingate, *Last Campaign*, 29; *OR* 27(3):593.

59. Park, *Twelfth Alabama Infantry*, 55.

60. Michael W. Taylor, *To Drive the Enemy*, 295.

61. Lumpkin was hospitalized in Williamsport after arriving with Rodes's trains. He died in Hagerstown on 11 September 1863. Henry W. Thomas, *Doles-Cook Brigade*, 485.

62. Generals Pender and Scales would have been ferried across the river immediately.

63. Hughes and Lucas would have arrived in the wee hours of 6 July after their escape at Cunningham's Crossroads.

64. Julius Lineback Diary, 6 July 1863, Lineback Papers, vol. 2, UNC-SHC.

65. Ibid.; Imboden, "Confederate Retreat," 425-26.

66. LeGrand Wilson Jr., *Confederate Soldier*, 126-31.

67. Julius Lineback Diary, 7, 8 July 1863, Lineback Papers, vol. 2, UNC-SHC; John Cabell Early, "Southern Boy," 41; C. E. H. Bonwill illustration number 100 for *Frank Leslie's Illustrated Newspaper*, entitled "Retreat of Gen. Lee's Army, July 13, 1863, Crossing the Potomac above Williamsport, Md.," Photographic Collection, NYPL. The illustration in Leslie's paper shows wagons fording the river alongside a ferry far upstream from Williamsport and lines of wagons stretched out along the towpath of the C&O Canal heading toward the fording and ferry sites upstream.

68. Edward E. Moore, *Story of a Cannoneer*, 206.

69. Belo, *Memoirs*, 22.

70. Black, *Crumbling Defenses*, 48, 51-53.

71. Hood, *Advance and Retreat*, 80; John Cabell Early, "Southern Boy," 41.

72. Charles Moore Jr. Diary, 6, 7, 8 July 1863, Moore Jr. Papers, TU.

73. Bowie, *Descriptive List*, 52-54.

74. *OR* 27(2):581; James B. Clifton Diary, 6, 7, 8, 9 July 1863, Clifton Papers, NCDAH.

75. Baker, "Diary and Recollections," 99; William Alexander Gordon Memoirs, 143, Gordon Papers, WLU.

76. Bowie, *Descriptive List*, 53; Worsham, *One of Jackson's Foot Cavalry*, 108.

77. *Raleigh News-Observer-Chronicle*, 11 May 1894. Although the newspaper states that Elijah took Avery's body back to North Carolina, it was actually buried in Williamsport. The remains were later exhumed and reinterred in the Confederate section of Rose Hill Cemetery in Hagerstown. Bowie, *Descriptive List*, 53.

78. Bowie, *Descriptive List*, 52-54.

79. Rozier, *Granite Farm Letters*, 118-19.

CHAPTER TWELVE

1. Edward Porter Alexander, *Fighting for the Confederacy*, 269-70; Koogle Diaries, 8 July 1863, HWCHS. Koogle's diaries are most useful, as he meticulously recorded the weather in Washington County, Maryland, every day.

2. *OR* 27(3):506, 587, 601-2, 606.

3. Weygant, *One Hundred and Twenty-fourth Regiment*, 197.

4. Ibid., 196.

5. *OR* 27(1):86, 27(3):568, 590; Headquarters, Army of the Potomac, Office of Chief Quartermaster to Montgomery C. Meigs, 11 September 1863, Office of the

Quartermaster General, Consolidated Correspondence File, NA. In his testimony before the Joint Committee on the Conduct of the War, Meade discussed the difficulty he encountered getting his trains and the supplies they carried to the troops. Hyde, *Union Generals Speak*, 114-15.

6. Edward Porter Alexander, *Fighting for the Confederacy*, 269.

7. *OR* 27(2):703, 27(3):985.

8. *OR* 27(2):703.

9. *OR* 27(1):928, 935-36, 940-41, 944, 1033; Receipts for Impressment of Hay, KMB. The old stone Washington Monument still stands in Washington Monument State Park across Route 40A from the South Mountain Inn near Boonsboro.

10. *OR* 27(2):703, 761; Neese, *Three Years*, 196-97; Charles William McVicar Diary, 8 July 1863, McVicar Papers, VSL.

11. *OR* 27(2):703, 27(1):935-36, 940-41, 944.

12. *OR* 27(1):935, 941, 998-1001.

13. *OR* 27(1):998-1001, 1033; Bliss Diary, 7, 8 July 1863, KL.

14. Bliss Diary, 8 July 1863, KL.

15. Hard, *Eighth Cavalry Regiment, Illinois Volunteers*, 262-63; Bliss Diary, 8 July 1863, KL.

16. *OR* 27(2):704.

17. Ibid.; Koogle Diaries, 9 July 1863, HWCHS; J. Willard Brown, *Signal Corps*, 375.

18. Hotchkiss, *Make Me a Map*, 159-60; Edward Porter Alexander, *Fighting for the Confederacy*, 269-70. Salisbury Ridge is still a dominant feature of the landscape between Hagerstown and Downsville. It may be best observed by looking west from St. James School.

19. Edward Porter Alexander, *Fighting for the Confederacy*, 270.

20. James B. Clifton Diary, 9 July 1863, Clifton Papers, NCDAH.

21. Julius Lineback Diary, 8 July 1862, Lineback Papers, vol. 2, UNC-SHC.

22. Shotwell, *Papers*, 2:36.

23. Charles Edward Lippitt Diary, 8 July 1863, Lippitt Papers, UNC-SHC.

24. Ibid., 9 July 1863; Julius Lineback Diary, 9 July 1863, Lineback Papers, UNC-SHC; John Cabell Early, "Southern Boy," 41; C. E. H. Bonwill illustration number 100 for *Frank Leslie's Illustrated Newspaper*, entitled "Retreat of Gen. Lee's Army, July 13, 1863, Crossing the Potomac above Williamsport, Md.," Photographic Collection, NYPL.

25. Shotwell, *Papers*, 2:36-37.

26. *Philadelphia Inquirer*, 11 July 1863.

27. Florence McCarthy to Sister, 10 July 1863, McCarthy Family Papers, VHS; Baker, "Diary and Recollections," 99-100.

28. Bowie, *Descriptive List*, 52-54; Charles Moore Jr. Diary, 9 July 1863, Moore Jr. Papers, TU.

29. Whitehorne Diary, 36, FLE; Bond Memoir, CSA "Core Collection": Regiments and Soldiers, MOC.

30. *OR* 27(1):146, 207-14, 27(3):603-4, 606, 616-17; Luther A. Rose Diary, 6, 7,

8 July 1863, Rose Papers, LC. The Mountain House still stands along Route 40A in Turner's Pass. It is now the South Mountain Inn, a very fine restaurant.

31. Edward Porter Alexander, *Fighting for the Confederacy*, 271.

32. Wingate, *Last Campaign*, 35-36; Billett, "Department of the Susquehanna," 41.

33. *OR* 27(2):220-47, 280-81, 27(3):576-79, 595-96, 748; Wainwright, *Diary*, 261-62.

34. *OR* 27(2):361, 370, 704; Driver, *First and Second Maryland Cavalry*, 35, n. 11; Thomas T. Munford to Joseph B. Kershaw, 10 July 1863, Kershaw Papers, folder 5, USC-SCL.

35. *OR* 27(3):616-17; Luther A. Rose Diary, 8, 9 July 1863, Rose Papers, LC.

36. Waddell Diary, 8, 9, 10 July 1863, CSA "Core Collection": Regiments and Soldiers, MOC.

37. *OR* 27(1):663, 667, 672; 27(2):704; Koogle Diaries, 10 July 1863, HWCHS.

38. The land east of Funkstown remains almost exactly like it was in 1863. Even the large bank barns still stand. Only the construction of Interstate 70, south of the actual battlefield, interrupts the original contours of the adjacent land.

39. *OR* 27(2):704.

40. *OR* 27(2):361, 381, 398, 704; Stonebraker, *Rebel of '61*, 53; "More about the Battle of Funkstown," Bierly Notes, HWCHS.

41. *OR* 27(2):398; Quartermaster Records, Articles Purchased, Impressed and Confiscated, Anderson's Brigade, ANV Collection, MOC. The stone Antietam bridge in Funkstown still stands.

42. *OR* 27(2):398.

43. Ibid.; Neese, *Three Years*, 197.

44. *OR* 27(1):692, 694, 936, 941-42, 944, 1033; "More about the Battle of Funkstown," Bierly Notes, HWCHS.

45. Hard, *Eighth Cavalry Regiment, Illinois Volunteers*, 254.

46. *OR* 27(2):361, 370, 383; Quartermaster Records, Articles Purchased, Impressed and Confiscated, Semmes's Brigade, ANV Collection, MOC.

47. *OR* 27(2):398.

48. *OR* 27(1):692, 694; Stonebraker, *Rebel of '61*, 54; "More about the Battle of Funkstown," Bierly Notes, HWCHS. The Stonebraker barn still stands.

49. *OR* 27(2):398; Stonebraker, *Rebel of '61*, 54.

50. "More about the Battle of Funkstown," Bierly Notes, HWCHS.

51. Shoemaker, *Shoemaker's Battery*, 47; Daniel W. Pullis to Parents, 11 July 1863, Pullis Papers, RPL.

52. Neese, *Three Years*, 197. The Jacob Hauck barn still stands on the old National Road, now U.S. 40A.

53. Sams, *With Unabated Trust*, 177-79; Austin, *Georgia Boys*, 65-66; Flavius Josephus Bellamy to Brother Frank, 11 July 1863, and Bellamy Diary, 10 July 1863, Bellamy Papers, ISL.

54. *OR* 27(1):931, 27(2):399, 716; Bowie, *Descriptive List*, 55.

55. "More about the Battle of Funkstown," Bierly Notes, HWCHS; Bowie, *Descriptive List*, 55. The Chaney house still stands on Baltimore Street in Funkstown.

56. "More about the Battle of Funkstown," Bierly Notes, HWCHS; Sams, *With Unabated Trust*, 177–79; Austin, *Georgia Boys*, 65–66; Lillian Henderson, *Roster . . . of Georgia*, 2:615; Stonebraker, *Rebel of '61*, 55. The German Reformed Church and the Keller house still stand on Baltimore Street in Funkstown.

57. Stonebraker, *Rebel of '61*, 55; Sams, *With Unabated Trust*, xvi, 177–79.

58. *OR* 27(2):361, 448, 472, 505, 558, 609; Edward Porter Alexander, *Fighting for the Confederacy*, 271; Henry Heth to James Lane, 12 July 1863, and Lane to George H. Stewart, 12 July 1863, Heth Papers, MC-3, File H-481, Confederate Military Leaders Collection, MOC; Charles Edward Lippitt Diary, 8, 9 July 1863, Lippitt Papers, UNC-SHC; Robert E. Lee to Richard S. Ewell, Archives Collection, USAMHI. From his headquarters in Hagerstown, Lee wrote to Ewell outlining the placement of the three corps in the defense lines.

59. Henry Heth to James H. Lane, 12 July 1863, and Lane to George H. Stewart, 12 July 1863, Heth Papers, MC-3, File H-481, Confederate Military Leaders Collection, MOC. According to his after-action report, Lane was in command of Pender's Division from the time General Trimble was wounded on 3 July until battle lines were formed south of Hagerstown on 12 July, when Pender's and Heth's Divisions were consolidated under Heth. Two contemporaneous letters indicate that Lane remained in command of Pender's Division through 12 July and most likely until after the division crossed the Potomac the next day. Heth to Lane, 12 July 1863, and Lane to Stewart, 12 July 1863, ibid. Both letters discuss the alignment of Heth's and Pender's Divisions in the defenses of Williamsport, and both refer to Lane as commander of Pender's Division. It is unlikely that such an arrangement would have been changed until after the army had recrossed the Potomac.

60. *OR* 27(2):377, 383, 385, 610, 674, 676, 679.

61. Ibid., 377, 428, 430, 433.

62. Ibid., 448, 472, 505, 558, 704–5.

63. *Gospel Visitor*, September 1863; Purifoy, "In Battle Array," 371; Scheibert, *Seven Months*, 121.

64. dePeyster, *Gettysburg and After*, 95–97; Wainwright, *Diary*, 261–62; Edward Porter Alexander, *Fighting for the Confederacy*, 270; *Gospel Visitor*, September 1863.

65. *Gospel Visitor*, September 1863.

66. dePeyster, *Gettysburg and After*, 96; *Gospel Visitor*, September 1863; Wainwright, *Diary of Battle*, 261–62.

67. Wainwright, *Diary*, 260; Koogle Diaries, 4, 7, 8 July 1863, HWCHS.

68. Franklin Gardner Walter Diary, 6, 7, 8 July 1863, Walter Papers, VSL.

69. *Gospel Visitor*, September 1863.

70. Quartermaster Records, Articles Purchased, Impressed and Confiscated, Longstreet's Corps, Hood's Division, Law's Brigade, Barksdale's Brigade, Anderson's Brigade, Texas Brigade, First Corps Reserve Artillery Battalion, ANV Collection, MOC.

71. Ibid.; Quartermaster Records, Articles Purchased, Impressed and Confiscated, Thirteenth Mississippi, ANV Collection, MOC.

72. Williams, *Washington County, Maryland*, 1:350; Coit, "Civil War Diary," 257; Johnson, *Maryland*, 336–37; Bevan, "Fountain Rock," 19–29. Fountain Rock was built

by Samuel Ringgold, a prominent landowner and political figure in Maryland. It is said that Henry Clay and Presidents James Madison and James Monroe were frequently entertained there. Ringgold was a friend of Benjamin H. Latrobe Jr. The house was known as "Claggett Hall" after it became the main building of St. James College. Although Fountain Rock no longer stands, the college remains in operation as St. James School, an Episcopal preparatory academy.

73. Williams, *Washington County, Maryland*, 1:350; Eisenschiml, *Case of Fitz John Porter*, 18-19.

74. *OR* 27(1):146-47.

75. *OR* 27(2):301.

76. Stiles, *Four Years*, 223-24.

77. Julius Lineback Diary, 11, 12 July 1863, Lineback Papers, UNC-SHC.

78. *OR* 27(2):534.

79. Barlow, *Company G*, 139-42.

80. Ibid., 142-43; *OR* 27(3):671.

81. *OR* 27(1):489, 27(3):626-30; dePeyster, *Gettysburg and After*, 95-97; Purifoy, "In Battle Array," 372.

82. *OR* 27(3):657-60; J. Willard Brown, *Signal Corps*, 377.

83. *OR* 27(3):656-57, 660.

84. *OR* 27(1):91, 27(3):669; Luther A. Rose Diary, 9-14 July 1863, Rose Papers, LC.

CHAPTER THIRTEEN

1. Harris, "Civil War Diary," 1773.

2. Scheibert, *Seven Months*, iii–v, 119–20.

3. Ibid., 120; Casler, *Four Years*, 179.

4. *OR* 27(2):361; Scheibert, *Seven Months*, 120; Harris, "Civil War Diary," 1773.

5. Harris, "Civil War Diary," 1773; Scheibert, *Seven Months*, 120; Casler, *Four Years*, 179.

6. Casler, *Four Years*, 179; Scheibert, *Seven Months*, 120.

7. Harris, "Civil War Diary," 1773; Casler, *Four Years*, 179; Jackson, *First Regiment, Engineer Troops*, 9.

8. Jackson, *First Regiment, Engineer Troops*, 9. Although Jackson claims that a dam was built over the canal, there is no evidence of that in any contemporary account or illustration of the crossing. The bridge was strong enough to handle the army so long as it had additional supports. Edwin Forbes's contemporary illustration of the crossing shows the army using the bridge. There is also no evidence at the site of the crossing that a dam was constructed there.

9. Harris, "Civil War Diary," 1773; Scheibert, *Seven Months*, 120.

10. Harris, "Civil War Diary," 1773. According to the current owner of the two-story farmhouse near Pettigrew's lines, J. M. Downey acquired the farm in 1863 at a courthouse sale from a prominent landowner named D. Donnelly. Although the current owner did not share any written documentation of these facts, he did recite to me the findings of his title examination; moreover, the *Illustrated Atlas of Washing-*

ton County, Maryland, states that Downey owned the property in 1877. The house still stands and has been fully restored.

11. *OR* 27(2):301–2, 309–10, 323, 27(3):669.

12. *OR* 27(3):705; Robert E. Lee to John D. Imboden, 13 July 1863, Lee Papers, WLU.

13. Longstreet, *Manassas to Appomattox*, 429–30.

14. James B. Clifton Diary, 13 July 1863, Clifton Papers, NCDAH.

15. Imboden, "Confederate Retreat," 428–29.

16. *OR* 27(2):448–49, 558–59.

17. Ibid., 361, 609.

18. *OR* 27(1):78–94, 27(3):519, 567; Basler, *Works of Abraham Lincoln*, 6:327–28; John Hay diary, quoted in Coddington, *Gettysburg Campaign*, 572.

19. *OR* 27(1):91–92, 27(3):700; Meade, *With Meade at Gettysburg*, 185–88; Hyde, *Union Generals Speak*, 116–21, 199–201, 328–30.

20. J. B. Clifton Diary, 13 July 1863, Clifton Papers, NCDAH; Charles Moore Jr. Diary, 12, 13 July 1863, Moore Jr. Papers, TU. Clifton knew that the army was falling back to Virginia when he observed cattle herds being driven across the river at Williamsport.

21. Folkes, *Confederate Grays*, 21.

22. Quartermaster Records, Articles Purchased, Impressed and Confiscated, Longstreet's Corps, Hood's Division, Semmes's Brigade, Benning's Brigade, Anderson's Brigade, Texas Brigade, First Corps Reserve Artillery Battalion, Cabell's Artillery Battalion, ANV Collection, MOC.

23. *OR* 27(2):448–49, 472, 505, 558–59.

24. *OR* 27(3):1001 (Robert E. Lee to J. E. B. Stuart, 13 July 1863, 4:15 P.M.), 27(2): 705.

25. Parks, "Young Man's Glimpse," 67–68.

26. *OR* 27(2):448–49, 472, 505, 558–59; Samuel Pickens Diary, 14 July 1863, Pickens Papers, UA.

27. Samuel Pickens Diary, 14 July 1863, Pickens Papers, UA.

28. *OR* 27(2):448–49; Long, *Memoirs of Robert E. Lee*, 301; Purifoy, "In Battle Array," 372.

29. *OR* 27(2):449; Long, *Memoirs of Robert E. Lee*, 301; C. E. H. Bonwill illustration number 100 for *Frank Leslie's Illustrated Newspaper*, entitled "Retreat of Gen. Lee's Army, July 13, 1863, Crossing the Potomac above Williamsport, Md.," Photographic Collection, NYPL; Samuel Pickens Diary, 14 July 1863, Pickens Papers, UA.

30. *OR* 27(2):448–49, 558–59; Purifoy, "In Battle Array," 372; Samuel Pickens Diary, 14 July 1863, Pickens Papers, UA; W. W. Blackford, *War Years with JEB Stuart*, 234–35.

31. Samuel Pickens Diary, 14 July 1863, Pickens Papers, UA. The aqueduct of the C&O Canal over Conococheague Creek still stands.

32. *OR* 27(2):558–59.

33. Samuel Pickens Diary, 14 July 1863, Pickens Papers, UA.

34. W. W. Blackford, *War Years with JEB Stuart*, 234–35.

35. Gordon, *Reminiscences*, 172–73.

36. *Daily Richmond Examiner*, 21 July 1863.

37. Berkeley, *Four Years*, 54.

38. *OR* 27(2):361, 609, 705.

39. M. V. Smith, *Reminiscences*, 39.

40. Scheibert, *Seven Months*, 122.

41. Everson and Simpson, *Far, Far from Home*, 225; Alexander McNeill to Wife, 15 July 1863, McNeill Papers, USC-SCL.

42. Giles, *Rags and Hope*, 189.

43. *OR* 27(2):609, 640, 705.

44. Riley, *Grandfather's Journal*, 151–52.

45. Folkes, *Confederate Grays*, 23–24; Robert G. Evans, *16th Mississippi Infantry*, 181.

46. *OR* 27(2):639–40.

47. Welch, *Letters to His Wife*, 70; *OR* 27(2):639–40; Heth, *Memoirs*, 178.

48. *OR* 27(2):653.

49. Sorrel, *Recollections*, 166.

50. *OR* 27(2):640; Louis G. Young, "Death of . . . Pettigrew," 31; Fulton, *War Reminiscences*, 81.

51. *OR* 27(2):640, 648; Louis G. Young, "Death of . . . Pettigrew," 29–30.

52. Louis G. Young, "Death of . . . Pettigrew," 29–30.

53. Fulton, *War Reminiscences*, 81.

54. Louis G. Young, "Death of . . . Pettigrew," 29–30.

55. Holographic Memoir of Gen. James J. Pettigrew, Pettigrew Family Papers, UNC-SHC; Clyde N. Wilson, *Carolina Cavalier*, 3, 135, 170–201.

56. *OR* 27(2):640.

57. Statement of Andrew Alexander Werts, Company H, Third South Carolina, Werts Papers, ANMP.

58. Giles, *Rags and Hope*, 190.

59. Folkes, *Confederate Grays*, 25–26.

60. *OR* 27(1):997–1001; Luther S. Trowbridge to J. Allen Bigelow, n.d., GNMP.

61. Luther S. Trowbridge to J. Allen Bigelow, n.d., GNMP.

62. Ibid.; Kidd, *Personal Recollections*, 183–84.

63. Louis G. Young, "Death of . . . Pettigrew," 30; McCall, "7th Tennessee—Battle of Falling Waters," 406.

64. Kidd, *Personal Recollections*, 184–86.

65. *OR* 27(2):640–41; Louis G. Young, "Death of . . . Pettigrew," 30–31; McCall, "7th Tennessee—Battle of Falling Waters," 406.

66. *OR* 27(2):640–41; Holographic Memoir of Gen. James J. Pettigrew, Pettigrew Family Papers, UNC-SHC; Fulton, *War Reminiscences*, 82.

67. Dunaway, *Reminiscences*, 98; Rollins, "*Damned Red Flags*," 217.

68. Ibid.; Louis G. Young, "Death of . . . Pettigrew," 30–31; Dunaway, *Reminiscences*, 98.

69. Louis G. Young, "Death of . . . Pettigrew," 31; Holographic Memoir of Gen.

James J. Pettigrew, Pettigrew Family Papers, UNC-SHC; Clyde N. Wilson, *Carolina Cavalier*, 202.

70. Louis G. Young, "Death of . . . Pettigrew," 30–31; McCall, "7th Tennessee—Battle of Falling Waters," 406.

71. Sorrel, *Recollections*, 166–67.

72. McCall, "7th Tennessee—Battle of Falling Waters," 406.

73. Holographic Memoir of Gen. James J. Pettigrew, Pettigrew Family Papers, UNC-SHC; *OR* 27(2):664–72; Welch, *Letters to His Wife*, 71–72.

74. Louis G. Young, "Death of . . . Pettigrew," 30–31; Kidd, *Personal Recollections*, 186; J. Jones to E. Jones, 17 July 1863, Pettigrew Family Papers, UNC-SHC.

75. Holographic Memoir of Gen. James J. Pettigrew, Pettigrew Family Papers, UNC-SHC; Louis G. Young, "Death of . . . Pettigrew," 30–31; Clyde N. Wilson, *Carolina Cavalier*, 202–3; Underwood, "Twenty-sixth Regiment," 376–77.

76. Underwood, "Twenty-sixth Regiment," 376.

77. Kidd, *Personal Recollections*, 186; Private Victor E. Compte to Elise, 16 July 1863, Compte Papers, UM-MHC.

78. *OR* 27(2):641, 648, 664, 667; Krick, *Lee's Colonels*, 80, 293–94; Gaines, "Sick and Wounded." According to Gaines's list, the largest number of those wounded on 14 July who were left at Williamsport and Hagerstown were from Davis's and Brockenbrough's Brigades on Heth's right flank.

79. *OR* 27(1):1001.

80. Giles, *Rags and Hope*, 190–91.

81. Holographic Memoir of Gen. James J. Pettigrew, Pettigrew Family Papers, UNC-SHC.

82. Paul Turner Vaughan Diary, 12, Vaughan Papers, UA.

83. James B. Clifton Diary, 14 July 1863, Clifton Papers, NCDAH.

84. *OR* 27(2):353, 603, 636, 653, 676.

85. Long, *Memoirs of Robert E. Lee*, 301.

86. Clyde N. Wilson, *Carolina Cavalier*, 204; Underwood, "Twenty-sixth Regiment," 378.

87. Paul Turner Vaughan Diary, 12, Vaughan Papers, UA.

88. *OR* 27(2):355–56.

89. Ibid., 323; Roll of Prisoners of War at Point Lookout, Md., Desirous of Taking the Oath of Allegiance, KMB.

90. Paul Turner Vaughan Diary, 12, Vaughan Papers, UA; Harris, "Civil War Diary," 1773.

91. Sorrel, *Recollections*, 173; Wood, "History of the Shearer Houses," 38–39.

92. Clausewitz, *On War*, 271.

CHAPTER FOURTEEN

1. *OR* 27(1):147.

2. *OR* 27(3):567.

3. *OR* 27(1):91–92.

4. Ibid., 92.

5. Ibid., 93-94.

6. Ibid., 147-48.

7. Gaines, "Sick and Wounded"; Joseph Jones, "Medical Officers . . . of Tennessee," 176, 194.

8. Apperson, *Repairing the "March of Mars,"* 473.

9. Don C. Wood, "Early Hedges"; Mrs. Hugh Holmes Lee Diary, 433, WFCHS.

10. Wayland, *Twenty-five Chapters*, 335-37; Gardiner and Gardiner, *Chronicles*, 103-4.

11. Gardiner and Gardiner, *Chronicles*, 161; J. William Jones, *Christ in the Camp*, 312-20.

12. Gardiner and Gardiner, *Chronicles*, 161.

13. Paul Jones Semmes to Wife, WT; Mary Oden to Mrs. Paul Jones Semmes, 10 July 1863, WT; James E. Taylor, *Sketchbook and Diary*, 185-89, 309.

14. Gardiner and Gardiner, *Chronicles*, 161. Susan Riddle notes in her diary that Colonel Morehead "was buried from Mrs. Staub's" on 28 June 1863. The Staubs owned the United States Hotel and lived there. Mary Oden to Mrs. Paul Jones Semmes, 10 July 1863, WT; William H. Staub Jr. to Martinsburg-Berkeley County Public Library, 23 August, 24 October 1994, Staub Family File, MBCPL.

15. Mary Oden to Mrs. Paul Jones Semmes, 10 July 1863, WT; Manarin and Jordan, *North Carolina Troops*, 4:10; Hill, *North Carolina*, 518-19.

16. *Charlotte Daily Bulletin*, 28 August 1863; Unknown newspaper, n.d., Scrapbook, Pettigrew Family Papers, NCDAH; Louis G. Young, "Pettigrew's Brigade," 557.

17. Michael W. Taylor, *To Drive the Enemy*, 295; Eighth U.S. Census, Berkeley County, Va.; Goldsborough, *The Maryland Line*, 159.

18. Paul Jones Semmes to Wife, WT; Mary Oden to Mrs. Paul Jones Semmes, 10 July 1863, WT; Eighth U.S. Census, Berkeley County, Va., NA.

19. Mary Oden to Mrs. Paul Jones Semmes, 10 July 1863, WT; Semmes, *The Semmes and Allied Families*, 111, 114.

20. Mary Oden to Mrs. Paul Jones Semmes, July 10, 1863, WT; J. William Jones, *Christ in the Camp*, 530. Semmes's remains were later exhumed and taken to Columbus, Ga., where they were buried in Linwood Cemetery.

21. Gardiner and Gardiner, *Chronicles*, 162.

22. Whitehorne Diary, 14 July 1863, FLE.

23. Morton, *Story of Winchester*, 143-78; Quarles, *Occupied Winchester*, 51-100.

24. *OR* 27(3):916. That fecal contamination of the water system produced the typhoid fever epidemic was confirmed by David V. Young, M.D., of Washington, D.C., whose expertise in diseases and their treatments has been utilized throughout this text.

25. Colt, *Defend the Valley*, 253-54; Mrs. Hugh Holmes Lee Diary, 394, 678, 690, 695, 741, WFCHS; "Diary of Lucy Cobb."

26. *OR* 27(3):916. Grier, Hofstra, and Whitehorne, "Sheridan Military Field Hospital Complex." Confederate correspondence sometimes refers to the Shawnee Springs hospital as the Garden Springs hospital. Samuel P. Moore to William A. Carrington, 20 June 1863, Records of Medical Department, ANV, Letters Sent and Received, NA.

27. *OR* 27(3):916; Cohen, *Historic Springs*, 70-72; Laura Lee Diary, 124, L. Lee

Papers, CWM; Muster Roll of the Hospital Department, 18 June–23 July 1863, Records of Hospitals in Virginia, Jordan White Sulphur Springs, NA; Blanton, *Medicine*, 404. The springhouse, a three-story hotel, and one of the frame cottages are still standing at Jordan White Sulphur Springs. The site is located on County Road 664, northwest of Winchester.

28. Muster Roll of the Hospital Department, 18 June–23 July 1863, Records of Hospitals in Virginia, Jordan White Sulphur Springs, NA; Quarles, *One Hundred Old Homes*, 44; *Winchester Evening Star*, 25 October 1913, 4 July 1913, WFCHS-BR.

29. Mrs. Hugh Holmes Lee Diary, 435, 442–43, WFCHS; Riggs, *13th Virginia Infantry*, 117; Hume, *Diary*, 15; Andrew B. Booth, *Records of Louisiana Confederate Soldiers*, 2:638, 3(1):937.

30. *OR* 27(3):916; Lafayette Guild to Joseph E. Claggett, 20 July 1863, Records of Medical Department, ANV, Letters Sent, NA; Mrs. Hugh Holmes Lee Diary, 432–33, 437, WFCHS; Newton, "Members of General Lee's Staff"; Hartzler, *Medical Doctors*, 26. Claggett was related to Otho Williams of Rose Hill Manor in Williamsport; he apparently had courted and earnestly wanted to marry Williams's daughter Mary Emma before the war. Mary Emma Williams Diary, 1–65, Williams Family Papers, JLH.

31. Lafayette Guild to William Barksdale, 21 June 1863, Guild to Joseph E. Claggett, 20 July 1863, and Guild to Samuel H. Moffitt, 5 June 1863, Records of Medical Department, ANV, Letters Sent, NA.

32. *OR* 27(3):916–17; Mrs. Hugh Holmes Lee Diary, 437, WFCHS; Newton, "Members of General Lee's Staff."

33. *OR* 27(2):464, 487–88; Buck, *With the Old Confeds*, 89–91; Walker, *Memorial*, 512; Kemp, *Alumni Directory*, 442.

34. *Richmond Daily Dispatch*, 10 July 1863.

35. Laura Lee Diary, 126, L. Lee Papers, CWM; Mrs. Hugh Holmes Lee Diary, 430, WFCHS.

36. Mrs. Hugh Holmes Lee Diary, 430, WFCHS.

37. Ibid.; Laura Lee Diary, 126, L. Lee Papers, CWM.

38. Whitehorne Diary, 37–41, FLE; Black, *Crumbling Defenses*, 48–53; Mrs. Hugh Holmes Lee Diary, 430–40, WFCHS; Charles Moore Jr. Diary, 13–16 July 1863, Moore Jr. Papers, TU.

39. Burnett, "Letters of a Confederate Surgeon," 164; McMullen, *A Surgeon with Stonewall Jackson*, 54–57.

40. "Surrender! Never Surrender!," 429, WFCHS; Norris, *History of the Lower Shenandoah Valley*, 680; Laura Lee Diary, 125, L. Lee Papers, CWM; Mrs. Hugh Holmes Lee Diary, 430–41, WFCHS.

41. LeGrand Wilson Jr., *Confederate Soldier*, 133–35.

42. Mrs. Hugh Holmes Lee Diary, 430–41, WFCHS; Whitehorne Diary, 37–41, FLE; "Surrender! Never Surrender!," 431–37, WFCHS; Black, *Crumbling Defenses*, 48–53; Charles Moore Jr. Diary, 14–16 July 1863, Moore Jr. Papers, TU.

43. Mrs. Hugh Holmes Lee Diary, 430, WFCHS; Black, *Crumbling Defenses*, 48–53; Russell, *What I Know*, 56, 66.

44. Laura Lee Diary, 130, L. Lee Papers, CWM.

45. Park, *Twelfth Alabama Infantry*, 55.

46. E. V. Turner, "Twenty-third Regiment," 238–39; Kerns, "Daniel Harvey Christie"; Oscar W. Blacknall Memoirs, 32, Blacknall Papers, NCDAH. Christie's remains were eventually reinterred in the Stonewall Jackson Cemetery in Winchester.

47. Black, *Crumbling Defenses*, 48–50; Macon and Macon, *Reminiscences*, 11–13.

48. Charles Moore Jr. Diary, 13–16 July 1863, Moore Jr. Papers, TU.

49. Whitehorne Diary, 37–41, FLE; Quarles, *Occupied Winchester*, 30.

50. Paxton Diary, 9, 10 July 1863, Civil War Miscellaneous Collection, USAMHI; Gantt, "The Gettysburg Prisoners," 9, 10 July 1863, KMB.

51. Henry T. Owen to Harriet, 18 July 1863, Owen Papers, VSL.

52. Wilson N. Paxton Diary, 12–18 July 1863, Civil War Miscellaneous Collection, USAMHI; Gantt, "The Gettysburg Prisoners," 12–18 July 1863, KMB.

53. Gardiner and Gardiner, *Chronicles*, 161–62; Frye, *2nd Virginia Infantry*, 112, 121.

54. Gardiner and Gardiner, *Chronicles*, 161–62.

55. Don C. Wood, "Bunker Hill Area."

56. Sarah Morgan McKown Diary, ANMP (typescript), MBCPL (microfilm).

57. *OR* 27.(2):362, 448–49, 615.

58. Holographic Memoir of Gen. James J. Pettigrew, Pettigrew Family Papers, UNC-SHC; McDonald, *Diary*, 178.

59. Holographic Memoir of Gen. James J. Pettigrew, Pettigrew Family Papers, UNC-SHC.

60. Wayland, *Shenandoah County*, 149; Rosen, Jordan, and Moomaw, *Our Soldiers' Cemetery*, 3; Quint, *Potomac and the Rapidan*, 136.

61. Wayland, *Shenandoah County*, 149, 311; *Rockingham Register*, 1 November 1861; Report of Sick and Wounded, Months Ending 31 October 1861, 30 November 1862, and 31 December 1862, and Discharges on Surgeon's Certificates and Deaths, December 1862, Records of Hospitals in Virginia, Mount Jackson, NA.

62. The earliest known record filed by Mount Jackson Hospital with the Confederate Medical Department was signed by Dr. Andrew Russell Meem on 31 October 1861. Report of Sick and Wounded, Month Ending 31 October 1861, Records of Hospitals in Virginia, Mount Jackson, NA. No one else signed any official forms for the hospital until after 1 July 1863. Dr. Meem's house, Mt. Airy, still stands on the east side of U.S. Route 11 south of Mount Jackson. Macon and Macon, *Reminiscences*, 13; Gilmore, *Four Years in the Saddle*, 125.

63. Wayland, *Shenandoah County*, 311–12; *Rockingham Register*, 1 November 1861. A monthly statement of the Hospital Fund at the Mount Jackson Hospital for the month of February 1862 (signed by Andrew Russell Meem) is found in Records of Hospitals in Virginia, Mount Jackson, NA.

64. Andrew Russell Meem to T. H. Williams, 2 December 1862, Records of Hospitals in Virginia, Mount Jackson, NA; George Washington Miley to T. A. Baker, 14 June 1863, Miley Papers, VHS, commenting on Dr. Meem's presence at Mount Jackson in June 1863; Miley to Baker, 28 June 1863, Miley Papers, VHS; William A. Carrington to Robert F. Baldwin, 20 July 1863, and Carrington to Meem, 20 July 1863, Records of Medical Department, ANV, Letters Sent and Received, 163–65, NA.

65. *OR* 27(3):916–17.

66. William A. Carrington to Robert F. Baldwin, 1 July 1863, and Carrington to Andrew Russell Meem, 20 July 1863, Records of Medical Department, ANV, Letters Sent and Received, 151–52, 165–66, NA.

67. Muster Roll of the Hospital Department, Pay Period Ending 30 June 1863, Records of Hospitals in Virginia, Mount Jackson, NA.

68. William A. Carrington to Robert F. Baldwin, 1 July 1863, Records of Medical Department, Letters Sent and Received, 151–52, NA.

69. Report of Sick and Wounded, July 1863, Records of Hospitals in Virginia, Mount Jackson, NA; Rosen, Jordan, and Moomaw, *Our Soldiers Cemetery*, 15.

70. Heneberger, *Harrisonburg*, 9 July 1863.

71. *Richmond Sentinel*, 25 July 1863.

72. Wise, *Virginia Military Institute*, 248–49. Major Latimer's grave remains in Woodbine Cemetery, Harrisonburg.

73. Peyton, *Augusta County*, 255–57; Hotchkiss, *City of Staunton*, 39, Imboden Papers, UK; Charles Turner, "Virginia Central Railroad," 510–12, 522–23.

74. Charles Turner, "Virginia Central Railroad," 510–12, 522–23.

75. Ibid., 524; Anderson, "Train Running for the Confederacy," Anderson Papers, UVA. Troops were transported by the Virginia Central for two cents per mile, while army munitions, provisions, and materials were carried for one-half the regular freight rates. Charles Turner, "Virginia Central Railroad," 524.

76. Hotchkiss, *City of Staunton*, 7–8, 22–24, 26–29, Imboden Papers, UK; Peyton, *Augusta County*, 260–61, 528; Waddell, *Annals*, 268, 311.

77. Waddell, *Annals*, 286. The diary of Joseph A. Waddell published in *Annals* states that the institute was occupied by sick and wounded as early as July 1861. The main dormitory building of the Virginia Institute for the Deaf, Dumb and Blind still stands.

78. Whitehorne Diary, 41–42, FLE; Park, *Twelfth Alabama Infantry*, 55.

79. Waddell, *Annals*, 311; Hotchkiss, *Virginia*, 721.

80. William A. Carrington to Samuel P. Moore, 20 June 1863, Records of Medical Department, ANV, Letters Sent and Received, 150–51, NA; Hotchkiss, *Virginia*, 927–28; Hay, "Surgeons of the Confederacy."

81. Return of the Medical Officers of the Regular Army, Volunteer Corps and Militia, including Physicians Employed under Contract, Staunton, for the Month of July 1863, Records of the Hospitals in Virginia, Staunton, NA; Blanton, *Medicine in Virginia*, 393–420.

82. Subscribers for Pay, etc., Pay Period Ending 30 June 1863, and Return of Hospital Stewards, Month of August 1863, General Hospital, Records of Hospitals in Virginia, Staunton, NA; Marion Smith, "Passing of a War Nurse"; Muster Roll of Stewards, Wardmaster, Cooks, Nurses, Matrons, and Detached Soldiers, Sick, General Hospital, Pay Periods Ending 27 September and 18 October 1862, Records of Hospitals in Virginia, Staunton, NA.

83. Report of Sick and Wounded, General Hospital, June 1863, Records of Hospitals in Virginia, Staunton, NA.

84. Waddell, *Annals*, 311; Francis McFarland Diary, 6–10 July 1863, McFarland

Papers, WLU. Rev. Dr. McFarland left copious entries in his diary of the weather conditions in Augusta County, Va. He even included a list of all high and low temperatures and the direction of the winds each day.

85. Waddell, *Annals*, 311.

86. *Raleigh News-Observer-Chronicle*, 11 May 1894; Hassler, *The General to His Lady*, 260–61; Francis McFarland Diary, 6–10 July 1863, McFarland Papers, WLU.

87. Hood, *Advance and Retreat*, 60; Wade Hampton to Sister, 18 July 1863, Hampton Family Papers, folder 80, USC-SCL.

88. *Staunton Spectator*, 4 August 1863.

89. Charles Moore Jr. Diary, 20–22 July 1863, Moore Jr. Papers, TU.

90. Whitehorne Diary, 42–43, FLE.

91. Report of Sick and Wounded, General Hospital, July 1863, Records of Hospitals in Virginia, Staunton, NA.

92. Ibid., August 1863.

93. *OR* 27(2):448–49; G. W. Nichols, *A Soldier's Story*, 123.

EPILOGUE

1. Robert E. Lee to Jefferson Davis, 16 July 1863, *OR* 27(2):302; J. T. Hardy to Mr. Houser, 21 October 1863, KMB. Private Hardy of the Eleventh Virginia of Kemper's Brigade, Pickett's Division, claimed that sixteen men in his company were shoeless; he asked all of his friends in Rockbridge and Botetourt Counties to send shoes.

2. Krick, *Confederate Death Roster*, 17; Edward Perry Vollum to Montgomery C. Meigs, 17 August 1863, Records of the Quartermaster General, Consolidated Correspondence File, NA; *OR* 27(1):224.

3. *Richmond Messenger*, n.d.; Wise, *Virginia Military Institute*, 244–45.

4. Edward Perry Vollum to Montgomery C. Meigs, 17 August 1863, Records of the Quartermaster General, Consolidated Correspondence File, NA; *OR* 27(1):25–28.

5. *OR* 27(1):187, 27(2):346; *New York Herald*, 24 July 1863.

6. *Richmond Enquirer*, 14 August 1863; Roll of Prisoners of War at U.S. General Hospital, Chambersburg, 21 July 1863, Papers Relating to Union Hospitals, NA; Simpson, *Hood's Texas Brigade: A Compendium*, 90; Coco, *Wasted Valor*, 30.

7. Gaines, "Sick and Wounded"; Kirkland, *Broken Fortunes*, 250; Bond Memoir," 190–96, CSA "Core Collection": Regiments and Soldiers, MOC; Sams, *With Unabated Trust*, 179–85; Henry W. Thomas, *Doles-Cook Brigade*, 485. Lumpkin's remains were buried in the Confederate section of Rose Hill Cemetery, Hagerstown. Bowie, *Descriptive List*, 54.

8. Green, Kenan, Hancock, Lewis, Bond, and Wheeler remained in prisons until the end of the war. Boyd and Blacknall were exchanged and returned to duty. Colonel Leventhorpe was exchanged but never rejoined the army because of his wounds. Colonel Boyd died at Spotsylvania Courthouse on 19 May 1864, two days after returning to duty. Major Blacknall died of wounds received at the Third Battle of Winchester on 19 September 1864; his remains were buried in the Stonewall Jackson Cemetery, Winchester. They rest there today beside those of his old commander, Colonel Daniel

Harvey Christie, whose remains were reinterred in the Stonewall Jackson Cemetery after the war. Green, *Recollections*, 179–83; Manarin and Jordan, *North Carolina Troops*, 3:264, 319, 5:6, 9:5–6, 10:293, 11:7; London, "Daniel-Grimes Brigade," 518; Charles C. Blacknall to Jinnie, 27 July 1863, Oscar W. Blacknall Memoirs, 4–5, Blacknall Papers, NCDAH.

9. Edward Perry Vollum to Montgomery C. Meigs, 17 August 1863, Records of the Quartermaster General, Consolidated Correspondence File, NA; Henry Heinzer to Cousin, KMB; T. Langstroth to Wife, MAG; Henry Boyden Blood Diary, 6–24 July 1863, Blood Papers, LC.

10. *Richmond Enquirer*, 21 July 1863; *Daily Richmond Examiner*, 17 July 1863; Robert E. Lee to Jefferson Davis, 31 July 1863, in Dowdey and Manarin, *Wartime Papers*, 564–65.

11. *Richmond Enquirer*, 21 July 1863.

12. G. W. Nichols, *A Soldier's Story*, 123. Private G. W. Nichols, of the Sixty-first Georgia, recalled seeing what he was told were "about twenty-six thousand head of cattle and twenty-two thousand head of sheep" being herded up the Shenandoah Valley to the Luray and Thornton Gaps to eventually rejoin Lee's army. The army must have taken some cattle and sheep with the troops as subsistence. The numbers are unknown, but to feed an army the size of Lee's for several weeks would have required at least ten thousand head of cattle and a similar number of sheep.

13. Westwood A. Todd Memoirs, 125–26, Todd Papers, UNC-SHC.

14. Quartermaster Records, Articles Purchased, Impressed and Confiscated, Longstreet's Corps, Hood's Division, Pickett's Division, McLaws's Division, First Corps Reserve Artillery, Cabell's Artillery Battalion, Law's Brigade, Semmes's Brigade, Benning's Brigade, Barksdale's Brigade, Anderson's Brigade, Texas Brigade, ANV Collection, MOC.

15. Robert E. Lee to Jefferson Davis, 31 July 1863, in Dowdey and Manarin, *Wartime Papers*, 564–65.

16. White, *West Virginia*, 181–82; Robertson, *4th Virginia Infantry*, 39; Burnett, "Letters of a Confederate Surgeon," 164–65; Mrs. Hugh Holmes Lee Diary, 440, WFCHS.

17. McDonald, *Diary*, 180.

18. *OR* 27(1):147–49, 489–90.

19. Noted historian Gary Gallagher has forcefully argued in the past that, although Gettysburg was a tactical defeat for Lee's army, the Pennsylvania campaign was not necessarily a strategic loss. Gallagher, "Lee's Army Has Not Lost Any of Its Prestige: The Impact of Gettysburg on the Army of Northern Virginia and the Confederate Home Front," *Third Day at Gettysburg*, 1–30. Although many of the facts in this text are presented for the first time and, consequently, Gallagher did not have access to them when he wrote his fine essay, the conclusion he reached was clearly on the mark.

Bibliography

ARCHIVAL SOURCES

Alabama
   University of Alabama Special Collection, Tuscaloosa
      Samuel Pickens Papers
      Paul Turner Vaughan Papers
Arkansas
   Gary Hendershott, Little Rock
      "The Civil War," catalog no. 109, September 2000
      Photographic Collection
Colorado
   University of Colorado at Boulder, Special Collection, Denver
      William Riddick Whitehead Papers and Photographic Collection
Connecticut
   Connecticut Historical Society, Hartford
      Norman C. Ball Papers and Journal
Georgia
   Emory University Special Collection, Atlanta
      Benjamin Wesley Justice Papers
   University of Georgia Special Collection, Athens
      William G. Delony Papers
      Photographic Collection
Indiana
   Indiana State Library, Indianapolis
      Flavius Josephus Bellamy Papers
Kentucky
   Kent Masterson Brown Collection, Lexington
      L. S. Figures to Ma, 21 June 1863
      George Gantt, "The Gettysburg Prisoners," July 1863: A Diary
      John R. Garden Diary
      William P. Garrett Diary
      J. T. Hardy to Mr. Houser, 21 October 1863
      Harry Heinzer to Cousin, 9 July 1863
      J. L. Hubbard to Uncle, 19 July 1863
      F. P. Miller Memoir

Receipts for Impressment of Hay to William Miller and George A. Custer, 10 July 1863, Boonsboro, Md.

Rev. Dr. Henry Reeves to My Dear Lizzie, 4 July 1863

Roll of Prisoners of War at Point Lookout, Md., Desirous of Taking the Oath of Allegiance, n.d.

General Orders No. 156, Adjutant and Inspector General's Office, 30 November 1863 (a Confederate imprint)

Photographic Collection

Fletcher L. Elmore Jr. Collection, Louisville

James E. Whitehorne Diary (Elmore is a descendant of Whitehorne.)

Hunt B. Jones, M.D., Louisville

Papers on the Life of Dr. Robert J. Breckinridge (Jones is a descendent of Breckinridge.)

James and Judy Philpot, Lexington

Harman and Cameron Family Papers (Judy Philpot is a direct descendant of Asher Harman, Major John Alexander Harman's brother.)

University of Kentucky Special Collection, Lexington

John D. Imboden Papers

Louisiana

Louisiana State University Special Collection, Baton Rouge

David E. Boyd Papers

Tulane University Special Collection, New Orleans

W. B. Bailey Papers

Charles Moore Jr. Papers

J. B. Walton Collection

Maine

Maine Historical Society Collection, Portland

John Parris Sheahan Papers

Maryland

Antietam National Military Park, Sharpsburg

George to Dear Father, 22 July 1863

Franklin Huff to Hetty Zeilinger, 7 August 1863

A. E. Matthews to Hetty Zeilinger, 21 July 1863

Sarah Morgan McKown Diary, 6–15 July 1863 (typescript)

Allen Price to Abram Wear, 25 August 1863

Andrew Alexander Werts Papers

William C. Blackwell Collection, Hagerstown

George Washington Miley Papers (Blackwell is a descendant of Miley.)

Clear Spring Historical Society, Clear Spring

Otto Nesbitt Diary

Hagerstown–Washington County Historical Society, Hagerstown

William C. Bierly Notes, 5 March 1942

John Koogle Diaries

Jane L. Hershey Collection, Williamsport

Williams Family Papers

1850 Diary of Mary Emma Williams of Rose Hill Manor
Last Will and Testament of Otho Williams
Photograph of Rose Hill Manor (Hershey resides at Rose Hill Manor.)
William Turner Collection, Lanham
   Mary Oden to Mrs. Paul Jones Semmes, 9, 10 July 1863
   Paul Jones Semmes to Wife, 9 July 1863
   Photographic Collection
Massachusetts
  American Antiquarian Society, Worcester
    Charles M. Monroe Papers
Michigan
  Detroit Public Library Collection
    Chamberlain Family Papers
    William W. Stewart Papers
  Michigan State University Special Collection, Lansing
    Edwin P. Havens Papers
    G. W. Mattoon Papers
  University of Michigan, Michigan Historical Collection, Ann Arbor
    Russell A. Alger Papers
    Victor E. Compte Papers
    James Harvey Kidd Papers
    Joseph Jessup Papers
    John R. Morey Papers
    Photographic Collection
  Western Michigan University Special Collection, Kalamazoo
    Mrs. Monroe Geneau Collection, A-284
    Mr. and Mrs. Ed Ridgeway Collection, A-1154
New York
  New York Public Library
    Photographic Collection
  Rochester Public Library Collection, Rochester
    Daniel W. Pullis Papers
North Carolina
  Duke University Special Collection, Durham
    Collett Leventhorpe Papers
    Marcus J. Wright Papers
  Greensboro Historical Museum, Greensboro
    Photographic Collection
  John H. Krohn Jr. Collection, Wilmington
    John Stewart Hard Papers (Krohn is a descendant of Hard.)
  North Carolina Division of Archives and History, Raleigh
    Henry Clay Albright Papers
    Oscar W. Blacknall Papers
    James B. Clifton Papers
    James E. Green Papers

Pettigrew Family Papers
Photographic Collection
Old Salem/Salem Museum of Early Southern Decorative Arts, Winston-Salem
　J. A. Leinbach, "Scenes at the Battle of Gettysburg: Paper Read Before the
　　Wachovia Historical Society"
　Photographic Collection
University of North Carolina, Southern Historical Collection, Chapel Hill
　Burgwyn Family Papers
　Campbell-Colston Papers
　Samuel W. Eaton Papers
　George Phifer Erwin Papers
　Samuel Angus Firebaugh Papers
　Thomas S. Kenan Papers
　Francis Milton Kennedy Papers
　Robert Goodloe Lindsay Papers
　Julius E. Lineback Papers
　Charles Edward Lippitt Papers
　John Paris Papers
　William Dorsey Pender Papers
　Pettigrew Family Papers
　Ruffin-Roulhac-Hamilton Papers
　Westwood A. Todd Papers
　Samuel H. Walkup Papers
　Photographic Collection
Ohio
　Michael A. Gureasko, M.D., Collection, Cincinnati
　　Thomas Langstroth to My Dear Wife, 7 August 1863
　Ken Lawrence, M.D., Collection, Orwell
　　Henry Gordon Bliss Diary and Photographs
　B. F. Moore Collection, Cincinnati
　　Jacob Hinshaw, "The Society of Friends during the Late Rebellion"
　Western Reserve Historical Society, Cleveland
　　James K. Taylor Sketchbook and Illustration Collection
Pennsylvania
　Gettysburg College Special Collection, Gettysburg
　　John Reed et al. v. Gettysburg Battlefield Mem. Ass'n, Ct. of Common Pleas,
　　　Adams County, In Equity, January Term 1889, Transcript of Testimony
　Gettysburg National Military Park Collection, Gettysburg, Pa.
　　Homer Baldwin to Father, 7 July 1863
　　William Hamilton Bayly Diary
　　Charles Blinn Diary
　　Kathleen Georg, Collation of Damage Claim Applications, 1862–90, Adams
　　　County, Pa., for July 1863 for the author, 15 January 2003
　　——, "Confederate and Union Field Hospitals of the Gettysburg Campaign
　　　in Adams County, Pennsylvania"

Isaac Harris Diary

W. B. Jenkins Journal

Mrs. Hugh McIlhenny Sr. Memoir

John W. C. O'Neal, M.D., Journal

Elizabeth Plank Memoir

Isaac Seymour Journal

W. R. Stillwell to Mollie, 10 July 1863

Luther S. Trowbridge to J. Allen Bigelow, n.d.

Newspaper Clippings File

Historical Society of Pennsylvania, Philadelphia

Charles Everet Cadwalader Papers

John D. Follmer Papers

William Gamble Papers

Pennsylvania Historical and Museum Commission, Harrisburg

Damage Claim Applications, Record of Board of Claims, 1862–90, Adams
   County

William H. Egle Journal

Loring Schultz, Gettysburg

Photographic Collection

Sam and Wes Small Collection, The Horse Soldier, Gettysburg

R. N. Martin to My Dear Aunt and Cousin, 9 October 1863

"Report of Ordnance Stores on Hand in the Reserve Ordnance Train," Army of
   Northern Virginia, 29 June 1863

U.S. Army Military History Institute, Carlisle Barracks

Civil War Times Illustrated Collection

John Blue Reminiscence

Isaac H. Resser Diary

John G. Robinson Diary

Archives Collection

J. P. Coburn Diary

Circular from Brigadier General Rufus Ingalls, 6 July 1863

Robert E. Lee to Richard S. Ewell, 11 July 1863

John B. Linn, "Journal of My Trip to the Battlefield at Gettysburg, 6 July
   1863–11 July 1863"

Jonah Yoder Diary

Civil War Miscellaneous Collection

Wilson N. Paxton Diary

Harrisburg Civil War Roundtable Papers

Romain Octave Landry Diary

Michael Winey Collection

Newell Burch Diary

Photographic Collection

Rhode Island

Brown University Special Collection, Providence

John B. McIntosh Papers

Michael S. Saks Collection, Providence
  William R. Aylett to Brother, 16 July 1863
South Carolina
  Camden Public Library
    Simon Baruch Papers
  J. J. Fraboni Collection, Myrtle Beach
    Royal N. Joy Diary and Papers
    George W. Whipple Diary
  South Carolina Confederate Relic Room and Museum, Columbia
    Simon Baruch Papers and Photographs
  Medical University of South Carolina, Waring Historical Library, Charleston
    Simon Baruch Papers and Photograph
  University of South Carolina, South Caroliniana Library, Columbia
    David Wyatt Aiken Papers
    David Ballenger Papers
    Hampton Family Papers
    James F. Hart Papers
    Kerrison Family Papers
    Joseph Brevard Kershaw Papers
    Alexander McNeill Papers
Virginia
  College of William and Mary Special Collection, Williamsburg
    Laura Lee Papers
  Richard Keith Irish Collection, Marshall
    William Porter Wilkin Papers and Diary (Irish is a descendant of Wilkin.)
  Lewis Leigh Jr. Collection, Leesburg
    Eugene Blackford Papers
    Walter Kempster to My Dear Best-Beloved One, 10 July 1863
  Museum of the Confederacy, Richmond
    Army of Northern Virginia Collection
      Robert E. Rodes Papers
      Quartermaster Records, Army of Northern Virginia, Articles Purchased,
        Impressed and Confiscated, June and July 1863, Longstreet's Corps,
        Pickett's Division, Hood's Division, McLaws's Division, Law's Brigade,
        Semmes's Brigade, Benning's Brigade, Barksdale's Brigade, Anderson's
        Brigade, the Texas Brigade, Cabell's Artillery Battalion, First Corps
        Reserve Artillery Battalion, Twenty-first Mississippi Infantry Reserve
        Regiment
      Quartermaster Records, Army of Northern Virginia, Certificates of
        Purchased Property Given to Jacob Deardorff, Henry Deardorff, and
        John A. Scholl, 1 July 1863, by Captain Charles D. Hall, Quartermaster,
        Scales's Brigade
      Quartermaster Records, Army of Northern Virginia, Statements of Property
        Impressed for the Public Service While in the Enemy's Country, June to
        August 1863, Scales's Brigade

Quartermaster Records, Army of Northern Virginia, Statement of Forage
    Issued to and Consumed by the Public Animals, July 1863, Scales's Brigade
Photographic Collection
Confederate Military Leaders Collection
    Henry Heth Papers
CSA "Core Collection": Bound Volumes
    Frank Bond Memoir
CSA "Core Collection": Regiments and Soldiers
    Lawson Morrissett Diary
    Robert P. Myers Diary
    John O'Farrell Diary
    Edward Owen Diary
    Charles E. Waddell Diary
CSA "Core Collection": Soldiers Letters
    Smith-Johnson Family Collection
Charles B. Hill Collection
    R. L. Christian and First Regiment Virginia Artillery Papers
David Schwartz, Staunton
Photographic Collection
General William A. Tidwell, Fairfax
    Emack Family Papers
    The Emack Family (typescript)
    George M. Emack Letters
    Emack Photographic Collection
University of Virginia Special Collection, Charlottesville
    C. S. Anderson Papers
    Berkeley Family Papers
    Booker Family Papers
    John Warwick Daniel Papers
    Washington Hands Papers
    George K. Harlow Papers
    Jasper Hawse Papers
    Robert Thruston Hubbard Jr. Papers
    Imboden Family Papers
    William Henry Redman Papers
    William Wells Papers
Virginia Baptist Historical Society, Richmond
    Henry H. Harris Diary
    Photographic Collection
Virginia Historical Society, Richmond
    John Warwick Daniel Papers
    Watkins Kearns Papers
    Florence McCarthy Family Papers
    George Washington Miley Papers
    David Washington Pipes Papers

John S. Shipp Papers
Walter Taylor Papers
Photographic Collection
Virginia Military Institute Special Collection, Lexington
    Alumni Records, "John Hyde Cameron in the War between the States, John
        Hyde Cameron '57 File
    Alumni Records, Waller Tazewell Patton '56 File
Virginia Polytechnical Institute Special Collection, Blacksburg
    Harvey Black Papers and Photograph
Virginia State Library Special Collection, Richmond
    Charles William McVicar Papers
    Henry T. Owen Papers
    Franklin Gardner Walter Papers
Washington and Lee University Special Collection, Lexington
    William Alexander Gordon Papers
    Robert E. Lee Papers
    Francis McFarland Papers
    Photographic Collection
Winchester–Frederick County Historical Society, Winchester
    Miss Julia Chase Diary
    Mrs. Hugh Holmes Lee Diary
    "Surrender! Never Surrender!": Kate S. Sperry Jr. Diary
    Photographic Collection
    Ben Ritter Collection, Winchester
        "Diary of Lucy Cobb," *Saturday Evening Post*, 22 July 1961
        Winchester Evening Star, 4 July, 25 October 1913
Washington, D.C.
    Library of Congress
        Charles Albert Papers
        Henry Boyden Blood Papers
        Adm. John A. Dahlgren Papers
        Samuel J. B. V. Gilpin Papers
        David McMurtrie Gregg Papers
        George Washington Hall Papers
        Haupt Family Papers
        Jedediah A. Hotchkiss Papers
        Henry Hunt Papers
        Robert E. Lee Papers
        Edward A. O'Neal Papers
        Alfred M. Pleasonton Papers
        Luther A. Rose Papers
        William H. Shriver Papers
        Charles Winder Squires Papers
        Thaddeus Stevens Papers

Gilbert Thompson Papers
Photographic Collection
National Archives and Records Administration
Compiled Service Records of Confederate General and Staff Officers and
Non-regimental Enlistedmen, RG 109, roll 38
Eighth U.S. Census, Berkeley County, Va., 1860, roll 1335
Letters and Orders Issued and Received, Chief Surgeon's Office, General
McLaws's Division, 1862-64, RG 109, chap. VI, vol. 646
Papers Relating to Union Hospitals, 1861-65, Pennsylvania, RG 109
Pennsylvania Hospital Registers, Seminary Hospital, Gettysburg, Pa., RG 94,
entry 544, nos. 540-62
Quartermaster Department, Records of Quartermaster Stores Issued to and
Condemned in Units of the Army of Northern Virginia, May to July 1863,
RG 109, chap. V, vol. 204
Records of Hospitals in Virginia, Jordan White Sulphur Springs, RG 109,
box 25
Records of Hospitals in Virginia, Mount Jackson, RG 109, box 27
Records of Hospitals in Virginia, Staunton, RG 109, box 29
Records of Medical Department, Army of Northern Virginia, Letters Sent and
Received, Medical Director's Office, Richmond, Va., 1862-63, RG 109,
chap. VI, vol. 416
Records of Medical Department, Army of Northern Virginia, Letters Sent,
Medical Director's Office, Richmond, Va., 1862-63, RG 109, chap. VI,
vol. 641
Records of the Quartermaster General, Consolidated Correspondence File,
1795-1915, RG 109, box 663
Photographic Collection
West Virginia
Martinsburg–Berkeley County Public Library, Martinsburg
Sarah Morgan McKown Diary, 6-15 July 1863 (microfilm)
Staub Family File
Watkins Ferry File

NEWSPAPERS

Baltimore Sun
Charleston Mercury
Charlotte Daily Bulletin
Daily Richmond Examiner
Gettysburg Compiler
Gettysburg Times
Gospel Visitor
Greencastle (Pa.) Echo-Pilot
Lancaster (Pa.) Daily Express

Mercersburg (Pa.) Journal
New York Herald
New York Times
Philadelphia Inquirer
Philadelphia Weekly Times
Raleigh Daily Progress
Raleigh News and Observer
Raleigh News-Observer-Chronicle
Richmond Daily Dispatch

Richmond Enquirer   *St. Mary's (Md.) Beacon*
Richmond Messenger   *Staunton (Va.) Spectator*
Richmond Sentinel   *Winchester (Va.) Evening Star*
Rockingham Register

MISCELLANEOUS SOURCES

Borries, Frank B. von. "General John Buford." Master's thesis, University of Kentucky, 1956
TopoZone.com UTM Zone 18

PRINTED SOURCES
Books

Adams, Charles R., Jr. *A Post of Honor: The Pryor Letters, 1861–1863: Letters from Capt. S. G. Pryor, Twelfth Georgia Regiment, and His Wife, Penelope Tyson Pryor*. Fort Valley, Ga.: Garrett Publications, 1989.
Alexander, Edward Porter. *Fighting for the Confederacy: The Personal Recollections of General Edward Porter Alexander*. Edited by Gary Gallagher. Chapel Hill: University of North Carolina Press, 1989.
Alexander, Ted, ed. *Southern Revenge: Civil War History of Chambersburg, Pennsylvania*. Shippensburg, Pa.: White Mane Pub. Co., 1989.
The Annals of the War Written by Leading Participants North and South Originally Published in the Philadelphia Weekly Times. Dayton, Ohio: Press of Morningside, 1988.
Apperson, John Samuel. *Repairing the "March of Mars": The Civil War Diaries of John Samuel Apperson*. Edited by John Herbert Roper. Macon, Ga.: Mercer University Press, 2001.
Austin, Aurelia. *Georgia Boys with "Stonewall Jackson": James Thomas Thompson and the Walton Infantry*. Athens: University of Georgia Press, 1967.
Ayers, Edward L. *In the Presence of Mine Enemies: War in the Heart of America, 1859–1863*. New York: W. W. Norton and Co., 2003.
Bachelder, John B. *John Bachelder's History of the Battle of Gettysburg*. Edited by David L. Ladd and Audrey J. Ladd. Dayton, Ohio: Press of Morningside, 1997.
Barlow, A. R. *Company G: A Record of the Services of One Company of the 157th N.Y. Vols. in the War of the Rebellion*. Syracuse, N.Y.: A. W. Hall Pub. Co., 1899.
Barnet, James. *The Martyrs and Heroes of Illinois in the Great Rebellion*, Chicago: Press of J. Barnet, 1865.
Bartlet, Arthur W., Jr. *Guide to Louisiana Confederate Military Units, 1861–1865*. Baton Rouge: Louisiana State University Press, 1989.
Bartlett, Napier. *A Soldier's Story of the War*. New Orleans: L. Graham and Co., 1875.
Basler, Roy P., ed. *The Collected Works of Abraham Lincoln*. 10 vols. New Brunswick, N.J.: Rutgers University Press, 1953.
Beach, William H. *The First New York (Lincoln) Cavalry*. New York: Lincoln Cavalry Assoc., 1902.

Beale, G. W. *A Lieutenant of Cavalry in Lee's Army*. Boston: Gotham Press, 1918.

Beale, R. T. L. *History of the Ninth Virginia Cavalry in the War between the States*. Richmond: B. F. Johnson Pub. Co., 1899.

Bean, William G. *Stonewall's Man: Sandie Pendleton*. Chapel Hill: University of North Carolina Press, 1959.

Beaudry, Louis N. *Historic Records of the Fifth New York Cavalry, First Ira Harris Guard*. Albany, N.Y.: J. Munsell Pub. Co., 1868.

―――. *War Journals of Louis N. Beaudry, Fifth New York Cavalry*. Edited by Richard N. Beaudry. Jefferson, N.C.: McFarland and Co., 1996.

Beers, D. G. *Atlas of Franklin County, Pennsylvania*. Philadelphia: Pomeroy and Beers Pub. Co., 1868.

Belo, Alfred Horatio. *Memoirs of Alfred Horatio Belo: Reminiscences of a North Carolina Volunteer*. Edited by Stuart Wright. Gaithersburg, Md.: Olde Soldier Books, n.d.

Berkeley, Henry Robinson. *Four Years in the Confederate Artillery: The Diary of Private Henry Robinson Berkeley*. Edited by William H. Runge. Chapel Hill: University of North Carolina Press, 1961.

Betts, A. D. *Experiences of a Confederate Chaplain, 1861–1865*. Edited by W. A. Betts. Sanford, N.C.; Francis Wilkins Muse and Banks Muse, n.d.

Black, John Logan. *Crumbling Defenses, or Memoir and Reminiscences of John Logan Black, Colonel, C.S.A.* Edited by Eleanor D. McSwain. Macon, Ga.: Privately published, 1960.

Blackford, Charles Minor. *Letters from Lee's Army: Memoirs of Life in and out of the Army in Virginia during the War between the States*. 2 vols. Edited by Susan Leigh Blackford. Lynchburg, Va.: J. P. Bell Pub. Co., 1894.

Blackford, L. Minor. *Mine Eyes Have Seen the Glory: The Story of a Virginia Lady, Mary Berkeley Minor Blackford, 1802–1896, Who Taught Her Sons to Hate Slavery and to Love the Union*. Cambridge: Harvard University Press, 1954.

Blackford, W. W. *War Years with Jeb Stuart*. New York: Charles Scribner's Sons, 1945.

Blanton, Wyndham B., M.D. *Medicine in Virginia in the Nineteenth Century*. Richmond: Garrett and Massie Pub. Co., 1933.

Board of Trustees. *Antietam National Cemetery: Program of Ceremonies and Descriptive List*. N.p., 1867.

Boatner, Mark Mayo, III. *The Civil War Dictionary*. New York: David McKay Co., 1959.

Booth, Andrew B., ed. *Records of Louisiana Confederate Soldiers and Commands*. 3 vols. Spartanburg, S.C.: Reprint Co., 1984.

Booth, George Wilson. *Personal Reminiscences of a Maryland Soldier in the War between the States, 1861–1865*. Baltimore: Privately published, 1898.

Bowie, Oden. *A Descriptive List of the Burial Places of the Remains of Confederate Soldiers Who Fell in the Battles of Antietam, South Mountain, Monocacy, and Other Points in Washington and Frederick Counties in the State of Maryland*. Hagerstown: Free Press, 1867.

Bradwell, Gordon. *Under the Southern Cross: Soldier Life with Gordon Bradwell and the Army of Northern Virginia*. Edited by Pharris Delouch Johnson. Macon, Ga.: Mercer University Press, 1999.

Brooks, O. R. *Stories of the Confederacy*. Columbia, S.C.: State Co., 1912.

Brown, Campbell. *Campbell Brown's Civil War: With Ewell and the Army of Northern Virginia*. Edited by Terry L. Jones. Baton Rouge: Louisiana State University Press, 2001.

Brown, J. Willard. *The Signal Corps, U.S.A. in the War of the Rebellion*. Boston: U.S. Veteran Signal Corps Assoc., 1896.

Brown, Maud Morrow. *The University Greys: Company A, Eleventh Mississippi Regiment, Army of Northern Virginia, 1861–1865*. Richmond: Garrett and Marsie Pub. Co., 1940.

Buck, Samuel D. *With the Old Confeds: Actual Experiences of a Captain in the Line*. Baltimore: H. E. Houck Pub. Co., 1925.

Buford, Thomas, Thomas H. Chilton, and Ben Price Jr. *Lamar Rifles: A History of Company G, Eleventh Mississippi Regiment, C.S.A., May 1861 to April 1865*. Oxford, Miss.: Survivors Assoc. of Lamar Rifles, 1901.

Busey, John W., and David G. Martin, *Regimental Strengths at Gettysburg*. Baltimore: Gateway Press, 1982.

Butterfield, Julia Lorrilard, ed. *A Biographical Memorial of General Daniel Butterfield*. New York: Grafton Press, 1904.

Byrne, Frank L., and Andrew T. Weaver, eds. *Haskell of Gettysburg: His Life and Civil War Papers*. Madison: State Historical Society of Wisconsin, 1970.

Caffey, T. E., John. *Battlefields of the South, from Bull Run to Fredericksburg; With Sketches of Confederate Commanders, and Gossip of the Camps, by an English Combatant*. New York: John Bradburn, 1864.

Carter, Robert Goldthwaite. *Four Brothers in Blue, or Sunshine and Shadows of the War of the Rebellion: A Story of the Great Civil War from Bull Run to Appomattox*. Austin: University of Texas Press, 1978.

Carter, W. H. *From Yorktown to Santiago with the Sixth U.S. Cavalry*. Baltimore: Lord Baltimore Press, 1900.

Casler, John O. *Four Years in the Stonewall Brigade*. Dayton, Ohio: Press of Morningside, 1981.

Chamberlaine, William W. *Memoirs of the Civil War between the Northern and Southern Sections of the United States of America, 1861 to 1865*. Washington, D.C.: Press of Byron S. Adams, 1912.

Chapman, Sarah Bahnson, ed. *Bright and Gloomy Days: The Civil War Correspondence of Captain Charles Frederic Bahnson, a Moravian Confederate*. Knoxville: University of Tennessee Press, 2003.

Cheney, Newel. *History of the Ninth Regiment, New York Volunteer Cavalry, War of 1861 to 1865*. Jamestown, N.Y.: Martin Merz and Son, 1901.

Clark, George. *A Glance Backward, or Some Events in the Past History of My Life*. Houston: Privately published, 1914.

Clark, Walter, ed. *Histories of the Several Regiments and Battalions from North Carolina in the Great War, 1861–1865*. 5 vols. Raleigh: E. M. Uzzell, 1901.

Clausewitz, Carl von. *On War*. Edited and translated by Michael Howard and Peter Paret. Princeton: Princeton University Press, 1984.

Coco, Gregory A. *Gettysburg's Confederate Dead*. Gettysburg: Thomas Publications, 2003.

———. *A Strange and Blighted Land, Gettysburg: The Aftermath of a Battle*. Gettysburg: Thomas Publications, 1995.

———. *A Vast Sea of Misery: A History and Guide to the Union and Confederate Field Hospitals at Gettysburg, July 1–November 20, 1863*. Gettysburg: Thomas Publications, 1988.

———. *Wasted Valor: The Confederate Dead at Gettysburg*. Gettysburg: Thomas Publications, 1990.

Coddington, Edwin B. *The Gettysburg Campaign: A Study in Command*. New York: Charles Scribner's Sons, 1968.

Cohen, Stan. *Historic Springs of the Virginias: A Pictorial History*. Charleston, W.Va.: Pictorial Histories Pub. Co., 1981.

Coles, R. T. *From Huntsville to Appomattox: R. T. Coles's History of the 4th Regiment, Alabama Volunteer Infantry, C.S.A., Army of Northern Virginia*. Edited by Jeffrey D. Stocker. Knoxville: University of Tennessee Press, 1996.

Colt, Margaretta Barton. *Defend the Valley: A Shenandoah Family in the Civil War*. New York: Orion Books, 1994.

Coltrane, Daniel Branson. *The Memoirs of Daniel Branson Coltrane, Co. I, 63rd Reg., N.C. Cavalry, C.S.A.* Raleigh: Edwards and Broughton Pub. Co., 1956.

Coté, Richard N. *Mary's World: Love, War, and Family Ties in Nineteenth-Century Charleston*. Mount Pleasants, S.C.: Corinthian Books, 2001.

Crute, Joseph H., Jr. *Confederate Staff Officers, 1861–1865*. Powhatan, Va.: Derwent Books, 1982.

C.S. War Department. *Regulations for the Army of the Confederate States, 1863*. Richmond: J. W. Randolph, 1863.

Dahlgren, Rear Admiral John A. *Memoir of Ulrich Dahlgren*. Philadelphia: J. B. Lippincott Pub. Co., 1872.

Davis, Archie K. *Boy Colonel of the Confederacy: The Life and Times of Henry King Burgwyn, Jr*. Chapel Hill: University of North Carolina Press, 1985.

Davis, Sidney Morris. *Common Soldier, Uncommon War: Life as a Cavalryman in the Civil War*. Edited by Charles Dyker. Bethesda, Md.: John H. Davis Jr., 1994.

Davis, William C. *Jefferson Davis: The Man and His Hour*. New York: Harper Collins Publishers.

Delauter, Roger U. *18th Virginia Cavalry*. Lynchburg, Va.: H. E. Howard, 1985.

dePeyster, J. Watts. *Gettysburg and After: Battle of Gettysburg and at Williamsport and Falling Waters*. New York: MacDonald and Co., 1867.

Dickert, D. Augustus. *History of Kershaw's Brigade with Complete Roll of Companies, Biographical Sketches, Incidents, and Anecdotes, etc*. Dayton, Ohio: Press of Morningside, 1976.

Dickinson, Jack L. *Jenkins of Greenbottom: A Civil War Saga*. Charleston, W.Va.: Pictorial Histories Pub. Co., 1988.

Dooley, John. *John Dooley, Confederate Soldier: His War Journal.* Edited by Joseph T. Durkin. Georgetown, D.C.: Georgetown University Press, 1945.

Douglas, Henry Kyd. *I Rode with Stonewall.* Chapel Hill: University of North Carolina Press, 1940.

Dowdey, Clifford, and Louis H. Manarin, eds. *The Wartime Papers of R. E. Lee.* Boston: Little, Brown and Co., 1961.

Driver, Robert J., Jr. *58th Virginia Infantry.* Lynchburg, Va.: H. E. Howard, 1990.

———. *First and Second Maryland Cavalry, C.S.A.* Charlottesville, Va.: Rockbridge Pub. Co., 1999.

———. *The 1st and 2nd Rockbridge Artillery.* Lynchburg, Va.: H. E. Howard, 1987.

———. *The Staunton Artillery—McClanahan's Battery.* Lynchburg, Va.: H. E. Howard, 1988.

Dunaway, Wayland Fuller. *Reminiscences of a Rebel.* New York: Neale Pub. Co., 1913.

Duncan, Louis C. *The Medical Department of the United States Army in the Civil War.* Gaithersburg, Md.: Old Soldier Books, 1987.

Early, Jubal A. *War Memoirs: Autobiographical Sketch and Narrative of the War between the States.* Edited by Frank E. Vandiver. Bloomington: Indiana University Press, 1960.

Eisenschiml, Otto. *The Celebrated Case of Fitz John Porter: An American Dreyfus Affair.* Indianapolis: Bobbs-Merrill Co., 1950.

Evans, Clement A., ed. *Confederate Military History: A Library of Confederate States History . . . Written by Distinguished Men of the South.* 13 vols. Atlanta: Confederate Pub. Co., 1889.

Evans, Robert G., ed. *The 16th Mississippi Infantry.* Jackson: University of Mississippi Press, 2002.

Everson, Guy R., and Edward H. Simpson Jr., eds. *Far, Far from Home: The Wartime Letters of Dick and Tally Simpson, 3rd South Carolina Volunteers.* New York: Oxford University Press, 1994.

Fleming, C. Seton. *Memoir of Capt. C. Seton Fleming of the Second Florida Infantry, C.S.A.* Jacksonville, Fla.: Times-Union Pub. House, 1881.

Fletcher, William Andrew. *Rebel Private, Front and Rear.* Austin: University of Texas Press, 1954.

Folkes, Joseph E. *The Confederate Grays.* Richmond: Kate Folkes Minor, 1947.

Fonderen, C. A. *A Brief History of the Military Career of Carpenter's Battery.* New Market, Va.: Henkel and Co., 1911.

Frassanito, William A. *Early Photography at Gettysburg.* Gettysburg: Thomas Publications, 1995.

———. *Gettysburg: A Journey in Time.* New York: Charles Scribner's Sons, 1975.

Freeman, Douglas Southall, and Grady McWhiney, eds. *Lee's Dispatches: Unpublished Letters of General Robert E. Lee, C.S.A., to Jefferson Davis and the War Department of the Confederate States of America, 1862–1865.* New York: C. P. Putnam's Sons, 1957.

Fremantle, Arthur J. L. *The Fremantle Diary: Being the Journal of Lt. Col. Fremantle, Coldstream Guards, on His Three Months in the Southern States.* Boston: Little, Brown and Co., 1954.

Frey, Donald J. *Longstreet's Assault—Pickett's Charge*. Shippensburg, Pa.: Burd Street Press, 2000.

Frye, Dennis E. *2nd Virginia Infantry*. Lynchburg, Va.: H. E. Howard, 1984.

Fulton, William Frierson, II. *The War Reminiscences of William Frierson Fulton, II, 5th Alabama Battalion, Archer's Brigade, A. P. Hill's Light Division, A.N.V.* Gaithersburg, Md.: Butternut Press, 1986.

Gallagher, Gary, ed. *The Third Day at Gettysburg and Beyond*. Chapel Hill: University of North Carolina Press, 1994.

Galloway, Tammy Harden, ed. *Dear Old Roswell: The Civil War Letters of the King Family of Roswell, Georgia*. Macon, Ga.: Mercer University Press, 2003.

Gardiner, Matt, and A. H. Gardiner. *Chronicles of Old Berkeley: A Narrative History of a Virginia County from Its Beginnings to 1926*. Durham, N.C.: Seeman Press, 1938.

Georg, Kathleen R., and John W. Busey. *Nothing but Glory: Pickett's Division at Gettysburg*. Hightstown, N.J.: Longstreet House, 1987.

Giles, Val C. *Rags and Hope: The Memoirs of Val C. Giles, Four Years with Hood's Brigade, Fourth Texas Infantry, 1861–1865*. Edited by Mary Lasswell. New York: Coward-McCann Pub. Co., 1961.

Gill, John. *Reminiscences of Four Years as a Private Soldier*. Baltimore: Sun Printing Office, 1904.

Gillespie, Samuel L. *A History of Company A, First Ohio Cavalry, 1861–1865*. Washington Court House: Press of Ohio State Register, 1898.

Gilmore, Harry. *Four Years in the Saddle*. New York: Harper and Brothers Pub. Co., 1866.

Glazier, Willard. *Three Years in the Federal Cavalry*. New York: R. H. Ferguson and Co., 1872.

Goff, Richard D. *Confederate Supply*. Durham, N.C.: Duke University Press, 1969.

Goldsborough, W. W. *The Maryland Line in the Confederate Army, 1861–1865*. Baltimore: Guggenheimer, Weil and Co., 1900.

———. *The Maryland Line in the Confederate States Army*. Baltimore: Kelly, Piet and Co., 1869.

Gordon, John B. *Reminiscences of the Civil War*. New York: Charles Scribner's Sons, 1904.

Gracey, S. L. *Annals of the Sixth Pennsylvania Cavalry*. Philadelphia: E. H. Butler and Co., 1868.

Graham, C. E., ed. *Under Both Flags: A Panorama of the Civil War*. Chicago: Monarch Book Co., 1896.

Green, Wharton, Jr. *Recollections and Reflections: An Auto of Half a Century and More*. N.p.: Edwards and Broughton, 1906.

Hahn, Thomas F. *Towpath Guide to the C&O Canal: Georgetown (Tidelock) to Cumberland*. Shepherdstown, W.Va.: American Canal and Transportation Center, 1985.

Hale, Laura Virginia. *Four Valiant Years in the Lower Shenandoah Valley, 1861–1865*. Front Royal, Va.: Hathaway Pub., 1986.

Hale, Laura Virginia, and Stanley S. Phillips. *History of the Forty-ninth Virginia Infantry, C.S.A., "Extra Billy Smith's Boys."* Lanham, Md.: S. S. Phillips and Assoc., 1981.

Hall, James E. *The Diary of a Confederate Soldier: James E. Hall*. Edited by Ruth Woods Dayton. N.p.: Elizabeth Teter Phillips, 1961.

Hard, Abner. *History of the Eighth Cavalry Regiment, Illinois Volunteers, during the War of the Rebellion*. Dayton, Ohio: Press of Morningside, 1984.

Hartley, Chris, Jr. *Stuart's Tarheels: James B. Gordon and His North Carolina Cavalry*. Baltimore: Butternut and Blue, 1996.

Hartzler, Daniel D. *Medical Doctors of Maryland in the C.S.A*. Gaithersburg, Md.: Olde Soldier Books, 1988.

Haskell, John. *The Haskell Memoirs: The Personal Narrative of a Confederate Officer*. Edited by Gilbert E. Govan and James W. Livingood. New York: G. P. Putnam's Sons, 1960.

Hassler, William Woods, ed. *The General to His Lady: The Civil War Letters of William Dorsey Pender to Fanny Pender*. Chapel Hill: University of North Carolina Press, 1965.

Haupt, Herman. *Reminiscences of General Herman Haupt*. New York: Arno Press, 1981.

Haynes, Draughton Stith. *The Field Diary of a Confederate Soldier While Serving with the Army of Northern Virginia*. Darien, Ga.: Ashantilly Press, 1963.

Haynes, E. M. *A History of the Tenth Regiment, Vermont Volunteers*. Lewiston, Maine: Tenth Vermont Regimental Assoc., 1870.

Hege, John B. *Marion and Environments, Franklin County, Pa.: Historical and Reminiscent*. Marion, Pa.: Privately published, 1900.

Heitman, Francis B. *Historical Register and Dictionary of the United States Army, from Its Organization, September 19, 1789 to March 2, 1903*. 2 vols. Washington, D.C.: U.S. Government Printing Office, 1903.

Henderson, Lillian, ed. *Roster of the Confederate Soldiers of Georgia, 1861–1865*. 7 vols. Hapeville, Ga.: Longino and Porter, 1955–62.

Henderson, William D. *12th Virginia Infantry*. Lynchburg, Va.: H. E. Howard, 1984.

Heneberger, E. R. Grymes, ed. *Harrisonburg, Virginia: A Diary of a Citizen from May 9, 1862–August 22, 1864*. Harrisonburg: Privately published, 1961.

Heth, Henry. *The Memoirs of Henry Heth*. Edited by James L. Morrison, Jr. Westport, Conn.: Greenwood Press, 1974.

Hewett, Janet B., ed. *The Roster of Confederate Soldiers, 1861–1865*. 16 vols. Wilmington, N.D.: Broadfoot Pub., 1995–96.

Hewett, Janet B., Noah Andre Trudeau, and Bryce A. Suderow. *Supplement to the Official Records of the Union and Confederate Armies*. 39 vols. Wilmington, N.C.: Broadfoot Pub. Co., 1994.

Hill, D. H., Jr. *North Carolina*. Vol. 5 of *Confederate Military History*, edited by Clement A. Evans. Atlanta: Confederate Pub. Co., 1899.

Hoke, Jacob. *The Great Invasion of 1863, or General Lee in Pennsylvania, Embracing an Account of the Strength and Organization of the Armies of the Potomac and Northern Virginia*. Dayton, Ohio: W. J. Shuey Pub., 1887.

———. *Reminiscences of the War: Of Incidents Which Transpired in and about Chambersburg during the War of the Rebellion*. Chambersburg, Pa.: M. A. Foltz Pub., 1884.

Holt, David. *A Mississippi Rebel in the Army of Northern Virginia: The Civil War Memoirs of Private David Holt*. Edited by Thomas D. Cockrell and Michael Ballard. Baton Rouge: Louisiana State University Press, 1995.

Hooker, Charles E. *Mississippi*. Vol. 9 of *Confederate Military History*, edited by Clement A. Evans. Atlanta: Confederate Pub. Co., 1899.

Hopkins, Donald A. *The Little Jeff: The Jeff Davis Legion Cavalry, Army of Northern Virginia*. Shippensburg, Pa.: White Mane Press, 1999.

Hopkins, Luther W. *From Bull Run to Appomattox: A Boy's View*. Baltimore: Fleet-McGinley Co., 1908.

Hotchkiss, Jedediah. *The City of Staunton, Augusta County, Virginia, and the Surrounding Country: Their Condition, Resources and Advantages, and The Inducements They Offer to Those Seeking Homes or Places for Business, Investments, Etc.* Staunton: N. E. Strasburg, 1878.

———. *Make Me a Map of the Valley: The Civil War Journal of Stonewall Jackson's Topographer*. Edited by Archie P. McDonald. Dallas: Southern Methodist University Press, 1973.

———. *Virginia*. Vol. 4 of *Confederate Military History*, edited by Clement A. Evans. Atlanta: Confederate Pub. Co., 1899.

Houghton, W. R., and M. B. Houghton. *Two Boys in the Civil War and After*. Montgomery, Ala.: Paragon Press, 1912.

Howard, McHenry. *Recollections of a Maryland Confederate Soldier and Staff Officer under Johnston, Jackson and Lee*. Baltimore: Williams and Wilkins Pub. Co., 1914.

Howard, Wiley C. *Sketch of Cobb's Legion Cavalry and Some Incidents of Scenes Remembered*. Atlanta: Privately published, 1901.

Hume, Fanny. *The Fanny Hume Diary of 1862: A Year in Wartime Orange, Virginia*. Edited by J. Randolph Grymes Jr. Orange, Va.: Orange County Historical Society, 1994.

Hunton, Eppa. *Autobiography of Eppa Hunton*. Richmond: William Byrd Press, 1933.

Hyde, Bill, ed. *The Union Generals Speak: The Meade Hearings on the Battle of Gettysburg*. Baton Rouge: Louisiana State University Press, 2003.

Iobst, Richard W., and Louis H. Manarin. *The Bloody Sixth: The Sixth North Carolina Regiment, Confederate States of America*. Raleigh: North Carolina Confederate Centennial Commission, 1965.

Isham, Asa B. *An Historical Sketch of the Seventh Regiment Michigan Volunteer Cavalry*. New York: Town Topics Pub. Co., 1893.

Jackson, Harry L. *First Regiment, Engineer Troops, P.A.C.S.: Robert E. Lee's Combat Engineers*. Louisa, Va.: R. A. E. Design and Pub., 1998.

Johnson, Bradley T. *Maryland*. Vol. 2 of *Confederate Military History*, edited by Clement A. Evans. Atlanta: Confederate Pub. Co., 1899.

Johnson, Robert Underwood, and Clarence Clough Buel, eds. *Battles and Leaders of the Civil War*. 4 vols. New York: Century Co., 1884–87.

Johnston, David E. *The Story of a Confederate Boy in the Civil War*. Portland, Ore.: Glass and Prudhomme Co., 1914.

Jomini, Baron Antoine Henri de. *The Art of War*. London: Greenhill Books, 1992.

Jones, John B. *A Rebel War Clerk's Diary*. Edited by Earl Schenk Miers. New York: Sagamore Press, 1958.

Jones, J. William. *Christ in the Camp, or Religion in the Confederate Army*. Harrisonburg, Va.: Sprinkle Publications, 1986.

Jones, J. William, R. A. Brock, et al., eds. *Southern Historical Society Papers*. 52 vols. Richmond: Southern Historical Society, 1876-1959.

Keller, S. Roger, ed. *Crossroads of War: Washington County, Maryland, in the Civil War*. Shippensburg, Pa.: Burd Street Press, 1997.

———. *Events of the Civil War in Washington County, Maryland*. Shippensburg, Pa.: White Mane Pub. Co., 1995.

Kemp, Vernon E., ed. *The Alumni Directory and Service Record of Washington and Lee University*. Lexington, Va.: Alumni, Inc., 1926.

Kidd, J. H. *Personal Recollections of a Cavalryman, with Custer's Michigan Cavalry Brigade in the Civil War*. Iona, Mich.: Sentinel Printing Co., 1908.

King, John R. *My Experience in the Confederate Army and in Northern Prisons*. Clarksburg, W.Va.: Stonewall Jackson Chapter, U.D.C., 1917.

Kirkland, Randolph W., Jr., ed. *Broken Fortunes: South Carolina Soldiers, Sailors & Citizens Who Died in the Service of Their Country and State in the War for Southern Independence, 1861-1865*. Charleston: South Carolina Historical Society, 1995.

Klein, Frederic Shriver, ed. *Just South of Gettysburg: Carroll County Maryland in the Civil War*. Westminster, Md.: Historical Society of Carroll County, 1963.

Krick, Robert E. L. *Staff Officers in Gray: A Biographical Register of the Staff Officers in the Army of Northern Virginia*. Chapel Hill: University of North Carolina Press, 2003.

Krick, Robert K. *The Gettysburg Death Roster: The Confederate Dead at Gettysburg*. Dayton, Ohio: Press of Morningside, 1981.

———. *Lee's Colonels: A Biographical Register of the Field Officers of the Army of Northern Virginia*. Dayton, Ohio: Press of Morningside, 1979.

Lake, D. J. *Atlas of Adams Co., Pennsylvania*. Philadelphia: I. W. Field and Co., 1872.

Lake, Griffing, and Stevenson. *An Illustrated Atlas of Washington County, Maryland*. Philadelphia: Lake, Griffing and Stevenson, 1877.

Lee, William O., ed. *Personal and Historical Sketches and Facial History of and by Members of the Seventh Regiment, Michigan Volunteer Cavalry, 1862-1865*. Detroit: 7th Michigan Cavalry Assoc., 1902.

Livermore, Thomas L. *Days and Events, 1860-1866*. Boston: Houghton Mifflin Co., 1920.

Long, A. L. *Memoirs of Robert E. Lee: His Military and Personal History Embracing a Large Amount of Information Hitherto Unpublished*. New York: J. M. Stoddart and Co., 1886.

Longstreet, James. *From Manassas to Appomattox: Memoirs of the Civil War in America*. Philadelphia: J. B. Lippincott Co., 1869.

Lord, Francis A. *Civil War Collector's Encyclopedia*. Harrisburg, Pa.: Stackpole Co., 1963.

Macon, Emma Cassandra, and Reuben Conway Macon. *Reminiscences of the Civil War*. Cedar Rapids, Iowa: The Torch Press, 1911.

Malone, Bartlett Yancey. *Whipt 'Em Everytime: The Diary of Bartlett Yancey Malone, Co. H, 6th N.C. Regiment.* Edited by William Whatley Pierson Jr. Jackson, Tenn.: McCowat-Mercer Press, 1960.

Manarin, Louis H., and Weymouth T. Jordan Jr., eds. *North Carolina Troops, 1861–1865: A Roster.* 13 vols. Raleigh: North Carolina Division of Archives and History, 1966–89.

Marbaker, Thomas D. *History of the Eleventh New Jersey Volunteers from Its Organization to Appomattox to Which Is Added Experiences of Prison Life and Sketches of Individual Members.* Trenton, N.J.: MacCrellish and Quigley, 1898.

McClellan, Henry B. *The Life and Campaigns of Major-General J. E. B. Stuart, Commander of the Cavalry of the Army of Northern Virginia.* Boston: Houghton Mifflin Co., 1885.

McDonald, Cornelia. *A Diary with Reminiscences of the War and Refugee Life in the Shenandoah Valley, 1860–1865.* Edited by Hunter McDonald. Nashville, Tenn.: Cullon and Ghertner Co., 1934.

McKim, Randolph H. *A Soldier's Recollections: Leaves from the Diary of a Young Confederate.* New York: Longmans, Green and Co., 1911.

McMullen, Glenn L., ed. *A Surgeon with Stonewall Jackson: The Civil War Letters of Dr. Harvey Black.* Baltimore: Butternut and Blue, 1995.

McMurry, Richard M. *John Bell Hood and the War for Southern Independence.* Lexington: University Press of Kentucky, 1982.

———. *Virginia Military Institute Alumni in the Civil War, in Bello Praesidium.* Lynchburg, Va.: H. E. Howard, 1999.

Meade, George Gordon, Jr., ed. *The Life and Letters of George Gordon Meade, Major General, United States Army.* 2 vols. New York: Charles Scribner's Sons, 1913.

———. *With Meade at Gettysburg.* Philadelphia: War Library and Museum, MOLLUS, 1930.

Merrill, Samuel H. *The Campaigns of the First Maine and First District of Columbia Cavalry.* Portland, Maine: Bailey and Noyes, 1866.

Miers, Earl Schenck, and Richard A. Brown. *Gettysburg.* New Brunswick, N.J.: Rutgers University Press, 1948.

Mohr, James C., ed. *The Cormany Diaries: A Northern Family in the Civil War.* Pittsburgh, Pa.: University of Pittsburgh Press, 1982.

Moore, Edward E. *The Story of a Cannoneer under Stonewall Jackson in Which Is Told the Part Taken by the Rockbridge Artillery in the Army of Northern Virginia.* Lynchburg, Va.: J. P. Bell Co., 1910.

Moore, Frank, ed. *The Rebellion Record: A Diary of American Events.* 12 vols. New York: G. P. Putnam, 1861–68.

Moore, Robert A. *A Life for the Confederacy: From the War Diary of Robert A. Moore, Pvt., C.S.A.* Edited by James W. Silver. Jackson, Tenn.: McCowat-Mercer Press, 1959.

Morgan, W. H. *Personal Reminiscences of the War of 1861–5.* Lynchburg, Va.: J. P. Bell Co., 1911.

Morton, Frederic. *The Story of Winchester in Virginia: The Oldest Town in the Shenandoah Valley.* Strasburg, Va.: Shenandoah Pub. House, 1925.

Moyer, H. P. *History of the Seventeenth Regiment Pennsylvania Volunteer Cavalry, or One Hundred and Sixty-Second in the Line of Pennsylvania Volunteer Regiments*. Lebanon, Pa.: Sowers Printing Co., 1911.

Murray, Alton J. *South Georgia Rebels: The True Wartime Experiences of the 26th Regiment Georgia Volunteer Infantry, Lawton-Gordon-Evans Brigade, Confederate States Army, 1861–1865*. St. Marys, Ga.: Alton J. Murray, 1976.

Myers, Frank M. *The Comanches: A History of White's Battalion, Virginia Cavalry, Laurel Brigade, Hampton Div., A.N.V., C.S.A.* Baltimore: Kelly, Piet and Co., 1871.

Neese, George M. *Three Years in the Confederate Horse Artillery*. Dayton, Ohio: Morningside House, 1983.

Nicholas, Richard L., and Joseph Servise. *Powhattan, Salem and Courtney Henrico Artillery*. Lynchburg, Va.: H. E. Howard, 1997.

Nichols, G. W. *A Soldier's Story of His Regiment (61st Georgia) and Incidentally of the Lawton-Gordon-Evans Brigade, Army of Northern Virginia*. Kennesaw, Ga.: Continental Book Co., 1961.

Nichols, James L. *Confederate Engineers*. Tuscaloosa, Ala.: Confederate Pub. Co., 1959.

Norris, J. E. *History of the Lower Shenandoah Valley Counties of Frederick, Berkeley, Jefferson and Clarke*. Chicago: A. Warner and Co., 1890.

Norton, Henry. *Deeds of Daring, or History of the Eighth N.Y. Volunteer Cavalry*. Norwich, N.Y.: Chenango Telegraph, 1889.

Nye, Wilbur S. *Here Come the Rebels*. Dayton, Ohio: Press of Morningside, 1984.

Oates, William C. *The War between the Union and the Confederacy and Its Lost Opportunities with a History of the 15th Alabama Regiment and the Forty-Eight Battles in Which It Was Engaged*. Dayton, Ohio: Press of Morningside, 1974.

Oeffinger, John C., ed. *A Soldier's General: The Civil War Letters of Major General Lafayette McLaws*. Chapel Hill: University of North Carolina Press, 2002.

Opie, John N. *A Rebel Cavalryman with Lee, Stuart and Jackson*. Chicago: W. B. Conkey Co., 1899.

Owen, William M. *In Camp and Battle with the Washington Artillery of New Orleans: A Narrative of Events during the Late Civil War from Bull Run to Appomattox and Spanish Fort*. Boston: Ticknor and Co., 1885.

Park, Robert Emory. *Sketch of the Twelfth Alabama Infantry of Battle's Brigade, Rodes' Division, Early's Corps, Army of Northern Virginia*. Richmond: Wm. Ellis Jones Co., 1906.

Parker, Eddy R., ed. *Touched by Fire: Letters from Company D, 5th Texas Infantry, Hood's Brigade, Army of Northern Virginia, 1862–1865*. Hillsboro, Tex.: Hill College Press, 2000.

Patrick, Marsena Rudolph. *Inside Lincoln's Army: The Diary of General Marsena Rudolph Patrick, Provost Marshal General, Army of the Potomac*. Edited by David S. Sparks. New York: Thomas Yoseloff, 1964.

Penfield, James. *The 1863–1864 Diary of Captain James Penfield, 5th New York Cavalry, Company H*. Ticonderoga, N.Y.: Press of America, 1999.

Pettijohn, Dyer B. *Gettysburg and Libby Prison*. Edited by Harriet Pettijohn Crawford. N.p., 1970.

Peyton, J. Lewis. *History of Augusta County, Virginia*. Staunton, Va.: Samuel M. Yost and Son, 1882.

Poague, William Thomas. *Gunner with Stonewall: Reminiscences of William Thomas Poague*. Edited by Monroe F. Cockrell. Jackson, Tenn.: McCowat-Mercer Press, 1957.

Polley, J. B. *Hood's Texas Brigade: Its Marches, Its Battles, Its Achievements*. Dayton, Ohio: Press of Morningside, 1976.

———. *A Soldier's Letters to Charming Nellie*. New York: Neale Pub. Co., 1908.

Potter, Harry Clay. *Memoirs of the Civil War*. N.p., Mathilda Potter, n.d.

Preston, N. D. *History of the Tenth Regiment of Cavalry, New York State Volunteers, August 1861 to August 1865*. New York: D. Appleton and Co., 1892.

Publications Committee. *History of the Eighteenth Regiment of Cavalry, Pennsylvania Volunteers (163d Regiment of the Line), 1862–1865*. New York: Wynkoop Hallenbeck Crawford Co., 1909.

Pyne, Henry R. *The History of the First New Jersey Cavalry, Sixteenth Regiment, New Jersey Volunteers*. Trenton, N.J.: J. A. Beecher, 1871.

Quarles, Garland R. *Occupied Winchester, 1861–1865*. Winchester, Va.: Farmers and Merchants National Bank, 1976.

———. *Some Old Homes in Frederick County, Virginia*. Winchester, Va.: Winchester-Frederick County Historical Society, 1990.

———. *The Story of One Hundred Old Homes in Winchester, Virginia*. Winchester: Winchester-Frederick County Historical Society, 1996.

Quint, Alonzo H. *The Potomac and the Rapidan: Army Notes, from the Failure at Winchester to the Reinforcement of Rosecrans, 1861–3*. Boston: Crosby and Nichols, 1864.

Regimental History Committee. *History of the Third Pennsylvania Cavalry, Sixtieth Regiment Pennsylvania Volunteers, 1861–1865*. Philadelphia: Franklin Printing Co., 1905.

Rhodes, John H. *The History of Battery B, First Rhode Island Light Artillery, in the War to Preserve the Union, 1861–1865*. Providence, R.I.: Snow and Farnham, 1894.

Riggs, David F. *7th Virginia Infantry*. Lynchburg, Va.: H. E. Howard, 1982.

———. *13th Virginia Infantry*. Lynchburg, Va.: H. E. Howard, 1988.

Riley, Franklin Lafayette. *Grandfather's Journal: Company B, Sixteenth Mississippi Infantry Volunteers, Harris' Brigade, Mahone's Division, Hill's Corps, A.N.V., May 27, 1861–July 15, 1865*. Edited by Austin C. Dobbins. Dayton, Ohio: Press of Morningside, 1988.

Robertson, James I. *4th Virginia Infantry*. Lynchburg, Va.: H. E. Howard, 1982.

Rollins, Richard. *"The Damned Red Flags of the Rebellion": The Confederate Battleflag at Gettysburg*. Redondo Beach, Calif.: Rank and File Pub., 1997.

Rosen, D. Coiner, Dewey W. Jordan, and Richard A. Moomaw, eds. *Our Soldiers Cemetery, Mount Jackson, Shenandoah County, Virginia*. Mount Jackson, Va.: Rinkerton Pub., 1998.

Rowe, James D. *Camp Notes of a Union Soldier*. N.p.: Privately published, n.d.

Rozier, John, ed. *The Granite Farm Letters: The Civil War Correspondence of Edgeworth & Sallie Bird*. Athens: University of Georgia Press, 1988.

Russell, William Greenway. *What I Know about Winchester: Recollections of William Greenway Russell, 1800–1891*. Winchester, Va.: McClure Pub. Co., 1984.

Salley, A. S., Jr., ed. *South Carolina Troops in Confederate Service.* 3 vols. Columbia, S.C.: R. L. Bryan Co., 1913.

Sams, Anita B., ed. *With Unabated Trust: Major Henry McDaniel's Love Letters from Confederate Battlefields as Treasured in Hester McDaniel's Bonnet Box.* Monroe, Ga.: Walton Press, 1977.

Scheibert, Justus. *Seven Months in the Rebel States during the North American War, 1863.* Translated by Joseph C. Hayes. Tuscaloosa, Ala.: Confederate Pub. Co., 1958.

Sears, Stephen W. *Gettysburg.* New York: Houghton Mifflin Co., 2003.

Semmes, Raphael Thomas. *The Semmes and Allied Families.* Baltimore: Sun Book Co., 1918.

Shaw, Maurice F. *Stonewall Jackson's Surgeon: Hunter Holmes McGuire: A Biography.* Lynchburg, Va.: H. E. Howard, 1993.

Shoemaker, John J. *Shoemaker's Battery: Stuart Horse Artillery, Pelham's Battalion, Army of Northern Virginia.* Memphis, Tenn.: S. C. Toof and Co., n.d.

Shotwell, Randolph Abbott. *The Papers of Randolph Abbott Shotwell.* 3 vols. Edited by J. G. de Roulhac Hamilton. Raleigh: North Carolina Historical Commission, 1929.

Simpson, Harold B. *Hood's Texas Brigade: A Compendium.* Hillsboro, Tex.: Hill Junior College Press, 1977.

———. *Hood's Texas Brigade: Lee's Grenadier Guard.* Dallas: Alcor Pub. Co., 1983.

Skelly, Daniel Alexander. *A Boy's Experiences during the Battles of Gettysburg.* Gettysburg: Privately published, 1932.

Smith, M. V. *Reminiscences of the Civil War.* N.p.: Privately published, n.d.

Smith, Timothy H. *The Story of Lee's Headquarters, Gettysburg, Pennsylvania.* Gettysburg: Thomas Publications, 1995.

Sorrel, G. Moxley. *Recollections of a Confederate Staff Officer.* Edited by Bill Irvin Wiley. Jackson, Tenn.: McCowat-Mercer Press, 1958.

Stegman, John F. *These Men She Gave: Civil War Diary of Athens, Georgia.* Athens: University of Georgia Press, 1964.

Stevens, John W. *Reminiscences of the Civil War: A Soldier in Hood's Texas Brigade, Army of Northern Virginia.* Hillsboro, Tex.: Hillsboro Mirror Print, 1902.

Stewart, George R. *Pickett's Charge: A Microhistory of the Final Attack at Gettysburg, July 3, 1863.* Boston: Houghton Mifflin Co., 1959.

Stewart, William H. *A Pair of Blankets: War-time History in Letters to the Young People of the South.* Edited by Benjamin H. Trask. Wilmington, N.C.: Broadfoot Pub., 1990.

Stiles, Robert. *Four Years under Marse Robert.* New York: Neale Pub. Co., 1903.

Stoeckel, Carl, and Ellen Battelle, eds. *Correspondence of John Sedgwick, Major-General.* 2 vols. Norfolk, Conn.: DeVine Press, 1902.

Stonebraker, Joseph R. *A Rebel of '61.* New York: Wynkoop Hallenbeck Crawford Co., 1899.

Stoner, J. H. *Fifteen Days under the Confederate Flag.* Edited by W. J. Davis. Waynesboro, Pa.: Greater Waynesboro Chamber of Commerce, 1963.

Storrick, W. C. *Gettysburg: The Place, the Battle, the Outcome.* Harrisburg, Pa.: J. Horace McFarland Co., 1932.

Stubbs, Steven H. *Duty, Honor, Valor: The Story of the Eleventh Mississippi Infantry Regiment.* Philadelphia, Miss.: Dancing Rabbit Press, 2000.

Tanner, W. R. *Reminiscences of the War between the States.* Cowpens, S.C.: Julia Tanner, 1931.

Taylor, James E. *With Sheridan up the Shenandoah Valley in 1864: Leaves from a Special Artist's Sketchbook and Diary.* Dayton, Ohio: Press of Morningside, 1989.

Taylor, Michael W. *The Cry Is War, War, War: The Civil War Correspondence of Lts. Burwell Thomas Cotton and George Job Huntley, 34th Regiment North Carolina Troops.* Dayton, Ohio: Press of Morningside, 1994.

———, ed. *To Drive the Enemy from Southern Soil: The Letters of Col. Francis Marion Parker and the History of the 30th Regiment North Carolina Troops.* Dayton, Ohio: Press of Morningside, 1998.

Terrill, John. *Campaign of the Fourteenth Regiment, New Jersey Volunteers.* New Brunswick, N.J.: Daily Home News Press, 1884.

Thomas, Emory M. *Robert E. Lee: A Biography.* New York: W. W. Norton and Co., 1995.

Thomas, Henry W. *History of the Doles-Cook Brigade, Army of Northern Virginia, C.S.A.* Dayton, Ohio: Press of Morningside, 1981.

Tilney, Robert. *My Life in the Army: Three Years and a Half with the Fifth Corps, Army of the Potomac, 1862–1865.* Philadelphia: Ferris and Leach, 1912.

Tobie, Edward P. *History of the First Maine Cavalry, 1861–1865.* Boston: Press of Emery and Hughes, 1887.

Trescott, William Henry. *Memorial of the Life of J. Johnston Pettigrew, Brig. Gen. of the Confederate States Army.* Charleston, S.C.: John Russell, 1870.

Trout, Robert J. *Galloping Thunder: The Stuart Horse Artillery Battalion.* Mechanicsburg, Pa.: Stackpole Books, 2002.

Tucker, Spencer C. *Brigadier General John D. Imboden: Confederate Commander in the Shenandoah.* Lexington: University Press of Kentucky, 2003.

Turner, George Edgar. *Victory Rode the Rails: The Strategic Place of the Railroads in the Civil War.* Indianapolis: Bobbs-Merrill Co., 1953.

U.S. War Department. *The War of the Rebellion: A Compilation of the Official Records of the Union and Confederate Armies.* 128 vols. Washington, D.C.: U.S. Government Printing Office, 1880–1901.

Waddell, Joseph A. *Annals of Augusta County, Virginia, with Reminiscences. . . .* Richmond: Wm. Ellis Jones Pub., 1886.

Wainwright, Charles S. *A Diary of Battle: The Personal Journals of Colonel Charles S. Wainwright, 1861–1865.* Edited by Allan Nevins. New York: Harcourt, Brace and World, 1962.

Walker, Charles D. *Memorial, Virginia Military Institute: Biographical Sketches of the Graduates and Élèves of the Virginia Military Institute Who Fell during the War between the States.* Philadelphia: J. B. Lippincott, 1875.

Wallace, Robert C. *A Few Memories of a Long Life.* Edited by John M. Carroll. Fairfield, Wash.: Ye Galleon Press, 1988.

Walters, John. *Norfolk Blues: The Civil War Diary of the Norfolk Light Artillery Blues.* Edited by Kenneth Wiley. Shippensburg, Pa.: Burd Street Press, 1997.

War Department. *Regulations for the Army of the Confederate States, 1863.* Richmond: J. W. Randolph, 1863.

Ward, James A. *That Man Haupt: A Biography of Herman Haupt*. Baton Rouge: Louisiana State University Press, 1973.

Ward, Patricia Spain. *Simon Baruch: Rebel in the Ranks of Medicine, 1840–1921*. Tuscaloosa: University of Alabama Press, 1994.

Warner, Beers and Co. *1886 History of Adams County, Pennsylvania*. Chicago: Warren, Beers and Co., 1886.

———. *History of Franklin County, Pennsylvania*. Chicago: Warder, Beers and Co., 1887.

Warner, Ezra J. *Generals in Blue: Lives of the Union Commanders*. Baton Rouge: Louisiana State University Press, 1964.

———. *Generals in Gray: Lives of the Confederate Commanders*. Baton Rouge: Louisiana State University Press, 1959.

Wayland, John W. *A History of Rockingham County, Virginia*, Dayton, Va.: Ruebush-Elkins Co., 1912.

———. *A History of Shenandoah County, Virginia*. Strasburg, Va.: Shenandoah Pub. House, 1969.

———. *Twenty-five Chapters on the Shenandoah Valley*. Harrisonburg, Va.: C. J. Carrier Co., 1989.

Welch, Spencer Glasgow. *A Confederate Surgeon's Letters to His Wife*. New York: Neal Pub. Co., 1911.

Wellman, Manley Wade. *Giant in Gray: A Biography of Wade Hampton of South Carolina*. Dayton, Ohio: Press of Morningside, 1988.

———. *Rebel Boast: First at Bethel—Last at Appomattox*. New York: Henry Holt and Co., 1956.

West, John C. *A Texan in Search of a Fight: Being the Diary and Letters of a Private Soldier in Hood's Texas Brigade*. Waco, Tex.: Press of J. S. Hill and Co., 1901.

Weygant, Charles H. *History of the One Hundred and Twenty-fourth Regiment, N.Y.S.V.* Newburgh, N.Y.: Journal Printing House, 1877.

White, Robert. *West Virginia*. Vol. 3 of *Confederate Military History*, edited by Clement A. Evans. Atlanta: Confederate Pub. Co., 1899.

Whitehead, William Riddick. *A 19th Century Memoir: Adventures of an American Surgeon*. Bethesda, Md.: Whitehead Books, 2002.

Williams, Thomas J. C. *A History of Washington County, Maryland, from the Earliest Settlements to the Present Time, Including a History of Hagerstown*. 2 vols. N.p.: John M. Runk and L. R. Titsworth, 1906.

Williamson, James J. *Mosby's Rangers: A Record of Operations of the Forty-third Battalion Virginia Cavalry, from Its Organization to the Surrender*. New York: Ralph B. Kenyon Publisher, 1896.

Williamsport Chamber of Commerce. *Williamsport and Vicinity: Reminiscences*. Williamsport, Md.: Chamber of Commerce, 1933.

Wilson, Clyde N. *Carolina Cavalier: The Life and Mind of James Johnston Pettigrew*. Athens: University of Georgia Press, 1990.

Wilson, LeGrand, Jr. *The Confederate Soldier*. Edited by James W. Silver. Memphis, Tenn.: Memphis State University Press, 1973.

Wingate, George W. *The Last Campaign of the Twenty-second Regiment, N.G.S.N.Y., June and July 1863*. New York: C. S. Westcott and Co., 1864.

Wise, Jennings Cropper. *The Long Arm of Lee: The History of the Artillery of the Army of Northern Virginia*. New York: Oxford University Press, 1959.

———. *Virginia Military Institute: Military History*. Lynchburg: J. P. Bell Co., 1915.

Woman's Club of Mercersburg, Pennsylvania. *Old Mercersburg*. 2 vols. Williamsport, Pa.: Grit Publishing Co., 1949.

Wood, James H. *The War: "Stonewall" Jackson, His Campaigns and Battles, The Regiment, as I Saw Them*. Cumberland, Md.: Eddy Press, 1910.

Wood, Thomas Fanning. *Doctor to the Front: The Recollections of Confederate Surgeon Thomas Fanning Wood, 1861–1865*. Edited by Donald B. Koonce. Knoxville: University of Tennessee Press, 2000.

Woodward, Harold R., Jr. *Defender of the Valley: Brigadier General John Daniel Imboden, C.S.A.* Berryville, Va.: Rockbridge Pub. Co. 1996.

Worsham, John H. *One of Jackson's Foot Cavalry*. Edited by James I. Robertson. Jackson, Tenn.: McCowat-Mercer Press, 1964.

Young, Mel, ed. *Last Order of the Lost Cause: The Civil War Memoirs of a Jewish Family in the Old South*. Lanham, Md.: University Press of America, 1995.

Articles in Journals, Periodicals, and Collected Works

Alexander, Edward Porter. "The Great Charge and Artillery Fighting at Gettysburg." In Johnson and Buel, *Battles and Leaders of the Civil War*, 3:360–68.

Alexander, Ted. "A Regular Slave Hunt: The Army of Northern Virginia and Black Civilians in the Gettysburg Campaign." *North & South* 4(7) (September 2001): 82–89.

Baker, I. Norval. "Diary and Recollections of I. Norval Baker." *Winchester–Frederick County Historical Papers*, 3:96–128.

Barnes, Ruffin. "The Confederate Letters of Ruffin Barnes of Wilson County." *North Carolina Historical Review* 31 (January 1954): 75–99.

Baruch, Simon. "Bernard Baruch's Father Recounts His Experiences as a Confederate Surgeon." *Civil War Times Illustrated* 4 (October 1965): 40–47.

———. "A Surgeon's Story of Battle and Capture." *Confederate Veteran* 22 (1914): 545–48.

Bean, William Gleason. "A House Divided: The Civil War Letters of a Virginia Family." *Virginia Magazine of History and Biography* 59 (July 1951): 397–422.

———. "John A. Harman: Jackson's Logistical Genius." *Ironworker* 35 (Summer 1971): 2–10.

Bevan, Edith Rossiter. "Fountain Rock: The Ringgold Home in Washington County." *Maryland Historical Magazine* 47 (March 1922): 19–28.

Bigelow, Edwin. "Edwin Bigelow: A Michigan Sergeant in the Civil War." Edited by Frank L. Klement. *Michigan History* 38 (1954): 193–227.

Bigelow, John A. "Draw Saber, Charge! The Michigan Cavalry Brigade at Gettysburg." *National Tribune*, 27 May 1886.

————. "Flashing Sabers: Chasing Lee's Columns after Gettysburg." *National Tribune*, 10 November 1887.

Billett, Glenn E. "The Department of the Susquehanna." *Journal of the Lancaster County Historical Society* 66 (Winter 1962): 1–66.

Boon, H. P. "The Charge at Monterey, 4 July 1863." *National Tribune*, 16 August 1888.

Bright, Robert A. "Pickett's Charge: The Story Told by a Member of His Staff." In Jones, Brock, et al., *Southern Historical Society Papers*, 31:228–36.

Burnett, Edmund Cody, ed. "Letters of a Confederate Surgeon: Dr. Abner Embry McGarity, 1862–1865." *Georgia Historical Quarterly* 24 (September 1945): 159–89.

Campbell, John T. "Sights at Gettysburg: Appearance of the Battlefield Two Weeks After." *National Tribune*, 17 September 1908.

Capehart, Henry. "Fighting His Way: The Night Passage of Kilpatrick through Monterey Pass." *National Tribune*, 3 January 1895.

Coit, Joseph H. "The Civil War Diary of Joseph H. Coit." Edited by James McLachlan. *Maryland Historical Magazine* 60 (September 1965): 245–60.

Collins, John L. "A Prisoner's March from Gettysburg to Staunton." In Johnson and Buel, *Battles and Leaders of the Civil War*, 3:429–33.

Cooke, Charles M. "Fifty-fifth Regiment." In Walter Clark, *Regiments and Battalions from North Carolina*, 3:287–312.

Cumming, C. C. "A Tribute to the Man in Black." *Confederate Veteran* 3 (1896): 153.

Early, John Cabell. "A Southern Boy at Gettysburg." *Civil War Times Illustrated* 9 (June 1970): 35–41.

Flowers, George W. "Thirty-eighth Regiment." In Walter Clark, *Regiments and Battalions from North Carolina*, 2:675–97.

Foster, Catherine. "The Story of the Battle: By a Citizen Whose Home Was Pierced by Shells." *Gettysburg Compiler*, 29 June, 6 July 1904.

Freeman, Douglas S., ed. "The Confederate Congress, First Congress—Third Session, Tuesday, March 24, 1863." In Jones, Brock, et al., *Southern Historical Society Papers*, 49:12–17.

Gaines, John Mutius. "Sick and Wounded Confederate Soldiers at Hagerstown and Williamsport." In Jones, Brock, et al., *Southern Historical Society Papers*, 27:241–50.

Gallagher, Gary. "Lee's Army Has Not Lost Any of Its Prestige: The Impact of Gettysburg on the Army of Northern Virginia and the Confederate Home Front." In Gallagher, *The Third Day at Gettysburg and Beyond*, 1–30.

Galloway, Felix Richard. "Gettysburg—The Battle and the Retreat." *Confederate Veteran* 21 (1913): 388–89.

Green, Fletcher M. "A People at War: Hagerstown, Maryland, June 15–August 31, 1863." *Maryland Historical Magazine* 40 (December 1945): 251–59.

Grier, Clarence, Warren Hofstra, and Joseph Whitehorne. "The Sheridan Military Field Hospital Complex at Shawnee Springs." *Winchester-Frederick County Historical Society Journal* 7 (1993): 17–32.

Harris, H. H. "H. H. Harris Civil War Diary." Edited by W. Harrison Daniel. *Virginia Baptist Register* 35 (1966): 1766–86.

Hart, William L. "Hanged at Frederick City." *National Tribune*, 2 February 1888.

Hay, James. "Surgeons of the Confederacy: William Hay, Surgeon, C.S.A." *Confederate Veteran* 34 (1926): 9.

Herbert, Hilary. "Colonel Hilary Herbert's History of the Eighth Alabama Volunteer Regiment, C.S.A." Edited by Maurice S. Fortin. *Alabama Historical Quarterly* 39 (1977): 5–131.

Hering, J. W. "Dr. Hering Describes Wagon Trains and Prisoners." In Klein, *Just South of Gettysburg*, 101–3.

Heyser, William. "The William Heyser Diary." In Ted Alexander, *Southern Revenge*, 85–92.

Imboden, John D. "The Confederate Retreat from Gettysburg." In Johnson and Buel, *Battles and Leaders of the Civil War*, 3:420–29.

———. "Incidents of the First Bull Run." In Johnson and Buel, *Battles and Leaders of the Civil War*, 1:229–39.

Jacobs, W. W. "Custer's Charge: Little Hagerstown, the Scene of Bloody Strife." *National Tribune*, 27 August 1896.

Jones, Archer. "The Gettysburg Decision." *Virginia Magazine of History and Biography* 68 (July 1960): 331–43.

———. "The Gettysburg Decision Reassessed." *Virginia Magazine of History and Biography* 76 (January 1968): 64–66.

Jones, B. F. "No Terrors There." *National Tribune*, 6 June 1895.

Jones, Joseph, M.D. "Roster of the Medical Officers of the Army of Tennessee." In Jones, Brock, et al., *Southern Historical Society Papers*, 22:165–280.

Kelly, John. "The Spy at Frederick, Md." *National Tribune*, 9 February 1888.

Kenan, Thomas S. "Forty-third Regiment." In Walter Clark, *Regiments and Battalions from North Carolina*, 3:1–18.

Kerns, Donna. "Daniel Harvey Christie." *UDC Magazine* 61 (October 1998): 14–15.

Krepps, John. "Regular Cavalry at Gettysburg." *National Tribune*, 15 July 1909.

Lokey, J. W. "Wounded at Gettysburg." *Confederate Veteran* 22 (1914): 400.

London, William L. "The Daniel-Grimes Brigade." In Walter Clark, *Regiments and Battalions from North Carolina*, 4:513–19.

Longstreet, James. "Lee in Pennsylvania." In *Annals of the War*, 414–46.

Lovejoy. "The Charge at Monterey." *National Tribune*, 12 October 1899.

Martin, W. J., and E. R. Outlaw. "Eleventh Regiment." In Walter Clark, *Regiments and Battalions from North Carolina*, 1:583–604.

McCall, John T. "7th Tennessee—Battle of Falling Waters." *Confederate Veteran* 6 (1898): 406.

McGarity, Abner E. "Letters of a Confederate Surgeon: Dr. Abner Embry McGarity, 1862–1865." Edited by Edmund Cody Burnett. *Georgia Historical Quarterly* 29 (September 1945): 159–89.

Mills, George H. "Supplemental Sketch, Sixteenth Regiment." In Walter Clark, *Regiments and Battalions from North Carolina*, 4:137–219.

Minor, Berkeley. "The Night after Gettysburg." *Confederate Veteran* 33 (1925): 140–41.

Mish, Mary. "Maidstone-on-the-Potomac." *Berkeley Journal* 2 (Fall 1970): 38–45.

Mitchell, Frances Letcher. "A Georgia Henry of Navarre." *Confederate Veteran* 23 (1915): 363.

Newton, E. D. "Members of General Lee's Staff." *Confederate Veteran* 16 (1908): 336–37.

"Opposing Forces at Gettysburg." In Johnson and Buel, *Battles and Leaders of the Civil War*, 3:437–39.

Parks, Leighton. "A Young Man's Glimpse of the Civil War." In Keller, *Crossroads of War*, 56–68.

Peters, Winfield. "Lost Sword of General Richard B. Garnett." In Jones, Brock, et al., *Southern Historical Society Papers*, 33:26–31.

Phillips, John W. "Hanover, Gettysburg and Hagerstown." In Publications Committee, *History of the Eighteenth Regiment of Cavalry, Pennsylvania Volunteers*, 77–86.

Poindexter, James. "General Armistead's Portrait Presented." In Jones, Brock, et al., *Southern Historical Society Papers*, 37:144–51.

Popkins, W. A. "Imboden's Brigade at Gettysburg." *Confederate Veteran* 22 (1914): 552–53.

Porter, John W. H. "The Confederate Soldier." *Confederate Veteran* 24 (1916): 460.

Purifoy, John. "In Battle Array at Williamsport and Hagerstown." *Confederate Veteran* 33 (1925): 371–73.

———. "The Retreat from Gettysburg." *Confederate Veteran* 33 (1925): 338–39.

———. "A Unique Battle." *Confederate Veteran* 33 (1925): 132–35.

Risch, John W. "The Frederick Spy Again." *National Tribune*, 22 March 1888.

Rodenbough, T. F. "Historical Sketch." In Publications Committee, *History of the Eighteenth Regiment of Cavalry, Pennsylvania Volunteers*, 13–30.

Schaff, Philip. "The Gettysburg Week." In Woman's Club, *Old Mercersburg*, 1:167–75.

Schuricht, Hermann. "Jenkins' Brigade in the Gettysburg Campaign." In Jones, Brock, et al., *Southern Historical Society Papers*, 24:339–50.

Shepherd, H. E. "Wounded and Captured." In Graham, *Under Both Flags*, 76–77.

Shotwell, Randolph Abbott. "Virginia and North Carolina in the Battle of Gettysburg." *Our Living and Our Dead* 4(1) (March 1876): 80–97.

Smith, Marion. "Passing of a War Nurse." *Confederate Veteran* 28 (1920): 31.

St. Clair, Samuel. "The Fight at Hagerstown." In Publications Committee, *History of the Eighteenth Regiment of Cavalry, Pennsylvania Volunteers*, 94–98.

Suddath, James B. "From Sumter to the Wilderness: Letters of Sergeant James Buttler Suddath, Co. E, 7th Regiment, S.C.V." Edited by Frank B. Williams, Jr. *South Carolina Historical Magazine* 63 (April 1962): 93–104.

Taylor, William H. "Some Experiences as a Confederate Surgeon." *Transactions of the College of Physicians of Philadelphia* 28: 91–121.

Torrence, Leonidas. "'The Road to Gettysburg'—The Diary and Letters of Leonidas Torrence of the Gaston Guards." Edited by Haskell Monroe. *North Carolina Historical Review* 36 (October 1959): 476–517.

"Tribute to Henry DeSaussure Fraser." *Confederate Veteran* 3 (1895): 217.

Trimble, Isaac R. "The Civil War Diary of General Isaac Ridgeway Trimble." *Maryland Historical Magazine* 17 (March 1922): 1–20.

Tucker, John S. "The Diary of John S. Tucker: Confederate Soldier from Alabama." Edited by Gary Wilson. *Alabama Historical Quarterly* 43 (Spring 1981): 5–33.

Turner, Charles. "The Virginia Central Railroad at War, 1861–1865." *Journal of Southern History* 12 (February–November 1942): 510–33.

Turner, E. V. "Twenty-third Regiment." In Walter Clark, *Regiments and Battalions from North Carolina*, 2:180–268.

Underwood, George C. "Twenty-sixth Regiment." In Walter Clark, *Regiments and Battalions from North Carolina*, 2:303–423.

Vaughan, E. H. "Battle of Fairfield, Pa." *National Tribune*, 16 August 1891.

Vermilyea, Peter C. "The Effect of the Confederate Invasion of Pennsylvania on Gettysburg's African American Community." *Gettysburg Magazine* 7: 112–28.

White, William S. "A Diary of the War." In *Contributions to a History of the Richmond Howitzer Battalion*, 2:89–304.

"Whitfield." *Confederate Veteran* 17 (1909): 416.

Williams, J. Marshall. "Fifty-fourth Regiment." In Walter Clark, *Regiments and Battalions from North Carolina*, 3:267–85.

Wingfield, H. W. "Diary of Capt. H. W. Wingfield." Edited by H. R. McIlwaine. *Bulletin of the Virginia State Library: Two Confederate Items* 16 (July 1927): 9–47.

Wood, Don C. "The Bunker Hill Area." *Berkeley Journal* 8 (1979): 20–49.

———. "The Early Hedges: Their Land and Homes." *Berkeley Journal* 3 (1974): 48–65.

———. "History of the Shearer Houses." *Berkeley Journal* 5 (1976): 33–41.

Wright, Gilbert. "Some Letters to His Parents by a Floridian in the Confederate Army." *Florida Historical Quarterly* 36 (April 1958): 353–72.

York, Herbert. "The Falling Waters Mill." *Berkeley Journal* 5 (1976): 43–44.

Young, Bennett H. "Col. John R. Lane and His Regiment." *Confederate Veteran* 17 (1909): 110–11.

Young, Louis G. "Death of Brigadier General J. Johnston Pettigrew." *Our Living and Our Dead* 1 (September 1874): 29–32.

———. "Pettigrew's Brigade at Gettysburg." *Our Living and Our Dead* 1 (February 1875): 552–58.

Index